TERRORISM

Documents of International and Local Control

VOLUME 92

TERRORISM

Documents of International and Local Control

VOLUME 92

LEBANON AND HEZBOLLAH

Douglas C. Lovelace Jr., Esquire
Senior National Security Strategist

Oceana®
NEW YORK

OXFORD
UNIVERSITY PRESS

Oxford University Press, Inc., publishes works that further Oxford University's objective of excellence in research, scholarship, and education.

Published by Oxford University Press, Inc.
198 Madison Avenue, New York, New York 10016

Cataloging-in-Publication information is available from the Library of Congress.

ISSN 1062-4007
Terrorism: Documents of International and Local Control

ISBN: 978-0-19-538278-5 (v. 92)

Note to Readers:
This publication is designed to provide accurate and authoritative information in regard to the subject matter covered. It is based upon sources believed to be accurate and reliable and is intended to be current as of the time it was written. It is sold with the understanding that the publisher is not engaged in rendering legal, accounting, or other professional services. If legal advice or other expert assistance is required, the services of a competent professional person should be sought. Also, to confirm that the information has not been affected or changed by recent developments, traditional legal research techniques should be used, including checking primary sources where appropriate.

(Based on the Declaration of Principles jointly adopted by a Committee of the American Bar Association and a Committee of Publishers and Associations.)

TABLE OF CONTENTS

VOLUME 92

LEBANON AND HEZBOLLAH

DOCUMENTS

INTRODUCTORY NOTE

The editors of *Terrorism: Documents of International and Local Control* are pleased to present in this volume a collection of English-language documents pertaining to Lebanon, Hezbollah, the Israel-Lebanon War of 2006, and the aftermath of that conflict. These documents encompass a wide range of sometimes conflicting perspectives, including viewpoints from the government of Lebanon, from the Congressional Research Service in the United States, and from NGOs such as Israel's Intelligence and Terrorism Information Center and Amnesty International. Also included are United Nations Security Council resolutions, agreements, and transcripts, reports of the UN Secretary General, and agreements between Lebanon and the European Union.

Because the institutional authors of many of the documents in this volume unapologetically advocate for the objectives of the governments or organizations which they represent, it is important to note that we are providing those documents to you not as assertions of fact but rather as a tour of current positions taken by those governments and private groups. We believe that all of these documents, when evaluated together, will serve to enhance the reader's understanding of the many issues relating to terrorism in Lebanon and the Lebanon-Israel War.

A. IN GENERAL

DOCUMENT NO. 1

LEBANON: THE ISRAEL-HAMAS-HEZBOLLAH CONFLICT

CRS Report
RL33566

September 15, 2006

Jeremy M. Sharp, Coordinator Foreign Affairs, Defense, and Trade Division

Christopher Blanchard, Kenneth Katzman, Carol Migdalovitz, Alfred Prados, Paul Gallis, Dianne Rennack, John Rollins, Steve Bowman, and Connie Veillette
Foreign Affairs, Defense, and Trade Division

Summary

This report analyzes the conflict between Israel and two U.S. State Department-designated Foreign Terrorist Organizations (FTOs), the Lebanese Shiite Muslim group Hezbollah and the radical Palestinian Hamas organization. On July 12, 2006, what had been a localized conflict between Israel and Palestinian militants in the Gaza Strip instantly became a regional conflagration after Hezbollah captured two Israeli soldiers in a surprise attack along the Israeli-Lebanese border. Israel responded by carrying out air strikes against suspected Hezbollah targets in Lebanon, and Hezbollah countered with rocket attacks against cities and towns in northern Israel. In order to push Hezbollah back from its border, Israel launched a full-scale ground operation in Lebanon with the hopes of establishing a security zone free of Hezbollah militants. Meanwhile, Israeli clashes with Hamas and other Palestinian militants have continued in the Gaza Strip.

A United Nations-brokered cease-fire came into effect on August 14, 2006. Based on United Nations Security Council Resolution 1701 passed a few days earlier, the cease-fire is intended to be monitored by the Lebanese Armed Forces in conjunction with an expanded U.N. peacekeeping force in Lebanon. The international community initially hesitated to contribute troops, though it appears now that enough countries have stepped forward to significantly expand the existing U.N. force (UNIFIL).

On July 18, 2006, the Senate passed S.Res. 534, which, among other things, calls for the release of Israeli soldiers who are being held captive by Hezbollah or Hamas; condemns the governments of Iran and Syria for their continued support for Hezbollah and Hamas; urges all sides to protect innocent civilian life and infrastructure; and strongly supports the use of all diplomatic means available to free the captured Israeli soldiers. On July 20, 2006, the House passed H.Res. 921, which also condemns Hezbollah's attack on Israel and urges the President to bring sanctions against the governments of Syria and Iran for their alleged sponsorship of Hezbollah.

The extension of the Israeli-Palestinian conflict into the Lebanese arena created a multifaceted crisis that cut across a number of U.S. policy issues in the Middle East. This report provides an assessment of the month-long war and its implications for regional stability and other key U.S. policy issues. This report will be updated periodically. A number of CRS analysts have contributed to this report. For additional questions, please contact the individual specialist listed under each section of the report. For more information on the major countries in the current conflict, please see CRS Report RL33476, *Israel: Background and Relations with the United States*; CRS Report RL33509, *Lebanon*; CRS Report RL33487, *Syria: U.S. Relations and Bilateral Issues*; CRS Report RL32048, *Iran: U.S. Concerns and Policy Responses*; and CRS Report RL33530, *Israeli-Arab Negotiations: Background, Related Developments, and U.S. Policy*.

Introduction

A Multi-Dimensional Conflict[1]

Hezbollah's[2] July 12, 2006, attack in northern Israel, in which two Israeli soldiers were kidnapped, elicited an Israeli military response that again embroiled the region in a multi-dimensional conflict. The month-long war touched upon an array of critical U.S. foreign policy issues in the Middle East, ranging from the continued instability arising from the lack of a comprehensive settlement to the Arab-Israeli peace process, to the preservation of Lebanon's sovereignty and independence which remains hampered by the inability to disarm Hezbollah. Though the primary combatants were part of a triangular dynamic in which Israel was (and still is) at war with Hezbollah in Lebanon and with Palestinian militants, including Hamas, in

[1] Prepared by Jeremy M. Sharp, Analyst in Middle East Policy.

[2] For the purposes of this report, "Hezbollah" is used in referring to the Lebanese Shiite Muslim group. Common alternate spellings include Hizballah, Hizbullah, and Hizb`allah.

the Gaza Strip, there were secondary players who added additional layers of complexity to the conflict, namely Iran and Syria.[3] Both countries have played significant roles in arming, training, and financing Hezbollah (and to a lesser extent Hamas) and have used the Lebanese Shiite organization as a proxy to further their own goals in the region. Iran may have aspirations to become the dominant power in the Middle East, and many in the international community are closely focused on its potential weapons of mass destruction capability. In this light, the fighting in southern Lebanon was viewed by some as a contest between two of the Middle East's most bitter rivals and most powerful actors, Israel and Iran (via Hezbollah by proxy), and it could be a harbinger of future indirect confrontations between two possibly nuclear-armed nations.

The "Root Causes" of the Conflict

Hezbollah's July 2006 attack inside Israeli territory and repeated Israeli-Palestinian clashes in the Gaza Strip and West Bank illustrated not only the risk posed by terrorist groups operating along Israel's borders, but more importantly, the risk to regional security in the absence of comprehensive peace agreements between Israel and the Palestinians, Lebanon, and Syria. Particularly along Israel's northern front, achieving peace between the major parties has been an elusive goal. The task has grown even more complex with the rising influence of non-state political movements/terrorist organizations, such as Hezbollah and Hamas, on Lebanon's southern border. Neither organization recognizes Israel's right to exist as a nation-state.

The 2006 war in Lebanon is the latest manifestation of conflict along the Israeli-Lebanese-Syrian border, the final demarcation of which has long been in dispute and is exacerbated by the technical/formal state of war (not active) that exists between Israel and its two northern neighbors. On the Lebanese side of the border, historically weak, usually Christian/Sunni-led governments paid scant attention to the southern portion of the country, a predominately Shiite area. Without much of an economy or government military presence in the south, the region was prone to penetration by outside groups (mainly Palestinian) opposed to Israel until the Shiites residing there formed their own militias. Since the earliest days of Jewish settlement in what was then the British-controlled Palestine-Mandate, militants could operate with impunity over a porous border. Before Hezbollah came on the scene, the Palestinian Liberation Organization (PLO) used Lebanon as a base to wage a guerrilla war against Israel. Repeated PLO-Israeli clashes in Lebanon helped ignite the 15-year long Lebanese civil war. To eliminate the PLO threat from its border, Israel occupied a buffer zone in southern

[3] There also are tertiary actors with an interest in the war in Lebanon. The European Union, other Arab states, and the United Nations all have been closely involved in trying to resolve the crisis.

Lebanon for 18 years, a policy which many observers believe accelerated the politicization of Lebanese Shiites there and, with significant assistance from Iran, led to the creation of Hezbollah.[4]

Today, with the PLO long expelled from Lebanon and the Syrian armed forces no longer in Lebanon and at a major technological disadvantage vis-à-vis Israel's conventional forces, it is Hezbollah that has stepped in to fill the power vacuum in southern Lebanon and continue to threaten Israel with the full support of its foreign patrons—Syria and Iran. Syria seeks the return of the Golan Height which it lost to Israel in the June 1967 Six Day War and finds non-state groups like Hezbollah and other Palestinian terrorist organizations based in Damascus as useful proxies. Most analysts believe the Israeli-Lebanese-Syrian tri-border area will remain a tinderbox that could spark future conflicts so long as territorial disputes remain unresolved. While Syria and Israel have at times come close to an agreement, most recently in 1999, significant differences between the two sides remain, notably control over the shores of the Sea of Galilee, a critical source of fresh water with symbolic importance as well for both countries.

The Cease-Fire

U.N. Security Council Resolution 1701[5]

After more than four weeks of fighting between Israel and the Lebanese Shiite Muslim militia Hezbollah, on August 11, 2006 the U.N. Security Council unanimously adopted Resolution 1701, calling for a "full cessation of hostilities based upon, in particular, the immediate cessation by Hezbollah of all attacks and the immediate cessation by Israel of all offensive military operations." The resolution provides: expansion of the existing U.N. Interim Force in Lebanon (UNIFIL) from 2,000 to a maximum of 15,000; deployment of UNIFIL plus a Lebanese Army force[6] to southern Lebanon to monitor the cease-fire; withdrawal of Israeli forces in southern Lebanon "in parallel" with the deployment of U.N. and Lebanese forces to the south; a ban on delivery of weapons to "any entity or individual" in Lebanon, except the Lebanese Army. The resolution requested the U.N. Secretary General to develop proposals within 30 days for delineation of Lebanon's international borders, including the disputed Shib'a Farms enclave located near the Lebanese-Syrian-Israeli tri-border area. The resolution's preamble also emphasizes the need to address the issue of prisoners on both sides. The resolution also calls upon the international community

[4] For an account of the creation of Hezbollah and the role of Iran see, Magnus Ranstorp, *Hizbollah in Lebanon*, St. Martin's Press, 1997, pp. 30–40.
[5] Prepared by Alfred Prados, Specialist in Middle Eastern Affairs.
[6] The Lebanese Prime Minister offered to deploy 15,000 military personnel. (See below.)

to extend financial and humanitarian assistance to the Lebanese people, including facilitating safe return of displaced persons.

The agreement entered into force on August 14. Factors critical to the effectiveness of the peacekeeping measures adopted by Resolution 1701 and the likelihood of a sustainable cease-fire include acceptance of the arrangements by Israel, Hezbollah, and the Lebanese population; training and motivation of peacekeeping forces; rules of engagement that allow for a military response to challenges; and cooperation among the various organizations involved in peacekeeping under Resolution 1701.

An Expanded UNIFIL. The U.N. Interim Force in Lebanon (UNIFIL), created in 1978 initially to monitor an earlier Israeli withdrawal, has fluctuated in size over the years, comprising approximately 2,000 military personnel as of mid-2006. As noted above, Resolution 1701 envisions increasing UNIFIL to a maximum of 15,000, of which approximately 7,000 would come from Italy, France, Spain, and other European countries. Turkey and Qatar have agreed to participate, thus providing Arab/Muslim representation and Indonesia has been approached as well. U.N. planners are hopeful that more Arab or at least other Muslim forces may participate as well to broaden support for UNIFIL. There has been talk of deploying the expanded UNIFIL not only in southern Lebanon but also along the Syrian-Lebanese border. Syria objects to this proposal as a hostile act. (See below.)

International Contributions to UNIFIL Peacekeeping Force

Country	Troop Pledges
Italy	3,000
Germany	2,400 (exclusively for naval patrol)
France	1,800–2,200
Spain	1,000–1,200
Turkey	1,000
Indonesia	500–1,000
Poland	500
Belgium	300
Qatar	250–300
Finland	250

Country	Troop Pledges
*Others (Sweden, Greece, Denmark, Britain,)	Offered ships, naval assets, engineers, and aircraft
Totals:	**11,00–12,150 est.**
W/ Existing UNIFIL Force (2,000)	**13,000–14,150 est.**

Source: Troop figures are only estimates based on media reports; not all of these are firm commitments.

*Some countries, such as Russia, are sending troops and rebuilding teams to Lebanon independent of the U.N. peacekeeping mission there.

Lebanese Armed Forces. Resolution 1701 also welcomes a decision by the Lebanese Government to deploy 15,000 personnel from the Lebanese Armed Forces to southern Lebanon as the Israeli forces withdraw. There are questions, however, about the likely effectiveness of Lebanese troops in maintaining stability. The 70,000-member Lebanese Armed Forces have limited capabilities and largely obsolescent equipment. Moreover, they are divided along religious sectarian lines, although Lebanon's leaders have tried in recent years to build a professional and more integrated force. Although the government does not release figures on the sectarian composition of the Lebanese Armed Forces, according to former Lebanese army general Elias Hanna, the army's officer corps is predominantly Christian and Sunni Muslim while the rank and file is about 70% Shiite.[7] Deployment of Lebanese military contingents could help break the deadlock over monitoring the Lebanese-Syrian border, however, since the various parties have not objected to the presence of Lebanese troops.

Unresolved Issues

The Difficulty of Disarming Hezbollah. Some analysts believe that Resolution 1701, while it may succeed in creating a temporary calm and end to the fighting, will probably fail to change the fundamental political and military dynamics on the ground that started the war in the first place—the presence of a well-armed Hezbollah militia on Israel's borders. Although Resolution 1701 calls for an expanded UNIFIL, it will not be operating in accordance with Chapter VII of the U.N. Charter, which allows the Security Council to "take such action by air, sea, or land forces as may be necessary to maintain or restore international peace and security." According to U.S. Secretary of State Condoleezza Rice, "I don't think there is an expectation that this [U.N.] force is going to physically disarm Hezbollah. . . . I think it's a little bit of a misreading about how you disarm

[7] "Lebanese Armed Forces May Play Bigger Role in War," *USA Today*, August 2, 2006.

a militia. You have to have a plan, first of all, for the disarmament of the militia, and then the hope is that some people lay down their arms voluntarily."

While Israel has demanded that peacekeepers be deployed along the Lebanese-Syrian border to prevent Hezbollah's re-armament by Syria and Iran, Lebanese Prime Minister Fouad Siniora stated on August 28, 2006 that the Lebanese Armed Forces have already been deployed along the border and that there is no need for an international presence there. Syria's President Bashar al-Asad had threatened earlier to close the border should peacekeepers take up positions close to Syria. In an interview with Dubai television, Asad stated that a possible peacekeeping force along the border "is an infringement on Lebanese sovereignty and a hostile position." Most analysts believe that the Lebanese army can do little to prevent the smuggling of arms to Hezbollah.

Release of Prisoners.[8] International mediators have been working through diplomatic channels to free the Israeli corporal kidnapped by the Hamas military wing and two other groups on June 25 almost from that date. The kidnappers and their supporters have insisted that the Israeli soldier be exchanged for some of the thousands of Palestinian prisoners being held by Israel. Although the kidnappers initially and specifically demanded the release of women and minors in Israeli custody, their subsequent demands have been less precise. The mediators' efforts have been hampered by Hamas's demand (specifically Damascus-based Hamas Political Bureau Chief Khalid al-Mish'al's demand) for a simultaneous prisoner swap and by Israel's reluctance to agree to any actions that would appear to be an exchange or a concession to the "blackmail" of kidnapings. Egyptian officials are said to be mediating and there are unconfirmed reports that a prisoner exchange is in the works. According to these reports, the soldier would be released and, subsequently, Palestinian prisoners would be released in three groups, totaling about 800.[9] The Egyptians' interlocutor is not known. Neither Palestinian President Mahmud Abbas nor Prime Minister Ismail Haniyah of Hamas is in control of the kidnapped Israeli soldier. The Hamas military wing may answer to Mish'al, who in turn may need the approval of his Syrian hosts or Iranian supporters for any deal.

U.N. Secretary General Kofi Annan announced on September 5 that Israel and Hezbollah had agreed to have him mediate an exchange of prisoners for the release of the two Israeli soldiers kidnapped on the northern border of Israel by Hezbollah on July 12 and that he would appoint an envoy to conduct "secret" negotiations. Israeli officials immediately reacted by saying

[8] Prepared by Carol Migdalovitz, Specialist in Middle Eastern Affairs.

[9] "Israeli Sources Confirm Prisoner Exchange Contacts, PM Office Denies Knowledge," *Yedi'ot Aharonot*, September 3, 2006, Open Source Center Document GMP20060903741001. Before the kidnaping, Israeli Prime Minister Ehud Olmert reportedly had been considering the release of a substantial number of Palestinian prisoners as a goodwill gesture toward Palestinian President Mahmud Abbas.

that they would not negotiate a prisoner release, but they have taken actions which contradict their statements and indicate that they expect an exchange. In addition to holding several Lebanese prisoners, one of whom has been in jail as a convicted murderer since 1979, Israeli forces reportedly captured about a dozen Hezbollah fighters and brought the corpses of others to Israel during the recent war specifically in order to exchange them for the captured soldiers after the war.[10] Israel has exchanged many Hezbollah prisoners for a few Israeli captives and corpses via third party mediators on past occasions. While the current Israeli government would prefer not to follow that precedent and apparently launched the recent war partly to end it, the captives' families and much of the Israeli public demand the return of the abductees, which appears to require an exchange.

Continued Fighting in Gaza.[11] While fighting continues in the Gaza Strip, it has abated somewhat in Lebanon since August as rockets have been launched less frequently. The Israeli Defense Forces have taken over some former settlements in Gaza and deployed just beyond the Gaza border in order to make sporadic incursions into Palestinian areas to attack terrorists, rocket launching sites, and tunnels used to smuggle arms into Gaza. However, their use of air and artillery strikes appears to have been curtailed somewhat. This may have been due to a shifting of regular Israeli forces and resources to the northern front against Lebanon and their replacement by reservists. It is not yet clear if hostilities will re-escalate in Gaza with the cessation of hostilities in Lebanon. Some 200 Palestinians have been killed since these operations began after the June 25 kidnaping of an Israeli soldier. A prisoner exchange might continue to constrain the fighting.

Much of the fighting in Gaza is intramural, i.e., between supporters and opponents of the Hamas-led government. The well-armed Palestinian security forces, manned largely by Fatah opponents of the government, have repeatedly confronted the Hamas military wing and other armed groups loyal to government. Crime rates also reportedly have risen.[12] Violence also may be attributed to the dire economic straits into which Gaza has fallen since the international community and Israel cut the transfer of funds to the Palestinian Authority (PA) after Hamas assumed leadership of the PA government in March. Palestinian security forces and other government employees hold the Hamas-led government responsible for the resulting non-payment of salaries. Israel also has sealed off the Gaza Strip, only allowing in sufficient humanitarian aid shipments to stave off

---

[10] Eliot Jager, "For the Good of the Many," *Jerusalem Post*, September 5, 2006.
[11] Prepared by Carol Migdalovitz, Specialist in Middle Eastern Affairs.
[12] Doug Struck, "Israel Siege Leaves Gaza Isolated and Desperate," *The Washington Post*, August 28, 2006.

a disaster. Thus, the domestic climate is considered chaotic and highly combustible.

As a result, pressure was exerted on Hamas to accept President Mahmud Abbas to form a national unity government in order to allow foreign aid to flow again. Hamas was reluctant to concede the premiership and insisted that ministries be distributed in proportion to a party's strength in parliament, ensuring continued Hamas domination in the cabinet. It has also firmly resisted the idea of a government of technocrats. Moreover, Hamas will not accede to the January 2006 demand of the "Quartet" (United States, United Nations, European Union, and Russia) that it accept principles of non-violence, recognize Israel, and prior agreements and obligations, including the Road Map to a two-state solution to the Israeli-Palestinian conflict. If Hamas is not in a position to compromise, the conditions which produced the international pressure will not change and violence will likely continue.

Shib'a (Shebaa) Farms.[13] A small 10-square-mile enclave near the Lebanon-Syria-Israel tri-border area known as the Shib'a Farms continues to exacerbate tensions in southern Lebanon and complicate implementation of cease-fire terms. Earlier, the withdrawal of Israeli forces from southern Lebanon in May 2000 left several small but sensitive border issues unresolved, including the Shib'a Farms. Israel did not evacuate this enclave, arguing that it is not Lebanese territory but rather is part of the Syrian Golan Heights, which Israel occupied in 1967. Lebanon, supported by Syria, asserted that this territory is part of Lebanon and should have been evacuated by Israel when the latter abandoned its self-declared security zone in southern Lebanon in 2000. On June 16, 2000, the U.N. Secretary General informed the Security Council that the requirement for Israel to withdraw from southern Lebanon had been met, thereby implying that the Shib'a Farms are not part of Lebanon.[14] The Secretary General did point out, however, that the U.N. determination does not prejudice the rights of Syria and Lebanon to agree on an international boundary in the future.

Leaders of Hezbollah immediately seized upon the Shib'a Farms issue as justifying Hezbollah's refusal to relinquish its weapons, arguing that the weapons were needed to confront Israel while the latter continued to occupy the Shib'a Farms. Hizbollah also argued that it was justified in continuing to launch periodic rocket attacks on Israeli military units in or near the Shib'a Farms area to counter alleged threats posed by Israeli forces in the area. For the next half-decade, this area remained a focal point for violence

[13] Prepared by Alfred Prados, Specialist in Middle Eastern Affairs.

[14] The U.N. Secretary General noted that the Shib'a Farms comes under the mandate of the U.N. Disengagement Observer Force (UNDOF), which is monitors the Israeli-occupied Syrian Golan Heights. UNDOF has no role in Lebanon. For more information, see CRS Report RL31078, *The Shib'a Farms Dispute and Its Implications.*

and border violations. Among the more serious incidents was the seizure by Hezbollah guerrillas in October 2000 of three Israeli soldiers, whose bodies were handed over to Israel in return for the release of a group of Hezbollah prisoners in January 2004. This incident, which anticipated the July 2006 kidnaping that triggered the recent Israeli-Hezbollah fighting, was followed by further unrest, including border violations, Hezbollah attacks by fire (e.g., rocket and mortar attacks), occasional Israeli air strikes, and frequent Israeli overflights of Lebanon.

The situation is made more complex by the fact that Syria and Lebanon have never demarcated a common border nor established formal diplomatic relations. The two countries, which were twin protectorates under a French "mandate" (trusteeship) between World Wars I and II, never established diplomatic structures or agreed boundaries upon graining independence in 1943. This was due in part to the influence of some factions in both Syria and Lebanon who regarded the two as properly constituting a single country. Advocates of a "Greater Syria" in particular were reluctant to establish diplomatic relations and boundaries, fearing that such steps would imply formal recognition of the separate status of the two states.

The Shib'a Farms emerged into the limelight once again after political upheavals in Lebanon in 2005 and the fighting that erupted in July 2006. As government leaders and diplomats sought to find ways to end the fighting and pursue more lasting peace efforts, it became obvious that the status of the Shib'a Farms territory would likely arise. At an inconclusive international conference on Lebanon held in Rome on July 26, Lebanese Prime Minister Fouad Siniora presented a seven-point proposal which called, among other things, for placing the Shib'a Farms and some adjacent areas under U.N. jurisdiction "until border delineation and Lebanese sovereignty over them are fully settled." The proposal also provided that the Shib'a Farms would be open to property owners during the period of U.N. custody.

U.N. Security Council Resolution 1701 of August 11, 2006, which brought about a cessation of active hostilities, did not specifically endorse the seven-point plan and its proposals for dealing with the Shib'a Farms question. However, in preambular language, the resolution referred to "the proposals made in the seven point plan regarding the Shebaa (variant spelling) farms area." Later on, in paragraph 10, the resolution requested the U.N. Secretary-General to develop proposals to implement terms of various agreements including, "delineation of the international borders of Lebanon, especially in those areas where the border is disputed or uncertain, *including by dealing with the Shebaa farms area* [emphasis added], and to present to the Security Council those proposals within thirty days." On September 1, 2006, during a follow-on trip to the region, Secretary-General Annan said Syrian President Bashar al-Asad informed him that "Syria is prepared to go ahead with the delineation of its border with Lebanon." According to the press article that reported the meeting, the process of delineation could include the Shib'a Farms area.[15] At the same time, President Asad ruled out formal *demarcation* (as distinguished from *delineation*) of the Shib'a Farms' boundaries pending Israeli withdrawal from the area.[16]

The status of the Shib'a Farms could be an important factor, not only in the stability of Lebanon but also in any future agreements involving Israel, Lebanon, and Syria. If the Shib'a Farms area forms part of Lebanese territory occupied by Israel in 1982, it would come under the provisions of U.N. Resolutions 425 and 426, which addressed Israeli withdrawal from Lebanon. If it forms a part of the Syrian Golan Heights territory occupied by Israel in 1967, it would come under the provisions of other U.N. resolutions (242 and 338), which address the Golan territory and other broader aspects of the Arab-Israeli conflict. In the latter case, the issue would be moot as long as Israel remains in occupation of the Golan Heights. For more background information on the Shib'a Farms issue, see CRS Report RL31078, *The Shib'a Farms Dispute and Its Implications.*

The War's Aftermath

Assessing Hezbollah[17]

The relative success of Hezbollah in the recent conflict can be credited to a variety of factors. In the six years since the Israeli withdrawal from southern Lebanon, Hezbollah devoted considerable efforts to constructing an extensive defensive infrastructure, providing substantial training to its personnel, establishing distributed stockpiles of supplies throughout the area, and preparing operational plans. All of these activities are reported to have received a very high level of support from Iran in the form of funds, equipment, and personnel.[18]

Perhaps the most significant factor in Hezbollah's ability to withstand the Israeli Defense Forces (IDF) is an the extensive network of fortified sites and underground facilities. These provided protection for both personnel and equipment against repeated Israeli air attacks, forcing the IDF to move to ground operations. Fighting from prepared positions and very

---

15 "Annan says Assad [variant spelling] will respect Hezbollah arms embargo," AFP News Wire, September 1, 2006.

16 Interview with Syrian President Bashar al-Asad carried by Dubai TV on August 23, 2006.

17 This section was prepared by Steve Bowman, Specialist in National Defense.

18 "Arming of Hezbollah Reveals U.S. and Israeli Blindspots," *The New York Times*, July 19, 2006; "Best Guerrilla Force in the World," *The Washington Post*, "The Iranian Connection," *Aviation Week and Space Technology*, August 14, 2006. Other sources include Robin Hughes, "Iran answers Hizbullah call for SAM systems," *Jane's Defence Weekly*, August 9, 2006; Alon Ben-David, "Iran 'supplied Zelzal-2 rockets to Hizbullah,'" *Jane's Defence Weekly*, August 16, 2006; *Jane's Terrorism & Security Monitor*, "Hizbullah's Islamic Resistance," September 13, 1006.

well equipped with a range of modern weaponry that included antitank and anti-ship missiles, night vision equipment, and computer assisted targeting, relatively small Hezbollah units were able to maintain stiffer resistance than expected. Hezbollah's stockpiled supplies and local support significantly mitigated the Israeli interdiction efforts. Though isolated by the IDF air and ground offensive, Hezbollah units were often sufficiently provisioned to continue fighting without immediate need for re-supply. Close familiarity with their area of operations, widespread support among the population, and effective communication networks enhanced Hezbollah's ability to slow Israeli advances, often conducting ambushes and rapidly withdrawing in classic guerrilla style warfare.

Though Hezbollah units did attempt limited incursions into Israeli territory, they were all successfully repulsed. Nevertheless, throughout the conflict Hezbollah was able to maintain its campaign of rocket attacks on Israeli territory. An estimated 4,000–5,000 rockets were fired; however, this represents only a third of Hezbollah's estimated rocket/missile arsenal.[19] Though Israeli retaliation against rocket launch sites came in a matter of minutes in some cases, the mobility of the rocket launchers continued to make them difficult targets. The rockets/missiles supplied to Hezbollah by both Iran and Syria carried a variety of conventional warheads and had ranges of up to 120 miles. Though most are of relatively low accuracy by modern standards, they remain effective terror weapons against urban populations.

Though Hezbollah's military capabilities may have been substantially reduced, and re-supply from Syria and Iran could be hampered by the presence of international peacekeepers in Lebanon, Hezbollah's long-term potential as a guerrilla movement appears to remain intact. Observers note that Hezbollah's leaders have been able to claim a level of "victory" simply by virtue of not having decisively "lost".

Debate Within Israel[20]

Israelis overwhelmingly supported the war as a legitimate response to an attack on sovereign Israeli territory and as a long overdue and decisive reaction to six years of Hezbollah rocket attacks against northern Israel. As the conflict progressed, however, the public and media increasingly questioned the government's and the military commanders' prosecution of the war. After the war, critics noted that the kidnapped soldiers had not been

[19] "Israeli Commandos Raid Tyre," *USA Today*, August 5, 2006; "Hezbollah Launches Rocket Barrage," *BBC News*, August 6, 2006. More recent source: Interview with Under Secretary of State for Political Affairs Nicholas Burns, "Assessing Hezbollah's Post-Conflict Power," *National Public Radio: Morning Edition*, August 18, 2006.

[20] Prepared by Carol Migdalovitz, Specialist in Middle Eastern Affairs, September 6, 2006.

freed and that Hezbollah had retained its arms and may have been strengthened politically; and they found fault with a government that had produced what they viewed as poor results. The charges levied against the government and the military leaders include hesitant decision-making; excessive reliance on air power; delayed launch of a ground offensive, which, once begun, was seen as deficient; launching an unnecessary and costly final ground action during the weekend after the U.N. passed the cease-fire resolution; poor intelligence concerning Hezbollah locations, arms, tactics, and capabilities; deficient training and equipment for mobilized reservists; tactics unsuitable for terrain and enemy; ill-prepared home front defenses, which left many poor and elderly who were unable to escape in the north; an inadequate presentation of the Israeli view to international audiences; and harm to future Israeli deterrence.

The government counters that the war succeeded in forcing Hezbollah from the border and in degrading its arms, particularly in eliminating a substantial number of its long- and mid-range missiles. It also sees success in forcing the Lebanese government, aided by international forces, to assert control over the south, which had been an unfilled demand made by Israel since it withdrew from the region in 2000. Most notably, Israeli officials took Hezbollah leader Sheikh Hassan Nasrallah's admission that he would not have authorized the July 12 action if he had known how strongly Israel would react as confirmation that Hezbollah has been weakened and that Israel's deterrence has been strengthened.[21]

Public opinion polls indicate that support for the government has fallen sharply and that a much of the public favor the resignations of Prime Minister Ehud Olmert, Defense Minister Amir Peretz, and Israeli Defense Forces (IDF) Chief of Staff Gen. Dan Halutz.[22] Critics claim that Olmert and Peretz's lack of military command experience make them unqualified to head the state during a war. Both had held only low-level positions during required military service and neither had served beyond that time. Some critics blame Gen. Halutz, a former head of the air force, for having made too many appointments to the general staff from the air force and for ignoring reportedly well-developed plans for a ground campaign. The revelation that Halutz had engaged in personal stock market transactions in the early hours of the war sparked additional questions about his priorities.[23] Reservists and families of those killed in action have been in the forefront of demonstrations demanding accountability.

---

[21] Nasrallah's August 27, 2006 interview with Lebanon television, cited by Joshua Mitnick, "Hezbollah Says Its War with Israel Was a Mistake," *Washington Times*, August 28, 2006.

[22] Dahaf poll results published in "Israel: Majority Favor Inquiry Commission," *Yedi'ot Aharonot*, August 16, 2006, Open Source Center Document GMP 20060816738001.

[23] Halutz claims that the stock sale was made before he learned of the kidnapings in northern Israel. Halutz interview by Sima Qadmon, "Clipped Wings," *Yedi'ot Aharonot*, August 18, 2006, Open Source Center Document GMP 20060818738004.

However, Prime Minister Olmert rejected demands for an independent state commission of inquiry, such as were headed by Supreme Court justices after past controversial conflicts, saying it would take too long and paralyze the military when it needs to attend to more vital tasks. Instead, he at first named former Mossad (Institute for Intelligence and Special Operations) Director Nahum Admoni to head a government investigatory committee to examine wartime decision-making. This move failed to satisfy critics, who charge that a government-appointed committee would lack independence and produce a white-wash; and they continued to demand a state inquiry. Attorney-General Menahem Mazuz then disqualified two of the Admoni committee's five members due to conflicts of interests. Olmert also approved Defense Minister Peretz's appointment of former Chief of Staff Gen. (Res.) Ammon Lipkin-Shahak to head a committee to investigate how the military and the Defense Ministry had performed during the war. Accusations of lack of independence and white-wash also were made against Lipkin-Shahak, who had advised Peretz during the war. Lipkin-Shahak suspended his activities and Peretz later came out in support of a state commission of inquiry. Despite these developments, Olmert persisted in his efforts to avoid a state commission. On September11, he announced that, instead of Admoni, retired judge Eliahu Winograd would head a committee to examine the conduct of both political and military leaders during the war. It will have two civilian and two retired military members and the power to subpoena witnesses and grant immunity for testimony. In addition, State Comptroller Micha Lindenstrausse will probe failings in home front preparedness.[24]

Domestic Political Repercussions in Israel. Politically, support for Olmert's Kadima and Peretz's Labor parties, the two main coalition partners, has plummeted, while that for the rightist Likud and Yisrael Beiteinu parties and their respective leaders, Benjamin Netanyahu and Avigdor Lieberman, has increased. There has been some speculation that the governing coalition might be reconfigured to bring in one or both of these larger opposition parties, although Olmert professes to have no interest in change. Lieberman disavows interest in joining the government, claiming that it will be short-lived. Netanyahu has been less categorical. Few in parliament, save Lieberman, appear to favor bringing down the government immediately and in sparking an early election as they have been in their seats only a few months. Likud has already struck a deal with the government to support the 2007 budget and budget votes have been used as vehicles for producing no-confidence votes and bringing down a government. Netanyahu may not believe that he has sufficiently repaired his public

[24] Aluf Ben and Yuval Yo'az, "Ex-judge Winograd Tapped to Head Government War Probe," *Ha'aretz*, September 12, 2006.

image from that of a Finance Minister whose policies harmed the aged and the poor to contest another election at this time. Such allegations contributed to Likud's poor showing in the March 2006 election.

Many Kadima Members of the Knesset (MKs) know that their political fate is tied to Olmert's and have a vested interest in his political survival. Hence, he does not face an imminent challenge to his party leadership, although polls indicate that Foreign Minister Tzipi Livni is more popular. Kadima had been formed in late 2005 in order to pursue unilateral disengagement from the West Bank. Many Israelis now believe that unilateral withdrawals from south Lebanon in 2000 and from Gaza in 2005 had transformed those regions into terrorist bases, and neither the public nor Kadima still supports disengagement from the West Bank. As a result, some observers say the party lacks a *raison d'etre*. Olmert has said that rebuilding a north devastated by the war is his highest priority, but few would consider this goal to be a new platform for the party.

Amir Peretz is facing greater challenges from within Labor. Since the government was formed, a block of party dissidents who did not receive cabinet portfolios have taken every opportunity to criticize their party leader and his actions. They are led by former Ben Gurion University President Avishay Braverman and former head of Shin Bet (Israeli counterintelligence and internal security service) Ami Ayalon, two strong personalities, and their voices have grown louder since the war. At the present time, the budget process is providing them with ammunition. Budget cuts to pay for the war are subordinating Labor's social and economic agenda; and the proposed 2007 budget contains more of the same. Defense Minister Peretz is in the awkward position of having to support the military's demands, while conceding championship of social causes to his intra-party opposition. As a former successful union leader who wrested control of Labor from an entrenched old guard, Peretz's abilities as an infighter should not be underestimated.

Most Israeli governments last less than two years. The current government is not threatened by imminent demise, but many believe that it will not survive two year years.

The Race to Rebuild Lebanon

While fighting has come to a halt, Iran and Hezbollah are vying with the United States and its international and Arab partners over which side can help rebuild southern Lebanon the fastest and win the "hearts and minds" of many distraught Lebanese civilians who have lost homes and businesses due to the war. Hezbollah militants and party members, perhaps as an implicit acknowledgment that the war they began brought much suffering to Lebanon, reportedly have been handing out $12,000 in cash payments to anyone who lost their home during the war. The money is meant to pay for rent and furniture while Hezbollah builds new homes for the displaced. Reportedly, the bulk of Hezbollah's largesse comes from Iran, which may have allocated hundreds of millions in aid to be channeled through Hezbollah to Lebanon.[25] According to the governor of Lebanon's Central Bank, Hezbollah was distributing banknotes that had not gone through the formal banking system implying that they may have been transported across the border by land. According to *Time*, Hezbollah has pledged to rebuild apartment buildings and entire villages within three years and has sent civil-affairs teams wearing hats that read Jihad For Reconstruction.[26] Lebanon's Prime Minister Fouad Siniora is reportedly offering a government compensation package of $33,000 for Lebanese whose homes were destroyed in the fighting between Hezbollah and Israel. At this time, it is unclear whether the Lebanese government will be able to follow through on such a commitment. Overall, the Lebanese government estimates that damage to the country's infrastructure from the war is approximately $3.5–$4 billion.

To counter Hezbollah's efforts, President Bush announced on August 21, 2006 that the United States would provide $230 million to Lebanon (an additional $175 million on top of an earlier pledge of $55 million). According to the U.S. State Department, the President's initial $55 million pledge came from various reprogrammed FY2006 foreign aid funds, including $24 million from the International Famine and Disaster Assistance account, $21 million from the Emergency Refugee and Migration Account (ERMA), $10 million from the P.L.480 fund (food aid), and $420,000 from the Non-proliferation, Anti-terrorism, De-mining, and Related Programs account (NADR). At this time, it is unclear where the second tranche of $175 million will come from.

According to Director of U.S. Foreign Assistance Ambassador Randall Tobias, U.S. aid to Lebanon will be focused on the following projects:

- Reconstructing the Fidar Bridge in Jbeil, a key link in Lebanon's coastal highway between Beirut and the northern city of Tripoli;
- Removing debris from the southern road between Marjeyoun and Nabatyeh;
- Procuring materials and hiring local workers to repair damaged homes;
- Cleaning and repairing schools in preparation for the coming school year;
- Providing new nets, hooks and other trade material to fishermen whose equipment was damaged; and

[25] David R. Sands, "Hezbollah takes lead in rebuilding," *The New York Times*, August 17, 2006; and Daniel Steinvorth, "The Footrace to Rebuild Lebanon," *The New York Times*, September 4, 2006.

[26] "The War for Hearts and Minds, *Time*, August 27, 2006.

- Supporting local fishermen working to clean up the oil slick that now pollutes 90 miles of the Lebanese coastline.[27]

The international community also has recognized Lebanon's urgent need for reconstruction assistance, and on August 31, 2006, donors convened in Stockholm, Sweden for a conference to raise reconstruction funds for Lebanon. A total of $940 million in early reconstruction aid was committed and earmarked for rebuilding. Some observers contend that countries opposed to Iranian influence in Lebanon have already fallen behind due to the slow pace of international financial and security commitments and the lack of adequate personnel on the ground to dispense aid.

International Contributions to Rebuilding Lebanon

Country	Pledge (Grants only)
Saudi Arabia	$500 million (also provided $1 billion in loans to Lebanon's Central Bank)
Kuwait	$300 million (also provided $500 million in loans to Lebanon's Central Bank)
Qatar	$300 million
United States	$230 million
European Union	$117 million
International Monetary Fund (IMF)	$112 million
United Arab Emirates	$50 million
United Kingdom	$40 million
Italy	$38 million
Spain	$34 million
Germany	$28 million
France	$25 million
Canada	$22 million
Switzerland	$20 million
Sweden	$20 million
Australia	$10.5 million
Turkey	$10 million
Japan	$1.9 million
Totals	**$ 1.8584 billion (est.)**

Sources: Estimates based on various media reports and U.S. State Department figures.

[27] David Shelby, "United States Extends Loan Guarantees to Israel," *Washington File*, August 31, 2006.

The War's Impact on Lebanese Internal Politics

For almost 30 years prior to 2005, Lebanon's internal politics were dominated by Syria, which maintained a large military presence in Lebanon ostensibly as part of an Arab League peacekeeping force. Though supported by some Lebanese, including much of the Shiite Muslim community, the Syrian presence was increasingly resented by other elements of the Lebanese population including Maronite Christians, Sunni Muslims, and Druze (followers of a small sect derived from Islam). The assassination in February 2005 of former Lebanese Prime Minister Rafiq Hariri, widely blamed on Syrian agents because of Hariri's opposition to Syrian policies, led to a dramatic chain of events that profoundly altered the Lebanese political scene. Under heavy domestic and international pressure, Syria withdrew its forces from Lebanon in April 2005; relatively free parliamentary elections were held in May and June without direct Syrian interference in the balloting process; a cabinet headed by a member of the anti-Syrian bloc was installed; and the U.N. Security Council passed Resolution 1595, which established an independent commission to investigate the circumstances of Hariri's murder. Initial reports of the commission seemed to implicate Syria or pro-Syrian Lebanese but findings remain inconclusive so far.

At the time, many observers interpreted Syria's unexpectedly rapid withdrawal and the subsequent election of an anti-Syrian majority in the Lebanese parliament as a major setback for Syria's ambitions in the region, and some even predicted that the regime of Syrian President Bashar al-Asad had been seriously weakened. However, Syria maintained significant assets in Lebanon: a mixed government in Lebanon comprising both pro- and anti-Syrian elements (see below); a possible residual presence of Syrian intelligence assets in Lebanon;[28] and Hezbollah, which has refused so far to relinquish its arms and apparently continued to support Syria's agenda by periodically attacking Israeli military positions near the Israeli-Syrian border.

The Lebanese government itself is far from monolithic. On one hand, parliamentary elections gave a majority (72 out of 128 seats) to a large anti-Syrian bloc headed by the late Prime Minister's son; on the other hand, the Lebanese Shiite Hezbollah leads a 33-seat minority bloc, and a third 21-seat

[28] In an interview with Lally Weymouth published in the May 1, 2006 edition of *Newsweek*, Prime Minister Siniora "Syria has its men and people in the country: supporters, some politicians and quite a number of Syrian intelligence." According to the U.N. Secretary-General, a U.N. team attempting to verify the withdrawal of all foreign armies from Lebanon under Security Council Resolution 1559 noted that the government of Lebanon "is confident that, by and large, Syrian intelligence has withdrawn," but allegations of "ongoing Syrian intelligence activity in Lebanon have continued to surface on occasion." United Nations Security Council, Document S/2006/248, Letter dated 18 April 2006 from the Secretary-General addressed to the President of the Security Council, Paragraph 19.

bloc headed by an independent former army officer is cooperating with the Hezbollah bloc on some issues. President Emile Lahoud was elected with strong support from Syria and currently enjoys the support of Hezbollah as well; he refuses to retire before his term ends in 2007. Prime Minister Fouad Siniora, though a member of the anti-Syrian bloc, nonetheless heads a mixed cabinet which, for the first time in Lebanese history, contains two members of Hezbollah. Disputes over disarmament of Hezbollah, the status of President Lahoud, and relations with Syria have already created several cabinet crises and severely limited the ability of the government to deal with domestic and regional issues.

The 34-day military confrontation between Hezbollah and the Israeli Defense Force in July and August 2006 greatly enhanced the prestige of Hezbollah at the expense of the Lebanese government. Hezbollah's leader Sheikh Hassan Nasrallah acquired a folk-hero status as his organization was widely hailed both for its military prowess in the conflict with Israel and for its perceived ability to initiate disaster relief projects far more quickly and efficiently than the regular governmental organizations. Even those Lebanese who might be inclined to criticize Hezbollah for precipitating a crisis that devastated much of southern Lebanon have been muted, at least temporarily, by Nasrallah's soaring popularity and Hezbollah's success in delivering aid to large numbers of displaced persons and other homeless or destitute Lebanese.[29] Similarly, he finds himself in a strong position to withstand pressures to disarm Hezbollah. Syria too, as a major sponsor of Hezbollah, finds that it has more maneuver room in dealing with Lebanese issues. Notably, the earlier enthusiasm among some Lebanese to pursue investigations designed to uncover a possible Syrian role in the Hariri assassination has dissipated, to a considerable extent.

The inevitable comparisons being drawn between Hezbollah effectiveness and Lebanese government ineptitude raise questions about the future of the Siniora government and its ability to withstand domestic criticism over its leadership during the current crisis. To some extent, the answers to these questions depend on the interaction of Lebanon's diverse religious sectarian and political groups. Lebanon is the most religiously diverse country in the Middle East and its political system is based on a careful distribution of governmental posts by religious sect. Shiite Muslims constitute a plurality, though not a majority, of the population, and in recent years they have increased their influence in the Lebanese body politic as their numbers have continued to grow. While not all Lebanese Shiites support Hezbollah, many observers believe Sheikh Nasrallah is likely to be heeded to a greater

[29] Sharon Behn, 'U.S., Hezbollah vie to rebuild for Lebanese; Hope to win public opinion," *The Washington Times*, August 18, 2006; Paul Richter, "Cease-Fire in the Middle East," *Los Angeles Times*, August 17, 2006.

degree in the post conflict environment in Lebanon; he benefits from his ability to play multiple roles including military leader, reconstruction czar, and political participant. Despite his currently favorable image, however, Nasrallah may prefer to enhance his role in the present government including participation by Hezbollah (albeit at a junior level) in the cabinet and leadership of a strong parliamentary bloc rather than to mount an uncertain challenge that could galvanize currently dormant opposition to the Shiite leadership in Lebanon.

In the meantime, the interaction of government offices and agencies in Lebanon remains somewhat awkward, complicating the national decision-making process. For example, Prime Minister Siniora, who maintains a dialogue with the United States and the international community, has not had direct dealings with Hezbollah, which the United States lists as a foreign terrorist organization, since the war began. Rather, Siniora and Nasrallah have communicated through the speaker of parliament, Nabih Berri, who is aligned with the Hezbollah-led bloc, but is a member of the more moderate Shiite faction known as Amal.[30] At the same time, Siniora has gained some stature by negotiating some of the wording to Lebanon's advantage in the final version of Resolution 1701. Realignments within the three somewhat amorphous blocs in parliament are also possible, if not likely, as the political situation continues to evolve in the aftermath of the July-August fighting.

Issues for U.S. Policy and Congress

U.S. Foreign Assistance to the Middle East[31]

As a result of the Israeli-Lebanon/Hezbollah conflict, the United States has pledged $230 million in humanitarian and reconstruction assistance to Lebanon. While some parts of Israel were also affected by the war, no additional assistance has been announced with the exception of an extension of existing loan guarantees.[32] The United States has longstanding aid programs to countries in the Middle East,[33] including both Israel and Lebanon. Foreign assistance has been used to promote the peace process, spur economic development, and in the case of Israel, to strengthen its defense capabilities through military assistance.

---

[30] Edward Cody, "Italian Troops Land in Southern Lebanon," *The Washington Post*, September 3, 2006, p. A15.

[31] Prepared by Connie Veillette, Analyst in Foreign Policy.

[32] Herb Keinon, "U.S. to Israel: No Financial Aid for War," *The Jerusalem Post*, August 22, 2006, and "Finance Minister: U.S. Loan Guarantee Extension Shows 'Faith' in Israeli Economy," *Tel Aviv Ynetnews*, August 20, 2006.

[33] For more information, see CRS Report RL33222, *U.S. Foreign Aid to Israel*, by Jeremy M. Sharp. And RL32260, *U.S. Foreign Assistance to the Middle East: Historical Background, Recent Trends, and the FY2007 Request*, by Jeremy M. Sharp.

Israel's Loan Guarantees. Loan guarantees are a form of indirect U.S. assistance to Israel, since they enable Israel to borrow from commercial sources at lower rates and not from the United States government. Congress directs that appropriated or other funds be set aside in a U.S. Treasury account for possible default. These funds, which are a percentage of the total loan (based in part on the credit rating of the borrowing country), come from the U.S. or the Israeli government. Israel has never defaulted on a U.S.-backed loan guarantee, as it needs to maintain its good credit rating in order to secure financing to offset annual budget deficits.

P.L. 108-11, the FY2003 Emergency Wartime Supplemental Appropriations Act, authorized $9 billion in loan guarantees over three years for Israel. P. L. 108-11 stated that the proceeds from the loan guarantees could be used only within Israel's pre-June 1967 borders, that the annual loan guarantees could be reduced by an amount equal to the amount Israel spends on settlements in the occupied territories, that Israel would pay all fees and subsidies, and that the President would consider Israel's economic reforms when determining terms and conditions for the loan guarantees. On November 26, 2003, the Department of State announced that the $3 billion loan guarantees for FY2003 were reduced by $289.5 million because Israel continued to build settlements in the occupied territories and continued construction of the security barrier separating the Israelis and Palestinians.

The Bush Administration reportedly plans to submit a request to Congress to extend the authorization of Israel's loan guarantees through FY2010.[34] To date, Israel has $4.6 billion in U.S.-backed commercial credit left to draw on.

Lebanon.[35] The United States provides modest amounts of assistance to Lebanon, including economic (ESF) and military assistance (FMF),[36] and humanitarian de-mining funds (NADR). Annual funding for Lebanon has been maintained at roughly $35 to $40 million since FY2001 with the objectives of promoting economic growth, strengthening democracy and good governance, and protecting the environment.

In addition, Lebanon may be eligible for $10 million in Department of Defense funds under Section 1206 of the FY2006 National Defense Authorization Act (PL 109-163), which authorizes funds for the training and equipping of foreign military forces conducting counter-terrorist operations. Reportedly, this aid would help modernize the Lebanese Armed forces (LAF) by providing funds for the procurement of spare parts to

[34] "United States Extends Loan Guarantees to Israel," *Jerusalem Post*, August 19, 2006.

[35] See also CRS Report RL33509, *Lebanon*, by Alfred B. Prados.

[36] FMF to Lebanon has moderately increased since the withdrawal of Syrian troops from Lebanon. U.S. officials would like to improve the capabilities of Lebanon's Internal Security Forces and the Lebanese Armed Forces which protect the country from external threats. See, "U.S. Pledges More Aid to Lebanon in '07," *DefenseNews.com*, July 10, 2006.

upgrade and repair the LAFs 5-ton military trucks, M113 armored personnel carriers, and UH-1H utility helicopters. The Pentagon may attach conditions to the $10 million aid package if appropriated, requiring the LAF to use the equipment provided to contain Hezbollah's militia.[37]

As stated earlier, the United States has pledged $230 million in aid to Lebanon for reconstruction. Of the total U.S. pledge, $55 million has been committed and reprogrammed from various FY2006 foreign operations accounts. The makeup of the remaining $175 million pledge had not been announced as of September 2006, but it is expected that the Administration will send a request to Congress to reprogram existing FY2006 funds for at least part of the total.

On September 14, 2006, the *Washington Post* reported that Representative Tom Lantos, ranking Minority Member of the House International Relations Committee, put a hold on any assistance to Lebanon until the Lebanese Armed Forces and international peacekeepers deploy along the Lebanese-Syrian border. At this point, it is unclear how long the delivery of aid will be suspended.

Humanitarian Issues[38]

During the war, partisans on both sides of the conflict and some independent human rights activists alleged that the warring parties were targeting each other's civilian populations by employing inaccurate munitions that are designed to saturate wide areas with shrapnel or explosive sub-munitions.

Condemning Hezbollah. Observers have condemned Hezbollah's indiscriminate firing of rockets into northern Israeli towns and cities in order to terrorize the population and cause extensive damage to infrastructure. According to the *Jerusalem Post*, many of the rockets fired contained anti-personnel munitions such as steel ball bearings.[39] Israeli civil defense agencies continue to identify, disarm, and remove unexploded ordnance (UXO) fired by Hezbollah into northern Israel during the conflict.

On September 14, 2006, Amnesty International accused Hezbollah militants of war crimes and "serious violations of international humanitarian law" during the Lebanon war. In a report that attempted to balance earlier accusations against Israel's bombing of civilian areas in Lebanon, Amnesty noted that Hezbollah's Katyusha rockets "cannot be aimed with accuracy, especially at long distances, and are therefore indiscriminate."[40]

---

[37] "Pentagon Aid Package For Lebanon Designed To Counter Hezbollah,"*Inside the Pentagon*, August 31, 2006.

[38] Prepared by Christopher M. Blanchard, Middle East Policy Analyst.

[39] "Expert Views Effect, Breakdown of Hizballah Rocket Attacks on Northern Israel," *Jerusalem Post*, September 6, 2006.

[40] "Amnesty International Says Hezbollah Committed War Crimes," *New York Times*, September 14, 2006.

Israel's Use of Cluster Weapons. Observers have decried Israel's use of cluster weapons to counter Hezbollah's rockets attacks. Since the United States is a major provider of military aid to Israel, the cluster weapons issue received media attention during and since the war and has reportedly become the subject of an Administration investigation.

Field and press reports suggest that large numbers of cluster weapon sub-munitions (commonly referred to as "cluster bombs") remain scattered across areas of southern Lebanon in the aftermath of fighting between Hezbollah and the Israel Defense Forces (IDF). The sub-munitions in southern Lebanon are the unexploded remnants of a range of Israeli ground- and air-launched cluster weapons, including bombs, artillery shells, and rockets. The United States apparently supplied some of the cluster weapons that Israel used in the conflict.[41] Officials from the United Nations, non-governmental organizations, and foreign governments have criticized Israel for its use of cluster weapons in populated areas because of the known high rate of failure for the cluster weapons' sub-munitions and the potential for these so-called "bomblets" to kill and injure civilians. Israel reportedly fired many of the cluster weapons in question during the final days of the conflict.[42] As of September 7, the United Nations had catalogued 12 deaths and 61 reported injuries from UXO in Lebanon, all but five of which were linked to cluster sub-munitions. Up to 448 cluster weapon strike sites from the recent conflict have been identified, and U.N. experts estimated that 12 to 15 months will be needed to clear the sites of cluster sub-munitions.[43] According to Human Rights Watch, 57 countries maintain stockpiles of cluster weapons, and nine countries have used them in combat, including the United States in Iraq and Afghanistan.[44]

Israeli Reaction. Israeli officials maintain that the IDF carefully considered the potential for civilian casualties both during and following their military operations, and that IDF use of cluster weapons, as well as the IDF's

[41] David S. Cloud, "Inquiry Opened into Israeli Use Of U.S. Bombs," *New York Times* August 25, 2006. An August 26, 2006, presentation by United Nations Mine Action Coordination Center (UNMAS) South Lebanon office catalogued the following numbers of U.S.-manufactured cluster weapon sub-munitions during surveys in southern Lebanon (source weapons in parentheses): 715 M-42's (105-millimeter artillery shells), 820 M-77's (M-26 rockets), and 5 BLU-63's (CBU-26 cluster bombs). The UNMAS teams also reported 631 M-85 Israeli-produced sub-munitions had been found. See, UNMAS South Lebanon, "Cluster Bomb Situation - South Lebanon July/August 2006," August 26, 2006. Available at [http://www.stopclustermunitions.org/files/CB%20South%20Lebanon.pdf].

[42] *Agence France Presse*, "Israel Spewed Cluster Bombs over Lebanon in Last Days of War: UN," August 30, 2006.

[43] UNMAS, "Lebanon Unexploded Ordnance Fact Sheet, September 7, 2006." Response to CRS Inquiry.

[44] See, Human Rights Watch, "Memorandum to Delegates to the Convention on Conventional Weapons Group of Governmental Experts On Explosive Remnants of War," March 2003; and, Paul Wiseman, "Cluster Bombs Kill in Iraq, Even After Shooting Ends," *USA Today*, December 11, 2003. According to the U.S. Defense Department, the U.S. military used air and ground launched cluster weapons during Operation Enduring Freedom in Afghanistan and Operation Iraqi Freedom, including in urban combat during the fall of Baghdad. Civilian casualties have been reported from unexploded U.S. cluster weapon sub-munitions in both countries.

broader methods during the southern Lebanon campaign, "are legal under international law and their use conforms with international standards."[45] Israel has identified Hezbollah's use of civilian homes for rocket launching and munitions storage as the primary explanation for IDF targeting of some populated areas during the conflict. IDF sources reported during the conflict that the predominant targets for their cluster weapons were Hezbollah-manned Katyusha rocket launch sites in open areas. Following the conclusion of the cease-fire agreement, the IDF transferred maps to UNIFIL forces showing likely locations for UXO and distributed warning notices to residents in conflict zones advising them to delay their return to their villages and homes until UXO had been cleared.[46]

Administration Response. The U.S. Department of State's Office of Weapons Removal and Abatement has announced plans to expand an ongoing landmine and unexploded ordnance (UXO) humanitarian clearance program in Lebanon in the aftermath of the Israel-Hezbollah conflict. The expansion of the program will consist of an emergency grant of $420,000 in reprogrammed FY2006 funds to a non-governmental UXO removal organization and greater support for the United Nations Joint Logistics Center UXO data collection and mapping operations in Lebanon.[47] The Department of State also is seeking congressional approval for the allocation of up to $2 million to continue UXO clearing activity in Lebanon during FY2007.[48]

Munitions Shipment Hold and Investigation. According to press reports citing unnamed Administration officials, the Department of State has held up a shipment of M-26 cluster munitions to Israel and initiated an investigation of the Israel Defense Force's use of cluster munitions during the recent fighting. In early August, Israel reportedly requested that a pre-ordered shipment of U.S. M-26 rockets be expedited for IDF use in Multiple Launch Rocket System (MLRS) counterfire strikes against Hezbollah rocket launch sites in southern Lebanon. Initial reports suggested the shipment

---

[45] *Agence France Presse*, "Israel Says Arms Used in Lebanon Keep by International Law," August 31, 2006. No treaty or international convention specifically governs the deployment or use of cluster munitions in war. However, unexploded ordnance (UXO) removal specialists and advocates for moratoria and bans on the use of cluster munitions argue that the articles of the Geneva Conventions relating to the differentiation and protection of civilian populations prohibit the use of cluster munitions in civilian areas. For example, this view is advanced by the Cluster Munition Coalition, an anti-cluster weapon network that advocates on behalf of sub-munition victims and campaigns to ban use of the weapons.

[46] See Israel Ministry of Foreign Affairs, "Behind the Headlines: Legal and operational aspects of the use of cluster bombs," September 5, 2006; and, Meron Rapoport, "IDF: No Prohibition on Cluster Bombs," *Ha'aretz* (Tel Aviv), September 8, 2006.

[47] The United Nations Joint Logistics Center (UNJLC) works in partnership with the Vietnam Veterans of America Foundation. For more information, see UNJLC, "Mine-UXO in Lebanon," August 2006. Available at [http://www.unjlc.org/lebanon/infosheets/mine/index_html/view].

[48] The grants will support the activities of the Mines Advisory Group (MAG). U.S. Department of State Office of the Spokesman, Fact sheet: "United States Emergency Aid to Lebanon to Clear Explosive Remnants of War," August 23, 2006. Available at [http://www.state.gov/r/pa/prs/ps/2006/71047.htm].

was delayed out of concern over the weapons' potential use, and subsequent press reports suggest the shipment has been placed on hold.[49] In addition to this reported hold, the Department of State's Directorate of Defense Trade Controls also reportedly is conducting an investigation focused on whether Israel violated confidential agreements with the United States that restrict Israel's use of U.S.-supplied cluster munitions to certain military targets in non-civilian areas.[50] Administration officials have declined to comment specifically on these reports. President Bush repeatedly characterized Israel's military actions as "self-defense" during the conflict. The Arms Export Control Act requires that U.S.-supplied weapons can be used only in "legitimate self-defense."

Congressional Responses. In Congress, Senators Feinstein and Leahy introduced an amendment to the FY2007 Department of Defense Appropriations bill (S.Amdt.4882 to H.R.5631) that would have prevented FY2007 funds from being spent "to acquire, utilize, sell, or transfer any cluster munition unless the rules of engagement applicable to the cluster munition ensure that the cluster munition will not be used in or near any concentrated population of civilians, whether permanent or temporary, including inhabited parts of cities or villages, camps or columns of refugees or evacuees, or camps or groups of nomads."[51] The amendment failed to pass during Senate floor consideration on September 6, 2006 by a vote of 30 to 70 (Vote No. 232). Some opponents of the amendment argued that its language would unduly restrict the options available to U.S. military commanders in battle. Others called for hearings to further discuss the subject.[52]

U.S. Efforts and Other Efforts to Combat Hezbollah

U.S. Terrorism Designations and Related Effects. In December 2004, the U.S. State Department added Al-Manar to the Terrorist Exclusion List (TEL). Applicable criteria for adding Al-Manar to the TEL included inciting to commit a terrorist act and providing material support to further terrorist activity. The effects of an entity being placed on the TEL could include the possible deportation and exclusion from the United States of individuals found belonging to or supporting the TEL designated organization. Concurrent with the State Department's placement of Al-Manar on the TEL, the organization was no longer allowed a satellite feed into the United States. Though Al-Manar is banned from broadcasting its satellite signal into the United States, the station does upload its television programs and

[49] David S. Cloud, "Israel Asks U.S. to Ship Rockets With Wide Blast," *New York Times*, August 11, 2006.
[50] David S. Cloud, "Inquiry Opened Into Israeli Use Of U.S. Bombs," *New York Times* August 25, 2006.
[51] S.Amdt.4882 to H.R.5631; and, Office of Senator Dianne Feinstein, Press Release: "Senators Feinstein and Leahy Call for New Policy on Use of Cluster Bombs," September 5, 2006.
[52] See Congressional Record, Senate, September 6, 2006, Department of Defense Appropriations Act, 2007 pp. S8992–S8996.

other like material on its website, which is accessible to any individual with an internet connection.[53]

On March 23, 2006, the Department of the Treasury designated Al-Manar as a Specially Designated Global Terrorist (SDGT) entity. In making this designation, Stuart Levey, Treasury Under Secretary for Terrorism and Financial Intelligence, stated, "Any entity maintained by a terrorist group—whether masquerading as a charity, a business, or a media outlet—is as culpable as the terrorist group itself."[54] The effects of an entity being designated as a SDGT include the blocking of access to all assets under U.S. jurisdiction by the organization, its parent companies, and individuals who have materially supported the entity's terrorist activities. Future transactions between U.S. persons or corporations and Al-Manar are also prohibited consistent with the provisions of the SDGT.

Recent Al-Manar Related Activity in the United States. In December 2002, Salim Boughader, an owner of a Lebanese restaurant in Mexico, was arrested by Mexican authorities on human-smuggling charges, as he is suspected of trafficking up to 200 Lebanese nationals into the United States. During post arrest questioning, Mr. Boughader reportedly admitted to knowingly providing assistance to an employee of Al-Manar in gaining unlawful entrance into the United States. Mr. Boughader also stated that he assisted individuals with ties to Hezbollah, as he and other Lebanese people "did not see Hezbollah as terrorists."[55]

On August 23, 2006, Javed Iqbal was arrested on charges of offering live broadcasts of Al-Manar programming to potential customers in New York. Through selling equipment from his home and his Brooklyn-based company, HDTV Ltd., Mr. Iqbal is suspected of offering customers access to the Al-Manar signal. It is reported that in the instances Mr. Iqbal installed the necessary equipment and attempted to retrieve the Al-Manar transmission, he ultimately was not successful in obtaining the desired signal.[56]

U.S. and Israeli Action Against Hezbollah Finances.[57] On August 29, 2006, the U.S. Department of the Treasury designated the Islamic Resistance Support Organization (IRSO) of Lebanon as a Specially Designated Global

53 Lebanese Communications Group—Al-Manar TV. Available online at [http://www.manartv.com.lb/NewsSite/News.aspx?language=en].

54 U.S. Designates Al-Manar as a Specially Designated Global Terrorist Entity Television Station is Arm of Hizballah Terrorist Network, 23 March, 2006, The Department of Treasury website [http://www.treas.gov/press/releases/js4134.htm].

55 "Terror Linked Migrants Channeled Into U.S.," *Fox News*, July 03, 2005, [http://www.foxnews.com/story/0,2933,161473,00.html].

56 Walter Pincus, "New Yorker Arrested for Providing Hezbollah TV Channel," *The Washington Post*, August 25, 2006.

57 Prepared by Christopher M. Blanchard, Middle East Policy Analyst.

Terrorist entity for serving as "a key Hezbollah fund-raising organization."[58] According to Treasury officials, the organization openly raised funds for Hezbollah via direct solicitation and advertisements on Hezbollah's Al-Manar television network. The IRSO reportedly allowed its donors to specify whether or not they wished their funds to be used for military equipment or weapons purchases, in addition to a range of other services. As a result of the designation, the IRSO is prohibited from operating in the United States, and any of its assets under U.S. jurisdiction were frozen.

The action against IRSO has been followed by two actions against Lebanese and Iranian financial entities suspected of providing support to Hezbollah. On September 7, 2006, Treasury's Under Secretary for Terrorism and Financial Intelligence (TFI) Stuart Levey announced the designation of Bayt al-Mal and the Yousser Company for Finance and Investment of Lebanon for serving "as Hezbollah's unofficial treasury, holding and investing its assets and serving as intermediaries between the terrorist group and mainstream banks." Bayt al-Mal director Husayn al-Shami also was designated.[59] On September 8, 2006, Treasury officials announced that Iran's Bank Saderat would be prohibited from conducting direct or indirect financial transactions with the U.S. financial system, in part because the Government of Iran has used the bank to fund Hezbollah and other terrorist organizations.[60] Prior to the U.S. legal action, Israel reportedly conducted a series of military strikes during July 2006 on Hezbollah financial centers and banks in Lebanon alleged to conduct business for Hezbollah operatives. Brigadier General Dani Arditi, advisor to the Israeli Prime Minister for Counterterrorism, confirmed that the strikes were meant to serve as a message "for all the Lebanese banks. . . . Assistance to Hezbollah is direct assistance to terrorist organizations."[61]

Al-Manar: Hezbollah's Satellite Television Station.[62] Al-Manar, a satellite television station controlled by Hezbollah, broadcasts into most areas of the world. Al-Manar refers to itself as the "station of resistance" and has a stated mission of conducting "psychological warfare against the Zionist enemy."[63] The station, with a reported budget of $20 million,[64] started transmitting limited programming in June 1991.

---

58 U.S. Department of the Treasury, "HP-73: Treasury Designates Key Hizballah Fundraising Organization," August 29, 2006.

59 U.S. Department of the Treasury, "HP-83: Treasury Designation Targets Hizballah's Bank," September 7, 2006.

60 U.S. Department of the Treasury, "HP-87: Treasury Cuts Iran's Bank Saderat Off From U.S. Financial System," September 8, 2006.

61 Adam Ciralsky and Lisa Myers, "Hezbollah Banks Under Attack in Lebanon," *MSNBC News*, July 25, 2006.

62 This section was prepared by John Rollins, Specialist in Terrorism and International Crime.

63 Al-Manar TV on the web at [http://web.manartv.org/html/about.html].

64 "Hizbullah's Al-Manar TV Budget More than Israel's PR Outlay," *Arutz Sheeva*, 28 August, 2006.

On two occasions during the recent conflict, Israel bombed the main Al-Manar facility located in southern Beirut. Though buildings on the complex caught fire, transmission satellite antennas were destroyed, and the station's signal went through brief periods of intermittent transmission, the network returned to broadcasting at full capacity shortly after these attacks.[65] Al-Manar's public relations chief Ibrahim Farhat stated that the organization developed contingency plans to allow for broadcasting from remote locations after the U.S. designated it a terrorist organization in December 2004.[66]

Islam, Al Qaeda, and the Global War on Terrorism[67]

The conflict in Lebanon challenged many Sunni Islamists, including jihadist Al Qaeda leaders such as Ayman Al Zawahiri, to reconcile their documented animosity toward Shiite Muslims with their desire to appear to be in solidarity with anti-Israeli and anti-American sentiment and activity that emerged around the Islamic world in response to the crisis. During the fighting, debate over the legitimacy of providing support for Hezbollah, a Shiite Lebanese militia, was particularly pointed on many extremist Internet fora and in a series of public statements issued by conservative Sunni Islamic leaders. Some condemned Hezbollah's actions as part of a Shiite conspiracy to gain regional power or a leadership bid by Hezbollah leader Hassan Nasrallah, while others argued that Sunni and Shiite Muslims should have united to confront Israel and its supporters.[68] To the extent that these debates may have inspired unity or division within and across religious and political communities in the Arab world and beyond, they may have important implications for the success of U.S. foreign policy initiatives in the region, and for U.S. counterterrorism policy objectives in particular.

The airing of diverse perspectives toward the crisis across the Arab and wider Islamic worlds brought the competing religious and political priorities of some important figures and groups into contrast and conflict. Conservative Sunni Islamic leaders, such as Qatar-based cleric and international Muslim Brotherhood figure Yusuf Al Qaradawi argued that Muslims should support the activities of Hezbollah and Hamas as legitimate "resistance" activities, based on Quranic injunctions to defend Muslim territory invaded by outsiders.[69] Similarly, Egypt's Grand Mufti Ali Gomaa

---

65 "Hizbollah Rockets Hit Haifa", *Reuters UK*, July 16, 2006.

66 "Hezbollah's Al-Manar TV survived attacks", *Examiner*, August 25, 2006.

67 This section was prepared by Christopher Blanchard, Middle East Policy Analyst.

68 For discussions of these competing views, see Bernard Haykel, "The Enemy of My Enemy Is Still My Enemy," *New York Times*, July 26, 2006; and, Annia Ciezadlo, "Sheikh Up," *New Republic*, August 7, 2006.

69 "Islamic Cleric Al-Qaradawi Supports Hizballah, HAMAS," *Al-Jazirah Television* (Doha), OSC Document GMP20060730638004, July 30, 2006.

stated that Hezbollah was "defending its country" and its actions were "not terrorism."[70] Saudi sheikh Salman Al Awda called for Sunnis to set aside their "fundamental and deep disagreement" with Hezbollah and Shiites in order to confront "the criminal Jews and Zionists."[71] While many of the strongest statements that were issued appeared to primarily serve rhetorical purposes, they may have continuing political implications: many religious figures sought to distance themselves from the more nuanced positions of Arab political leaders during the crisis, some of whom have otherwise been characterized as detached from public opinion and vulnerable to revolt. Moreover, groups or individuals may utilize religious figures' judgments and statements to justify future attacks on the interests or personnel of Israel, the United States, or their own governments should the crisis flare up again.

Disagreements also emerged among violent Sunni Islamist extremists, including Al Qaeda and its affiliates. In a July 31 Internet posting, an Al Qaeda in the Arabian Peninsula representative seemingly rejected any unitarian sentiment between violent Sunni groups and Hezbollah by characterizing Hezbollah as "the head of the Iranian spear in the Arab region," and arguing that "any support to Hezbollah in Lebanon is indirect support for the Iranian objectives."[72] The view of Al Qaeda leadership figures, as expressed by Ayman Al Zawahiri first in a video released on July 27, and again on September 11, remains somewhat ambiguous with regard to sectarian issues. On July 27, Al Zawahiri stated that "our nation will get together to fight [Israel and its allies]," but he refrained from directly urging Sunni-Shiite unity or advocating direct Sunni support for Hezbollah.[73] A Hezbollah official interviewed on Al Jazeera television following the release of Al Zawahiri's July tape stated that Al Zawahiri's statement should have been "clearer in its reference to the ideological and political dimensions of unity among Muslims, and that, in the future, "there should be clear and direct references to Hizballah and Shiites in a positive sense."[74] In September, Zawahiri addressed his advice and urgings to "Muslims" around the world and in Lebanon rather than addressing the sectarian questions raised by Hezbollah and others. He specifically called on "the Muslim nation" to aid "its Muslim brothers in Lebanon and Gaza," and

[70] Reuters, "Egypt's Mufti Defends Hizbollah Operations," July 28, 2006.

[71] Sheikh Abdallah Bin-Jibrin, "Is It Permissible to Support the So-Called Rafidi [Shiite] Hizballah?" *Nur al-Islam* (website), OSC Document GMP20060721827005, July 19, 2006; and, Abdallah al-Rashid, "Al-Awdah: We Disagree with Hizballah, But We Reject Israel's Aggression," *Islam Today* (Riyadh), OSC Document GMP20060724837002, July 24, 2006.

[72] "Al-Qa'ida in Saudi Arabia Urges Countering Hizballah," OSC Document - FEA20060802025964, August 2, 2006.

[73] "Al-Zawahiri Comments on Lebanon, Gaza" OSC Document - FEA20060727025705, July 27, 2006.

[74] Interview with Hezbollah Political Council member, Hasan Hudruj, "Al-Jazirah TV: Hizballah Official Comments on Al-Zawahiri's New Videotape," *Al-Jazirah Television* (*Doha*), OSC Document—GMP20060727648002, July 27, 2006.

urged Lebanese Muslims "to reject international resolutions, particularly the recent Security Council Resolution 1701."[75] Any resolution of the ongoing Sunni jihadist debate regarding the appropriate stance toward Shiites will likely have broader implications for any potential intervention in future conflict involving Shiites by Sunni jihadist cells and others who look to Al Qaeda leaders for guidance.

Conclusion

There are many divergent interpretations of the July-August war in Lebanon and its implications for U.S. policy in the Middle East. On the one hand, some consider this conflict to be just the latest battle in a global war on terror pitting the democracies of the West and Israel against terrorist organizations backed by radical regimes. Others view the war less in terms of an overall effort against Islamic extremism and more of a battle between powerful nation-states, seeing Lebanon as the battleground in an "opening round" of an Iranian-Israeli struggle for regional preeminence. Still, some observers assert that the war is simply another chapter in a long history of localized Arab-Israeli violence spurred by the lack of any discernable progress in a peace process. In reality, there may be elements of truth within all of these perspectives.

The conflict has posed its own set of challenges for U.S. policy toward Lebanon. In a broader sense, the war has jeopardized not only the long-term stability of Lebanon but has presented the Bush Administration with a basic dilemma. On one hand, the Administration is sympathetic to Israeli military action against a terrorist organization; President Bush has spoken in favor of Israel's right of self-defense. On the other hand, the fighting dealt a setback to Administration efforts to support the rebuilding of democratic institutions in Lebanon. One commentator suggested "the two major agendas of his [Bush's] presidency—anti-terrorism and the promotion of democracy—are in danger of colliding with each other in Lebanon."[76]

If Lebanon disintegrates through a return to communal civil strife or becomes closely aligned with Syria or Iran, U.S. goals could be seriously affected. The United States would lose a promising example of a modernizing pluralist state moving toward a resumption of democratic life and economic reform and quite possibly face a return to the chaos that prevailed in Lebanon during the 15-year civil war. Such conditions would be likely

[75] "Jihadist Website Posts Al-Zawahiri 9/11 Anniversary Video," OSC Document - FEA20060912027565, September 11, 2006.
[76] Michael Hirsh, "The Legacy On the Line," *Newsweek*, July 24, 2006, p. 30.

to foster terrorism, unrest on Israel's border, and other forms of regional instability. Moreover, the growth of Syrian or Iranian influence or some combination of the two could strengthen regional voices supporting extremist and likely anti-Western views associated with clerical regimes (Iran), totalitarian models (Syria), or a militant stance toward Israel. A viable cease-fire, on the other hand, could be an initial step toward further progress in the long quest for regional peace.

With Hezbollah deeply ingrained in Lebanese Shiite society, the movement has become a fixture in the political system, though whether or not its militia and terrorist wings can be disarmed remains to be seen. Many Israelis remain deeply skeptical over international efforts to disarm Hezbollah, as the real work of preventing rearmament over land, sea, and air will take place behind the scenes in the months ahead. Israeli sources are already reporting the renewal of Syrian and Iranian shipments to Hezbollah though such reports are difficult to confirm.

A key aspect of Hezbollah's possible re-armament is the role of Syria. Many questions remain concerning Syria: the willingness of the United States and Israel to bring Syria into the diplomatic mix, Syria's influence over Hezbollah in a Lebanon free of Syria's military occupation, and what demands Syria may make in exchange for its possible cooperation. Some observers suggest a variety of theoretical incentives that the West could provide Syria, including the end of its isolation by the United States and the removal of Syria from the State Department's terrorism list and the relaxation of economic sanctions; the tacit recognition of its influence in Lebanese politics; the ratification of the EU Association Agreement with Syria that provides it with certain trade benefits; diminished international pressure regarding the U.N.-led investigation into the murder of former Lebanese Prime Minister Rafiq Hariri; increased financial support, possibly from Arab Gulf states; and finally (though less likely), a resumption of negotiations over the Israeli-occupied Golan Heights—a longstanding Syrian goal since its defeat in the June 1967 Six-Day War. Others believe that U.S. refusal to reward Syria for its intransigence should continue and that any U.S. engagement would undermine Western efforts to strengthen Lebanese independence and sovereignty, even if the unspoken reality is one in which Syria's special role in Lebanese affairs is widely recognized. After the recent attack on the U.S. embassy in Damascus, some observers have asserted that the United States and Syria share an interest in combating Islamic extremism and should renew limited security cooperation and intelligence sharing.

Finally, speculation over the winners and losers of the war will most likely be debated for some time. Israeli officials believe that their overwhelming response to Hezbollah's provocation caught it and Iran off-guard and that Israel's subsequent operations have eroded its opponents' deterrent capabilities along the Israeli-Lebanese borders. Nevertheless, there are many Israelis both in and out of the government who believe that the war was poorly managed, did not achieve its goals, or was simply ill-conceived. Hezbollah claimed that by merely surviving, it gained a symbolic victory over the more powerful Israeli army and that it continued to threaten Israel with rocket attacks after weeks of Israeli attempts to destroy its arsenal. Iran may believe that it achieved an ideological victory against Israel, seeing the conflict as producing increased Arab and Muslim support for Lebanese Shiites and for overall Iranian opposition to Israel. Analysts caution that increased Arab and Muslim support for Hezbollah may simply be a temporary phenomenon in response to solidarity with the Lebanese people and sympathy for Lebanese civilian casualties. Others see increasing domestic political pressure in moderate Arab states and elsewhere, such as Egypt, Jordan, Saudi Arabia, and even Turkey to condemn Israel and hold the United States partially responsible for civilian casualties in Lebanon as a way to deal with popular anger and their own Islamists.

Appendix A: Prelude to the Crisis

The following was originally the opening section of this report and has been included in the Appendix for use a resource on background to the July-August war. It will not be updated.

Although Hezbollah's July 12, 2006, kidnaping of two Israeli soldiers initiated the conflict in southern Lebanon, tensions in the region had grown since the Hamas electoral victory in Palestinian legislative elections in January 2006. Over the course of the next six months, Israeli-Palestinian relations deteriorated rapidly, culminating in renewed fighting in the Gaza Strip, only months after Israel withdrew entirely from the territory and evacuated its settlements. Most observers assert that Hezbollah used the clashes between Hamas and Israel as a pretext and justification for its July 12 attack. The following sections provide background on how the region was transformed over six months from one of relative calm to full-scale war.

Palestinian Elections and the Hamas-led PA Government[77]

On January 25, 2006, candidates of the "Change and Reform" party associated with the Islamic Resistance Movement (Hamas)[78] won a majority in Palestinian Legislative Council (PLC) elections, defeating Fatah, the prior ruling party of the PLC and of Palestinian Authority President (PA) Mahmoud Abbas. In response, the Quartet (i.e., the United States, European Union, United Nations, and Russia) stated that "there is a fundamental contradiction between armed group and militia activities and the building of a democratic state."[79] Subsequent Quartet statements established clear principles for reviewing further engagement and assistance with the Hamas-led Palestinian government, namely "that all members of a future Palestinian government must be committed to non-violence, recognition of Israel, and acceptance of previous agreements and obligations, including the Roadmap."[80] President Abbas endorsed Hamas' platform and cabinet candidates while expressing his demand that Hamas comply with the Quartet's principles and support his efforts to achieve a two-state solution to the Israeli-Palestinian conflict.[81] Since January 2006, Hamas leaders have largely rejected and refused to discuss the Quartet principles, arguing that

77 The following sections were prepared by Christopher Blanchard, Middle East Policy Analyst.

78 Hamas is an acronym for its full name in Arabic, *Harakat al-Muqawamah al-Islamiyyah* (the Islamic Resistance Movement).

79 Quartet Statement on Palestinian Legislative Council Elections, January 26, 2006.

80 Quartet Statements released January 30, 2006, and March 30, 2006. "The Roadmap" refers to the Performance-Based Roadmap to a Permanent Two-State Solution to the Israeli-Palestinian Conflict, which was presented to Israel and the Palestinian Authority on April 30, 2003, by the Quartet as a plan to achieve a comprehensive settlement of the conflict in three phases by 2005.

81 The PLC approved the majority Hamas-bloc on March 28, 2006.

while President Abbas may decide to negotiate with Israel, ultimately the Palestinian people would decide what to accept.

The Isolation of Hamas and Internecine Palestinian Violence

The electoral victory of Hamas surprised many outside observers and created a series of policy challenges for the Bush Administration, which had supported the election process as part of its efforts to reform the Palestinian Authority and its broader Middle East democracy promotion agenda. Israel and members of the Quartet took steps to limit the provision of non-humanitarian aid and financial resources to the Hamas-controlled Palestinian Authority based on Hamas leaders' refusal to accept the Quartet principles. Israel ceased its monthly transfers of approximately $55 million in taxes and customs revenue collected monthly on behalf of the PA, and two leading Israeli banks announced plans to sever their commercial relationships with financial institutions in the West Bank and Gaza Strip.[82] The Bush Administration suspended U.S.-funded development projects in the Palestinian territories and prohibited any and all U.S. persons from engaging in any unauthorized transactions with the Palestinian Authority because of its control by Hamas, a designated terrorist entity.[83] The European Union—the PA's largest donor—also suspended its direct aid to the Palestinian Authority and, at the Quartet's behest, has subsequently spearheaded efforts to develop an international mechanism to deliver assistance to the Palestinian people without transfers to or through Hamas or the elements of the PA under its control.

The loss of customs revenue and direct foreign aid created crippling budgetary shortfalls for the PA and significant derivative economic hardship for many Palestinian citizens. President Abbas referred to the steps as a "siege," and throughout April, May, and June 2006, tensions over unpaid salaries and disagreements over command responsibilities flared between the Hamas-led government and armed security force personnel loyal to Fatah. Palestinian leaders, including President Abbas, engaged in several efforts to end the intra-Palestinian violence and bring closure to open questions of official Palestinian support for the Quartet principles (see discussion of the National Accord Document below). However, before these efforts could bear fruit, fresh violence between Israel and Hamas erupted in the Gaza Strip and has escalated.

---

[82] Press reports suggested that Israel's Bank Discount and Bank Hapoalim have agreed to postpone their plans until August 15, 2006. The proposals would directly affect Palestinian civilians by severely complicating or preventing most Palestinian commercial financial transactions in Israeli shekels, the principal currency used in the West Bank and Gaza Strip.

[83] For more information see CRS Report RS22370, *U.S. Foreign Aid to the Palestinians*.

Israeli-Palestinian Fighting[84]

For many months prior to the late spring/summer 2006 outbreak of fighting, violence had been somewhat subdued due to some self-imposed restraint by the major players involved. In March 2005, Hamas and 12 other Palestinian groups agreed to extend an informal truce or "calm" (referred to in Arabic as a *hudna*) with Israel for one year. Some call the agreement a cease-fire even though it was a unilateral Palestinian declaration to which Israel was not a party. Palestine Islamic Jihad (PIJ) did not agree to the calm and was responsible for several suicide bombings within Israel in the period that followed. Hamas, which had been responsible for many suicide bombings during the second *intifadah* (Palestinian uprising against Israeli occupation) that had begun in September 2000, refrained from such attacks after declaring the *hudna*. It did, however, continue to fire mortars and rockets against Israeli settlements in the Gaza Strip before Israel's summer 2005 withdrawal from the region and into southern Israel after Israel's withdrawal. Israel usually responded with air and artillery strikes, but it also carried out what it terms targeted killings of terrorists.

On June 9, 2006, a Palestinian family was killed on a Gaza beach. The Palestinians claimed that the victims had been struck by Israeli artillery fire, but Israel denied responsibility for the deaths. Nonetheless, the incident provoked Hamas to call off its truce and intensify rocket fire into southern Israel.

Also in June, Palestinian factions held an intense national dialogue in the West Bank and Gaza in which they ultimately agreed on a National Accord Document (also known as the Prisoners' Document because Hamas and Fatah leaders imprisoned by Israel had collaborated on the first draft) to reconcile their positions and goals. Hamas leaders in Damascus, notably political bureau chief Khalid Mish'al, reportedly did not agree with the National Accord Document because it might be seen as suggesting that Hamas had moderated its views regarding Israel and the peace process. On June 25, members of the Hamas military wing (Izz ad-Din al-Qassam Brigades) and two other groups attacked Israeli forces in Israel, just outside of Gaza, killing two Israeli soldiers, wounding four, and kidnaping one. The perpetrators demanded the release of Palestinian women and minors from Israeli prisons. Some analysts suggest that Mish'al was behind the attack in order to assert his power over more "moderate" Hamas officials in the territories and to undermine the National Accord.

On June 27, after unsuccessful diplomatic efforts to secure the kidnapped soldier's release, Israeli forces began a major operation which Israel

[84] The following sections were prepared by Carol Migdalovitz, Specialist in Middle Eastern Affairs, on August 3, 2006.

explained as an effort to rescue the soldier, to deter future Hamas attacks including rocket launches from Gaza into southern Israel, and to weaken, bring down, or change the conduct of the Hamas-led Palestinian Authority government. Israeli officials claimed that Hamas had crossed a "red line" with the kidnaping and attack within pre-1967 Israel, but said that Israel did not intend to reoccupy Gaza.

On June 28, Hamas officials in the Palestinian Authority allied themselves with the kidnappers by adopting their demands. Israeli officials responded by insisting on the unconditional release of the soldier. On June 29, Israel forces arrested 64 Palestinian (Hamas) cabinet ministers, parliamentarians, and other Hamas officials in the West Bank and Jerusalem in what the Foreign Ministry described the action as a "normal legal procedure" targeting suspected terrorists.

In early military operations, Israeli planes bombed offices of PA ministries headed by Hamas, weapons depots, training sites, and access roads; ground forces entered Gaza to locate tunnels and explosives near the border and targeted Hamas offices in the West Bank. After Hamas militants fired an upgraded rocket at the Israeli port city of Ashkelon on July 4, the Israeli cabinet approved "prolonged" activities against Hamas; air and artillery strikes and ground incursions are still occurring. Meanwhile, Palestinian militants continue to fire rockets into southern Israel.

International mediators have tried to calm the recent upsurge in violence. The Egyptians have reportedly proposed a resolution in which Hamas would release the soldier in exchange for an Israeli promise to release prisoners at a later date. On July 10, however, Khalid Mish'al insisted on the mutual release or "swap" of prisoners. On the same day, Israeli Prime Minister Ehud Olmert reportedly said that trading prisoners with Hamas would cause a lot of damage to the future of the State of Israel, perhaps because it would continue a precedent that he seeks to break.[85] He later observed that negotiating with Hamas also would signal that moderates such as Palestinian Authority (PA) President Mahmud Abbas are not needed.

Abbas told a visiting U.N. team that he wanted to "de-link" the crisis in the Palestinian areas from the crisis that developed subsequently between Israel and Hezbollah in Lebanon in order to prevent non-Palestinian extremists (Hezbollah) from hijacking the leadership of the Palestinian issue.[86] Yet, neither President Abbas nor the Hamas-led PA government officials represent the kidnappers and can bring about a resolution. Hamas leader Mish'al appears to be in control of key elements in Hamas and

[85] "Olmert Says No Deal With 'Bloody' Hamas," *FoxNews.com*, July 10, 2006.
[86] As reported to the U.N. Security Council, July 21, 2006, meeting record S/PV.5493.

emphasizes the importance of cooperation between Hamas and Hezbollah and specifically calls for not separating the Palestinian and Lebanese issues.[87]

Enter Hezbollah

On July 12, under cover of massive shelling of a town in northern Israel, Hezbollah forces crossed the international border from Lebanon into northwestern Israel and attacked two Israeli vehicles, killing three soldiers and kidnaping two. Hezbollah thereby opened a second front against Israel ostensibly in support of Hamas. Sheikh Hassan Nasrallah, Hezbollah's leader, suggested that the Hezbollah operation might provide a way out of the crisis in Gaza because Israel had negotiated with Hezbollah indirectly in the past even though it refuses to negotiate with Hamas now. He said that the only way the soldiers would be returned would be through a prisoner exchange.[88] Although Hezbollah and Hamas are not organizationally linked, Hezbollah provides military training as well as financial and moral support to the Palestinian group and has acted in some ways as a mentor or role model for Hamas, which has sought to emulate the Lebanese group's political and media success. Hamas's kidnaping of the Israeli soldier follows a different Hezbollah example. Moreover, two groups share the goal of driving Israel from occupied territories and ultimately eliminating it; both maintain close ties with Iran.

Possible Explanations for Hezbollah's Attack. Nasrallah has publicly espoused an intention to kidnap Israelis to effectuate a prisoner exchange. Hezbollah, however, has the capacity to decide to act on its own and could have done so in the spirit of "Shi'a triumphalism" spurred by the Iraqi Shiites' ascension to power and Iran's pursuit of nuclear weapons. It also may have acted in solidarity with the besieged Palestinians or with its Syrian and Iranian supporters. Another explanation is that Hezbollah may have wanted to prevent a resolution of the Gaza crisis. Egyptian President Hosni Mubarak and Palestinian Authority President Mahmud Abbas have claimed that an agreement for a prisoner exchange had almost been reached, immediately before the Hezbollah attack, but Hezbollah's action complicated or prevented it.[89]

Some observers question Hezbollah's autonomy and offer other explanations for the July 12 action. Much speculation focuses on whether Hezbollah acted at the behest of or with the approval of Iran, its main sponsor, because

[87] Reported on Al-Jazirah Satellite Channel Television, July 31, 2006, Open Source Center Document GMP20060731635002.

[88] "Lebanon: Hezbollah Leader Holds News Conference on Captured Israeli Soldiers," *Al-Manar Television*, July 12, 2006, Open Source Center Document, GMP 20060712617001.

[89] "PA's Abbas Speaks to Journalists on Palestinian, Lebanese Develoopments," *Al-Hayah al-Jadidah*, July 16, 2006, Open Source Center Document, GMP 200607116620002.

Iran also supports Hamas or may have wanted to divert international attention from the impasse over its nuclear program. If the latter is the case, it gained only a limited time when the U.N. Security Council postponed consideration of the nuclear issue due to the Lebanon situation because, on July 31, the Council approved a resolution demanding that Iran suspend its uranium enrichment program by August 31 or face sanctions. Others suggest that Syria may be using its Hezbollah allies to resurrect its influence in Lebanon, from which it had been forced to withdraw in 2005.[90]

Other experts give a more nuanced appraisal. U.S. CENTCOM Commander General John Abizaid observed that it is more likely that Syria and Iran are exploiting the situation created by the kidnaping than that they ordered it.[91] U.S. State Department Coordinator for Counterterrorism Henry Crumpton reportedly asserted that Syria and Iran do not control Hezbollah, but added that Hezbollah asks Iranian permission if its actions have broader international implications.[92] In this case, Hezbollah may not have foreseen the implications of its July 12 operation and expected "the usual, limited" Israeli response characteristic of the period since 2000.[93] Therefore, it may not have asked permission from Teheran.

Appendix B: Chronology of Conflict on the Israeli-Lebanese-Syrian Border

December 1968	Israeli commandos destroy 13 passenger planes at the Beirut airport, in reprisal for attack by Palestinian terrorists trained in Lebanon on an Israeli airliner in Athens.
March 1978	Israel invades south Lebanon and sets up a roughly 10-km (6-mile) occupation zone. Most troops withdraw within weeks, leaving a security area held by Israel's Lebanese largely Christian allies, the South Lebanon Army (SLA).
January 1979	Israeli agents detonate a car bomb in west Beirut, killing Ali Hassan Salameh, security chief of the Black September group. Salameh, known as Abu Hassan, was one of the plotters of the Munich Olympics attack against Israeli athletes in 1972.

90 Syria already has benefitted somewhat from the conflict as the U.N. envoy investigating the assassination of former Lebanese Rafiq Hariri, and possible Syrian involvement in that killing, was evacuated from Beirut.

91 Greg Myre and Jad Mouawad, "Israel: Build up at Lebanese Lines as Fight Rages," *The New York Times*, July 22, 2006.

92 Sarah Baxter and Uzi Mahnaimi, "Iran's President Recruits Terror Master," *Sunday Times (London)*, April 23, 2006.

93 Observation of Mahmoud Komati, an Hezbollah political official, quoted by Greg Myre and Helene Cooper, "Israel to Occupy Area of Lebanon as a Security Zone," *New York Times*, July 26, 2006.

June 1982	Terrorist and rocket attacks by Lebanon-based Palestinian groups and Israeli counter-strikes culminate in Israeli invasion of Lebanon. Syrian army ousted from Beirut and thousands of Palestinian guerrillas under Yasser Arafat depart for Tunisia by sea.
September 1982	Israel captures Beirut after pro-Israel Christian leader Bashir Gemayel, who had been elected president, is assassinated. Hundreds of civilians in Palestinian refugee camps of Sabra and Shatila are killed by Christian militiamen allied with Israel.
May 1983	Israel and Lebanon sign peace agreement under U.S. patronage. Syria opposes it, and it is never ratified.
March 1984	Peace agreement with Israel is cancelled and Lebanese President Amin Gemayel breaks with Israel under Syrian pressure.
June 1985	Israel pulls back to a self-declared 15-km (9-mile) border security zone in south Lebanon controlled by Israeli forces and their Lebanese militia allies.
February 1992	Israeli helicopter gunships rocket car convoy in south Lebanon, killing Hezbollah leader Sheikh Abbas Musawi, his wife and six-year-old son.
July 1993	Hezbollah launches rocket attacks on northern Israel. Israel unleashes "Operation Accountability," a week-long air, artillery and naval operation.
April 1996	After Hezbollah began shelling towns in northern Israel, Israel launched "Operation Grapes of Wrath," a 17-day campaign against Hezbollah positions in south Lebanon. On April 18, Israeli artillery fire targeting Hezbollah rocket crews falls in and around a U.N. refugee camp near the village of Qana, killing 91 civilians and sparking international calls for an immediate ceasefire, achieved on April 26.
June 1999	The South Lebanon Army retreats from the Jezzine enclave north of the Israeli zone it held for 14 years.
May 2000	Israel ends 18-year occupation of south Lebanon. On June 18, 2000, the U.N. Security Council certifies Israel's withdrawal in accordance with U.N. Security Council Resolution 425 (1978). Lebanon and Syrian governments maintain that withdrawal is not complete since it did not include the disputed Shib'a Farms enclave.
October 2003	After a suicide bombing in Haifa killed 20 Israelis, Israel launches air strikes against an alleged terrorist training camp at Ain Saheb, northwest of Damascus, Syria.
September 2004	Months before the assassination of former Lebanese Prime Minister Rafiq Hariri, which was widely blamed on Syrian agents, the U.N. Security Council passed Resolution 1559 calling for withdrawal of "foreign forces" from Lebanon (Syria) and disarming of militia, such as Hezbollah.

Source: Reuters, "Chronology—Israel's interventions in Lebanon," July 19, 2006.

Appendix C: Recent Legislation

Congressional Oversight

In response to the current crisis, Congress took swift steps to express its support of Israel and that country's "right to take appropriate action to deter aggression by terrorist groups and their state sponsors," and to urge "the President to continue fully supporting Israel as Israel exercises its right of self-defense in Lebanon and Gaza." Some Members of Congress called on the President to appeal to all parties for an immediate cessation of violence, to commit to multi-party negotiations, and expressed support for an international peacekeeping mission in southern Lebanon. Others called for "the cessation of targeting . . . of infrastructure vital to noncombatants"; establishment of "a secure humanitarian corridor" for purposes of evacuation and transporting of food and medicine to the civilian population; an immediate cease-fire; and a "comprehensive and just solution". House Resolution 954 called on the President to appoint a Special Envoy for Middle East Peace. A Senate resolution, SRes 548, called on Syria and Iran to end their support for Hezbollah, for the warring parties to reach a cessation of hostilities, and for reconstruction to find international support.[94]

Legislation providing oversight (in order of introduction)

S./H.	Primary Sponsor	Introduced/ Referred	Intent	Status
S. Res. 534[95]	Sen. Frist	July 18, 2006 directly to floor	Congress' support of Israel, support of the President	Agreed to by voice vote, July 18, 2006
H.Res. 921	Rep. Boehner	July 18, 2006 directly to floor	Similar to S. Res. 534	Agreed to by vote of 410–8 (with 4 voting "present"). July 20, 2006
H.Res. 922	Rep. Ackerman	July 18, 2006 HIRC	Similar to S. Res. 534	No further action
H.Res. 923	Rep. Shaw	July 18, 2006 HIRC	Similar to S. Res. 534	No further action

94 The following section was prepared by Dianne Rennack, Specialist in Foreign Policy Legislation.

95 It was reported that some Members drafted a resolution that would have cast Lebanon's responsibility differently than those resolutions agreed to, and would have called for restraint from all sides. See Flaherty, Anne Plummer. "House on Track to Voice Support for Israel's Military Campaign in Lebanon," *Associated Press*, July 20, 2006. By contrast, S.Res. 534 "urges all sides to protect innocent civilian life and infrastructure . . . ". H.Res. 921 "recognizes Israel's longstanding commitment to minimizing civilian loss and welcomes Israel's continued efforts to prevent civilian casualties".

S./H.	Primary Sponsor	Introduced/ Referred	Intent	Status
H.Res. 926	Rep. Issa	July 19, 2006 HIRC	Similar to S. Res. 534	No further action
H.Con. Res. 450	Rep. Kucinich	July 19, 2006 HIRC	Support international peacekeeping mission in Lebanon	No further action
H.Res. 945	Rep. Jackson-Lee	July 25, 2006 HIRC	Cease targeting infrastructure, establish humanitarian corridor, cease-fire	No further action
H.Res. 954	Rep. Leach	July 26, 2006 HIRC	Establish envoy for Middle East Peace	No further action
H. Res. 955	Rep. Farr	July 26, 2006 HIRC	Cease-fire, and recognize Israel's right to exist	No further action
S. Res. 548	Sen. Dodd	Aug. 3, 2006 directly to floor	Calls on Syria and Iran to end support to Hezbollah; international community to support lasting solution and reconstruction	Agreed to by Unanimous Consent, Aug. 3, 2006

Evacuation Costs for U.S. Citizens

In the early stages of U.S. government-supported evacuations of Americans from Lebanon, the State Department required evacuees to sign promissory notes to assume financial liability of the costs of their evacuation. Several Members of Congress objected to this, noting that the law is ambiguous at best, and called on the U.S. Secretary of State to waive the statutory requirements for reimbursement.[96] On July 18, 2006, after the Secretary of State consulted with some Members, the State Department announced that such fees would be waived. Congress adopted two measures increase funding available to the Social Security Administration to provide temporary assistance to U.S. citizens returned from foreign countries (Public Law 109-250),

96 § 4(b)(2)(A) of the State Department Basic Authorities Act of 1956, as amended (22 U.S.C. 2671), authorizes the Secretary of State to expend funds to evacuate "U.S. citizens or third-country nationals, on a reimbursable basis to the maximum extent practicable" "when their lives are endangered by war, civil unrest, or natural disaster."

to authorize the Secretary of State to redistribute funds within the State Department's budget to cover the costs of evacuations, and to increase funding available to the State Department for such evacuations (Public Law 109-268). Other legislation, as yet not enacted, proposed to change permanently the statutory basis under which the State Department requests reimbursements, or replenish funds in the budget of the Department of Health and Human Services that are expended once evacuees have returned to the United States.

Legislation relating to evacuations (in order of introduction)

S./H.	Primary Sponsor	Introduced/ Referred	Intent	Status
H.R. 5828	Rep. Dingell	July 18, 2006 HIRC	Amends the State Department Basic Authorities Act of 1956 to remove the reimbursement requirement from permanent law.	No further action
S. 3690	Sen. Stabenow	July 19, 2006 SFRC	Authorizes the Secretary of State to cover the costs of evacuation related to the Israel-Hezbollah crisis without amending the underlying statute.	No further action
H.R. 5865	Rep. Thomas	July 24, 2006 Ways and Means	Amends the Social Security Act to increase near-term funding for assistance to newly evacuated U.S. citizens.	**P.L. 109-250** July 27, 2006
H.R. 5873	Rep. Smith	July 24, 2006 HIRC	Seeks to enact an amendment similar to that in H.R. 5828.	No further action
H.R. 5869	Rep. McDermott	July 24, 2006 Ways and Means	Similar to H.R. 5865.	No further action

S./H.	Primary Sponsor	Introduced/ Referred	Intent	Status
S. 3741	Sen. Lugar	July 26, 2006	Authorizes the Secretary of State to move funds from one account to another to cover the costs of evacuations. Increases funding available to the State Department for evacuation expenses (Wolf amendment).	**P.L. 109-268** Aug. 4, 2006
H. Res. 972	Rep. Hastings	July 28, 2006 HIRC	Expresses the House's appreciation to Cyprus and Turkey for the roles each played in sheltering evacuees.	No further action

Appendix D: U.S. Sanctions[97]

Syria, Iran, Hamas, and Hezbollah—the states and entities that Congress has noted for aggression against Israel, support for terrorism, or terrorist activities in the current crises—are currently subject to fairly comprehensive U.S. economic sanctions. The Secretary of State designated Syria and Iran as state sponsors of acts of international terrorism, in 1979 and 1984 respectively, thus triggering a myriad of statutorily required restrictions and prohibitions on aid, non-emergency agricultural aid, trade, support in the international banks, and other economic transactions.[98] Such a designation

[97] Prepared by Dianne Rennack, Specialist in Foreign Policy Legislation. For more on U.S. economic sanctions imposed on Iran, see CRS Report RL32048, *Iran: U.S. Concerns and Policy Responses*, by Kenneth Katzman. For Syria, see CRS Report RL33487, *Syria: U.S. Relations and Bilateral Issues*, by Alfred B. Prados.

[98] § 6(j) of the Export Administration Act of 1979 (P.L. 96-72; 50 U.S.C. 2405(j)), under which the state sponsor of acts of international terrorism designation is made, authorizes the curtailment of commercial trade in dual-use goods and technology to named countries. § 620A of the Foreign Assistance Act of 1961 (P.L. 87-195; 22 U.S.C. 2371) prohibits most foreign aid, non-emergency agricultural aid, Peace Corps programs, or Export-Import Bank funding to designated countries. § 40 of the Arms Export Control Act (P.L. 90-629; 22 U.S.C. 2780) prohibits government sales or leases of defense goods or defense services to named countries. § 505 of the International Security and Development Cooperation Act of 1985 (P.L. 99-83; 22 U.S.C. 2349aa-9) authorizes the President to ban the importation of goods and services from any state found to support acts of international terrorism. § 1621 of the International Financial Institutions Act (P.L. 95-118; 22 U.S.C. 262p-4q), § 6 of the Bretton Woods Agreements Act amendments, 1978 (P.L. 95-435; 22 U.S.C. 286e-11) each state similar prohibitions relating to international bank programs. § 502(b)(2)(F) of the Trade Act of 1974 (P.L. 93-618; 19 U.S.C. 2462)

generally triggers a prohibition on all but the most basic of humanitarian exchanges.[99]

Iran. Iran is also denied investment dollars intended for development of its petroleum industry under the Iran and Libya Sanctions Act of 1996.[100] Sanctions available under this Act, to be imposed on those who engage in unlawful investment in Iran, include a prohibition on Export-Import Bank funds, prohibition on exports, denial of loans from U.S. financial institutions, denial of rights to financial institutions to participate as a dealer in U.S. debt instruments, denial of procurement contracts, and any other transaction the President wishes to restrict if the authority to do so also is stated under the International Emergency Economic Powers Act (IEEPA). Petroleum-related investments are restricted also by Executive Order, and all new investments, regardless of the industry, are also restricted under the IEEPA.[101]

Syria. Although Syria has been identified as a state sponsor of acts of international terrorism since 1979, regulations that implement restrictions on trade and transactions with that country are less restrictive than those that pertain to other designated countries, reportedly because Syria is considered instrumental in the Middle East peace process. Congress took this into account when it sent the Syria Accountability and Lebanese Sovereignty Restoration Act of 2003 to the President.[102] The act, triggered by increasingly organized and forceful efforts in Lebanon to shed itself of foreign forces, and reflecting recent statements from the Bush Administration targeting Syria's involvement with terrorism, development and trade of weapons of mass destruction, and support of the insurgency in Iraq, requires the President to curtail trade and transactions until certain conditions are met. The act requires the denial of export licenses for any item on the U.S.

---

requires the withholding of favorable trade terms with cited countries. Annual foreign operations appropriations measures usually restrict or prohibit most forms of aid to designated countries. Other legislation prohibits certain transactions with countries found to be not cooperating with U.S. antiterrorism efforts, and still other legislation prohibits or curtails economic relations with third countries that aid terrorist-designated states.

99 Some trade, albeit highly restricted, is allowed with Iran and Syria. U.S. exporters may, for example, market agricultural commodities, medicines, and medical supplies to countries designated as supporters of international terrorism under terms of the Trade Sanctions Reform Act of 2000 (P.L. 106-387; 22 U.S.C. 7201 *et seq*.). Suppliers may provide spare parts related to civil air safety. U.S. persons may import and export informational material and propaganda. And since 2000, in an attempt through trade diplomacy to open relations with Iran, one may import nuts, dried fruit, caviar, and carpets from that country.

100 P.L. 104-172 (50 U.S.C. 1701 note). This Act no longer applies to Libya, following the President's determination that the country was in compliance with terms of the Act (Presidential Determination No. 2004-30; 69 F.R. 24907; May 5, 2004).

101 Petroleum-related investments in Executive Order 12957 (March 15, 1995; 60 F.R. 14615; 50 U.S.C. 1701 note); other new investments in Executive Order 12959 (May 6, 1995; 60 F.R. 24757; 50 U.S.C. 1701 note); and a consolidation of earlier orders in Executive Order 13059 (August 19, 1997; 62 F.R. 44531; 50 U.S.C. 1701 note).

102 P.L. 108-175 (22 U.S.C. 2151 note).

Munitions List (USML) or Commerce Control List (CCL). The act also requires the President to impose two or more of the following restrictions:[103]

- prohibit export of all products (except food and medicine, as made exempt by the Trade Sanctions Reform Act of 2000);
- prohibit investment in Syria;
- restrict travel of Syrian diplomats to only the environs of Washington, DC and the United Nations in New York;
- prohibit Syrian-owned air traffic in or over the United States;
- reduce diplomatic contact; and
- block transactions in property.

The President implemented terms of the Syria Accountability and Lebanese Sovereignty Restoration Act on May 11, 2004, by complying with the mandatory restrictions on USML and CCL exports, and by prohibiting U.S. exports and restricting Syrian air traffic.[104]

Lebanon. For FY2003 and each fiscal year thereafter, of any Economic Support Funds allocated or obligated to Lebanon, $10 million shall be withheld:

> unless and until the President certifies . . . that
>
> (1) the armed forces of Lebanon have been deployed to the international recognized border between Lebanon and Israel; and
>
> (2) the Government of Lebanon is effectively asserting its authority in the area in which such armed forces have been deployed.[105]

To date, the President has not certified that these conditions have been met. Congress, however, has ensured that the $10 million would be made available each year by overriding the restriction. Annual foreign operations appropriations measures have provided assistance to Lebanon "notwithstanding any other provision of law."[106]

Hamas and Hezbollah. In 1995, the President identified Hamas and Hezbollah as Specially Designated Terrorists (SDT) that threaten to disrupt the Middle East peace process and authorized the blocking of all assets and

---

103 The act provides the President the authority to waive the application of sanctions if he finds it in the national security interest of the United States to do so (§ 5(b)).

104 Executive Order 13338 (69 F.R. 26751; May 13, 2004). The Order also cited the National Emergencies Act and the International Emergency Economic Powers Act as its underlying statutory basis.

105 § 1224 of the Security Assistance Act of 2002 (division B of the Foreign Relations Authorization Act, Fiscal Year 2003; P.L. 107-228; 22 U.S.C. 2346 note).

106 Most recently, in sec. 534(a) of the Foreign Operations, Export Financing, and Related Programs Appropriations Act, 2006 (P.L. 109-102).

of transactions with persons associated with either organization.[107] Subsequent legislative and executive initiatives led to the creation of several other lists. Enactment of the Anti-Terrorism and Effective Death Penalty Act of 1996, which also authorizes deportation or exclusion from entry into the United States, generated the Foreign Terrorist Organization (FTO) list.[108] The President issued an executive order to create the Specially Designated Global Terrorists (SDGT) list in the wake of events of September 11, 2001.[109] All these lists were subsequently consolidated into one Specially Designated Nationals and Blocked Persons list (the "SDN list"), administered by the Department of the Treasury's Office of Foreign Assets Control in 2002.[110] Hamas and Hezbollah, or individuals associated with each, are on each of the lists.

107 Executive Order 12947 (January 23, 1995; 60 F.R. 5079; 50 U.S.C. 1701 note). Each of the executive orders cited in this paragraph are issued under the authority vested in the President in the National Emergencies Act (P.L. 94-412; 50 U.S.C. 1601 *et seq.*), and § 203 of the International Emergency Economic Powers Act (P.L. 95-223; 50 U.S.C. 1702).

108 Anti-Terrorism and Effective Death Penalty Act of 1996 (P.L. 104-132), particularly as it amends the Immigration and Nationality Act at § 219 (8 U.S.C. 1189).

109 Executive Order 13224 (September 23, 2001; 66 F.R. 49079).

110 Office of Foreign Assets Control SDN list: [http://www.treas.gov/offices/enforcement/ ofac/sdn/index.shtml].

DOCUMENT NO. 2

HEZBOLLAH: A CASE STUDY OF THE BATTLE FOR HEARTS AND MINDS

Intelligence and Terrorism Information Center at the Israel Intelligence Heritage & Commemoration Center (IICC) Report

June, 2007

Dr. Reuven Erlich and Dr. Yoram Kahati[1]

Overview

1. Hezbollah, "the party of Allah," is a Lebanese Muslim terrorist organization, established with Syrian support in 1982 during the first Lebanon war (Operation Peace for the Galilee). Hezbollah's ideology is radical Shi'ite Islam, and the organization serves as a tool to promote the goals of Iran and Syria, while at the same time it is an integral part of the Lebanon's political and social fabric.

2. During the 25 years of its existence Hezbollah, with massive support from Iran, established an **extensive military infrastructure** in Lebanon. Equipped with advanced weapons, it was activated against Israel in the second Lebanon war. In addition to its military infrastructure, Hezbollah also established a **civilian framework** which supports Lebanese Shi'ites in the fields of education, health care, religion and provides various social

Editor's note: The original version of this document included some color images that could not be adequately reproduced in this publication. Where necessary, captions, headings, and/or footnotes specifically relating to any omitted images have also been left out of the version reprinted herein. The main text of the document has not been affected by these omissions, but the footnote numbering has been changed where necessary to remove gaps between the footnote numbers.

[1] This study is one in a series of Intelligence and Terrorism Information Center articles dealing with various aspects of the battle for hearts and minds and a continuation of Dr. Reuven Erlich's February 14, 2006 article entitled "The battle for hearts and minds: The ongoing Israeli-Palestinian confrontation as a case study," http://www.terrorism-info.org.il/malam_multimedia/English/eng_n/pdf/i_p_conflict_e.pdfat. **Dr. Erlich** is the director of the Intelligence and Terrorism Information Center at the Israel Intelligence Heritage and Commemoration Center; **Dr. Kahati** is deputy director and the Center's head researcher. **Other researchers of the ITIC also participated in writing this study.**

services. Operated together, the two systems turned Hezbollah from a local Lebanese terrorist organization, with limited guerilla and terrorist capabilities, into an organization with military and civilian capabilities which go far beyond those of the other terrorist organizations both in the Middle East and the rest of the world.

3. Hezbollah, like other terrorist organizations, is fully aware of the importance of the battle for hearts and minds, whose objective is to influence the insights and perceptions of various target audiences in Lebanon and abroad. The battle is waged in many different ways, from information and propaganda to "education" and indoctrination. Alongside its **vast network of educational and cultural institutions,** the organization, with massive financing from Iran, built a media empire and learned (as did the other terrorist organizations) how to exploit the possibilities presented by the communications and information revolution.

4. The flagship of Hezbollah's **media empire** is its TV satellite channel, **Al-Manar,** which was set up in 1991 with aid from the Iranian Revolutionary Guards. The channel's broadcasts are slanted toward propaganda and reflect Hezbollah's Iranian-inspired ideology and political agenda. From the very beginning Hezbollah specialized in mixing propaganda with factual information, including **visual material from the battlefield.** To that end, it established a body called **"battle information,"** which embedded professional photographers in the squads attacking the IDF and the South Lebanese Army. Al-Manar is professional and effective, and it is extremely popular not only in Lebanon but throughout the entire Arab-Muslim world, the Middle East (including the Palestinian Authority) and abroad.

5. In addition to Al-Manar, Hezbollah owns a radio station (Radio Nur), newspapers, Internet sites in several languages (including English, French, Spanish and even Hebrew) and publishing houses (the most notable of which is Dar al-Hadi, named for Hassan Nasrallah's son Hadi, killed in south Lebanon). All of the above, in addition to the organization's extensive network of religious, "educational" and cultural institutions, and its internal indoctrination system, have a uniform strategic propaganda base determined by Hassan Nasrallah, with neither internal criticism nor leaks to the media.

6. Hezbollah's battle for hearts and minds employs terminology expressing Iran's extremist Shi'ite Islamic worldview. Special emphasis is put on fostering the values *of jihad* (holy war) and ***shahadah*** (death as a martyr for the sake of Allah) to justify the campaign of terrorism and guerilla warfare waged by Hezbollah (and the Palestinian terrorist organizations) against Israel. At the same time, Hezbollah does not hesitate to use Western terminology unrelated to Islam, such as ***muqawamah,*** a modern secular Arabic

term meaning "active resistance," or to adopt anti-Semitic European Christian motifs to encourage hatred for Israel and the Jewish people.

7. The **principal messages** sent by Hezbollah to its target audiences at home, in the Arab-Muslim world and the Western world are the following: the organization is Lebanese-nationalist in character and non-sectarian; it plays a role as Lebanon's "defender," which legitimizes its military infrastructure; hatred for Israel and denying its right to exist, which justify the terrorist campaign waged by Hezbollah and the Palestinians against it, and it uses its communications empire to encourage anti-Semitism and hatred for the Jewish people; hatred for the United States, by representing it as the source of evil and terrorism; Hezbollah's image of might, its "glorious successes" against Israel and Hassan Nasrallah as a role model; radical Shi'ite Islamic ideology and Iranian "leader Ali Khamenei" as a role model.

8. However, all of the above messages are rife with **internal contradictions and weaknesses.** Hezbollah's complete dependence on Iran (and Syria) and its regarding Khamenei as the source of authority contradict the image of "Lebanese nationalism" the organization tries to create; its clearly Shi'ite identity contradicts its non-ethnic stance; the radical Islamic Iranian ideology it represents contradicts the basic pragmatism which is characteristic of most of the Lebanese population, regardless of ethnic affiliation; its militant jihadist character contradicts Lebanon's national interests and even the interests of the Shi'ites themselves, who bear the burden of the results of Hezbollah's terrorism and guerilla tactics against Israel.

9. During the second Lebanon war Hezbollah waged a shrewd, successful propaganda campaign against Israel by using the media empire it had built over the years. The campaign was aimed primarily at Lebanese and Arab-Muslim audiences, but was also intended to influence Western and Israeli public opinion. **Hezbollah strove to delegitimize the IDF's actions in Lebanon** by inculcating the message that Israel was harming innocent Lebanese civilians, while ignoring the fact that it had established its military infrastructure within the midst of Lebanon's dense civilian population and was using them as human shields. At the same time, the organization waged a propaganda campaign and used psychological warfare to attack its Israeli target audience to lower morale, cause panic, increase fear of its rocket fire and strengthen Hezbollah's image as a strong organization possessing impressive operational capabilities.

10. The battle for hearts and minds in the second Lebanon war was spearheaded by Al-Manar TV, which survived and remained on the air, even after the Israeli air force bombed its building in a southern suburb of Beirut. It regularly broadcast factual information mixed with propaganda about its rocket fire and the successes it achieved in battle, and its broadcasts served as a source for many other media. Hassan Nasrallah was interviewed

six times during the war (four times by Al-Manar) and his statements were often quoted, especially in Lebanon, other Middle Eastern countries and around the world. To a great extent, during the war he succeeded in taking over TV screens (even in Israel), thus achieving an enormous advantage.

11. Hezbollah's propaganda achievements were also the result of **its ability to prevent foreign journalists, Arab and Western alike,** from accessing combat zones and to keep information away from them, making it impossible for them to cover topics which were incompatible with the organization's propaganda strategy. In general, foreign correspondents in Lebanon could not visit military sites (weapons' depots, bases, facilities) or interview organization operatives in the field. They were channeled into covering Lebanese civilians harmed by Israeli attacks and the damage done to Lebanon's civilian infrastructure. Reports by foreign correspondents show that only a few of them succeeded in evading supervision and the limitations placed on them by Hezbollah, and in operating in ways other than those dictated by the organization.

12. After the war Hezbollah launched another extensive propaganda campaign, whose objective was to inculcate its target audiences with the myth of the "divine victory." The campaign was based on three main elements:

A. The IDF's failure to stop or significantly reduce Hezbollah rocket fire throughout the war;

B. The harsh internal criticism expressed for the IDF and the government when the war ended: the many failures and mistakes exposed were used and are still being used by Hezbollah as grist for its propaganda mill.

C. Israel's achievements and Hezbollah's failures in the war were not sufficiently emphasized within Israel itself because of internal criticism. Therefore, they were not always picked in Lebanon and the Arab world, with the result that they did not succeed in undermining Hezbollah's victory myth.

13. However, as the dust settled in the months following the war, and as the Lebanese internalized the destruction wrought upon their country, the myth of the "divine victory" began to crack, and internal criticism increased because of the high price Lebanon was forced to pay for Hezbollah's military escapade. Therefore the organization was forced to switch to defensive tactics and must now face the accusations of its opponents in Lebanon for having dragged the country into an unnecessary war, and to fend off demands to disarm and implement UN Security Council Resolution 1701. The fierce dispute between Hezbollah and the opposition camp created an on-going political crisis in Lebanon, which is apparently far from being resolved.

A Portrait of Hezbollah

1. Hezbollah[2] ("the party of Allah," in modern political terminology) is a Lebanese Shi'ite Muslim terrorist organization. It was established by Iran with Syrian support in the summer of 1982 during the first Lebanon war (Operation Peace for the Galilee). Hezbollah's ideology is the radical Islam preached by Iran's Khomeini. **The organization is a strategic tool in Iranian and Syrian hands, and at the same time an integral part of Lebanon's political and social fabric.** Its radical Islamic identity and complete dependence on Iran and Syria dictate its jihadist militant stance towards Israel, against which it has waged a terrorist campaign and guerilla warfare since its inception (for the difference between terrorism and guerilla warfare, see below).

2. Hezbollah was established in the Baalbek region of Lebanon's Beqa'a Valley, from whence it spread to Shi'ite population concentrations in south Lebanon and Beirut's Southern Suburb. Within those areas Hezbollah established an **extensive military infrastructure,** aided and supported by the Iranian Revolutionary Guards. The infrastructure has the military capabilities of a sovereign state, which on the eve of the second Lebanon war included more than 20,000 rockets and advanced anti-tank missiles. Relying on Shi'ites throughout the world, Hezbollah also maintains an operational infrastructure outside Lebanon and has created a real potential for terrorist attacks abroad.

3. The terrorist and guerilla operations undertaken by Hezbollah since its inception have focused on Israel, although occasionally it has acted against the United States and other Western countries, as well as against Israeli and Jewish targets abroad. While conducting its routine, on-going terrorist and guerilla activities, it also built up a military infrastructure, which was upgraded after the IDF left the security zone in south Lebanon in May 2000. The infrastructure's resources were used against Israel following the abduction of two IDF soldiers near the Lebanese border on July 12, 2006 (the event which led to the second Lebanon war).

4. With massive Iranian aid and support, Hezbollah also established **an extensive civilian infrastructure.** With facilities and institutions for **education, health, religion, social services and propaganda,** it helps the traditionally deprived Shi'ite Lebanese community to advance its sectarian interests politically, economically, and socially. Hezbollah's civilian activities have enabled it to establish a broad power base within the Shi'ite community and to become an influential factor in Lebanon's internal politics.

---

[2] The name Hezbollah is taken from the Qur'an, Surah 5, Verse 56: "As to those who turn (for friendship) to Allah, His Messenger, and the (fellowship of) believers, it is the party of Allah that must certainly triumph," http://www.isna.net/library/quran/quran_e/5.html.

5. Hezbollah is motivated by radical Iranian Shi'ite Islamic ideology, exported from Iran and inculcated into the local Shi'ite population. The Ayatollah Khomeini, who instigated and led the Islamic revolution in Iran in 1979, and his heir, Leader Ali Khamenei, are two key personalities, both revered and acclaimed. They were turned by Hezbollah into role models, and in the second Lebanon war their pictures and sayings were found in Hezbollah offices and bases in south Lebanon. **It should be noted that Hezbollah did not develop its own unique Islamic ideology, but rather adopted the Iranian ideology *in toto*.**

6. Since its establishment, Hezbollah has succeeded in converting from a local terrorist organization to one with broad military, social and communications capabilities which surpass those known to be possessed by terrorist organizations in the Middle East and even beyond. That was made possible by the massive military and financial support and political backup provided by Iran and Syria, which view Hezbollah as an important strategic tool for waging their campaign against the United States and Israel, for increasing their influence in Lebanon and for advancing their regional interests.

The Battle for Hearts and Minds in Hezbollah Strategy

1. "Members of the resistance have come to the conclusion that while a bullet can wound a soldier or two, a picture can wound all of Israeli society, which is the most significant aspect of the conflict" (a senior member of Hezbollah's battle information department to *Al-Diyyar*, Lebanon, October 25, 1997).

2. The confrontation between Hezbollah, the Palestinian terrorist organizations[3] and Israel waged during the past decades is fought on three fronts:

A. **On the ground,** between the organizations initiating terrorism and those who carry it out, and the security forces which try to prevent terrorist attacks;

[3] **Terrorist organizations** wage a politically-oriented campaign with the deliberate use of various forms of violence, usually accepting no moral or legal limitations. They more often **target civilians** rather than at army and security forces, with the objective of forcing governments to change their policies in various fields. The acts of violence are carried out by terrorist organizations supported in many instances, directly or indirectly, by sovereign states ("terrorism supporting countries"). The international community regards terrorism as illegitimate and heinous because its perpetrators attack innocent civilians to promote their national interests, as opposed to guerilla warfare, whose targets are army and security forces.

B. **On the political front,** as both sides try to rally support from the international community and the Arab-Muslim world;

C. **In the battle for hearts and minds,** in which both the terrorist organizations and Israel, using a variety of means and methods, try to bring their positions and perceptions to the attention of the relevant target audiences.

Success or failure on one of the fronts can influence, and sometimes determine, the events in the other two.

3. In the battle for hearts and minds rival sides use many methods to try to influence, directly or indirectly, the perceptions and insights of their various target audiences. The methods used include education, indoctrination, information, propaganda and psychological warfare. The battle is waged not only to reinforce the positions of supporters but to win over neutral and hostile target audiences.

4. The terrorist organizations fighting Israel regard the battle for hearts and minds as extremely important. Hezbollah and Hamas, which are radical-Islamic in nature,[4] are particularly prominent. Both devote enormous resources to the battle and use it extensively when dealing with their rivals at home, as well as against Israel and the West. The weapons used are virtual: pictures shown on television, the written word, hard-copy media, the Internet, radio broadcasts, the sermons of the preachers in the mosques.

5. However, the harm done by such virtual weapons and their long- and short-term influence on morale are no less than those of real bullets. For better or worse, they influence the motivation, will and determination of both sides to continue the battle, despite the difficulties and the harm done to morale. In the battle for hearts and minds each side tries to create a positive image for itself and a negative image for its enemy and to draw favorable public opinion to its cause.

6. The terrorist campaign and accompanying battle for hearts and minds are waged on the backdrop of the communications revolution, especially exploiting satellite television channels and the enormous vistas opened by the Internet. The terrorist organizations, aware of the critical importance of the battle for hearts and minds, have chalked up impressive successes by using the media to transmit their messages, create public interest in their doings, generate support and sympathy for their causes and increase the influence of terrorism.[5]

---

4 The Islamic version of the battle for hearts and minds appears in the Hamas charter (Article 15), "... the propagation of Islamic awareness among the masses."

5 See the article (in Hebrew) by Boaz Ganor, "Communications and the strategy of terrorism," in *Security and Communications, the Dynamics of Relations,* The Ben Gurion Heritage Institute and Research Center, 2005, pp. 219–235.

7. Among the radical Islamic terrorist organizations which learned how to exploit the possibilities presented by the communications and information revolution, most prominent are Hezbollah, Hamas and Al-Qaeda. All three completely reject the messages spread by Western television and the Internet and at the same time use both media to spread their own messages and support for their terrorist campaigns. In a recent article about the second Lebanon war, American journalist Marvin Kalb related to the issue by quoting an Austrian expert and noting that "If Bin Laden didn't have access to global media, satellite communications and the Internet, he'd just be a cranky guy in a cave.' Maybe, but in fact Bin Laden does understand the enormous power of modern communications."[6]

8. **The Iranian regime invests great efforts to export its Khomeini-inspired radical Islamic ideology.** Hezbollah, inspired by Iran, established a broad network of educational, cultural (including publishing houses) and religious institutions, all intended to shape the Shi'ite mindset to the ideology of the Iranian Islamic revolution. Hezbollah also acts as the vanguard in exploiting the potential of mass communications in the battle for hearts and minds. Hezbollah is exceptional in that it is the only terrorist organization to possess a satellite television channel, a radio station and a vast Internet presence, all of which reach the organization's various target audiences. They are based on a uniform propaganda strategy, with no internal criticism and no leaks to the media. Thus Hezbollah has become a model for the Palestinian terrorist organizations, especially Hamas, in the battle for hearts and minds as well as in terrorism.

Hezbollah's Terminology

1. Hezbollah, having adopted the Islamic radical Shi'ite Iranian ideology, often employs specific terminology to express it. Hatred is fostered for Israel by calling it "the Zionist entity," and for the United States by calling it "the enemy of Islam" and "the source of world evil." The **tenets of *jihad* and *shahadah*** are also glorified and used to justify terrorist campaign waged by the organization against Israel.[7] At the same time, Hezbollah does not hesitate to employ Western terminology completely unrelated to

[6] Marvin Kalb, "The Israeli-Hezbollah War of 2006: The Media as a Weapon in an Asymmetrical Conflict," Harvard University, John F. Kennedy School of Government, February 28, 2007, p. 6. The Australian expert is Col. David Kilcullen, now on loan to the American State Department.

[7] For an in-depth study of the issue see our Bulletin entitled "Suicide bombing terrorism during the current Israeli-Palestinian confrontation (September 2000 - December 2005)" at http://www.terrorism-info.org.il/malam_multimedia/English/eng_n/pdf/suicide_terrorism_ae.pdf, pp. 4–10.

Islam. For example, it makes extensive use of the term **"resistance"** (see below), nor does it hesitate to exploit Christian European anti-Semitic motifs for its own purposes.

2. The terminology used by Hezbollah, like that of the Palestinian terrorist organizations, represents terrorist attacks as **legitimate actions** which cannot be surpassed. It glorifies the various types of terrorism, making no distinction between suicide bombing attacks and rockets fired into civilian populations, and turns the suicide bombers into role models for the younger generation. At the same time, the terminology negates the right of the State of Israel to exist. It makes free use of anti-Semitic slogans, sometimes with no distinction between Israel, the Zionist movement and the Jewish people. Two examples follow, one of Hezbollah's use of terminology borrowed from the West, and the other of Islamic terminology:

A. First, Hezbollah often uses the term ***muqawamah* ("active resistance"),** which is in effect a modern secular Arabic term. Hezbollah and its operatives are often called "the Islamic resistance in Lebanon."[8] The term was borrowed from the French *résistance* and was intended to imbue terrorism with the cachet of self defense against a foreign occupier. However, the French Resistance in the Second World War did not operate against civilians but rather against soldiers and military facilities with the objective of driving the Nazis out of France (and is therefore considered a guerilla movement). In addition, *muqawamah,* which is the translation of *résistance,* also expresses general resistance to an enemy arising from disgust related to non-military aspects, such as culture, economy and society, and not just narrow terrorist-operational activities.

B. **Secondly, Hezbollah uses the term *istishhad,* cognate with *shaheed*** (a martyr for the sake of Allah). It means "dying the death of Muslim martyr for the sake of Allah through self-sacrifice on the battlefield against an enemy," and has been attached principally to suicide bombing attacks. That is done to justify suicide bombing terrorism, since suicide is forbidden by Islam if its motive is personal, in which case it is called *intihar.* Hezbollah (and the Palestinian terrorist organizations) use the term freely and the message is that death as a martyr through self-sacrifice (i.e., a suicide bombing attack) is a transcendent, heroic action done first and foremost for the sake of Allah, and also for the sake of all Muslims. Its objective is to advance the Islamic terrorist organizations' political agenda, but also to provide the suicide bomber and his or her family with bonuses both in this world and the next, which "ordinary"

[8] The full name of Hamas in Arabic is the **Islamic Resistance Movement.** Both Hezbollah and Hamas took names integrating an Islamic motif with the term *resistance.* The Hezbollah faction in the Lebanese parliament is called Loyalty to Resistance.

Muslims usually do not receive. Thus the suicide bomber is glorified, and it is no surprise that **suicide bombing terrorism has spread from Lebanon throughout the entire Arab-Muslim world,** fomented especially by propaganda in the media and mosques.

Hezbollah's Target Audiences

1. Hezbollah is a terrorist organization that specializes, among other things, in the battle for hearts and minds, supported and inspired by Iran. That component of the organization's strategy enables it to upgrade its terrorist-operational and political activities. Hezbollah's battle for hearts and minds is directed at many target audiences, each of which is ranked differently in importance, and each receives unique and specially suited messages, some of them sometimes contradictory.

2. The classic propaganda is aimed at three types of audiences: the home audience, the neutral audience and the audience identified with the enemy. Hezbollah, although it is a Lebanese Shi'ite organization, is not satisfied with the home audience and makes a great effort to spread its propaganda to the other two. The various target audiences in Lebanon, the Middle East and the West are the following:

A. **The Lebanese,** whom Hezbollah regards as of supreme importance: Its power base is among the Lebanese Shi'ites and they are Hezbollah's first priority. The organization places special emphasis on children, adolescents and university students, whom it views as its future. In addition to the Shi'ites, there are various other sectarian groups, parties and organizations that Hezbollah regards as important, even if they are not necessarily among its supporters. Hezbollah works to increase their support and to be more effective with its opponents.

B. **Arabs and Muslims:** Hezbollah also regards the support of neutral target audiences in the Arab-Muslim world as important. It tries to gloss over the rivalry and contradictions between Shi'ites and Sunni Muslims and to stress what it views as common denominators, especially political and cultural factors, such as hostility toward Israel and the West, particularly the United States, support for the Palestinians, rejection of modern Western values and the preservation of the values of traditional Islam. Sometimes if does so by appealing directly to the Arab street, bypassing the heads of the pro-Western Arab regimes hostile to Hezbollah and the Iranian-Syrian axis (i.e., Egypt, Saudi Arabia and Jordan).[9] Hezbollah also regards the Palestinian target audience as

[9] Despite their basic hostility, both Saudi Arabia and Egypt permit Hezbollah to broadcast Al-Manar TV using communications satellites which they control, while Hezbollah conpensates them by avoiding blatant direct attacks on pro-Western Arab regimes (see below).

particularly important and pays it a great deal of attention to **encourage** the Palestinian terrorist organizations to escalate their campaign against Israel (see below).

C. **Western countries,** and concentrations of Lebanese and Muslim Arabs in Western countries: When dealing with the West, Hezbollah tries to play down its image as a terrorist organization in order to win justification for its military-terrorist attacks against Israel, to vilify Israel and its policies, and to make it difficult for the IDF to operate in Lebanon. Aware of the difficulties it faces in the West (as a terrorist organization operated by Iran), Hezbollah uses terminology specially adapted to Western ears, sometimes even glossing over or even hiding the radical rhetoric it usually employs when dealing with Israel, the Jewish people and the West.[10]

D. **The enemy target audience, Israeli public opinion:** Hezbollah attempts to manipulate Israeli public opinion with propaganda in Arabic and sometimes even Hebrew.[11] That is done to increase the impact of its terrorist activities, to widen the schisms within Israeli society and to turn Israeli public opinion against government policy makers. Its influence was felt both during the years of the IDF's presence in the security zone in south Lebanon and during the second Lebanon war, when Hassan Nasrallah used mass communications to hold a kind of dialogue with the Israeli public, employing propaganda and psychological warfare. He represented Hezbollah as an organization which was reliable and faithful to its word, as opposed to the Israeli leadership, which he claimed was hiding the truth from the Israeli public. The issue of the abducted Israelis and the corpses of IDF soldiers were exploited to humiliate the IDF and the State of Israel, to reinforce Hezbollah's achievement,[12] and to transmit the message that the Israeli government was not doing enough to release the Israelis held by Hezbollah. It was also intended to drive a wedge between the government and the people and to exert pressure on the government to comply with Hezbollah's demands.

---

[10] For example, in view of the fact that its broadcasts are forbidden in the United States and France (see below), at the beginning of April 2005 Al-Manar TV launched a news site on the Internet in Arabic and English (www.manartv.com.lb). It claims to focus on religious tolerance, strengthening culture and dialog, unity and cooperation between members of monotheistic religions and world cultures, a complete contradiction of the hate propaganda and encouragement of terrorism which are spread by Al-Manar TV.

[11] Hezbollah sometimes uses Hebrew texts or subtitles in its Al-Manar broadcasts and Websites. The language is usually fairly inarticulate and it is obvious that Hezbollah does not invest much effort in preparing them.

[12] For example, after the abduction of three IDF soldiers in 2000, Al-Manar TV broadcast a clip advising then-prime minister Ehud Barak to "count his soldiers every morning."

3. Hezbollah employs many methods to send the following messages to different target audiences, mainly to the internal Lebanese one:

A. **"Hezbollah is a popular, national-Lebanese non-sectarian movement which conducts political, social and cultural activities and is well-integrated into the fabric of Lebanese life."** Hezbollah attempts to play down its Shi'ite sectarian character and to deny its being a cat's paw for Iran and Syria, which provide it with massive military and financial aid and use it promote their own interests. The organization is also very sensitive to attempts to undermine that message (see below).

B. **"Hezbollah is the shield of Lebanon and its military activity against Israel is undertaken for the sake of Lebanese national interests"** (i.e., the "liberation" of the security zone, and, after the IDF withdrew, of the Shebaa Farms, and the release of the Lebanese prisoners in Israeli jails).[13] Hezbollah claims that its role as "Lebanon's shield" will exist as long as the country is weak and does not have its own "strong national army" to defend it.[14] The message, which is backed up by Hezbollah's supporters in the Lebanese government, is intended to allow the organization to claim that its military infrastructure terrorist and guerilla actions against Israel are legitimate, and to fend off the demands of opponents in Lebanon and abroad that it disarm.

C. **"Israel and the United States seek to harm Lebanon and they are behind all the ills and problems plaguing the country."** Hezbollah fosters hatred for Israel, denies its right to exist, strives to destroy it, justifies terrorism against it and disseminates anti-Semitic propaganda, sometimes without making a distinction between Israel, the Zionist movement and the Jewish people. Hezbollah also spreads hate propaganda against the United States and the American administration, representing them as a source of evil and terrorism, and accusing them of bloodshed, worldwide oppression, attempts to cause a split between Shi'ites and Sunni Muslims, etc.

D. **The image of Hezbollah's military might is nurtured, its successes against Israel are glorified and Hassan Nasrallah's personality cult is fostered** (as is that of Ali Khamenei, who serves Hezbollah as a source of religious authority). The organization represents itself as being unconquerable: "We have never suffered a defeat, never at any time . . . we will never be defeated, if Allah so wills it" (Hassan Nasrallah speaking before

[13] Hezbollah's communications media often deal with the Lebanese prisoners serving terms in Israeli jails for murder, and praise them and their actions. Samir al-Kuntar, who led a squad of terrorist-operatives and on April 22, 1979 murdered three members of the Haran family in Nahariya, receives special attention. Hezbollah continually promises the prisoners' families that it is working to secure their release and that they will be set free in the near future.

[14] To his opponents Hassan Nasrallah says: "Build that [strong Lebanese national] army and then we will be able to settle the issue of resistance" (Al-Manar TV, April 8, 2007).

students and their families, Al-Manar TV, April 8, 2007). **On the other hand, it exposes what it views as weaknesses and claims Israel's army[15] and leadership are weak, and its social fiber is disintegrating.** That is done to reinforce the claim that Israel's social, economic and political foundations can be undermined through adhering to a strategy of violence and terrorism (i.e., "resistance"). Nasrallah has many stock phrases which reappear in his speeches, such as claiming Israel is "weaker than a spider's web" (after the IDF's withdrawal from the security zone).

4. In addition to the above, and despite its claim as being a Lebanese organization, Hezbollah's propaganda department **also deals with fostering the personality cult of Iranian Leader Ali Khamenei** (since, with the exception of Hassan Nasrallah, it does not view any Lebanese figure as worthy of being called a leader). Cultivating the image of Khamenei and representing him as a worthy model result from Hezbollah's complete identification with the ideology of Iran's Muslim revolution, from its dependence on Iran and essentially from the fact that it is Iran's Shi'ite Muslim vanguard at the heart of the Arab Sunni Muslim world.

5. Moreover, Khamenei is represented as Nasrallah's patron, who in the past served (and who in the present sometimes serves) as Khamenei's senior legal emissary in Lebanon. It should be noted that in Shi'ite Islam, especially that represented by Khomeini, the leader always has a personality cult, a custom rooted in the high religious status of the Shi'ite Islamic Imam, who is considered both a religious and political leader.[16]

7. Since May 2000, when the IDF withdrew from the security zone in south Lebanon, and September 2000, when the Palestinian terrorist campaign ("second *intifada*") broke out, **Hezbollah has invested an enormous effort in the battle for the hearts and minds of the Palestinians. That is part of its commitment to the Palestinian cause and its desire to emphasize its identity as a radical jihadist Islamic organization.**

8. Hezbollah's media empire (at the center of which is Al-Manar TV) encourages the Palestinian terrorist organizations to escalate their campaign against Israel, praises the suicide bombing attacks and opposes agreements

---

[15] Hezbollah follows the Israeli media closely and exploits reports on the IDF's shortcomings in its battle for hearts and minds. For example, sheikh Nasim Qassem, Hezbollah's deputy secretary general, said: " Imagine a group from the Golani Brigade, about 200 of them, demonstrating because those in charge of them refused to allow them to be examined by an Israeli entity psychiatrist. That shows . . . the loss, the tension and the nervous breakdowns that plague them . . . [and] indicates the low fighting level of the soldiers of the elite units of the Israeli army" (Hezbollah publication Al-Intiqad Website, March 16, 2007). As of this writing (June 2007), Hezbollah has made intensive propaganda use of the Winograd Committee's Report regarding its investigation of the second Lebanon war.

[16] For the status of the imam in Shi'ite Islam, see Eitan Kolberg, "Shi'a: Ali's Faction," in *Protest and Revolution in Shi'ite Islam,* (Hebrew), ed. Martin Kramer, Tel Aviv University, pub. Hakibbutz Hameuchad, 1985, pp. 11–30; Nehemiah Levzion, "Islamic Factions, in *Chapters in the History of the Arabs and Islam,* (Hebrew), ed. Hava Lazarus-Yafeh, Chapter 9, pub. Reshafim, Tel Aviv, 1968, 2nd ed., pp. 180–189.

and arrangements brokered to calm the situation and bring an end to terrorist activity. Al-Manar TV serves as an important channel through which responsibility for the terrorist attacks carried out in the Palestinian Authority (including suicide bombing attacks) can be claimed and its broadcasts provide a stage for vicious incitement and anti-Israeli (and sometimes anti-Semitic) propaganda.

Weak Spots in Hezbollah Propaganda

1. The messages Hezbollah sends to its target audiences **have internal contradictions and weaknesses** which, when exposed in the past, caused the organization to react with anger. Hezbollah's Lebanese enemies often make use of the weaknesses.

2. The most important are the following:

A. **Hezbollah's overwhelming dependence on Iran (and Syria), and its global aspirations (symbolized by the globe on its emblem), which are in direct contradiction to the national-Lebanese image Hezbollah tries to create for itself:**[17]

1) For those reasons, many Lebanese, the Arab-(mostly Sunni) Muslim world and the international community do not consider Hezbollah an independent organization with its own policies and agenda, but rather one operated by extra-Lebanese forces which use it to advance their own interests and goals, which are far different from those of Lebanese nationalism.

2) In the face of Hezbollah's attempts to stress its independence and to minimize or obscure its overwhelming dependence on the support, aid and instructions it receives from beyond the Lebanese borders, there are nevertheless the massive amounts of visible military, financial and political aid it receives from Iran and Syria, and its radical Iranian Shi'ite Islamic ideology.

3) All of the above contradict Hezbollah's Lebanese nationalism and its independence propaganda, and make it more difficult for the organization to wage the battle for hearts and minds. That has been especially true during recent years, when in both the West and the Arab world fears have grown regarding Iran's aspirations for regional hegemony, and there has been increasing criticism of Bashar Assad's regime in Syria, Iran's strategically.

[17] In an unusual admission, Hezbollah's deputy secretary general sheikh Na'im Qassem said that the organization's policies, especially those relating to attacks, need religious authorization from the leader in Iran. He said that even the organization's activities in the last war, including firing rockets at Israeli civilians in the north of the country, received religious authorization from Iran (Iranian television channel Al-Kawthar, April 15, 2007).

The Revolutionary Guards emblem

Hezbollah emblem

Left: the emblem of the Iranian Revolutionary Guards. Right: the emblem of Hezbollah, established by the Revolutionary Guards and operated by the Quds Force. The similarity between them is obvious, and includes an upraised arm holding an assault weapon, the symbol of the revolution; militant verses from the Qur'an, which lend an air of radical Islam; the globe of the earth in the background gives militant Islam a global aspect; a book, most probably the Qur'an; and leaves sprouting form it, possibly a symbol of peace, perhaps intended to soften its militant message.

B. **Hezbollah's inability to transcend its sectarian Shi'ite roots, a situation diametrically opposed to the non-sectarian image it tries to project.** The social infrastructure upon which the organization rests is the Shi'ite community; Hezbollah's internal Lebanese interests are a function of Shi'ite interests; its concepts were taken from Shi'ite Islam and its ideology is radical Shi'ite Islam; its leadership and operatives are Shi'ite and it operates under the aegis of Shi'ite Iran. Therefore the Lebanese government and members of other ethnic and religious groups in Lebanon (Maronite Christians, Druze and Sunni Muslims) regard Hezbollah as an obviously Shi'ite sectarian organization. As a result, they are not willing to join its ranks (Hezbollah attempts to include other communities have met with resounding failure).[18] They view Hezbollah and its

[18] At the end of the 1990s, during the military confrontation in the security zone in south Lebanon, Hassan Nasrallah appealed to members of all the other sectarian groups to join forces with the

activities as endangering, in the long run, their interests and Lebanon's sectarian balance. The organization's radical Shi'ite Islam also creates fundamental difficulties when it comes to marketing its propaganda to pro-Western Arab countries like Saudi Arabia, Egypt and Jordan, and even to pragmatic secular sectors in Palestinian society. They regard both radical Shi'ite and Sunni Islamic movements as dangerous and threatening.

C. **The contradiction between the radical revolutionary Islamic ideology Hezbollah represents and the fundamental pragmatism characteristic of most of the Lebanese population, regardless of sectarian affiliation.** The pragmatism, bourgeois outlook and love of the good life of many Lebanese of all sects are fundamentally opposed to Hezbollah's Iranian ideology and its strict behavior codes. That contradiction exists not only between Shi'ite Hezbollah and the other communities in Lebanon, but also within the Shi'ite community itself, and it is manifested by the ideological and political rivalries between Hezbollah and the Amal movement, which represents pragmatic Shi'a in Lebanon. There is also clear contraction between the broad criminal activity undertaken by Hezbollah operatives (drugs, counterfeiting, smuggling cars, etc.), and the organization's ideology.

D. **The contradictions between Hezbollah's militant jihadism and the national interests of Lebanon and of the entire Shi'ite community:**

1) There are fundamental contradictions between jihad, "resistance" *(muqawamah)* and martyrdom *(shahadah)*, and the interests of Lebanon as an independent, sovereign state:

2) Between Hezbollah's desire to continue its existence as a military organization, and the provision of the Taif Agreement of 1989 according to which all ethnic militias are to be disarmed;

3) Between the Lebanese government's aspirations for the country's economic rehabilitation and Hezbollah's military operations, which create insecurity and political instability and drive away foreign investors and tourists;

4) Between the Lebanese government's interest in maintaining a stable regime and a national army to enforce its rule over all of Lebanon, along with the Shi'ites (especially in south Lebanon) who want to live a routine, tranquil life without poverty and distress, and Hezbollah's interests to maintain a military force as an alternative to

---

Islamic Resistance to turn it into the "Lebanese Resistance," not limited to the Shi'ite community. Hezbollah announced the establishment of the "Lebanese companies for resistance to the Israeli occupation" and called upon members of all religions to join. It was a feeble attempt to increase Hezbollah's power base and gain legitimacy, and it failed miserably.

a Lebanese army, to preserve its militant character, to control large areas in Lebanon and to prepare for the next round with Israel;

5) Between the fact that there is no real conflict of interests between Israel and Lebanon, and the fact that Hezbollah is militant and, inspired by Iranian ideology and policy, aspires to destroy Israel;

6) Between Lebanon's interest (especially among the Maronite Christians) to maintain good relations with the United States, France (which has traditionally been Lebanon's patron) and other Western countries, a situation anchored in centuries of history, and Hezbollah's anti-Western ideology, inspired by Iran and not by Lebanese interests.

3. **Another weakness is that according to Western public opinion, Hezbollah is a terrorist organization.** Despite its integration into internal Lebanese politics, Hezbollah is not regarded by Western public opinion as a legitimate Lebanese political organization, especially not by the United States. The reasons for that include its past involvement in deadly attacks against American and French targets and the abduction of Western hostages; its building an extensive military infrastructure with Iranian and Syrian aid, including the enormous rocket arsenal which was used against Israeli civilians in the second Lebanon war; the anti-Semitic statements it makes and its avowed striving to destroy the state of Israel. All of the above **reinforce its image as a terrorist organization** and an obvious emissary of the Iranian and Syrian regimes, both considered repellant not only by the United States but also large sectors of the international community.

4. Hezbollah is fully aware of its weaknesses and makes an effort to find responses for them in its battle for hearts and minds. Two of them are to gloss over inconvenient aspects and to avoid relating to problematical issues. **Hezbollah is especially sensitive to attempts to attack its image as independent and Lebanese-nationalist, and its image as Lebanon's shield.** Two examples are:

A. On June 1, 2006, Lebanese TV LBC, affiliated with the Christian Lebanese Forces, broadcast a satirical program which attacked Hezbollah's image as Lebanon's shield and questioned its reliability. The program showed an actor playing the part of Hassan Nasrallah being interviewed by a man dressed as a woman, and poked fun at Hassan Nasrallah's boasting about Hezbollah's ability to maintain a balance of terror with Israel. According to the script, liberating the Shebaa Farms was nothing more than an excuse for attaining long-term goals, and the launching of rockets from Lebanon into Israel while refraining from taking responsibility was irresponsible. The program incited a wave of riots within the pro-Hezbollah Shi'ite population in Beirut and the series was quickly taken off the air on the grounds that the station's broadcasting schedule was full.

B. **According to an ITIC Special Bulletin about Hezbollah's scout movement (the Iman Al-Mahdi Scouts),**[19] based on material seized during the second Lebanon war, the scout movement is a tool for radical Shi'ite Islamic indoctrination and is used to inculcate **Hezbollah's "battle legacy" in Shi'ite youth to prepare the next generation of Hezbollah operatives** (see below). After the Bulletin appeared, Hezbollah instituted a media counterattack which described it as a compilation of "fabrications and mistakes." An announcement issued by the Al-Mahdi Scout Movement stated that the movement was cultural and multi-sectarian in nature and membership was open to all Lebanese and not specifically to Shi'ites. However, it also stated that "Israel is a cancerous growth . . .We will continue to educate [our children on the basis of] the culture of resistance . . ." until the liberation of Jerusalem and all Palestine.

Weapons in the Battle for Hearts and Minds

Overview

1. During the 25 years of its existence, Hezbollah has devised **a variety of tools and methods to wage its battle for hearts and minds,** depending on the target audience. Some of them are the following:

A. **A direct appeal to Shi'ite supporters, using Hassan Nasrallah's undeniable talents as a speaker and propagandist:** Nasrallah, with the aid of other senior Hezbollah members, customarily appeals to the organization's supporters (especially Shi'ites) on political, religious or social occasions and during ceremonies. The events are routinely held in halls, religious and social institutions, and are attended by hundreds of participants. [20]In exceptional circumstances Hezbollah holds mass rallies (such as the "victory rally" after the second Lebanon war) with hundreds of thousands of supporters.

B. **A widespread media empire:** In the 1980s and 90s Hezbollah, with massive funding from Iran, constructed a media empire for disseminating propaganda to its various target audiences. **The network includes Al-Manar TV, Radio Nur, newspapers, Websites and publishing houses.** Hezbollah is an extraordinary example of a terrorist organization which has constructed a communications empire for propaganda purposes.

[19] For further information see our September 11, 2006 Bulletin entitled "Hezbollah's Shi'ite youth movement, 'The Imam al-Mahdi Scouts,' has tens of thousands of members Hezbollah's Shi'ite youth movement, 'The Imam al-Mahdi Scouts,' has tens of thousands of members. According to captured documents, they are indoctrinated with the principles of radical Iranian Islam. That indoctrination includes the personality cult of Iranian Leader Ali Khamenei and Hezbollah's 'battle legacy . . .'" at http://www.terrorism-info.org.il/malam_multimedia/English/eng_n/pdf/hezbollah_scouts_e.pdf.

[20] One of Nasrallah's favorite venues is the Sayyid al-Shuhada' Complex, in the Shi'ite Southern Suburb of Beirut.

C. **Clever use of Lebanese, Arab and Western communications:** Hezbollah either manages to insert its "news" into the broadcasts of other media or blocks information from reporters who are not willing to accept the rules Hezbollah dictates. "Factual information," the product of the organization's spokesmen and propaganda network, is selective and laced with propaganda. Hezbollah exploits Lebanese and foreign media to reach foreign target audiences outside Lebanon.

D. A **cultural-educational system** for the indoctrination of radical Islam among Shi'ites in Lebanon, especially the younger generation: to that end Hezbollah (with Iranian support) established a vast network of educational, religious and cultural institutions, including kindergartens, elementary schools, religious and trade high schools, religious colleges, teachers' seminaries, etc. The organization's most important target audience is its own operatives, regardless of rank and level, to whom internal memoranda are sent with exclusively tailored information. The memoranda deal with topics on the organization's agenda, both military and political, in which various aspects of the given issue are analyzed from both Israel's position and Hezbollah's.

Hezbollah's Media Empire

2. Lebanon has traditionally been an important center of Arab media. Thus Hezbollah faces stiff competition from the dozens of other newspapers, television channels and radio stations operating in Lebanon, some of whose professional level is high. That competition, and Hezbollah and Iran's awareness of the importance of propaganda, have forced Hezbollah to continually upgrade its communications capabilities, especially television and the Internet.

3. Hezbollah's entire communications network has **a common, uniform propaganda strategy determined by Hassan Nasrallah.** It is centralized and no allowance is made for differences of opinion or their expression. Senior Hezbollah members and the organization's functionaries (such as members of the Lebanese parliament) are often interviewed, and **express only such opinions as have been predetermined by Nasrallah.**

4. Most often interviewed are **Sheikh Na'im Qassem,** Hezbollah's deputy secretary general; **Sheikh Nabil Qaouk,** responsible for Hezbollah's southern sector; **Nawaf al-Mousawi,** responsible for international relations; **Mahmoud Komati,** a member of the political bureau; **Mohammed Yazbek,** a member of the Shura Council, Hezbollah's its top decision-making authority; **Hashem Safi al-Din,** head of the Political Council; **Mohammed Ra'ed,** head of the Resistance Faithful faction, and other faction members.

Al-Manar TV

5. The flagship of Hezbollah's media empire is its satellite television channel, **Al-Manar** ("the beacon"). It began on June 3, 1991, as a small land-based television station, and initially operated with the help of the Iranian Revolutionary Guards. During its first years it operated illegally. In 1997 it was officially listed as **The Lebanese Media Group—Al-Manar.**

6. **Al-Manar TV is propagandist in nature and its broadcasts reflect Hezbollah's ideology and political agenda.** It is both professional and effective, and popular not only in Lebanon but throughout the entire Arab-Muslim world, including the Palestinian Authority. It broadcasts news in Arabic, English and French, documentary series, various talk shows, music, etc. Its headquarters are in Beirut and it has offices in several Middle Eastern countries, including in the Palestinian Authority-administered territories, and an international network of reporters.

7. Al-Manar TV developed during the 1990s, at the height of Hezbollah's terrorist-guerilla campaign against Israel. It served the campaign's needs by broadcasting directly from the battlefield. Al-Manar photographers were embedded in the organization's squads operating in the security zone in south Lebanon as part of Hezbollah's battle information department. That was done even if it meant risking their lives. They brought the Lebanese, Arab and Israeli viewer photographs of attacks on IDF and South Lebanese Army posts and showed how land mines were laid. The pictures raised Hezbollah operatives' morale and upgraded the image of the organization's military achievements. The broadcasts were received in Israel and contributed to disagreements in Israeli society over the continued policy of maintaining the security zone.[21] Today as well Hezbollah battle information photographers and reporters accompany Hezbollah operatives on military actions.

8. Al-Manar TV began to bloom in 2000, after the IDF withdrew from Lebanon. **On May 25, 2000, the day the IDF left the security zone and nine years after the establishment of Al-Manar, its satellite channel was launched,** and since December 2000 it has broadcast 24 hours a day. The new satellite capabilities meant its broadcasts were received further afield. In addition, it had more air time, the studios were renovated and its news programs were given a facelift. **It was transformed from a local Lebanese station to a pan-Arab channel, popular throughout the Arab-Muslim world and among Muslim communities in the West.**

[21] Hezbollah's **battle information** department began its operations on September 18,1986. It became fundamental to Hezbollah and is part of the indoctrination received by children and adolescents (see below).

9. Hezbollah holds the stocks in the communications company operating Al-Manar TV, whose chairman of the board of directors and director general is **Abdallah Kassir.** Hezbollah uses **Al-Manar to disseminate the organization's radical Islamic worldview and its hostility toward Israel and the West.** In 1992 a high-ranking Ali Dahir, the station's first general manager, stated that "Hezbollah had founded the station to express the views of the oppressed . . . and advocate a mass media that respects Islamic moral and Muslim traditions." Therefore, he continued, "the goal of our station is to show the facts, focus on our hostility and hatred for Israel and its racist government system, whose downfall we see as one of our fundamental principles."[22]

10. **Al-Manar's broadcasts systematically provide backing and publicity for the terrorist campaign waged by Hezbollah and the Palestinian terrorist organizations against Israel.** Since the inception of the terrorist campaign against Israel (the second *intifada)* in September 2000, Al-Manar has served as a source of inspiration for the terrorist organizations (the "Palestinian resistance") and even calls itself "the resistance channel." Much of its programming is devoted to the Palestinian issue. It gives detailed coverage of the terrorist attacks carried out by the Palestinian terrorist organizations, enables them to use it as a forum to claim responsibility for attacks, including suicide bombing attacks, and also broadcasts anti-Israeli propaganda to Israeli Arabs.[23]

11. Brent Sadler, CNN's Beirut bureau chief, who visited Al-Manar TV in Beirut shortly after the beginning of the terrorist campaign against Israel, was deeply impressed by its anti-Israeli propaganda capabilities. He wrote that Al-Manar was meticulous in its choice of photographs dealing with the Israeli-Palestinian conflict and the violence in the Gaza Strip and West Bank, and edited them to make them dramatic and one-sided.

12. Al-Manar's objective is to enlist popular support for the Palestinians and to incite the Palestinians to take the path Hezbollah took, which led to Israel's withdrawal from south Lebanon. **The station employees claimed to be the first Arabs to use effective psychological warfare against the Israelis.** One of them said they tried to plant the idea in the minds of those living in the PA-administered territories that the successes of Lebanon could be repeated to liberate their land in Gaza and the West Bank (Brent Sadler for CNN, October 26, 2000).

---

[22] Jorisch, p. 20. For further information see our October 2004 Bulletin entitled "The Al-Manar TV station as a powerful instrument in Hezbollah's campaign over public perception," at http://www.terrorism-info.org.il/malam_multimedia//ENGLISH/MARKETING%20TERR0RISM/PDF/OCT3_04.PDF.

[23] Jorisch, pp. 14–15, 26.

13. In its prime-time broadcasts (including music), Al-Manar is not only blatantly anti-Israeli and expresses its desire to destroy the "Zionist entity," but it is also virulently **anti-Semitic,** which has let a number of countries (among them the United States, France and Spain) to ban its broadcasts (see below). In addition, it disseminates **anti-American propaganda** and encourages suicide bombing attacks, especially since March 2003, when the Americans and their allies invaded Iraq. A year and half before, on September 11, 2001, Al-Manar closely covered the attack on the World Trade Center and helped spread the calumny that the terrorist attacks in the United States were carried out by the Jews, Israel and the Israeli intelligence service (Mossad).

Al-Manar Broadcasts During the Second Lebanon War

14. **During the second Lebanon war Al-Manar TV spearheaded Hezbollah's battle for hearts and minds.** Its broadcasts, which were rife with propaganda and psychological warfare, accompanied the organization's rocket fire into Israel and the war on the ground in south Lebanon, and resounded throughout the Arab-Muslim world, even in Israel and the West. The Israeli Air Force bombed a building housing Al-Manar but it **continued on the air** using alternate broadcasting sites which had been prepared in advance (for further information see below, "The battle for hearts and minds during and after the second Lebanon war").

European and American Measures Taken Against Al-Manar

15. Between 2000 and 2004 Al-Manar TV uninterruptedly disseminated anti-Israeli, anti-Semitic and anti-American propaganda to the Arab-Muslim communities throughout the world. **Its programs were broadcast globally by means of a multi-national satellite system: Telestar 5** to North America; **NSS (New Skies Satellites)** 806 to South America; **Arabsat 3A** to the Middle East, North America and parts of Europe; **Hotbird 4** (a subsidiary of **Eutelsat)** to North Africa and Europe, including France; **NSS 803** to Africa and parts of Europe; **Nilesat** to the Middle East, and parts of North Africa and Europe; **Hispasat** to Spain, various other European countries and South America; and **Asiasat** to the Asian countries.

16. The last straw, and what led Western countries, especially France, to take practical steps against Al-Manar, was **an anti-Semitic series called "The Diaspora," which was broadcast during October and November 2003**, and viewed by Muslim communities in Europe.[24] Following the

[24] For further information see our November 2003 Bulletins entitled "Terror and anti-Semitism: additional episodes of the anti-Semitic TV series "The Diaspora," broadcast by Al-Manar, the Hezbollah television station in Lebanon," at http://www.terrorism-info.org.il/malam_multimedia//ENGLISH/IRAN/PDF/AL_MANAR.PDF and "Terror and anti-Semitism: additional episodes of the anti-Semitic TV series "The Diaspora," broadcast by Al-Manar, the Hezbollah television station in

broadcasts France's television and radio authority decided, as of March 17, 2004, to ban Al-Manar's programs from French TV. Attempts made by the Lebanese government through diplomatic channels to have the ban revoked were unsuccessful. It was ratified by the French supreme court on December 13, 2004, when it was determined that the channel's programming violated French anti-incitement laws and thereby endangered public order.

17. France was followed by other European Union countries and by the United States:

A. On March 17, 2005, the representatives of more than 25 of the national boards of radio and television supervision of European Union countries decided to act against television channels broadcasting incitement to hatred, racism and xenophobia. Following the decision, on March 17, 2005, **Holland** banned the satellite company NSS 803, whose head offices are in the Hague, from airing Al-Manar's programs. In July 2005 **Spain** ordered the cessation of Hezbollah's broadcasts via Hispasat.

B. On March 23, 2006, the Treasury Department of the United States announced it was activating Executive Order 13224 against Al-Manar TV, Radio Nur and the Lebanese Media Group, the Lebanese corporation of which Al-Manar and Radio Nur are subsidiaries. According to Stuart Levy, Treasury Undersecretary for Terrorism and Financial Intelligence, **Al-Manar TV and Radio Nur are Hezbollah's media wing, supporting the organization's terrorist activities.**[25] The Executive Order gave the Treasury Department and American law enforcement agencies the legal tools it needed to combat Al-Manar TV and Radio Nur, including confiscating their assets in the United States.

The Heading of the Treasury Department Announcement

18. The rationale behind the measures taken by the United States against Al-Manar TV and Radio Nur:

A. According to Stuart Levy, **"Any entity maintained by a terrorist group—whether masquerading as a charity, a business, or a media outlet is as culpable as the terrorist group itself."**[26] That is, as far as the American administration is concerned, there is no essential difference

Lebanon," at http://www.terrorism-info.org.il/malam_multimedia//ENGLISH/HATE-ANTI%20 SEMITISM/PDF/DIASPORA.PDF.

25 For further information see our Bulletin entitled "Another limitation placed by the international community on broadcasts emanating from Hezbollah's Al-Manar TV station The American Department of the Treasury designated Hezbollah's Al-Manar TV and Radio Al-Nour as terrorist entities pursuant to Executive Order 13224, which gives it the tools to enforce sanctions against their activities in the United States," at http://www.terrorism-info.org.il/malam_multimedia/English/eng_n/pdf/almanar_e0306.pdf.

26 From http://www.omedia.org/Show_Article.asp?DynamicContentID=1795&MenuID=681&ThreadID=1014003.

between Hezbollah (and other terrorist organizations) and the media, social and financial bodies belonging to it.

B. **The American announcement was accompanied by a kind of "indictment" of Al-Manar and Radio Nur,** and its main points were: Hassan Nasrallah and Hezbollah's operational council are in charge of the budgets for both Al-Manar TV and Radio Nur; prominent Hezbollah activists hold stock in the company operating them; Al-Manar TV employs Hezbollah operatives and one of them was even involved in collecting intelligence for the organization; Al-Manar and Radio Nur are involved in raising funds for Hezbollah. In addition to supporting Hezbollah, Al-Manar TV supports the Palestinian terrorist organizations on the American list of designated terrorist groups, and provides funds for a Palestinian Islamic Jihad "charitable society."

19. For France, Holland, Spain and the European Union, the scales were tipped toward banning Al-Manar by the **anti-Semitic content** of its broadcasts. **The American considerations were different and more a matter of principle:** Al-Manar was an integral part of Hezbollah, designated as a terrorist organization, directed by Iran and responsible, before September 11, 2001, for **the deaths of more Americans than any other such organization**.

20. The steps taken by the international community beginning in 2005 were a severe blow, although not a decisive one, to Al-Manar's ability to market its programs beyond Lebanon and the Middle East. The two remaining weak spots in the ban on Al-Manar's broadcasts are the **Arab satellite companies. Arabsat** (a pan-Arab company, most of whose shareholders are Saudi Arabians) and **Nilesat** (owned by Egyptians) enable their subscribers in the Middle East and southern Europe to receive Al-Manar's broadcasts. Since Saudi Arabia and Egypt **do not prevent Al-Manar's** propaganda programs from being received by subscribers, Hezbollah is very careful not to broadcast anything that might offend either regime. At the beginning of the second Lebanon war Egypt and Saudi Arabia were critical of Hezbollah, but did nothing to keep Al-Manar off the air.

Hezbollah's Internet Presence

21. **The Iranian regime** makes extensive use of the Internet, which it regards as an effective tool for spreading information and propaganda to various target audiences in the Middle East and around the world. To that end Iran has developed an impressive Internet presence of sites in Farsi, Arabic and English, and their uniform editorial policy is tailored to serve Iranian strategic needs.[27]

[27] For further information see our December 18, 2008 Bulletin entitled "The Iranian regime operates many Arabic-language Internet sites to spread its radical Islamic ideology to the Arab and Muslim populations around the world The Iranian regime makes a great effort to export Khomeini's radical Islamic ideology," at http://www.terrorism-info.org.il/malam_multimedia/English/eng_n/pdf/iran_int_e.pdf.

(The Palestinian and Islamic terrorist organizations also use the Internet as an important tool to spread their ideology.[28])

22. In addition to Websites directly under its control, Iran also supports Hezbollah's Internet network, where preference is given to sites in Arabic. The network is another component indirectly operated in the propaganda-indoctrination campaign being waged by the Iranian regime.

23. Hezbollah appeared on the Internet for the first time in 1997. It has been inspired, funded and given technical support by Iran. At first the organization had two sites, one affiliated with Al-Manar TV and the other called "Support for the Islamic Resistance." Immense resources were invested in expanding both of them during the past decade and turning them into a vast Internet network. The network is an important weapon in Hezbollah's battle for hearts and minds, since it can reach audiences in the Middle East and beyond.

24. **All 15–20 of Hezbollah's Websites are operated according to a uniform information-propaganda strategy integrated into Iran's battle for hearts and minds.** As can be expected, the sites emphasize what the organization is interested in inculcating. Hezbollah's target audiences are located in the Middle East (primarily Lebanon but even including Israel) and around the world, especially the Arab-Muslim communities in Western countries. The sites appear in a number of languages: **Arabic** (the organization's top priority), **English** (its second priority), and **French, Farsi and Hebrew.**

25. A study performed by the ITIC and published in December 2006[29] showed that the Webhosts of most of Hezbollah's leading Websites were in Arab-Muslim countries in the Middle East (Syria, Iran, Lebanon, Kuwait, Qatar). A number of hosts were also found in the United States and Sweden. Prominent among them was the **Syrian Telecommunications Establishment,** which hosted the "Islamic Resistance" site, Hezbollah's leading news site.

26. **Hezbollah's internet network can be divided into five main groups:**

A. Central news sites: The leading site is *Al-Muqawamah [al-Islamiyyah]* (The [Islamic] Resistance). It can be accessed through other addresses, among them *Ghaliboun* ("victors," a word in the Qur'an verse which

---

[28] For the importance of the use of the Internet for the dissemination of terrorist organization ideology, especially the Islamic organizations, including Al-Qaeda, see Matti Steinberg, "The Theology and Strategy of Al-Qaeda and the Global Jihad," (Hebrew), Part 1, *Keshet Hahadasha*, No. 12 (Summer 2005), pp. 66-75; also see Gabriel Weimann, *Terror on the Internet: the New Arena, the New Challenges*, United States Institute of Peace Press, 2006 (Foreword by Bruce Hoffman,Washington); for the influence of the Internet on Muslims to join the jihad, see "Online Fatwas Incite Young Muslims to Jihad," MEMRI (Middle East Media Research Institute), October 26, 2006, http://memri.org/bin/articles.cgi?Page=archives&Area=sd&ID=SP133506.

[29] For further information see our December 2003 Bulletin entitled "Terrorism and Internet: Hezbollah's widespread use of the Internet as a means to distribute anti-Israeli, anti-Jewish, and anti-American incitement," at http://www.terrorism-info.org.il/malam_multimedia/English/eng_n/pdf/hezbollah_int_e.pdf.

appears in Hezbollah's motto), **Al-'udwan al-Isra'ili ala'-Lubnan** ("Israeli aggression toward Lebanon"), *Moqavemat* ("resistance" in Farsi[30]), *Hezbollah TV, Nasrallah.* The addresses change every so often.

B. **Hezbollah media sites:** Al-Manar TV, Radio Nur, Al-Intiqad (a Hezbollah publication).

C. **Additional Hezbollah news sites:** *Wa'ad* (The promise), *Sumoud* (Steadfastness).

D. **Local town and village sites in south Lebanon:** Bint Jbeil, Deir Qanoun al-Nahar, Houleh.

E. **Sites belonging to social organizations and designated sites:** *Mua'ssasat al-shaheed* (The shaheed institution), *Kashafat* (Scouts of) *Imam al-Mahdi,* Jihad and Shahadah, Samir al-Kuntar (a site for the purposes of promoting the release of a convicted murderer currently in an Israeli prison), and the Dar al-Hadi publishing house site (recently inactive).

27. Using the above, Hezbollah reports the activities of its leaders, shows video clips and operational activities, and relates and responds to reports about activities or incidents considered relevant to the organization. The sites are used to foster Hassan Nasrallah's personality cult, to praise and glorify terrorist attacks and the shaheed myth, to spread hate propaganda against Israel and call for its destruction, and to disseminate anti-Semitic propaganda and hatred for the United States. The sites are also used for purposes of **psychological warfare.**[31] It should be noted that Hezbollah's media have their own Websites (especially Al-Manar), enabling the organization to spread its propaganda directly to the West, circumventing the limitations placed on it when Al-Manar TV's broadcasts were banned in Europe and the United States.

28. Most of Hezbollah's Websites crashed or were crashed during the second Lebanon war. However, after the war the organization upgraded its Websites significantly and added **new, technologically improved sites with frequent updating.**[32] Local Websites have been launched to reinforce the relationship between Hezbollah headquarters in Beirut and its supporters in south Lebanon, and to glorify the *shaheeds* who came from south Lebanon villages.

---

[30] An exceptional Website with an Iranian address appearing in four different languages, none of which is Farsi.

[31] For example, in 1997, when Hezbollah's Internet network was taking its first steps, it posted a picture of a soldier holding a Lebanese child with a subtitle reading "Israeli terrorism." The Israeli media reported that the soldier belonged to the IDF even though it was not specifically stated. It was a deliberate - and successful - piece of Hezbollah disinformation. An examination of the facts showed that the man was a member of the Lebanese civil defense force in the village of Qana and not an IDF soldier.

[32] Some of the sites are interactive. The Radio Nur and Wa'ad sites allow surfers to listen to their broadcasts. The Al-Manar site makes it possible to view its programs.

29. Hezbollah's Internet network is exceptional in its extent and quality, and far exceeds those of local terrorist organizations. It is another expression of the support Iran gives Hezbollah expressed, in our assessment, by the enormous sums of money needed to operate it at a high technological level in several languages.

30. In our assessment, Iran provides the necessary support because it views Hezbollah's Internet network as an additional means of spreading the ideology of Tehran's radical Islamic regime into Lebanon, the Middle East and throughout the world. Tehran has left its fingerprints on several Hezbollah Websites along with echoes of its anti-Israeli, anti-Semitic and anti-American propaganda. However, Hezbollah, as opposed to Hamas, has no Website (or other media) in Farsi, most likely, in our assessment, to hide its identification with Iran.

31. In addition to Hezbollah's Websites, there are sites and blogs which identify (or are identified) with Hezbollah in **Spanish** in Latin America. Their orientation is clearly South American, but they also call themselves "Hezbollah," use its symbols and terminology and identify with its messages of violence and hatred. Among them are a number of Websites and blogs in Latin America and Venezuela, and one in El Salvador.

Radio Nur

32. Almost from its inception Hezbollah established a radio station called Sawt al-Islam (The Voice of Islam), and sometimes Sawt al-Iman (The Voice of Faith) or Sawt al-mustadh'afin (The Voice of the Oppressed). In 1991 it changed its name to Sawt al-Nur (The Voice of Light). It complements Al-Manar TV and targets the Lebanese.

Journalism

33. In 1983 Hezbollah began publishing a Friday paper called **Al-Ahed** (The Covenant). The paper, which always features the portrait of the Ayatollah Khomeini (and after his death, that of his heir, Ali Khamenei), became the organization's main ideological tool. By means of its political and religious editorials, its Shi'ite worldview in day-to-day affairs, and columns about culture, religion and politics, Hezbollah shaped the opinions of its members.

34. Today the newspaper is still published on Fridays but is called **Al-Intiqad al-Ahed.** It is sometimes quoted as Al-Ahed and sometimes as Al-Intiqad (Criticism). Its editor-in-chief is **Ibrahim al-Musawi.** Since 1991 the organization has also published a Shi'ite Islamic monthly called **Baqiyyat Allah** (The legacy of Allah), which deals with matters of religion.

Books, Pamphlets and Information and Guidance Material

35. Hezbollah often publishes books, pamphlets and information and guidance material which are distributed throughout Lebanon and the Arab-Muslim world. Their objective is to spread Iran's brand of radical Islam, to encourage terrorist attacks and to foster hatred for Israel, the Jewish people, the United States and the West. Some of the publications are meant for the general Lebanese and Arab-Muslim public and some only for members of the organization.

36. Some of the books and other publications are **Iranian Shi'ite Islamic ideological material** translated into Arabic and distributed by publishers in Lebanon, some of them belonging to Hezbollah and some of them institutions and publishers affiliated with Hezbollah and Iran. Some of the publications do not specifically refer to Lebanon, and when there is a reference, it is modest and marginal compared with those of an overall Islamic character.[33]

The Dar al-Hadi Publishing House

37. Hezbollah's most important publishing house is **Dar al-Hadi,** which does not connect itself formally with the organization. It is named after Hadi Nasrallah, son of Hassan Nasrallah, who was killed by the IDF in south Lebanon in September 1997. Dar al-Hadi publishes books about Hezbollah, religion and the legacy of the Ayatollah Khomeini, as well as anti-Israeli, anti-Zionist and anti-Semitic propaganda.

38. One of its most important books was an authorized study of Hezbollah written by sheikh Na'im Qassem, Hassan Nasrallah's second in command, and published in Beirut in 2002, called ***Hezbollah—Methods, the Experience, the Future;*** it was also translated in English.[34] Sheikh Na'im Qassem devoted an entire chapter to suicide bombing terrorism and analyzing the *fatwa* (religious Muslim edict) enabling them to be carried out. He viewed them as "the main source of strength on which [we can] rely, and their effectiveness has already proven itself." He praised the achievements gained by suicide bombing attacks in Lebanon, however, he noted that the "weapon" should be used selectively, and only when they will cause the enemy heavy losses. They should not be used, he said, in "routine" activities.

---

[33] For further information see our October 10, 2006 Bulletin entitled "Hezbollah publications found during the second Lebanon war in south Lebanon inculcate the radical ideology of the Islamic revolution in Iran," at http://www.terrorism-info.org.il/malam_multimedia/English/eng_n/pdf/hezbollah_e_pub.pdf.

[34] *Hizbullah, The Story from Within,* Saqi Books, London, 2005. The cover of the English edition was changed to play down its Islamic message, and shows a demonstration of Hezbollah supporters waving the organization's flag.

39. Dar al-Hadi often publishes pro-Iranian Shi'ite Islamic books fostering the image of the Iranian Leader Ali Khamenei side by side with anti-Israeli and anti-Semitic books. Some examples are:

A. The Exalted of the Nation [i.e., true Muslims] and the Fateful Moments

The book, which was seized by IDF forces in the town of Ainata on August 15, 2006, was written by Ali Khamenei himself, and published by Dar al-Hadi in Beirut in 2000 (first printing). It deals with his philosophy. Pages 17–19 deal with the idea of *jihad* in the sense of fighting on the battlefield for the sake of Islam, devotion to Allah and every action which takes place as part of the confrontation with the enemy.

B. The Secrets of the Evil Ones

The book was published in Beirut by Dar al-Hadi in 2004. It is blatantly anti-Semitic and presents a ridiculous and wholly imaginary hypothesis about Jewish plots to corrupt and take over the world by means of secret organizations based on the Kabbala.[35] Its objective is to make the reader aware of the Jewish "plots" to increase hatred of the Jews and justify acts of violence against them.

C. Jewish Zionist Racism and its Religious Ideological Perspective: A study of the religious and historical background of the racist acts of the Zionist entity in Palestine, Lebanon, etc.

The book was written by Ali Hassan Tahe and published by Dar al-Hadi in 2002 (first printing). It repeats a routine claim found in anti-Semitic Islamic literature that Judaism is not a monotheistic religion, with the implication that Jews are infidels and **may therefore be killed freely.** The implication is that Muslims must fight a war to the death against them, as is customary regarding infidels.

D. Our Campaign against the Jews, Past and Present

The book was published by Dar al-Hadi in 2005 (first printing) and deals with anti-Semitic hate propaganda. Its central claim is that the Jewish religion is corrupt, and that is the reason for the confrontation between Judaism and Islam. The book is also anti-American and anti-Christian.

Other Publishing Houses

40. In Lebanon there are other cultural centers and publishing houses operated by Iran and Hezbollah or closely connected with them. They publish radical Iranian-inspired ideological material and foster Khamenei's personality cult. Prominent among them is the Iman **Khomeini Cultural Center** which publishes, among other things, ideologically oriented books.

[35] What is the Kabbala, find it.

Hezbollah's scout organization, the Imam al-Mahdi scouts, also issues books and other publications. For example:

A. ***Qaa'di*** (My Leader)[36]

Qaa'di was published by the Imam al-Mahdi Scouts, Hezbollah's youth movement, and includes biographical information about 'Ali Khamenei. He is represented as a **role model for youth and an example of a dedicated *jihad* fighter** who made a major contribution to the first stages of the Islamic revolution in Iran.

B. *A Reappraisal of The* Path of Eloquence[37]

The booklet, which was seized by IDF forces in the village of Kila on August 7, 2006, was published by the Markaz Bequiyyat Allah al-'Azam lil-Dirasat[38] in Beirut in 2000. It contains three speeches by Khamenei and is one of his 14 books issued by the publishing house which were translated into Arabic. *A Reappraisal of The* Path of Eloquence was translated in Qom, an Iranian city holy to Shi'ite Muslims.

C. America [is] the Source of Terrorism

The pictures are meant to show that Iran and Hezbollah protect the Palestinian people and defend it against the "injustices" inflicted on it by Israel because of American policy.

The booklet was published by Hezbollah and seized by the IDF in the eastern sector of south Lebanon on August 12, 2006. It contains the text of the speech Khamenei gave on March 17, 2002, reflecting the Ayatollah Khomeini's perception of the United States as the source of oppression, corruption, imperialism and terrorism in the world. Israel, as an American ally, participates in its policies.

D. The Mosque in the Reflections of the Imam Khomeini

The booklet, which was seized by IDF forces in the village of Maroun al-Ras on July 26, 2006, was published by the Imam Khomeini Cultural Center in Beirut in 2002. It surveys the importance of prayer, of the religious man and of meeting in the mosque to spread the ideology of the Islamic Revolution. It notes the political, social, educational and *jihad* roles of the mosque which is regarded, among other things, a means of disseminating the spirit *of jihad* and of meeting for the sake of the Islamic wars.

[36] The term *Ca'adi* designates, especially in the current context, i.e., Ali Khamenei, both a political and military leader.

[37] The term *nahj al-balagha* ('the path of eloquence) refers to a collection of Shi'ite religious books, including the sayings of 'Ali bin Abu Talib, the fourth Caliph and first Shi'ite Imam of Islam. He was famous for his eloquence.

[38] A publishing house specializing in Shi'ite religious books and which promotes books about Iran's Islamic Revolution, especially the works of the Ayatollah Khomeini and Ali Khamenei. It apparently also has connections with Hezbollah. See http://baabooks.com/index.php?language=ar.

E. Milestones in the Life of the Imam Khomeini and his Holy War

The booklet was seized by the IDF in the village of Dir Sirhan on August 24, 2006 and published by the Imam Khomeini Cultural Center in Beirut in 1999. It is an illustrated biography of the Ayatollah Khomeini and was apparently intended to provide adolescents with information about his deeds. It describes a series of events in which Khomeini participated, the most important of which were the overthrow of the Shah and the Iran-Iraq war. **The booklet ends by referring to the work of the Ayatollah Khomeini as being continued by the Leader 'Ali Khamenei.**

Leaflets, Flyers and Pamphlets

41. Among the material seized during the second Lebanon war were leaflets calling for contributions to Hezbollah and indoctrination pamphlets intended especially for Lebanese Shi'ite youth. The material was issued by a Hezbollah institution called The Islamic Resistance Support Association. It was founded in 1989 as a permanent fund-raising institution. **It also plays an important role in the battle for hearts and minds, especially among the younger generation, by distributing leaflets and collection boxes printed with Hezbollah propaganda.**

42. In the village of 'Aita al Sha'ab a kind of kit for children was found. It contained a quiz with prizes for the correct answers and **a call to contribute to Hezbollah.** The quiz was called **"The competition of the youth of victory - 2006"** and the six-part kit was produced by the Islamic Resistance Support Association. The center is a call for contributions, illustrated by coins dropping into a collection box and turning into bullets. The Arabic reads, "You support [with your contribution means] you show resistance."

43. The kit includes a 10-question quiz for **indoctrinating youth.** The questions read as follows:

1) To what did the honorable Sayyid Hassan Nasrallah compare the heroic confrontation, during which the Islamic resistance completely destroyed the two [Israeli] posts, al-'Abassiya and al-Ghajar?

2) Who is the most senior Lebanese [imprisoned] in the jails of the Israeli enemy.

3) Who said: "[Our] position is the weapon, but a handshake means recognition [of Israel]?"

4) Where did the Zionist enemy planes hit sheikh 'Abbas Musawi, his wife and baby son Hussein?

5) Which farm [of those mentioned] does not belong to the Sheba'a Farms?

6) When did the heroic battle of Maidun take place?

7) Where did the *istishhadi* [suicide bomber], sheikh Ass'ad Bero, carry out his heroic action?[39]

8) Who said: "We defeated Hezbollah" [just] after 13 Zionist soldiers were killed in the Shihin [a village in south Lebanon] action?

9) When did the Islamic resistance execute the high-ranking collaborator 'Akel Hashem [head of the western brigade of the South Lebanese Army, murdered by Hezbollah]?"

10) On September 18, 1986, the Islamic resistance penetrated an enemy post, and for the first time [in Hezbollah attacks] a battle information camera was used for filming operational footage.[40] What was the name of the post?

A Calendar with Radical Iranian Shi'ite Islamic Messages

44. During the second Lebanon war **calendars** for 2006 were seized which had also been distributed by Hezbollah's Iman Al-Mahdi Scouts, containing radical Iranian Shi'ite Islamic messages. For example, the main events for the month of April were Islamic Unity Week and **Leader's Day** (honoring Leader Ali Khamenei).

A Shaheed Instruction Booklet for Writing a Will

45. The booklet, which was seized by IDF forces in the village of Maroun al-Ras on July 16, 2006, was published by Hezbollah and intended to serve as **a guide for Hezbollah operatives in writing their wills.** There is a form to be filled out which asks for personal details, the name of the heir and the requested burial place. It also contains an appeal to parents and siblings, an appeal to *jihad* fighters in general and thoughts about *jihad,* as well as praise for *jihad* and self-sacrifice for the sake of Islam.

Fostering Khamenei's Personality Cult

46. **The text of a speech of the honorable imam, the commander al-Sayyid Ali Khamenei, may he have a long life, relating to recent events**[41]

The leaflet, which was seized by the IDF in the village of Rajamin on August 10, 2006, was published by Hezbollah. Publisher and date are not noted, but according to the contents it was written in 2003 or possibly later. In his speech Khamenei condemns the mass murders carried out throughout the world in which he includes what he calls "the actions of the Zionist enemy

[39] Assad Bero was a suicide bomber who blew himself up next to an IDF convoy near the Fatma Gate in the Metulla region on August 19, 1988,, killing seven IDF soldiers. Hezbollah turned him into a role model.

[40] Hezbollah embeds teams of battle information photographers in the squads which attack Israel, aware of the great importance of visual material in the battle for hearts and minds.

[41] "May he have a long life," literally, "May we take refuge in his shadow for a long time," an expression of honor and awe for an admired Shi'ite Muslim leader.

Left: The front cover, with Khanmenei's picture. Right: The back cover, showing the Hezbollah emblem

The Hezbollah emblem

in Palestine." Regarding the United States, he says that the terrorist attacks against it were a response to its striving to rule the world.

Exploiting Lebanese, Arab and Western Media

47. Hezbollah makes extensive use of the technique of **news-based propaganda,** that is, reporting what seems to be news, sometimes even attractive news, so that its neutral and hostile target audiences will accept it and in turn use it themselves. However, the information distributed by Hezbollah is clearly **selective and rife with propaganda** (see below, "The battle for heats and minds during and after the second Lebanon war").

48. Hezbollah's news-based propaganda is systematically distributed to the Lebanese, Arab and Western media by the organization's "information" department, its senior members and skilled spokesmen. The use made of the propaganda by Arab and Western media enables Hezbollah to increase the volume of its messages beyond what its own media can provide. Hezbollah works with the various media in the following ways:

A. **The Lebanese Media:** Hezbollah continually and systematically supplies the written and electronic Lebanese media with its own information. It provides them with speeches and statements made by Hassan Nasrallah and with announcements from its information department. Lebanese newspapers sympathetic to Hezbollah, or with pro-Syrian leanings, often give the organization a forum to express itself (for example, **Al-Akhbar,**[42] **Al-Safir** and **Al-Diyyar).** The Lebanese media, including

[42] A Lebanese daily supporting Iran and Hezbollah which began publishing during the second Lebanon war and which has become the most important mouthpiece of Hezbollah journalism in Lebanon. **Ibrahim al-Amin,** a journalist who expresses Hezbollah positions, moved to Al-Akhbar from Al-Safir.

those belonging to Hezbollah's opponents, often give Hezbollah a forum when the issue is **its fighting against the IDF.** That could be clearly seen during the second Lebanon war, when Lebanon's written and electronic media (LBC TV, for instance) gave Hezbollah propaganda prominent coverage and in general refrained from criticizingthe organization. (Only **after the war** was anti-Hezbollah criticism in the rival media renewed, and even increased.)

B. **The Arab Media:** Hezbollah makes extensive use of the Arab media, exploiting their correspondents stationed in Beirut. The written and electronic Arab media, most prominently popular Al-Jazeera TV, frequently provide a forum for Hezbollah's propaganda and interview its leaders, especially on topics touching upon the campaign against Israel. How Hezbollah exploits Al-Jazeera TV through Ghassan bin Jiddoo, the channel's Beirut chief, was made obvious during the second Lebanon war. Hezbollah gave Al-Jazeera an exclusive interview and allowed its correspondent to tour south Lebanon and interview Hezbollah operatives. During the war Hezbollah spokesmen often appeared all the Arab news channels, including Al-Jazeera TV, Al-Arabiya TV, the pro-American Al-Hura, Al-'Alam (an Arabic-language Iranian channel) and others. Thus Hezbollah had an important media stage which it exploited to represent Israel's "aggression" against Lebanon, and which enabled it to spread its messages throughout the Arab-Muslim world, giving it a significant media advantage. The Arab press, including newspapers published in London, also gave Hezbollah a great deal of coverage. [43]

C. **The Western Media:** Hezbollah habitually feeds "information" to the Western media, often through correspondents stationed in Beirut. Representatives of Hezbollah's propaganda department are in contact with journalists, arrange their visits to south Lebanon and make it possible for them to interview Hassan Nasrallah and organization operatives (in line with his interests). During the second Lebanon war, Hassan Nasrallah appointed an English-speaking press officer named **Hussein Nablusi,** who briefed the Western press corps in Beirut and gave them a guided tour of Beirut's Southern Suburb to illustrate the harm done to the civilian population (while glossing over the fact that the military infrastructure had been located within that population and that Hezbollah used them as human shields). Western correspondents stationed in Lebanon often relay information from Hezbollah without having the tools necessary to verify it. It can be assumed that the narrow angle of vision of the local Western correspondents, their fears for their

[43] For example, the popular Arab newspaper **Al-Sharq al-Awsat,** which is printed in London, between July 13 and August 16, published photographs from the war on the front page. With the exception of two, every picture showed the death and destruction in Lebanon caused by Israeli attacks. (From Marvin Kalb's article on the media war between Israel and Hezbollah in 2006, p. 13.)

own safety and their interest in keeping the lines of communication with Hezbollah open were what often made them give an unbalanced and biased picture of the organization.

49. **One of Hezbollah's strongest levers of influence is its sometimes exclusive access to information about events in Lebanon** and the confrontation between Lebanon and Israel. That was exploited by Hezbollah to **supervise the correspondents stationed in Beirut and to influence what they wrote.** They did so by preventing or granting access to information, sometimes exclusively, that Hezbollah was interested in spreading.

50. Marvin Kalb described the way Hezbollah used foreign correspondents during the second Lebanon war:[44]

> "Reporters always complain about access; specifically in this war they complained about not having had enough access to the battlefield. Their complaints were directed primarily at Israel, which tried to accommodate the needs of hundreds of foreign correspondents attempting to cover the conflict. **Complaints were rarely directed at Hezbollah, which controlled media access with a bookkeeper's rigidity.** Once, Hezbollah conducted a media tour of Beirut's Southern Suburb, inhabited by Shiite supporters whose homes and apartments had been badly damaged during Israeli air strikes.[45] The point was to again use the media as a weapon in the propaganda war for public approval, **and the media did not mind being used, though they were forced to pay a price.** Foreign correspondents were warned, on entry to the tour, that they could not wander off on their own or ask questions of any of the residents. **They could only take pictures of sites approved by their Hezbollah minders.** Violations, they were told, would be treated harshly. Cameras would be confiscated, film or tape destroyed, **and offending reporters would never again be allowed access to Hezbollah-controlled areas.**
>
> "So far as we know, of all the reporters taken on this guided tour, reminiscent of the Soviet era, only CNN's Anderson Cooper described the rigid ground rules for what they were—**an attempt to create and control a story.**[46] **And Hezbollah succeeded.** All of the other reporters followed the Hezbollah script: Israel, in a cruel, heartless display of power, bombed innocent civilians. Casualties were high. Devastation was everywhere. So spoke the Hezbollah spokesman; so wrote many in the foreign press corps . . ."

---

[44] Marvin Kalb, pp. 18–19. The boldface type was inserted by the authors of this study.

[45] Marvin Kalb quoting Anderson Cooper, "Hezbollah Remains Secretive Organization," Anderson Cooper 360 on CNN, August 9, 2006.

[46] Anderson Cooper.

51. Another description of the degree to which Hezbollah controlled the foreign press in Lebanon during the second Lebanon war was given by Captain Avihai Edri, head of the Arab media desk for the IDF spokesman:[47]

> "I heard about Hezbollah control of the media from one of the foreign correspondents, [who said] that every foreign correspondent in Lebanon had two Hezbollah members guarding him. I don't know [how] true that was, but [during the war] one of them was talking to one of his journalists [in Lebanon] through a microphone in her ear, and he said to her: **'Why do you keep whispering to me?'** Later on she told him, **'There were Hezbollah members sitting next to me, and I didn't want to get into trouble.'"**

The Differences Between Education and Indoctrination

52. **Education** is an activity designed to change human behavior (in the widest sense of the term) through a system of values, opinions, beliefs and (critical) thought processes which it desires to impart.[48] **Indoctrination** is an educational system designed to inculcate a doctrine[49] while preventing the target audience of the inculcation from making a critical evaluation of claims or independently making up its own mind.[50]

53. During the Cold War, when education became an arm of government propaganda, especially in the Soviet Union and the satellite countries, the term *indoctrination* was censured (and aroused disgust) in the liberal Western democratic countries. The censure was of its biased and one-sided teaching and educating methods, whose objective was to influence people's desires, actions and thoughts. Such educational methods were designed to ensure a **slanted result in accordance with a preordained worldview** (as opposed to democratic educational methods, which allow for self-criticism and a search for proof).

54. **Indoctrination** is one of the main tools used by the terrorist organizations in their battle for hearts and minds, and is part of their campaign against Israel and the Western world. The tool is intended is **to shape the perceptions of the internal target audience** in accordance with the ideologies and doctrines of the various organizations. Iran and Hezbollah carry out a wide variety of activities in Lebanon, especially among the Shi'ites (with the emphasis

[47] Comments made during a symposium held at the Israel Intelligence Heritage and Commemoration Center on December 26, 2006, called "The second Lebanon war, open intelligence and the media, open and hidden" (from *Mabat Malam* (Hebrew), a periodical dealing with intelligence and security, No. 48, March 2007 (henceforth "Open intelligence").

[48] Yosef Avinun, *The Philosophical Fundamentals of Education*, Part 1, (Hebrew), Dekel Academic Publishers, Tel Aviv, 1978, p. 84.

[49] **Doctrine:** a system of unproven but cohesive rulings used as the basis in principle for a belief or ideology. Doctrines are usually religious, political or military and their application is linked to an active plan of action.

[50] Aharon Kleinberger, *An Introduction to the Philosophy of Education*, (Hebrew), Yahdav Publishers, Tel Aviv, 1980, p. 109.

on the younger generation) **to indoctrinate radical Iranian Shi'ite Muslim ideology and its activist, militant anti-Israel, anti-Western values.**

55. **To that end, Iran established a broad network of educational, religious and cultural institutions in Lebanon,** which it views as the **primary means** of enlisting the younger generation into the Hezbollah's ranks and of shaping an Islamic Lebanese society at some time in the future. Its institutions import radical Iranian Shi'ite Muslim ideology in its entirety into Lebanon. **Hezbollah serves as its exclusive contractor, having no significant ideological input of its own.** Iran's emissaries were involved in establishing the network: the Revolutionary Guards, the cultural attaches in the Iranian embassies in Damascus and Beirut and the Imam Khomeini Cultural Center, whose home base is in Iran.

56. Sheikh **Subhi Tufayli,** who was a high-ranking Hezbollah figure when Hezbollah was established, testified as to the place and importance of education in Hezbollah's path of indoctrination. In an interview printed in a Lebanese paper he said that education begins at a very early age, when children visit the mosques where they learn the Qur'an, Islamic law, and to pray and fast. Later they take courses in [Islamic] culture. The mature students receive guidance, direction and training in the use of weapons, since Muslims live in "a world full of wolves at a time when a great attack is being waged on Islam and on the honor of Muslims by the whole world."[51]

57. Hezbollah's indoctrination system, which began in the 1980s in the mosques and the *husseiniyahs* (a kind of religious Shi'ite community center for cultural, religious, educational and social activities take place) and it was soon enlarged. By the end of the 1980s it included kindergartens, elementary schools and religious and technical high schools, religious colleges and teachers' seminaries.[52] All of them were built with generous funding from Iran, which carried over into their day-to-day activities as well (Iran even paid student tuitions and provided scholarships). Descriptions of some of the institutions and bodies dealing with indoctrination follow:

Religious Institutions *(khawzas)*

58. A *khawza* is a Shi'ite religious institution, many of which were established in Shi'ite centers in Iraq (such as Najaf) and Iran (such as Qom). By the beginning of the 1970s the *khawzas* began to be built in Lebanon in the Shi'ite population centers in Beirut, the Bequa'a Valley and south Lebanon. They instructed students in the fundamentals of activist Shi'ite Islamic ideology, and after the Islamic Revolution in Iran became institutions for

[51] From an interview printed in Al-Kifah al-Arabi, a Beirut daily newspaper, November 26, 1983, quoted by Shimon Shapira in *Hezbollah between Iran and Lebanon,* (Hebrew), Hakibbutz Hameuchad Publishers, Tel Aviv, 2000, p. 140.

[52] Shapira, pp. 140–141.

teaching the ideology of the Ayatollah Khomeini.[53] Some of those active in establishing the *khawzas,* among them Abbas al-Musawi and Muhammad Yazbek, later became high-ranking Hezbollah members.[54]

59. The *khawza* in Sidiqin, a village south of the Litani River, received special attention from Iran and was named for the Imam al-Mahdi ("the hidden imam"). In his book *Hezbollah between Iran and Lebanon,* Shapira has the following to say:[55]

> "Judging from appearances one might think that [the *khawza* in the village of Sidiqin] was in Iran: enormous pictures of Khomeini and his then heir-apparent, Montazeri, decorated the building and could be seen from afar, as if to display those to whom the students and teachers gave their loyalty. However, it was in south Lebanon and stood on the front line with Israel, damaged in bombardments more than once. For Iran, the *khawza* in Sidiqin was the model for the Islamic struggle . . ."[56]

The Imam Khomeini Cultural Center

60. **The Imam Khomeini Cultural Center** was founded in 1991 and **its head office is in Iran.** The main branch in Lebanon is in the Shi'ite neighborhood of Haret Hreik, Hezbollah's stronghold, in Beirut's Southern Suburb, and it has other branches throughout the country. The Center deals with translating and spreading the religious legacy of the Ayatollah Khomeini and the Iranian Islamic Revolution, and with fostering the "culture of resistance" (i.e., the culture of terrorism).

61. The Center has four departments: The library, which is composed of two separate areas, one for men and the other for women. Each area has several thousand titles and a reading room. There is also a computerized archive and a collection of video tapes and CDs containing various religious and cultural lessons, including those dealing with activist Iranian Shi'ite ideology. There are books about Islamic culture, especially those focusing on Khomeini's ideology. The public relations department maintains connections with other cultural centers, researchers, writers and academician. The center includes an exhibition of books by Khomeini and Khamenei and about the Islamic Revolution in Iran.

62. The Imam Khomeini Educational Center issues books and other publications of an ideological nature and books written to enhance the images of the

---

[53] Sheikh Abd al-Muni'm Mihna, head of the *khawza* in Sidiqin in south Lebanon, one of the most prominent *khawzas* in the country, testified that the "*khawza* is committed to the teaching of Khomeini, adheres to his path and graduates aware students loyal to Khomeini's Islam and the perception of an Islamic state. Their role is to lead the rest of society in that direction . . ." *Ibid.,* p. 142.

[54] *Ibid.,* p. 101.

[55] *Ibid.,* pp. 141–142.

[56] According to the *khawza* director Sheikh Abd al-Muni'm Mihna, more than 30 of its students were killed "in the struggle for Islam." (Shapira, p. 230)

Ayatollah Khomeini and his heir, Leader Khamenei (for a detailed description see above, "Books, pamphlets, and information and guidance material").

Hezbollah's Scout Movement

63. As part of the investment made in the education of the younger generation, Hezbollah has a scout movement called the **Imam al-Mahdi Scouts.** The movement is one of the means used by Hezbollah to indoctrinate Khomeini's radical Shi'ite Islam and the personality cults of Khomeini and Khamenei. Its ideology is based on hostility to Israel to the point of destroying it, the importance *of jihad* and the willingness of its followers to sacrifice themselves for the sake of Allah as part of *the jihad* against Israel.

64. The objective of the indoctrination is to prepare the Imam al-Mahdi scouts to join the operative ranks of Hezbollah when they reach the age of 17. In point of fact, more than 120 former al-Mahdi scouts have become *shaheeds* (including suicide bombers) during Hezbollah's violent campaign against Israel.

Fostering the Personality Cults of Nasrallah and Khamenei Among Children and Adolescents

65. Hezbollah even uses computer games for indoctrination. For example, on March 14, 2007, Al-Manar broadcast a program called Open Studio. Its subject was the development of computer games which would send the message that the second Lebanon war was a realization of Hassan Nasrallah's promise to secure the release of Lebanese soldiers held by Israel by means of abducting IDF soldiers (Al-Manar TV, March 14).

66. The name of the game was **The Kept Promise**[57] (Hezbollah's name for the second Lebanon war), which participants in the program claimed had been developed by young residents of south Lebanon. They also stated that the company producing the game would issue a beta version by the end of March 2007, and it would include all the battles fought by Hezbollah and the IDF day by day during the 33 days of fighting. In addition, they said that the game would have a "toned-down" version for young children and one for adults which would include pictures of blood and killing.

Fostering Contact with Student Organizations

67. Another channel through which Iranian and Hezbollah shape the perception of the Shi'ite Lebanese younger generation is **student organizations,** reflecting Iran's interest in student welfare. In a special ceremony held in the Iranian embassy in Beirut, sheikh Na'im Qassem, one of the heads of Hezbollah and Hassan Nasrallah's deputy, bid farewell to

[57] That is, his promise to secure the release of Lebanese prisoners by abducting IDF soldiers.

students with outstanding grades by telling them to "integrate your Islamic studies with modern scientific research . . ." "Your brothers in Iran," he reminded them "have great hopes for you because **you represent the line of the Islamic resistance."**[58]

68. In April 2007 Hassan Nasrallah spoke before 1,700 male and female students who had finished their university studies (in our assessment, most of them Shi'ites). The ceremony was held at the Sayyid al-Shuhadaa center Beirut's Southern Suburb, and its theme was "The graduating class of the martyrs of the kept promise [Hezbollah's name for the second Lebanon war]." Nasrallah handed out diplomas to some of the graduates. He congratulated their parents on their having made the effort, in spite of the war, to enable their children to finish their studies, and in particular praised the families of the students who had died in the war. To the students he said: "Your success is a message, in every sense of the word, expressing the genuine aspects of the **jihad path** you have chosen to tread . . ." (Al-Manar TV, April 8, 2007).

Indoctrinating Hezbollah Operatives

69. Hezbollah operatives, regardless of rank and status, are the organization's most important target audience. The organization customarily sends them **internal memoranda for their eyes only**.

70. One of the documents seized during the second Lebanon war was a "weekly political analysis," issued by Hezbollah for limited distribution to important functionaries within the organization ("members of the councils and those assigned to head departments and sections"). **Hezbollah is scrupulous in its field security:** every "weekly political analysis" recipient is required to destroy the memorandum after it has been read and the recipients' names are in code.

71. The June 1, 2006 issue of the **"weekly political analysis"** was distributed to Hezbollah operatives about a month and a half before the beginning of the second Lebanon war. It is written tersely and to the point and analyzes, from Hezbollah's point of view, the developments occurring on the three fronts most important to both Hezbollah and Iran: the Lebanese, Palestinian and Iraqi. It also relates to internal Israeli developments and their implications for Hezbollah and Lebanon in general.

72. The main points of the analysis are:

A. **Lebanon:**

1) The analysis begins with what it calls "the despicable crime committed by the intelligence services of the Israeli enemy in the heart of Sidon against two jihad warriors, the brothers Mahmoud and Nidal al-Majzoub . . ."

[58] Shapira, p. 143.

The reference was to the death of Mahmoud Majzoub, a senior Palestinian Islamic Jihad terrorist operative and his bodyguard who were killed when a charge in their car blew up. **The memorandum notes that the event was considered "a security success for the Israeli enemy" and that it exposed "a grave security breach" that had to be examined seriously.** A connection is made between the deaths and the revival of the activities of Hezbollah opponents in Lebanon (The February 14th group).

2) The memorandum goes on to analyze the "day of battle" between the IDF and Hezbollah on May 28, 2006, which began with rocket fire at an Israeli Air Force base on Mt. Meiron and ended with exchanges of fire between the IDF and Hezbollah along the Lebanese border.[59] While Hezbollah spokesmen **publicly denied** any connection between the organization and the rocket fire, **in an internal memorandum Hezbollah took responsibility for the event and even explained to its operatives the logic of the strategy behind it and Israel's logic.**

3) "Bombing the air control base at Mt. Meiron, near Safed, sent an exceptional message to the Israeli entity . . . **[one] with strategic importance. The bombing clearly showed the extent of our ability and willingness to reach targets deep within the Israeli entity and to hit them with precision. In that respect, bombing Safed was a decisive experience in re-emphasizing the balance of deterrence,** especially in all respects of the defense of the security heart of Lebanon . . ."

4) " . . .the response of the resistance [Hezbollah] **preserves the existing equation:** the shelling of northern Palestine (i.e., northern Israel] in retaliation for turning Lebanese civilians into targets [i.e., by implication in retaliation for the deaths of the Majzoub terrorist brothers, represented as Lebanese "civilians"]. In addition, it at least forced [Israel] to obey the international efforts relating to the cease fire."

5) The analysis claimed the anti-Syrian camp which opposes Hezbollah (the February 14 group) was trying to make political capital out of the confrontation between Israel and Hezbollah by raising the demand that the Palestinians and Hezbollah disarm. That was the context, according to Hezbollah, in which the letter sent by Lebanese prime minister Fuad Siniora to the Arab rulers should be viewed. In his letter, Siniora asked them to support him and his followers in pressuring Syria to deal with the issue of Palestinian weapons outside the refugee camp. The memorandum stated that:

"The Israeli [enemy] tried to provide fire support for The February 14 group's negative stance [both] in relation to the weapons [in the hands of]

[59] For further information see our May 29, 2006 Bulletin entitled "Katyusha rockets fired deep into the Galilee led to a day of exchange of heavy fire between the IDF and Hezbollah, the most significant since Israel withdrew from Lebanon (May 2000)," at http://www.terrorism-info.org.il/malam_multimedia/English/eng_n/pdf/hezbollah_be0506.pdf.

the resistance [Hezbollah] [and] the Palestinians. **In addition, the Israeli [enemy] tried to send a message regarding the necessity to strictly preserve the ceasefire and to prevent the resistance's weapons from being used in any possible confrontation with Iran . . ."**

B. The Palestinian arena: The memorandum analyzes Israel's intensive operational activity in the West Bank and Gaza Strip and the military and political struggle being waged between Hamas (and the organizations supporting it) and Fatah/Abu Mazen. Hezbollah's stated interpretation of the cause of the struggle is that "The current fierce conflict between Hamas and Fatah focuses on political options. That is because Fatah, Mahmoud Abbas and their allies, in coordination with . . .the international committee of four [the Quartet] and some of the Arabs sides, especially Egypt and Jordan, strive to extort concessions from Hamas and its government . . . regarding recognition of Israel, abandoning [the path of] resistance and adherence to agreements [already] signed, which Hamas refuses to do . . ."

C. Israel:

1) The response to the rocket fire **(which according to the internal memorandum was in fact carried out by Hezbollah)** the Israeli Air Force attacked two targets belonging to the Popular Front for the Liberation of Palestine - General Command, a pro-Syrian Palestinian terrorist organization headed by Ahmad Jibril. Hezbollah's interpretation of the attack on the PFLP-GC bases was that Israel was trying to assert its authority over the organization (and not over Hezbollah) to cause internal dissention among the organizations, and to raise the problem of the Palestinian weapons located outside the refugee camps, but without bringing about a counter-reaction from Hezbollah.

2) Hezbollah, for its part, responded with artillery and sniper fire and May 28, 2006, was a day of battle between Israel and Hezbollah, during which the IDF attacked about 20 Hezbollah strongholds along the border with air and artillery fire. Hezbollah interpreted the Israeli response as an attempt by Israeli Prime Minister Ehud Olmert to strike at Hezbollah and have it viewed as an achievement. According to the memorandum, "the Israeli enemy's new prime minister needs that achievement to provide himself with the aura his personality lacks, for he is not a member of the [narrow] circle of historic Zionist prime ministers . . .[60]

D. **Iraq:** The analysis gives a short survey of the deteriorating security situation in Iraq despite the establishment of a permanent government, and

[60] Following Hezbollah's logic, the organization should have expected Israel to respond aggressively to the provocative attack on July 12, 2006, in which two IDF soldiers were abducted. That is in **opposition** to Hassan Nasrallah's post-war claim that had he known that there was a one percent chance that the abduction of the soldiers would lead to the war he would not have had it carried out (see below).

poses questions regarding the security services of Iraq and the American army (called "the occupation army") to control the situation. **Most of the analysis is devoted to praise for the visit of Mottaki, the Iranian foreign minister in Iraq,** which "clearly overshadowed the political arena in Iraq during the past week . . ." His visit was designed "to emphasize the importance and might of the presence and role of the Islamic Republic [of Iran] in Iraq, as opposed to the reduction of the Arab role in Iraq." Iran is "a central player in the Iraqi arena" and part of the **solution** for Iraq, not part of its problem, as the Americans have tried to show. Thus **the war in Iraq is viewed through Iranian eyes and the memorandum does not provide an independent Hezbollah analysis.**

The battle for hearts and minds during and after the second Lebanon war

Hezbollah's Main Propaganda Messages During and After the Second Lebanon War

1. The second Lebanon war, like that which preceded it, was also a virtual war, fought with equal intensity on the field and in the media, on TV screens and in human perception. During and after the war Hezbollah waged an intensive and successful propaganda campaign against Israel, making shrewd use of the media empire it had built up over the years, **especially Al-Manar TV. The battle for hearts and minds was primarily directed at the Lebanese and Arab-Muslim target audiences, but it was also meant to influence Western and Israeli public opinion.**

2. Hezbollah sent a number of messages to its various target audiences:

A. **The delegitimization of IDF actions in Lebanon:** Israel was harming innocent Lebanese civilians and destroying civilian infrastructures in Lebanon. What was glossed over was that Hezbollah was using Lebanese civilians as human shields by situating their military infrastructures within densely populated civilian areas. The message was picked up and repeated by Arab and Western media and by human rights' organizations, which devoted a great deal of attention to the suffering of Lebanese civilians and the foreign nationals who fled from Lebanon.

B. Psychological warfare directed at the Israeli target audience: Its objectives were to lower morale, cause panic, increase fears of Hezbollah's rocket fire and reinforce Hezbollah's image as an organization that both does what it says it will and has impressive operational capabilities. That was done by monitoring the results of the rocket fire, providing wide media coverage for those results, making continuous reference to the places in the heart of Israel "still" not bombarded and to Hezbollah's intention to bombard them in the future.

C. Emphasizing the legitimacy of Hezbollah's continued existence as an organization with a military infrastructure which "defends Lebanon," especially in view of UN Security Council Resolution 1701 and the growing internal Lebanese criticism of its existence as an armed organization: That was done by claiming that Israel's "aggression" against Lebanon showed the need for an armed "resistance" which would defend it. That would be done while avoiding confrontation with the Lebanese Army and UNIFIL, which were deployed n south Lebanon after the war in accordance with Resolution 1701.

D. Justifying the abduction of the two IDF soldiers which led directly to the war[61] and shrugging off Hezbollah's responsibility for the war and the destruction wrought on Lebanon. That was done in view of the scenes of ruin and the accusations hurled at Hezbollah after the war by its opponents in Lebanon: they argued that the war did not break out because of the abduction of the two soldiers but rather was a move planned by Israel in advance. The abduction, according to Hezbollah's argument, was not intended to lead to a crisis and war but was rather a legitimate action, and it was Israel's response which was out of proportion. The Israeli response was not what Hezbollah had expected.

Al-Manar TV Spearheads Hezbollah's Media

3. **Spearheading the battle for hearts and minds has been Al-Manar TV,** which survived and continued broadcasting even after the Israeli Air Force had hit its building in the Shi'ite neighborhood Haret Hreik in Beirut's Southern Suburb. Al-Manar had a large viewing audience in Israel and in the Arab-Muslim world, and broadcast interviews with Hassan Nasrallah during and after the war. Its broadcasts of factual information (such firing on the Israeli warship across from the Beirut shore) were accompanied by large amounts of propaganda including elements of psychological warfare.

4. **Al-Manar TV's broadcasts during the second Lebanon war included:**

A. Frequent reports of the fighting in south Lebanon and the rocket fire into Israel: The commentators boasted of Hezbollah's success in launching long-range rockets into Israeli population centers, equating the Israeli and Hezbollah threats. They also boasted of the "surprises" the organization had in store for Israel. Al-Manar often showed offensive pictures of the dead and wounded, and scenes of the destruction of Israeli buildings (sometimes with fractured Hebrew subtitles) to reinforce

[61] As noted above, Hezbollah calls the war "the promise that was kept," that is, Hassan Nasrallah's promise to secure the release of Lebanese [terrorist] prisoners by means of abducting IDF soldiers to use as bargaining chips.

the psychological effect of the rocket fire and fighting in south Lebanon on Israeli morale.

B. Hassan Nasrallah as media star: During the war Nasrallah granted six interviews, four of them to Al-Manar, one to Al-Jazeera TV and one to a Lebanese channel called New TV. He apparently did not go to the TV studios but rather recorded the interviews in advance or used a cell phone. In any case, the interviews received broad coverage not only from Lebanese media but from Arab, world and Israeli media as well. **In point of fact, Nasrallah (and Al-Manar TV) to a great extent succeeded in taking over the TV tubes, even in Israel, thereby gaining an advantage in the battle against Israel for hearts and minds.**[62]

C. Horrific pictures of dead and wounded Lebanese civilians: Al-Manar showed many grisly pictures, giving extensive coverage to funerals and scenes of bombed houses and facilities. **On the other hand, only on rare occasions were Hezbollah operatives, bases and weapons shown.** That was done to represent Israel as "aggressive" and thus to cause the international community to exert pressure on it, while ignoring Hezbollah's extensive military infrastructure, the broad use the organization made of Lebanese civilians as human shields and the deliberate firing of rockets at Israeli population centers.[63]

D. **Broadcasts from an open studio:** Al-Manar TV often enabled Lebanese civilians and citizens of the Arab countries to come on camera and praise Hassan Nasrallah and Hezbollah, and call for the leaders of the Arab world to support the Lebanese. Every day it broadcast a large number of songs praising Hezbollah and its operatives. They were accompanied by scenes of Hezbollah's operational activity and calls for the struggle against Israel to be continued through the "resistance" (terrorism).

E. **Film clips as part of Hezbollah's psychological warfare aimed at the Israeli viewing public:** Al-Manar TV broadcast films emphasizing Hezbollah's ability to hit Israel's sensitive spots. To make the message clearer and stronger Hezbollah integrated successful rocket and missile hits (the attack on the warship opposite Beirut's shore, the hits in Haifa). The films were subtitled in Hebrew, sometimes ungrammatical and incorrect.

During the war Hezbollah added **new correspondents** to its ranks of commentators who surveyed the developments in Lebanon. They were

[62] The advantage was made even greater by the lack of an Israeli commentator of sufficient stature to provide the various audiences with an answer to the attractiveness of Hassan Nasrallah.

[63] For further information see our December 5, 2006 Bulletin entitled "Hezbollah's use of Lebanese civilians as human shields: the extensive military infrastructure positioned and hidden in populated areas," at http://www.terrorism-info.org.il/malam_multimedia/English/eng_n/pdf/human_shields.pdf.

deployed throughout the country and reported events in real time. Al-Manar often transmitted special news flashes, exploiting its advantage of being in control of the Shi'ite areas in which its military infrastructure was located and where the fighting was going on in south Lebanon.[64]

Blocking Access to Information from Foreign Correspondents

5. During the war Hezbollah managed to focus world attention on "Israeli aggression" and the destruction it caused to Lebanon, and at the same time to gloss over the use it made of Lebanese civilians as human shields by locating its military infrastructure among them and launching rockets close to residential dwellings. It was successful because it prevented the press corps stationed in Beirut from taking photographs of Hezbollah operatives, its military infrastructure and rocket fire from populated areas.

6. Marvin Kalb writes the following:[65]

> **"Rarely did the media use photographs to show that Hezbollah fired its weapons from residential neighborhoods in clear violation of international law. This was rare, because Hezbollah did not allow reporters to film such military activity.** Yet, on July 30, the Sunday Herald Sun in Australia did just that.[7] It published photos that, in its own words, 'damn Hezbollah' for conducting military operations in populated suburbs. In one photo of a 'high density residential area,' 'Hezbollah was shown preparing launch pads for 'rockets and heavy caliber weapons.' In another men were firing an anti-aircraft gun 'meters from an apartment block' where laundry was drying on a balcony. The newspaper said that the photos were 'exclusive,' shot by a 'visiting journalist and smuggled out by a friend.' The photos had to be smuggled out of Beirut, because Hezbollah would never have allowed them to be shot**- they proved that Hezbollah was in fact conducting military operations from heavily populated Beirut suburbs, which was considered a war crime."**

[64] In a discussion which took place at the Israel Intelligence Heritage and Commemoration Center, Oded Granot, Israeli TV Channel 1's senior Arab commentator said: " . . .my conclusions are extremely unpleasant. I remember that during the war I listened to the other side not only to find out what they were saying but also to learn what was going on, and where things were headed . . . Nasrallah announced the attack on the warship. I tried to find out if it had really happened, and I was told that it was just nonsense . . ." ("Open Intelligence and the Media"). Nevertheless, the information received by the Israeli, Arab and Western correspondents was selective and reflected Hezbollah's viewpoints. Oded Granot gave an example of an announcement by Nasrallah that another warship had been attacked, that one off Tyre, which was untrue, but reports of it appeared as breaking news headlines on the Arab stations for hours afterwards.

[65] Marvin Kalb, pp. 27–28.

[7] Chris Link, "Photos that Damn Hezbollah," Australia Herald Sun, July 30, 2006, http://www.news.com/au/heraldsun/story/0,,19955774-5007220,00.html.

The "Divine Victory" Myth Campaign

7. To indoctrinate its various target audiences with the myth of the "divine victory," even before the war had ended (and more so afterwards), Hezbollah began an extensive propaganda campaign. Its themes were praise for the organization's military capabilities, justification for the abduction of the IDF soldiers and a glossing over of Israel's achievements.

8. The campaign was waged in Hezbollah's written and electronic media, with an active part taken by Hezbollah supporters in Lebanon. Giant signs and posters in Arabic, English and French were hung throughout the country, praising the "divine victory."[66] Al-Manar TV and Radio Nur often lauded the "victory" and played songs of praise for Nasrallah and Hezbollah (for example, one called "Your victory shook the world").

9. The campaign had three main components:

A. **Israel's operational failures, which contributed to the success of Hezbollah's battle for hearts and minds:** The one Hezbollah boasted of most was Israel's failure to stop (or even significantly reduce) the rocket fire up to the last day of the war. To that were added the IDF's military failures in south Lebanon and in taking care of the Israeli civilian population. Thus Hassan Nasrallah boasted: "The July war was a world war against the resistance, but we won it, defeating all those who hoped in vain that we would be defeated, destroyed, exterminated . . ." (Al-Manar TV, April 8, 2007).

B. **The harsh internal criticism of the IDF and political leadership in Israel after the war:** The criticism and failures served as grist for Hezbollah's propaganda mill. It contributed to the myth of the **"divine victory"** and the claim that Israeli Prime Minister Ehud Olmert was "drowning in a sea of defeat." Hezbollah also made similar intensive use of the Winograd Committee Report and its echoes in Israeli society.

C. **The whitewashing of Israel's achievements during and after the war:** Israel successfully hit Hezbollah's long-range rocket launchers; Israeli Air Force capabilities were made known; the Lebanese Army and an upgraded UNIFIL were deployed throughout south Lebanon, making it difficult for Hezbollah to operate; Hezbollah's posts along the border in south Lebanon were destroyed; Hezbollah's infrastructure in Beirut was damaged; Hezbollah received serious criticism in both Lebanon and the Arab world. **Those achievements were not sufficiently emphasized in Israel (because of the enormous amount of criticism of the IDF and the government) and thus were not always picked up in**

[66] Beyond its religious connotations, the term also sounds like praise for Hassan Nasrallah, since "*nasr min allah*" ("divine victory") sounds like "Nasrallah."

Lebanon and the Arab world, and were not sufficient to undermine the myth of the "divine victory."

Arguments with Internal Criticism

10. As the dust settled after the second Lebanon war, and as the Lebanese internalized the pictures of ruin and destruction of their country, criticism increased **regarding the price Lebanon was forced to pay for Hezbollah's military escapade.** The organization has been forced more and more often to face the accusations of its opponents in Lebanon for having dragged the country into a needless war, and to deflect the demands that it disarm and implement UN Security Council Resolution 1701.

11. Because of the accusations hurled against Hezbollah by its Lebanese opponents, Hassan Nasrallah was forced to switch to **defensive propaganda** and to provide a response to their criticism, then and now. He admitted that he had been mistaken in his assessment of Israel's reaction to the abductions, saying that had he known the action (legitimate in his view) would lead to a war, he would not have carried it out. He also made the false claim that the abduction upset an Israeli-American plan to attack Lebanon in October 2006 and forced Israel to move against Hezbollah before it had finished its preparations. The defensive propaganda was accompanied by a political initiative (manipulated by demonstrations and protests) to overthrow the Lebanese government and hold early elections, or, to establish a government in which Hezbollah would have the power to veto decision.

Appendix

A Selection of ITIC Bulletins Dealing with the Various Aspects of Hezbollah's Battle for Hearts and Minds[67]

1. "Terrorism and Internet: Hezbollah's widespread use of the Internet as a means to distribute anti-Israeli, anti-Jewish, and anti-American incitement as part of the war for the hearts and minds," December 3, 2006, at http: // www.terrorism-info.org.il/malam_multimedia/English/eng_n/pdf/hezbollah_int_e.pdf.

2. "Hezbollah publications found during the second Lebanon war in south Lebanon inculcate the radical ideology of the Islamic revolution in Iran," October 10, 2006, at http://www.terrorism-info.org.il/malam_multimedia/English/eng_n/pdf/hezbollah_e_pub.pdf.

3. "Hezbollah indoctrination for the younger generation: book and coloring books captured in the second Lebanon war designed to inculcate children and adolescents with the organization ideology," September 21, 2006, at http://www.terrorism-info.org.il/malam_multimedia/English/eng_n/pdf/hezbollah_e_ind.pdf.

4. "Hezbollah's Shi'ite youth movement, The Imam al-Mahdi Scouts, has tens of thousands of members," August 25, 2006, at http://www.terrorism-info.org.il/malam_multimedia/English/eng_n/pdf/hezbollah_scouts_e .pdf.

5. "Documents captured during the second Lebanon war reveal how Hezbollah raises funds and at the same time furthers its propaganda and indoctrination campaign, stressing the younger generation," August 25, 2006, at http://www.terrorism-info.org.il/malam_multimedia/English/eng_n/pdf/hezbollah_funds.pdf.

6. "Terrorism and humor: a satirical show severely criticizing Hezbollah was shown on Lebanese LBC-TV," June 25, 2006, at http://www.terrorism-info.org.il/malam_multimedia/English/eng_n/pdf/lbc_e_tv.pdf.

7. "The fight against Hezbollah's inciting broadcasts: the French authorities reject Al-Manar's request to allow the resumption of its broadcasts in France," January 10, 2006, at http://www.terrorism-info.org.il/malam_multimedia/English/eng_n/pdf/al_manar_e0106.pdf.

8. "Further limitations on Al-Manar broadcasts: The Spanish government ordered the banning of Hezbollah TV station's broadcasts to Latin America via its satellite company, Hispasat," July 11, 2005, at http://www.terrorism-info

[67] All the Information Bulletins appear on the ITIC Website. The list is accurate to April 2007.

.org.il/malam_multimedia//ENGLISH/MARKETING%20TERRORISM/PDF/JULY12_05.PDF.

9. "Publishing and distributing anti-Semitic literature in the Arab world: the Hezbollah publishing house issues *Secrets of the Evildoers,*" May 19, 2005, at http://www.terrorism-info.org.il/malam_multimedia//ENGLISH/HATE-ARAB/PDF/JUNE1 05.PDF.

10. "France closes down Al-Manar TV channel," December 15, 2004, at http://www.terrorism-info.org.il/malam_multimedia//ENGLISH/MARKETING%20TERRORISM/PDF/DEC 7 04.PDF.

11. "Hezbollah, portrait of a Lebanese Shi'ite terrorist organization," Part A at http://www.terrorism-info.org.il/malam_multimedia/English/eng_n/pdf/heazbollah_p1.pdf, Part B at http://www.terrorism-info.org.il/malam_multimedia//ENGLISH/IRAN/PDF/JULY 03.PDF.

12. "Analysis of a Popular Resistance Committees' poster showing clear influence of Hezbollah, Hamas and radical Islam in general," August 1, 2004, at http://www.terrorism-info.org.il/malam_multimedia//ENGLISH/IRAN/PDF/JULY_03.PDF.

13. "Terror and Anti-Semitism: The Disapora: a featured anti-Semitic television series produced in Syria, is being broadcast for Ramadan by al-Manar, the Hezbollah TV channel in Lebanon," October 2004, Part 1 at http://www.terrorism-info.org.il/malam_multimedia//ENGLISH/IRAN/PDF/AL_MANAR.PDF, Part 2 at http://www.terrorism-info.org.il/malam_multimedia//ENGLISH/HATE-ANTI%20SEMITISM/PDF/DIASPORA.PDF.

14. "The Al-Manar TV station as a powerful instrument in Hezbollah's campaign over public perception," October 2004, at http://www.terrorism-info.org.il/malam_multimedia//ENGLISH/MARKETING%20TERRORISM/PDF/OCT 3 04.PDF.

DOCUMENT NO. 3

ISRAEL/LEBANON UNDER FIRE: HIZBULLAH'S ATTACKS ON NORTHERN ISRAEL

Amnesty International Report

September, 2006

Introduction

On the morning of 12 July 2006, Hizbullah fighters (known as al-muqawama al-islamiyya, Islamic Resistance) crossed the border into Israel and attacked an Israeli patrol near the village of Zarit. A number of Israeli military vehicles and a tank got involved in the clashes, at the end of which Hizbullah fighters returned to Lebanon with two captured Israeli soldiers. Eight other soldiers were killed. At the same time Hizbullah carried out diversionary attacks along the border. Hizbullah officials told Amnesty International that no civilian was targeted on 12 July, although according to press accounts a number were injured in these other attacks.[1]

Hizbullah named its "Operation True Promise" after a "promise" by its Secretary General, Hasan Nasrallah, to capture Israeli soldiers in order to exchange them for Lebanese prisoners in Israeli jails. Israeli Prime Minister Ehud Olmert declared Hizbullah's attack an "act of war" and promised Lebanon a "very painful and far-reaching response".

For the next month—until 14 August—a major military confrontation took place between Hizbullah and Israel. Israel's "Operation Change of Direction" involved widespread attacks across Lebanon from land, sea and air, killing some 1,000 civilians. Hizbullah launched thousands of Katyusha and other rockets on northern Israel, killing 43 civilians. Several hundred thousand Israeli civilians and approximately one million Lebanese civilians were displaced. UN Security Council resolution 1701 brought about a ceasefire and provided for the deployment of a reinforced UN peacekeeping

[1] See, for example, Amos Harel, "Hezbollah kills 8 soldiers, kidnaps two in offensive on northern border", *Haaretz*, 13 July 2006, http://www.haaretz.com/hasen/pages/ShArt.jhtml?itemNo=737825.

mission in south Lebanon, one of several measures aimed at consolidating the end of the fighting.

The briefing that follows summarizes Amnesty International's assessment of and concerns about violations of international humanitarian law by Hizbullah in its attacks on northern Israel. It is based on first-hand information from visits to Israel and Lebanon; interviews with dozens of victims; official statements; discussions with Israeli and Lebanese military and government officials, as well as senior Hizbullah officials; information from non-governmental groups; and media reports.

This briefing does not address Israeli charges that Hizbullah used the civilian population as a cover for its military activities and that it must therefore be held responsible for the harm caused to civilians by Israeli attacks. Specifically, Israel accuses Hizbullah of having bases in tunnels and other facilities within towns and villages; of storing Katyusha rockets and other weapons there; of firing Katyusha rockets from close proximity to civilian houses; and of having prevented civilians from fleeing their villages.

Hizbullah denies any policy of endangering civilians and accuses Israel of deliberating targeting civilians in Lebanon. Hizbullah officials deny that their fighters launched Katyusha rockets into Israel from populated areas or that they stored their rockets in such areas. They acknowledge that other weapons and facilities are present in towns and villages and argue that they are needed for their fighters to defend their communities against Israeli attacks. Hizbullah strongly denies that it prevented civilians from fleeing.

Amnesty International is conducting further research into these issues and intends to address them separately. It will also be addressing the issue of attacks by Israeli forces that Israel says were directly aimed at Hizbullah fighters and their bases and resulted in heavy civilian casualties, and the impact of such attacks on civilians in Lebanon.

Israeli attacks on the infrastructure in Lebanon were the subject of the briefing, *Israel/Lebanon: Deliberate destruction or "collateral damage"? Israeli attacks on civilian infrastructure*, AI Index: MDE 18/007/2006, August 2006.

This briefing highlights one aspect of the conflict, one of several that underline the need for an urgent and comprehensive international inquiry into the conduct of the hostilities by both parties.

During and after the conflict, Amnesty International conducted in-field research in both Israel and Lebanon. It has repeatedly appealed to both Hizbullah and the Israeli government to abide by the principles and rules of international humanitarian law. During the conflict, Amnesty International members and supporters around the world campaigned for a ceasefire, called for safe passage for trapped civilians, and have urged Israel and

Lebanon to consent to a comprehensive investigation by an independent and impartial international body into the pattern of attacks by both Hizbullah and Israel.

International Humanitarian Law and War Crimes

International humanitarian law (the laws of war) governs the conduct of war. It seeks to protect civilians, others not participating in the hostilities, and civilian objects (all objects that are not military objectives).

Hizbullah is bound by a number of rules and principles of international humanitarian law. Some of these obligations, including the requirement to treat humanely at all times people taking no active part in hostilities, are contained in common Article 3 of the four 1949 Geneva Conventions. Other principles and rules specific to the conduct of hostilities have been accepted by the international community—including Israel, Lebanon and most other states—as binding on all parties to international and non-international armed conflicts. These rules are encapsulated in the Additional Protocol I of 1977 to the Geneva Conventions.

Some serious violations of international humanitarian law, including many of those addressed in this report, are war crimes and give rise to international criminal responsibility for the perpetrators. These crimes are subject to universal jurisdiction (they may be prosecuted by any state in its national courts) and fall within the statute of the International Criminal Court.

A core principle of the rules governing the conduct of hostilities is the principle of distinction. The rules require that combatants at all times distinguish between civilians, the civilian population and civilian objects on the one hand, and military objectives on the other.

Military objectives are those that: "by their nature, location, purpose or use make an effective contribution to military action and whose total or partial destruction, capture or neutralization, in the circumstances ruling at the time, offers a definite military advantage."[2] Objects that are normally considered "civilian objects" may, under certain circumstances, become legitimate military objectives if they are "being used to make an effective contribution to military action". However, in case of doubt, the object must be presumed to be civilian.

Directing attacks at civilians or civilian objects is a violation of international humanitarian law, and doing so with intent constitutes a war crime.

Indiscriminate attacks too contravene the principle of distinction and are also a war crime. Indiscriminate attacks include those that involve a method

[2] Additional Protocol I to the Geneva Conventions (Article 52).

or means of combat that cannot be directed at specific military objectives and are therefore "of a nature to strike military objectives and civilians or civilian objects without distinction."

Parties to an armed conflict are required to protect civilians and civilian objects by adopting a number of precautionary measures in preparing and carrying out their attacks. In addition, combatants must not place themselves or other military objectives within the civilian population in an attempt to shield military objectives from attacks or to shield, favour or impede military operations.

Attacks against the civilian population or civilians or against civilian objects by way of reprisals are expressly prohibited by international humanitarian law and are widely held to be prohibited by customary international law.[3] The fact that one party may have violated the laws of war cannot therefore serve as a basis for an opposing party to engage in such unlawful acts, whether as a deterrent to bring the offending party into compliance, or as a means of retaliation or retribution. Amnesty International believes that the prohibition on reprisals must be respected in all circumstances.

Hizbullah's Bombardment of Northern Israel

"As long as the enemy undertakes its aggression without limits or red lines, we will also respond without limits or red lines."

Hasan Nasrallah, Hizbullah's Secretary General, 16 July 2006

For more than four weeks, rockets launched by Hizbullah fell on northern Israel on a daily basis—usually more than 100 per day, as many as 240 one day towards the end of the hostilities. Many landed in heavily populated areas, damaging homes and killing and injuring civilians.

According to the Israeli authorities, 3,970 rockets fired by Hizbullah landed in Israel between 12 July and 14 August, 901 of them in urban areas.[4] More than 1,000 landed in the Kiryat Shmona area, 808 in or near Nahariya, 471 in or near Safed, 176 in or near Carmiel, 106 in or near Acre, 93 in or near Haifa, and 81 in or near Tiberias. Almost a third of Israel's population—more than 2 million people—were within range of the rockets launched from south Lebanon.

[3] According to the 2005 International Committee of the Red Cross (ICRC) study of customary international humanitarian law, "the vast majority of states have . . . committed themselves not to make civilians the object of reprisal." While noting that a few countries maintain that reprisal may be lawful under certain stringent conditions, the ICRC study concludes that there is "a trend in favour of prohibiting such reprisals."

[4] Israeli Ministry of Foreign Affairs website, http://www.mfa.gov.il/MFA/Terrorism-+Obstacle+to+Peace/Terrorism+from+Lebanon-+Hizbullah/Hizbullah+attack+in+northern+Israel+and+Israels+response+12-Jul-2006.htm. One senior Hizbullah official told Amnesty International that the number of rockets fired was around 8,000.

The Israeli authorities reported that most of the rockets fired were Katyusha-type rockets with a calibre of 122mm and a maximum range of 20–40km. They said that a few hundred others were improved versions of Katyushas with a longer range and higher calibre. Those fired included rockets with warheads packed with thousands of metal ball bearings intended to maximize harm to people. Once the rockets struck, the ball bearings sprayed out, inflicting death and injury for 300 metres or more if in the open. Katyusha rockets cannot be aimed with accuracy, especially at long distances, and are therefore indiscriminate.

Other places affected by Hizbullah rocket attacks included Nazareth, Afula, Beit She'an and Ma'alot-Tarshiha. Dozens of settlements and agricultural villages were also hit. Hizbullah told Amnesty International that it had targeted military facilities, for example in Hadera and Meron.

Hizbullah's Justification

Hizbullah's Secretary General Hasan Nasrallah and other senior leaders in the party or associated with it have asserted that the shelling of northern Israel was a reprisal for Israeli attacks on civilians and the infrastructure in Lebanon, and was aimed at stopping such attacks. Senior Hizbullah officials told Amnesty International that it is a policy of the party not to target civilians, and for that reason Hizbullah remains committed to an agreement reached in April 1996 aimed at sparing civilians while pursuing hostilities with Israel in south Lebanon.[5] However, it is clearly also Hizbullah policy to resort to attacks against Israel's population centres, with the declared aim of forcing Israel to stop its attacks and return to a situation where civilians would be spared by both sides.

On 14 July, in his first broadcast address after the beginning of the hostilities two days earlier, by which time some 50 civilians in Lebanon and four Israeli civilians had been killed, Hasan Nasrallah addressed the issue of Hizbullah's attacks on northern Israel and threatened to hit Haifa:

> "You wanted open warfare, and we are going into open warfare. We are ready for it, a war on every level. To Haifa, and, believe me, to beyond Haifa, and to beyond Haifa. Not only will we be paying a price. Not only will our

[5] The agreement ended another outbreak of hostilities and formally involved France, Israel, Lebanon, Syria and the USA. It prohibited attacks against civilians in Israel and Lebanon, stipulating also that "civilian populated areas and industrial and electrical installations will not be used as launching grounds for attacks". As part of the agreement, a monitoring group was set up to adjudicate on complaints by either Israel or Lebanon that the agreement had been violated. The working group ceased to operate in February 2000 and Israel withdrew from Lebanon in May that year. http://telaviv.usembassy.gov/publish/peace/documents/ceasefire_understanding.html. See also Adir Waldman, *Arbitrating Armed Conflict: Decisions of the Israel-Lebanon Monitoring Group*, Juris 2003, p. 27.

houses be destroyed. Not only will our children be killed. Not only will our people be displaced."[6]

On 16 July 2006, by which time more than one hundred civilians in Lebanon and 12 Israeli civilians had been killed, he said that Hizbullah had begun by targeting military objectives and avoiding hitting "any Israeli colony or settlement in occupied northern Palestine". He accused Israel of targeting civilians and civilian infrastructure from the first day, and said that, despite this, Hizbullah had continued to focus its attacks on Israeli military facilities. "We were patient", he said, and still did not feel compelled to "bomb civilian targets" and "therefore did not resort to bombing civilian targets". However, he then added:

> "Today we had no choice but to reject the pledge we had made to ourselves and proceeded to bomb the city of Haifa, knowing the importance and significance of this city . . . As long as the enemy undertakes its aggression without limits or red lines, we will also respond without limits or red lines."

Later in the same speech, he confirmed that Hizbullah intended to continue targeting civilians as a form of reprisal:

> "In the next phase we will continue this open war, as they have chosen. We will be very careful to avoid civilians unless they force us to [target them]. During the past period, even when we were forced to target civilians, we focused on the major settlements and cities. We are still capable of reaching any settlement, any village or any city in northern occupied Palestine, at the least, but we have preferred to use matters within the limits of pressuring the government of this enemy. Even in this context, when the Zionists act on the principle that there are no principles, no red lines and no limits to the confrontation, it is our right to act accordingly."[7]

In further public statements on 29 July and 3 August, Hasan Nasrallah suggested that Hizbullah would continue to inflict destruction and force people to flee or take refuge in shelters for as long as Israel continued with its attacks on Lebanon. On 3 August he stated:

> "If you bomb the city of Beirut, the Islamic Resistance will bomb the city of Tel Aviv . . . I would like to confirm that our shelling of the settlements, in the north or beyond Haifa or Tel Aviv, and since the issues are now clearer, is a reaction and not an action. If you attack our cities, villages and capital, we will react. And any time you decide to stop your attacks on our cities, villages and infrastructure, we will not fire rockets on any Israeli settlement

[6] Speech broadcast by *Al-Manar* TV station, Arabic text: *Ad-Diyar* website, 15 July 2006 pdf edition, English text: www.islamicdigest.net/v61/content/view/1870/0/ and www.aimislam.com/forums/index.php?showtopic=457.

[7] Speech broadcast by *Al-Manar* TV station, Arabic text: *Ad-Diyar* website, 17 July 2006 pdf edition, English text [extract]: www.aimislam.com/forums/index.php?showtopic=457.

or city. Naturally, we would rather, in case of fighting, fight soldier to soldier on the ground and battlefield."[8]

On 9 August 2006, Hasan Nasrallah publicly appealed to Arabs in Haifa to leave the city. Hizbullah officials told Amnesty International that this was a warning that could have been heeded by Israeli Jews as well. However, the appeal clearly implied that Hizbullah's continuing bombardment was targeted at Israeli Jews, and showed no concern for distinguishing between civilians and the military:

> "To the Arabs of Haifa, I have a special message. We have grieved and we are grieving for your martyrs and wounded people. I beg you and turn to you asking you to leave this city. I hope you will do so. Over the past period, your presence and your misfortune made us hesitant in targeting this city, despite the fact that the southern suburbs [of Beirut] and the rest of the heart of Lebanon were being shelled, whether Haifa was being shelled or not. Please relieve us of this hesitation and spare your blood, which is also our blood. Please leave this city."[9]

Other influential personalities close to Hizbullah made similar statements throughout the conflict. For example, on 21 July 2006 senior Shi'a cleric Sheikh Muhammad Hussein Fadlallah declared:

> "The resistance is repelling the army which was said to be unvanquishable by dropping victorious blows onto its settlements and cities. This has driven the people there into shelters and paralysed economic and political activity."[10]

Several statements broadcast on television or on websites and attributed to "The Islamic Resistance" also reiterated that rocket attacks were being launched deliberately on civilian areas in reprisal for Israeli attacks. For example, on 12 August the Hizbullah-backed television station *Al-Manar* broadcast:

> "In response to Zionist attacks against the southern suburbs [of Beirut] and the rest of the Lebanese territory throughout Friday, the Islamic Resistance this morning bombarded the city of Haifa with two rounds of rockets."[11]

The scale of the rocket attacks on cities, towns and villages in northern Israel, the indiscriminate nature of the weapons used, together with official statements, specifically those of Hizbullah's leader, show that Hizbullah has committed serious violations of international humanitarian law. These include deliberately attacking civilians and civilian objects, and indiscriminate

---

[8] Speech broadcast by *Al-Manar* TV station, 3 August 2006, English text: www.islamicdigest.net/v16/content/view/1887/0/.

[9] 9 August 2006: speech broadcast by *Al-Manar* TV station, Arabic text: www.manartv.com.lb/NewsSite/NewsDetails.aspx?id=1002, English text: www.aimislam.com/forums/index.php?showtopic=457&st=40.

[10] Lebanese national news agency, 21 July 2006, www.ghaliboun.net/newsdetails.php?id=189.

[11] *Al-Manar* TV, 12 August 2006, www.manartv.com.lb/NewsSite/NewsDetails.aspx?id=1123.

attacks, both of which are war crimes, as well as attacking the civilian population as reprisal.

The fact that Israel in its attacks in Lebanon also committed violations of international humanitarian law amounting to war crimes, including indiscriminate and disproportionate attacks, is not an acceptable justification for Hizbullah violating the rules of war, whether as a deterrent or as a means of retaliation or retribution.

The underlying reason for the prohibition on reprisal attacks is plain: civilians and other non-combatants should not be made to pay the price for the unlawful conduct of armed forces. The very concept of violations as reprisal must be emphatically rejected, if the goal of containing the devastation caused by war on non-combatants is ever to be achieved.

The Impact of the Rocket Attacks

"We do everything in fear. We eat in fear, we sit in fear. We shower in fear. We sleep in fear."

An occupant of a shelter in Nahariya, northern Israel, 6 August 2006

Casualties

During the conflict, Hizbullah's rocket attacks dominated the lives of the civilian population of northern Israel. In total, 43 civilians died as a result of rocket strikes.[12] Seven of them were children,[13] of whom four were younger than eight years old. Some died in their homes, some in the streets, some in cars, one while riding a bicycle. At least 4,262 civilians were treated in hospitals. Of these, 33 were seriously wounded, 68 moderately, and 1,388 lightly. Some 2,773 were treated for shock and anxiety.[14] Twelve Israeli soldiers were also killed, all of them in a single strike, as they were about to enter Lebanon.[15]

The first reported deaths of Israeli civilians as a result of Katyusha rockets fired by Hizbullah occurred on 13 July. Monica Seidman, 40, of Nahariya

[12] Israeli Ministry of Foreign Affairs website, http://www.mfa.gov.il.

[13] Israeli Ministry of Foreign Affairs website, http://www.mfa.gov.il/MFA/Terrorism-+Obstacle+to+Peace/Terrorism+from+Lebanon+Hizbullah/Israel-Hizbullah+conflict+Victims+of+rocket+attacks+and+IDF+casualties+July-Aug+2006.htm. Also, Jacob Blaustein Institute for the Advancement of Human Rights, *Israel Under Rocket Attack: A Profile of Destruction and Displacement*, August 2006.

[14] Health Ministry cited in Eli Ashkenazi, Ran Reznick, Jonathan Lis, and Jack Khoury, "The Day After / The War Numbers—4,000 Katyushas, 42 civilians killed", *Haaretz*, 15 August 2006.

[15] Israeli Ministry of Foreign Affairs website, http://www.mfa.gov.il/MFA/Terrorism±Obstacle+to+Peace/Terrorism+from+Lebanon-+Hizbullah/Israel-Hizbullah+conflict-+Victims+of+rocket+attacks+and+IDF+casualties+July-Aug+2006.htm.

was killed in her home and Nitzo Rubin, 33, of Safed, was killed on his way to visit his children.[16]

Amnesty International delegates in Israel heard from officials and inhabitants of towns and villages affected by the rocket attacks that the flight of many people from these areas and the protracted use by those who stayed of shelters and secure rooms contributed significantly to the relatively low casualty figures compared to the number of rockets that fell on populated areas. In places close to the border with Lebanon, there was virtually no time to sound the sirens between when the rockets were launched and when they struck.

Amnesty International delegates spoke to several people directly affected by rocket attacks. Terez Levy described the day when her husband Reuven Levy, 46, was killed by a direct hit on Haifa's railway maintenance depot. The attack, on 16 July, caused the highest civilian death toll of any single Hizbullah rocket. The rocket, which the Israeli authorities said was packed with steel ball bearings, killed Reuven Levy, chief mechanic, and seven other employees of Israel Railways—Shmuel Ben Shimon, Asael Damti, Nissim Elharar, David Feldman, Rafi Hazan, Dennis Lapidos and Shlomi Mansura.[17] Dozens more were reportedly injured. It was the first attack on Haifa during the war.

Mounira Saloum described what happened to her brother, Don (Hamudi) Saloum, a 40-year-old lifeguard. On 6 August he was standing by the family house on Caesarea Street in Haifa when the sirens went off. Simultaneously, a rocket fell on the house, which began to collapse. Hamudi Saloum tried to enter it to rescue his sister and mother, but as he did so domestic gas cylinders attached to the house exploded. He was severely burned and his leg was crushed (it was subsequently amputated). Weeks later he was still in a coma on a life support machine in hospital. Mounira Saloum said: "Everyone loses in war, on this side and over there."

In Tel Aviv's Haim Sheba Medical Centre, Amnesty International delegates met distraught members of the Assadi family who had survived a rocket attack on their house. Ahmed Assadi described how on 10 August his home in the village of Dir el-Asad was directly hit by a Katyusha rocket while his family was eating breakfast. The blast killed his wife Mariam and their five-year-old son Fathi, and left his three-year-old son Faris with serious injuries, requiring amputation of his right leg below the knee.

Amnesty International also spoke to Linda Zaribi, whose family had been devastated by rocket attacks on the northern Israeli coastal town of Acre on 3 August. Her husband Shimon and 15-year-old daughter Mazal were

[16] Israeli Ministry of Foreign Affairs website, see footnote 15.

[17] Israeli Ministry of Foreign Affairs website, see footnote 15,

killed, and her 17-year-old son Raz suffered shrapnel wounds. Three other civilians died in the attack. Linda Zaribi said that on the day of the attack her family and some neighbours had gone to a nearby bomb shelter after a siren sounded. After hearing rockets landing nearby, some of those in the shelter went to see what had happened. Soon after, more rockets landed. One of them killed five people, including her husband and daughter. She said: "[Their] bodies weren't so damaged. I saw them on the ground holding hands . . . I keep seeing in my mind the terrible images on the lawn that day."

The town of Maghar experienced two fatal attacks during the war. The first occurred at around 2pm on 25 July, when a Katyusha rocket smashed through the roof of the home of the Abbas family. Doaa Abbas, a 15-year-old schoolgirl who was sitting reading in a chair by the window of the family's living room, was killed instantly when the rocket ricocheted off the floor and hit her. Her mother Emtiyaz and sister Hana, who were sitting in the same room, received light shrapnel wounds. Wassim Abbas, Doaa's brother, told Amnesty International that the sirens only sounded several minutes after the rocket strike had happened.

The second fatal attack occurred on 4 August. Manal Azzam, a 28-year-old housewife, was at home with her daughter Kanar, aged six, and son Adan, aged two, when a Katyusha rocket hit a house immediately adjacent to hers and rebounded at an angle, piercing a wall of her home. She was struck in the head and died immediately. At the time, she had been waiting for her husband Shadi Azzam to return from the textile factory where he worked to take her and their children to the wedding of a relative in the town. The children were in their mother's arms when she died, having rushed to their mother when they heard the sirens. Both were lightly wounded by shrapnel.

Internal Displacement

In a region with a population of about 1.2 million inhabitants, between 350,000 and 500,000 people fled their homes and became internally displaced. The towns north of Nazareth were described as ghost towns, inhabited only by the elderly, sick or those without the means to flee.[18] Of those who stayed, many were too old, too ill or too poor to travel. Some left the area but returned after a few days or weeks when they ran out of funds. Those who remained spent much of their time sheltering in overcrowded basements or underground shelters.

[18] Jacob Blaustein Institute for the Advancement of Human Rights, *Israel Under Rocket Attack: A Profile of Destruction and Displacement*, August 2006.

In Kiryat Shmona, for example, only about 6,000 of its 24,000 residents stayed in the town.[19] Many left through private arrangements, either staying with relatives in southern Israel or moving into hotel rooms as long as their financial resources allow them to. Others found places to stay through charitable initiatives by wealthy individuals or non-governmental organizations (NGOs).[20] Those who remained told Amnesty International delegates that most shops were closed, and those that were open soon ran short of supplies.

Some returned to find they had lost their home or business or both. Maurice Maman told Amnesty International delegates at his ruined home in September that he and his family left Kiryat Shmona on 14 July to stay with relatives in Tel Aviv, where they spent a week, before staying in hotels in central Israel. When they returned to Kiryat Shmona after the ceasefire, they found that their home had been hit by a Katyusha rocket. The office in the house, from which Maurice Maman operated a small business installing air-conditioning units, was destroyed.

The NGO Migdal Or evacuated 5,000 children from northern Israel.[21] By 6 August, at least 23,000 children had been moved to emergency summer camps in central Israel.[22] Oren Yirmiyahu, coordinator of the youth community centre of Kol Nidrei in Kiryat Shmona, told Amnesty International delegates:

> "For young children, under six for instance, the experience was especially traumatic as this was the first time they experienced a massive rocket attack. They are being treated by professionals. They exhibit symptoms of anxiety—lack of sleep, sensitivity to noise, and crying out of fear."

Life in Shelters

Hundreds of thousands of people moved into basements or air raid shelters underground for days or weeks. Conditions in many were poor, with inadequate toilet facilities, and no facilities for food preparation. Shelters were often crowded, stuffy and dirty.[23]

During the conflict, Amnesty International delegates visited two public shelters in Nahariya, where many of the city's residents had spent the previous 26 days mostly underground. In the first, most people spent the entire day there, when the majority of rockets were launched, but went home

---

19 Eli Ashkenazi, Ran Reznick, Jonathan Lis, and Jack Khoury, "The Day After / The War Numbers—4,000 Katyushas, 42 civilians killed", *Haaretz*, 15 August 2006.

20 Jacob Blaustein Institute for the Advancement of Human Rights, *Israel Under Rocket Attack: A Profile of Destruction and Displacement*, August 2006.

21 Ruth Sinai, *Haaretz*, 8 August 2006.

22 http://www.Jewishagency.org/JewishAgency/English/Home.

23 *TV Channel 23*, News, 8 August 2006, cited in Jacob Blaustein Institute for the Advancement of Human Rights, *Israel Under Rocket Attack: A Profile of Destruction and Displacement*, August 2006.

at night. In the second, there were around 40 people, including 10 children, most of whom had been living in the shelter around the clock since the first rockets hit Nahariya on the second day of the conflict. They said that because they were so close to the border, the sirens often went off after the bombs hit or simultaneously, which made many of them too afraid to step outside.

Damage to Buildings

Hizbullah rockets damaged houses, apartment blocks, schools, kindergartens, synagogues, public buildings, factories and shops in towns and villages across northern Israel.

According to the estimates of Israel's Ministry of Building and Housing, and its Property Tax department, rocket attacks by Hizbullah damaged about 12,000 buildings, some 400 of which were public buildings.[24] Based on interviews in August and September 2006 with local administration officials and residents of a number of Israeli cities, towns and villages, as well as visits to dozens of affected buildings, Amnesty International understands that the figure of 12,000 includes the full range of buildings damaged. A small percentage received a direct hit from a Katyusha rocket and were seriously damaged, sometimes evidently beyond repair. Most were located in the vicinity of a building which was hit directly and suffered lighter damage, such as broken windows, shrapnel marks in the walls or cracked tiles.

Kiryat Shmona and its surrounding communities, for example, were hit by more than 1,000 rockets, of which 372 fell inside the town. The municipality said that the rockets injured 25 residents and damaged 2,003 housing units and dozens of public buildings, including schools, factories, businesses, and synagogues.[25] In early September Amnesty International delegates visited a number of sites where rockets had fallen inside the town. These included several houses and apartment buildings which had received a direct hit and were seriously damaged such that they would require extensive structural repair work to render them habitable again. These also included the main high school, which had been hit by four rockets.

At least four hospitals were badly affected. A rocket hit a hospital in Safed, northern Galilee on 18 July, wounding eight people. The Western Galilee hospital in Nahariya was hit on 28 July, causing serious damage to the third floor but no casualties as all the patients had been moved to its fully

[24] The Chief Scientist, Ministry of the Environment, "Assessment of the environmental damage caused by the war in the north, Summer 2006", 27 August 2006.

[25] Eli Ashkenazi, Ran Reznick, Jonathan Lis, and Jack Khoury, "The Day After / The War Numbers—4,000 Katyushas, 42 civilians killed," *Haaretz*, 15 August 2006, and "Preparing to rebuild the north", *Ynet News*, 14 August 2006.

equipped and purpose-built shelter. Rambam hospital in Haifa had to repeatedly move patients to unsatisfactory conditions in the basement because of rockets in the vicinity.

Many hospitals in the north moved some or all of their patients into basement areas, together with their respirators, oxygen tanks and IV drips. However, facilities underground were far from ideal, with some equipment unavailable, few curtains to provide privacy, and toilets located far from the beds.[26]

Other Consequences

According to the Federation of Israeli Chambers of Commerce, about 70 per cent of businesses in northern Israel closed during the conflict, losing revenues of 5.9 billion shekels (US$1.4 billion).[27] About a quarter of the region's small businesses had to be saved from bankruptcy by emergency government support.[28] Much of the region's fruit harvest rotted on the trees because farm labourers could not go to work.[29] The Bank of Israel estimated the direct economic damage in lost tourism and industrial activity at 5 billion shekels (US$1.14 billion).[30]

Hizbullah rockets also severely damaged forests and open land, burning thousands of acres. Officials estimated that up to 12,800 acres of land had been burned by more than 450 fires ignited by rockets.[31] One forest had reportedly lost about 75 per cent of its trees.[32]

The Need for an International Investigation

Over the many years of conflict between Hizbullah and Israel, both sides have repeatedly committed serious violations of international humanitarian law without any accountability. The Israeli authorities have investigated a few incidents, and have stated that they are still investigating some of the incidents in the latest outbreak of hostilities, but the methods and outcomes of these investigations have never been properly disclosed. They fall far short of the standards required. No investigation into violations of international humanitarian law by Hizbullah is known to have been conducted by the Lebanese authorities or by Hizbullah commanders. If respect

[26] Delphine Matthieussent and Matti Friedman, "Israeli Hospitals Working Under Fire", *Associated Press*, 7 August 2006.
[27] http://news.bbc.so.uk/go/pr/fr/-/1/hi/world/middle_east/5257128.stm.
[28] http://www.guardian.co.uk/international/story/0,,1850823,00.html.
[29] http://www.guardian.co.uk/international/story/0,,1850823,00.html.
[30] *Reuters*, 14 August 2006.
[31] The Chief Scientist, Ministry of the Environment, "Assessment of the environmental damage caused by the war in the north, Summer 2006", 27 August 2006.
[32] Dina Kraft, "Dry Forests in Northern Israel Are Damaged as Hezbollah's Rocket Attacks Ignite Fires", *New York Times*, 8 August 2006.

for the rules of war is ever to be taken seriously, a proper investigation of their violation by both parties to the recent conflict is imperative.

Amnesty International welcomes the visit to Lebanon and Israel in early September of four independent experts of the UN Human Rights Council to investigate the impact of the conflict on the right to life, health and housing, and the situation of the internally displaced. It also expects that the Commission of Inquiry created by the Human Rights Council in August 2006 and comprising three independent experts will look impartially at violations by both sides.[33] These investigations are important and should feed into a broader inquiry.

Amnesty International calls for a comprehensive, independent and impartial inquiry to be conducted by the UN into violations of international humanitarian law by both sides in the conflict. The inquiry should examine in particular the impact of this conflict on the civilian population, and should be undertaken with a view to holding individuals responsible for crimes under international law and ensuring that full reparation is provided to the victims.

Amnesty International has asked the UN Secretary-General to establish a panel of independent experts to conduct this inquiry. They should include experts with proven expertise in investigating compliance with international humanitarian and human rights law, in military matters, as well as in forensics and ballistics. The experts should receive all necessary assistance and resources. The outcome of the inquiry should be made public and include recommendations aimed at ending and preventing further violations.

[33] Amnesty International expressed deep regret that the resolution of the Human Rights Council setting up this inquiry was exclusively focused on Israel and did not address the conduct of Hizbullah (see *Lebanon/Israel: Human Rights Council members put politics before lives*, AI Index MDE 02/014/2006).

B. 2006 LEBANON WAR

DOCUMENT NO. 4

ISRAEL/LEBANON: OUT OF ALL PROPORTION—CIVILIANS BEAR THE BRUNT OF THE WAR

Amnesty International Report

November 2006

Preface

From the outbreak of the war between Hizbullah and Israel in July 2006, Amnesty International called on both sides to respect their obligations under international humanitarian law (the rules of war), particularly those relating to the protection of civilians. In July Amnesty International published *Israel/Lebanon: Israel and Hizbullah must spare civilians—Obligations under international humanitarian law of the parties to the conflict in Israel and Lebanon,* a reminder to the parties of their legal obligations.[1]

Amnesty International delegates visited both Israel and Lebanon during the fighting to research serious violations by both sides. As the conflict escalated, with both sides repeatedly violating international humanitarian law, Amnesty International joined the call for a ceasefire made by UN Secretary-General Kofi Annan and other world leaders, and its members continued to appeal specifically for the protection of civilians.

Following the end of the hostilities, Amnesty International delegates again visited both countries for further research and discussions with officials. As a result, the organization issued two publications covering some aspects of the conflict. In August it published *Israel/Lebanon: Deliberate destruction or "collateral damage"? Israeli attacks against civilian infrastructure.*[2] Amnesty International found that Israeli forces had committed indiscriminate and disproportionate attacks, pursuing a strategy which appeared

[1] AI Index: MDE 15/070/2006.
[2] AI Index: MDE 18/007/2006.

intended to punish the people of Lebanon and their government for not turning against Hizbullah, as well as harming Hizbullah's military capability.

In September, Amnesty International published *Israel/Lebanon: Under fire: Hizbullah's attacks on northern Israel*.[3] This concluded that Hizbullah's bombardment amounted to direct attacks on civilians as well as indiscriminate attacks. The attacks also violated the prohibition under international humanitarian law on attacking the civilian population as reprisal, regardless of what abuses the enemy may be carrying out.

This new report covers further aspects of the conduct and consequences of Israeli military actions in Lebanon, and looks into allegations that Hizbullah's fighters used civilians as "human shields". The report recalls standards of international human rights, humanitarian and criminal law relevant to the conflict. It analyses patterns of Israeli attacks and a number of specific incidents in which civilians were killed in Lebanon. It highlights the impact on civilian life of other Israeli attacks, including the legacy of the widespread cluster bomb bombardment of south Lebanon by Israeli forces in the last days of the war. The final chapter summarizes Amnesty International's conclusions with regard to the overall conduct of both Israel and Hizbullah, and makes recommendations addressed to the parties to the conflict as well as to the international community.

The report is based on field research conducted in Lebanon and Israel in July, August and September 2006, including interviews with victims; a briefing by a senior Israeli commander in September 2006 and other discussions with Israeli and Lebanese military and government officials, as well as senior Hizbullah officials; information from non-governmental groups; and official statements and media reports. In September and October Amnesty International sought from the Israeli authorities specific information on attacks by Israeli forces included in this report, but received no such information.

Amnesty International has examined the conduct of each party to the conflict, in light of the standards laid down by international law and binding on those parties, as it does in other conflicts. Each side in this conflict has committed serious violations of international law, including war crimes. These are addressed on their own merit, seeking accountability, redress and the prevention of future violations.

3 AI Index: MDE 02/025/2006.

Chapter 1
Introduction

"I have lost all my children, my mother, my sisters. My wife is in a very serious condition . . . How do you tell a mother that she has lost all her children?"

Ahmad Badran spoke these words to Amnesty International delegates in al-Ghazieh village in south Lebanon after watching the bodies of eight members of his family being dug from under a pile of rubble. On 7 August an Israeli missile hit his home, killing his four children, his mother, his two sisters and his niece, and critically injuring his wife.

The 34-day war that destroyed his family and so many others in Lebanon and Israel began on 12 July after Hizbullah's military wing (known as *al-muqawama al-islamiyya,* Islamic Resistance) crossed into Israel and attacked an Israeli patrol, killing eight Israeli soldiers and capturing two. Almost immediately, a major military confrontation ensued between Israeli forces and Hizbullah fighters.

Within the first 24 hours Israeli attacks killed at least 38 civilians in their homes, many of them children. Among the victims were 12 members of the Bze'a family, killed as the family was having breakfast in Zibqin village; nine members of the Zein family in Baflay village; and 12 members of the Akash family in al-Dweir village.

Hizbullah rockets also killed a 40-year-old woman in her home in Nahariya in northern Israel and another civilian in the town of Safed.

The scale of the attacks and the high death toll among civilians within 24 hours prompted concern at the international level. Lieutenant General Dan Halutz, Chief of Staff of the Israel Defense Forces (IDF), vowed at a press conference in Tel Aviv on 14 July to continue the offensive. He said that Israel wanted to deliver a clear message to:

"both greater Beirut and Lebanon that they've swallowed a cancer and have to vomit it up, because if they don't their country will pay a very high price."[4]

In the following days, Israeli air strikes intensified and the number of civilian casualties continued to rise. Many among south Lebanon's half a million people quickly realized it was too dangerous to stay in their homes and fled northwards. However, more than 120,000 people remained effectively trapped and continued to face Israel's bombardments in Tyre and in other towns and villages.[5] Some were too poor, sick or elderly to flee. Many knew that it had already become too hazardous to travel to safety. Israeli

[4] "Israel Vows to Crush Militia; Group's Leader is Defiant", by Steven Erlanger, *New York Times,* 14 July 2006.

[5] In addition to some 500,000 inhabitants of south Lebanon, many Lebanese who reside abroad, including nationals of other countries, were in south Lebanon for their summer vacation when the war broke out. According to the UN Office of the Coordinator for Humanitarian Affairs (OCHA) on

forces had bombed roads, bridges, airports, petrol stations and other infrastructure in the first days of the war, and the continuing bombardment made movement treacherous or impossible. Civilians were killed when vehicles crammed with people obeying Israeli orders to leave their villages in south Lebanon were hit in Israeli strikes.

By the time of the ceasefire on 14 August, 1,191 people—hundreds of them children—had been killed and more than 4,400 injured in Israeli attacks.[6]

The death and destruction spread far beyond the confines of southern Lebanon. Israeli strikes focused on the south, where tens of thousands of homes were destroyed or damaged, but also targeted the capital Beirut and the Beqa'a valley, including the town of Ba'albek.[7] In the predominantly Shi'a Muslim neighbourhood of Dhahiyeh in south Beirut, where Hizbullah had its headquarters, some 250 multi-storey buildings containing at least 4,000 apartments were destroyed. In Ba'albek and the Beqa'a valley, a key agricultural area of Lebanon, dozens of people were killed, some 400 homes were destroyed and extensive damage was caused to orchards, agricultural estates, factories and infrastructure.

According to Israeli official figures, in the course of the war Israel's air force attacked some 7,000 targets throughout Lebanon and the navy carried out 2,500 bombardments on areas near the coast.[8] However, the Israeli authorities have not provided a total figure of their forces' strikes against Lebanon, including the sustained artillery barrage against villages in south Lebanon. According to the ground assessment by the UN Mine Action Coordination Centre (UNMACC), Israeli aerial and ground strikes during the first weeks of the war used up to 3,000 bombs, rockets and artillery rounds daily, with the number rising to 6,000 towards the end of the war.[9] Israeli forces also used cluster bombs and white phosphorous munitions in civilian areas. Up to one million unexploded cluster bomblets now litter south Lebanon and continue to kill and injure civilians. They also hinder the return of displaced residents and the relief and reconstruction efforts.[10]

---

26 July, some 115,000 "Third Country Nationals" from some 20 countries were in Lebanon, http://www.reliefweb.int/rw/rwb.nsf/db900SID/SODA-6S42E2?OpenDocument.

6 http://www.lebanonundersiege.gov.lb/english/F/Main/index.asp. Lebanese internal security sources told Amnesty International that the identities of 129 bodies had not been established by early September 2006 and that 56 of those killed were not Lebanese nationals.

7 See, among other sources, Israeli and Lebanese government websites, the *Report of four Special Rapporteurs on their mission to Lebanon and Israel*, 2 October 2006. Amnesty International also received information directly from Israeli and Lebanese official sources.

8 Report of four Special Rapporteurs on their mission to Lebanon and Israel, 2 October 2006, para. 33.

9 OCHA Situation Report No. 35, 31 August 2006, http://iys.cidi.org/humanitarian/hsr/ixl79.html. The report provided no figure for the total number of strikes, including artillery and navy.

10 See UNMACC at: http://www.maccsl.org/War%202006.htm.

The widespread bombardment led to the displacement of around a million people in Lebanon, nearly a quarter of the country's population. Some 500,000 of them ended up in Beirut. An estimated 200,000 Lebanese are believed to be still displaced.[11]

Hizbullah fighters fired an estimated 4,000 rockets into northern Israel, including rockets armed with ball-bearings for maximum damage to people and rockets reportedly armed with cluster weapons. These attacks led to the deaths of 43 civilians, led to the displacement of some 300,000 residents of northern Israel and caused widespread damage to buildings.[12]

Among combatants, the Israeli authorities have given the figure of 117 Israeli soldiers killed. Israel maintains it has the names of 500 Hizbullah fighters killed, although it has not released these names. According to Hizbullah, 74 of its fighters were killed; a smaller number of fighters belonging to other groups who fought Israel were also killed.[13] Four members of Lebanon's internal security forces and some 40 Lebanese soldiers were killed in Israeli strikes, even though the Lebanese security and armed forces did not participate in the fighting.

It was civilians, however, who overwhelmingly bore the brunt of the conflict—not just in terms of being killed or physically disabled for life, but also as a result of forced displacement, destruction of homes, psychological trauma and the long-term impact on the economy and environment.

Hostilities between the two sides ended on the morning of 14 August following UN Security Council resolution 1701, adopted on 11 August, which spelled out the terms of a ceasefire and enlarged the role of the UN Interim Force in Lebanon (UNIFIL). On 17 August the Lebanese army moved into south Lebanon. On 7 and 8 September Israel lifted the air and sea blockades imposed at the start of the war. On 1 October the Israeli army announced that it had completely withdrawn from Lebanon, although as of early November it still had a presence in the Lebanese part of the border village of al-Ghajar.

Hizbullah forces continue to hold the two Israeli soldiers captured on 12 July.[14] Although they are reported to be alive, the International Committee of the Red Cross (ICRC) has not been allowed access to them. Israeli forces captured at least 20 Lebanese nationals during the conflict. They continue to detain at least three of them who have reportedly been charged in Israel

[11] "Up to 200,000 still displaced after war, UN says", IRIN News, http://www.irinnews.org/report.asp?ReportID=56142&SelectRegion=Middle_East&SelectCountry=LE BANON, accessed 4 November 2006.

[12] Israeli Foreign Affairs Ministry website, http://www.mfa.gov.il/MFA/Terrorism+Obstacle+to+Peace/Terrorism+from+Lebanon+Hizbullah/Hizbullah+attack+in+northern+Israel+and+Israels+response+12-Jul-2006.htm.

[13] *Report of four Special Rapporteurs on their mission to Lebanon and Israel*, 2 October 2006, footnote 53.

[14] The soldiers are Ehud Goldwasser and Eldad Regev.

with offences including membership of Hizbullah.[15] They have been visited by the ICRC. In addition, the bodies of at least 13 Hizbullah fighters were taken to Israel by Israeli forces and, according to Israeli military sources cited in Israeli media, "could potentially be used in negotiations over the return of [the] two soldiers abducted".[16]

During and after the conflict, both parties have sought to justify their resort to force and the way they fought the war. Hizbullah launched its "Operation True Promise" on 12 July with the declared aim of obtaining the release of Lebanese and other Arab prisoners held in Israel by exchanging them with captured Israeli soldiers—as "promised" by its Secretary General, Hasan Nasrallah. After the war Hasan Nasrallah stated that had he known that Israel was going to respond so harshly he would not have ordered the 12 July raid.[17]

However, Hizbullah still sees itself as defending Lebanon, as well as Arabs and Muslims in general, against a long-standing aggression by Israel and its allies, specifically the USA. In particular, Hizbullah maintains that its conflict with Israel did not end in 2000 when Israel withdrew from Lebanon, as it considers Israel's withdrawal incomplete. Hizbullah, and the Lebanese government, assert that the border area known as Sheba'a Farms is Lebanese even though the UN considers it to be Syrian territory occupied by Israel. They also object to the frequent overflights of Lebanon by the Israeli Air Force, and are still seeking from Israel full disclosure of the location of minefields left from the previous occupation of south Lebanon.

Israeli Prime Minister Ehud Olmert declared Hizbullah's attack of 12 July an "act of war" and promised Lebanon a "very painful and far-reaching response" when he launched "Operation Change of Direction".[18] Israel maintains that the attack by Hizbullah combatants was unprovoked, as Israel had withdrawn from Lebanon in 2000 and the border demarcation between it and Lebanon was recognized by the UN. Israeli officials also see Hizbullah as part of a broader anti-Israel front, which includes the Palestinian organization Hamas, as well as Syria and Iran. They view with particular concern the close alliance between Hizbullah and Iran, whose President has repeatedly made statements threatening to the Israeli state. For Israel, the military campaign against Lebanon was an act of self-defence.

---

15 The three confirmed detainees are Muhammed Srour, Maher Kourani and Hussein Suleiman (also named as Mahmoud 'Ali Suleiman).

16 "Thirteen corpses of gunmen held for possible swap", *Jerusalem Post*, 23 July 2006.

17 "Nasrallah sorry for scale of war", *BBC* web news, http://news.bbc.co.uk/1/hi/world/middle_east/5291420.stm?ls.

18 http://www.msnbc.msn.com/id/13827858/.

The Lebanese government said it did not have advance warning of the attack by Hizbullah, did not condone it, and sought a ceasefire from the outset. Hizbullah's leader said that he ordered the 12 July operation to seize Israeli soldiers and that the Lebanese government was not party to that decision.

The relationship between the Lebanese state and Hizbullah is complex. Politically, at the time of the conflict Hizbullah was represented as a party in both parliament and the government of Prime Minister Fouad Siniora. Socially, Hizbullah provides substantial medical, educational and other services to Lebanon's people, particularly the traditionally marginalized Shi'a Muslim population. Hizbullah, whose armed wing led the fighting against Israeli troops in Lebanon until they withdrew in 2000, maintains its military capability even though UN Security Council resolution 1559, passed in September 2004, had called for the "disbanding and disarmament" of all militias in Lebanon.

Amnesty International takes no position on the broad ideological and political issues underlying the hostilities between Hizbullah and Israel, nor on Hizbullah's status within Lebanon. The organization has not condemned Hizbullah for carrying out a military attack against Israel on 12 July, nor Israel for launching a military campaign against Hizbullah in Lebanon. However, from the beginning of the war Amnesty International has appealed to both sides to respect international humanitarian law. These rules apply to both aggressors and defenders, to organized armed groups such as Hizbullah as well as to states.

Since the end of the conflict, there has been an ongoing public debate in Israel and Lebanon on the conduct of the war. In Israel, official inquiries have been initiated into various aspects of Israel's preparations for the war and response to Hizbullah's attacks, but none is mandated to look into how the conduct of hostilities complied with Israel's obligations under the laws of war. To Amnesty International's knowledge, no official inquiry is being conducted by the Lebanese government or by Hizbullah.

The conflict shattered innumerable lives and caused devastation in Lebanon and Israel that will take years to overcome. Much of this could have been avoided had both sides respected the rules of war. Amnesty International has looked into the conduct of both sides in light of their obligations under international law with the aims of seeking to ensure accountability for the perpetrators, justice for the victims, and the prevention of further similar abuses.

War inevitably results in personal tragedies, but any life lost or harmed as a result of a violation of the rules of war demands that those responsible be held to account and that victims receive reparations.

Chapter 2
International Law as it Applies to the War

The legal framework elaborated below sets out key rules and principles relevant to the conflict between Hizbullah and Israel. In certain instances, Amnesty International has identified clear violations of these rules and principles by one or other of the parties to the conflict. A comprehensive international inquiry, as set forth in the recommendations at the end of this report, is required to assess more fully the conduct of the parties and the extent of the violations.

Several bodies of international law apply to this conflict. International humanitarian law, also known as the laws of war, binds all parties to an armed conflict, including armed groups. International human rights law remains applicable in conflict and is binding on states. Under international criminal law, individuals incur criminal responsibility for certain violations, such as war crimes. Further, the law of state responsibility provides a framework to address the issue of reparations for victims of violations.

International Humanitarian Law

International humanitarian law contains the rules and principles that seek to protect those who are not participating in hostilities, notably civilians but also certain combatants, including those who are wounded or captured. It sets out standards of humane conduct and limits the means and methods of conducting military operations. Its central purpose is to limit, to the extent feasible, human suffering in times of armed conflict.

The four Geneva Conventions of 1949 and their two Additional Protocols of 1977 are the principal instruments of international humanitarian law. Israel is a party to the 1949 Geneva Conventions but is not a party to Protocol I relating to the Protection of Victims of International Armed Conflicts. Lebanon is a party to the Geneva Conventions as well as Protocol I.

Hizbullah has itself accepted some of the core rules of international humanitarian law, for example when it accepted the April 1996 agreement which ended a previous outbreak of fighting with Israel. The agreement was aimed at sparing civilian lives while allowing for the hostilities to continue in south Lebanon.[19] Hizbullah reiterated its commitment to this agreement after the recent war.

---

[19] The agreement formally involved France, Israel, Lebanon, Syria and the USA. It prohibited attacks against civilians in Israel and Lebanon, stipulating also that "civilian populated areas and industrial and electrical installations will not be used as launching grounds for attacks". As part of the agreement, a monitoring group was set up to adjudicate on complaints by either Israel or Lebanon that the agreement had been violated. The working group ceased to operate in February 2000 and Israeli forces withdrew from Lebanon in May 2000. http://telaviv.usembassy.gov/publish/peace/documents/

The fundamental provisions of Protocol I, including the rules cited below, are considered part of customary international law and are therefore binding on *all* parties to a conflict.[20] Grave breaches of the Geneva Conventions and of Protocol I amount to war crimes. The accepted definitions of these crimes under customary international law are contained in the Rome Statute of the International Criminal Court.

Prohibition on Direct Attacks on Civilians and Civilian Objects—the Principle of Distinction

Article 48 of Protocol I sets out the "basic rule" regarding the protection of civilians—the principle of distinction. This is a cornerstone of international humanitarian law.

> "In order to ensure respect for and protection of the civilian population and civilian objects, the Parties to the conflict shall at all times distinguish between the civilian population and combatants and between civilian objects and military objectives and accordingly shall direct their operations only against military objectives."

According to the Rome Statute, intentionally directing attacks against the civilian population as such or against individual civilians not taking direct part in hostilities is a war crime.[21] Under Article 51(3) of Protocol I, civilians remain protected "unless and for such time as they take a direct part in hostilities".

Article 52(1) of Protocol I stipulates that:

> "Civilian objects are all objects which are not military objectives."

Article 52(2) defines military objectives as:

> "those objects which by their nature, location, purpose or use make an effective contribution to military action and whose total or partial destruction, capture or neutralization, in the circumstances ruling at the time, offers a definite military advantage."

Objects that do not meet these criteria are civilian objects. In cases where it is unclear whether a target is used for military purposes, "it shall be presumed not to be so used" (Article 52(3)).[22] Intentionally directing attacks against civilian objects constitutes a war crime.

Military advantage may not be interpreted so broadly as to render the rule ineffective. To justify under this provision attacks aimed at harming the

---

ceasefire_understanding.html. See also Adir Waldman, *Arbitrating Armed Conflict: Decisions of the Israel-Lebanon Monitoring Group*, Juris, 2003, p. 27.

20 *Customary International Humanitarian Law*, ICRC, 2005.

21 Article 8(2)(b)(i).

22 The authoritative ICRC Commentary on the Additional Protocols to the Geneva Conventions (para. 2024) interprets the expression "definite military advantage" by stating that "it is not legitimate to launch an attack which only offers potential or indeterminate advantages."

economic well-being of a state or demoralizing the civilian population in order to weaken the ability to fight would be to distort the legal meaning of military advantage, undermine fundamental principles of international humanitarian law, and pose a severe threat to civilians.

Prohibition on Indiscriminate or Disproportionate Attacks

Article 51(4) of Protocol I prohibits indiscriminate attacks, which are those:

> "of a nature to strike military objectives and civilians or civilian objects without distinction."

Disproportionate attacks, a type of indiscriminate attack, are also those that:

> "may be expected to cause incidental loss of civilian life, injury to civilians, damage to civilian objects, or a combination thereof, which would be excessive in relation to the concrete and direct military advantage anticipated." (Article 51(5))

Intentionally launching a disproportionate attack is a war crime.[23] Launching an indiscriminate attack resulting in loss of life or injury to civilians or damage to civilian objects is also a war crime.[24]

In addition, incidental losses and damage should never be extensive.[25] The extensive destruction and appropriation of property, not justified by military necessity and carried out unlawfully and wantonly, is a war crime.[26]

Precautions in Attack

Article 57 requires all parties to exercise constant care "to spare the civilian population, civilians and civilian objects." Article 57(2) stipulates that those intending to attack shall:

> "(i) do everything feasible to verify that the objectives to be attacked are neither civilians nor civilian objects and are not subject to special protection but are military objectives within the meaning of paragraph 2 of Article 52 and that it is not prohibited by the provisions of this Protocol to attack them;
>
> "(ii) take all feasible precautions in the choice of means and methods of attack with a view to avoiding, and in any event to minimizing, incidental loss of civilian life, injury to civilians and damage to civilian objects;

[23] Rome Statute of the International Criminal Court, Article 8(2)(b)(iv).

[24] *Customary International Humanitarian Law*, ICRC, 2005, Vol. I: rules; Rule 156, p. 589. Article 8(2)(b)(i).

[25] The ICRC Commentary explains (para. 1980): "The idea has also been put forward that even if they are very high, civilian losses and damages may be justified if the military advantage at stake is of great importance. This idea is contrary to the fundamental rules of the Protocol . . . The Protocol does not provide any justification for attacks which cause extensive civilian losses and damages. Incidental losses and damages should never be extensive."

[26] Rome Statute of the International Criminal Court, Article 8(2)(a)(iv).

"(iii) refrain from deciding to launch any attack which may be expected to cause incidental loss of civilian life, injury to civilians, damage to civilian objects, or a combination thereof, which would be excessive in relation to the concrete and direct military advantage anticipated;

"(b) an attack shall be cancelled or suspended if it becomes apparent that the objective is not a military one or is subject to special protection or that the attack may be expected to cause incidental loss of civilian life, injury to civilians, damage to civilian objects, or a combination thereof, which would be excessive in relation to the concrete and direct military advantage anticipated;

"(c) effective advance warning shall be given of attacks which may affect the civilian population, unless circumstances do not permit."

Precautions in Defence

Warring parties also have obligations to take all feasible precautions to protect civilians and civilian objects under their control against the effects of attacks by the adversary. Protocol I requires each party to avoid locating military objectives within or near densely populated areas (Article 58(b)).

Protocol I also expressly prohibits the use of tactics such as using "human shields" to prevent an attack on military targets. Article 51(7) states:

"The presence or movements of the civilian population or individual civilians shall not be used to render certain points or areas immune from military operations, in particular in attempts to shield military objectives from attacks or to shield, favour or impede military operations. The Parties to the conflict shall not direct the movement of the civilian population or individual civilians in order to attempt to shield military objectives from attacks or to shield military operations."

Intentionally shielding a military objective using civilians is a war crime.[27]

However, the Protocol also makes it clear that even if one side is shielding itself behind civilians, such a violation "... shall not release the Parties to the conflict from their legal obligations with respect to the civilian population and civilians."

Furthermore, Article 50(3) states that:

"The presence within the civilian population of individuals who do not come within the definition of civilians does not deprive the population of its civilian character."

As indicated by the ICRC in its authoritative commentary:

"In wartime conditions it is inevitable that individuals belonging to the category of combatants become intermingled with the civilian population, for

[27] Rome Statute of the International Criminal Court, Article 8(2)(b)(xxiii).

> example, soldiers on leave visiting their families. However, provided that these are not regular units with fairly large numbers, this does not in any way change the civilian character of a population."

Prohibition on Reprisal and Collective Punishment

Under Articles 51(6) and 52(1), attacks against the civilian population or civilians or against civilian objects by way of reprisals are expressly prohibited by international humanitarian law and are widely held to be prohibited by customary international law. The fact that one party may have violated the laws of war cannot therefore serve as a basis for an opposing party to engage in unlawful acts, whether to bring the offending party into compliance, or as a means of retaliation or retribution.

According to Article 33 of the Fourth Geneva Convention:

> "No protected person may be punished for an offence he or she has not personally committed. Collective penalties and likewise all measures of intimidation or of terrorism are prohibited."

Protection of the Environment

Under Article 55 of Protocol I, care must be taken to protect the natural environment "against widespread, long-term and severe damage". Methods or means of warfare that are intended or may be expected to cause such damage are forbidden.

Article 8(2)(b)(iv) of the Rome Statute of the ICC provides that the following is a war crime:

> "Intentionally launching an attack in the knowledge that such an attack will cause incidental loss of life or injury to civilians or damage to civilian objects or widespread, long-term and severe damage to the natural environment which would be clearly excessive in relation to the concrete and direct overall military advantage anticipated."

Survival of the Population and Humanitarian Access

Attacking, destroying, removing or rendering useless objects indispensable to the survival of the civilian population is prohibited (Protocol I, Article 54(2)). The parties to the conflict must allow and facilitate rapid and unimpeded passage of impartial humanitarian relief (Protocol I, Article 70). They must respect and protect medical personnel and their means of transport (Protocol I, Articles 15 and 21).

Weapons

International humanitarian law prohibits the use of weapons that are by nature indiscriminate and weapons that are of a nature to cause superfluous injury or unnecessary suffering. The ICRC Commentary to the Protocols mentions "long-range missiles which cannot be aimed exactly at the objective" as an example of indiscriminate weapons.

Other weapons used in indiscriminate attacks during this conflict included cluster weapons. Cluster bombs or shells scatter scores of bomblets, or submunitions, over a wide area, typically the size of one or two football fields. These can be dropped by aircraft, or fired by artillery or rocket launchers. Depending on which type of submunition is used, between 5 and 20 per cent of cluster bomblets fail to explode. They are then left behind as explosive remnants of war, posing a threat to civilians similar to anti-personnel landmines. The use of these bombs in areas where there is a concentration of civilians violates the prohibition of indiscriminate attack, because of the wide area covered by the numerous bomblets released and the danger posed to all those, including civilians, who come into contact with the unexploded bomblets.

White phosphorous was also used in this conflict by Israeli forces, reportedly in areas where civilians were present. White phosphorous is used in grenades and shells to mark targets, to provide smokescreens for troop movement, to "trace" the path of bullets, and as an incendiary.[28] Protocol III on Prohibitions or Restrictions on the Use of Incendiary Weapons (a Protocol additional to the 1980 UN Convention on the Prohibition or Restrictions on the Use of Certain Conventional Weapons) prohibits the use of such weapons against civilians. This is a rule of customary international law, therefore binding on Israel and Lebanon even if they are not parties to Protocol III. According to the ICRC, it is a rule of customary international law that the use of incendiary weapons against combatants is prohibited unless it is not feasible to use a less harmful weapon to render a person *hors de combat* (out of the fight). This rule is not included in Protocol III.

International Human Rights Law

As affirmed by the International Court of Justice and the UN Human Rights Committee, human rights law remains applicable during times of international armed conflict, in a position complementary to international humanitarian law.[29] Both legal regimes are essential to ensure the protection of people during armed conflict.

---

[28] For an explanation of the uses and effects of white phosphorous in weapons, see Federation of American Scientists, "White Phosphorous Fact Sheet", available on http://www.fas.org/biosecurity/resource/factsheets/whitephosphorus.htm.

[29] "[T]he Court considers that the protection offered by human rights conventions does not cease in case of armed conflict, save through the effect of provisions for derogation of the kind to be found in Article 4 of the International Covenant on Civil and Political Rights", *Legal Consequences of the Construction of a Wall in the Occupied Palestinian Territory*, Advisory Opinion of 9 July 2004, ICJ reports 2004. See also Human Rights Committee, General Comment 31, para. 11: "[T]he Covenant applies also in situations of armed conflict to which the rules of international humanitarian law are applicable.

Lebanon and Israel are both party to major human rights treaties, including the International Covenant on Civil and Political Rights (ICCPR) and the International Covenant on Economic, Social and Cultural Rights (ICESCR). As the UN Human Rights Committee has made clear, the human rights obligations of states in respect of the ICCPR apply extraterritorially.[30] The ICESCR provides for no explicit limitations with respect to territorial jurisdiction.

Among the obligations relevant to the conflict that were breached are the right to life (ICCPR, Article 6); the right to adequate food and housing (ICESCR, Article 11); the enjoyment of the highest attainable standard of physical and mental health (ICESCR, Article 12), which also includes the right to water; and the right to education (ICESCR, Article 13).[31] Actions that were aimed towards or were likely to result in the destruction or impairment of infrastructure necessary for the enjoyment of those rights, including hospitals and schools, are violations for which the parties can be held responsible.

With respect to the right to housing, certain actions in the war—namely the widespread destruction of tens of thousands of homes—may constitute unlawful forced evictions, a breach of Article 11 of the ICESCR. The Committee on Economic, Social and Cultural Rights defines "forced evictions" as "the permanent or temporary removal against their will of individuals, families and/or communities from the homes and/or land which they occupy, without the provision of, and access to, appropriate forms of legal or other protection."[32] The Committee includes among such evictions those resulting from "international armed conflicts, internal strife and communal or ethnic violence."[33]

The ICESCR does not allow for derogation, even in times of emergency, and allows for only those limitations "as are determined by law only in so far as this may be compatible with the nature of these rights and solely for the purpose of promoting the general welfare in a democratic society." As the Committee has made clear, any limitations must be proportionate and

While, in respect of certain Covenant rights, more specific rules of international humanitarian law may be especially relevant for the purposes of the interpretation of Covenant rights, both spheres of law are complementary, not mutually exclusive." General Comment 31: The Nature of the General Legal Obligation Imposed on States Parties to the Covenant. UN Doc. CCPR/21/Rev.1/Add.13.

30 Human Rights Committee, General Comment 31, para. 10.

31 Committee on Economic, Social and Cultural Rights, General Comment 15, The right to water, UN Doc. E/C. 12/2002/11(2002).

32 Committee on Economic, Social and Cultural Rights, General Comment 7, Forced evictions, and the right to adequate housing (Sixteenth session, 1997), UN Doc. E/1998/22, annex IV at 113 (1997), para. 4.

33 Committee on Economic, Social and Cultural Rights, General Comment 7, op cit, para. 7.

"the least restrictive alternative must be adopted where several types of limitations are available."[34]

International Criminal Law

Grave breaches of the Geneva Conventions and Protocol I and other serious violations of international humanitarian law are war crimes. The list of war crimes in Article 8 of the Rome Statute of the International Criminal Court reflected customary international law at the time of its adoption.

Article 86 of Protocol I requires that, "'Parties to the conflict shall repress grave breaches, and take measures necessary to suppress all other breaches, of the [1949 Geneva] Conventions or of this Protocol which result from a failure to act when under a duty to do so."

Individuals, whether civilians or military, regardless of rank, can be held criminally responsible for such violations. Commanders can be held responsible for the acts of their subordinates. In the words of Article 86(2):

> "The fact that a breach of the Conventions or of this Protocol was committed by a subordinate does not absolve his superiors from penal or disciplinary responsibility, as the case may be, if they knew, or had information which should have enabled them to conclude in the circumstances at the time, that he was committing or was going to commit such a breach and if they did not take all feasible measures within their power to prevent or repress the breach."

Superior orders cannot be invoked as a defence for violations of international humanitarian law although they may be taken into account in mitigation of punishment. This principle has been recognized since the Nuremberg trials which followed World War II and is now part of customary international law.

There are several possible mechanisms for investigating and bringing to justice perpetrators of violations of international humanitarian law, in trials which must be fair and without the death penalty:

(a) By the parties themselves

Each party to the conflict must bring to justice any of their nationals suspected of being responsible for serious violations of international humanitarian law. Israel and Lebanon are under such an obligation.

[34] Committee on Economic, Social and Cultural Rights, General Comment 14: The right to the highest attainable standard of health (Article 12), para. 29. Adopted at the Twenty-second session (2000). UN Doc. E/C. 12/2000/4 (2000).

(b) By other states

Other states should exercise their obligations to conduct criminal investigations of anyone suspected of grave breaches of international humanitarian law during the conflict. If there is sufficient admissible evidence and the suspect is within their jurisdiction, such states should prosecute or extradite the suspects to another state willing and able to try them.

In addition to being obliged to exercise universal jurisdiction for grave breaches of the Geneva Conventions and Protocol I, states are permitted to exercise universal jurisdiction for other serious violations of international humanitarian law. If there is sufficient admissible evidence and the suspect is within their jurisdiction, states should prosecute or extradite the suspects to another state willing and able to try them.

(c) By the International Criminal Court

Neither Israel nor Lebanon has ratified the Rome Statute of the International Criminal Court. However, Israel and Lebanon could recognize the Court's jurisdiction on their territories by making a declaration under Article 12(3) of the Rome Statute, or the situation in Israel and Lebanon could be specifically referred to the Court by the UN Security Council, in accordance with Article 13(b) of the Rome Statute.

Reparations and State Responsibility

The principle that states are responsible before the international community for "internationally wrongful acts" has been incorporated into the 2001 International Law Commission's Articles of Responsibility of States for Internationally Wrongful Acts. These Articles codify the law on state responsibility and were commended to governments by the UN General Assembly in 2002.[35] Article 31 states:

> "The responsible State is under an obligation to make full reparation for the injury caused by the internationally wrongful act . . . Injury includes any damage, whether material or moral, caused by the internationally wrongful act of a State."

Internationally wrongful acts include violations of a state's obligations under customary and conventional international law. For example, Article 91 of Protocol I makes clear that each party to the conflict "shall be responsible for all acts committed by persons forming part of its armed forces." Accordingly, "A Party to the conflict which violates the provisions of the

[35] General Assembly Resolution, Responsibility of States for Internationally Wrongful Acts, UN Doc: A/Res/56/83 (28 January 2002), para. 3.

Conventions or of this Protocol shall, if the case demands, be liable to pay compensation."

The right to reparation of individual victims is also well established in international human rights law as a key element of the right to a remedy contained in international and regional human rights treaties.[36] The Customary International Humanitarian Law[37] study by the ICRC concludes in Rule 150: "A state responsible for violations of international humanitarian law is required to make full reparations for the loss or injury caused." In addition, the Basic Principles and Guidelines on the Right to Remedy and Reparation for Victims of Gross Violations of International Human Rights Law and Serious Violations of International Humanitarian Law, adopted by the UN General Assembly in 2005 (Resolution 60/147 of 16 December 2005) enshrines the duty of states to provide effective remedies, including reparation to victims. This instrument sets out the appropriate form of reparation, including, in principles 19–23, restitution, compensation, rehabilitation, satisfaction, and guarantees of non-repetition.

Armed Groups and Reparations

Under the law of state responsibility, an armed group can only be required to provide reparations if it subsequently becomes the new government of a state, or succeeds in establishing a new state in part of the territory of a pre-existing state or in a territory under its administration.

International human rights law focuses primarily on the obligations of states and therefore does not create obligations in respect to armed groups, except the obligation of the state to exercise due diligence to prevent, punish, investigate or redress the harm caused by such actors. In this context, Lebanon would have such an obligation with regard to Hizbullah.

The ICRC notes that armed groups are themselves required to respect international humanitarian law. While the question as to whether armed groups are under an obligation to make full reparation for violations of international humanitarian law is unsettled,[38] practice indicates that such groups are required to provide a measure of appropriate reparation.[39]

[36] See, for example, the ICCPR, Article 2(3), and the Arab Charter on Human Rights, Article 9.
[37] *Customary International Humanitarian Law*, ICRC, Volume I Rules.
[38] *Customary International Humanitarian Law*, ICRC, Volume I, Rules, Rule 150.
[39] *Customary International Humanitarian Law*, ICRC, Volume I, Rules, Rule 139.

Chapter 3
Israel's Attacks and Their Rationale

Israel has repeatedly maintained that it complied with international law throughout the conflict in launching its attacks on Lebanon, including by respecting the principle of distinction (distinguishing between civilian and military targets) and the requirements of proportionality (ensuring that attacks do not cause excessive civilian damage in relation to the concrete and direct military advantage anticipated). Israeli officials told Amnesty International that all targets were vetted prior to attack by international humanitarian law advisers, and that civilian deaths and the destruction in Lebanon were either legitimate collateral damage or the result of mistakes.

Ultimately, however, the Israeli authorities blame Hizbullah for starting the conflict and hold it responsible for the civilian casualties that resulted from attacks by Israeli forces. They allege that Hizbullah fighters deliberately used civilians as "human shields", which made it particularly difficult for Israeli forces to avoid killing and injuring civilians in Lebanon. For example, in the immediate aftermath of the attack that killed at least 28 civilians in a house in Qana on 30 July (see below), Brigadier General Amir Eshel, Israel's Air Force Chief of Staff, gave an overview of Israeli military operations:

> "Operations are very complicated. We are talking about hundreds of launchers and a great number of missiles dispersed throughout Lebanon, with everything from short range to long range. We are trying to hit the elements of these capabilities wherever possible, to create an effect that ultimately results in a reduction in the number of launches and their accuracy. This is what we are concentrating on. The attack on the chain of the missile-launching activities is focused on the launchers, on the people operating them, on the logistics rear of the launchers, and on the command centers that operate these launcher forces. Here we are talking about highly organized military organizations that operate different types of weapons; in fact, I would say, almost a regular army. Additional elements that we are dealing with are disruption of their operational capacity by hitting the routes they use, and by firing into the launch zones to prevent or disrupt their smooth operation as much as possible."[40]

Amnesty International is aware that fighting a guerrilla group based among the civilian population poses specific challenges—for example, identifying and destroying weapons located in civilian houses while minimizing harm to civilians. However, the rules of international humanitarian law take such challenges into account. This means that the challenges of fighting

---

[40] Israel Defense Forces (IDF) press conference following the Qana incident, 30 July 2006, http://www.mfa.gov.il/MFA/Terrorism+Obstacle+to+Peace/Terrorism-+from+Lebanon-+Hizbullah/IDF+press+conference+following+the+Kafr+Qana+incident+30-Jul-2006.htm.

irregular forces may never be used to justify indiscriminate or disproportionate attacks, the failure to adopt precautionary measures to protect civilians, or other serious violations.

The rules also set limits on the tactics that guerrilla groups may lawfully employ. Again, the challenges posed for armed groups when fighting more powerful, better equipped and organized state forces cannot excuse serious violations of international humanitarian law.

In a briefing with Amnesty International in September 2006, Israeli military officials stated that only two major mistakes were made by their forces during the campaign—an attack on a UN post near al-Khiam that killed four UN observers, and an attack on a building in Qana which killed 28 civilians. However, the explanations offered by the Israeli authorities in both cases, seemingly in response to concerns and interest at the international level, were inadequate, leaving key questions unanswered.

Attacks on a UN Post Near al-Khiam and a House in Qana

A UN observation post near al-Khiam was destroyed on 25 July by a direct hit from the air by Israeli forces after a day of close artillery shelling. The UN said that its staff had repeatedly contacted Israeli officials over several hours, asking that Israeli forces cease shelling near the UN building. UNIFIL reported that there were 21 strikes within 300 metres of the base and 12 artillery rounds fell within 100 metres, four of which hit the base directly.[41]

The following day, the UN Security Council stated that it was "deeply shocked and distressed" by the attack and called on the Israeli government to conduct a comprehensive inquiry into it. Also on 26 July, the Israeli forces stated that they were operating in the area of al-Khiam "from which Hezbollah has been launching missile attacks against Israel." They expressed regret for the incident and said that they were "launching a full investigation in close co-ordination with the UN."[42] However, Israel refused to conduct a joint investigation with the UN and did not disclose what kind of inquiry it was conducting nor its outcome.

[41] Briefing by Assistant Secretary-General for Peacekeeping Operations Jane Holl Lute, 26 July 2006, during which she specified: "To our knowledge, unlike in the vicinity of some of our other Patrol Bases, Hezbollah firing was not taking place within the immediate vicinity of the Patrol Base." http://www.un.org/News/dh/infocus/jane.htm.

[42] IDF website, "Regarding the UN post near al Khiyam", 26 July 2006, http://www1.idf.il/DOVER/site/mainpage.asp?sl=EN&id=7&docid=55107&Pos=27&last=0&bScope=False.

Following the UN's own Board of Inquiry investigation into the incident, the UN Secretary-General's Office stated:

> "The Board of Inquiry notes that the Israeli authorities have accepted full responsibility for the incident and apologized to the United Nations for what they say was an 'operational level' mistake. The Board did not have access to operational or tactical level IDF commanders involved in the incident, and was, therefore, unable to determine why the attacks on the UN position were not halted, despite repeated demarches to the Israeli authorities from UN personnel, both in the field and at Headquarters."[43]

On 30 July an Israeli air attack on a three-storey house in Qana killed at least 28 civilians, most of them children, who were sheltering in it (see Chapter 4 for full details).

At first Israeli officials said that they were responding to the firing of Katyushas from the area of the village and that the collapse of the house may have been caused by the explosion of Hizbullah's weapons stored there rather than by the Israeli attacks.[44]

Announcing the completion of an inquiry three days later, on 2 August, Israeli officials stated that "the building was targeted in accordance with the military's guidelines regarding the use of fire against suspicious structures inside villages whose residents have been warned to evacuate, and which were adjacent to areas from where rockets are fired towards Israel." They said that their information was that "the building was being used as a hiding place for terrorists" and that there were no civilians in it. The statement also announced that the IDF's Chief of Staff had "instructed that guidelines for opening fire against suspicious targets be evaluated and updated immediately."[45]

In both cases the Israeli authorities have not provided information on the methods and full findings of the inquiries they conducted, including the nature of the mistakes they consider were made or whether they have identified any responsibility for the mistakes. Also, the Israeli authorities have not indicated whether the review of the guidelines for opening fire announced on 2 August took place and, if so, what was the outcome.

---

[43] UN Secretary-General, Department of Public Information, "Secretary-General receives report on attacks that killed observers at Khiam, Lebanon", SG/SM/10666, http://www.un.org/News/Press/docs/2006/sgsm10666.doc.htm.

[44] Brigadier General Amir Eshel, Air Force Chief of Staff, quoted in the Israeli news website *YNet*, 30 July 2006, http://www.ynetnews.com/articles/0,7340,L-3283816,00.html.

[45] "Completion of inquiry into July 30th incident in Qana", 2 August 2006, Israel Foreign Affairs Ministry website, http://www.mfa.gov.il/MFA/Government/Communiques/2006/Completion+of+inquiry+into+July+30+incident+in+Qana+2-Aug-2006.htm.

In relation to other incidents, the Israeli authorities regularly expressed regret for civilian casualties resulting from attacks by Israeli forces and provided statements of general policy. However, in virtually all other cases, they have given no specific information relating to each incident, such as the intended target, considerations of proportionality and any precautionary measures taken. These are all essential elements for assessing the lawfulness of an attack, particularly where the evidence on the ground—as far as Amnesty International has been able to determine in the cases included in this report—does not point to any military activity by Hizbullah in the areas attacked at the time of the attack.

Particularly disturbing are Israeli officials' denials of knowing that civilians were present at locations under attack, given that the Israeli forces employed sophisticated surveillance systems, particularly pilotless drones which they used extensively over Lebanon during the conflict.

> In the village of 'Ainata, the Wehbe family home was hit twice on 19 July, killing 85-year-old Mousa Wehbe and his elderly neighbour Hussein Samhat. Soon after, another house was hit, killing Mousa Darwish, his 17-year-old daughter Amal and his two nieces, Zainab, 17, and Salwa, 20; and the family's Ethiopian domestic worker, Alawiya Muzammal Awali. Mousa Darwish's son and daughter were seriously injured in the attack; 18-year-old Himyam was in a coma for 10 days and suffered memory loss, and her younger brother Mahmoud lost the use of his legs.
>
> The house was outside the immediate centre of the village in a group of single-storey houses separated by orchards. Mousa Darwish's half brother, Samih, who lives next door to the destroyed house, told Amnesty International:
>
> > "There was nothing here, we have no Resistance here. Only we from the family live here and the road ends here so there are not even passers-by. So we know what goes on and there was nothing happening here, no reason to bomb us."

General explanations of policy and interpretation of international law which the Israeli authorities have published or discussed with Amnesty International also raise serious concerns.

For example, at the briefing by Israeli military officials in September 2006, Amnesty International was told that if Israeli soldiers saw a man fire a rocket and then enter a house, the soldiers would be allowed to attack the house without asking further questions. Amnesty International believes such a response would be disproportionate. The mere fact that a combatant enters a house does not automatically make lawful an attack on the house: attacking it in order to kill one combatant without trying to establish whether civilians are in the house violates the prohibition on disproportionate attacks.

Also of serious concern are several public statements from Israeli political and military leaders indicating that Israeli forces considered the civilians who did not flee south Lebanon as legitimate targets. On 27 July Israel's Justice Minister Haim Ramon said: "All those now in south Lebanon are terrorists who are related in some way to Hizbullah".[46] He also said: "A village like Bint Jbeil, whose residents were alerted to evacuate and had left the place, and in which only Hizbullah gunmen remained, should be pounded from the air and with artillery before ground troops enter."[47] The same day IDF Chief of Staff Dan Halutz said in a press conference: "Bint Jbeil was bombed from the air and by artillery to the extent that we calculated to be sufficient. This is not a humanitarian issue, as Bint Jbeil was empty of citizens and surrounded by terrorists both inside and out."[48]

However, the village of Bint Jbeil was not "empty of citizens". On 31 July and 1 August, when journalists and the ICRC were able to visit Bint Jbeil during a two-day suspension of air strikes by Israeli forces, the media showed bodies as well as survivors being pulled from the rubble of their houses. Three journalists told Amnesty International that they had come across a distressed woman digging with her bare hands and pleading with them to help her find her sister under the rubble. They helped her and eventually found two elderly women, one of them disabled and bedridden, and their elderly brother still alive. The three, all in their seventies, had been trapped under the rubble of their home in the centre of Bint Jbeil for over a week.

Similar concerns are raised by the content of leaflets that Israeli forces repeatedly dropped on south Lebanon, warning of forthcoming attacks and ordering the population to evacuate. Particularly disturbing is a leaflet of 7 August which announced that "any vehicle of any kind travelling south of the Litani river will be bombarded, on suspicion of transporting rockets, military equipment and terrorists". This flagrantly breaches the principle of distinction and the presumption of civilian status: an attack

---

46 http://www.ctv.ca/servlet/ArticleNews/story/CTVNews/20060725/Israel_lebanon_fighting_060727/20060727?hub=CTVNewsAt11, and: http://www.jpost.com/servlet/Satellite?cid=1153292014162&pagename=JPost%2FJPArticle%2FShowFull.

47 Israeli daily *Yedioth* at: http://www.ynetnews.com/articles/0,7340,L-3282314,00.html.

48 http://www.mfa.gov.il/MFA/Terrorism-+Obstacle+to+Peace/Terrorism+from+Lebanon-+Hizbullah/Chief+of+Staff+Halutz+No+intention+of+hurting+Syria+or+citizens+of+Lebanon+27-Jul-2006.htm.

carried out in implementation of this threat would have been an indiscriminate attack and may also have been a direct attack on civilians.

Other leaflets and patterns of attack suggest that Israeli forces were targeting certain types of vehicles such as trucks, vans and motorcycles on the presumption that they were being used by Hizbullah fighters. A leaflet of 25 July stated that "pick-up trucks" or "trucks" may be bombed on these grounds. Amnesty International has documented (see Chapter 4) two fatal air strikes on a baker's van and on a man on a motorcycle, both of which took place on 6 August close to a UN humanitarian convoy travelling north of Tyre.

When asked by Amnesty International in September 2006 about these kind of attacks, Israeli officials said that in most cases there was intelligence that the targeted vehicles were "on a Hizbullah mission". However, they also indicated that they considered trucks still on the road after the population had been warned, and in the main had left, to be a legitimate target, particularly on locations such as the main road linking Lebanon to Syria. Amnesty International believes that any attack which does not fully take into consideration the specific circumstances of each case violates the presumption of civilian status and would amount to an indiscriminate attack and possibly a direct attack on civilians.

At any rate, escaping was no guarantee of safety. Israeli forces attacked civilians who had left their villages and were travelling north in response to instructions from the Israeli military authorities, delivered through air-dropped leaflets and other means. Israel has provided no adequate explanation for specific instances of the killing of unarmed civilians in such circumstances.

Attacked While Fleeing

> "The army told us to leave the village but those who did leave were bombarded and killed. Why? A car full of children!"

This was how a member of the 'Abdallah family who survived an Israeli attack on a convoy of families fleeing the village of Marwahin described his despair and bewilderment. The attack, on 15 July, left 23 civilians dead, most of them children. The residents of Marwahin had only evacuated their village after they were ordered to do so by Israeli soldiers using loudspeakers. The survivor said:

> "Israeli soldiers from near the border fence accused us of helping the Resistance and said we must leave, but we don't have anything to do with the Resistance. There was only one Hizbullah fighter from the village and we made it clear to him that we oppose any attacks from near the village or any weapons in the village."

As the convoy reached the area between Shama'a and Bayada, it came under sustained assault apparently from an Israeli navy warship and helicopter missiles. The death toll from just this one incident makes grim reading:

Zahra Fares 'Abdallah, aged 45, mother of 10, her son Hedi, 6, and her daughter Mirna, 12; Sana' Muhammad 'Abdallah, 30, and five of her children—'Ali, 15, Muhammad, 13, Hussein, 12, Hassan, 10, and Lama, 2; Muhammad Mousa Ghannam, 47, his 35-year-old wife Suha, and their six children—Qasem, 16, Mustapha, 15, Hussein, 11, Fatima, 14, Zainab, 10, and Do'a, 7; Mariam Brahim 'Abdallah, 27; and 'Ali Kamil 'Abdallah, 55, his 17-year-old son Muhammad and his elderly mother Subha Hassan 'Abdallah; and two elderly sisters, Latifa and Fawzia Abu Hadla.

Many others were seriously injured, including an elderly man, Mousa Touhan Seif, who lost both his legs.

Another area of serious concern is Israel's interpretation of the concept of "military advantage" in considering proportionality. Israel maintains that the military advantage "is not of that specific attack but of the military operation as a whole".[49] Israeli officials indicated to Amnesty International that the simple fact that certain objects, such as electricity and fuel installations, could offer a military advantage would in their view make them a legitimate target.

This interpretation is too wide. A legitimate military advantage cannot be one that is merely a potential or indeterminate advantage, otherwise this interpretation could be used effectively to justify any attack since just about all civilian objects can potentially have a military use, even food and water. Instead, a balance must always be struck between military advantage and anticipated harm to civilians, and military forces must refrain from an attack if the latter outweighs the former.

The pattern and scope of Israeli attacks on the infrastructure in Lebanon, coupled with statements by Israeli officials, reflected this overbroad interpretation of the concept of military advantage. These attacks seem to have been aimed at inflicting a form of collective punishment on Lebanon's people in order to induce the Lebanese government to turn against Hizbullah, as well as harming Hizbullah's military capability.[50] In this context, Israeli

[49] Israel Ministry of Foreign Affairs, Responding to Hizbullah attacks from Lebanon: Issues of proportionality, 25 July 2006, http://www.mfa.gov.il/MFA/Government/Law/Legal+Issues+and+Rulings/Responding+to+Hizbullah+attacks+from+Lebanon-Issues+of+proportionality+July+2006.htm.

[50] See *Deliberate destruction or "collateral damage"? Israeli attacks against civilian infrastructure*, op. cit.

forces appear to have carried out direct attacks on civilian objects, such as the destruction of factories and of the small port of al-Ouza'i and its fishing boats (see Chapter 5).

The possible punitive nature of the attacks on the infrastructure was highlighted by official Israeli statements. Early in the conflict, after the capture by Hizbullah of the two Israeli soldiers, the IDF's Chief of Staff threatened: "If the soldiers are not returned, we will turn Lebanon's clock back 20 years."[51] According to the *Jerusalem Post* newspaper, a high-ranking IDF officer threatened that Israel would destroy Lebanese power plants if Hizbullah fighters fired long-range missiles at strategic installations in northern Israel.[52] On 24 July, at a briefing by a high-ranking Israeli Air Force officer, reporters were told that the Chief of Staff had ordered the military to destroy 10 buildings in Beirut for every Katyusha rocket strike on Haifa.[53] According to the *New York Times*, the Chief of Staff said the air strikes were aimed at keeping pressure on Lebanese officials, and delivering a message to the Lebanese government that it must take responsibility for Hizbullah's actions.[54]

In any case, it appears that much of Israel's destruction of Lebanon's infrastructure mainly hindered civilians in flight and humanitarian convoys, rather than preventing Hizbullah fighters from moving fighters or equipment.

Jiyye—An Environmental Catastrophe

The Israeli bombing of the Jiyye power station on 13 and 15 July had a devastating impact on the environment, as well as on the economy and the livelihoods of many.

Between 10,000 and 15,000 tons of fuel oil spilled into the sea. A further 55,000 tons burned, sending thick smoke and depositing droplets of oil across a large area.

The spill coated some 120km of the Mediterranean coast with oil to varying degrees, and large areas of the seabed were polluted. Damage was caused to the coastal and marine eco-systems, including to birds and fish.[55]

The power station's Director, 'Abd al-Razaq al-Eitani, told Amnesty International that the first tank, containing 10,000 tons of fuel, was hit in

[51] http://www.cnn.com/2006/WORLD/meast/07/12/mideast/.
[52] *Jerusalem Post*, "IAF continues attack on Lebanon", 17 July 2006.
[53] *Jerusalem Post*, "High-ranking officer: Halutz ordered retaliation policy", 24 July 2006.
[54] *New York Times*, "Israel Vowing to Rout Hezbollah", 15 July 2006.
[55] A report sponsored by the World Conservation Union's Commission on Environmental, Economic and Social Policy and Green Line (Beirut), written by Professor Richard Steiner, *Lebanon Oil Spill Rapid Assessment/Response Mission*, 11 September 2006.

an air strike on 13 July. Two days later the 15,000-ton fuel tank was hit and caused a 25,000-ton fuel tank to catch fire. He said one person was slightly injured in the attacks, and that several people, including himself, had suffered from smoke inhalation.

The Lebanese government estimated it would take 10 years for the area to recover completely; the UN estimated the cost for the initial clean-up at US$64 million.

As the power station and its fuel tanks are located right beside the sea, it was highly likely that targeting them would have a devastating immediate and long-lasting effect on the marine environment. Such risks clearly exceeded any anticipated military advantage. Amnesty International believes that the attacks on Jiyye power station were disproportionate. They also violated the prohibition on methods or means of warfare that may be expected to cause widespread, long-term and severe damage to the environment.

Among the Israeli attacks which appear to have been grossly disproportionate are those on the Dhahiyeh neighbourhood in south Beirut, where Hizbullah had its headquarters.

Dhahiyeh was extensively and heavily bombarded from the sea and air, including long after most of the residents had fled. The bombardment caused massive damage—around 250 multi-storey buildings containing at least 4,000 apartments are reported to have been destroyed.[56] Between 30,000 and 60,000 people are estimated to have lost their homes.[57] While military command centres located in Hizbullah's headquarters would have been a legitimate target, the extent of the damage suggests that Israeli strikes were aimed at any building that may have housed any activity associated with Hizbullah, including non-military activities. As such they would have been direct attacks on civilian objects, and may also have been carried out as a form of collective punishment of Dhahiyeh's residents.

Throughout the war Israeli forces pounded south Lebanon, from the air, ground and sea, firing thousands of shells virtually every day. This bombardment killed civilians and destroyed or rendered unusable thousands of homes and other buildings. It may have been part of the tactic described

[56] The Government of Lebanon, *Setting the stage for long term reconstruction: The national early recovery process, Stockholm Conference for Lebanon's Early Recovery,* 31 August 2006, p. 10; and Amnesty International interview with Hizbullah's Jihad al-Bina. The UN Development Programme (UNDP) estimates that a total of 35,000 Lebanese homes and businesses were destroyed.

[57] *Report of four Special Rapporteurs on their mission to Lebanon and Israel,* 2 October 2006, footnote 68, which refers to the assessment made on the ground by Hizbullah's Jihad al-Bina.

by the IDF as "firing into the launch zones to prevent or disrupt their [Hizbullah's] smooth operation as much as possible".[58]

However, the artillery bombardment of south Lebanon was indiscriminate. "In the recent war in Lebanon we fired like madmen, without adhering to any safety ranges," an artillery officer is reported to have said.[59] One Israeli soldier told Amnesty International that his artillery unit was given target co-ordinates in early August commensurate with "flooding"—dense shelling—of a number of Lebanese villages, one of which he believed was Tayyabah (see Chapter 4).

In the overwhelming majority of destroyed or damaged buildings it examined, Amnesty International found no evidence to indicate that the buildings were being used by Hizbullah fighters as hide-outs or to store weapons. In most cases, the pattern of destruction suggested that the properties had been targeted to put them out of use rather than to kill individual fighters or destroy weapons stored there. The pattern of damage caused to buildings by this artillery barrage would not usually have impeded the retrieval by Hizbullah of weapons if they had been kept there. In the many buildings surveyed, Amnesty International delegates did not observe conflagrations that would have resulted if a munitions dump had been struck, even when fires had resulted from the use of incendiary projectiles or other factors.

In the last three days of the conflict, after the ceasefire had been agreed, Israeli air and artillery strikes intensified and included widespread use of cluster weapons across residential areas. Some four million bomblets, of which around a quarter did not explode, were scattered over south Lebanon, landing in villages, homes, fields, roads and orchards, as illustrated in Chapter 5.

> Marwa and Sikne Me'ri, both aged 12, and 10-year-old Hassan Tehini, were injured when a cluster bomblet exploded near their home in the village of 'Ait al-Sha'b on 17 August 2006. Marwa told Amnesty International that she, Sikne and Hassan were playing on the rubble of a relative's home, which had been destroyed by Israeli forces, when she noticed a small object:
>
> > "I picked up the bomb but I didn't know it was a bomb. Hassan said to throw it away and when I threw it, it exploded."

[58] IDF press conference following the Qana incident, 30 July 2006, op. cit.

[59] The officer was commenting on an artillery barrage that killed 19 civilians in Beit Hanun, the Gaza Strip, on 8 November 2006. *Haaretz*, 9 November 2006.

All three children were injured. Hassan sustained serious stomach injuries. Marwa and Sikne had shrapnel injuries all over their bodies. The doctor who first saw Hassan said:

> "The boy's injuries were horrendous; his guts were hanging out and we were very worried that we may lose him. Luckily he survived."

Marwa's mother told Amnesty International:

> "The day after the war started I took the children and we fled because the Israeli army was bombing the village. We spent a month away from home and only returned on 15 August, the day after the end of the war, but we found that our home had been destroyed and now we are staying with relatives. I thought that at least we would be safe now that the war is over but there are unexploded bombs everywhere. Now we don't even have a home and school will start later this year because the schools and everything has been destroyed in the village, so the children are out playing more and I am terrified every time the children are out of my sight."

Cluster bombs constitute a grave threat to the civilian population. The bomblets they scatter are small and of different shapes—some like a tennis ball and others like a torch battery. This makes them attractive to children and much more difficult to detect than other unexploded ordnance.

The huge number of unexploded bomblets continue to kill and maim indiscriminately and can be expected to do so for years to come. Israel defended its use of cluster bombs, saying such weapons are legal under international law and that it had made "strenuous efforts" to avoid civilian casualties. However, cluster weapons are subject to the rules of international humanitarian law in the same way as any other weapons, and in this respect their massive use over populated areas clearly amounted to an indiscriminate attack.

Amnesty International also noted a pattern of destruction by Israeli attacks that indicated that Israeli forces had targeted objects that are indispensable to the survival of the civilian population, including supermarkets and other food distribution points, petrol stations and water pumping stations. The effect of this pattern of destruction was compounded by the naval and air blockade Israel imposed from the beginning of the conflict until nearly four weeks after the ceasefire. Israel maintained that the blockade was necessary to cut off weapons and supplies to Hizbullah and, after the ceasefire, it delayed lifting the blockade on the basis that international peacekeeping forces should first be deployed to prevent the rearmament of Hizbullah from sea and air.

Although blockades are not prohibited by international humanitarian law, they must not prevent food and other essential supplies from reaching civilians. The Israeli blockades did prevent or hinder vital supplies and humanitarian assistance reaching people in need, and may have been imposed as a form of collective punishment as well as a means of hampering Hizbullah's military operations.

It is vitally important that information pointing to violations of international humanitarian law—such as the evidence presented in this report—be properly investigated. Such an investigation is needed if those responsible for the violations, including war crimes, are to be brought to justice; full reparations provided to the victims; and new policies and other necessary measures implemented to prevent a repeat of such violations.

Chapter 4
Civilians Under Fire

Trapped and Terrorized

"It was dangerous to travel on the roads, but it was also dangerous to stay in our homes." A surviving member of the 'Awada family, nine of whom were killed in their home by an Israeli missile on 17 July.

The intensity of the Israeli bombardment from the outset of the war meant that within a few days, most of south Lebanon's half a million residents and tens of thousands of visitors had fled northwards. However, many were trapped for days and weeks, and up to 120,000 people remained in villages and towns in south Lebanon throughout the conflict, facing Israel's bombardments.[60]

Some could not flee because of their age or infirmities. Some wanted to leave but feared it was too dangerous to travel or had no means to do so. Some did not want to abandon their homes.

People had started to leave their villages from the first days of the war. However, the Israeli attack on vehicles fleeing the village of Marwahin on 15 July (see Chapter 3), as well as the widespread attacks on roads and other infrastructure, appeared to deter many from leaving. On 30 July, Israel announced a 48-hour suspension of air strikes to start the following day. Many inhabitants of the southern villages who had not yet left took the opportunity to flee. By the end of the 48-hour period on 1 August, many villages in south Lebanon had been largely abandoned.

In the second week of the conflict Israeli forces dropped leaflets over south Lebanon instructing residents to leave. In general, the leaflets did not mention specific villages but rather ordered people to evacuate the entire area south of the Litani river.

---

60 http://www.reliefweb.int/rw/rwb.nsf/db900SID/SODA-6S42E2?OpenDocument.

By this point, however, it had become extremely difficult for residents to leave. Many roads were impassable and the targeting by Israeli forces of moving vehicles made travelling on roads that were still open increasingly dangerous.

There was also a fuel shortage caused by the blockade and the targeting by Israeli forces of fuel depots and petrol stations. Most of the petrol stations that had not run out of petrol or been destroyed were closed by their owners out of fear that they would be targeted. This meant that even those who had cars often could not find petrol.

For those without cars, the price of even short journeys increased dramatically because of the fuel shortage and dangers involved, putting the cost of flight beyond most people's means. Even those who could afford the journey often had no way of communicating with the cities to arrange for transport because by this time telephone and electricity networks had been put out of use by Israeli bombardments and people could not use landlines or charge their mobile telephones as they had no power.

The leaflets dropped by Israeli forces initially ordered everyone to leave the entire area south of the Litani river, home to some 500,000 people. Subsequent leaflets said that any vehicle of any kind in the area would be attacked. Civilians were thus put in an impossible situation, risking their lives whether they stayed or they left. Even leaving in convoys co-ordinated with the Israeli forces was no guarantee of safety, as shown by the attack on those who had fled Marjayoun on 11 August (see below).

To residents of villages living south of the Litani River

Because of the terrorist operations which are executed against the state of Israel from your villages and homes the Israel Defense Forces are obliged to retaliate immediately against these acts even inside your villages.

For your safety!!!

You are asked to evacuate your villages immediately in the direction north of the Litani[61]

[61] Leaflet dropped on 21 July—Amnesty International translation from Arabic.

> ***To the people of Lebanon***
>
> *Pay attention to these instructions!!*
>
> *The IDF [Israel Defense Forces] will intensify its activities and will heavily bomb the entire area from which rockets are being launched against the State of Israel.*
>
> ***Anyone present in these areas is endangering his life!***
>
> ***In addition, any pickup truck or truck travelling south of the Litani River will be suspected of transporting rockets and weapons and may be bombed.***
>
> *You must know that anyone travelling in a pickup truck or truck is endangering his life.*
>
> *The State of Israel*[62]
>
> *To the Lebanese civilians south of the Litani River*
>
> ***Read this announcement carefully and follow the instructions***
>
> The IDF will escalate its operations, and will strike with great force the terrorist groups which are exploiting you as human shields, and which fire rockets from your homes at the State of Israel.
>
> *Any vehicle of any kind travelling south of the Litani River will be bombarded, on suspicion of transporting rockets, military equipment and terrorists.*
>
> *Anyone who travels in any vehicle is placing his life in danger.*
>
> *The State of Israel*[63]

Such leaflets did not reach all villages and there were areas where leaflets were only dropped after the places had already been bombed.[64] In the villages visited by Amnesty International many people said that they had not seen any. The leaflets were widely mentioned on Lebanese and international radio and television stations, but in many villages residents quickly lost access to the media and communication with the outside world because Israeli attacks destroyed electricity, broadcast and communication networks.

[62] Leaflet of 25 July, Israel Ministry of Foreign Affairs—http://www.mfa.gov.il/MFA/Terrorism-+Obstacle+to+Peace/Terrorism+from+Lebanon-+Hizbullah/IDF+warns+Lebanese+civilians+to+leave+danger+zones+3-Aug-2006.htm.

[63] Leaflet of 7 August—also accompanied by radio broadcasts issuing the same warning. Ibid.

[64] Israeli leaflets calling on people to evacuate the al-Shiyah, Hay Selloum and Bourj al-Barajneh areas of Beirut were only dropped days after the al-Shiyah area had been bombed.

Others who had seen or heard about leaflets announcing that Israeli forces would bomb the areas from which rockets were being launched concluded that it was safer to remain at home if they knew that rockets were not being launched from nearby. They also thought that if they travelled they could inadvertently enter areas from which rockets were being launched or where there were confrontations on the ground between Israeli forces and Hizbullah fighters.

In some villages, such as 'Ainata, 'Aitaroun and Bint Jbeil, around which Israeli forces had been present since early in the conflict, residents had quickly become trapped by the fighting raging around their villages. In other villages, people were aware that Israeli troops had entered south Lebanon to fight Hizbullah on the ground, but did not know precisely the location of these forces, so were afraid to move.

Killed in Their Homes

"None of us had anything to do with the war. I don't understand why they bombed our house." Fatima al-Akhras, who lost 12 members of her family when their house in 'Aitaroun village was hit in an Israeli attack on 16 July.

From the first day of the conflict, 12 July, there were reports of Israeli army artillery strikes on villages across south Lebanon. On the second day, air strikes hit houses in many villages, killing dozens of civilians.

In the cases highlighted in this chapter, Amnesty International found no evidence of Hizbullah military activity in or near the sites that were hit. Amnesty International has requested information from the Israeli authorities regarding most of these cases, particularly the reasons for the attacks in which civilians were killed and injured, and their justification under the laws of war. The Israeli authorities told Amnesty International that targets were assessed and approved after legal advice but did not provide further details. To date, they have not provided the additional information requested by Amnesty International which could indicate whether these attacks comply with international humanitarian law. Based on the available evidence, and in the absence of the specific information requested, Amnesty International considers that the civilian deaths and injuries were likely to have been the result of violations of international humanitarian law by Israeli forces.

Zibqin—13 July

Twelve members of the Bze'a family were killed and two others were seriously injured by an Israeli air strike on the home of 78-year-old Fatima Ahmad Bze'a in the centre of Zibqin on 13 July as they were having breakfast. Several members of the family who lived in houses elsewhere in the village were staying with the grandmother to keep her company or because they feared that their homes on the outskirts of the village, which had been shelled the previous day, would be more dangerous.

Those killed were: Fatima Ahmad Bze'a; her 60-year-old sister Thania; her 44-year-old daughter Amal and her three daughters, Khouloud, 18, Farah, 14, and 'Aziza, 12; her 45-year-old daughter-in-law Mariam al-Husseini Bze'a and her three sons, 17-year-old twins Malik and Mohammed, and 12-year-old Hussein; her daughter-in-law Sou'ad Nassour Bze'a, 40; and her 18-year-old grandson Na'im Wa'el Bze'a.

Fatima's two sons, 'Ali and Darwish Bze'a, told Amnesty International in Lebanon:

> *"We were sitting on the veranda drinking coffee . . . It had been quiet for a few hours; we had heard some shelling around the village at about 5 am but not after that. There had also been shelling the previous evening, at around 7pm, also around the village, not in the village itself. We had gone to our mother's house to be with her. The house was an old and sturdy house; a second floor had been added on to the old one-floor house . . . We don't know if the bomb came in from the roof or from the side. It felt like two explosions; we were thrown off, away from the house."*

Both 'Ali and Darwish were seriously injured. 'Ali, who lost his wife Mariam and his three children (Malik, Mohammed and Hussein) in the attack, suffered a head injury and his nose and right ankle were broken. Darwish, who lost his wife Sou'ad, suffered a head injury, severe burns, shrapnel injuries all over the right side of his body, and severed tendons in his left foot. He spent 27 days in hospital, four of them in intensive care.

Zahra Bandar, a neighbour of the Bze'a family, told Amnesty International:

> *"I went over to my neighbour Fatima's house at around 8am to borrow some flour to make bread . . . They invited me to stay and have breakfast with them but I just stayed a few minutes and came back home to make breakfast. I had only been home a short while when their house was bombed. It was terrible, indescribable; some of the bodies were thrown outside the house, far away. The bodies of the five I left in the bedroom were found in the same place. The body of Fatima was in pieces, the bodies of Farah and Na'im were thrown into the fields, and 'Ali was also thrown far; I could not believe that anyone survived. Mariam's body could not be found for days."*

Zahra Bandar explained the ordeal that she and her relatives endured in the weeks following the attack:

> "After Fatima's house was bombed things became very difficult in the village. People who lived in the outskirts of the village were scared. Many relatives came to my house, because it is less exposed. We were about 20. On Friday, in the early evening there was a lot of shelling and more relatives and others from the village came, we were 60 or 70 altogether, mostly women and children and old people. Doors were blown off by the blasts, it was very scary and we did not have enough food for everyone but it was too

dangerous to go out to look for food. On Saturday we all moved to the garage of another house nearby which seemed to be in a more sheltered place but there was not even water.

"Some UNIFIL armoured vehicles also passed and we tried to stop them to ask them to evacuate us but they could not. Some of us moved again to another house; every time we moved to a place which seemed to be safer but then the bombardments came nearby. We again saw a UNIFIL patrol, this time with a vehicle of the Lebanese army, but again they could not evacuate us. We kept moving from house to house. Once after we left the house we were in and crossed the road to go to an empty house of a lady who had died some time before, a shell fell on the road just after we had crossed, in exactly the same place we crossed two minutes before. We felt that we were being targeted."

Baflay, al-Dweir and Srifa—13 July

Also on 13 July pre-dawn Israeli aerial attacks killed at least 25 civilians, many of them children, in three other villages—Baflay, al-Dweir and Srifa.

- Nine members of the Zein family were killed in their home in Baflay—Mounir Zein, a farmer, his wife Najla and their five children; and their daughter's husband and his father.
- Twelve members of the Akash family were killed in their home in al-Dweir, some 15km north of Tyre: 'Adil Akash, a religious cleric, his wife Rabab and their 10 children, aged between two months and 18 years. The family's maid, a Sri Lankan national, was also killed. 'Adil Akash was reportedly linked to Hizbullah's political wing, but there is no indication that either he or anyone else in the house had been involved in military activities.
- An air strike at about 4am on a two-storey house in Srifa killed four members of the Mer'i family—'Aqil Mer'i, his wife Ahlam, their nine-year-old son Hedi and their six-year-old daughter Fatima. Hedi and Fatima were heard crying until 8am. All were Brazilian nationals who had gone to Lebanon on vacation to visit relatives. They were staying with their cousins, who were asleep in another part of the house and survived the attack unharmed. The victims' cousin told Amnesty International:

  "Our cousins were on vacation; they had been in Lebanon less than a month. They came all the way from Brazil to be killed in their sleep. The bomb or the missile, I don't know, I think it was a missile, hit the side of the house where they were sleeping, on the second floor, and killed them. The other cousins who were sleeping in the other side of the house almost died of shock . . . It was impossible to take the bodies out from under the rubble until much later in the day because there continued to be bombing."

The high civilian death toll in Lebanon within the first 24 hours of the conflict prompted concern at the international level. Speaking at the UN Security Council, Israel's ambassador stated on 14 July that Israel targeted "Hizbullah strongholds and infrastructure, not civilian targets",[65] and Israeli officials indicated that the bombing campaign would continue as it had started.

In the following days, Israeli air strikes and civilian casualties continued to grow.

'Aitaroun and Tyre—16 and 17 July

More than 30 civilians—again many of them children—were killed and several others were injured in three aerial attacks on 16 and 17 July on 'Aitaroun village and on Tyre, the largest town in the south.

Twelve members of the al-Akhras family were killed by an Israeli air strike on the family's two-storey house in the centre of 'Aitaroun on 16 July. Those killed included several children and elderly people. The victims were: Ali Ahmad al-Akhras; his wife Amira Raslan and their four young children, Saja, 7, Zeinab, 5, Ahmad, 3, and Salam, 1—all six of them Canadian nationals; Ali al-Akhras' aunts Fadda and Haniya, both in their sixties; his grandfather Hassan Mahmoud, 82, and his uncles Muhammad Mahmoud, 86, and Ali Hassan, 65; and Amira Raslan's sister, 16-year-old Manal Raslan. Ali al-Akhras' father, 65-year-old Ahmad Hassan, also a Canadian national, and his sister Fatima Hassan, were injured.

Fatima and Sikne al-Akhras, daughters of Muhammad Mahmoud al-Akhras, were in a different part of the house and survived unharmed. Fatima told Amnesty International:

> "I was in the house with the family, it was 17:45 on Sunday [16 July]; there had been one strike the previous day in an empty area of the village and that day there had not been any strikes in the village. And then suddenly our house was bombed and everybody was killed. My father, who was 86 years old, was killed in front of me. My cousin Ali Ahmad had never even lived in Lebanon. He and his wife and children lived in Canada and came to visit for the summer holiday and they were caught up in the war. None of us had anything to do with the war. I don't understand why they bombed our house.
>
> "When the bomb hit the house Sikne and I were across the courtyard and everyone else was in the kitchen except for Amira and two of the children, Saja and Salam, who were outside near the well. Their bodies remained in the well for 35 days because a bulldozer was needed to dig for the bodies and it was impossible for a bulldozer to come; it was dangerous, any such

[65] UN Security Council, 14 July 2006, http://www.un.org/News/Press/docs/2006/sc8776.doc.htm.

vehicle would be bombed. Eventually we were able to take their bodies out after we came back, after the ceasefire.

"We stayed in the village in terror for two days after the massacre of our family and then we fled to Rmeish [a nearby village] and stayed there for 12 days; there were tens of thousands of refugees from many villages and there was hardly any food and it was very overcrowded. Eventually we were able to leave in a convoy of hundreds of cars and went to Sidon."

The following day, another house full of civilians was hit by Israel's air force in the same village, killing nine members of the 'Awada family, including six children under 12 years old, and injuring three other children and their mother. Those killed were: Musa Naif 'Awada; his wife Jamila and their five children, 'Ali, 12, 'Abir, 11, Hassan, 7, Mariam, 6, and Muhammad, 5; and Hassan Mahmoud 'Awada and his 18-month-old son Hussein. Hassan Mahmoud 'Awada's wife, Mayada Mansour, and three of their children (Katia, 13, Jana, 8, and 'Ali, 4) were injured in the attack.

Twelve other family members were in an adjacent house and survived the attack. One of them told Amnesty International:

"This was the second air strike on 'Aitaroun; the one before was the previous day on the home of the al-Akhras family. There had been some shelling, mostly around the village. We were scared, and that is why we stayed in the inside rooms of the houses, on the ground floor to be away from the outer walls and the roof. The bombardment was at 11.45pm. Some of the bodies were thrown more than 20 metres away. After the massacre all of us who survived fled and our neighbours also fled, even though it was dangerous to travel on the roads, but it was also dangerous to stay in our homes."

Nabil Baidoun told Amnesty International that his wife had been visiting her family (the 'Awada family) in 'Aitaroun with their two young children when the war broke out on 12 July and she had been trapped there. She only found the courage to flee after the attack which killed her relatives.

"For days I did not know if my wife and my children were alive or dead. Once we were reunited I found my wife deeply traumatized by the ordeal she lived through. She was in the next door house when the massacre happened and she lost so many of her family. And she and the children could have died too. It was lucky that they survived but she cannot forget what happened. She is still in a terrible condition; she mostly does not speak and cannot function."

In the afternoon of 16 July, Israel's air force struck a 13-storey building in Tyre, where tens of thousands of villagers from the south had sought refuge. The building also housed the offices of the Lebanese Civil Defence. After the building was hit, the top six floors collapsed, killing those inside and sending debris cascading down onto those in a café below. At least 11 civilians were killed. Residents told Amnesty International that Hizbullah was not active in the area and the organization found no indication that the building had been used for military purposes.

Within the first week of the conflict, more than 200 civilians were killed and more than 500 injured by Israeli air strikes. Concerns were again raised by the international community.[66] Israeli officials continued to repeat that their forces were only attacking military targets, but offered no explanation for the specific attacks that had resulted in civilian deaths.

As the conflict went on, more and more homes in other areas of Lebanon felt the full force of Israeli missiles, including the capital Beirut.

'Ainata—28 July

Seventy-five-year-old Zeinab Khanafer lived alone in the centre of 'Ainata. She was in poor health and had mobility difficulties. Her close relatives in Beirut felt it was too dangerous for them to try to go to 'Ainata to take her out of the village, and lost contact with her when telephones stopped working in the village. When Amnesty International delegates tried to enter 'Ainata on 1 August they had to do so on foot as all the roads into the village had been rendered impassable by Israeli strikes. When they reached Zeinab's house they found that it had been destroyed by an air strike. There were no remains of spent munitions or other evidence that there had been any military activity in or around the house.

Two weeks later, the body of Zeinab was found under the rubble of the nearby house of a distant relative, which had been bombed on 28 July. In that attack, on a family home in the centre of 'Ainata next to the mosque, 15 members of the Khanafer and Fadlallah families were killed, 12 of them women and children. They were Almaza Fadlallah, 68; Mariam Shbiti Fadlallah, 60; Zahra Fadlallah; Zeinab Khanafer, 75; Kamila Khanafer, 70; Fayez Khanafer, 33, and his wife Rima Samhat and their four children, Ali, 8, Abdallah, 6, Muhammad, 3, and Dumu'a, 1; Um Khader Fadlallah, 28, and her son Khader Amir, 3; 'Afif Fayes Khanafer, 47; and Muhammad Ali Wehbe, 75.

There were reports that two injured men who had arrived at the house looking for help shortly before the strike were also killed. The two men, who were not from the village, were said to have been unarmed and in civilian clothes. Amnesty International delegates found no evidence that there had been any military activity or any weapons stored in or near the house.

Qana—30 July

On 30 July an Israeli air strike killed at least 28 civilians, most of them children, in the village of Qana—already known for the killing in April 1996 of

[66] *UN: Security Council must adopt urgent measures to protect civilians in Israel–Lebanon,* Amnesty International (AI Index: IOR 41/012/2006), 18 July 2006; and *UN agencies express "serious concern" over civilian casualties in Lebanon and Israel,* UN News Centre, 19 July 2006, http://www.un.org/apps/news/story.asp?NewsID=19243&Cr=Leban&Cr1.

102 civilians in Israeli artillery strikes a UNIFIL compound where they had been sheltering.[67]

At about 1am on 30 July Israeli forces launched an air strike on a three-storey house in the Khraibe district of Qana where some 60 members of the Shalhoub and Hashem families were sheltering in the basement. The description of the survivors and fragments found at the scene indicate that a laser-guided precision bomb was used, penetrating the building and exploding in the lowest level, the only part of the house that was occupied.

Among those killed were Khadija 'Ali Younes, her five children: Haura', 11, Ali, 10, Yahia, 8, Qasem, 6, and Zahra, 2; and her 70-year-old mother-in-law, Hasna Hazme. Her husband, Mohamed Qasem Shalhoub, was injured but survived. He told Amnesty International from his hospital bed:

> "Those near me all died except me and another one. I felt as if the ground beneath me was lifted and as if I was spinning; then I heard people screaming, as if for an instant I had gone deaf before that; then I took a boy out, I think it was Hassan Mohammad Shalhoub, aged 5, but I am not sure; it was the first child I could grab; and I put him by a tree about 50 metres outside the house and I went back to the house and as I was approaching to enter there was a second explosion and I was thrown and I started to shout to the people in the other house for help and ran toward the other house. When I reached there I collapsed."

Other people killed included Maryam Brahim Hashem, 60, several children of the Shalhoub family—Samih, 8, Husan, 10, Brahim, 6, 'Ali 2, Jaafar, 11, Zainab, 6, her aunt Nabila Shalhoub, aged about 40, and her uncle (Nabila's brother), Taysir Ali Shalhoub, 38; Ahmad Mahmoud Shalhoub, 50, his wife Afaf Zabat, aged in her forties, their daughter Ola, 25, and their son 'Ali, 17.

At a press conference on 30 July, Israeli senior military officials said that 150 missiles had been fired from Qana and its surroundings since the beginning of the war, and that the Israeli forces were trying to disrupt the "chain of the missile-launching activities". The Israeli authorities suggested that the house may have collapsed as a result of an explosion of weapons stored in it rather than because of the strike, and again accused Hizbullah fighters

[67] Israel maintained at the time that the artillery shelling of the UNIFIL compound was a mistake made while trying to rescue Israeli soldiers who had come under Hizbullah mortar fire from the vicinity of the compound—but again no other findings or details of the methods used to establish them were disclosed. A UN investigation concluded that "While the possibility cannot be ruled out completely, it is unlikely that the shelling of the United Nations compound was the result of gross technical and/or procedural errors." On the basis of all the information available, Amnesty International concluded that the IDF intentionally attacked the UNIFIL compound, although the motives for doing so remain unclear. See Israel/Lebanon, Unlawful killings during Operation "Grapes of Wrath" (AI Index: MDE 15/042/1996), July 1996.

of using civilians as "human shields" and thus being responsible for any harm suffered by them.[68]

On 2 August the Israeli authorities announced that, according to an inquiry they had conducted, the house was attacked from the air at 12.52am with two missiles. The first exploded, the second was apparently a dud. They said that the house "was targeted in accordance with the military's guidelines regarding the use of fire against suspicious structures inside villages whose residents have been warned to evacuate, and which were adjacent to areas from where rockets are fired towards Israel." They added that their information was that the building "was being used as a hiding place for terrorists" and that "[h]ad the information indicated that civilians were present in the building the attack would not have been carried out."[69] They did not repeat the suggestion that the house may have been destroyed by the explosion of weapons stored there.

Air surveillance footage provided by the Israeli authorities shows rockets being launched from an area apparently some distance from the house. The footage is not dated. The existence of surveillance images of the area and testimonies of survivors and of relatives who were sheltering in a house nearby indicate that Israeli forces should have known that there was a high concentration of civilians in the targeted house and in houses next to it. The victims and their relatives, more than 100 people, had been sheltering in these houses for between 10 and 18 days, during which Israeli surveillance drones (unmanned aircraft) had been constantly present.

Najwa Shalhoub, who was seriously injured in the attack, told Amnesty International:

> "There were surveillance planes hovering overhead every day. We were outside a lot during the day, giving showers to the children and the children were playing outside; just the normal daily chores. It is impossible that the planes would not have seen that the place was full of women and children."

In a briefing to Amnesty International in September, a senior Israeli commander said that the building where the civilians died had been hit by mistake, and that the Israeli Air Force had hit empty buildings and a rocket launcher nearby. He again cast doubt on Israel's responsibility and alleged that Hizbullah fighters had closed the area for a few days, only allowing media in to see what they wanted to show.

[68] IDF press conference following the Qana incident, 30 July 2006, op cit.

[69] "Completion of inquiry into July 30th incident in Qana", 2 August 2006, Israel Foreign Affairs Ministry,http://www.mfa.gov.il/MFA/Government/Communiques/2006/Completion+of+inquiry+into+July+30+incident+in+Qana+2-Aug-2006.htm.

This does not tally with Amnesty International's findings on the ground. The organization's delegates were in and near Qana on 30 and 31 July. They did not encounter Hizbullah fighters and nobody imposed any restrictions on their movements in and around the bombed house or anywhere else in the area. Scores of journalists were also on the ground filming, taking photographs and interviewing survivors. No evidence was found of rockets, rocket launchers or other weapons in or around the bombed house or in nearby houses.

The ICRC spoke out about the incident, describing it as "emblematic for others". ICRC spokesperson Roland Huegenin said:

> "The fact that it was practically exclusively women and children who were killed in a residential building, which was actually an unfinished building where they had taken shelter, was so obviously the wrong target. There were no fighters, there were no weapons available. Only women and children . . ."[70]

By early November the Israeli authorities had not provided information on the method and full findings of the inquiry they conducted, nor have they disclosed whether they have identified any responsibility for the mistakes they consider were made in this fatal attack.

Al-Shiyah Neighbourhood, Beirut—7 August

At least 39 people, including 11 children, were killed by an Israeli air attack on a six-storey apartment building and a nearby house in the densely populated al-Shiyah neighbourhood of Beirut, near a school and shopping centre, at around 7pm on 7 August. Israeli forces had not issued any warning that they intended to attack the area. Leaflets calling on residents to leave al-Shiyah, Hay Selloum and Bourj al-Barajneh suburbs were dropped by Israeli aircraft over Beirut only on 10 August.

Until the bombardment, al-Shiyah was considered a safe neighbourhood and many people who had been forced to flee the Dhahiyeh suburb of Beirut and villages in south Lebanon were staying there. Some of those who died were displaced people.

Huda Rmeiti, her husband and her son were all injured in the bombing. She told Amnesty International:

> "Life in the neighbourhood was almost normal; no leaflets had been dropped telling us to leave and during the day nobody was particularly worried. At night we used to go down to sleep in one of the rooms that was more protected than others on the ground floor. At the time of the shelling we were

[70] "Roland Huegenin ICRC Interview", Four Corners, *Australian Broadcasting Corporation,* 18 September 2006.

sitting in the evening on the balcony. We heard the Israeli surveillance airplanes then suddenly the house was bombarded."

Ma'roub—7 August

On 7 August, 34-year-old Najma Hassan Moussa was killed with her three children, Zahra, 16, Hyder, 14, and Ousra, 3, by an Israeli air strike on the basement of a school in Ma'roub where the family had been sheltering.

Najma's husband, 40-year-old Abu Ali Ahmed Moussa, had been the caretaker of the School for Orphans in Ma'roub for 12 years and the family had been living on the premises, in the caretaker's house at the main entrance of the school, some 50m from the school building. When the war started, the family took shelter in the concrete basement of the school, where they had enough food and water. Some 10 other members of the family had joined them and virtually no one left the basement until the 48-hour suspension of air strikes on 31 July.

At that time, relatives offered the Moussa family the chance to go with them to Tyre. However, there was not enough room in the van for five more people, so the family decided to stay.

On 7 August at 11.30am, Abu Ali left the basement to go to the family home, near the school main entrance, to wash, change clothes and pray. He had just left the school building when four Israeli planes and a surveillance drone suddenly appeared in the sky and launched eight missiles on the school. Two additional missiles reportedly did not explode. Abu Ali watched in horror as the school where his wife and children were sheltering collapsed. He tried to call for help on the main road but there was nobody. The next day an ambulance took him to Tyre but he could not go back to Ma'roub until 11 August because of continuous air strikes. He looked in the rubble for the bodies of his wife and children but did not have any equipment to dig, so went back to Tyre. He eventually returned to Ma'roub after the ceasefire and only then could the bodies of his family be retrieved.

Al-Ghazieh—7–8 August

At least 20 civilians were killed in al-Ghazieh, outside Sidon, in two days of Israeli attacks in the area. Eight members of the Badran family, four women and four children, were killed at around 8am on 7 August when Israeli forces bombed a four-storey building in the Hay Badran area in the centre of al-Ghazieh. When Amnesty International delegates arrived at the scene a few hours later, the bodies of the victims were being dug from under the rubble by rescue workers. Ahmed Badran lost his four children—Hanin, 16, Manal, 14, 'Ali, 12, and Hassan, 11—his mother Ruqaya Nasser,

67; his sisters Zeinab, 44, and Leila, 46, and her daughter Mariam, 28. His wife, Basima Nasser was gravely injured. She remained in intensive care for over a month. Ahmed Badran told Amnesty International:

> "When the bombardment happened I was outside. I was shocked by the bombing. Why our house? We are just ordinary civilians, we have nothing to do with the party [Hizbullah] or with anything. Why my family? I have lost all my children, my mother, my sisters. My wife is in a very serious condition, I don't know if she will ever recover; how can she recover? How do you tell a mother that she has lost all her children?"

Neighbours told Amnesty International that the strike on the house surprised everyone because it was the first air strike on a house in al-Ghazieh (previously bridges were bombed around al-Ghazieh) and because the family has no links to Hizbullah.

The following day at about 2.30pm, an air strike on a house in the Hay Bashroun area of al-Ghazieh killed seven members of the Khalife family: Mahmoud Khalife, a 32-year-old chemist, his wife Ibtisam, 30, and their three children: Hussein, 10, Fatima, 6, and Ahmad, 2; and his wife's mother and father. When the house was bombed Mahmoud Khalife had just returned home from work and the whole family was having lunch. No one survived.

His brother, Ahmad Khalife, and his wife Ibtisam, were killed in a separate air strike launched the same day on their house and neighbouring houses, including the house of a third brother who is reportedly linked to Hizbullah but who was not at home.

Later on 8 August Israeli forces launched air strikes on the cemetery in the Hay Ruwais district of al-Ghazieh during the funeral of the members of the Khalife family. A two-year-old girl who lived next to the cemetery, Malak al-Jbeili, was killed and another young girl who also lived in the area was seriously injured.

Attacked in Flight

In the first few days of the conflict Israeli orders to evacuate were directed at residents of some border villages. Residents of 'Ait al-Sha'b, for example, told Amnesty International that in the afternoon of 14 July Israeli forces used a loudspeaker to order them to leave the village. Many fled to nearby Rmeish, a village inhabited by Christians and therefore thought to be safer.

However, some villagers who heeded the order to leave were attacked by Israeli forces on the road. The killing of people in the convoy fleeing Marwahin on 15 July (see Chapter 3) received wide media coverage. Another similar incident happened on 11 August.

That day, residents of Marjayoun, having remained in their homes throughout the war despite severe hardship, decided to leave after Israeli troops entered the town and took over the local headquarters of the Lebanese army and several civilian houses. A large convoy of vehicles, accompanied by Lebanese forces and a UNIFIL patrol, was given permission to leave by the Israeli authorities.[71] Negotiations to obtain Israeli clearance and an agreed route out of Marjayoun were lengthy and the convoy only left Marjayoun at around 4pm. The convoy travelled extremely slowly also because of the condition of the roads (some had been bombed by Israeli forces and were only partially usable) and the circuitous route agreed by the Israeli army. The UNIFIL escort could only accompany the convoy for a few kilometres, until it reached the limit of UNIFIL's area of operation.[72]

Several hours later, when the convoy reached an area between the villages of Joub Jenine and Kefraya, Israeli aircraft—reportedly unmanned drones—launched several missiles at the vehicles. Seven people were killed, including Colette Rashid, Ely Salame, Khaled Abdallah, Kamil Tahtah and Red Cross volunteer Mikhail Jabaili who was killed while assisting one of the wounded.[73] Thirty-two others were injured. One of the injured, 28-year-old 'Abir Abla, told Amnesty International:

> "On 10 August, Marjayoun was shelled by Israeli army tanks, which were stationed in the town. Our house was damaged but nobody was wounded. People had been wounded and brought to the hospital. Many decided to leave the town, even though the Israeli army had not told the population to leave the area. There were no telephone lines anymore and no communication with the outside was possible. The hospital was closed and the wounded people were taken out of town with the convoy.
>
> "On 11 August, some 1,000 cars were ready to leave Marjayoun, filled with residents fleeing the Israeli army presence in the town. The cars were following Lebanese Red Cross and Lebanese army vehicles. Negotiations between the Israeli army and Lebanese army had been going on from the morning and the cars had waited from 8am until 4pm before they could start moving.
>
> "I was in one car with my aunt and my mother in the middle of the convoy and I was driving the car. The cars were moving very slowly and the convoy

[71] UNIFIL said that it approached the IDF at the request of the Lebanese government to facilitate the withdrawal of Lebanese forces from Marjayoun and that "Israeli forces informed UNIFIL that they agree to such a request". UNIFIL press release, 12 August 2006, http://www.un.org/Depts/dpko/missions/unifil/pr027.pdf.

[72] The convoy was reported to include around 465 civilian vehicles and nearly 100 vehicles of Lebanese forces. UNIFIL press release, 12 August 2006, op cit.

[73] "Lebanon – Israel: ICRC deplores increasing number of civilian casualties and lack of respect for medical mission", ICRC press release, 12 August 2006, http://www.icrc.org/web/eng/siteeng0.nsf/htmlall/lebanon-news-120806?opendocument.

> could not take the normal road as the Israeli Army had instructed us to take a different, slower road. Around 10pm, we were reaching the town of Kefraya on the way to Beirut when Israeli planes launched seven missiles against the convoy. Fifteen minutes later, the Lebanese Red Cross from Kefraya came to the rescue and when they arrived they were also targeted and one missile killed a Red Cross volunteer. I was wounded in the hand, face and chest and had a lot of shrapnel in my chest."

The following day the Israeli authorities said that Israeli forces "identified suspicious movement along a route forbidden for travel which had been used by Hizbullah to transport rockets and other weaponry. Acting on the suspicion that these were Hizbullah terrorists transporting weaponry an aerial attack was carried out." The Israeli authorities denied that the convoy had been authorized and recalled that "a curfew has been placed on any non-authorized vehicular movement south of the Litani river several days ago".[74] The village of Kefraya is north-west of the river.

Medical Vehicles and Humanitarian Convoys

The intensity of the conflict created significant difficulties for humanitarian operations. Ambulances were attacked in Israeli strikes and humanitarian organizations frequently had to abandon attempts to rescue people or deliver humanitarian assistance even after receiving clearance from the Israeli authorities.

On 23 July, for example, two Red Cross ambulances in Qana were struck by missiles launched by Israeli aircraft just after 11pm. Six Red Cross ambulance workers and three patients were wounded. The vehicles were hit on the roof, which in both cases was clearly marked by a large red cross and illuminated by a spotlight. At the time of the air strike, the crews of the ambulances were transferring three patients, all of them civilians, from one ambulance to the other. The three patients, one of them a child, had been injured in earlier attacks and suffered additional wounds.

Following this attack, the ICRC Delegate-General for the Middle East and North Africa, Balthasar Staehelin, said:

> "The ICRC is gravely concerned about the safety of medical staff . . . We have raised this issue with the Israeli authorities and urged them to take the measures needed to avoid such incidents in the future."

[74] "IDF response on convoy hit in south Lebanon", 12 August 2006, http://www.mfa.gov.il/MFA/Government/Communiques/2006/IDF+response+on+convoy+hit+in+south+Lebanon+12-Aug-2006.htm.

Another ICRC spokesperson, Roland Huegenin, in response to a general question on such attacks, said:

> "Destroying an ambulance and killing the people inside whether it's a casualty or whether it is a driver or whatever is never going to achieve any military aim, so why should it happen at all?"[75]

Civil Defence and Lebanese Red Cross volunteers reported air strikes, probably from drones, very close to their clearly marked vehicles when there were no signs of Hizbullah activity nearby and sometimes no other vehicles on the road or even any buildings. They believe that such strikes were aimed at intimidating them.

For example, on 22 July, after the ICRC had notified the Israeli authorities, a convoy of four Lebanese Red Cross ambulances was evacuating eight people using an improvised crossing of the Litani river some 9km north of Tyre. Just beyond, the road separated into two before converging again. The convoy took the less used but more passable road. Amnesty International was told that shortly afterwards a rocket fired from a drone landed in fields some 200m from the convoy. There were no buildings or other vehicles in sight nor was there any sign of Hizbullah activity. There was a steep drop by the narrow road and the ambulances were fortunate to stay on the road.

In another incident, during the afternoon of 3 August, a Lebanese Red Cross minibus was evacuating nine people from the Salah Ghandour hospital in Bint Jbeil. Elias Diab, a volunteer who was in the minibus, told Amnesty International that as they approached Tibnin, a drone that had been overhead disappeared. Shortly after, bombs started landing in the fields some 500m from the vehicle. Again, there were no buildings or other vehicles in sight nor was there any sign of Hizbullah activity.

One humanitarian convoy organized by the World Food Programme found itself close to vehicles that were targeted by Israeli forces on 6 August. The convoy was moving from Beirut to Tyre using eight trucks from the UN Relief and Works Agency for Palestine Refugees in the Near East (UNRWA), plus lead and rear escort vehicles. The convoy had Israeli military clearance. Some 15km north of Tyre, the convoy neared a baker's van, which was hit by a missile believed to have been fired from an Israeli drone. The van careered towards the lead vehicle of the convoy, just missing it, before crashing into a wall. Two people in the van were killed. On the convoy's return journey, a motorcyclist who had just overtaken the convoy was hit and killed by a missile, also believed to have been fired from an Israeli drone. The convoy team leader and four drivers resigned on return to Beirut. In any event, the Israeli authorities reportedly did not clear UN convoys to Tyre in the following days.

---

[75] "Roland Huegenin ICRC Interview", Four Corners, *Australian Broadcasting Corporation*, 18 September 2006.

Four UN Special Rapporteurs who visited Lebanon and Israel concluded that the bombardment of roads and other infrastructure "had a particularly debilitating effect on the . . . provision of humanitarian assistance and access to medical care".[76]

UNIFIL told Amnesty International that UNIFIL had been required by the Israeli army to seek clearance for humanitarian and other movements, and that it had encountered difficulties in obtaining such clearance. For example, on 17 July UNIFIL reported that a response to a request to transport humanitarian assistance from Tyre to two border villages had been pending since 14 July.[77] On 9 August UNIFIL reported that a humanitarian convoy to distribute food had been delayed for four days "due to the denial of consent by the IDF".[78] Such consent was not received before the cessation of hostilities on 14 August. The report said that sometimes only late and partial clearances were given, forcing UNIFIL to cancel convoys.

Destruction of Homes

Thousands of civilian homes were destroyed and even more were damaged. Most were in villages and towns south of the Litani river, but many were in the Dhahiyeh suburb of Beirut (see Chapter 3), and Ba'albek and its environs. Around a million people had to seek shelter, many ending up in overcrowded and often rank shelters that lacked basic services such as water and electricity.

Amnesty International delegates visited some of the worst hit residential areas and spoke to some of the survivors.

The town of Bint Jbeil, for example, in the far south of the country, was largely destroyed. In many areas, virtually every building had been flattened or was damaged, many beyond repair.

Huseyn Sa'id Bazzi, aged 72, showed Amnesty International delegates the pile of stones that had been his two-storey house about 100 metres from the centre of Bint Jbeil. "It was my parents' house and my grandparents' house. My father was born here and died here", he said. All the buildings in the vicinity were badly damaged or destroyed.

In southern Lebanon, some 7,500 homes were destroyed and 20,000 damaged. Some 400 homes were also reportedly destroyed and 5,000 damaged in Ba'albek and the Beqa'a Valley. Other houses were destroyed and damaged in the north.

[76] *Report of four Special Rapporteurs on their mission to Lebanon and Israel*, op cit, para 49.
[77] UNIFIL press release, 17 July 2006 (http://www.un.org/Depts/dpko/missions/unifil/pr01.pdf).
[78] UNIFIL press release, 9 August 2006 (http://www.un.org/Depts/dpko/missions/unifil/pr024.pdf).

According to UNIFIL assessments, 80 per cent of the civilian houses were destroyed in Tayyabah and al-Ghanduriyah villages, 60 per cent in Zibqin, 50 per cent in al-Markaba, al-Qantarah, Jabal al-Butm and Bayada, 30 per cent in Meis al-Jebel and Beit Leif, 25 per cent in Kafra, 20 per cent in Hula, and 15 per cent in Talusha.[79]

Sidiqin and Srifa suffered extremely high levels of damage from both artillery shelling and Israeli air force bombings. The targeting of Zibqin and Sidiqin was particularly severe in the 60 hours before the ceasefire.

In many of these cases, it is not clear what, if any, was the anticipated concrete and direct military advantage of the attack.

After the ceasefire, people quickly returned to the dusty sites that used to be their homes. When Amnesty International visited, many were sifting through the rubble or were waiting, as the bulldozers cleared the heavy debris, for an opportunity to salvage some of their belongings.

Mariam al-Shuqeiri and her husband Muhammad Akram al-Shuqeiri, a Palestinian writer and poet, were two of those watching the clearing up process in Dhahiyeh when Amnesty International delegates arrived. Muhammad al-Shuqeiri said it was the third time he had lost his home since 1948. He had salvaged a few of his poems and his ID card. At night the couple stayed with their daughter's family north of Sidon.

The home of Mustafa Wazni, an information technology merchant, his wife and seven children was badly damaged when blocks of flats opposite in 'Obayni Street, Dhahiyeh, were destroyed in an Israeli attack on or around 10 August. The front of his building was ripped off and the flats within were wrecked by the blasts. At the time of the attack, the inhabitants were not there—the Waznis, for example, had fled to Tripoli in the north. When Amnesty International visited, Mustafa Wazni was back in his apartment, which still had no front, with his two sons Hasan, 12, and Rida', 10, trying to clear up. "There were no guns, no rifles, nothing [in the area]", said Mustafa Wazni.

Chapter 5
Impact on Civilians

The war had a profound impact on virtually everyone in Lebanon. The air and sea blockade deprived the country of vital supplies and stopped all commercial imports and exports. The destruction of infrastructure and the bombardment of key industrial sites and agricultural areas devastated the economy. Humanitarian assistance could not reach people desperate

[79] http://www.un.org/Depts/dpko/missions/unifil/pr030.pdfandhttp://www.un.org/Depts/dpko/missions/unifil/pr031.pdf.

for help. Damage to hospitals, combined with the disruption of power and water supplies, severely restricted access to health care. Schools were destroyed or closed. A million or more unexploded cluster bomblets fired by Israeli forces in effect created a vast minefield in south Lebanon, as a result of which civilians there are still being killed and maimed, and many will not be able to return to their homes, fields or orchards for months or even years to come.

The Blockade

"Our aid operation is like a patient starved of oxygen facing paralysis, verging on death." Zlatan Milisic, the UN's World Food Programme emergency co-ordinator for Lebanon, 10 August 2006[80]

From the moment the war started, Israeli forces disabled Beirut's international airport by bombing its runways, sealed off Lebanon with a sea and air blockade, and bombed roads and bridges leading in and out of the country. The declared aim was to hamper Hizbullah's operations, including by preventing weapons from reaching Hizbullah fighters. With air, sea and land routes blocked or severely disrupted, supply channels were few and far between. The economy plunged into crisis.

Badly needed food and emergency assistance was often delayed. Damaged roads and bridges meant vehicles had to take lengthy detours along minor roads or dirt tracks, some of which were too narrow for lorries.

For at least a week in early August neither the ICRC nor any other humanitarian or relief organization could reach villages in south Lebanon under siege. The UN Food and Agriculture Organization (FAO) warned that damage to roads and bridges had interrupted the food supply chain, risking a "major food crisis". On 4 August Israeli jets severed Lebanon's last major road link to Syria. This blocked a convoy carrying 150 tons of relief and cut what the UN called its "umbilical cord" for aid supplies. The blockade and bombardment caused disruption in the north of Lebanon too.

When the ceasefire came into effect on 14 August, Israel refused to lift the blockade arguing that sufficient UNIFIL forces should be deployed first to prevent the rearmament of Hizbullah from sea and air. UN Secretary-General Kofi Annan warned that this risked being seen as "collective punishment" of the Lebanese people.[81] The continuation of the air and sea blockades until 7 and 8 September respectively severely hampered Lebanon's reconstruction and recovery efforts.

---

[80] "UN attacks Lebanon aid 'disgrace', *BBC News,* http://news.bbc.co.uk/1/hi/world/middle east/4778591.stm.

[81] "Annan says Israeli blockade must not be a 'collective punishment'," UN News Centre, http://www.un.org/apps/news/story.asp?NewsID=19688&Cr=Leban&Cr1=.

Amnesty International met many people in Lebanon who had been badly affected by the blockade, including representatives of the fishing, construction, agricultural and medical sectors.

Among the worst hit were the country's fishermen. Unable to fish since the start of the war, the boats of some 8,000 fishermen remained idle and many of the men and their families had become destitute. In addition, an Israeli air force attack on 4 August destroyed the fishermen's port at al-Ouza'i in south-west Beirut. Fishermen told Amnesty International that between 300 and 400 boats, each worth between US$5,000 and US$50,000, were badly damaged or destroyed in repeated air raids. The fishermen's Co-op offices, the cafe, the steel repair garage, carpentry workshop, net repair workshop and market—as well as a three-storey Lebanese army building—were also all destroyed. Jamal' Allama, Head of the Co-op, said that Hizbullah combatants could not have been using the port given the sensitive and well-monitored location—just metres from the perimeter fence of Beirut's international airport and with an army checkpoint to pass through to enter the port.

The fishermen also explained the hardships caused by the blockade, which had already stopped them earning anything for six weeks. Khalil Taha, head of the Fishermen's Syndicate for the South, said there were about 1,300 fish workers in the south—620 fishermen in Tyre, 100 fishermen in al-Naqoura and around 600 in al-Sarafand—as well as many retired fishermen who make the nets, ropes and iron weights, and the market traders. He said that all these people work on the basis of a daily income and few have savings. "Even our nets came apart by having been left out of water in the sun for so long. Some boats' engines cannot restart after being idle for so long."

One of the fishermen from Tyre, 50-year-old Rida Qassaab, had used up all his savings up. He has four children. "We eat bread, cheese and drink tea. Little else. Yesterday I ate a tin of tuna for one of the first times in my life—it should be fresh fish we eat."

Even after the sea blockade was lifted, the fishermen's lives did not return to normal because of the oil spill caused by the Israeli bombing in mid-July of the coastal Jiyye power station (see Chapter 3).

Other areas of Lebanon's economy were also particularly hard hit by the blockade because they rely heavily on the free movement of goods and people. The Lebanese authorities estimate that the blockade cost the country US$30–50 million a day in trade.[82]

[82] Israel ends blockade of Lebanon, BBC, http://news.bbc.co.uk/1/hi/world/middle_east/5327244.stm.

Economic Devastation

"Twenty-five years' hard work was destroyed in 10 minutes . . . there was no military, nothing military here, nothing at all. Not even the guards had pistols." George Hanna, General Manager of Dalal Steel Industries in Ta'nayel, Beqa'a, which was destroyed in Israeli air strikes on 23 July.

The 34-day bombardment of Lebanon caused extensive damage to the country's infrastructure and devastated large parts of its commercial and agricultural sectors.

The destruction had a direct and indirect impact on the economy. Some 900 commercial enterprises were damaged and more than 30,000 residential properties, offices and shops were completely destroyed.[83] Lebanon's trade, heavily dependent on importing and exporting goods, collapsed for the month of the conflict. Many families lost their only source of income when their small businesses were destroyed. Thousands of companies could barely function because the destruction of infrastructure left them without power and without any way of importing supplies or selling their produce. Hotels and other tourism-related businesses were devastated as tourists fled the country or cancelled trips, largely wiping out the whole season's income.[84]

The air strikes also targeted communications networks, including telephone and television centres. For example, aerial attacks on 22 July hit the *LBC TV* station installation in Satqa, east Beirut, killing technician Sliman Shidiac. The same day television transmission antennae in Terbel, in the north of the country, including that of *Avenir* and *al-Manar*, were struck in aerial attacks.

In a report published in August 2006, Amnesty International summarized its initial findings on the Israeli attacks on Lebanon's infrastructure.[85] Amnesty International delegates subsequently visited commercial and agricultural sites that had been attacked, finding no evidence that they had been used by Hizbullah fighters or had any other military purposes. Nor has any information been made available by the Israeli authorities explaining why any of them was attacked.

---

[83] Figures of the Engineers Syndicate, released in Lebanese media 17 August 2006.

[84] Most hotels lost almost their whole summer season because of the conflict. Having been on the verge of being full and remaining so for the rest of the summer when the conflict started on 12 July, the conflict escalated and the hotels quickly emptied. One hotelier told Amnesty International that his hotel was typical in having been over 80 per cent full on 11 July and expecting to be 100 per cent full within a few days. Instead, the hotel had less than 5 per cent occupancy and a decision was taken that all staff would have to take unpaid holiday for the foreseeable future. The catering and hospitality sectors were similarly affected.

[85] *Israel/Lebanon: Deliberate destruction or "collateral damage"?* op cit. The government said that 31 "vital points" (such as airports, ports, water and sewage treatment plants and electrical facilities) were completely or partially destroyed, as were at least 70 bridges and 94 roads.

Commercial Properties

At least 30 factories were completely or partially destroyed in Israeli attacks during the conflict,[86] knocking out around 5 per cent of Lebanon's industrial sector.[87] More than 700 industrial enterprises reportedly suffered extensive damage.[88] Productive capabilities of companies in key industrial sectors that were damaged or destroyed include those of Liban Lait in Ba'albek, the country's largest dairy farm; the Maliban glass works in Ta'nayel, Beqa'a; the Safieddin plant in Bazouriye, south Lebanon, that manufactured medical supplies; the Fine tissue paper mill in Kafr Jara, near Sidon; Musawi Building Supplies near Ba'albek; and the Dalal Steel Industries factory in Ta'nayel, Beqa'a, that made prefabricated houses.

Amnesty International visited the Liban Lait milk and derivatives factory, which was destroyed in an air strike at about 3am on 17 July. The control room, processing plant and canning and cheese-making sections were all left in ruins. Liban Lait had produced over 90 per cent of Lebanon's long-life pasteurized milk, as well as fresh milk, yoghurt, cheese and lebneh. Its chief engineer, Hisham Oraybi, told Amnesty International at the end of August that the company had employed 160 workers at the factory, of whom only 18 now had work. The destruction of Liban Lait disrupted the provision of fresh milk to schoolchildren that was co-ordinated by nongovernmental and intergovernmental organizations.[89] Hisham Oraybi said the attack had cost the company an estimated US$20 million in damage alone and that "while we paid the staff for the first half of the war we don't know when we'll next be able to do so."

The Maliban factory that produced glass bottles and jars and its warehouse were destroyed in an air strike at around 12.30pm on 19 July. One worker, Devesh Kumar Swain, was killed and a number of others were injured, including one whose neck was broken and another who was in a coma for 15 days. The factory, owned by a British citizen of Indian origin, was reportedly the largest in the Beqa'a valley and produced 190 tons of bottles and jars every day, exporting them to the Middle East and Europe. Roy Chowdhury, the manager, said that the factory was beyond repair: "It has to be rebuilt, although whether we are able to do so depends on the shareholders. We estimate it will require US$60–70 million to rebuild, and more for the clean up." He said that the company had not paid its 350 workers beyond 19 July and that the 400 suppliers would be similarly affected.

---

86 *The Government of Lebanon, Setting the stage for long-term reconstruction: The national early recovery process*, Stockholm Conference for Lebanon's early recovery, 31 August 2006.

87 Nabil Itani, head of the Investment Development Authority of Lebanon, quoted in *Reuters* article, "Lebanon sees investment boom if truce holds", published in *Daily Star*, 24 August 2006.

88 *The Government of Lebanon, Setting the stage for long-term reconstruction*, op cit.

89 *Report of the Special Rapporteur on the right to food, Jean Ziegler, on his mission to Lebanon*. 29 September 2006.

The factory and warehouse of Dalal Steel Industries in Ta'nayel were attacked and destroyed on 23 July. Heavy machinery including steel hangers and overhead cranes were left in ruins. General Manager George Hanna said Dalal, which employed 650 workers, had suffered losses of US$25 million.

On 4 August, the Elektra Company, which made electrical goods, and the adjacent café, in al-Ouza'i, Beirut, were completely destroyed when the site was hit by about nine missiles at around 5am on 4 August. Three workers sleeping at the site were injured: 'Abd al-Karim Khalaf, an Iraqi national, was injured in the leg by shrapnel and has lost hearing in one ear; Musa al-'Abud al-'Attiyeh, a Syrian national, had his arm broken; and Haytham 'Abd al-Rasul Marhum Muhammad, a Sudanese national, was buried under the rubble and spent five days in intensive care with a head wound. The three men said that 35 families had depended on the work provided by the site and that they themselves were in limbo—they could neither earn money nor afford to return home to their families.

In addition to the factories, many hundreds of small- and medium-sized commercial properties were damaged or destroyed across Lebanon.

Among the sites inspected by Amnesty International delegates was a one-storey building containing Samar Pharmacy, a fruit and vegetable market and al-Kawthar car wash, on the main road about 1km south of al-Nabatiyeh, which was seriously damaged in an air strike at around 3.30am on 26 July. There were no casualties. The market had been closed since 17 July and local residents had vacated the area.

In south Beirut, the nine-storey Kazma Mu'awadh building in Mar Mikhail was completely destroyed in an Israeli air strike at about 4pm on 6 August. The building housed shops, offices, a gold and diamond workshop, and a furniture storage area. "This building was our life, our future", Fadia Kazma told Amnesty International. "All our family lives from the income it generates." The family estimate that the attack cost them US$3 million. "We've no idea why they wanted to destroy the building. Of course there was nothing [military] there, and we have no political affiliations."

Amnesty International also visited 15 of the 25 petrol stations that were reportedly destroyed or severely damaged by Israeli air strikes, most of them in south Lebanon and in the Ba'albek area. The Daghr petrol station, for example, as well as the adjacent tyre repair shop and a small house, just north of Sidon, were destroyed and one person was killed in a missile attack, reportedly at around 5am on 18 July. Hani 'Omar al-Habash, a 28-year-old Syrian who worked at the tyre repair shop, told Amnesty International: "One missile hit the station itself, one of the petrol tanks, and Abu 'Ali Ibrahim was killed."

Agricultural Sector

People whose livelihoods depend on Lebanon's agricultural sector were deeply affected by Israel's strikes. The attacks killed dozens of farm workers; caused thousands of others to flee or stop working, leaving crops untended; and damaged or destroyed greenhouses, farm buildings, reservoir pumps, vehicles and other equipment vital for agriculture.

Lebanon's agriculture is concentrated in south Lebanon and the Beqa'a valley, two of the three areas (in addition to south Beirut) targeted most by Israeli forces during the conflict.

Among the farm workers killed were at least five members of the Syrian Shibli family in the Beqa'a village of al-Jamaliye on 2 August. Two days later at least 23 Syrian Kurdish workers were killed in an air strike on a fruit-packing warehouse in the north-eastern village of al-Qa'a, near the Syrian border.

A priest who witnessed the attack told Amnesty International:

> "At 2pm there was the first bombardment. I saw it from the roof of my church compound. The sky was black with smoke. I quickly got ready to go over to see if I could help. As I was leaving, within about seven minutes, there was a second air strike. I left immediately and got to the site of the bombardment a few minutes later. It was a terrible scene. I counted 23 bodies, five of them women, horribly burned. There were also several injured. It was absolute panic as we feared that there could be more bombardments. The victims were having lunch when the bombardment happened, so they were all grouped together and that is why so many were hit. They were sitting in the open with just a tin roof; they had no protection. These were poor vulnerable people; labourers, who came to work for a small wage to feed their families and they died for this."

The air strikes caused thousands of Syrian workers to flee Lebanon and prevented other workers, including Lebanese nationals, from tending to crops.

According to UNIFIL's veterinary officer, around 60 per cent of the country's farm animals died during the conflict.[90] Jihad Bakir, director of eight Tenmiye Chicken Farms in the Beqa'a valley, told Amnesty International that their chickens had steadily starved and dehydrated, and that farm workers had been forced to cull those that had not died. A total of 72,000 had died or were culled after weeks of Israeli attacks on vehicles in the area—including on a company truck—had made it impossible to bring feed to the chickens. "We have nothing now. We can't pay our workers.

[90] *Reuters*, "Indian U.N. vet treats animal victims of Lebanon war", 25 October 2006.

We've had to dismiss them without pay," he said. Of 400 employees before the conflict, only 20 were in work afterwards.

Seba' Tahtuh, a goat herder, told Amnesty International that four of his 21 goats had died during the Israeli attacks because he could not get them to water. Since the ceasefire, he said, he had faced continuing problems trying to feed them as their normal pasture was littered with unexploded cluster bomblets.

Hajj 'Adnan 'Abd al-Satr, a 70-year-old farmer, along with his family and around 10 other people, work collectively in fields in Aya'at, near Ba'albek. They grow tobacco, watermelons and cucumbers. "All are wasted," he told Amnesty International, waving at the dry and yellowed crops around him. "What can I do? Everything is ruined." These crops are harvested once a year, so nearly the whole year's harvest was lost.

Fatima and Sikne al-Akhras, who lost 12 members of their family in an Israeli air strike on their home in 'Aitaroun (see Chapter 4), told Amnesty International about the losses suffered by the family tobacco business they ran:

> "We have lost more than two-thirds of the harvest. July and August are crucial months for the tobacco cultivation. A lot of it had to be harvested just at the time of the war and it went to waste in the fields, and the leaves which had been picked could not be processed and were also spoiled. And now whatever is left in the fields is also going to waste because it is not safe to go to the fields, as there are unexploded Israeli bombs everywhere, mostly cluster bombs but also large ones."

Among those also affected by the Israeli attacks on the agricultural sector were people working in markets, shops and stores selling the produce. In Tyre's fruit and vegetable market a number of stall holders told Amnesty International that the market had been closed during the bombings, with the exception of one or two stalls, and consequently no income was received for over a month. Farmers were also unable to sell by the side of the road what little produce they did gather, since the roads had been almost deserted through the vital summer period.

Access to Health Care

Access to health care services was seriously undermined by Israel's bombing of hospitals and other health care facilities, the destruction of other infrastructure, and shortages of fuel, power and water supplies. The dramatic reduction in health care provision came at precisely the time when more people needed health care services because of the war.

The Lebanese Ministry of Public Health estimated that around 60 per cent of the country's hospitals had ceased to function by 12 August due to fuel shortages. According to a report by the Lebanese Ministry of Health and the World Health Organization, 12 health facilities were destroyed in Israeli attacks and a further 38 severely damaged.[91]

Amnesty International visited a number of the affected sites. The Bahman Hospital in Beirut's Dhahiyeh neighbourhood, for example, suffered widespread external damage and destruction of much of its equipment during a succession of Israeli air attacks between 15 July and 13 August. Among the losses were six of the hospital's 10 baby incubators and 5,000 litres of oxygen. The hospital's director, 'Ali Krayem, estimated that the damage was worth some US$1 million.[92]

The Dar al-Hawra health facility in Dhahiyeh, which mainly served women and children, was severely damaged by Israeli shelling. Its laboratory and X-ray room, as well as its gynaecology, paediatrics, dentistry and administrative departments, were destroyed.

In the village of Tibnin in south Lebanon, only hours before the ceasefire on 14 August, Israeli forces fired cluster bombs all around the government hospital, where hundreds of civilians were sheltering.

The report of the four UN Special Rapporteurs stated that the Israeli attacks had "a major impact on service delivery throughout the districts affected". It said that following the conflict, only one in four health care facilities could provide pre-natal care; only one in 10 could support proper delivery and emergency obstetric care; only one in three could store vaccines; and only one in eight could provide some mental health services.[93]

Israeli attacks on water and electricity facilities dramatically reduced people's access to water.[94] Human waste and other refuse disposal systems were also damaged and disrupted. This coincided with an increased need for such services, given the levels of dirt, dust, injuries and heightened risks of infection.

In south Lebanon "the water infrastructure was destroyed", according to UNICEF in August.[95] The same month the ICRC expressed concern:

> *"Villagers have no access to water. The large pumping station in the mountains has been destroyed beyond repair. People are having to rely on wells, but to pump the water from the wells they need electricity and the electricity stations have been destroyed."*[96]

[91] http://www.who.int/hac/crises/international/middle_east/Lebanon_2Sept2006/en/index.html.
[92] He described the hospital as "a non-profit making hospital that does not belong to any religious group or political party".
[93] *Report of four Special Rapporteurs on their mission to Lebanon and Israel*, op cit, footnote 42.
[94] For further information, see *The Government of Lebanon, Setting the stage for long-term reconstruction: The national early recovery process*, 31 August 2006; *http://www.reliefweb.int/library/documents/2006/govlbn-lbn-31aug.pdf*, and Israel/Lebanon: Deliberate destruction or "collateral damage"? op cit.
[95] "UNICEF and UN partners step up humanitarian aid in southern Lebanon", UNICEF, 28 August 2006, http://www/unicef.org/emerg/index 35455.html.
[96] "Red Cross courage in Lebanon", British Red Cross, August 2006, http://www.redcross.org.uk/news.asp?id=58445.

Most people met by Amnesty International delegates in August across south Lebanon and in south Beirut were having to buy bottles of water for their daily needs.

Doctors at the hospital in Meis al-Jebel told Amnesty International that the lack of water supplies, as well as lack of fuel and electricity, had contributed to their decision to close the newly opened hospital a fortnight into the conflict. The water tower around 100m from the hospital was hit and rendered useless by a single missile on or shortly before 27 July, when the hospital was closed. The water tower is near no other building and there were no signs of military activity in the area.[97]

Access to Education

Up to 50 schools in south Lebanon were reported to have been completely destroyed in Israeli attacks and some 300 suffered major damage.[98] As a result, hundreds of thousands of schoolchildren missed their first few weeks of the new academic year—delayed from mid-September until 16 October. Many schoolchildren have had to find places in other schools.

Amnesty International delegates visited several of the destroyed and badly damaged schools in south Lebanon, southern Beirut and Ba'albek. In Ma'roub, the school was flattened. In north-western Bint Jbeil, 'Oweyna girls school was severely damaged—its desks and chairs were visible from the street as one of the main walls had been ripped off. Kawnin's government school on the main road to Tibnin suffered severe external and internal damage, including partial destruction of walls—there was little or no sign of destruction in the surrounding area, indicating that the school was the target. Three of al-Khiam's five schools were severely damaged. In Beirut's Dhahiyeh neighbourhood, al-Mustaqbal school was completely destroyed, and Ashbel Sahel primary and secondary school was badly damaged.

Lethal Legacy of Cluster Bombs

"In Lebanon, we covered entire villages with cluster bombs... What we did there was crazy and monstrous." Israeli commander quoted in *Haaretz* newspaper[99]

---

[97] In the briefing, *Deliberate destruction or "collateral damage"? Israeli attacks against civilian infrastructure,* Amnesty International reported that the state hospitals in Bint Jbeil and Meis al-Jebel were "completely destroyed", citing as its source the Council for Development and Reconstruction. This was incorrect. Amnesty International delegates visited the hospitals in August and found that they had not been destroyed but rather could not function because of the attacks. There was unexploded ordnance visible around the Bint Jbeil hospital grounds, and a private hospital nearby had received extensive damage.

[98] UNICEF press statement, "The long road back to school for children in southern Lebanon", 7 September 2006.

[99] "When rockets and phosphorous cluster" by Meron Rapaport, *Haaretz* newspaper, 14 September 2006, http://www.haaretz.com/hasen/spages/761910.html.

Six-year-old 'Abbas Yousef Shibli was playing with three friends in the southern village of Blida on 26 August when they spotted what they thought was a perfume bottle. One of them went to pick it up and it exploded, leaving 'Abbas with devastating injuries—a ruptured colon and gall bladder, a perforated lung and a torn medial nerve. When 'Abbas spoke to Amnesty International delegates from his bed in Najde hospital in al-Nabatiyeh a few days later, he wailed over and over again, "Take the bombs away from my village."

His three friends—eight-year-old Ahmed Shibli, 11-year-old 'Ali Hasan and his nine-year-old sister Sahar—were also injured. 'Ali suffered a broken leg and both he and Sahar sustained shrapnel injuries. Sahar told Amnesty International:

> "Ali's leg has to stay in a cast for one and a half months and he can't go to play outside. And now it's better to play in the house because of the bombs. I told other children not to touch anything outside, not even a stone, and even under a leaf there could be a bomb."

In the last three days of the conflict, Israel showered cluster bombs over large areas of south Lebanon, depositing bomblets over residential areas, roads, orchards and fields. Many of the bomblets failed to explode. As a result, for hundreds of thousands of people in Lebanon, the war did not end with the ceasefire. In the first fortnight after the ceasefire, an average of one person a day was killed and five were injured by bomblets.[100] By 2 November, 22 people had been killed and 134 wounded in civilian areas, according to the UN Office for the Coordination of Humanitarian Affairs.[101]

An Israeli commander of a Multiple Launch Rocket System unit told the Israeli daily newspaper *Haaretz* that the army had fired 1,800 cluster bombs during the war, each containing hundreds of bomblets. "In Lebanon, we covered entire villages with cluster bombs," he said. "What we did there was crazy and monstrous."[102] The same newspaper reported that Israeli forces had also used 155mm artillery cannons to fire cluster shells.

UN Mine Action Coordination Center (UNMACC) estimated in September that around a million unexploded cluster bomblets remained scattered across Lebanon. Each has the potential to destroy lives, particularly those of curious children. It also estimated that it would take at least a year to clear the unexploded munitions.[103]

---

[100] *Lebanon: Cluster-bombs threaten civilian lives* (AI Index: MDE 02/024/2006).

[101] "See: http://www.maccsl.org/War%202006.htm.

[102] "When rockets and phosphorous cluster" by Meron Rapoport, *Haaretz* newspaper, 14 September 2006, http://www.haaretz.com/hasen/spages/761910.html.

[103] http://www.maccsl.org/reports/Leb%20UXO%20Fact%20Sheet%204%20November,%202006.pdf. There are also an estimated 15,000 unexploded ordnance of various kinds, mostly 155m tank shells but also grenades and air-delivered bombs.

UNMACC's spokesperson said that many of the cluster bomblets it had found were "in civilian areas, on farmland and in people's homes . . . We're finding a lot at the entrances to houses, on balconies and roofs . . . Sometimes windows are broken and they get inside the houses."[104] Amnesty International's delegates in Lebanon made similar findings, coming across many unexploded cluster bomblets in villages and inside homes.

In early November, UNMACC said it had cleared some 58,000 cluster bomblets and other pieces of unexploded ordnance.[105] Earlier it had said that around 200,000 people still could not return to their homes due to the level of destruction and contamination by cluster bomblets and other unexploded ordnance.[106]

Jan Egeland, UN Under-Secretary-General for Humanitarian Affairs, condemned Israel's use of cluster bombs in residential areas in Lebanon as "completely immoral". He added: "Every day, people are maimed, wounded and killed by these weapons. It shouldn't have happened."[107]

Israeli forces used cluster bombs made in the USA and Israel, and fired them from the air and by artillery. They included the 58B CBU (Cluster Bomb Unit) containing around 650 BLU 63 bomblets (shaped liked tennis balls), many of them produced in the Viet Nam war era. This old stock was apparently used overwhelmingly in the three days before the ceasefire.[108]

Amnesty International delegates in Lebanon talked to dozens of children and adults recovering from injuries inflicted by cluster bombs, and to relatives of those killed or wounded by such weapons.

On 14 August several members of the Hattab family were eating breakfast in front of their house in Habboush, near al-Nabatiyeh. A cat walking on the other side of the road detonated an explosive device and three consecutive explosions took place. Two people were killed—Hadi Mohammed al Hattab, who died instantly, and Moussa Hussein al Hattab, 34, who died three days later in hospital. Five people were injured.

The following day, Ali Turkiye, 20, was with a group of young men in a field in Zawtar al-Gharbiyeh on 15 August. He stretched up to pick some grapes from a vine above his head, disturbing a cluster bomb stuck in the leaves. It exploded, killing him instantly. Mahmoud Darwish, 24, was wounded in the knee and foot.

---

[104] US probes Israel cluster bomb use, http:/news.bbc.co.uk/1/hi/world/middle_east/5286352.stm.
[105] http://www.maccsl.org/reports/Leb%20UXO%20Fact%20Sheet%204%20November,%202006.pdf.
[106] UN News Centre, 29 September 2006.
[107] UN denounces Israel cluster bombs, 30 August 2006, http://news.bbc.co.uk/1/hi/world/middle_east/5299938.stm.
[108] Interview with Andrew Gleeson of the Mines Advisory Group.

Hussein Qaduh, a 19-year-old accountancy student at the Beirut Islamic Technical Institute, was walking on a path beside a football field in the southern village of al-Sultaniyeh on 28 August, two weeks after the cease-fire. What should have been a peaceful day was shattered by an explosion that ripped through his body. He was rushed to hospital in the nearby village of Tibnin and later transferred to hospital in Tyre as his injuries were so severe. Amnesty International delegates saw him there the following day after he had undergone extensive surgery and was still in a critical condition. The delegates then visited the area where he had been injured and found it was littered with unexploded cluster munitions, some of them just centimetres from the path he had been walking on. Blood was still visible on the ground.

Children have featured disproportionately in the long list of casualties. For example, Hassan Hussein Hamadi, aged 13, picked up a canister-type cluster bomb on 27 August while playing with his brothers and sisters in the front yard of his home in Deir Qanoun village, south of Tyre. It exploded, blowing off four fingers of his right hand and causing him major shoulder and abdominal injuries.

Jean Ziegler, UN Special Rapporteur on the right to food, said that he feared the long-term effects of unexploded ordnance on the livelihoods of hundreds of thousands of people would be severe as it will prevent irrigation, harvesting and planting.[109] In parts of Lebanon there is barely an orchard, olive grove, tobacco field or pasture that is not littered with cluster bomblets waiting to explode. As a result, the country's shepherds and farmers face a deadly dilemma—whether to let their animals starve and their harvests rot, or do they risk life and limb by entering areas infested with bomblets.

Unexploded bomblets have affected many other commercial concerns by disrupting repairs to blocked water supplies and broken power lines, as well as to destroyed buildings, roads and other infrastructure.

Wafiq Kishan, a 45-year-old school teacher from Sammaaiye village in the Ras al-'Ein district south of Tyre, told Amnesty International that the banana and orange trees in the groves around the family home were withering and damaged, partly because they were littered with cluster bomblets so the family could not water or prune the trees as required. He said that even if the unexploded bomblets were cleared quickly from the groves, it would be too late for the crops this year.

Khalil Badawi, 64, was injured on 24 August by a cluster bomb as he worked in an orchard in Sammaaiye village in the Ras al-'Ein district. He said that the bomb exploded when the hoe he was using touched it. He said he had

[109] http://www.un.org/apps/news/story/asp?NewsID=19900&Cr=leban&Cr1=.

no choice but to go into the field before it was de-mined: "We have to feed our families. Every morning we say goodbye to our families because we know we may not return . . . We try to be as careful as we can."

When the Heriz family returned home on 14 August, they saw that their animals lay dead in a nearby field. Ali Heriz, 26, went to try and move one of the cows and apparently triggered a cluster bomb. His chest and stomach bore the brunt of the blast, although his face was also injured. The family said that many of their fields could not be worked because of the cluster bomblets. The family did not know how it would survive.

'Abd al-Mohsen Heriz, a relative of 'Ali Heriz, told Amnesty International:

> "I've never seen anything like this. The presence of these cluster bombs force us now to fight another war. They are even more dangerous than the war itself, and this war may last for 20 years."

The bombing of Lebanon did not just kill and wound people. It also left deep scars on the mental and psychological well-being of civilians, especially in the south and in the southern suburbs of Beirut. Médecins Sans Frontières reported during the conflict that up to a third of its work was related to mental health problems.[110]

The long-term impact on the children of Lebanon is likely to be severe and health professionals fear for their future. A recognized way to help children overcome trauma is through play. However, in many parts of south Lebanon, playgrounds and other areas where children used to go are littered with cluster bomblets. As a result, outdoor play is a dangerous activity.[111]

Chapter 6
'Human Shields'

The protection of civilians on either side of a conflict is a shared responsibility of the parties at war. All parties to a conflict are obliged to take precautions to ensure that civilians under their control are not harmed by the dangers of military operations. They also have an obligation not to use the civilian population as a cover for their military activities—a war crime often referred to as using "human shields".

The Israeli authorities argue that Hizbullah must be held responsible for the harm caused to civilians by Israeli attacks, accusing Hizbullah fighters of intentionally using the civilian population as a cover for their military activities by having bases in tunnels and other facilities within towns and

[110] Médecins Sans Frontières, "Humanitarian corridor into South Lebanon is a delusion", 1 August 2006.

[111] *Daily Star*, "Good clean fun helps the youngest victims overcome stresses of war", 26 September 2006.

villages; storing Katyusha rockets, their launchers and other weapons in populated areas; firing Katyusha rockets from close proximity to civilian houses and often seeking cover in such houses after firing; and preventing civilians from fleeing their villages. Hizbullah denies any policy of endangering civilians. Hizbullah officials openly acknowledge that their fighters and military facilities are present in towns and villages in south Lebanon and elsewhere, but argue that the role of their fighters is to defend their communities against Israeli attacks. However, it denies that its fighters stored Katyusha rockets in populated areas or that they fired them from such areas. Hizbullah also denies that it prevented civilians from fleeing.

Military Facilities in Civilian Areas

As a political party, a social organization and an armed group, Hizbullah is based among the Shi'a Muslim population in Lebanon, particularly in the south. Hizbullah does not dispute that it built a network of tunnels and other military hide-outs in the vicinity of and inside towns and villages in south Lebanon, and used them to ambush Israeli troops once they entered Lebanon.[112] Hizbullah points out that Israeli forces invaded Lebanese territory, moving with tanks and troops into villages in south Lebanon, occupying civilian homes and launching attacks from these homes. It maintains that the armed confrontations that took place in or near certain villages were aimed at resisting Israeli ground attacks, and that its fighters were themselves from these villages.

In the course of its field research, Amnesty International found remains of short-range weapons, such as PK-type machine guns and anti-tank missiles, in the rubble of two buildings that had been destroyed by Israeli forces, in an uninhabited house on the edge of Marwahin and in a building on the outskirts of Bint Jbeil known to local residents as belonging to Hizbullah. In Marwahin, villagers confirmed to Amnesty International that a van parked next to a mosque—and seen in footage provided by the Israeli army to contain anti-tank missiles—had been used by Hizbullah during the conflict. In the village of Rmeish, Amnesty International delegates were shown two seemingly unused launchers for anti-tank missiles, which villagers said had been left by Hizbullah fighters near an unfinished building on a hill on the outskirts of the village.

As confirmed by Israeli infantry soldiers interviewed by Amnesty International, both Israeli troops and Hizbullah combatants fought each other with similar tactics, often in house-to-house fighting in villages that were largely abandoned by civilians. Amnesty International found evidence of

[112] See, for example, "Hiwar maftuh" ("Open Dialogue"), *al-Jazeera* programme about the Islamic Resistance fighting the Israeli army in Lebanon, broadcast on 19 August 2006.

the presence of Israeli troops in homes in several villages, including 'Aitaroun, 'Ait al-Sha'b, 'Ainata and Mheibib. Food wrappers and other items with Hebrew writing, as well as large numbers of spent cartridges and used rocket launchers with Hebrew markings, littered such houses. Israeli soldiers had also vandalized these houses, including with insulting graffiti.

The close proximity of the military to civilian areas is also not unusual in Israel. According to reports, military installations are located in Kiryat Shimona and Metulla, and military border posts are near or within a number of other northern Israeli towns and villages. During the war there were more Israeli military positions and activities close to and within civilian areas in north Israel than usual. The Israeli army is reported to have installed bases near Arab towns and villages, including Fassuta, 'Arab al-'Aramshe and Tarshiha—in this last village three residents were killed by a Hizbullah rocket attack. The Israeli army also reportedly carried out training exercises inside Israeli Arab villages because their landscape resembled that of villages in south Lebanon.[113]

Following the killing of 12 Israeli soldiers "outside the entrance" to the kibbutz of Kfar Giladi, where their battalion had been stationed for a week, it was reported that "during the war hundreds of soldiers were on the kibbutz, including a medical company, special units and artillery troops".[114] A number of other northern towns and villages with large Arab populations reportedly have munitions factories near to them.[115] Finally, while Hizbullah's headquarters are indeed in an area of Beirut that was heavily bombed by Israeli forces, Israel's Ministry of Defense is itself located in the heart of Tel Aviv.

While the presence of Hizbullah's fighters and short-range weapons within civilian areas is not contested, this in itself is not conclusive evidence of intent to use civilians as "human shields", any more than the presence of Israeli soldiers in a kibbutz is in itself evidence of the same war crime. Such conduct may, however, amount to a violation of the obligation of each party to the conflict to take the necessary precautions to protect civilians under its control from the dangers of military operations "to the maximum extent

113 Arab Association for Human Rights (AAHR), *Weekly Review*, No.286, 4–11 August 2006, http://www.arabhra.org/publications/wrap/wraphome2006.htm. Majd al-Krum residents told UN Special Rapporteurs that artillery was located near their town during the conflict, http://www.ohchr.org/english/bodies/hrcouncil/docs/2session/A.HRC.2.7.pdf.

114 According to *Haaretz* newspaper, "The rocket hit an area where logistics and headquarters officials from the reserve paratroopers battalion . . . were stationed". Also, "Three military trucks filled with ammunition were parked" at the site. "Reservists failed to take cover after siren", *Haaretz,* 7 August 2006, http://www.haaretz.com/hasen/pages/ShArt.jhtml?itemNo=747042; "During war, troops needed permission to enter communities", *Haaretz,* 20 September 2006.

115 Jonathan Cook, *The Human Shields of Nazareth,*19 July 2006, http://www.jkcook.net/Articles2/0261.htm#Top.

feasible", and in particular "avoiding locating military objectives within or near densely populated areas".

In any case, by placing combatants and a variety of weapons within towns and villages, Hizbullah and Israel remain responsible for rendering such locations lawful targets and therefore exposing civilians who may have been present to risk. Israeli forces and Hizbullah fighters, however, were obliged at all times to apply the principle of distinction and proportionality, and take the precautions required by international humanitarian law, when launching attacks.

Storing and Firing Katyushas

Israel accuses Hizbullah of storing Katyushas and other missiles and their launchers in civilian areas, specifically homes but also schools and mosques. An Israeli infantry officer told Amnesty International that his platoon found 15 Katyushas—without their launchers—in the lower floor of a two-storey house in the village of 'Ait al-Sha'b in August. Photographic evidence produced by the IDF shows what appears to be a damaged Katyusha-type rocket in the courtyard of a mosque in Marwahin, next to the van with anti-tank missiles referred to earlier. Hizbullah told Amnesty International that it does not store Katyushas in towns and villages, but in woods or other natural areas providing cover.

Israel published or provided Amnesty International with a few samples of air surveillance footage showing the firing of Katyusha-type rockets and short-range antitank missiles from near civilian houses. One such incident was recorded on 7 August, the footage showing rockets taking off from between two houses in the village of Sidiqin.[116] However, in most of the other footage, crucial co-ordinates, such as date, time and location, are not provided and the few incidents that are dated, such as the one above, took place long after much of the civilian population had left some of the villages. Other footage shows what appear to be trucks with mounted Katyusha launchers taking refuge inside buildings.

The Israeli senior commander who briefed Amnesty International in September also said that Hizbullah forces fired rockets from places only 30–40 metres from UNIFIL bases, seeking to avoid Israeli counter-fire, and that on occasion Hizbullah fighters had sought refuge in UNIFIL bases.

UNIFIL reported more than 20 instances of rockets being fired by Hizbullah "from the vicinity" (up to 500m) of UN positions in south Lebanon, as well as a number of cases of Hizbullah small arms and mortar fire from "close

---

[116] See *Hizbullah's exploitation of Lebanese population centers and civilians: Photographic evidence,* http://www.mfa.gov.il/MFA/MFAArchive/2000_2009/2006/Operation+Change+of+Direction+Video+Clips.htm.

to" (up to 100m) UNIFIL positions and several cases of UN positions and vehicles being hit by Hizbullah mortars, small arms fire or rockets. UNIFIL maintains that Hizbullah fighters were never allowed into any of its bases.[117]

Hizbullah denies using civilian areas to launch Katyushas, stating that such attacks were launched from woods, plantations, riverbeds and other places outside villages, far from populated areas.

In 'Ein Ebel and Rmeish, villagers told Amnesty International that on some occasions, mostly at the beginning of the war, Hizbullah fighters did fire rockets from villages, though not from inside or near their homes. They did not know whether the attacks were aimed at Israeli troops near the villages or at Israeli territory. They said that after villagers complained to Hizbullah, such practices generally stopped. In 'Ein Ebel, a resident who remained in the village throughout the war told Amnesty International that Israeli forces bombarded the village, including the church, at times when there was no Hizbullah presence or activity anywhere in the village.

It is not clear from the handful of examples made available by the Israeli authorities whether any civilians were present in buildings from which, or close to which, rockets were launched. If civilians were not present, Hizbullah fighters launching rockets in those circumstances would not have violated the prohibition on using "human shields". However, buildings used as launching bases for Katyushas would have been a legitimate target for Israeli forces, and buildings close to launching areas would have been exposed to possible incidental damage. Again, Israeli forces would still have needed to apply the principles of distinction and proportionality and take the precautions required by international humanitarian law.

In conclusion, had Hizbullah fighters stored Katyushas or launched them from close proximity to civilians in the hope of deterring Israeli attacks, this would have amounted to the crime of using civilians as "human shields". The available evidence suggests that in at least some cases Katyushas were stored within villages and fired from civilian areas, but it is not apparent that civilians were present and used as "human shields". With almost 4,000 rockets fired on Israel and very little undisputed information about where they were actually stored and fired from, the extent of such conduct and its qualification in terms of international humanitarian law remains unclear.

[117] See UNIFIL press releases during the conflict at http://www.un.org/depts/dpko/missions/unifil/unifilpress.htm and conversation with Milos Strugar, UNIFIL Senior Advisor, 6 November 2006. According to UNIFIL, Israeli forces often fired tank and artillery shells, aerial bombs and machine-gun fire into UN positions or in their "immediate vicinity". For example, during the last 24 hours before the cessation of hostilities on 14 August, a total of 85 artillery shells impacted inside UNIFIL positions, 35 of them inside the headquarters of the Ghanaian battalion in the Tibnin area. A further 10 impacted within 70m of the base.

Preventing Civilians from Fleeing?

Israeli officials alleged that Hizbullah prevented civilians from leaving certain areas by blocking roads or even firing over their heads, in order that the civilians would shield the fighters. However, the Israeli authorities provided no evidence of this, beyond suggesting that Amnesty International investigate one such alleged incident in Marwahin. Amnesty International did so and found no evidence to substantiate the allegations. Villagers in Marwahin—including those known for political affiliations rival to Hizbullah—denied that any such event happened. Indeed, many of the villagers fled at the beginning of the hostilities, only for their convoy to be attacked by Israeli forces (see Chapter 3).

None of the people interviewed by Amnesty International in towns and villages in south Lebanon and elsewhere in the country alleged that Hizbullah prevented or tried to prevent them from leaving their town or village, or reported cases where others had been so impeded. Some stated that Hizbullah had warned residents of the likelihood of Israeli attacks in their areas. In some cases, notably during the 48-hour suspension of air strikes by Israel on 31 July and 1 August, Hizbullah activists in certain areas are said to have encouraged or assisted people who had been unable to leave their villages in south Lebanon to do so. Civilians resident in the Beirut neighbourhood of Dhahiyeh, where Hizbullah had its headquarters as well as other offices relating to its media, social, medical and educational activities, were also evacuated before Israeli attacks began. Hizbullah reportedly led the evacuation efforts.

In conclusion, the evidence available to Amnesty International does not substantiate the allegations that Hizbullah prevented civilians from fleeing, and in several cases points to the contrary.

Chapter 7
Conclusions and Recommendations

The 34-day war between Hizbullah and Israel in July and August 2006 caused death and devastation on a large scale, with civilians on both sides bearing the brunt of military operations.

Based on its research and analysis, including a review of Israeli interpretation of the laws of war, Amnesty International has concluded that Israeli forces committed serious violations of international human rights and humanitarian law, including war crimes. In particular, Amnesty International has found that Israeli forces carried out indiscriminate and disproportionate attacks on a large scale. These include the sustained artillery bombardment of south Lebanon and, in particular, the widespread use of cluster bombs in civilian areas in the last days of the war.

As shown in an initial briefing published in August[118] and illustrated further in this report, such attacks also included those on civilian infrastructure—for example, the bombing of the Jiyye power station which also caused massive environmental damage. In this context Israeli forces also appear to have carried out direct attacks on civilian objects, such as the destruction of factories and of the small port of al-Ouza'i and its fishing boats.

The attacks on the infrastructure, on objects indispensable to the survival of the population, as well as the air and sea blockade imposed throughout the war and beyond, seem to have been intended to inflict a form of collective punishment on Lebanon's people, in order to induce them and the Lebanese government to turn against Hizbullah, as well as to cause harm to Hizbullah's military capability.

Finally, based on the available evidence and in the absence of an adequate or any explanation from the Israeli authorities for so many attacks by their forces causing civilian deaths and destruction, when no evidence of Hizbullah military activities was apparent, it seems clear that Israeli forces consistently failed to adopt necessary precautionary measures. As seen in threats expressed in public statements by senior political and military leaders and in leaflets dropped into Lebanon, Israeli forces effectively considered any civilian travelling in south Lebanon as a military target, in flagrant violation of the principle of distinction. Any attack carried out in this context would have been an indiscriminate attack if not a direct attack against civilians.

In a briefing published in September 2006, Amnesty International looked into Hizbullah's rocket bombardment of northern Israel and concluded that Hizbullah also committed serious violations of international humanitarian law, including war crimes. In particular, the scale of Hizbullah's rocket attacks on towns and villages in northern Israel, the indiscriminate nature of the weapons used, together with statements by Hizbullah's leader, showed that Hizbullah carried out direct attacks on civilians as well as indiscriminate attacks and attacks on the civilian population as reprisal.

Hizbullah fighters also appear not to have taken necessary precautions to protect civilians in Lebanon from the effects of Israeli attacks. The evidence suggests that, in at least some cases, Katyusha rockets were stored within villages and fired from civilian areas, although the extent of such conduct is not clear. It is also not clear from the handful of examples made available by the Israeli authorities and other evidence whether civilians were present in buildings close to the firing areas. If Hizbullah fighters stored Katyushas in, or fired them from, close proximity to civilians in the hope of deterring

[118] See *Deliberate destruction or "collateral damage"? Israeli attacks against civilian infrastructure,* op cit.

Israeli attacks, this would amount to the war crime of using civilians as "human shields". The evidence available to Amnesty International does not substantiate the allegations that Hizbullah prevented civilians from fleeing, and in several cases points to the contrary.

The scale and nature of the violations committed by both Israeli forces and Hizbullah fighters in their latest war calls for accountability and remedial action. Over the many years of conflict between Hizbullah and Israel, both sides have repeatedly committed serious violations of international humanitarian law without any accountability.[119]

Prompt, independent, impartial and thorough investigations in accordance with international standards for such investigations and bringing to justice perpetrators of serious violations are essential to build respect for international humanitarian law.

The Israeli authorities maintain that they carry out investigations into incidents, but these investigations fail to conform to international standards, including the obligation of transparency. For example, they have never disclosed the methods of such investigations—whether in fact they differ, for example, from routine battlefield debriefings which in no way can amount to a proper investigation—and to which incidents they relate.

As in previous conflicts relating to Lebanon, the Israeli authorities have in general provided no specific explanation for attacks that led to civilian deaths. In the few such cases where the authorities have offered some explanations, these were inadequate. When they indicated that civilian deaths and injuries were the result of mistakes, they provided no indication that anyone had been or would be held accountable for the mistakes.

No investigation into violations of international humanitarian law by Hizbullah is known to have been conducted by Hizbullah commanders or by the Lebanese authorities.

At the international level, two inquiries have been conducted. In early September, four UN independent experts of the UN Human Rights Council examined the impact of the conflict on the right to life, health and housing, and the situation of the internally displaced.[120] In August 2006 a Commission of Inquiry was set up by the Human Rights Council, comprising three independent experts. However, these inquiries were limited in scope to the specific mandates of the UN experts, and in the case of the Commission of Inquiry by a mandate which related only to violations by Israel, not Hizbullah. In addition, both inquiries operated under significant restrictions in terms of time and resources.

---

[119] See *Israel/Lebanon: Attacks on Lebanese civilians in south Lebanon by Israeli forces*, June 2000 (AI Index: MDE 02/006/2000), and *Israel/Lebanon: Unlawful killings during Operation - "Grapes of Wrath"*, op cit.

[120] *Report of four Special Rapporteurs on their mission to Lebanon and Israel*, 2 October 2006.

Amnesty International has been calling for a comprehensive and impartial inquiry by independent experts into the conduct of both sides to be set up by the UN Secretary-General, the outcome of which should be made public and include recommendations aimed at ending and preventing further violations. Such an inquiry should look at all the available evidence, including Amnesty International's findings in this and previous reports. It should also be empowered to decide on the form of reparation for the victims of violations, including financial compensation.

In addition, while international investigations play a crucial role in establishing facts and responsibilities, and thus seek to implement the right to truth of the victims and the public, the parties to the conflict and the international community have the primary responsibility to ensure the right to justice, with judicial determinations of guilt or innocence and reparations.

Amnesty International calls on the Israeli government to:

- Investigate promptly, independently, impartially and thoroughly, in accordance with international standards, the evidence indicating that its forces committed serious violations of international human rights and humanitarian law during the conflict, including war crimes.
- Wherever there is sufficient admissible evidence, prosecute anyone suspected of serious violations in proceedings that fully respect international fair trial standards.
- Revise its interpretation of the rules and principles relating to the concepts of military objective, military advantage and proportionality, to ensure that these concepts are fully consistent with international humanitarian law.
- Ensure that the Israeli military complies fully with the duty to take precautionary measures when carrying out attacks, as well as in defence, and does not carry out attacks as a form of collective punishment.
- Announce a moratorium on the use of all cluster weapons and, in any event, declare that it would not, under any circumstances, use such weapons to target military objectives in civilian areas.
- Provide without delay detailed maps of the areas of Lebanon into which cluster bombs were fired, to facilitate clearance and prevent further civilian casualties.
- Provide without delay maps of the minefields established in southern Lebanon during previous conflicts.
- Announce that it will not use white phosphorous weapons in civilian areas.
- Provide full reparations for the consequences of its unlawful acts and omissions.

- Co-operate fully with an international commission empowered to investigate such acts and omissions by all the parties to the conflict, and decide on the form of reparation, including financial compensation. It should provide such a commission with information on any investigations undertaken, as required under international standards.
- Ratify Protocol I of the Geneva Conventions without reservations and make a declaration under Article 90 accepting the competence of the International Humanitarian Fact-Finding Commission.
- Ratify the Rome Statute of the International Criminal Court, without making a declaration under Article 124—which would exclude for seven years the jurisdiction of the Court over war crimes—and making a declaration pursuant to Article 12(3) that its jurisdiction encompasses the 2006 war.

Amnesty International calls on Hizbullah to:

- Publicly renounce its unlawful policy of reprisal rocket attacks against the civilian population of Israel.
- Carry out an investigation into any violations of international humanitarian law by its own forces, and hand over to the Lebanese authorities anyone suspected of such abuses for further investigation and prosecution if appropriate.
- Ensure that Hizbullah's fighters comply fully with the need to take precautionary measures in attacks and in defence, including the need to distinguish themselves from non-combatants to the maximum extent possible.
- Provide full reparations for the consequences of its unlawful acts and omissions.
- Co-operate fully with an international commission empowered to investigate such acts and omissions by all the parties to the conflict, and decide on the form of reparation, including financial compensation.

Amnesty International calls on the Lebanese government to:

- Investigate promptly, independently, impartially and thoroughly, in accordance with international investigation standards, the evidence indicating that Hizbullah forces committed serious violations of international humanitarian law during the conflict, including war crimes.
- Wherever there is sufficient admissible evidence, prosecute anyone suspected of serious violations in proceedings that fully respect international fair trial standards and do not lead to the imposition of the death penalty.

- Ensure that no armed group operating within its territory carries out abuses of international human rights and humanitarian law.
- Provide full reparations for the consequences of unlawful acts or omissions by Lebanese officials and by Hizbullah.
- Co-operate fully with an international commission empowered to investigate such acts or omissions by all the parties to the conflict, and decide on the form of reparation, including financial compensation.
- Ratify the Rome Statute of the International Criminal Court, without making a declaration under Article 124—which would exclude for seven years the jurisdiction of the Court over war crimes—and making a declaration pursuant to Article 12(3) that its jurisdiction encompasses the 2006 war.

Amnesty International calls on the international community to:

- Ensure that the UN sets up an international commission empowered to investigate the evidence of violations of international human rights, humanitarian and criminal law by all the parties to the conflict; make recommendations for addressing impunity for violations committed and preventing future violations; and make recommendations on the form of reparation, including financial compensation. All states and the parties to the conflict must co-operate with such an inquiry.
- Exert pressure on all those involved in the conflict to co-operate with such a commission and implement its recommendations.
- Ensure that UNIFIL includes a component that would monitor any violations of international human rights and humanitarian law.
- Declare and enforce an arms embargo on both Israel and Hizbullah until effective mechanisms are in place to ensure that weapons will not be used to commit serious violations of international humanitarian law. This must include ensuring that a thorough investigation of violations in this conflict takes place and anyone found responsible is brought to justice in fair trials. The USA, Lebanon, Iran, Syria and other states should ensure that no weapons that may be used to commit violations are sent by them to any of the parties or transits through their territory.
- Announce an immediate moratorium on the use of all cluster weapons, end the transfer of such weapons to other states, and support initiatives by the UN and the ICRC to develop a new international humanitarian law agreement which will effectively address the threat that cluster weapons pose to civilians.
- Ensure that states exercise jurisdiction including, where necessary, universal jurisdiction, over suspects of crimes under international law, including war crimes.

DOCUMENT NO. 5

CESSATION OF HOSTILITIES IN LEBANON

UN Security Council
S/RES/1701 (2006)

August 11, 2006

The resolution calls for a cessation of hostilities in Lebanon.

The Security Council,

Recalling all its previous resolutions on Lebanon, in particular resolutions 425 (1978), 426 (1978), 520 (1982), 1559 (2004), 1655 (2006), 1680 (2006) and 1697 (2006), as well as the statements of its President on the situation in Lebanon, in particular the statements of 18 June 2000 (S/PRST/2000/21), of 19 October 2004 (S/PRST/2004/36), of 4 May 2005 (S/PRST/2005/17), of 23 January 2006 (S/PRST/2006/3) and of 30 July 2006 (S/PRST/2006/35),

Expressing its utmost concern at the continuing escalation of hostilities in Lebanon and in Israel since Hizbollah's attack on Israel on 12 July 2006, which has already caused hundreds of deaths and injuries on both sides, extensive damage to civilian infrastructure and hundreds of thousands of internally displaced persons,

Emphasizing the need for an end of violence, but at the same time emphasizing the need to address urgently the causes that have given rise to the current crisis, including by the unconditional release of the abducted Israeli soldiers,

Mindful of the sensitivity of the issue of prisoners and encouraging the efforts aimed at urgently settling the issue of the Lebanese prisoners detained in Israel,

Welcoming the efforts of the Lebanese Prime Minister and the commitment of the Government of Lebanon, in its seven-point plan, to extend its authority over its territory, through its own legitimate armed forces, such that there will be no weapons without the consent of the Government of Lebanon and no authority other than that of the Government of Lebanon, welcoming also its commitment to a United Nations force that is supplemented and enhanced in numbers, equipment, mandate and scope of operation, and bearing in mind its request in this plan for an immediate withdrawal of the Israeli forces from southern Lebanon,

Determined to act for this withdrawal to happen at the earliest,

Taking due note of the proposals made in the seven-point plan regarding the Shebaa farms area,

Welcoming the unanimous decision by the Government of Lebanon on 7 August 2006 to deploy a Lebanese armed force of 15,000 troops in South Lebanon as the Israeli army withdraws behind the Blue Line and to request the assistance of additional forces from the United Nations Interim Force in Lebanon (UNIFIL) as needed, to facilitate the entry of the Lebanese armed forces into the region and to restate its intention to strengthen the Lebanese armed forces with material as needed to enable it to perform its duties,

Aware of its responsibilities to help secure a permanent ceasefire and a long-term solution to the conflict,

Determining that the situation in Lebanon constitutes a threat to international peace and security,

1. Calls for a full cessation of hostilities based upon, in particular, the immediate cessation by Hizbollah of all attacks and the immediate cessation by Israel of all offensive military operations;

2. Upon full cessation of hostilities, calls upon the Government of Lebanon and UNIFIL as authorized by paragraph 11 to deploy their forces together throughout the South and calls upon the Government of Israel, as that deployment begins, to withdraw all of its forces from southern Lebanon in parallel;

3. Emphasizes the importance of the extension of the control of the Government of Lebanon over all Lebanese territory in accordance with the provisions of resolution 1559 (2004) and resolution 1680 (2006), and of the relevant provisions of the Taif Accords, for it to exercise its full sovereignty, so that there will be no weapons without the consent of the Government of Lebanon and no authority other than that of the Government of Lebanon;

4. Reiterates its strong support for full respect for the Blue Line;

5. Also reiterates its strong support, as recalled in all its previous relevant resolutions, for the territorial integrity, sovereignty and political independence of Lebanon within its internationally recognized borders, as contemplated by the Israeli-Lebanese General Armistice Agreement of 23 March 1949;

6. Calls on the international community to take immediate steps to extend its financial and humanitarian assistance to the Lebanese people, including

through facilitating the safe return of displaced persons and, under the authority of the Government of Lebanon, reopening airports and harbours, consistent with paragraphs 14 and 15, and calls on it also to consider further assistance in the future to contribute to the reconstruction and development of Lebanon;

7. Affirms that all parties are responsible for ensuring that no action is taken contrary to paragraph 1 that might adversely affect the search for a long-term solution, humanitarian access to civilian populations, including safe passage for humanitarian convoys, or the voluntary and safe return of displaced persons, and calls on all parties to comply with this responsibility and to cooperate with the Security Council;

8. Calls for Israel and Lebanon to support a permanent ceasefire and a long-term solution based on the following principles and elements:

- full respect for the Blue Line by both parties;
- security arrangements to prevent the resumption of hostilities, including the establishment between the Blue Line and the Litani river of an area free of any armed personnel, assets and weapons other than those of the Government of Lebanon and of UNIFIL as authorized in paragraph 11, deployed in this area;
- full implementation of the relevant provisions of the Taif Accords, and of resolutions 1559 (2004) and 1680 (2006), that require the disarmament of all armed groups in Lebanon, so that, pursuant to the Lebanese cabinet decision of 27 July 2006, there will be no weapons or authority in Lebanon other than that of the Lebanese State;
- no foreign forces in Lebanon without the consent of its Government;
- no sales or supply of arms and related materiel to Lebanon except as authorized by its Government;
- provision to the United Nations of all remaining maps of landmines in Lebanon in Israel's possession;

9. Invites the Secretary-General to support efforts to secure as soon as possible agreements in principle from the Government of Lebanon and the Government of Israel to the principles and elements for a long-term solution as set forth in paragraph 8, and expresses its intention to be actively involved;

10. Requests the Secretary-General to develop, in liaison with relevant international actors and the concerned parties, proposals to implement the relevant provisions of the Taif Accords, and resolutions 1559 (2004) and 1680 (2006), including disarmament, and for delineation of the international borders of Lebanon, especially in those areas where the border is disputed or uncertain, including by dealing with the Shebaa farms area, and to present to the Security Council those proposals within thirty days;

11. Decides, in order to supplement and enhance the force in numbers, equipment, mandate and scope of operations, to authorize an increase in the force strength of UNIFIL to a maximum of 15,000 troops, and that the force shall, in addition to carrying out its mandate under resolutions 425 and 426 (1978):

(a) Monitor the cessation of hostilities;

(b) Accompany and support the Lebanese armed forces as they deploy throughout the South, including along the Blue Line, as Israel withdraws its armed forces from Lebanon as provided in paragraph 2;

(c) Coordinate its activities related to paragraph 11 (b) with the Government of Lebanon and the Government of Israel;

(d) Extend its assistance to help ensure humanitarian access to civilian populations and the voluntary and safe return of displaced persons;

(e) Assist the Lebanese armed forces in taking steps towards the establishment of the area as referred to in paragraph 8;

(f) Assist the Government of Lebanon, at its request, to implement paragraph 14;

12. Acting in support of a request from the Government of Lebanon to deploy an international force to assist it to exercise its authority throughout the territory, authorizes UNIFIL to take all necessary action in areas of deployment of its forces and as it deems within its capabilities, to ensure that its area of operations is not utilized for hostile activities of any kind, to resist attempts by forceful means to prevent it from discharging its duties under the mandate of the Security Council, and to protect United Nations personnel, facilities, installations and equipment, ensure the security and freedom of movement of United Nations personnel, humanitarian workers and, without prejudice to the responsibility of the Government of Lebanon, to protect civilians under imminent threat of physical violence;

13. Requests the Secretary-General urgently to put in place measures to ensure UNIFIL is able to carry out the functions envisaged in this resolution, urges Member States to consider making appropriate contributions to UNIFIL and to respond positively to requests for assistance from the Force, and expresses its strong appreciation to those who have contributed to UNIFIL in the past;

14. Calls upon the Government of Lebanon to secure its borders and other entry points to prevent the entry in Lebanon without its consent of arms or related materiel and requests UNIFIL as authorized in paragraph 11 to assist the Government of Lebanon at its request;

15. Decides further that all States shall take the necessary measures to prevent, by their nationals or from their territories or using their flag vessels or aircraft:

(a) The sale or supply to any entity or individual in Lebanon of arms and related materiel of all types, including weapons and ammunition, military vehicles and equipment, paramilitary equipment, and spare parts for the aforementioned, whether or not originating in their territories; and

(b) The provision to any entity or individual in Lebanon of any technical training or assistance related to the provision, manufacture, maintenance or use of the items listed in subparagraph (a) above; except that these prohibitions shall not apply to arms, related material, training or assistance authorized by the Government of Lebanon or by UNIFIL as authorized in paragraph 11;

16. Decides to extend the mandate of UNIFIL until 31 August 2007, and expresses its intention to consider in a later resolution further enhancements to the mandate and other steps to contribute to the implementation of a permanent ceasefire and a long-term solution;

17. Requests the Secretary-General to report to the Council within one week on the implementation of this resolution and subsequently on a regular basis;

18. Stresses the importance of, and the need to achieve, a comprehensive, just and lasting peace in the Middle East, based on all its relevant resolutions including its resolutions 242 (1967) of 22 November 1967, 338 (1973) of 22 October 1973 and 1515 (2003) of 19 November 2003;

19. Decides to remain actively seized of the matter.

DOCUMENT NO. 6

THE ROAD TO THE SECOND LEBANON WAR: THE LEBANESE SCENE IN THE YEARS 2000–2006

Intelligence and Terrorism Information Center at the Israel Intelligence Heritage & Commemoration Center (IICC) Report

October 30, 2007

by Col. (Ret.) Reuven Erlich, PhD[1]

Events and Developments that Influenced Lebanon

1. The six years preceding the second Lebanon war saw great turmoil on the Lebanese scene and in the history of Syrian and Israeli involvement in Lebanon. The developments in that period of time were influenced by **three dramatic events that occurred both inside and outside of Lebanon in the year 2000:**

a. **The IDF's withdrawal from the security zone (May).** Israel had been dragged into the Lebanese civil war and was involved in the goings-on in Lebanon since the war had first started (1975). The IDF's withdrawal from the security zone marked the end of Israel's direct, intensive involvement in Lebanon. The security zone collapsed, the IDF positioned itself south of the "blue line", thus discrediting the international (and, to a great extent, the internal Lebanese) legitimacy of Hezbollah's continuing armed struggle against Israel.

Editor's note: The original version of this document included some color images that could not be adequately reproduced in this publication. Where necessary, captions, headings, and/or footnotes specifically relating to any omitted images have also been left out of the version reprinted herein. The main text of the document has not been affected by these omissions, but the footnote numbering has been changed where necessary to remove gaps between the footnote numbers.

[1] Based on a lecture by Reuven Erlich, PhD, given on September 6, 2007 during the "Lebanon 2000–2006" study day, being part of a seminar titled "The Second Lebanon War – 2006". The seminar was held in Ramat Efal by Yad Tabenkin, the Israeli Society for Military History at the Tel-Aviv University, and the Yisrael Galili Institute for the Study of the Defense Forces.

b. **The death of Syria's president Hafez Assad (June).** The Syrian president, who had reigned for thirty years, died of a disease and passed down the presidency to his inexperienced son, Bashar Assad. The government change in Damascus influenced not only Syria but also the "Syrian order" in Lebanon, which formed in Lebanon in the course of the last twenty-five years of the previous century.

c. **The outbreak of the Palestinian campaign of terrorism, referred to by the Palestinians as the "second intifada" (October).** As a result, Israel focused its attention on the struggle against the escalating Palestinian terrorism, making efforts not to be dragged once again into what was perceived as the "Lebanese swamp". Israel embraced a policy of containment vis-à-vis Hezbollah's terrorism, and avoided retaliatory actions that could have resulted in escalation on the Lebanese scene.

2. Those events were joined by dramatic developments on the international and regional scene, mainly the **September 11 attacks and the US takeover of Iraq.** Iran rushed to fill the void in the regional balance of power, caused by the collapse of Saddam Hussein's regime, and joined forces with Syria to achieve regional hegemony. These developments also influenced the Lebanese scene.

3. It is against this background that we can examine **Hezbollah's buildup** in the years preceding the second Lebanon war. Hezbollah was perceived by the Iranian regime and by Syria as an important means of entrenching their influence in Lebanon **(and all the more so** following the withdrawal of the Syrian forces) and as an important instrument for promoting their interests in the struggle against Israel. As a result, **the two countries accelerated Hezbollah's military buildup** while encouraging it to join the Lebanese government and further its integration into the Lebanese political system.

The Formation of the Opposing Camps in Lebanon

4. **After the Syrian forces were pulled out of Lebanon in March 2005, two opposing camps formed on the Lebanese interior scene:**

a. **The supporters of the "new order", or the March 14 Forces** (the date of a massive anti-Syrian rally in Beirut). A pro-Western, anti-Syrian, and anti-Iranian coalition, it is based on **Sunni Muslims** led by **Saad Hariri** (the son of Rafik Hariri, the assassinated prime minister) and **Fouad Siniora,** the Prime Minister of Lebanon. They were joined by part of the Christian camp **(Amin Gemayel, Samir Ja'ja')** and a significant portion of the Druze community **(led by Walid Jumblatt).**

b. **The supporters of Syria and Iran,** led by **Hezbollah. This camp** also includes the **Amal** movement led by **Nabih Berry, and some of the Christian camp** led by **Michel Aoun,** who returned from his exile in

France. Michel Aoun, who enjoys considerable support among the Christians, preferred to join the pro-Syrian camp (against which he fought in the past) out of his own self-serving interests (such as his desire to become president).

5. The Lebanese government, dominated by the March 14 Forces, enjoys a slight majority in the Lebanese parliament and is subjected to heavy political pressure by Hezbollah and the supporters of Syria and Iran. The internal Lebanese political struggles intensified following the second Lebanon war and sometimes even turned violent. However, the two opposing camps take great care not to be dragged into a civil war, such as the war that took place in the 1970s and 1980s of the previous century.

6. In the year that passed since the second Lebanon war, Fouad Siniora's government has showed impressive determination and ability to withstand the pressure exerted by the opposition. The government has succeeded in preserving its rule in spite of the resignation of Hezbollah ministers from the government and a series of protests and rallies organized by Hezbollah and the supporters of Syria and Iran. It can also boast some considerable achievements: the unprecedented deployment of the Lebanese army in south Lebanon and the strengthening of the Lebanese army in south Lebanon; the ratification of the international tribunal for the murder of Rafik Hariri; the deployment of the Lebanese army, for the first time, in the Nahr al-Bared refugee camp and the submission of Fatah al-Islam, the Al-Qaeda branch in Lebanon. However, **the government took care not to confront Hezbollah and did little to address the core issues of Security Council Resolution 1701:** preventing Hezbollah's military restoration; the demilitarization of south Lebanon and enforcing an effective embargo on arms smuggling from Syria and Iran.

7. An important test for both opposing camps is going to be the **process of the presidential elections,** beginning in late September 2007. The identity of the new president who will succeed pro-Syrian Emile Lahoud, and the manner in which he will be elected, will have a tremendous influence on the internal Lebanese scene in the coming years.

The Formation and Collapse of the Syrian Order in Lebanon

8. The last quarter of the previous century saw massive Syrian involvement in Lebanon and the formation of the Syrian order, which characterized the internal Lebanese scene from 1989 (the Taif Accord) and 2005 (the pullout of the Syrian forces from Lebanon). The Syrians' path to enforce the Syrian order was **long, arduous, and fraught with difficulties:**

a. In the summer of 1976, the year when the Lebanese civil war reached its peak, the Syrian army invaded Lebanon, after indirect dialog with

Israel brokered by the US. As part of the dialog, the two parties reached an understanding on the "red line", north of which the Syrian army enjoyed freedom of action. In 1976, the Syrian army took over the majority of Lebanese territory, except for south Lebanon (which remained under the control of Palestinian terrorist organizations) and the Christian enclave of Mount Lebanon (controlled by the Christian Lebanese Forces, led by Bashir Gemayel).

b. The Syrian army which invaded Lebanon subdued the Palestinian terrorist organizations and their allies from the Muslim-leftist camp, which would not accept the dictates imposed by Damascus. Later on it received inter-Arab legitimacy, turned into the "Arab Deterrence Forces", and acted against the Christian camp, led by Bashir Gemayel. The differences of opinion between Syria and the Christian camp escalated into a violent conflict. Israel was dragged into the struggles waged by Syria against the Christian militias (1978–1982) first by providing indirect military assistance to the Christian camp and then by direct involvement on the Lebanese scene.

c. **On June 6, 1982,** the IDF invaded Lebanon (the first Lebanon War) and destroyed the political–military infrastructure of the Palestinian terrorist organizations in south Lebanon and west Beirut. Syria, weak both politically and militarily, facilitated the establishment of Hezbollah by the Iranian Revolutionary Guards and assisted the organization in its terrorist activities and guerilla warfare against the Multinational Force (US, France) and the IDF. In January 1985, the IDF was forced to pull out of Lebanon without a political agreement after an intensive series of terrorist attacks by Hezbollah and the Shi'ite Amal movement, perpetrated with the encouragement of Syria and Iran.

9. The Syrians took advantage of the political vacuum formed after the IDF's withdrawal in order to entrench their control of Lebanon. In 1989–1991, the Syrian army overpowered the anti-Syrian Christian camp (led by Michel Aoun), occupied the Christian enclave on Mount Lebanon, disbanded the Christian militias, eliminated or exiled their leaders, and established a pro-Syrian Lebanese regime led by a pro-Syrian president. **Since then, Lebanon virtually became a Syrian protectorate,** which was reflected in the Taif Accord, which formally ended the civil war and the continuing crisis in Lebanon.

10. In the years **1989–2005,** during the "Taif Regime", the Syrians no longer needed to wage a sustained struggle to entrench their domination over Lebanon, and they managed to use their control of Lebanon **to their great benefit in the spheres of politics, defense, and economy**. The Syrian control of Lebanon was based not only on the presence of the army and security forces, but also on the **deep penetration of pro-Syrian Lebanese into the fabric of Lebanese politics, society, and economy**. The independence

of Lebanon, given lip service in the Taif Accord, has actually become null and void. Lebanon became a Syrian province of sorts, closely monitored by the man in charge of the security and intelligence apparatus, **General Ghazi Kanaan (who took his own life)** and his successor Lieutenant Colonel **Rustum Ghazali, suspected of involvement in the murder of Rafik Hariri.**

11. **The last decade of the previous century saw the stabilization** of an internal Lebanese system based on checks and balances between the large sects, set against the background of concerns over the renewed outbreak of another civil war, a possibility no one desires. Following the Taif Accord, **the Christian and Druze militias were disbanded and the pro-Syrian Lebanese regime grew stronger; the Lebanese economy was rebuilt;** the ruined capital city of **Beirut** was rebuilt by Rafik Hariri (who became a symbol of Lebanon's post-war recovery); **the Lebanese army and the Lebanese intelligence apparatuses were rebuilt and grew stronger** (under the close supervision of the Syrian intelligence apparatuses). An exception was the **Hezbollah** organization, which the Syrians did not disband under the pretext of the continuing "resistance" against Israel because of the continued existence of the security zone.

12. **The traditional opposition to the Syrian takeover of Lebanon, mainly among the Maronite Christians, was smashed to pieces following the anti-Syrian uprising of Michel Aoun.** In the age of the Taif regime, the heads of the Christian camp did not dare to go against the Syrian policy. On the eve of the death of Hafez Assad, Lebanon did not have an organized opposition capable of taking action against the Syrian order. The former leaders of the Christian camp **were either dead** (Bashir Gemayel, Dany Chamoun), **or in exile** (Michel Aoun, who attempted to mobilize his many supporters from his exile in France), or **sentenced to long prison terms** (Samir Ja'ja'), or allowed to return from exile to Lebanon, taking it upon themselves to maintain a low profile (Amin Gemayel). **That state of affairs changed dramatically in the years preceding the second Lebanon war due to events and developments analyzed above.**

13. **A highly significant event was the death of Hafez Assad and the rise of his son, Bashar, in June 2000, shortly after the IDF's withdrawal from Lebanon.** The government change in Syria had far-reaching effects on the Lebanese scene. Hafez Assad had established **a reign of terror** in Syria and Lebanon, **including by the use of brutal force against his opponents.** Such brutal force was occasionally reflected in the physical elimination of Syria's opponents in Lebanon (mostly through the Syrian intelligence services and various Lebanese proxies). The rise of his son, Bashar, lacking in experience and charisma, **gradually dissipated the fear entertained by the Lebanese of the Damascene ruler and his Lebanese henchmen.** It appears that the fear of the Syrian regime has dissipated not only among the opponents of

the Syrian order in Lebanon but also among Hezbollah and Syria's other supporters in Lebanon, which gained more independence and freedom of movement vis-à-vis Bashar Assad's regime.

14. **The new strategic situation formed in the Middle East after the September 11 attacks, the US takeover of Iraq** and the downfall of Saddam Hussein, put Syria **on the "axis of evil"** and increased the outside pressure exerted on it to relinquish its hold on Lebanon through an unusual **French–American joint diplomatic** effort, reflected in Security Council Resolution **1559**, dated September 2, 2004. The resolution expresses unequivocal support of Lebanon's sovereignty and independence, calls for the withdrawal of all non-Lebanese forces (i.e., the Syrian army) and calls to disband the Lebanese militias (i.e., Hezbollah) and non-Lebanese militias (i.e., the Palestinian terrorist organizations in the refugee camps).

15. The processes that had formerly weakened the Syrian order **came into dramatic fruition with the murder of Prime Minister Rafik Hariri, who refused to go along with the Syrian order**. After the murder, they were reflected in popular protests **of unprecedented scale** that broke out in Beirut ("Intifada of Independence"), **accompanied by anti-Syrian shows of solidarity between the various sects—Christians, Sunni Muslims, and Druze**. Hundreds of thousands of protesters took to the streets of Beirut, while Lebanese citizens appeared on Lebanese and international media and dared, for the first time, to demand the withdrawal of the Syrian army, the expulsion of the Syrian intelligence apparatuses, and the replacement of Syria's henchmen in the Lebanese government. **Inexperienced President Bashar Assad gave in to the pressure and quickly ordered the Syrian forces to pull out from Lebanon.**

16. Conspicuously absent in the anti-Syrian demonstrations were members of the Shi'ite community. The largest of Lebanon's sects, it also suffers from political, economic, and social discrimination. Hassan Nasrallah, the leader of Hezbollah, which grew out of the Shi'ite community, stepped forward as leader of the pro-Syrian camp and initiated a power display in a mass rally (attended by hundreds of thousands of people) in Beirut, on March 8, 2005. That rally (as well as the "counter rally" by Syria's opponents on March 14, also attended by hundreds of thousands), clearly demonstrate that the internal Lebanese schism runs very deep, and that the internal Lebanese scene in the era following the withdrawal of the Syrian forces is potentially highly explosive.

Hezbollah Gains Prominence Among the Shi'ite Community

17. A Lebanese Shi'ite organization, Hezbollah was founded by the **Iranian Revolutionary Guards** with the assistance of Syria, in the summer of 1982, at the height of the first Lebanon War. Hezbollah professes a Shi'ite radical Islamic ideology inspired by Khomeinist Iran. Throughout its entire existence,

it has enjoyed massive assistance from Iran and Syria, which consider it to be a **strategic asset** and an important tool of promoting their national goals in the struggle against Israel, in Lebanon, and in the entire Middle East.

18. In addition to serving as a strategic tool for Iran and Syria, Hezbollah is also an **inseparable part of the internal Lebanese political and social system** inside which it operates. Hezbollah therefore has **two identities: the Shi'ite Lebanese identity and the Iranian jihadist radical Islamic identity,** existing side by side in perpetual tension:

a. **The Lebanese identity:** being a Lebanese organization of ethnic character, Hezbollah enjoys considerable support from the Shi'ite community, the largest and most underprivileged among all Lebanese sects. To a great extent, the organization represents the Shi'ites' struggle for power on the internal Lebanese scene at the expense of the traditional alliance between the Christians and the Sunni Muslims. Hezbollah attempts to portray itself as an organization acting to promote Lebanon's national interests within the context of the struggle against Israel, in which framework it often presents itself as "Lebanon's defender" against Israel.

b. **The jihadist identity:** at the same time, Hezbollah is also an organization of radical Islamic character directed and supported by the Iranian Islamic regime, which has embraced a radical ideology rooted in Iran. That identity, coupled with its great dependence on Iran and Syria, impose on the organization a **jihadist ideology striving for the elimination of Israel,** similarly to the Iranian regime. Like Iran, Hezbollah's ideology is unmistakably **anti-Western** (and mostly anti-American), in stark contrast to Lebanon's long-standing history and tradition of relying on Western countries.

The Iranian Leadership as the Source of Hezbollah's Religious and Political Authority

19. In the two decades that passed from the first Lebanon war to the second Lebanon war, **Hezbollah entrenched itself** among **Shi'ite population centers** and, with the backing of Iran and Syria, achieved success in its struggle against Amal, a Lebanese movement holding nationalistic and more pragmatic views. The Amal movement was dominant among the Shi'ite community before 1982. However, in the early 1990s, Hezbollah managed to establish itself as the **most powerful, leading organization** among **the Shi'ite community,** at the expense of Amal. The non-compromising struggle it waged against the security zone, the existence of a powerful military infrastructure, the large amounts of money it received from Iran, the charismatic figure of Hassan Nasrallah, and most of all the Syrian and Iranian backing—**all of these factors combined allowed the organization to attain a dominant status it did not possess before.**

20. **The financial resources coming in from Iran help Hezbollah conduct extensive social and economic activities among the Shi'ite community,** taking advantage of the traditional discrimination and the neglect of Shi'ite needs by all Lebanese governments. Such activities cover numerous spheres, including education, healthcare, society, and religious services. **Hezbollah has therefore taken a firm hold among the Shi'ite community, for clearly internal Lebanese reasons** which are not necessarily related to the conflict with Israel. Such hold granted Hezbollah considerable support among the Shi'ite community, allowed it to **recruit its operatives** from the community's ranks, **allowed it to embed its military infrastructure inside of the community,** and helped it gain the community's support even after the suffering it underwent during the second Lebanon war.

The Buildup and Operation of Hezbollah's Military Force in the Years 2000–2006

Characteristics of the Military Activity Against Israel

21. Following the IDF's withdrawal from the security zone (May 2000), Hezbollah lost the international and, to a great extent, the internal Lebanese legitimacy for the continuation of the armed struggle against Israel. As a result of that, during the six years preceding the second Lebanon war Hezbollah scaled back its routine operative activity against Israel. **It did not, however, abandon it completely, continuing to carry out terrorist attacks against Israel based on "game rules" of its own design.**

22. Hezbollah's spheres of operative activity in the years 2000–2006 were:

a. **Abducting IDF soldiers.** The two noteworthy events were the abduction of three IDF soldiers on Har Dov (October 2000) and the abduction of two IDF soldiers, Eldad Regev and Ehud Goldwasser, which led to the second Lebanon war. Between those two incidents were other failed attempts (prominent among them was an attempt to abduct IDF soldiers in the village of Ghajar under the cover of a firing attack along Israel's northern border, which took place on November 21, 2005).

b. **Attacking IDF outposts and patrols,** primarily on Har Dov (Shabaa Farms), where Hezbollah claims its activity is still legitimate. Dozens of attacks were perpetrated during that period of time, including mortar fire, anti-tank fire, small arms fire, and setting roadside charges against IDF outposts and IDF patrols.

c. **Firing Katyusha rockets on Israel.** The most noteworthy event since the IDF's withdrawal from the security zone was a volley of eight 122-mm Katyushas on Mount Meron, resulting in a day of clashes between the IDF and Hezbollah (May 28, 2006). In several other incidents, rockets were fired by Palestinian terrorist elements. Such attacks were perpetrated with Hezbollah's tacit agreement.

d. **A firing attack inside Israeli territory through the activation of the Palestinian Islamic Jihad** (March 12, 2002). That terrorist attack took place on the Shlomi–Metzuba road, in the vicinity of the Israeli–Lebanese border. Perpetrated at the peak of the Palestinian terrorist campaign (the Intifada), it led to the deaths of five civilians and an IDF soldier. Hezbollah did not publicly claim responsibility for the terrorist attack.

23. As the terrorist attacks along the Lebanese–Israeli border continued, Hezbollah assisted Palestinian terrorist organizations, mostly by supplying arms and transferring money to fund acts of terrorism **in order to bring about an escalation in the Palestinian campaign of terrorism against Israel.**

The Military Buildup

24. Hezbollah's construction of an extensive military infrastructure in Lebanon was a **prolonged process,** which grew faster since the IDF's withdrawal from the security zone. Following the IDF's withdrawal, Hezbollah, for the first time since its foundation in 1982, could finally rid itself of the burden of day-to-day fighting and **focus** its attention on building up and upgrading its military force.

25. The buildup of the military force was done **with the unprecedented assistance and backing of Iran and Syria,** which assisted Hezbollah in the acquisition of high-quality advanced arms and ammunition, turning it **from a terrorist and guerilla organization to an organization with capabilities approaching (and at times even surpassing) those of a state.** An important figure in the buildup and operation of Hezbollah's military infrastructure is **Hajj Imad Fayez Mughniyah,** the military deputy of organization leader Hassan Nasrallah and the man behind many terrorist attacks against Israeli and Western targets.

26. The upgraded military infrastructure is designed to achieve the following goals:

a. **Gaining strategic resilience**, meaning:

1. **In the offensive aspect,** the ability to conduct a sustained campaign against Israel in order to inflict **massive, continuous damage** to civilian population, including on the Israeli home front.

2. **In the defensive aspect,** the ability to mount a coordinated, well-planned defense against a ground assault by the IDF, **allowing the organization to maintain its survivability, power, and status.**

b. **The creation of a balance of terror, which would deter Israel from entering another confrontation and allow Hezbollah to continue provoking it, based on the "game rules" the organization has been shaping since May 2000** (those game rules **no longer** exist since the second Lebanon war).

c. **Establishing Hezbollah's power and status on the internal Lebanese scene,** where it is a revolutionary force striving to establish the dominance of the Shi'ite community and radically change the existing traditional government system and the pro-Western orientation of the Lebanese regime.

Hezbollah's Concept of Deployment and Use of Military Force

27. Before the second Lebanon war, Hezbollah's **deployment** across Lebanon covered four different territorial divisions populated by the Shi'ite community:

a. **The "general headquarters" in Beirut,** which includes infrastructure in Shi'ite suburbs of southern Beirut. Most of it was set up in **Harat Hreik,** in an area nicknamed the "security square", which housed Hezbollah's military "nerve center". The "general headquarters" controlled Hezbollah's operative and regional units across Lebanon.

b. **The operative core in south Lebanon,** which, up until the war, included most of the organization's rocket arsenal. The operative core is designed to allow **sustained** rocket and artillery fire on Israel and resist possible IDF ground assaults.

c. **The rear combat zone in the Nabatiyeh region,** north of the Litani River. This zone, providing Hezbollah with defensive depth, is used for firing long-range rockets on Israel.

d. **The training and logistics division in the Bekaa Valley.** This is where Hezbollah receives arms and ammunition from Syria and Iran, subsequently storing or distributing them to other territorial divisions.

28. In these divisions, key among which is south Lebanon, Hezbollah has built **three combat arsenals:**

a. **The offensive arsenal:** before the second Lebanon war, it was based on a large rocket arsenal estimated at **over 20,000 rockets** of varying ranges. **Most** of the rockets were hidden in designated storehouses **in the villages of south Lebanon, and only some** were hidden outdoors.

b. **The defensive arsenal:** designed to allow Hezbollah to wage guerilla warfare against the IDF in south Lebanon while inflicting heavy casualties, in order to **make it difficult for IDF forces to take over south Lebanon.** The central components of that guerilla force are infantry, anti-tank fire (by means of advanced anti-tank missiles), sabotage, special forces, and anti-aircraft fire.

c. **The logistics infrastructure:** based on arms storehouses located in hundreds of residential buildings and social and religious institutions (including mosques). It is designed to provide Hezbollah with sustained fighting ability and makes it more difficult for the IDF to attack.

Figure 1: A Schematic Distribution of Hezbollah's Four Territorial Divisions

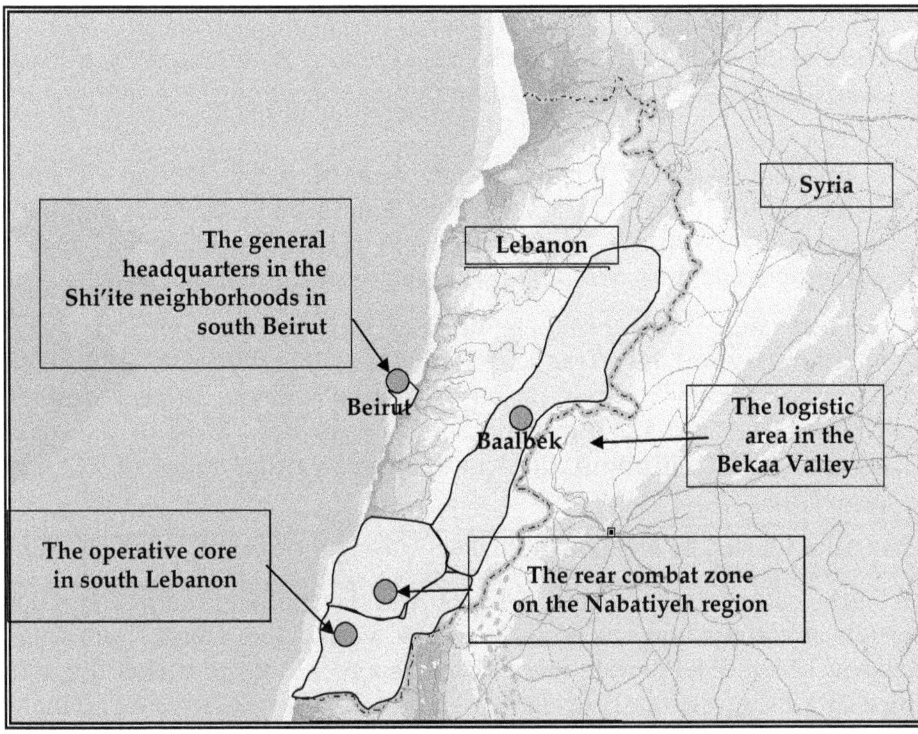

29. In order to operate those four divisions, Hezbollah, in our assessment, can recruit **more than 10,000 operatives in times of crisis.** During the second Lebanon war, **several thousands** of Hezbollah operatives served south of the Litani River, alongside several **hundreds of operatives on the Nabatiyeh region.** Of those operatives, the organization's **quality hardcore** included (before the war) **about 1,000 regular operatives** and the rest were reservists.

30. The majority of Hezbollah's offensive and defensive military arsenal was **concealed within densely-populated area** where the Shi'ite community resides, **using the local population as human shields.** Hezbollah's arms and ammunition were sometimes hidden inside residential buildings as well as in religious and social institutions. This was designed to increase

its **survivability** during wartime and provide Hezbollah with benefits in the sphere of media and propaganda, as happened in the second Lebanon war. Part of the military arsenal was hidden in non-populated areas (ditches, bunkers, tunnels, and so forth).

31. The most potent offensive threat to Israel from Hezbollah is the organization's extensive **rocket arsenal.** On the eve of the second Lebanon war, Hezbollah had **over 20,000 rockets** designed for various ranges. These rockets can be divided into **three types:**

a. **Rockets made by the Iranian arms industry: Fajr-3** (43 km), **Fajr-5** (75 km), **Falaq** with enhanced warhead (10–11 km), **Zelzal** (125–210 km), **Naze'at** (80–140 km). Those rockets are the source of the **strategic threat** posed by Hezbollah to the civilian population of northern and central Israel.

b. **Rockets produced by the Syrian arms industry:** 220mm (70 km), 302mm (over 100 km). **Of note are the 220mm rockets, equipped with metal pellets, which struck the city of Haifa.** These rockets caused numerous casualties in Haifa during the second Lebanon war.

c. **Short range, 122mm rockets made by Iran, Russia, and China, provided to Hezbollah by Iran and Syria:** Russian and Iranian **122 mm** HE (i.e., high explosive)-frag rockets, **122 mm** Chinese increased-range **Grad** rockets and **122 mm** Chinese cluster rockets. **Most of the rockets fired at Israeli population centers were various types of 122 mm projectiles.**

Casualties Caused by Hezbollah Rockets During the Second Lebanon War

32. In the course of the second Lebanon war, Hezbollah fired **nearly 4,000 rockets of various types** on Israeli territory. Most of them were short-range rockets (122mm). **53 people were killed as a result of the rocket fire, one third of all the war fatalities (159).** Among those killed were 41 civilians and 12 soldiers (as a result of a rocket which landed near Kibbutz Kfar Giladi). Most of the victims were residents of Israel's big cities. The leading city is **Haifa** (13 killed). No one was killed in **Kiryat Shmona,** hit by the largest number of rockets.

Other Arms and Ammunition Provided by Iran to Hezbollah

33. **Other advanced arms and ammunition provided by Iran to Hezbollah:**

a. **Upgraded Iranian-manufactured anti-tank missiles with a double tandem-type warhead which can penetrate armor even after reactive shielding:** the **Raad**, an Iranian version of the Sagger, has range of 3000 meters (1.86 miles) and can penetrate 400 mm; the **Raad-T**, an Iranian version of the Sagger with a tandem warhead, has a range of 3000 meters and can also penetrate 400 mm (16") after reactive shielding[2]; the **Toophan** is an Iranian version of the TOW, has a range of up to 3750 meters (2.33 miles) and can penetrate 550 mm (22") steel armor (these were coupled with **Kornet** and **Konkurs**, advanced antitank missiles made by the USSR). The advanced anti-tank missiles delivered to Hezbollah were used with a high degree of skill day and night, hitting dozens of armored IDF vehicles in south Lebanon.

b. **Chinese made coast-to-sea C-802 missiles,** such as the missile that hit the IDF Hanit missile boat off the coast of Beirut two days after the outbreak of the war (July 14). The hit killed four crewmen and the missile boat was severely damaged. The C-802 has a range of 65 nautical miles and carries a warhead weighing 165 kg (363 lbs).

c. **Ababil unmanned air vehicles (UAVs),** developed by the Iranian aeronautical industry. There are a number of different models, including reconnaissance and "attacker" UAVs carrying warheads weighing scores of kilograms, found in the possession of Hezbollah. During the war, Hezbollah launched a UAV, probably an "attacker", which was shot down off the coast of Haifa on August 7. Its remains were found in an open field near Kibbutz Kabri, about 4 km (2.1 miles) east of Nahariya (August 13).

d. **Motorized hang gliders,** to which a small piston motor can be attached, as they were used by Palestinian terrorists during "the night of the hang gliders" (November 25, 1987). The system preserves the form and operation of the hang glider, but gives it propulsion sufficient to raise it to a greater than usual height and assure it a prolonged stay in the air, **allowing it a range greater than 100** km (62 miles).

e. Russian made SA-7 and SA-14 **anti-aircraft** missiles.

f. **Night-vision goggles.**

The Post-War Restoration of Hezbollah's Military Infrastructure

34. In the year that has passed since the second Lebanon war, Hezbollah has restored its military infrastructure to the north and south of the Litani River, **without any effective attempt on part of the Lebanese government to prevent it from doing so,** as it is obliged by Security Council Resolution 1701. During that year, Hezbollah **smuggled** to Lebanon a large quantity of arms and ammunition in order to rebuild its military infrastructure. A special emphasis was placed on **rockets, anti-tank, and anti-aircraft weapons.**

[2] A new shielding for tanks causing the missile to explode before it even contacts the tank.

35. The arms and ammunition were provided to Hezbollah by **Iran and Syria.** The main smuggling route runs through Syria. Arms and ammunition are transported on vehicles to the Bekaa Valley, and then to other regions of Lebanon. In the year that has passed since the second Lebanon war, the Lebanese army stopped, on two separate occasions, vehicles that transported arms from Syria. However, those were uncharacteristic incidents rather than part of an overall policy.

36. As a result of the massive supply of rockets by Iran and Syria, **Hezbollah is completing the restoration of its rocket arsenal, hit during the second Lebanon war.** As already mentioned, the organization had over 20,000 rockets of various ranges on the eve of the war. It is our assessment that the number of rockets Hezbollah can currently fire on Israel **is similar to** the number it fired during the war, **and that the range of the rockets allows the organization to fire on population centers in northern and central Israel.**

37. In the region of the "operative core", south of the Litani River, Hezbollah has rebuilt most of its military infrastructure, while **adapting its activity to the new reality formed following the deployment of the Lebanese army and that of UNIFIL.** Following are the characteristics of its activity and deployment:

a. **Avoiding terrorist attacks against the IDF** (for the first time in a long period of time since the establishment of Hezbollah).

b. **Avoiding frontal confrontations with UNIFIL and the Lebanese army.**

c. **Low visibility:** the lack of an outpost line along the border, camouflaging the transportation of arms, appearing without Hezbollah uniform (with only flags and posters to indicate the organization's presence).

d. It is our assessment that Hezbollah currently has **thousands of 40–110 km rockets** in south Lebanon. South of the Litani River are **hundreds of anti-tank missiles and anti-tank rocket launchers, hundreds of anti-aircraft missiles and anti-aircraft cannons, and a large quantity of roadside charges.**

e. **Manpower:** to replace the well-trained operatives killed, Hezbollah recruited **new operatives, trained** them, and gradually brought them back to regular activity. It is our assessment that there are now **several thousands of operatives** south of the Litani River.

The Implementation of Security Council Resolution 1701 (Interim Account)

38. UN Security Council Resolution 1701 (August 12, 2006) marked the end of the second Lebanon war and forced Hezbollah to adapt to a **new reality in south Lebanon.** Following is an interim account of the resolution's implementation a year after it was first passed:

a. **On one hand,** it is the first time that a significant force of the Lebanese army, with the assistance of an upgraded UNIFIL force, is deployed south of the Litani River; **Hezbollah has lost its position as the sole key player in south Lebanon** and its freedom of action has been restricted. **A relative calm** has settled in south Lebanon. Hezbollah, busy restoring its military power and struggling to topple Fouad Siniora's government, has so far avoided (for the longest time since its foundation) perpetrating terrorist attacks against Israel. The void formed by Hezbollah **has been filled by global jihad elements, which attempted to act in south Lebanon as well** (the most prominent incident was the firing of three rockets from the Taybeh-Adeiseh region on Kiryat Shmona on June 17, 2007).

b. **On the other hand, the implementation of Security Council Resolution 1701 has only been partial and its main components have not been implemented:** the south Lebanon region has not been demilitarized of terrorist organizations. Hezbollah has not been disarmed, it continues the process of its military restoration with the assistance of Iran and Syria; no effective embargo has been imposed on arms smuggling from Syria to Lebanon; and there has been no significant progress on the issue of the two abducted IDF soldiers.

39. **The interim account a year after the second Lebanon war indicates that the achievements of Security Council Resolution 1701 are short-lived, and that they cannot create long-lasting calm and stability in south Lebanon and elsewhere in the country.** Hezbollah might change its policy of terrorist attacks and attempt to regain its status as "master of the south" once its restoration is complete or once there is a change in Hezbollah, Iran or Syria's set of considerations in internal Lebanese or regional contexts (such as a political crisis in Lebanon or a regional crisis).

C. HEZBOLLAH'S NON-MILITARY ACTIVITY

DOCUMENT NO. 7

HEZBOLLAH AS A STRATEGIC ARM OF IRAN

Intelligence and Terrorism Information Center at the Center for Special Studies (C.S.S) Report

September 8, 2006

Overview

This Bulletin deals with Hezbollah's place in Iranian strategy and the vast amounts of aid and support Iran has given the organization since its founding 24 years ago. Hezbollah, and the Lebanese Shi'ite community among whom it took root, are actually the only successful example of exporting the Islamic revolution. Hezbollah also demonstrates how Iran uses the concept to further its ambitions for regional hegemony and the struggle against Israel and the West.

The massive support Iran and it ally, Syria, have given Hezbollah since its founding increased during the past six years, turning it not only into a terrorist organization with military and political capabilities, but also an **Iranian stronghold in the heart of the Arab world.** Hezbollah's capabilities, which go far beyond those of a terrorist organization, are **a clear-cut threat to the population of Israel,** as was well illustrated in the second Lebanon War (which **took place earlier than Iran and Syria had planned).** The presence of an stronghold in Lebanon has given Iran cultural influence and political clout, increased its regional influence and enabled it to use terrorism against Israel without being linked involved. In addition, and more even importantly, it provides Iran with a **military option to both attack Israel and destabilize the region during a crisis** (for example, in response to an attack on its nuclear installation).

Editor's note: The original version of this document included some color images that could not be adequately reproduced in this publication. Where necessary, captions and/or headings specifically relating to any omitted images have also been left out of the version reprinted herein. The main text of the document has not been affected by these omissions.

The second Lebanon war **weakened** both Hezbollah's military capability and its political power in Lebanon. However, the organization was **not defeated** and its prewar capabilities can be **restored.** Therefore, Iran and its ally, Syria, can be expected to make an effort to rehabilitate the organization's capabilities, especially by smuggling arms in from Syria in spite of the embargo imposed on arms shipments to Hezbollah. At the same time, Iran can be expected to use Hezbollah to pour vast amounts of money into rebuilding Lebanon and compensating the local residents (the overwhelming majority of whom are Shi'ites) who were harmed by the war.

From the Israeli perspective, the Islamic regime in Iran presents a danger to its existence. The regime's ideology uncompromisingly and publicly calls for the destruction of the State of Israel, fosters the Palestinian terrorist organizations and systematically strives to attain unconventional nuclear capabilities while thumbing its nose at the demands of the international community. It also clearly presents a threat to American and Western interests in the Persian Gulf and the Middle East in general. Much of the Arab/Muslim world is also apprehensive of an Iranian threat.

For that reason, the State of Israel and the entire international community must make an effort to hamper the post-war rehabilitation of Hezbollah's strategic capabilities as part of a general struggle against the threat of Iran and its stronghold in Lebanon.

This Information Bulletin contains the following:

A. The concept of exporting the Islamic revolution

B. The establishment of Hezbollah by Iran during the Lebanon War, 1982–1985

C. Strengthening Hezbollah after the Lebanon War

D. Iranian aid and support for Hezbollah

1) Overview

2) Exporting Iranian ideology

3) Massive supplies of state-of-the-art weapons

4) Ways of bringing weapons into Lebanon

5) Training Hezbollah to use weapons

6) Supervising the build-up of Hezbollah's military strength and preparing it for a possible confrontation with Israel

7) Financing Hezbollah

8) The damage done to Hezbollah's military infrastructure during the war.

E. Summary and conclusions

Exporting the Islamic Revolution

The desire to export the Islamic revolution to the rest of the Muslim world (and even to non-Muslim societies) is an integral part of the philosophy of the Ayatollah Khomeini, who led the Islamic revolution in Iran in 1979. Khomeini and his confederates sought to ignore national division and the religious differences between Shi'ite and Sunni Muslims by creating a revolutionary Islamic power. That power, led by Iran, would stamp out the "root of evil," the superpowers which had, in their view, led to world corruption, especially the United States ("the big Satan") and its ally, Israel ("the little Satan").

For Khomeini (and his heir, Ali Khamenei), the concept of exporting the revolution served as a **means of advancing Iranian strategic interests, centering around the desire for regional hegemony and the battle against Israel and the West**, by intervening in the internal politics of other countries.

As part of its marketing strategy, Iran provided particularly **generous aid to subversive Islamic movements and terrorist organizations in the Middle East, the Balkans and Africa.** At the same time, it undertook an intensive propaganda campaign in various parts of the world to disseminate the principles of the Islamic revolution. That activity continues to this day. In practice, and in addition to Hezbollah, Iran provides support for the **Palestinian terrorist organizations** (particularly the Palestinian Islamic Jihad and Hamas) and the **Shi'ite militias in Iraq,** helping them to destabilize the country and hinder the democratization process the Americans are trying to advance.[1]

> Hezbollah is the most prominent terrorist organization receiving Iranian aid and is **clearly a priority for the regime's attention and allotment of resources,** and not by chance. During the 24 years which have passed since Hezbollah's founding, it has entrenched itself among the Lebanese Shi'ites, had impressive achievements and **become, in Iranian perspective, the most shining (albeit the only) example of its success in exporting the revolution.**

[1] The Iranians provide the Shi'ite militias in Iraq with weapons, ammunition, money and instructions for preparing explosive charges and even carrying out attacks.

The Establishment of Hezbollah by Iran During the Lebanon War (1982–1986)

The first Lebanon War, which began on June 6, 1982, reduced Syria's influence there, destroyed the Palestinian terrorist infrastructure and led to the collapse of the central Lebanese government. The Iranians correctly identified the opportunity presented by the political upheaval and exploited it to transport the Islamic struggle to the Lebanese arena, **in the heart of the Arab world,** and from there to wage its battle against Israel and the United States **without direct involvement.**[2] The Iranians were active mostly among the Shi'ites, the largest sect in Lebanon, which has traditionally suffered from political, economic and social deprivation.

Iran's strategy was compatible with the interests of Syria, which at that time struggled against Israel's presence in Lebanon from a position of military and political weakness. The meeting of Iranian and Syrian interests led to Syria's permitting 2,500 Iranian Revolutionary Guards to enter Lebanon and to set up a stronghold within the Shi'ite population in the Beqa'a Valley.

Although the Syrians prevented the Iranian force from participating in the fighting against Israel and large numbers of them returned to Iran, the remaining 1,000–1,500 Iranians entrenched themselves in Baalbek, which was under Syrian military control. They established a military-logistic infrastructure at the **Sheikh 'Abdallah camp in Baalbek,** which they took over from the Lebanese army, and at the **Zabadani camp in Syria,** northwest of Damascus. Intelligence and operational Revolutionary Guards elements were later installed in Beirut, Zahle and Mashgharah in the southern Beqa'a Valley. The military infrastructure set up in the summer of 1982 played an important part in establishing Hezbollah and using it to carry out terrorist missions.

The Revolutionary Guards' most conspicuous achievement was **successfully uniting** the various radical Shi'ite groups which objected to the Israeli presence and Western influence in Lebanon. The Revolution Guards established Hezbollah from among those groups and supported them by training their members, transmitting technical know-how, and providing weapons (through Damascus), ideological guidance and extremely generous funding.

The **key role** in establishing Hezbollah in Lebanon and dispatching its members on terrorist missions against Israel and the West was filled by **Hujjat al-Islam 'Ali Akbar Mokhtashemipour,** who was then the Iranian ambassador to Damascus (and is currently head of the Headquarters for

---

[2] Shimon Shapira, *Hizbullah between Iran and Lebanon,* (Hebrew) Hakibbutz Hameuchad Publishing House, (Tel Aviv, 2000), pp. 96–133.

Intifada Support, and important in providing Iranian support for Palestinian terrorism).

Guided by the Iranians, during its first years Hezbollah developed **two modes of action which became the trademarks of Iranian-directed Shi'ite terrorism:**

- **Suicide bombing attacks:** suicide bombing attacks in Lebanon were carried out by Shi'ite terrorists sent to sacrifice themselves for the sake of Allah as part of jihad, an important element in Khomeini's ideology (and that of his heirs).[3] **The first suicide bombing attacks were directed against Western targets,** and **later against Israeli targets** in Lebanon and Jewish and Israeli targets abroad (Argentina). During the first Lebanon War Hezbollah carried out a series of suicide bombing attacks against **American and French** targets, killing hundreds. As a result of the attacks, the multinational force was evacuated from Lebanon and the Palestinian terrorist organizations were **encouraged** to copy the Lebanese model, using the suicide bombing attack as the main weapon in their terrorist campaigns against Israel (in the middle 1990s and during the second intifada).
- **Abducting hostages:** During the 1980s Hezbollah abducted scores of Western civilians in Lebanon, murdering some of them. Abduction became its primary means exerting pressure on Western countries to change their policies regarding the Iran-Iraq war and the Arab-Israeli conflict, and to secure the release of Shi'ite terrorists in prisons all over the globe.[4]

Strengthening Hezbollah after the Lebanon War

During the second half of the 1980s and during the 1990s, Syria permitted Hezbollah to strengthen its position in the Shi'ite community in Lebanon and to set up an extensive military infrastructure in south Lebanon, **to a great extent at the expense of Amal,** the movement representing the pragmatic Shi'ite trend. The Syrians, Iran's allies, did not disarm Hezbollah after the other armed militias had turned in their weapons following the Taef Accord in 1989, which marked the end of the Lebanese civil war.

[3] For further information see our Information Bulletin entitled ""Exporting" the radical ideology of the Islamic revolution in Iran," at http://www.terrorism-info.org.il/malam_multimedia/English/eng_n/html/jihad0806e.htm and http://www.terrorism-info.org.il/malam_multimedia/English/eng_n/pdf/jihad0806e.pdf.

[4] For further information about Iranian and Shi"ite terrorism and about Iranian-directed Hezbollah attacks, see both parts of our Information Bulletin entitled "Hezbollah: profile of the Lebanese Shiite terrorist organization of global reach sponsored by Iran and supported by Syria," at http://www.terrorism-info.org.il/malam_multimedia/English/eng_n/html/hezbollah.htm and http://www.intelligence.org.il/eng/bu/hizbullah/pb/hezb_B.htm. Also see "Iran as a state sponsoring and operating terror," at http://www.terrorism-info.org.il/malam_multimedia/html/final/eng/iran.htm or http://www.terrorism-info.org.il/malam_multimedia/html/final/eng/iran.htm.

Thus Hezbollah's position was strengthened among the Shi'ites and within Lebanese politics in general, and it could continue its campaign against both the IDF and the Southern Lebanese Army in the security zone established by Israel, under the banner of "struggle against the occupation."

The IDF's complete withdrawal from the security zone in south Lebanon on May 24, 2000, and Israel's full implementation of UN Security Council Resolution 425 should have obviated Hezbollah's internal-Lebanese justification for the continued armed campaign against Israel. However, the above notwithstanding, Hezbollah, encouraged by Iran and Syria, refused to disarm and cease its terrorist attacks against Israel. During the past six years Hezbollah has carried out occasional attacks against IDF forces along the border, shooting and abducing soldiers, and establishing a broad military infrastructure in south Lebanon. It has found various new pretexts, such as the Sheba'a Farms and the release of Lebanese prisoners, to continue its military campaign against Israel. At the same time it has increased its support for the Palestinian terrorist organizations and encouraged them, in return for money, to carry out suicide bombing attacks within Israel, including during the second Lebanon war.

Iranian Aid and Support for Hezbollah

Overview

During the six years since the IDF withdrew from Lebanon, **Iran and Syria (under Bashar Assad) have increased their assistance and support of Hezbollah** Both countries regard Lebanon as their **front line** against Israel and Hezbollah as their **strategic proxy.** Iran, along with Syria, has upgraded **Hezbollah's military capabilities,** primarily by providing the organization with rockets and constructing **an arsenal of between 12,000 and 13,000 ground-to-ground missiles of various ranges. They also assisted in creating a well-planned and organized Hezbollah military deployment in south Lebanon, in accordance with Iranian military doctrine.**

The Iranians leading and directing the support of Hezbollah belong to an elite unit of the Revolutionary Guards know as **"the Jerusalem *[Qods]* Force."** The unit, headed by **Qassem Suleimani,** is responsible for Iranian military activity and for directing terrorist organizations in Lebanon and other places around the globe (including Palestinian terrorists). Iranian support for Hezbollah through the Qods Force includes financing (more than $100 million annually), training in Iran and Lebanon, and supplying state-of-the arts weapons and intelligence about Israel.

Exporting the Ideology of Iran's Islamic Revolution

Material captured from Hezbollah terrorists in south Lebanon during the second Lebanon war included material relating to Iranian ideology, clear evidence of the export of the Iranian Islamic revolution radical ideas to Lebanon. The materials were printed in Arabic by publishing houses connected to Hezbollah and distributed among Hezbollah and the Shi'ite community in Lebanon. Hezbollah has **adopted** Iranian ideology and like Iran, considers the destruction of the State of Israel its mission.

For example, in the village of Marun al-Ras (and others) copies of a booklet called *Jihad* were taken from Hezbollah terrorists. It was apparently initially meant for the Iranian armed forces, especially the Revolutionary Guards. It contains many quotations of statements made by Khamenei, who views jihad as a doctrine and plan of action by which every Muslim can "sacrifice his life for the sake of Allah and reach paradise." The height of jihad is *shahadah,* a martyr's death for the sake of Allah. Jihad and *shahadah* are two of the central themes in religious Islamic perception as conceived by the Ayatollah Khomeini and his heir, Khamenei.[5]

During the second Lebanon war, a booklet entitled "My **Leader"** was captured from Hezbollah operatives in the village of Yarun. It was published by Hezbollah's scouting movement ("the Imam al-Mahdi Scouts") and contained biographical information about Iranian leader Khamenei, around whom Hezbollah terrorist-operatives have formed a personality cult. Khamenei is represented in the booklet as admirable and worthy of emulation, and as an example of a devoted jihad fighter who contributed much to the Islamic revolution. 24.

Massive Supply of State-of-the-Art Weapons

During the past six years the supply of **high-quality weapons** from Iran and Syria to Hezbollah has been **accelerated,** and some of them were used by Hezbollah during the second Lebanon war. Prominent among them were the long range missiles **targeting civilian population centers in Israel** (such rockets cannot not be aimed with precision, and therefore they indiscriminately hit the civilian population).

Hezbollah's weapons threat to Israel's population centers: range of Iranian rockets in Hezbollah possession

There were three categories of weapons:

- **Weapons manufactured by Iran's military industry,** including long range Fajr-3 rockets, with a range of 43 km (miles) and Fajr-5, with a range of 75 km (47 miles). In our assessment, in some instances Hezbollah independently decided to fire the weapons in accordance with what it perceived as the needs of the war, and in some instances needed Iranian approval.

[5] See Footnote 4.

- **Weapons manufactured by Syria's military industry,** including 220 mm rockets with a range of up to 75 km (47 miles) and 302 mm rockets with a range of more than 110 km (68 miles). At least partial payment for the rockets came from Iran. Hezbollah preferred the Syrian rockets during the war.
- **Weapons manufactured in other countries and given to Hezbollah by Syria and Iran,** including 122 mm long range rockets made in China and furnished by Iran. For example, advanced Kornet and Metis anti-tank missiles, RPG-29s and SA-7 and SA-14 anti-aircraft missiles, all made in Russia and furnished by Syria, and Chinese C-802 land-to-sea cruise missiles given to Hezbollah by Iran.

The weapons furnished by Iran were mostly manufactured by the Iranian military industry, although some were manufactured elsewhere. They included:[6]

- **Long-range Zelzal ground-to-ground rockets,** which can reach targets 125-210 kms (78-130 miles) away, depending on the model.[7] **Zelzal-1** rockets have a range of 125 km and **Zelzal-2** rockets have a range of 210 km. Both have a diameter of 610 mm (2 ft) and carry a warhead weighing 600 kg (1320 lbs). In our assessment, such rockets were severely damaged during the second Lebanon war and were not used.
- Long-range **Fajr-3** and **Fajr-5** ground-to-ground missiles manufactured in Iran. The **Fajr-3** has a maximum range of 43 km (27 miles), a diameter of 240 mm (almost 10 inches) and carries a warhead weighing 90 kg (208 lbs). The **Fajr-5** has a maximum range of 75 km (47 miles). Their technology is very simple and they are inaccurate. **Strategically they were the main threat to Israel's northern population,** although they were used infrequently during the second Lebanon war (they were aimed at Haifa and hit the outskirts of the city). We are uncertain whether that was because they were damaged or because Hezbollah and/or Iran decided not to use them.
- **Iranian-manufactured Falaq rockets which carry a large warhead and are used to attack fortified targets.** The Falaq-1 has a range of 10 km (almost 6 miles), a diameter of 240 mm and carries a 50 kg (110 lb) warhead. The Falaq-2 has a maximum range of 11 km (almost 7 miles), a diameter of 333 mm (13 inches) and carries a 120 kg (264 lb) warhead.
- **Iranian-manufactured long-range Naze'at rockets of various models (4 through 10).** They have a maximum range of 80-140 km (50-87 miles),

[6] The list does not include weapons given to Hezbollah by Syria.

[7] In an exceptional statement, 'Ali Akbar Mohtashamipour admitted that Zelzal-2 rockets had been given to Hezbollah (in an interview with the reformist daily paper *Sharq*, August 3).

diameters varying from 356-450 mm (14-18 in) and carry warheads weighing between 240 and 430 kg (528-946 lbs). As far as can be ascertained, they were not used during the second Lebanon war.

- Upgrad Iranian-manufactured anti-tank missiles with a double tandem-type warhead which can penetrate armor even after reactive shielding:[8] the **Raad,** an Iranian version of the Sagger, has range of 3000 meters (1.86 miles) and can penetrate 400 mm; the **Raad-T,** an Iranian version of the Sagger with a tandem warhead, has a range of 3000 meters and can also penetrate 400 mm (16′) after reactive shielding; the **Toophan** is an Iranian version of the TOW, has a range of up to 3750 meters (2.33 miles) and can penetrate 550 mm (22′) steel armor. Iran and Syria delivered advanced anti-tank missile to Hezbollah and they were used with a high degree of skill day and night, hitting dozens of armored IDF vehicles in south Lebanon.
- **Chinese-manufactured land-to-sea C-802 cruise missiles,** such as the one which hit the Israeli gunboat off the coast of Beirut on July 14, two days after the war began. The missile killed four crewmembers and **Chinese C-802 land-to-sea missile** e damage to the boat. The C-802 has a range of 65 naval miles and carries a warhead weighing 165 kg (363 lbs).
- **Ababil unmanned air vehicles** (UAVs), developed and manufactured by the Iranian areonautical industry. There are a number of different models, including reconnaissance and "attacker" UAVs carrying warheads weighing scores of kilograms. The "attacker" UAVs have two guidance systems: a camera with a range of dozens of kilometers and GPS with a range of more than 100 km (62 miles). Hezbollah sent reconnaissance UAVs into Israel a number of times before the war.[9] On August 7 Hezbollah launched an "attacker" UAV which was shot down over the Haifa shore. On August 13, its remains were found in an open field near Kibbutz Kabri, about 4 km (2 V2 miles) east of Nahariya.
- **Motorized hang gliders,** to which a small piston motor can be attached, as they were used by Palestinian terrorists during "the night of the hang gliders," (November 25, 1987). The system preserves the form and operation of the hang glider but gives it propulsion sufficient to raise it to a greater than usual height and assure it a prolonged stay in the air, allowing it a range greater than 100 km (62 miles).

[8] A new type of tank armor which explodes a projectile before it comes into contact with the tank body.

[9] On the morning of November 7, 2004, Hezbollah sent a reconnaissance UAV which passed over Nahariya and crashed into the sea as it returned to south Lebanon, apparently because of a technical fault. On April 11, 2005, the organization sent another reconnaissance UAV which flew between Acre and Nahariya and landed safely in south Lebanon.

- Russian SA-7 and SA-14 **anti-aircraft missiles**
- **Various types of artillery and mortars.**
- **Improved Iranian-manufactured Nader RPGs,** an Iranian version of the RPG-7. It has range of 300 meters (328 yds), its main warhead has a diameter of 80 mm (3') and it can penetrate 280 mm (11') of steel.
- **Night-vision goggles.**[10]
- **Equipment and weapons for small-scale sea fighting. It is possible that Iran also sent Hezbollah vessels such as torpedo boats, miniature submarines, etc**

Ways of Smuggling Weapons into Lebanon

The Iranians smuggle most of the weapons into Lebanon **by a combination of air and overland routes.** They reach Lebanon in Iranian planes which **land at the Damascus international airport.** From there they are transported **overland** to Hezbollah in Lebanon. **The Syrians have studiously ignored repeated appeals from the United State, the international community and the UN to keep their territory from being used as an illegal Hezbollah weapons and ammunition supply route.**

During the past few years the Iranians have exploited the opportunities which presented themselves, such as the humanitarian aid flights for the victims of the earthquake at Bam in southeastern Iran (December 2003–January 2004). On at least nine separate occasions, the Qods Force used the Iranian and Syrian cargo planes bringing humanitarian aid, loading the return flights with large amounts of weapons and other equipment for Hezbollah.

During and after the second Lebanon war the Iranians continued sending Hezbollah weapons, disguising them as humanitarian aid.[11] In our assessment, some of the attempts were foiled by IDF activity. According to Security Council Resolution 1701, the Lebanese government is supposed to prevent the smuggling of weapons to Hezbollah (aided by UNIFIL, should it so desire). The Syrians have already made it clear that they will oppose UNIFIL action along the Syrian-Lebanese boundary.

[10] The spokesman for the British Foreign Office stated that the IDF had found British-made night vision goggles used by Hezbollah in south Lebanon. The *London Times* reported that the 250 pairs of goggles found in south Lebanon had been sent to Iran by Britain in 2003 as part of a British-Iranian joint effort to fight drug-smuggling.

[11] Some of the flights exploited for the transport of weapons went through Turkey. A spokesman for the Turkish Foreign Ministry confirmed a Turkish newspaper report which claimed that the authorities had forced two Iranian planes on their way to Syria to land because they suspected them of being used to smuggle weapons to Hezbollah.

Training Hezbollah

The Iranians instruct and train Hezbollah terrorists to use the new weapons at **designated training camps in Iran,** using Revolutionary Guard bases and installations. Additional instruction and guidance are provided by the Revolutionary Guards for Hezbollah terrorists in Lebanon.[12]

The two main camps used by the Qods Force to train foreign terrorist-operatives are the **Imam 'Ali camp in Teheran** and the camp at **Honar near Karaj, north of Teheran.** Two of the Hezbollah terrorists who were captured by the IDF during the second Lebanon war revealed during interrogation that they had been trained by the Revolutionary Guards at the training camp at Karaj. One of them even stated that in 1999 he had received anti-aircraft training and that his instructor had been a high-ranking Iranian named Hassan Irlu.

Hezbollah operatives have undergone varied training courses in Iran, from combined maneuvers through the use of anti-tank missiles (including Saggers and TOWs) to the use of anti-aircraft missiles. Special attention has been paid to Hezbollah units operating weapons perceived as strategic, such as ground-to-ground rockets with a range of more than 75 kms (46 miles) and UAVs. It should be noted those who helped Hezbollah launch the UAV into Israel in November 7, 2004 were Revolutionary Guards officers.

Hussein 'Ali Suleiman, a Hezbollah terrorist who was involved in the abduction of the two IDF soldiers on July 12, was captured during the second Lebanon war. During interrogation he said that he and 40–50 other Hezbollah members had undergone training in Iran. Their passports, he said, had not been stamped in Syria or Iran in order to hide the fact that they had been trained in Iran.

Supervising the Build-Up of Hezbollah's Military Strength and Preparing it for a Possible Confrontation with Israel

During the six years since the IDF withdrew from the security zone in south Lebanon, the Iranian Revolutionary Guards in Lebanon **upgraded Hezbollah's military operational capabilities while preparing for a possible confrontation with Israel.**

The Revolutionary Guards established **a well-organized and well-planned military deployment zone for Hezbollah in south Lebanon. It was more in the style of an Iranian division than the force of a terrorist organization.** Thus the Revolutionary Forces created the model of a terrorist organization

[12] Iran also supports the Palestinian terrorist organizations and members of the Qods Force train Palestinian terrorists in Lebanon and sometimes in Iran as well.

for Hezbollah with state capabilities. The Hezbollah "division" was constructed with the supervision and counsel of members of the Revolutionary Guards, who visited south Lebanon frequently and sometimes even approached the fence along the border with Israel.

That was confirmed by one of the Hezbollah terrorists captured during the war, who said that a year and a half previously, while he was on guard in south Lebanon, two Iranians and two Hezbollah commanders visited the post. He identified one of the Iranians as "Mahmoud," a member for the Revolutionary Guards who had been his instructor during anti-aircraft training he had had in Iran.

In effect, **the Hezbollah formation in south Lebanon was the direct product of Iranian doctrine and technology supplied by Iran and Syria.** Hezbollah's military zone in south Lebanon was composed of a number of territorial brigades and anti-tank, artillery, logistics, engineering and communications units. It was subordinate to a kind of Hezbollah "general staff" in the southern Beirut Shi'ite neighborhood of Dahia. The "general staff" had various functions such as a "strategic weapons" unit (ground-to-ground rockets) an aerial unit (UAVs), a marine unit and others.

Financing Hezbollah

The cost of supporting Hezbollah's vast military and social infrastructure is beyond the organization's resources. Its annual budget is estimated at about $100 million, most of which comes from Iran. The money finances the organization's terrorist-operative activities and infrastructures, purchases weapons, pays the operatives salaries, pays for training and is also invested in financing terrorist attacks in the Palestinian Authority.

In addition, the generous Iranian financial support pays for the organization's expenses and broad **social activities,** such as the operation of schools, hospitals and clinics, welfare institutions, etc., and also finances **propaganda and indoctrination activities.** These activities are aimed at deepening its penetration of the Shi'ite community and creating new generations of terrorists.

The Iranians transfer the funds to Hezbollah through the Revolutionary Guards' Qods Force, the foreign ministry, and its embassies in Damascus and Beirut. The Hezbollah budget is also paid by quasi-government institutions and charitable societies and organizations under Khamenei's control which have branches in Lebanon.

It should be noted that Iranian financial aid to Hezbollah increased after the IDF withdrew from the security zone, with the objectives of improving the organization's military capabilities and increasing support for the activities of the Palestinian terrorist organizations in the PA. After the second Lebanon war the Iranians can be expected to provide Hezbollah with massive amounts of money, in our assessment several hundred million dollars,[13] to repair the heavy damages caused to the Shi'ite populations in Beirut and south Lebanon.

The Damage Done to Hezbollah's Military Infrastructure During the War

During the second Lebanon war the IDF severely damaged Hezbollah's broad military infrastructures in south Lebanon, Beirut and the Beqa'a Valley. Weapons and headquarters were destroyed and more than **500** terrorists were killed. It will apparently take Hezbollah a great deal of time to rehabilitate its fighting force. The arsenal of rockets it stockpiled through the years was **significantly damaged,** especially its **long-range rockets.** However, the organization **still has the capabilities to fire rockets into the State of Israel.**

Despite the blows Hezbollah's military infrastructure suffered, and despite the blow to its standing in Lebanon, **it was not defeated and can be rehabilitated.** Thus it can be expected that Iran, supported by Syria, **will made the effort to repair the damage done to its front-line outpost in Lebanon** by supplying weapons (especially rockets) and pouring large sums of money into rebuilding civilian infrastructures.

Summary and Conclusions

Through the massive support given to Hezbollah by Iran and Syria since its inception, **the organization has turned from a local Lebanese terrorist organization, one of the many operating in Lebanon, into a military force with strong military operational capabilities and a great deal of influence both within the Shi'ite community and on the overall Lebanese political scene.** In the eyes of its sponsors, Hezbollah has become a strategic asset which serves their regional policies well.

Hezbollah's terrorist-operative capabilities, **which are those of a state, not a terrorist organization, were demonstrated during the second Lebanon war, earlier than what Iran and Syria had planned.** It was evident that the military infrastructure constructed in Lebanon permitted the Iranians and Syrians to **both attack and respond to Israel, and that its control was largely in Iranian hands**

Hezbollah's existence has made the Iranians, in their own eyes, a factor with the ability to escalate the destabilization of the region without direct intervention and to harm Israeli and Western interests in accordance with Iranian policy considerations. Thus in the near future the Iranians and Syrians **can be expected to make an effort to rebuild Hezbollah's military infrastructures** and ignore Security Council Resolution 1701.

[13] Hezbollah has publicly committed itself to pay $150 million in reparations for the destruction of houses, especially in south Lebanon and Dahia. Only from Iran can the organization receive such sums.

DOCUMENT NO. 8

TERRORISM AND INTERNET: HEZBOLLAH'S WIDESPREAD USE OF THE INTERNET

Intelligence and Terrorism Information Center at the Center for Special Studies (C.S.S) Report

December 3, 2006

Overview

1. As part of the **war for the hearts and minds** waged by Hezbollah, the organization, similarly to Hamas, makes **extensive use of the Internet.** After the second Lebanon war (in which many of Hezbollah's websites crashed or were shut down), the organization **rebuilt and even upgraded** its Internet infrastructure, adding new, heretofore non-existent websites. Compared to the websites run by Hezbollah before the war, the new websites show a marked **improvement both technology-wise and in terms of their update frequency**.

2. Hezbollah's network of Internet websites is run on the basis of a **uniform propaganda strategy** that serves the anti-Israeli, anti-Jewish, and anti-American incitement campaign **waged by Hezbollah and its sponsor, the Iranian regime.** The major themes on the organization's Internet websites are the personality cult of Hassan Nasrallah, glorification of terrorist attacks and suicide bombers, blatant anti-Israeli incitement and calls for the destruction of Israel, alongside vicious anti-Semitism and anti-Americanism. The criticism directed at the organization following the second Lebanon war compelled Hezbollah to make a propaganda effort to perpetuate the myth of "victory" over Israel and respond to internal critics.

Editor's note: The original version of this document included some color images that could not be adequately reproduced in this publication. Where necessary, captions, headings, and/or footnotes specifically relating to any omitted images have also been left out of the version reprinted herein. The main text of the document has not been affected by these omissions, but the footnote numbering has been changed where necessary to remove gaps between the footnote numbers.

3. The organization's **target audiences** are **varied** and include Lebanon and the Middle East (including Israel) on one hand, and other countries in the world on the other (mostly Arab and Muslim populations in Western countries). The websites are published in a **number of languages: Arabic** (first priority), **English** (second priority), and other languages such as **French, Spanish, and even Hebrew** (third priority).

4. **The scope and quality** of Hezbollah's **Internet infrastructure clearly exceed the capabilities of a terrorist organization, being one of the many forms of assistance the organization receives from Iran**. In our assessment, the Iranian aid is reflected in allocating substantial sums of money necessary for the operation of Hezbollah's extensive, multilingual Internet infrastructure, as well as in the high quality and frequency of updates. In our assessment, Iran considers Hezbollah's Internet infrastructure to be **yet another means for the dissemination of the Islamic regime's radical messages and ideology in Tehran, Lebanon, the Middle East, and the whole world.**[1] The Iranian regime's fingerprints and echoes of its propaganda are clearly visible on some of the websites.

5. Hezbollah's leading Internet websites can be divided into five main groups:

a. **Group A: Hezbollah's leading news websites, including** "Moqawama" (i.e., the Islamic resistance), "The Israeli Aggression on Lebanon", "Moqavemat" (i.e., the resistance, in Persian), "Shi'a Web".

b. **Group B: Hezbollah's media websites,** including Al-Manar TV, Al-Nour Radio, and Hezbollah publication Al-Intiqad.

c. **Group C: Hezbollah's other news websites, including** "Wa'ad" (i.e., the promise), "Islamic Digest", "Somod" (properly transliterated, *sumud* in Arabic means "firm stand").

d. **Group D: Hezbollah's local Internet websites in Lebanon, including** the websites of the towns and villages of Bint Jbeil, Taybeh, Deir Qanoun al-Nahr, and Houla.

e. **Group E: websites of Hezbollah's social organizations and designated websites, including** the Mu'assasat al-Shahid (shahid's organization) website, the Imam al-Mahdi Scouts website, and the Samir al-Kuntar website, promoting the release of the prisoner held in Israel (these websites have been inactive lately).

6. In addition to the above websites, **there are also Hezbollah-associated websites in Spanish in South America** (mostly in Venezuela). While possessing unmistakable South American characteristics, these websites

[1] At the same time, Iran censors and blocks access to external websites it does not approve of, such as YouTube.com (Ali Akbar Dareini, Associated Press, December 5, 2006).

refer to themselves as Hezbollah, use the organization's symbols and terminology, and sympathize with its messages of violence and hatred. Among these websites are a Hezbollah website in Latin America, a Hezbollah blog in Latin America, a Hezbollah website in Venezuela, a Hezbollah blog in Caracas, Venezuela, another website in Venezuela named after the native Wayuu tribe, and a Hezbollah website in El Salvador (see below).

7. The Hezbollah websites use the following web hosting companies:[2]

a. Most of Hezbollah's leading websites use Internet service providers located in Arab/Muslim countries in the Middle East **(Syria, Iran, Lebanon, Kuwait, Qatar)** and elsewhere **(Malaysia, Tanzania).**

b. Prominent among the Arab providers is **Syrian Telecommunication Establishment,** a company that provides Internet services to the [Islamic] Resistance website, Hezbollah's leading news website.

c. Additionally, there are several websites that use Internet service providers based in the **US** (where Hezbollah is considered a terrorist organization) and in **Sweden** (through local residents who appear to be Lebanese immigrants).

d. Three **South American** websites associating themselves with Hezbollah and its messages use the services of **American** Internet companies. Two of them use companies located in **Argentina** and in **Spain.**

8. What follows are details on the websites and technical information on the companies which they use.

Hezbollah's Leading News Websites

a. The "[Islamic] Resistance" Website, www.Moqawama.org

1. **The "[Islamic] Resistance" website is Hezbollah's leading news website. Its current address is www.moqawama.org.** It can also be reached at www.moqawama.tv, www.ghaliboun.net, www.hizbollah.org, www.nasrollah.org, and www.hizbollah.tv. Previously, it could also be accessed at www.moqawama.info and www.moqawama.net.

2. The **terminology** used by the website for its domain names is a cornerstone in Hezbollah's worldview: the term **"al-Moqawama"** refers to active resistance to one's adversary or enemy—that is, by violence and terrorism;[3] the term **"ghaliboun",** which appears in another address, means "victors"

[2] According to the Hagana and whois websites, as at November 21, 2006.

[3] Hezbollah often refers to itself as "Al-Muqawama al-Islamiyya fi Lubnan"—the Islamic Resistance in Lebanon.

or "conquerors", and is also a part of the Hezbollah slogan, taken from a verse in the Quran: *"Inna hizb allah humma al-ghaliboun"*—"The party of Allah is the party of the conquerors". Other terms that appear in the domain names are **Hizbollah** (the organization's name, Arabic for "Party of Allah"), **Nasrollah** (Arabic for "victory of Allah", also the name of Hezbollah leader Hassan Nasrallah).

3. **The website is available in Arabic and in English, reflecting its main target audiences.** The contents in both languages are more or less identical. The homepage of the website features the image of Hezbollah leader Hassan Nasrallah. The website publishes news focusing on Iran, Lebanon, and the Palestinians. Hezbollah's ideology clearly shows in the website's contents, which include anti-Israeli and anti-American messages. Since the second Lebanon war, the website focuses on perpetuating Hezbollah's "victory" in the war against Israel and nurtures the personality cult of Hezbollah leader Hassan Nasrallah (by the use of his photographs and citations).

4. **A sub-website accessible through this website is "The Israeli Aggression on Lebanon"** (www.moqawama.org/aggression/index.php). **The website also has an English version.** Recently opened, it features photographs of killed and wounded Lebanese children, with the purpose of nurturing hatred to Israel.

5. Following is technical information on the website:

   a. **http://www.moqawama.org**

   b. **IP address:** 82.137.205.249

   c. **Network access provider and web hosting service provider:** Syrian Telecommunication Establishment

   d. **Address:** 1 Mazza Autostrad Damascus Syria P.O.Box 11774, tel. +963 11 2311293, fax +963 11 2319975.

6. Following is technical information on the website's other addresses:

   a. **http://www.moqawama.tv**

      1. **IP address:** 82.137.205.247

      2. **Web hosting service provider:** Syrian Telecommunication Establishment

      3. **Contact:** Muhammad Hejazi, Harat Hreik, Beirut. Tel: 009613216933.

      4. E-mail: elco@cyberia.net.lb

   b. **www.ghaliboun.net**

      1. **IP address:** 202.75.42.155

      2. **Internet access provider:** Telecom Malaysia Berhad

      3. **Web hosting service provider:** Beirut, Lebanon (no details)

c. **www.hizbollah.org**

1. **IP address:** 205.178.189.131
2. **Internet service provider:** US-based Network Solutions

d. **www.nasrollah.org**

1. **IP address:** 82.137.205.247
2. **Web hosting service provider:** Syrian Telecommunication Establishment
3. **Contact:** Mohammad Hejazi, Hadeel.net, Harat Hreik, Beirut.

e. **www.hizbollah.tv**

1. **IP address:** 216.21.229.196
2. **Internet service provider:** Register.com, Inc, New York, USA
3. **The website is registered to** Mohammad Hejazi, Hadeel.net, Harat Hreik, Beirut.

b. The Moqavemat Website (www.moqavemat.com)

1. Yet another news website, **with unmistakable Iranian characteristics, is Moqavemat (Persian for "resistance",** the equivalent term for the Arabic "muqawama"). The address of the website is www.moqavemat.ir—**a domain name registered in Iran.** The website is also accessible at www.moqavemat.com. **It has versions in four languages: Arabic, English, French, and Hebrew.** The contents in the various languages are more or less identical. The top section of the first page features a photograph of Hezbollah leader Hassan Nasrallah.

2. The website publishes news stories similar to those which appear on the Moqawama website. The articles are rife with blatant anti-American and anti-Israeli contents and pro-Iranian views. The title of the homepage reads (October 26, 2006): "The [Iranian] Revolution leader [i.e., Ali Khamenei] calls upon peoples of the region to unite against the schemes of America and the Zionist entity".

3. Following is technical information on the website:

a. **http://www.moqavemat.ir**

b. **IP address:** 202.71.104.241

c. **Internet service provider:** Information Technology Company (ITC), P.O. Box 16315-737, Tehran, Iran.

c. The Shi'a Web website (www.shiaweb.org)

1. Shi'a Web (www.shiaweb.org) is a Hezbollah website combining religious Shi'ite themes and Hezbollah's political messages. The website contains a

link to another internal website located at http://www.shiaweb.org/hizbulla/index.html. The website contains speeches made by Nasrallah (in audio format), as well as a link to a website named Somod (see details below). The website makes extensive use of photographs of Hassan Nasrallah and distributes anti-Semitic and anti-American messages.

2. Following is technical information on the website:

a. **www.shiaweb.org**

b. **IP address:** 209.85.5.112

c. **Internet access provider:** Everyones Internet, based in Houston, Texas.

d. **Internet service provider:** USBHOST NET, based in Houston, Texas.

e. **The website is registered to** Malik al-Hashemi, Houston, Texas.

The Websites of Hezbllah's Media (Television, Radio, Newspapers)

a. The Al-Manar TV Website (www.manartv.com.lb)

1. This is the website of Hezbollah's television channel, Al-Manar ("the lighthouse"), the flagship of Hezbollah's propaganda. The two addresses of the website are www.manartv.com.lb and www.almanar.com.lb. The website is available both in Arabic and in English.

2. **The website draws its information from the Al-Manar TV channel.** Both the website and the television channel are permeated with anti-Israeli and anti-US incitement. The website's main areas of interest are Iraq, the Palestinian Authority-administered territories, and Lebanon.

3. **The English version of the website is accessible at** www.islamicdigest.net/almanar/start.php. It contains links to the Moqawama website and to Al-Manar's broadcasts. This website is part of Hezbollah's English-language website—**www.islamicdigest.net** (see below). **Using the Internet, Hezbollah can therefore circumvent the restrictions imposed by Europe and the US on the broadcasting of the Al-Manar TV channel through communications satellites.**[4]

4. Following is technical information on the website:

a. **www.manartv.com.lb**

[4] Within this context, see Information Bulletin published by the Intelligence and Terrorism Information Center: "Another limitation placed by the international community on broadcasts emanating from Hezbollah's Al-Manar TV station" (March 29, 20006).

b. **IP address:** 203.121.71.217

c. **Internet access provider:** Time Telecommunications Sdn Bhd Malaysia

d. **Internet service provider:** cyberia.net.lb, Beirut, Lebanon.

e. **Contact:** Ali al-Husni, Beirut.

b. The Al-Nour Radio Website

1. The Al-Nour radio website is the Arabic-language website of Hezbollah's radio station. The station disseminates anti-Israeli and anti-US incitement. The themes of the station are similar to those that appear on the Al-Manar TV channel. The website offers the station's news editions in audio format.

2. Following is technical information on the website:

a. **www.al-nour.net**

b. **IP address:** 82.137.205.249

c. **Internet access provider:** Syrian Telecommunication Establishment

d. **Internet service provider:** cyberia.net.lb, Beirut, Lebanon.

e. **The website is registered to** Hadi Abdallah Ja'far, Beirut.

c. The Website of Hezbollah's Publication Al-Intiqad (www.intiqadonline.com)

1. The Al-Intiqad (Arabic for "criticizing") newspaper is **Hezbollah's main publication.** The Internet addresses of the newspaper are **www.intiqadonline.com, www.alintiqad.com,** and **www.alahed.org** (another address, www.intiqad.net, is currently inactive). **The website is available in Arabic and in English.**

2. This is an important website, and it is updated in real-time. It contains news flashes, various channels (including the "Resistance" channel, the "Local Lebanese News" channel, the "Palestine" channel), and scanned copies of the Al-Intiqad newspaper in PDF format. The website disseminates messages of hatred against Israel and covers Lebanon and the Israeli-Palestinian conflict. **The website is also available in English.**

3. Following is technical information on the website:

a. **http://www.intiqadonline.com**

b. **IP address:** 82.137.205.249

c. **Internet access provider:** Syrian Telecommunication Establishment

d. **Internet service provider:** Terra.net.lb, Lebanon.

e. **The website is registered to** Mustafa Hazem, Lebanon.

f. **E-mail: officet@terra.net.lb**

4. Following is technical information on the website's other address:
   a. **http:// www.alintiqad.com**
   b. **IP address:** 69.10.136.210; 207.44.244.117
   c. **Internet access provider:** Everyones Internet, based in Houston, Texas.
   d. **Internet service provider:** Unknown.
   e. **The website is registered to** Intiqad Magazine, Harat Hreik, Beirut.

Other Hesbollah News Websites

a. The Wa'ad ("Promise") Website (http://www.wa3ad.org)

1. This is an important, up-to-date news website that recently became available. It only has an Arabic version. The choice of the name **Wa'ad** ("Promise") is not accidental. It is a widely-used term in the organization's terminology, referring to a Quran verse[5] that contains what modern Islamic scholars view as **Allah's promise to destroy the State of Israel.** Another expression espoused by Hezbollah is "the divine promise" *(al-wa'ad al-alihi)*—a promise that Islam will succeed and persevere.[6]

2.The themes of the Wa'ad website are reminiscent of those found on the Al-Intiqad website. The website has a channel that monitors the Israeli press, titled "Enemy Press", and another channel titled "History of Zionism", presenting the history of Israel from Hezbollah's hostile viewpoint in order to inspire hatred against Israel and the West. The upper section of the homepage as well as many articles feature photographs of Hezbollah leader Hassan Nasrallah as part of nurturing his personality cult.

3. Following is technical information on the website:
   a. **http://www.wa3ad.org**
   b. IP **address:** 66.98.225.220
   c. **Internet access provider:** Everyones Internet, based in Houston, Texas.
   d. **Internet service provider:** ALNA3I.NET, based in Kuwait.
   e. **The website is registered to** Sa'ad Mustafa.

---

[5] Sura 17, Al-Isra' ("The Night Journey").

[6] Hezbollah leader Hassan Nasrallah makes frequent use of this term. Thus, for example, speaking on Al-Manar on May 7, 1998, Nasrallah declared: "The hope grows stronger that the divine promise to destroy this cancer [i.e., Israel] will finally be fulfilled." Another related term is *"al-wa'ad al-sadeq"* ("the real promise [that was fulfilled]"), **a term popularized by Hezbollah to refer to the abduction of the two Israeli soldiers, the incident** which triggered the second Lebanon war. Yet another use of the term "promise" is to refer to Hezbollah's commitment to release Lebanese and Palestinian prisoners.

b. The Islamic Digest Website (www.islamicdigest.net)

1. **Islamic Digest is an English-language website that aims to deliver Hezbollah's messages to Western countries and to Arab/Muslim communities residing therein.** The website contains news, Islamic sermons, photographs, message boards, links to the organization's websites, and incitement videos against US President George Bush. **The website is available only in English.** Its address is www.islamicdigest.net.

2. Following is technical information on the website:

   a. **http://www.islamicdigest.net/almanar/start.php**

   b. **IP address:** 209.172.35.181

   c. **Internet access provider:** Group iWeb Technologies Inc., based in Montreal, Canada.

   d. **Internet service provider:** an unknown Tanzanian company.

   e. **The website is registered to** Sabbir and Fatma Hassanally, P.O.Box 19915 Dar es-Salaam, Tanzania.

c. The Somod ("Firm Stand") Website (www.somod.org)

1. Somod is a Hezbollah news site that is only available in Arabic. Like Wa'ad, the website went online after the second Lebanon war. The Arabic (properly transliterated) term *sumud* refers to a firm stand or perseverance, a constituent of the concept of "resistance"—the willingness to hold fast in face of difficulties. It is mainly used within the context of "occupation" (that is, to display staying power against the pressure exerted by Israel and the West).

2. The website provides regular news updates in like manner to Hezbollah's other news websites. It contains a news channel dedicated to the Israeli-Palestinian conflict.

3. Following is technical information on the website:

   a. **http://www.somod.org**

   b. **IP address:** 209.85.5.113

   c. **Internet access provider:** Everyones Internet, based in Houston, Texas.

   d. **Internet service provider:** USBHOST.NET, based in Dallas, Texas.

   e. **The website is registered to** Mohd Kumail, P.O. Box 133, US.

Locally-Oriented Internet Websites

Overview

1. Hezbollah has several Arabic-language websites of towns and villages in south Lebanon, **many of them of recent origin.** Their purpose is to

strengthen the bond between Hezbollah and important towns in south Lebanon, and to nurture the image of martyrs originating from those towns as role models. This bond became all the more important following the second Lebanon war, due to the massive destruction caused to population centers in south Lebanon which housed Hezbollah's military infrastructure[7] and due to the criticism the organization took because of that.

2. Following are the main characteristics of these websites.

1. The Website of the Town of Bint Jbeil (www.bintjbeil.com)

3. Relatively old, it boasts more content than all other Hezbollah's local websites. The website has highly active message boards, and it is available both in Arabic and in English.[8] It is fairly up-to-date, and it includes Hezbollah-oriented news such as praise of the "resistance" and of shahids. The website has a channel dedicated to Hezbollah's shahids and photographs from the town of Bint Jbeil.

4. Following is technical information on the website:

a. **www.bintjbeil.com**

b. **IP address:** 208.64.28.10

c. **Internet access provider:** versaweb.net, based in the US.

d. **Internet service provider:** Talal Nahle L02, from Stockholm, Sweden.

e. **The website is registered to** Yatim Yatim, from Nabatiyeh, Lebanon.

2. The Website of the Town of Taybeh (www.altaybeh.net)

5. A new website, it praises Hezbollah's shahids originating from the town.

6. Following is technical information on the website:

a. **http://www.altaybeh.net**

b. **IP address:** 208.64.28.10

c. **Internet service provider:** FullwebHosting.net from Sweden.

d. **Contact:** Talal Nahle, Sweden.

3. The Website of the Town of Deir Qanoun al-Nahr (www.deirqanounalnahr.jeeran.com)

7. The articles and photographs on the website address the destruction caused by Israel to the town during the second Lebanon war. On at least

[7] The Intelligence and Terrorism Information Center has recently published on its website a comprehensive study on the use of Lebanese civilians as a human shield.

[8] Many Lebanese originally from the town of Bint Jbeil reside in the United States.

some of the photographs, one can make out Hezbollah flags raised over the destroyed buildings. The website has links to other Hezbollah websites.

8. Following is technical information on the website:

   a. **www.deirqanounalnahr.jeeran.com**

   b. **Internet access provider:** Jeeran Co., based in Amman, Jordan. It is a company that provides free Internet services.

   c. **Internet service provider:** Electric Lightwave Inc., from the US.

4. The Website of the Town of Houla (www.houla.org)

9. The website praises the value of "resistance" (i.e., violence and terrorism) and Hezbollah shahids originating from the town, and nurtures hatred against Israel.

10. Following is technical information on the website:

   a. **www.houla.org**

   b. **IP address:** 66.199.236.147

   c. **Internet service provider:** Alameh Issam, P.O Box 20764, Doha, Qatar.

Websites of Hezbollah's Social Organizations and Designated Websites (Currently Inactive)

a. The Shahid's Institution (Mu'assasat Al-Shahid) Website, Currently Inactive (http://www.alshahid.org)

1. This website belongs to the Shahid's Institution (Mu'assasat al-Shahid), a Hezbollah institution involved in providing assistance to families of killed Hezbollah operatives. The website commemorates the organization's shahids—including photographs and biographies—and details the activities of the Shahid's Institution for the families of Hezbollah's shahids. The website praises the organization's shahids and their activities.

b. The Imam Al-Mahdi Scouts Website, Kashafat Al-Imam Al-Mahdi (www.almahdiscouts.org, presently inactive)

2. A presently inactive website, it was dedicated to the Hezbollah's youth movement: "Kashafat al-Imam al-Mahdi" (the Imam al-Mahdi Scouts).[9]

[9] Within this context, see "Hezbollah's Shi'ite youth movement, "The Imam al-Mahdi Scouts," has tens of thousands of members. According to captured documents, they are indoctrinated with the principles of radical Iranian Islam. That indoctrination includes the personality cult of Iranian leader 'Ali Khamenei and Hezbollah's "battle legacy;" national Lebanese symbols are minimized" (September 11, 2006).

c. The Jihad al-Binaa website (www.jihadalbinaa.org, presently inactive)

3. This is the website of a Hezbollah socio-economic organization currently involved in rebuilding post-war Lebanon. Jihad al-Binaa ("the jihad of building") is a term coined by Ayatollah Khomeini, signifying a social reform for Muslims that constitutes a holy war in its own right. The website is recently inactive.

d. The Samir Al-Kuntar Website (www.samirkuntar.org, presently inactive)

2. **This is a website advocating the release of the murderer Samir al-Kuntar,** a major issue on Hezbollah's list of demands. A Druze from Mount Lebanon and a notorious member of the Palestinian Liberation Front (a pro-Iraqi terrorist organization), he was sentenced to a long term of imprisonment in Israel for his participation in a terrorist attack in Nahariya.[10] Israel had refused to release Al-Kuntar during negotiations with Hezbollah. Hezbollah, referring to Al-Kuntar as "the most high-ranking Lebanese prisoner in Israeli prisons", has turned him into the symbol of the struggle for the release of Lebanese prisoners held in Israel. The organization claims that Al-Kuntar's release justifies the abduction of Israeli soldiers and civilians as bargaining chips.

3. **The website has versions in Arabic, English, French, and Hebrew.** It calls for the release of Samir al-Kuntar and portrays him as a hero. All the website's themes pertain to Al-Kuntar's release, and its ideology and messages match Hezbollah's anti-Israeli and anti-American rhetoric. The Hebrew version contains an interview with Al-Kuntar casting him in a human light and showing him grieving the death of the girl he had killed. The website is presently inactive.

Hezbollah-Associated (or Sympathetic) Websites in South America

Overview

1. Following are Spanish-language websites in South America, of South American character, not necessarily belonging to Hezbollah. However, these websites identify themselves as Hezbollah's, use the organization's symbols and terminology, and sympathize with its messages of violence and hatred. It is possible that (Shi'ite) Lebanese who immigrated to South America are involved in at least some of these websites.

---

[10] The terrorist attack was perpetrated on April 22, 1979, by a squad headed by Samir al-Kuntar that reached Nahariya by sea. Three members of the Haran family and officer Eliyahu Shachar were killed in the attack. Samir al-Kuntar killed the four-year-old daughter of Dani and Smadar Haran with his bare hands.

1. http://es.groups.yahoo.com/group/Hezboallah_latino

2. A Hezbollah-associated website in Latin America, it contains news in Spanish.

3. Following is technical information on the website:

a. **http://es.groups.yahoo.com/group/Hezboallah_latino**

b. **IP address:** 66.218.66.241

c. **Internet access provider:** Yahoo, California, US.

d. **Internet service provider:** Yahoo, California, US.

2. A Website in Venezuela Titled http://groups .msn.com/justiciadivinavenezuela

4. This is a Spanish-language website dedicated to Hezbollah. It includes articles and photographs inciting to violence.

5. There exists an organization in Venezuela calling itself **Hezbollah Venezuela,** led by "Teodoro Rafael Darnott". The organization, advocating social change in Venezuela, looks upon Hezbollah as its role model. The organization claims to possess "jihad warriors" *(mujahedin)* willing to die for the organization's goals (source: El Nacional, a newspaper published in Caracas, available online at www.El-Nacional.com).

6. **Ali Fayad,** a member of the Hezbollah Political Bureau and director of the Research and Documentation Center, gave the website an interview on the happenings in Lebanon (July 25, 2006). Ali Fayad may be a sort of Hezbollah contact to these sites (see below).

7. Following is technical information on the website:

a. **http://groups.msn.com/justiciadivinavenezuela**

b. **IP address:** 65.54.134.94

c. **Internet access provider:** Microsoft Inc, US.

d. **Internet service provider:** Microsoft Inc, US.

3. A Hezbollah Blog in Caracas, Venezuela (http://bloggy.com.ar/caracas)

8. The blog is built as a website and is available only in Spanish. The sponsor is a blog website from Argentina: http://bloggy.com.ar.

9. Following is technical information on the website:

a. **http://bloggy.com.ar/caracas**

b. **IP address:** 200.122.70.209

c. **Internet access provider:** prima.com.ar, Argentina.

d. **Internet service provider:** Bloggy.com.ar, Buenos Aires, Argentina.

4. Another Hezbollah Website in Venezuela: http://groups.msn.com/autonomiaislamicawayuu

10. The website was originally designed to disseminate Islamic ideology under the slogan "political activity is a religious duty". The website is named after a native tribe, Wayuu, residing on the Columbian-Venezuelan border, **where many former Lebanese Shi'ites live**.

11. An active participant in the website is the leader of Hezbollah in Venezuela, Teodoro Rafael Darnott, who uses it to detail Hezbollah's strategy in Venezuela. Yet another active participant is Ali Fayad, a member of the Hezbollah Political Bureau and director of the organization's Research and Documentation Center. He regularly updates the website on happenings in Lebanon.

12. Following is technical information on the website:

a. **http://groups.msn.com/autonomiaislamicawayuu**

b. **IP address:** 65.54.134.94

c. **Internet access provider:** Microsoft Inc, US.

d. **Internet service provider:** Microsoft Inc, US.

5. The Hezbollah Website in El Salvador: http://groups.msn.com/Hezbollahelsalvador

13. The website shares a similar format with the Venezuelan website, and it is also available only in Spanish.

14. Following is technical information on the website:

a. **http://groups.msn.com/Hezbollahelsalvador**

b. **IP address:** 65.64.134.94

c. **Internet access provider:** Microsoft Inc, US.

d. **Internet service provider:** Microsoft Inc, US.

6. A Hezbollah blog in Latin America: http://hezboallahpartidoislamico.blogspot.es/

15. This is a Spanish-language blog that contains photographs inciting to violence. The sponsor is a Spanish blog website: http://www.blogspot.es.

16. Following is technical information on the website:

a. **http://hezboallahpartidoislamico.blogspot.es/**

b. **IP address:** 213.228.192.182

c. **Internet access provider:** Blogspot.es San Sebastian, Spain.

d. **Internet service provider:** Blogspot.es San Sebastian, Spain.

DOCUMENT NO. 9

FUNDING TERRORISM: HEZBOLLAH USES ITS WEBSITES TO COLLECT DONATIONS

Intelligence and Terrorism Information Center at the Israel Intelligence Heritage & Commemoration Center (IICC) Report

May 26, 2008

Overview

1. Hezbollah collects donations using its websites and by various other means. The donations are collzected in Lebanon, Iran, and other countries in the world. A significant portion of the donations are collected in Shi'ite Lebanese communities, being the organization's primary support infrastructure. The donations are collected **to supplement the Iranian financial assistance,** which makes up most of Hezbollah's budget. The donations are used not only for social and cultural activities but also to support the restoration of Hezbollah's military infrastructure following the second Lebanon war (including the acquisition of weapons).

2. One of Hezbollah's main institutions involved in collecting donations is the **Support Association of the Islamic Resistance in Lebanon** (hereinafter: **the Support Association).** Founded by Hezbollah in 1989, it is associated with **Beit al-Mal** (an Islamic financial institution which fulfills some of the functions of a bank, an important component in Hezbollah's financial structure in Lebanon). The Support Association collects funds in **Lebanon** (in commerce sites, mosques, educational institutions, gas stations, roadblocks, etc.) **and also among Shi'ite Muslim communities in Arab countries and elsewhere in the world** (mostly in the Gulf States and

Editor's note: The original version of this document included some color images that could not be adequately reproduced in this publication. Where necessary, captions, headings, and/or footnotes specifically relating to any omitted images have also been left out of the version reprinted herein. The main text of the document has not been affected by these omissions, but the footnote numbering has been changed where necessary to remove gaps between the footnote numbers.

in Western countries).[1] **Pamphlets distributed by the Support Association make it perfectly clear that the donations are also used to support Hezbollah's military infrastructure.**

3. **Hezbollah's extensive network of websites, published in several languages,** is an important leverage for collecting donations for the organization and its various institutions. Using online ads, web surfers worldwide can call Hezbollah's numbers in Lebanon in order to transfer the donations to their destination in Lebanon. In some cases, donations can be transferred to bank accounts located in Lebanese and European banks mentioned in the websites.

4. Following are the methods used to collect donations using the various websites. It should be noted that some websites involved in raising funds are serviced by **US**-based Internet Service Providers (even though Hezbollah is considered a global terrorist organization by the American State Department).

a. Collecting Donations through the English-language Wa'ad Website

5. **Wa'ad** (Arabic for "promise") is one of Hezbollah's important news websites, available in Arabic and in English. Both versions are serviced by a **US**-based Internet service provider. The website was active until early April 2008, when the English version went offline. Past experience shows that it may be a temporary shutdown.

6. Using the Wa'ad website, Hezbollah collects donations for some of its institutions:

a. **The Support Association of the Islamic Resistance in Lebanon.**

b. **Jihad al-Bina' (the Reconstruction Campaign).**

c. ***Muassasat al-Shahid* (Al-Shahid Foundation).**

Details follow:

7. **Raising funds for the Support Association of the Islamic Resistance in Lebanon:** formerly, the Support Association had its own website for transferring donations to Hezbollah and Palestinian terrorist organizations. Now, the donations are transferred through the **Wa'ad** website, which publishes Lebanese telephone numbers (country code 961). The title reads: "Do not turn a blind eye to the holocaust in the Gaza Strip". Hezbollah, which combines the collection of donations with propaganda, has adopted the false Palestinian propaganda, claiming that Israel is perpetrating a "holocaust"

[1] For more details, see our Information Bulletin: "Documents captured during the second Lebanon war reveal how Hezbollah raises funds and at the same time furthers its propaganda and indoctrination campaign, stressing the younger generation" (August 25, 2006).

in the Gaza Strip while using a term which refers to the genocide of European Jewry.

8. Collecting donations for **Jihad al-Bina'**, a socio-economical organization which helps rebuild the infrastructure of Hezbollah and its supporters in Lebanon. The phone numbers mentioned in the ad are located in Lebanon.

9. Raising funds for **Al-Shahid Foundation**, an institution belonging to Hezbollah which helps the families of martyrs killed in the organization's activities. It is also involved in commemorating killed terrorists, glorifying them, and turning them into role models for the rest of Hezbollah's operatives and for the Lebanese. Since the second Lebanon war, Al-Shahid Foundation has been supporting some 2440 martyrs' families, compared to 1440 families before the war.[2]

10. **Details on the Wa'ad website (English version):**[3]

Website: www.english.wa3ad.org

IP address: 208.64.29.122

ISP: US-based versaweb.net

b. Raising Funds through the Al-Shahid Foundation Website

11. **The Al-Shahid Foundation** has its own website (www.alshahid.org), which is also used as a leverage for fundraising. The website features a Lebanese phone number for transferring funds to the "Mutual Solidarity *[takafful]* Program", that is, financial assistance to families of martyrs supported by Hezbollah.

12. **Website details:**

Website: www.alshahid.org

IP address: 82.137.205.251

Internet Service Provider: Syrian Telecommunication Establishment

c. Collecting Donations through the Shiaweb Website

13. Hezbollah's Shiaweb website calls to donate funds to an **Islamic charitable society** named **The Islamic al-Emdad Aid Association—Lebanon**[4] (or **Imam Khomeini Relief Organization).** That association (henceforth "Al-Emdad Association") is an **Iranian charitable society** which was established along with other Iranian charitable societies following Khomeini's revolution in 1979. The Iranian charitable societies are under the direct

[2] http://www.wa3ad.org/index.php?show=news&action=article&id=3302.

[3] For details on the website (and on other websites), we have used the whois websites and the manager of the American Haganah website.

[4] In Arabic: *Jam 'iyyat al-Imdad al-Khayriyya al-Islamiyya—Lubnan.*

control of the leader's office, they act in an independent, non-government context, and are mostly headed by senior figures in the regime. They are major economic corporations which serve as an important component in exporting the Islamic revolution and spreading Iranian radical Islam, inter alia, by providing financial and material assistance to Hezbollah and Palestinian terrorist organizations (including Hamas[5] and the PIJ).

14. Other than their social activity, the Iranian charitable societies are a channel through which donations intended to people in need are funneled to Hezbollah, Hamas, and other terrorist organizations. Ayatollah Khomeini, as stated above, has given a religious approval to such activities by issuing a *fatwa* (Islamic religious opinion) allowing charitable societies to transfer funds for the armed struggle waged by the Palestinians against Israel.

15. Iran's major foundations, including the Al-Emdad Association, have **branches in Lebanon** through which they implement Khomeini's concept. Starting 2001, those foundations, including Al-Emdad, have passed into the possession and management of **Hezbollah.** Accordingly, it is **Hezbollah which sets the policy of** the Al-Emdad Association in Lebanon and determines the allocation of its budget. In public interviews granted in 2001, Hassan Nasrallah noted that the Al-Emdad Association was one of Hezbollah's sources of funds in the social sphere (Hezbollah is engaged in extensive social activity among the population, particularly Lebanon's Shi'ites, to deepen its hold and recruit operatives).

16. Published on the Shiaweb website are bank account numbers through which donations can be transferred for the Al-Emdad Association, and phone numbers through which fund transfers can be arranged. Most of the bank account numbers and telephone numbers are in **Lebanon;** however, two bank account numbers are in **BLC Bank, Paris and in Dresdner bank, Frankfurt.** Those who donate to those bank account numbers are asked to make their transfers in Euros or in Dollars.[6]

17. **Website details:**

Website: shiaweb.org

Address: 66.207.161.14

Internet Service Provider: US-based cologuys.com

[5] The "charitable societies" of the Hamas movement are an important component of its civilian activities, and serve to support the military-terrorist wing.

[6] http://shiaweb.org/hizbulla/emdad.html. Details on these bank accounts were formerly published on the Al-Emdad Association website; however, they were taken off the website and, probably recently, republished on the Shiaweb website.

d. Collecting Donations through the Al-Emdad Website

18. The Al-Emdad Association has a website at www.alamdad.net. This website, too, is used to collect donations for the charitable association and, indirectly, for Hezbollah.

19. Published on the website are telephone numbers of Al-Emdad's various offices in Lebanon: the central management of the charitable association ("the center"), the Beirut branch, the Tyre office, the Jabal 'Amel office (south Lebanon), the Saida office, the Bint Jbeil office, the Al-Khayam office, the Central and North Beqaa offices, the Hermel office, the West Beqaa office. **All the offices are located inside Shi'ite population centers in Lebanon. Fax numbers** are listed, and there is an option to make a **Western Union** transfer to **Habib Amar in Beirut, or to the Middle East and Africa Bank in the Beirut neighborhood of Al-Shiyah**.

20. **Website details:**

Website: www.alamdad.net

IP address: 208.96.29.150

Internet Service Provider: US-based servepath.com

The website is registered with France-based bookmyname.com

The website's owner is Rehlah multimedia services from **Beirut**

The Imam Al-Mahdi Scouts Website

21. Imam al-Mahdi Scouts is Hezbollah's youth movement, which nurtures the values of Islamic revolution, violence, and hatred against Israel among generations of children and teenagers.[7] The scouts go on to become the new generations of Hezbollah's operatives. The organization's website shows telephone numbers and an email address through which donations can be made.

[7] See our Information Bulletin: "Hezbollah's Shi'ite youth movement, "The Imam al-Mahdi Scouts," has tens of thousands of members. According to captured documents, they are indoctrinated with the principles of radical Iranian Islam. That indoctrination includes the personality cult of Iranian leader 'Ali Khamenei and Hezbollah's "battle legacy;" national Lebanese symbols are minimized" (September 11, 2006).

D. LEBANON'S INTERNAL EFFORTS

DOCUMENT NO. 10

LEBANON'S 2001 REPORT TO THE UN ON ITS COUNTER-TERRORISM EFFORTS

United Nations Security Council
S/2001/1201

December 13, 2001

Distr.: General
13 December 2001
English
Original: French

Letter dated 13 December 2001 from the Chairman of the Security Council Committee established pursuant to resolution 1373 (2001) concerning counter-terrorism addressed to the President of the Security Council

The Counter-Terrorism Committee has received the attached report from Lebanon, submitted pursuant to paragraph 6 of resolution 1373 (2001) (see annex). I should be grateful if you would arrange for this letter and its annex to be circulated as a document of the Security Council.

(*Signed*) Jeremy **Greenstock**
Chairman of the Counter-Terrorism Committee

Annex

Note verbale dated 13 December 2001 from the Permanent Representative of Lebanon to the United Nations addressed to the Chairman of the Security Council Committee established pursuant to resolution 1373 (2001) concerning counter-terrorism

[Original: Arabic]

The Permanent Mission of Lebanon to the United Nations presents its compliments to the Security Council Committee established pursuant to resolution 1373 (2001) of 28 September 2001 concerning counter-terrorism (Counter-Terrorism Committee) and has the honour to submit to it herein the report requested in paragraph 6 of the same resolution, in accordance with the Committee's note of 29 [i.e. 26] October 2001 (SCA/20/01(6)).

In submitting this report to the Committee, the Mission is anxious to affirm at the outset the principles and premises set forth hereunder.

1. Lebanon reaffirms its condemnation of terrorism in all its forms and its fixed commitment to international legitimacy and to the implementation of the terms of Security Council resolution 1373 (2001). It further reaffirms its readiness to cooperate with the United Nations in the suppression of international terrorism in accordance with the norms of international law and the established principles of national sovereignty, first and foremost the distinction between terrorism and resistance to foreign occupation, and its commitment to strive constantly to promote the principles of right and justice.

2. In the preparation of the present report Lebanon has based itself on the distinction, as made in United Nations General Assembly resolution 46/51 of 19 January 1991 and in the 1998 Arab Convention for the Suppression of Terrorism, between terrorism on the one hand and the legitimate right of peoples to resist foreign occupation on the other, as well as on the international conventions relating to terrorism to which Lebanon has acceded and on the provisions of Security Council resolution 1333 (2000) of 19 December 2000.

On the basis of the foregoing and in accordance with the concepts mentioned, Lebanon addresses to the Committee its answers to [the questions corresponding to the relevant] operative paragraphs [of resolution 1373 (2001)].

Question 1 (a): What measures if any have been taken to prevent and suppress the financing of terrorist acts in addition to those listed in your responses to [the] questions on 1 (b) to (d)?

Such measures are included among the general measures adopted to combat money-laundering, as can be seen in Law No. 318 of 20 April 2001 and in decision of the Governor of the Bank of Lebanon No. 7818 of 18 May 2001, whether they relate to banks and financial institutions, to the requirement to monitor certain transactions or to the elaboration of means to combat money-laundering activities, including activities for the financing of terrorism.

Under Law No. 318, a special board of inquiry was formed with the task of conducting inquiries into transactions suspected of constituting money-laundering offences, including those involving the illegal proceeds of crimes, such as racketeering, that are internationally regarded as constituting organized crime, and the terrorist crimes stipulated in articles 314 to 316 of the Lebanese Penal Code.

On the basis of this law, the special board of inquiry has sought information from banks concerning any accounts held with them that belong to persons and entities included in the lists issued by the Security Council with a view to freezing or confiscating them. No accounts belonging to persons or entities included in the lists have been found.

Question 1 (b): What are the offences and penalties in your country with respect to the activities listed in this subparagraph?

Penalties for terrorist offences are provided by articles 314 to 316 of the Lebanese Penal Code. Articles 217 to 222 of the Code penalize anyone who incites, participates in or is an accessory to the commission of crimes, including terrorism. Lebanese jurisprudence regards the person who finances a crime as an accessory to it, and the penalty for the accessory is the same as for the perpetrator when it is evident that without his assistance the crime would not have been committed.

This rule is applied whether an act of terrorism is financed within or by way of Lebanese territory (such as bank financing through a bank in Lebanon). It is sufficient for this purpose for one of the elements of a crime of terrorism or attempted terrorism to be committed in Lebanese territory, or for a constitutive act of primary or secondary implication to occur there, or for its outcome to occur or be expected to occur there. It makes no difference whether the person providing funding is Lebanese or not (Penal Code, article 15).

The same provisions apply to Lebanese nationals who finance terrorist operations from abroad, even if the acts are committed outside Lebanese territory (Penal Code, article 20).

They also apply to all foreigners or stateless persons residing or present in Lebanon who finance terrorist activities abroad if extradition is not requested or not granted.

It should be noted that by Law No. 57/99 the Lebanese Government acceded to the Arab Convention for the Suppression of Terrorism. Under the Convention, the States parties undertake to suppress terrorist crimes in accordance with their domestic laws and internal measures and to prevent the financing of terrorist elements (article 3).

Question 1 (c): What legislation and procedures exist for freezing accounts and assets at banks and financial institutions? It would be helpful if States supplied examples of any relevant action taken.

Law No. 318 of 20 April 2001, which relates to the suppression of money-laundering, establishes an independent special board of inquiry that has a judicial character and may have banking secrecy waived with respect to accounts held with banks and financial assets with financial institutions if those holding them commit offences punishable under the same Law (including terrorist activities) and the funds in question may thus be frozen or confiscated (Penal Code, article 98; and Law No. 318/2001, article 14). The board may ask the Office of the Special Public Prosecutor to prosecute those responsible for committing such acts in the criminal courts.

Question 1 (d): What measures exist to prohibit the activities listed in this subparagraph?

On 15 May 2001, the Bank of Lebanon issued its decision No. 7818, on a system to monitor financial and banking operations in order to combat money-laundering. It establishes binding rules with which banks and financial institutions operating in Lebanon are required to comply in order to prevent money-laundering activities arising out of the offences stipulated in the aforesaid Law No. 318/2001, including, of course, crimes of terrorism. A staff of auditors and investigators has been provided to the special board of inquiry as well as a special administrative unit, and advocacy and information campaigns are being conducted among the public.

Question 2 (a): What legislation or other measures are in place to give effect to this subparagraph? In particular, what offences in your country prohibit (i) recruitment to terrorist groups and (ii) the supply of weapons to terrorists? What other measures help prevent such activities?

Lebanese laws, specifically article 314 of the Penal Code, the Arms and Ammunition Law (No. 137/59) and Law No. 318/2001, stipulate that anyone suspected of a punishable offence in the terrorism field or of illegal possession of arms and ammunition must be investigated, arrested and prosecuted. Penalties are applied whenever persons involved in terrorist activities commit acts that constitute terrorist offences as understood by Lebanese law, and the security agencies are authorized to assist the Office of the Public Prosecutor in preventing terrorist activities and thwarting the elaboration of schemes against the security and safety of the international community and local society.

Question 2 (b): What other steps are being taken to prevent the commission of terrorist acts and, in particular, what early-warning mechanisms exist to allow exchange of information with other States?

There is ongoing and direct coordination between the security services of the Ministry of the Interior and the security attachés accredited to Lebanon in the various embassies of other States. The exchange of information on terrorist activities was thus under way before 11 September 2001, and such cooperation still exists between Lebanese security agencies, especially the Interpol Division in the Office of the Director-General of the Internal Security Forces, and their counterparts in other States.

Question 2 (c): What legislation or procedures exist for denying safe haven to terrorists, such as laws for excluding or expelling the types of individuals referred to in this subparagraph? It would be helpful if States supplied examples of any relevant action taken.

The law promulgated on 10 July 1962 stipulates that entry to, residence in and departure from Lebanon will be regulated in such a way as to prevent entry unless a person is provided with the documents and visas required by law.

In accordance with the Code of Criminal Procedure, all security agencies are required to conduct the investigations necessary for the arrest of suspects against whom domestic or international arrest warrants or search and inquiry orders relating to terrorist or other offences have been issued.

Such persons are arrested in Lebanese territory or on attempting to enter or leave it by way of the posts maintained by General Security, and they are remanded to the relevant jurisdiction.

The provisions of the Criminal Code with respect to the punishment of the concealment of offenders against whom judicial orders or verdicts have been issued are applied to terrorist offenders, and the laws relating to aliens allow the Office of the Director of General Security to deport them from Lebanese territory.

The extradition of aliens charged with an offence regarded as a terrorist offence under Lebanese law may be requested in accordance with the terms for extradition laid down in the Penal Code and in keeping with the bilateral agreements, if any, on the extradition of offenders. Such persons may also be deported by administrative action of the Office of the Director of General Security.

If they have committed a terrorist crime in Lebanese territory they are tried by the Lebanese courts and must be expelled from the country after serving or discharging the penalty imposed.

In general, Lebanon does not provide a safe haven for those who finance, direct, support or commit acts of terrorism, especially those stipulated in Security Council resolution 1333 (2000), and it does not permit them to enter its territory.

Question 2 (d): What legislation or procedures exist to prevent terrorists acting from your territory against other States or citizens? It would be helpful if States supplied examples of any relevant action taken.

Lebanese laws require the investigation and arrest of any fugitive charged with or convicted of an offence punishable under Lebanese legislation or under the provisions of the international conventions to which the Lebanese State has acceded and which have come to have the force of law. The Lebanese State is committed to applying the provisions of the protocols and conventions in the domain of the suppression of terrorism to which it has acceded to date. The Arab Convention for the Suppression of Terrorism, to which Lebanon has acceded and which has been considered as the law since its entry into force, stipulates explicitly in its article 3 (i) that all the States parties undertake to prevent the use of their territory for the planning, organization or commission of terrorist offences and to prohibit terrorist elements from residing in their territory.

Question 2 (e): What steps have been taken to establish terrorist acts as serious criminal offences and to ensure that the punishment reflects the seriousness of such terrorist acts? Please supply examples of any convictions obtained and the sentence given.

Lebanese legislative enactments impose penalties for terrorism that can include the death penalty. The law promulgated on 11 January 1958 imposes for every terrorist act a penalty of hard labour for life, and the penalty becomes death if the terrorist act causes the death of a person, or the partial or total destruction of a building in which a person is present, or the destruction, even the partial destruction, of a public building, industrial establishment, ship or other installation, or the disruption of information, communications or transport.

Examples of the suppression of terrorist acts include Lebanon's past experience of a bloody clash with members of the Ansar group in northern Lebanon in early 2000 in which most of the members of the organization were arrested. They are currently being tried before the Judicial Council.

Many States have asked to be kept informed of the course of the investigations and proceedings, including the United States of America at the time, and their officials have been notified of the details.

Question 2 (f): What procedures and mechanisms are in place to assist other States? Please provide any available details of how these have been used in practice.

Under the supervision of the relevant jurisdiction, namely the Special Public Prosecutor, the services of the Judicial Police have mobilized all of their resources in order to give the requesting State all the information or data available to them on persons suspected of committing terrorist acts. They undertake the investigations necessary to obtain the information required in all fields (concerning travel documents, means of communication, movements, criminal records, etc.). It should be said that after the events of 11 September 2001 the central criminal research services and the international (Interpol) liaison division provided all those who submitted requests in many countries with the information requested in accordance with the letters addressed to them by Interpol divisions in those countries or by their diplomatic missions.

The Bank of Lebanon has also cooperated with the authorities in various foreign countries for the suppression of money-laundering, including the laundering of proceeds of terrorist crimes.

Question 2 (g): How do border controls in your country prevent the movement of terrorists? How do your procedures for issuance of identity papers and travel documents support this? What measures exist to prevent their forgery etc.?

The response to this question is similar to that given under 2 (c) above. The border control authorities, especially General Security, have to date dealt with many cases of forgery of other countries' passports. There are many examples of how action is taken in this matter. General Security arrests the bearer of a false passport and hands him over to the courts, and contact is made with the embassy of the country whose passport has been forged in order to inform it of the documents found and of the investigations under way in their regard.

Question 3 (a): What steps have been taken to intensify and accelerate the exchange of operational information in the areas indicated in this subparagraph?

The terms of this subparagraph have been implemented in accordance with the provisions of the Lebanese laws mentioned above with the direct coordination of security officials in Lebanon and the security attachés at the embassies accredited to the country and through the Interpol Division in the Office of the Director-General of the Internal Security Forces.

Question 3 (b): What steps have been taken to exchange information and cooperate in the areas indicated in this subparagraph?

In accordance with international law, the exchange of information takes place through Interpol in accordance with the principles set forth in the ICPO-Interpol Constitution. Cooperation in judicial matters takes place in accordance with the provisions of national law and pursuant to the principle of reciprocity and international cooperation in meeting requests for judicial assistance and the extradition of offenders in the event there is no bilateral agreement. Where there is a bilateral agreement, then extradition takes place in accordance with the provisions of that agreement.

Question 3 (c): What steps have been taken to cooperate in the areas indicated in this subparagraph?

In implementation of the Arab Convention for the Suppression of Terrorism, there is ongoing cooperation between the States parties and through the secretariat of the Council of Arab Ministers of the Interior in the exchange of information, in the investigation and arrest of suspects or convicts, in the extradition of offenders, and in meeting requests for judicial assistance and cooperation with respect to all the terrorist offences addressed in the Convention.

The case is the same with regard to the 10 international conventions on terrorism to which Lebanon has acceded, the country being anxious to implement all the provisions of these conventions in the field of cooperation in combating terrorist acts.

Question 3 (d): What are your Government's intentions regarding signing and/or ratifying the conventions and protocols referred to in this paragraph?

Lebanon has signed and has acceded to 10 of the 12 conventions for the suppression of terrorism adopted by the United Nations and its specialized agencies. It is now in the process of acceding to the two conventions that it did not sign at the time, namely the International Convention for the Suppression of Terrorist Bombings of 15 December 1997 and the International Convention for the Suppression of the Financing of Terrorism of 9 December 1999.

It should be said that the international protocols and conventions to which Lebanon has acceded have come to have the force of law in the country and take precedence over the provisions of national law.

By Law No. 57 of 31 March 1999 the National Assembly authorized the Government to ratify the Arab Convention on the Suppression of Terrorism, and the provisions of this convention have come to take precedence over the application of the provisions of national law.

Question 3 (e): Provide any relevant information on the implementation of the conventions, protocols and resolutions referred to in this subparagraph.

Lebanon is committed to implementing the conventions and protocols to which it has acceded or to which it is in the process of acceding in the knowledge that international cooperation can assist in the proper implementation of these conventions.

Question 3 (f): What legislation, procedures and mechanisms are in place for ensuring asylum-seekers have not been involved in terrorist activity before granting refugee status? Please supply examples of any relevant cases.

As stipulated in the Law promulgated on 10 July 1962, Lebanese laws on political asylum prohibit refugees admitted to Lebanon from engaging in any political activity whatever. Thus terrorist activities of whatever kind will cause them to forfeit their refugee status and make them subject to legal prosecution like any other resident of Lebanese territory.

The right of asylum is granted only by decision of a committee whose members represent the ministries of the interior, justice and foreign affairs, and its decision is taken by a vote to grant or deny asylum.

Question 3 (g): What procedures are in place to prevent the abuse of refugee status by terrorists? [Please provide details of legislation and/or administrative procedures which prevent claims of political motivation being recognized as grounds for refusing requests for the extradition of alleged terrorists. Please supply examples of any relevant cases.]

The response is similar to that given under 3 (f) above. The law mentioned there permits the extradition of a refugee in accordance with the provisions of articles 30 to 36 of the Penal Code, relating to extradition. In this case, the State that wishes to extradite a refugee must compile a judicial extradition dossier covering the legal aspects of the issue and submit it to the Lebanese judicial authorities, which are authorized to decide on the request.

The Permanent Mission of Lebanon to the United Nations takes this opportunity to convey to the Counter-Terrorism Committee the assurances of its highest consideration.

DOCUMENT NO. 11

LEBANON'S 2002 REPORT TO THE UN ON ITS COUNTER-TERRORISM EFFORTS

United Nations Security Council
S/2002/728

July 5, 2002

Distr.: General
5 July 2002

Original: English

Letter dated 2 July 2002 from the Chairman of the Security Council Committee established pursuant to resolution 1373 (2001) concerning counter-terrorism addressed to the President of the Security Council

I write with reference to my letter of 10 April 2002 (S/2002/406).

The Counter-Terrorism Committee has received the attached supplementary report from Lebanon (see annex) submitted pursuant to paragraph 6 of resolution 1373 (2001).

I would be grateful if you could arrange for this letter and its attachment to be circulated as a document of the Security Council.

(*Signed*) Jeremy **Greenstock**
Chairman
Security Council Committee established
pursuant to resolution 1373 (2002)
concerning counter-terrorism

Annex

[Original: Arabic]

Note verbale dated 21 June 2002 from the Permanent Mission of Lebanon to the United Nations addressed to the Chairman of the Security Council Committee established pursuant to resolution 1373 (2001) concerning counter-terrorism

The Permanent Mission of Lebanon to the United Nations in New York presents its compliments to the Counter-Terrorism Committee and, in reference to letter No. S/AC.40/2002/MS/OC.39 of the Chairman of the Committee, dated 1 April 2002, requesting clarification by the Government of Lebanon of certain points contained in Lebanon's report of 13 December 2002, submitted to the Committee pursuant to operative paragraph 6 of Security Council resolution 1373 (2001) of 28 September 2001, has the honour to submit a new report providing the requested clarifications and responses to the questions posed.

The Permanent Mission of Lebanon takes this opportunity to convey to the Counter-Terrorism Committee the assurances of its highest consideration.

Enclosure

The Lebanese Republic
Ministry of Foreign affairs and Emigrants

Subparagraph 1 (a) of Security Council Resolution 1373 (2001)

Question or request for clarification:

Could Lebanon please describe in more detail how Lebanese laws and regulations prevent the financing of terrorist activities?

Response:

The measures conducive to the prevention of the financing of terrorist activities adopted by the competent authorities under the Lebanese laws and regulations in force and the international conventions to which Lebanon is a party are as follows:

1. Cooperation and coordination with other States to detect operations for the financing of terrorist activities conducted through banks or financial institutions, through customs or across borders;

2. Development and strengthening of systems related to bank monitoring operations and security information activities with a view to discovering the objectives of terrorist groups and organizations and thwarting plans to finance them;

3. Creation of a database in the office of the International Criminal Police Organization (Interpol) and the Office to Combat Terrorism to collect information on terrorist elements, groups, movements and organizations; to exchange information with Interpol offices in other member States so as to prevent those elements, groups, movements and organizations from being financed or offered any facilities; and to provide the competent authorities in other States with such information upon request;

4. The arrest of persons committing crimes of complicity in the crime of terrorism through financing in accordance with the Lebanese Penal Code, which provides for the punishment of the crime of financing terrorism as constituting complicity in the crime of terrorism. Complicity in the perpetration of crimes, generally speaking, is governed by articles 219 to 221 of the said Code.

Pursuant to article 219, the following are considered accessories to a felony or misdemeanour:

- Anyone who, by any means, strengthens the intention of the perpetrator;
- Anyone who, for material or immaterial advantage, accepts an offer by the perpetrator to commit a crime;
- Anyone who assists or supports the perpetrator in acts that prepare or facilitate the crime;
- Anyone who agrees with the perpetrator of or any accessory to the crime prior to its commission or helps to conceal its character or to conceal or dispose of things derived from it;
- Anyone who is aware of the criminal conduct of wrongdoers who engage in brigandage or the perpetration of acts of violence against the State or public safety or against individuals or property and offers them food, shelter, a hiding place or a meeting place.

Under article 220, an accomplice without whose assistance the crime would not have been committed is subject to punishment as though he himself were the principal; all accomplices are sentenced to hard labour either for life or for a period ranging from 10 to 20 years if the principal receives the death sentence;

5. Cooperation at the international and regional levels in the fight against terrorism, including the adoption of all measures for the prevention and suppression of terrorist crimes and the prevention of the financing of terrorist elements and the offering of any facilities to them.

In addition, ways of preventing the financing of terrorist acts are included among the measures provided for in Law No. 318 of 20 April 2001 and decision No. 7818 of the Governor of the Bank of Lebanon of 18 May 2001, both of which relate to the suppression of money-laundering, including operations for the financing of terrorism.

Law No. 318 defines illicit funds as including, within the meaning of that Law, those connected with terrorist offences as provided in articles 314 to 316 of the Lebanese Penal Code, which also, in its articles 217 to 222, inclusive, provides penalties for the abetting of or participation or complicity in the commission of such offences. According to Lebanese precedent, whosoever finances a crime is considered an accessory thereto. We have dealt with this point in paragraph 4 above.

Law No. 318 makes it incumbent both on institutions not subject to the Banking Secrecy Law (article 4) and on banking institutions subject to that Law (article 5) to monitor the transactions carried out by them with their clients, with a view to the elimination of any involvement thereof in suspicious transactions, and to report immediately (article 7) to the special board of inquiry [officially: Special Investigation Commission ("the Commission")] created under the said Law (article 6), in detail, any transactions they suspect of concealing money-laundering operations, including operations for the financing of terrorism.

The Commission meets immediately upon receiving such information from the bodies mentioned above or from the official Lebanese or foreign authorities (article 8) and takes a temporary decision to freeze the suspicious account or accounts for a period of five days, renewable once. During that period the Commission carries out its inquiries through the persons designated by law, who conduct an investigation into the specified accounts and obtain all the necessary information concerning them or concerning their holders either from the reporting institutions or through the Financial Investigation Administrative Unit (article 10). Moreover, the Chairman of the Commission (article 9) or any Commission member delegated by him may contact any and all Lebanese or foreign judicial, administrative, financial or security authorities in order to request information or examine the details of any investigations already conducted by them on matters connected with or related to the investigations carried out by the Commission.

Upon the completion of the necessary inquiries and within the period of the temporary freeze on the suspected account, the Commission issues a final decision either to release the account, if the source of the funds has not been found illegal and, in the case in hand, if it has not been used for financing terrorist operations, or to remove the banking secrecy from the account and freeze it definitively, in the event that the Commission finds that the funds are being used to finance such operations.

The Commission transmits a copy of its final report to the reporting institution, the persons concerned and the Public Prosecutor at the Court of Cassation, who takes the requisite legal steps with respect to the operations and persons concerned.

Question or request for clarification:

Does Lebanon have any provisions for regulating alternative remittance arrangements? Please outline any such regulations.

Response:

The laws and regulations in force in Lebanon regulate money transfer operations, which may be effected only through banks and institutions having obtained prior authorization from the Bank of Lebanon, which has the discretionary power to grant or deny such authorization depending on whether it deems it in the public interest.

The statutory and regulatory provisions requiring institutions carrying out money transfer operations to obtain authorization from the Bank of Lebanon are as follows:

- Articles 128, 131, 179 and 181 of the Code of Money and Credit;
- Article 4 of Law No. 234 of 10 June 2000 (regulating the financial intermediary profession);
- Article 1 of Law No. 347 of 6 August 2001 (regulating the money-changing profession in Lebanon);
- Article 1 of Law No. 520 of 6 June 1996 (development of the financial market and fiduciary contracts);
- Article 3 of the Bank of Lebanon decision No. 7548 of 30 March 2000 (electronic banking and financial operations).

Question or request for clarification:

What acts constitute reasonable grounds for suspicion in Lebanese legislation and practice and how are they dealt with?

Response:

In accordance with Law No. 318 (articles 4 and 5) and decision No. 7818 of the Governor of the Bank of Lebanon, all the institutions concerned have been requested to apply a "know your client" policy and to make sure that the transactions effected by clients do not bear any signs of suspicious operations. Conditions constituting reasonable grounds for suspicion in the banking and finance sector include the following:

- The size and movements of the account are not commensurate with the client's financial position and business;
- Operations on the account are effected by third parties having no relationship to the account holder, or such relationship is not justified;
- The account is used basically to effect or receive transfers of large amounts, when the client's business does not warrant such transactions.

The manner of dealing with suspicious transactions that may be effected through the banking and finance sector has been touched upon in the response to the question of how Lebanese laws and regulations prevent the financing of terrorist activities.

Operations constituting reasonable grounds for suspicion in other sectors are governed by the general laws in force (the Penal Code, the Code of Criminal Procedure, the Judicial Police, etc.).

Subparagraph 1 (c)

Question or request for clarification:

Please provide a detailed outline of the Lebanese legal provisions which permit the freezing of funds as required by subparagraph 1 (c) (of Security Council resolution 1373 (2001)).

Response:

The Special Investigation Commission, which is an autonomous special body having a judicial character, created pursuant to article 6 of Law No. 318 of 20 April 2001, can take a temporary decision to freeze suspicious accounts for a period of five days, renewable once (article 8). Upon the completion of the investigation and within the period of the temporary freeze, the Commission issues a final decision either to release the account or to freeze it definitively, removing banking secrecy in respect of it. In addition, any movable or immovable property established pursuant to a final judgement as being related to any of the offences provided for in the said Law shall be forfeited to the State (article 14), unless its owners judicially prove their lawful entitlement thereto.

The Commission requests the office of the Public Prosecutor at the Court of Cassation to prosecute those responsible for the perpetration of such acts before the criminal courts in order that they may be tried and the penalties provided by law imposed.

In addition to Law No. 318, application may be made of the general Lebanese Penal Code, article 69 of which provides that, without prejudice to the rights of innocent third parties, all things derived from or used or prepared for the perpetration of an intentional misdemeanour or felony may be confiscated.

On the basis of that text, the judge may decide to confiscate assets prepared for the financing and perpetration of terrorist offences or crimes of complicity in the perpetration of such offences, as stipulated in articles 219 and 220 of the Penal Code, as well as all assets derived from or used for the perpetration thereof.

Moreover, article 98 of the Penal Code deals with the confiscation of things manufactured, acquired, sold or used illegally, even if not owned by the defendant or the person sentenced or if the prosecution does not result in a judgement, provided, however, that these provisions are applicable to illegal assets and weapons.

Given below are the texts of articles 8 and 14 of Law No. 318 and articles 69 and 98 of the Penal Code:

Article 8 of Law No. 318

"1. Upon receiving information from the concerned parties mentioned in Article 7, or from official Lebanese or foreign authorities, the Commission shall convene immediately to consider the case.

"2. After perusing the received information, the Commission shall, within a period of three working days, take a temporary decision to freeze the suspected account(s) for a one-time renewable period of five working days, when the source of funds remains unknown or suspected to proceed from a money-laundering offence. During the said period, the Commission shall continue the investigation of the suspected account(s) either directly or through a delegated member of the Commission or a designated concerned responsible, or through its Secretary or an appointed bank auditor. All designated persons shall discharge their duties under the obligation of confidentiality, but without being bound by the provisions of the Banking Secrecy Law of 3 September, 1956.

"3. After completing its investigations, the Commission shall take, during the temporary freezing period of the suspected account(s), a final decision on whether to free the said account(s) if the source of funds is not found to be illicit, or to lift banking secrecy regarding the account(s) and maintain the freezing. If, at the end of the period stipulated in Paragraph 2 above, the Commission does not render any decision, the said account(s) shall be automatically deemed free. The final decision of the Commission is not subject to any ordinary or extraordinary form of administrative or judicial recourse, including recourse against abuse of authority.

"4. In case of a decision on lifting banking secrecy, the Commission shall send a certified copy of its justified, final decision to the State Prosecutor of the Supreme Court, the Higher Banking Commission through its Chairman, the concerned party, the concerned bank, and the concerned foreign authority. This shall be effected either directly or through the official party through which the information has been received."

Article 14 of Law No. 318

"The State shall confiscate any movable or immovable assets that are proved, by a final court ruling, to be related to, or proceeding from, offences listed in Article 1 of this Law, unless the owners of the said assets prove in court their legal rights therein."

Article 69 of the Penal Code

"Without prejudice to the rights of innocent third parties, all things derived from or used or prepared for the perpetration of an intentional misdemeanour or felony may be confiscated.

"Such things may be confiscated in the case of an unintentional misdemeanour or a contravention if the law contains a clear provision in that regard.

"If what is to be confiscated has not already been seized, the person adjudged guilty shall be granted a respite for surrendering it, under penalty of payment of its value as assessed by the judge.

"The court may, if need be, have recourse to an expert to assess the amount payable and shall collect the assessed amount in the same manner in which it collects fines."

Article 98 of the Penal Code

"Things manufactured, acquired, sold or used illegally shall be confiscated, even if not owned by the defendant or the person sentenced or if the prosecution does not result in a judgement.

"If what is to be confiscated has not already been seized, the person adjudged guilty or the defendant shall be granted a respite for surrendering it, under penalty of payment of twice its value as determined by the judge.

"The court may, if need be, have recourse to an expert to assess the amount payable and shall collect the assessed amount in the same manner in which it collects fines."

Subparagraph 1 (d)

Question or request for clarification:

According to the report (submitted by Lebanon), *"a staff of auditors and investigators has been provided to the special board of inquiry [Special Investigation Commission] as well as a special administrative unit"*. Please elaborate on the work of the board and unit. In particular, it would be useful to know how these entities ensure that funds received by associations are not diverted from their stated purposes to terrorist activities.

Response:

The Special Investigation Commission carries out its investigations on the basis of information received from institutions required to report suspicious transactions, Lebanese or foreign authorities or the administrative unit for the collection of financial information.

The Commission charges its staff of auditors and investigators with investigating the operations concerned. They examine and analyse the suspicious accounts in order to ascertain the amounts paid into them and their sources and the amounts withdrawn from them and their destinations. Whenever necessary, they also request the administrative unit to gather financial information [and] furnish to them all information concerning the matter that can be obtained from the various local and international judicial, security or other sources. They submit to the Commission a report on the findings of the investigations conducted.

If the Commission feels that the sums paid into such accounts are transferred to persons or entities unrelated to the original stated activities of the account holders, and in particular to individuals or entities connected with terrorist activities and acts, it takes a decision to freeze the accounts definitively and deprive them of banking secrecy and informs the Public Prosecutor at the Court of Cassation of its decision. It should be borne in mind, however, that the field investigation to ascertain that associations have not transformed their activities or diverted them from their stated purposes to terrorist activities belongs to the competent judicial and security authorities.

At the field level, the competent security organs charged by the office of the Public Prosecutor at the Court of Cassation, on the basis of a request by national authorities, foreign judicial authorities or foreign judicial police, with carrying out investigations in a matter relating to funds received by associations suspected of covering the financing of terrorist acts and activities, proceed to comply with the request or letters rogatory under the supervision of the judges at the office of the Public Prosecutor. That office guides them in the detection of covert acts, thus enabling them to ascertain to what extent the suspicions in question are correct and whether or not such associations have deviated from their original stated purposes to terrorist acts and activities and to report the results of their investigations to the requesting authorities. In addition, local organs collect, through the Office to Combat Terrorism, information on religious, social and political associations that might be used as a cover for illegal acts, whereupon they place them under close scrutiny, instituting criminal prosecution in the event that they find them to have committed unlawful acts, including the financing of terrorism.

Question or request for clarification:

Please provide a copy of decision No. 7818 of the Governor of the Bank of Lebanon, referred to in the report.

Response:

The requested copy is annexed to the present report.*

Question or request for clarification:

Please outline how Lebanese legislation deals with the prohibition of financing of terrorism as distinct from money-laundering.

Response:

Lebanese legislation deals with the prohibition of financing of terrorism as distinct from money-laundering through the Penal Code, articles 217 to

* The annex is on file with the Secretariat and is available for consultation.

222 of which provide penalties for anyone who abets, participates in or is an accessory to the commission of crimes, including terrorist offences. The latter offences are defined by articles 314 to 316 of the Code, which sets the penalties to be imposed on their perpetrators. According to Lebanese precedent, anyone who participates in the financing of such offences is considered an accessory thereto and is given a penalty equal to that of the principal, provided that such financing proves to have been of assistance in the commission of the offence.

The investigations, inquiries and constant monitoring carried out by the competent security organs in coordination with the Interpol offices of other States in respect of elements and associations suspected of financing terrorism and terrorist activities are of help in ascertaining the nature of the case under consideration.

Subparagraph 2 (a)

Question or request for clarification:

Do those who buy or sell weapons require a licence to do so legally?

Response:

Pursuant to legislative decree No. 137 of 12 June 1959 (Arms and Ammunition Law), the purchase and sale of weapons in Lebanon requires a licence issued in advance by the competent authorities. In particular, article 3 of the decree provides as follows: "No person or entity shall have the right to perform, within Lebanese territory, commercial or manufacturing acts of any nature whatsoever related to materiel, arms or ammunition of any type without having first obtained a legal licence granted by decree on the basis of a proposal of the Ministers of the Interior and National Defence."

Question or request for clarification:

Are there legal provisions prohibiting the transport and procurement of weapons for terrorists and their organizations?

Response:

Some components of the response are provided by article 3 of the Arms and Ammunition Law referred to in the previous response. Other articles of the same Law also apply to the eventuality referred to in the question.

Article 24 of this Law prohibits any individual from transporting or possessing weapons and ammunition unless he has obtained a permit from the army command in accordance with specific conditions.

The penalties applicable to violators, provided for in articles 72 to 77 of the Law, are imprisonment for a term ranging from six months to three years, a pecuniary fine and the seizure of the weapons, ammunition and materiel.

In accordance with the principle of comprehensive, automatic, personal and regional jurisdiction provided for in articles 15, 19, 20 and 23 of the Lebanese Penal Code, the provisions of the aforementioned Law apply to all persons in Lebanese territory and to Lebanese nationals wherever they have committed the offence.

Article 17 of legislative decree No. 137 of 12 June 1959, mentioned above, makes the import, export and re-export of war materiel, weapons, ammunition and the related spare parts contingent on the prior obtainment of permission from the Ministry of National Economy upon the approval of the Ministry of National Defence (the army command) and of the Council of Ministers.

In addition, article 6 of the Law of 11 January 1958 on crimes against the internal security of the State or terrorism provides that anyone who proceeds, with the intention to commit or facilitate any felony mentioned in the Law or any other felony against the State, to manufacture, acquire or gain possession of explosive or inflammable materials, poisonous or incendiary products or the components used in their composition or manufacture shall be punished by hard labour for life.

Lastly, it should be mentioned that paragraph I.3 of article 3 of the Arab Convention for the Suppression of Terrorism, signed at Cairo on 22 April 1998, which the Government of Lebanon was authorized to enter into pursuant to Law No. 57 of 31 March 1999, provides as follows:

> "To develop and strengthen systems for the detection of the transport, importation, exportation, stockpiling and use of weapons, munitions and explosives and of other means of aggression, killing and destruction as well as procedures for monitoring their passage through customs and across borders in order to prevent their transfer from one Contracting State to another or to third-party States other than for confirmed lawful purposes".

Question or request for clarification:

Please specify whether there is any law that prohibits the recruitment of members of terrorist groups in Lebanon. Please outline the law.

Response:

There is no law specifically for that purpose. However, on the basis of the general Lebanese Penal Code, the fact that recruitment of members of terrorist groups is an act of incitement to the commission of a crime entails the application of the provisions of articles 335 to 339, which establish the act of forming an unlawful association as a crime, and article 316, which relates to crimes against the internal security of the State and terrorism, coupled with articles 217 and 218 of the Penal Code, which criminalize incitement to the commission of a crime and make the inciter subject to a penalty identical to the punishment for the crime which he induces or attempts to induce another person to commit.

Consequently, anyone who recruits members of terrorist groups in Lebanon for the purpose of committing the crimes enumerated above is subject to the same punishment as for the crime of terrorism.

Presented below, in succession, are the texts of article 316 of the Penal Code and article 314 referred to in the text of that article:

> Article 316
>
> "Any association established with intent to change the economic and social nature of the State or the fundamental conditions of society by any of the means referred to in article 314 shall be dissolved and its members condemned to a term of hard labour. The penalty for the founders and directors shall be not less than seven years."
>
> Article 314
>
> "'Terrorist acts' means all acts aimed at creating a state of terror which are committed by means such as explosive devices, inflammable materials, poisonous or incendiary products or infectious or microbial agents likely to create a public hazard."

Question or request for clarification:

Please outline the measures, both legislative and practical, preventing groups from recruiting, collecting funds or soliciting other forms of support for terrorist acts or terrorist activities to be carried out inside or outside Lebanon, in particular:

- The carrying out, within or from Lebanon, of recruiting, collecting of funds and soliciting of other forms of support from other countries; and
- Deceptive activities such as recruitment based on a representation to the recruit that the purpose of the recruitment is one (e.g., teaching) different from the true purpose and collection of funds through front organizations.

Response:

Part of the response has been provided in the response to the previous question of whether there is any law that prohibits the recruitment of members of terrorist groups in Lebanon.

Inasmuch as the formation of unlawful or secret associations constitutes an offence punishable under the Lebanese Penal Code, recruiting, collecting funds or soliciting other forms of support for terrorist acts or terrorist activities inside or outside Lebanon constitutes an offence, since such acts consist either in incitement to or complicity in the crime of forming an unlawful or secret association.

Let us refer to a number of relevant legal provisions contained in the Lebanese Penal Code or in the Arab Convention for the Suppression of Terrorism, signed at Cairo on 22 April 1998, to which Lebanon is a party:

- Article 335 of the Penal Code provides penalties for anyone who forms an association or makes a written or verbal agreement with the intent to commit felonies against persons or property or to detract from the authority or dignity of the State. Article 373 provides that an association shall be considered secret if its purpose is incompatible with the law and it carries out all or some of its acts in secret. Article 338 of the Code provides for the dissolution and the confiscation of the property of any and all secret associations. Article 3 of the Arab Convention for the Suppression of Terrorism provides that the "Contracting States . . . shall endeavour . . . to prevent the use of their territories as a base for planning, organizing, executing, attempting or taking part in terrorist crime in any manner whatsoever. This includes efforts to prevent terrorist elements from infiltrating into or taking up residence in their territories, either as individuals or in groups, and to prevent their being received, given refuge, trained, armed, financed or provided any facilitation";
- Regarding the collection of funds for use in terrorist activities, we have mentioned that the Special Investigation Commission conducts its investigations in the light of information obtained from certain bodies and takes the appropriate decisions based on the results of those investigations. The operating procedure of the Commission and the bodies subordinate to it is set forth in articles 8 to 10 of Law No. 318, referred to above.

As for practical measures, the various types of Lebanese security bodies, under the supervision of the competent judicial authority, and specifically the Office of the Public Prosecutor at the Court of Cassation, make all their capabilities available, in coordination with Interpol, for the exchange of information. These bodies, including the army and the internal security, public security and State security forces, each within its sphere of competence, monitor entities and individuals under suspicion, observe their movements and prevent them from carrying out any acts contrary to security or to the laws in force, establishing groups, recruiting members for secret associations, collecting funds or providing any support for terrorist activities to be carried out inside or outside Lebanon. The investigations and other procedures carried out by the security bodies on instructions from and under the supervision of the judicial authority comprise fact-finding and inquiries concerning individuals suspected of engaging in disguised or misleading activities such as recruiting under the guise of teaching or collecting funds by means of organizations that may be a front for terrorist acts. The competent authorities in the requesting States are informed of the results of such inquiries and the necessary steps are taken with regard to the suspects in the event that sufficient evidence is found to exist.

Any and all establishments subordinate to any group found to be involved in terrorist acts or activities are closed, even if civil or secular and irrespective of the name (such as "school") they may have adopted for the recruitment of members or the collection of funds through organizations serving as a front for terrorist activities.

Subparagraph 2 (c)

Question or request for clarification:

According to the report, *"In general, Lebanon does not provide a safe haven for those who finance, direct, support or commit acts of terrorism, especially those stipulated in Security Council resolution 1333 (2000), and it does not permit them to enter its territory". Please elaborate on what is meant by the term "in general"* in this context.

Response:

What is intended by the use of the term "in general" [in Arabic (and in the original French) literally: "in a general manner"] is "in a comprehensive manner".

Subparagraph 2 (d)

Question or request for clarification:

Please outline the relevant legal provisions which ensure the implementation of subparagraph 2 (d).

Response:

Part of the answer has been provided in the preceding response concerning the practical measures taken by the competent security bodies.

Provisions of Lebanese laws require investigation and the arrest of all suspects, fugitives and persons accused or convicted of an offence punishable under Lebanese law or the provisions of international conventions to which the Lebanese State is a party and which have acquired the force of law.

Those provisions are contained in the Code of Criminal Procedure, and specifically article 24 thereof, which charges the competent Office of the Public Prosecutor with the task of investigating offences classified as misdemeanours or felonies and prosecuting those indicted for committing them, having recourse to the security forces in the performance of its duties.

The fact-finding done by the judicial police upon being charged with the investigation of crimes provides it with an opportunity to learn if individuals are financing, plotting or facilitating terrorist acts, whereupon it becomes easy for it to prevent them from using Lebanese territory to realize those objectives.

If local measures based on the aforementioned legislation are coupled with the international bulletins and studies received via the Interpol offices, the judicial police in Lebanon has at its disposal the wherewithal to set up a defensive system to prevent terrorist groups from realizing their objectives and making Lebanon a springboard for terrorist acts. It is easy to keep suspect groups located in specific places under surveillance by means of the competent security organs and to learn about their movements if police informers are slipped in among them to discover criminal designs and report them to the police, which can in turn inform other States through the competent authorities so that precautions may be taken. Moreover, nipping such acts in the bud forestalls all anticipated or planned acts.

The feeling in Lebanese citizens of the importance of the idea of combating terrorism is an essential factor in preventing and controlling it. This requires the creation of greater awareness of the illegality of such acts and of how far removed they are from political motives that sometimes take on the character of noble motives.

Subparagraph 2 (e)

Question or request for clarification:

Are the relevant provisions of the Penal Code of Lebanon applicable in all of the following circumstances:

- Acts committed outside Lebanon by a person who is a citizen of, or habitually resident in, Lebanon (whether that person is currently present in Lebanon or not);
- Acts committed outside Lebanon by a foreign national who is currently in Lebanon?

Response:

1. Article 19 of the Lebanese Penal Code provides as follows:

> "Lebanese law is applicable to any Lebanese or foreign national who, whether as principal, abettor or accessory, proceeds, outside Lebanese territory or aboard a foreign vessel, to commit a felony against the security of the State, counterfeits the State seal, forges or counterfeits Lebanese or foreign banknotes or currency in circulation by law or by custom in Lebanon or falsifies Lebanese passports, entry visas, identity cards or extracts of records;
>
> "These provisions shall not apply, however, to a foreign national whose action is not in violation of the rules of international law."

2. Article 20 of the Code provides as follows:

> "Lebanese law is applicable to any Lebanese who, whether as principal, abettor or accessory, proceeds, outside Lebanese territory, to commit a misdemeanour punishable under Lebanese law.

> "This shall remain true even if the defendant loses or acquires Lebanese nationality subsequent to the commission of the felony or misdemeanour."

3. Article 23 of the Code provides as follows:

> "Lebanese law is applicable to any foreign national who is in Lebanese territory and who has proceeded, abroad, whether as principal, abettor or accessory, to commit a felony or misdemeanour not provided for in articles 19, 20 or 21, unless his extradition has been requested or agreed to."

Pursuant to the articles cited above, the Lebanese Penal Code applies to acts committed outside Lebanon by a Lebanese or a foreign national resident in Lebanon or currently in Lebanon within the conditions stipulated in those articles.

Subparagraph 2 (f)

Question or request for clarification:

Please outline the laws or international treaties which provide a legal basis for the implementation of this subparagraph in Lebanon.

Response:

The Lebanese State, as a member of Interpol, furnishes to requesting States, within the framework of that international organization and its regulations, information in its possession concerning persons suspected of providing support or financing for terrorist acts. The competent security organs proceed, under the supervision of the Public Prosecutor at the Court of Cassation, to conduct the necessary investigations for obtaining such information in accordance with the provisions of the Code of Criminal Procedure, referred to above.

Inasmuch as the Lebanese State promptly acceded to 10 international conventions and protocols relating to terrorism, it is bound to apply all their provisions which have acquired the force of law.

It is also bound by the Arab Convention for the Suppression of Terrorism, to which it became a party pursuant to Law No. 57/99 and which contains detailed provisions on cooperation between the Contracting States for the prevention and suppression of terrorist offences in the areas of information exchange, investigations, letters rogatory, judicial cooperation and the exchange of evidence.

The competent judicial and security organs, under the supervision of the Office of the Public Prosecutor at the Court of Cassation, engage in such cooperation in accordance with the provisions of the aforementioned international agreements and protocols and Lebanese national law.

Question or request for clarification:

How long does it take (on average) to implement a request for judicial assistance in criminal investigations or criminal proceedings relating to the financing or support of terrorist acts?

Response:

The security organs and judicial authorities provide the requested judicial assistance as quickly as possible. It is not possible, however, to specify the period in an all-inclusive manner because the time required for an investigation depends on the difficulty and complexity of the investigation.

As for legal actions, trials and other criminal proceedings, they differ from case to case depending on the number of accused persons and witnesses and the seriousness and complexity of the criminal acts.

The Lebanese State can exhort its judges, in cases involving terrorist acts and their financing, to expedite the related criminal investigations and court proceedings and to accord such cases priority in view of their seriousness and their bearing on the security of the international community.

It can be affirmed, however, that the security bodies, under the supervision of the judicial authorities, exert themselves to the utmost to comply with requests for judicial assistance and to complete criminal investigation procedures in connection with all offences, especially those affecting State security, including the crimes of financing and supporting terrorist acts.

Subparagraph 2 (g)

Question or request for clarification:

Please explain how the procedures for the issuance of identity papers and travel documents help prevent counterfeiting, forgery or fraudulent use of those documents.

Response:

The procedure for the issuance of a Lebanese passport requires the submission of certain proofs of identity (identity card, certificate of residence, declarations of witnesses) and the examination of judicial and administrative records. In this process extreme care is exercised, especially where doubt exists as to the authenticity of any document. Present passports exhibit advanced technical features that render falsification difficult; moreover, the General Directorate of Public Security is about to issue a new type of Lebanese passport incorporating advanced, internationally recognized technical characteristics that will reduce to the minimum the possibility of falsifying data entries.

With regard to the issuance of identity papers, the procedures followed in the General Directorate of Personal Status, which is subordinate to the Ministry of Interior and Municipalities and placed under the authority of the Minister, call for verification of the identity of the applicant by means of a form to be filled in, indicating the particulars of his identity, the manner in which he obtained Lebanese nationality (by birth or by virtue of a republican decree or a judgement of the competent court in Lebanon, etc.). All the information entered on the form, including a photograph and the signature of the applicant, prints of all the fingers of both hands and the signatures of two Lebanese witnesses, must be certified by the mayor of the locality, village or quarter. Next, the information entered on the form is verified, and once it has been ascertained that the identity elements match those of the applicant, the form is sent to the identity card facility of the Ministry of Interior and Municipalities. The facility, which is guarded by the Internal Security Forces, issues the dated, magnetized card, which comprises numerous security elements that make it difficult to falsify. It bears a unique number assigned to the cardholder and is delivered to him through the mayor of the quarter or village.

Question or request for clarification:

Could Lebanon please provide CTC with information on the mechanism for inter-agency cooperation between the authorities responsible for narcotics control, financial tracking and security, with particular regard to the border controls preventing the movement of terrorists?

Response:

Cooperation among the various Lebanese agencies in the field of counter-terrorism takes place in some cases through coordination activities required by law and in others through the centralized work of the Office of the Public Prosecutor at the Court of Cassation, which oversees all public prosecutors' offices and the security forces that operate under its authority as a judicial police.

The General Directorate of Public Security performs the tasks of monitoring the entry of foreign nationals and verifying the authenticity of the documents carried by them. Moreover, it is provided with all the files on wanted persons and persons for whom judicial investigation or search warrants or warrants of arrest have been issued. It can check such documents for authenticity and seeks to enforce warrants, thus making it difficult for delinquents to travel and enter Lebanese territory to carry out terrorist acts.

The General Directorate of Public Security makes use of all information available from security attachés at the embassies concerned and takes measures to be on the alert for the entry of individuals to whose activity attention has been drawn by those attachés. In addition, the General

Directorate cross-checks all information obtained concerning them and concerning possible Al-Qa'ida activity in Lebanon and reports the results to the embassies concerned.

The General Directorate of Public Security also stresses coordination with Interpol and the utilization of all information obtained from it, particularly with regard to visas and lost and falsified passports and travel documents, and circulates such information to all land, air and sea exit/entry posts, where such documents are checked and their bearers arrested and handed over to the judicial authorities.

Through the Office to Combat Terrorism, the Drug Control Office and the Office for the Control of Financial Crime, the Directorate of Internal Security Forces observes the actions of suspects and persons with prior records and establishes links between their movements into and out of Lebanese territory and their activities inside that territory. It monitors their accounts, once that has been made possible under the money-laundering law, and is furnished with information on the movements of their accounts and on whether any flows take place to terrorist groups under any external guise whatsoever.

The Intelligence Directorate of the Lebanese Army is very active in the surveillance of persons suspected of having committed crimes affecting the internal or external security of the State. It plays a prominent and active role in the arrest of members of terrorist groups in Lebanon.

The Customs Administration also plays a part in respect of the movement of suspicious goods and their entry into and exit from Lebanese territory to support or finance terrorist acts.

The money-laundering law opened the way for the Special Investigation Commission to freeze accounts connected with terrorist acts, drug-related crimes and arms trafficking after they are stripped of banking secrecy. The Office of the Public Prosecutor at the Court of Cassation is then notified, in order that it may conduct the necessary investigations to bring the delinquents to trial and obtain a judgement for the confiscation of assets relating to terrorist acts and the crimes specified in the money-laundering law.

Subparagraph 3 (a)

Question or request for clarification:

Please outline the legal provisions which implement this subparagraph.

Response:

The law of 10 July 1962 pertaining to entry into, residence in and exit from Lebanon prohibits entry into or exit from Lebanon otherwise than via points controlled by Public Security. Pursuant to that law, the General Directorate of Public Security issues, on instructions from the judicial authority, search and investigation warrants for wanted persons and persons suspected of terrorist or other offences and circulates them via computer and electronic mail to all offices, border crossing points, seaports and airports so that the necessary steps may be taken in respect of such persons immediately upon their arrival (denial of entry, arrest, etc.).

It should be noted that all border crossing points are equipped with computers containing the names of all persons wanted for arrest and for interrogation by the competent judicial and security authorities.

In addition, with respect to such matters the General Directorate of Public Security immediately coordinates with all the embassies in Lebanon, through their security attachés, the exchange of information on terrorists and terrorist networks with a view to detecting forged or falsified travel documents and corroborating information on trafficking in arms, explosives or sensitive substances, the use of communication technology by terrorist groups and the threat posed by terrorist groups possessing weapons of mass destruction.

All Public Security offices and posts and the Internal Security Forces are charged with monitoring the activities and movements of foreign nationals upon any violation by them of the laws in force throughout Lebanese territory and interrogating them in accordance with the laws in force, in particular the law of 10 July 1962 pertaining to entry into, residence in and exit from Lebanon, the Lebanese Penal Code and decision No. 115 of 12 August 1932 on combating crimes that violate public security in Lebanon, combating terrorism and the use by terrorist groups of weapons of mass destruction. In case of confirmed crime, the General Directorate of Public Security proceeds, under the supervision of the Public Prosecutors' offices, to issue search and investigation warrants and notices of denial of entry, to adopt other restrictive measures and to circulate them to all border posts and to the Interpol office, which in turn makes use of them and exchanges them with other States concerned.

Subparagraph 3 (c)

Question or request for clarification:

Please provide a list of bilateral agreements for the purpose of preventing and suppressing terrorist attacks and for taking action against perpetrators of such acts (such as extradition treaties or agreements on mutual legal assistance) to which Lebanon is a party.

Response:

Lebanon is a party to the bilateral agreements indicated below:

- Agreement on the extradition of criminals between Lebanon and Iraq, signed at Beirut on 6 May 1929 and at Baghdad on 23 May 1929;

- Agreement on the extradition of criminals between Lebanon and Yemen, permission for the ratification of which was granted by the Law of 15 February 1949;
- Judicial agreement concluded between Lebanon and Syria, signed at Damascus on 25 February 1951 (Law of 28 October 1951);
- Judicial agreement concluded between Lebanon and Jordan (law promulgated in April 1954);
- Agreement on the exchange of criminals between Lebanon and Kuwait (Decree No. 15743 of 13 March 1964);
- Agreement on the execution of judgements, concluded between Lebanon and Kuwait (Decree No. 15744 of 13 March 1964);
- Treaty on the extradition of criminals between Lebanon and Belgium (Law No. 33/64 of 17 November 1964);
- Agreement on judicial notices and letters rogatory, concluded with Kuwait (Decree No. 9795 of 4 May 1968);
- Agreement on judicial cooperation, reciprocal enforcement of judgements and extradition of criminals, concluded between Lebanon and Tunisia (Law No. 38/68 of 30 December 1968);
- Judicial agreement between Lebanon and Italy (Decree No. 3257 of 17 May 1972);
- Agreement supplementary to the judicial agreement concluded between Syria and Lebanon on 25 February 1951 (Law No. 630 of 23 April 1997);
- Judicial agreement between Lebanon and Egypt, permission for the conclusion of which was granted to the Government by Law No. 693 of 5 November 1998;
- Ten international conventions on terrorism to which Lebanon is a party and the Arab Convention for the Suppression of Terrorism, signed at Cairo on 22 April 1998, which will constitute a basis for the conclusion of any future bilateral agreements.

Subparagraph 3 (d)

Question or request for clarification:

Please provide a periodic report (progress report) on the signing by Lebanon of those relevant international conventions and protocols relating to terrorism to which Lebanon has not yet acceded.

Response:

We reaffirm what is stated in Lebanon's report to the Counter-Terrorism Committee dated 13 December 2001, i.e., that Lebanon has acceded to 10 of the 12 conventions for the suppression of terrorism and is in the process of acceding to the two conventions that it did not sign at the time, namely the International Convention for the Suppression of Terrorist Bombings of 5 December 1997 and the International Convention for the Suppression of the Financing of Terrorism of 9 December 1999. Letters have been sent to the competent administrations to initiate the appropriate legal procedures.

Subparagraph 3 (e)

Question or request for clarification:

Have the crimes set forth in the relevant international conventions and protocols relating to terrorism to which Lebanon is a party been included as extraditable offences in the bilateral treaties which Lebanon has concluded, as provided for in those international conventions and protocols?

Response:

At the time of drafting of this report, the official administrations took note of the need to include the crimes specified in the relevant international conventions and protocols relating to terrorism to which Lebanon is a party as extraditable offences in any bilateral agreements that may be concluded in the future. We shall inform you subsequently of any new developments in that regard.

Subparagraph 4

Question or request for clarification:

Has Lebanon addressed any of the concerns expressed in paragraph 4 of the resolution?

Response:

Under Law No. 318 of 20 April 2001 (money-laundering law) Lebanon established a link between the crimes referred to in the said paragraph 4 for the purposes of determining the sources of illegal funds. Combating those crimes involves close cooperation among the bodies of the Internal Security Forces competent in that regard (Drug Control Office, Office for the Control of Financial Crime, Office to Combat Terrorism and Crimes Affecting State Security, etc.), and coordination takes place through the related bilateral, regional and international agreements concluded by Lebanon and the exchange of information and consultations between the Lebanese security organs, Interpol and the military attachés accredited in Lebanon.

Other Matters

Question:

Could Lebanon please provide an organizational chart of its administrative machinery, such as police, immigration control, customs, taxation and financial supervision authorities, established to give practical effect to the laws, regulations and other instruments that are seen as contributing to compliance with the resolution?

Response:

Consultations take place on an ongoing basis among the organs referred to in the question, as well as periodically and as needed in the Council of Ministers or among the ministries and administrations concerned. Some aspects of this question have been dealt with in our response to the second question pertaining to subparagraph 2 (g).

DOCUMENT NO. 12

LEBANON'S 2003 REPORT TO THE UN ON ITS COUNTER-TERRORISM EFFORTS

United Nations Security Council
S/2003/451

April 25, 2003

Distr.: General
25 April 2003

Original: English

Letter dated 21 April 2003 from the Chairman of the Security Council Committee established pursuant to resolution 1373 (2001) concerning counter-terrorism addressed to the President of the Security Council

I write with reference to my letter of 13 November 2002 (S/2002/1251).

The Counter-Terrorism Committee has received the attached third report from Lebanon submitted pursuant to paragraph 6 of resolution 1373 (2001) (see annex).

I would be grateful if you could arrange for this letter and its annex to be circulated as a document of the Security Council.

(*Signed*) Inocencio F. **Arias**
Chairman
Security Council Committeeestablished pursuant to
resolution 1373 (2001) concerning counter-terrorism

Annex

[Original: Arabic]

Note verbale dated 31 March 2003 from the Permanent Mission of Lebanon to the United Nations addressed to the Chairman of the Security Council Committee established pursuant to resolution 1373 (2001) concerning counter-terrorism

The Permanent Mission of Lebanon to the United Nations in New York presents its compliments to the Counter-Terrorism Committee established pursuant to resolution 1373 (2001) and, in reference to letter No. S/AC.40/2002/MS/OC.175 of the Chairman of the Committee, dated 30 October 2002, has the honour to submit herewith a second supplementary report containing the responses of the Lebanese Government to the questions put by the Committee with regard to the supplementary report transmitted by the note verbale dated 21 June 2002 from the Permanent Mission of Lebanon (see S/2002/728).

The Permanent Mission of Lebanon takes this opportunity to convey to the Counter-Terrorism Committee the assurances of its highest consideration.

Enclosure[1]

The Lebanese Republic

Ministry of Foreign Affairs and Emigrants

Question:

No. 1.2. Effective implementation of paragraph 1 (b) of the resolution requires, in accordance with articles 2 and 4 of the Convention for the Suppression of the Financing of Terrorism that there are provisions in place specifically criminalizing the wilful provision or collection, by any means, directly or indirectly, of funds by the nationals of Lebanon or in its territory with the intention that the funds should be used, or in the knowledge that they are to be used, in order to carry out terrorist acts. The acts sought to be criminalized are thus capable of being committed without any specific act of terrorism actually occurring or being attempted, either within or outside Lebanon. As Lebanon intends to ratify the Convention for the Suppression of the Financing of Terrorism, is it the intention of Lebanon to include such provisions in its criminal law?

Reference: Paragraph 1 (b) of Security Council resolution 1373 (2001).

[1] The annexes are on file with the Secretariat and are available for consultation.

Response:

The articles of the Penal Code relating to terrorism provide for the prosecution of any person who is an accomplice in or an accessory to the crime of terrorism or who incites others to or perpetrates the crime of terrorism.

Moreover, in the context of the amendment to the Law on the Combating of Money-laundering, the Administration and Justice Committee decided at its session held approximately two months ago to introduce a provision that considers the deliberate or intentional funding of terrorist acts or such funding by any means an offence punishable by hard labour.

Lastly, this draft amendment to the Law on the Combating of Money-laundering will be put before the Chamber of Deputies at the next plenary session.

It should be mentioned that the Arab Convention on the Suppression of Terrorism, signed at Cairo on 22 April 1998, to which Lebanon became a party pursuant to Law No. 57 of 31 March 1999, criminalizes such acts.

Question:

No. 1.3. If not currently provided in the money-laundering laws or regulations of Lebanon, please provide information on how Lebanon intends to require financial institutions to record originator information on all financial transactions.

Reference: Paragraph 1 of resolution 1373 (2001).

Response:

The banking laws and regulations in effect in Lebanon make it incumbent upon banks and financial institutions operating in Lebanon to record on their books all banking and financial transactions. Law No. 318 of 20 April 2001 on the Combating of Money-laundering also makes it incumbent upon the institutions subject to its provisions to take measures to make available knowledge of the source of the transactions that they conduct with their clients.

Article 4 of Law No. 318 on the Combating of Money-laundering makes it incumbent upon institutions not subject to banking secrecy, including individual institutions, in particular money-changing offices, financial brokerage companies, leasing companies, mutual funds, insurance companies, companies promoting, building and selling real estate and merchants dealing in valuables (jewellery, precious stones, gold, works of art, antiques) to keep records of transactions with a value in excess of US$ 10,000. They must also, through official documents, verify the identity and address of each client and keep photocopies of these and transaction-related documents for a period of no less than five years.

Article 5 of the above-mentioned law makes it incumbent upon banks, financial institutions and all other institutions subject to the Banking Secrecy Law to monitor their transactions with clients in order to avoid any possible involvement of such institutions in the laundering of funds deriving from the offences specified by this Law, including the terrorist offences, set out in articles 314, 315 and 316 of the Penal Code. The principles of this monitoring are set out in the Regulations on the Monitoring of Financial and Banking Transactions to Combat Money-laundering issued by the Bank of Lebanon in Circular No. 83 of 18 May 2001 and the amendments thereto.

Question:

No. 1.4. Effective implementation of paragraph 1 of the resolution requires that the legal obligation to report suspicious transactions for banks and financial institutions should extend to all professions engaged in financial transactions (such as lawyers, accountants) and that they should all be subjected to penalties for non-compliance in order to enable the effective prevention of the financing of terrorism. Could Lebanon please comment on the action that it intends to take in this regard?

Reference: Paragraph 1 of resolution 1373 (2001).

Response:

In accordance with article 11 of the Regulations on the Monitoring of Financial and Banking Transactions to Combat Money-laundering issued by the Bank of Lebanon in Circular No. 83 of 18 May 2001, the auditor assigned to monitor the bank or financial institution is required to review internal auditing procedures in order to ascertain compliance by the bank or financial institution with the provisions of the Regulations, and to report immediately to the Governor of the Bank of Lebanon, in his capacity as Chairman of the Special Investigation Commission, any violation of these provisions, especially any transactions suspected of involving the laundering of funds deriving from any of the offences specified in Law No. 318 of 20 April 2001 on the Combating of Money-laundering, if it emerges that the bank or financial institution has omitted to make such a report.

Articles 8 and 18 of Decree No. 1983 of 25 September 1971 relating to the regulation of the profession of bank auditor require that such auditors exercise their powers in accordance with the provisions of the Code of Commerce and the Code of Money and Credit and such written instructions as may be issued by the Bank of Lebanon or the Banking Control Commission in circulars sent directly to the auditors. The same articles also stipulate that any auditor who fails to fulfil his professional obligations in the discharge of his functions shall be subject to administrative penalties, namely, warning, reprimand or being barred for a specific time from serving as a bank auditor.

The obligation incumbent upon bank auditors to report suspicious transactions and the penalties imposed should they fail in their professional duties applies also to auditors assigned to all other institutions subject to the control of the Bank of Lebanon. The same obligations are imposed upon the auditors assigned to monitor other financial institutions by articles 185 and subsequent articles of the Code of Money and Credit, article 21 of Law No. 160 of 27 December 1999 (regulation of commercial and financial transactions), article 11 of Law No. 234 of 10 June 2000 (regulation of financial brokerage) and article 20 of Circular No. 49 of 5 September 1999 issued by the Bank of Lebanon (mutual funds).

Question:

No. 1.5. Effective implementation of this paragraph also requires the existence of legal provisions or administrative measures that ensure that funds and other economic resources collected by non-profit organizations (e.g., religious, charitable or cultural organizations) are not diverted for other than the stated purposes, particularly for the financing of terrorism. Please explain whether such provisions or measures are in place in Lebanon and, if not, how Lebanon proposes to monitor the use of funds and so on by non-profit organizations.

Reference: Paragraph 1 and, in particular, 1 (d) of resolution 1373 (2001).

Response:

Some elements of the response were mentioned in the first report with regard to the question concerning the manner in which Lebanese laws and regulations prevent the financing of terrorist activities as well as the question on how Lebanese legislation prevents the financing of terrorism as distinct from or independent of money-laundering.

In addition, there are legal and regulatory provisions that aim to monitor the use of funds or other economic resources collected by non-profit organizations (e.g., religious, charitable and cultural organizations) in order to ascertain that they are not being diverted for purposes other than the stated purposes, particularly for the financing of terrorism.

Article 7 of the Law on Associations stipulates that it is incumbent upon associations to keep a record of their income, sources of income and details of the type and amount of expenditures, to be submitted at any time to the Government on request.

Law No. 318 of 20 April 2001 also makes it incumbent upon institutions not subject to the Banking Secrecy Law (article 4) and banking institutions subject to that Law (article 5) to monitor the transactions they conduct with their clients, with a view to avoiding the institution's involvement in suspicious transactions, and to report immediately (article 7) to the Special Investigation Commission established under the Law (article 6) any transactions they suspect of concealing money-laundering, including those for the financing of terrorism. Article 3 of the Regulations on the Monitoring of Financial and Banking Transactions to Combat Money-laundering states that "client" means any natural or legal person, whether a company, institution of any kind or a non-profit organization or association (such as a trust fund, cooperative, social care establishment, charitable association or club).

The Ministry of Interior and Municipalities, which is concerned with the affairs of political parties and associations in Lebanon, exercises financial control over the activities of parties and associations legally licensed under the provisions of article 7 of the law promulgated by Decree No. 10830 of 9 October 1962, which makes it incumbent upon each licensed association to submit in the first month of every year a list containing the names of its members, a copy of its annual budget and its previous end-of-year account and imposes a financial penalty for each violation or delay in submission of the said documents. This Ministry also exercises administrative control based on the provisions of article 6 of the Law on Associations, which absolutely prohibits the formation of secret associations, makes it incumbent upon each association to inform the department immediately of any change in its statutes, bye-laws, board of administration or headquarters and imposes penalties and fines in cases of non-compliance. In addition to the above, article 335 of the Lebanese Penal Code penalizes anyone who forms an association or enters into a written or verbal agreement with the intent to commit a serious offence against persons or property or to impugn the authority or dignity of the State or challenge its civil, military, financial or economic institutions. Article 373 of the Code provides that an association shall be considered secret if its purpose is incompatible with the law and it carries out all or some of its acts in secret.

Article 316 of the Penal Code penalizes any association established with intent to change the economic or social nature of the State or the fundamental conditions of society and stipulates that such an association shall be dissolved and its members condemned to a term of hard labour. The penalty for founders and directors shall be not less than seven years.

Moreover, the Lebanese security agencies, including the army and the internal security, general security and State security forces, each within its sphere of competence, monitor entities and individuals under suspicion, observe their movements and prevent them from carrying out any acts that disrupt security or contravene the laws in force, establishing groups, recruiting members for secret organizations, collecting funds or providing any support to terrorist acts carried out inside or outside Lebanon. The investigations and procedures carried out by the security forces are conducted on instructions from, and under the supervision of the judicial authority and are based on the provisions of the Code of Military Justice and the Code of Criminal Procedure; specific contraventions lead to revocation of the licence and dissolution of the association.

Non-profit associations are subject to monitoring by the supervisory authorities and, under the laws in force, may have their licences revoked if they use their funds for purposes other than the stated aims of the association, not to mention facing criminal prosecution.

Lastly, the Lebanese Government has recently approved two draft laws and transmitted them to the Chamber of Deputies for adoption and promulgation.

The first amends Law No. 318 of 20 April 2001 by adding to article 1 a provision whereby "funds relating or contributing to the funding of terrorism, terrorist acts or terrorist organizations" are to be deemed illegal.

The second adds to article 315 of the Penal Code a provision imposing the penalty of "a term of hard labour for a period of not less than three years and not exceeding seven years and a fine not less than the equivalent of the amount paid and not greater than three times that amount on every individual who, with intent, directly or indirectly finances or contributes to the financing of terrorism, terrorist acts or terrorist organizations".

Question:

No. 1.6. Please outline the existing or proposed legal provisions that criminalize the use of Lebanese territory for the purpose of financing, planning, facilitating or committing terrorist acts against other States or their citizens. Effective implementation of paragraph 2 (d) and (e) of the resolution requires that such provisions should be incorporated in the penal law of Lebanon.

Reference: Paragraphs 2 (d) and (e) of resolution 1373 (2001).

Response:

We enclose the legal provisions in the Penal Code that relate to crimes of terrorism and to the Arab Convention on the Suppression of Terrorism, signed at Cairo on 22 April 1998, which was approved by Law No. 57 of 31 March 1999 and has become part of Lebanese legislation.

Question:

No. 1.7. According to the supplementary report, Lebanese law is not applicable to a foreign national who, outside Lebanese territory or while aboard a foreign vessel, commits a felony against the security of the State of Lebanon, counterfeits the State seal, forges or counterfeits Lebanese or foreign banknotes or currency in circulation by law or by custom in Lebanon or falsifies passports, entry visas, identity cards or extracts of records, if that foreign national does not act in violation of the rules of international law. Please explain to which rules of international law article 19 of the Lebanese Penal Code refers.

Reference: Paragraph 2 (e) of resolution 1373 (2001).

Response:

Article 19 of the Penal Code states that Lebanese law does not apply to a foreign national who, outside Lebanese territory or while aboard a foreign vessel, commits a felony against the security of the State of Lebanon, counterfeits the State seal, forges or counterfeits Lebanese banknotes or currency in Lebanon or falsifies passports, entry visas, identity cards or extracts of records, if that foreign national does not act in violation of the rules of international law.

The words "rules of international law" in the last phrase of this article refer to the international treaties or agreements by which Lebanon is bound. The felonies referred to in the article in question do not constitute a violation of these treaties or agreements, given that article 2 of the Code of Civil Procedure lays down the principle of the hierarchy of rules, including the precedence of international treaties over internal law.

Question:

No. 1.8. Please provide the CTC with a copy of article 21 of the Lebanese Penal Code.

Reference: Paragraph 2 (e) of resolution 1373 (2001).

Response:

You will find attached the text of the article in question.

Question:

No. 1.9. Effective implementation of paragraph 2 (e) of the resolution requires that States ensure that persons who participate in the financing, planning, preparation or preparation of terrorist acts or support such acts are brought to justice either by submitting the case without undue delay to their respective competent authorities for the purpose of prosecution or by extraditing these persons. This applies without any exception whatsoever and whether or not the offence was committed in their respective territories. Please explain how, in order to comply with paragraph 2 (e), Lebanon would deal with a foreign national who is in Lebanon and has committed a terrorist act outside Lebanon against a State other than Lebanon or against that State's citizens. Is it possible under current or proposed law to prosecute that person in Lebanon if he or she is not extradited?

Reference: Paragraph 2 (e) of resolution 1373 (2001).

Response:

There is no legal provision that currently authorizes the prosecution of a foreign citizen who is in Lebanon and has committed a terrorist act outside

Lebanon, since this is outside the framework of extradition or bilateral agreements.

Question:

No. 1.10. What measures are in place to prohibit the black market sale of documentation, in particular identity papers and travel documents? How are such measures, if any, being enforced?

Reference: Paragraph 2 (e) and (g) of resolution 1373 (2001).

Response:

Lebanese law considers that official documentation—in particular identity papers and accompanying documents—is personal and must not be subject to commercial exchange or improperly used or forged.

However, despite the provisions it contains concerning the above, Lebanese law does not make provision for any measures specifically prohibiting commerce in such documents on the black market, given that the Lebanese Penal Code punishes anyone who forges official documents and facilitates the use of forged documents.

The Directorate-General for Public Security of the Lebanese Ministry of the Interior has adopted precise and stringent measures to verify the forgery or sale of any documentation, in particular identity papers and travel documents, and has taken radical measures in this connection with a view to arresting violators, seizing forged documents, handing them over to the competent judicial authorities and pursuing investigations in order to discover the manner in which the forgery operations were carried out and the techniques used in this connection.

The Directorate-General for Public Security of the Ministry of the Interior and of Municipal and Rural Affairs has, since the beginning of 2003, adopted a new Lebanese passport incorporating advanced techniques and meeting high specifications in order to prevent counterfeiting or the possibility of a Lebanese passport being used by any person other than its rightful holder.

Question:

No. 1.11. According to the supplementary report, Lebanon is bound to apply all the provisions of the relevant international conventions and protocols against terrorism to which it is a party. Please outline the legal provisions that provide for the imposition of penalties for the commission of the offences referred to in these international instruments.

Reference: Paragraph 2, in particular 2 (g) of resolution 1373 (2001).

Response:

Lebanon is committed to implementing all the provisions and articles of the international conventions and protocols against terrorism to which it is a party.

In response to the question, the following information is provided:

The Lebanese Penal Code imposes penalties for the illegal seizure of aircraft and on any person who carries out destructive acts in public places, including airport runways. The penalty is increased for individuals committing crimes against persons acting in an official capacity and enjoying international protection, such as diplomats, and penalties are imposed on anyone who takes hostages as a means of achieving his ends. Lebanon is currently considering amending the Penal Code of 1943 and will take into account all matters relating to the combating of terrorism.

Question:

No. 1.12. When does Lebanon intend to include the offences set forth in the relevant international conventions and protocols relating to terrorism as extraditable offences in the bilateral treaties to which Lebanon is a party?

Reference: Paragraph 3, in particular paragraph 3 (f) of resolution 1373 (2001).

Response:

1. When Lebanon becomes a party to international conventions and the protocols thereto pursuant to the authorization issued by the Chamber of Deputies, these provisions become an integral part of Lebanese legislation, without there being any need to amend it. Where its international commitments are incompatible with its internal legislation, the former take precedence over the latter.

2. The Ministry of Justice takes cognizance of requests for judicial assistance addressed to it by foreign States in extradition cases and studies and implements them according to the relevant rules.

It should be noted that Lebanon committed itself to cooperation with the European Union in combating terrorism when it signed the Association Agreement with the European Union in Luxembourg on 17 June 2002.

Question:

No. 1.13. Paragraph 3 (d) of the resolution requires all States to become parties as soon as possible to all the relevant international conventions and protocols relating to terrorism. The CTC would appreciate receiving information on the progress made regarding the ratification by Lebanon of the International Convention for the Suppression of Terrorist Bombings and the International Convention for the Suppression of the Financing of Terrorism.

Reference: Paragraph 3 (d) of resolution 1373 (2001).

Response:

In view of the importance of the two conventions in question and their various implications, more than one department must be consulted before the necessary decision is taken. The Lebanese Government is diligently following up this matter.

Question:

No. 1.14. Paragraph 3 (g) of the resolution requests States to ensure *"that claims of political motivation are not recognised as grounds for refusing requests for the extradition of alleged terrorists"*. Please clarify how Lebanese legislation meets this requirement.

Reference: Paragraph 3 (g) of resolution 1373 (2001).

Response:

The position of the Lebanese legislator, who has devoted a section to terrorism in the Penal Code, is clearly in favour of more stringent penalties, ranging from hard labour to the death penalty, for the perpetrators of acts of terrorism. Lebanon, which is aware of the requirements laid down in resolution 1373 (2001), is currently amending the Penal Code, taking into account all matters relating to the combating of terrorism, as well as matters contributing to the effective implementation of resolution 1373 (2001).

Note:

It is evident that, in order to ensure that claims of political motivation are not recognized as grounds for refusing requests for the extradition of alleged terrorists in accordance with the provisions of paragraph 3 (g) of resolution 1373 (2001), a uniform international definition of terrorism is necessary. In this context Lebanon has defined its basic position in the introduction to its first report which was transmitted to you on 13 December 2001.

DOCUMENT NO. 13

LEBANON'S 2004 REPORT TO THE UN ON ITS COUNTER-TERRORISM EFFORTS

United Nations Security Council
S/2004/877

November 1, 2004

Distr.: General
1 November 2004

Original: English

Letter dated 26 October 2004 from the Chairman of the Security Council Committee established pursuant to resolution 1373 (2001) concerning counter-terrorism addressed to the President of the Security Council

I write with reference to my predecessor's letter of 21 November 2003 (S/2003/1128). The Counter-Terrorism Committee has received the attached fourth report from Lebanon submitted pursuant to paragraph 6 of resolution 1373 (2001) (see annex). I would be grateful if you could arrange for the present letter and its annex to be circulated as a document of the Security Council.

(*Signed*) Andrey I. **Denisov** Chairman
Security Council Committee established pursuant to
resolution 1373 (2001) concerning counter-terrorism

Annex

Note verbale dated 14 October 2004 from the Permanent Mission of Lebanon to the United Nations addressed to the Chairman of the Counter-Terrorism Committee

[Original: Arabic]

The Permanent Mission of Lebanon to the United Nations presents its compliments to the Counter-Terrorism Committee and, with reference to letter No. S/AC.40/2003/MS/OC.349 of the Committee, dated 12 November 2003, has the honour to submit herewith, pursuant to paragraph 6 of resolution 1373 (2001), the fourth report of Lebanon on counter-terrorism.

The Permanent Mission of Lebanon to the United Nations takes this opportunity to renew to the Counter-Terrorism Committee the assurances of its highest consideration.

Enclosure*

[Original: Arabic]

The Lebanese Republic

Ministry of Foreign Affairs and Emigrants

Effectiveness in the Protection of the Financial System

Question No. 1.1:

Effective implementation of subparagraph 1 (a) of the resolution requires States to have in place efficient executive machinery for preventing and suppressing the financing of terrorist acts. In this context, the CTC would appreciate learning whether the Special Investigation Commission has sufficient resources (human, financial and technical) to carry out its mandate. Please provide appropriate data in support of your response. The CTC would be pleased to receive a description of the structure, staffing and powers of the Commission.

Response:

For 2003, the budget of the Special Investigation Commission of the Banque du Liban amounted to 2,889,700,000 Lebanese pounds, equivalent to approximately US$ 1.9 million. For 2004, that same budget amounted to 3,252,800,000 Lebanese pounds, equivalent to approximately US$ 2.1 million.

---

* Annexes are on file with the Secretariat and are available for consultation.

The Commission has a staff of 35 employees, mainly specialists with first-class university degrees who have the expertise required to audit bank accounts and monitor the procedures applied by banks, financial institutions, bureaux de change and gold businesses, inter alia, in order to combat money-laundering operations and the financing of terrorism.

The Commission also has at its disposal modern technologies for communicating directly with all concerned domestic bodies and departments (customs, police, the judiciary . . .) and all foreign financial intelligence units with a view to exchanging information on suspicious transactions.

As for its structure and powers, under article 6 of the Combating of Money-laundering Act No. 318/2000, an independent commission known as the Special Investigation Commission has been established at the Banque du Liban. It has a judicial character and a juridical personality and pursues its activities without being subject to the authority of the latter. Its function is to investigate money-laundering operations and monitor compliance with the rules and procedures provided for in the above Act.

The Special Investigation Commission is composed of:

- The Governor of the Banque du Liban as member and, if he is unable to attend, such member of the Commission as he may delegate;
- The chairman of the Banking Control Commission as member and, if he is unable to attend, such member of the Commission as he may delegate;
- The judge appointed to the Higher Banking Commission as member and, if he is unable to attend, an alternate judge appointed by the Supreme Judicial Council for a term equivalent to that of the full member;
- A full member and an alternate member appointed by the Council of Ministers at the proposal of the Governor of the Banque du Liban.

The function of the Special Investigation Commission is to investigate operations suspected of constituting money-laundering offences and determine the seriousness of the evidence for the commission of any such offence.

The Commission has the exclusive right to determine that banking secrecy should be lifted for the benefit of the competent judicial authorities and the Higher Banking Commission, in the person of its chairman, in cases where it is suspected that accounts opened at banks or financial institutions are being used for the purpose of money-laundering.

The Commission meets at the invitation of its chairman at least twice a month and as necessary. Its meetings are legal only if attended by a minimum of three members.

The Commission adopts its decisions by a majority of those present and, if votes are equal, the chairman has the casting vote.

The Commission appointed a full-time secretary, who implements its decisions and directly supervises the secretariat staff, consisting of 35 employees divided among four units, as follows:

- **The Audit and Investigation Unit:** Its tasks include those of gathering evidence on operations that may constitute money-laundering offences, checking information received by the Commission and reporting investigation findings to the Commission through its secretary;
- **The Financial Investigation Administrative Unit:** Its tasks include those of receiving and gathering information from various sources on suspected money-laundering operations, entering and archiving such information using approved programmes, analysing and comparing it with information already available and exchanging information with all concerned bodies and departments, both domestic and foreign;
- **The Compliance Unit:** Its tasks include the ongoing periodic investigation and auditing of banks, financial institutions and all concerned establishments, as mandated by the Commission, to ensure that, within their respective spheres of competence, they perform the obligations stipulated in the Combating of Money-laundering Act and such implementing regulations as may be issued in that connection by the Banque du Liban or the Commission;
- **The Information Technology and Security Unit:** Its tasks include those of installing and updating computer programmes, securing and maintaining computer equipment and preparing, maintaining and developing programmes for the work of the Units, the databank and security and monitoring equipment.

Question No. 1.2:

Effective implementation of subparagraphs 1 (a) and (d) requires States to have in place legal provisions to prevent informal money/value transfer systems from being used for the purpose of the financing of terrorism. The CTC notes from page 5 of the supplementary report that Lebanon has no such provisions. In this regard, could Lebanon indicate the steps it intends to take in order to comply fully with this aspect of the resolution?

Response:

Reference has already been made to this subject; we stated that informal money/value transfer systems in Lebanon, such as *hawalah,* for instance, are non-existent and that money transfer operations are governed by the laws and regulations in force in Lebanon. Such operations may be effected only through banks and financial institutions having obtained prior authorization from the Banque du Liban, which has the discretionary power to grant or deny such authorization depending on whether it deems it to be in the public interest.

The Regulations on the Monitoring of Financial and Banking Transactions to Combat Money-laundering, issued by the Banque du Liban pursuant to Decision No. 7818 of 18 May 2001, as amended, contain provisions pursuant to which banks and concerned financial institutions are required to verify the identity of the beneficiary of incoming or outgoing transfers. These institutions are under obligation to report any suspicious transfers without delay to the Special Investigation Commission, which, after auditing the bank accounts to or from which the transfers are made, may decide, as appropriate, to lift banking secrecy from the accounts in question, place an immediate freeze on the account balances and notify both local and foreign authorities accordingly.

Question No. 1.3:

With regard to the effective implementation of subparagraph 1 (d) of the resolution, the CTC would be grateful to know whether Lebanon has taken judicial action against non-profit organizations for suspected involvement in the financing of terrorism? If yes, could Lebanon outline the relevant procedures and provide information concerning the outcome of such action? The CTC would also welcome examples of cases in which sanctions were imposed against those organizations. Are there procedures in place to respond to requests from other Governments to investigate particular organizations which are suspected of being linked to terrorism?

Response:

(a) In 2003, at the request of national or foreign judicial authorities or of foreign police, the Office of the Public Prosecutor at the Court of Cassation instructed the security agencies which perform judicial enforcement functions to investigate a number of cases involving funds suspected of being linked to non-profit organizations (such as religious, charitable or cultural organizations) serving as a cover for the financing of terrorist acts and activities. The aim was to reveal the soundness and accuracy of those suspicions and learn whether the organizations were straying from their original stated objectives into terrorist acts and activities. The requesting authorities have been informed of the negative outcome of the investigations.

Moreover, through the Counter-Terrorism Office and at the request of the offices of the International Criminal Police Organization (Interpol), the competent local agencies gathered information on whether certain religious, social and political associations are engaged in activities on Lebanese territory that are suspected of being used as a cover for unlawful acts. The information, which turned out to be negative, was forwarded to the requesting Interpol offices.

(b) The judicial authorities in Lebanon have brought no legal prosecutions against non-profit associations or organizations suspected of financing terrorist activities, as the investigations carried out ultimately failed to confirm the accuracy of such suspicions about any of these associations or organizations. An example which can be cited, however, is the prosecution of persons for the offence of complicity in terrorist activities in that they financed the group which, in 2003, bombed restaurants in Lebanon with United States names; elements of the group were arrested and tried by the competent military court, which sentenced two Lebanese persons holding Australian passports to 15 years' imprisonment, it having been proved to the court that they had aided and abetted in the commission of those terrorist acts.

(c) For its part, the Banque du Liban informed us that it had received no reports of any suspicious non-profit organizations and had therefore taken no action against any such organization.

(d) As for procedures in place to respond to requests from foreign Governments, the procedures stipulated in the Combating of Money-laundering Act and in the regulations issued by the Banque du Liban and the Special Investigation Commission are applied.

Question No. 1.4:

Effective implementation of subparagraph 1 (a) of the resolution requires financial institutions and other intermediaries to identify their clients and report suspicious financial transactions to the relevant authorities. With reference to pages 4 and 5 of the third report of Lebanon, it is not clear whether its legal provisions require the reporting of suspicious transactions to all professionals engaged in financial transactions (such as lawyers and/or accountants)? The CTC would appreciate an outlining of the steps Lebanon intends to take in order to comply fully with this aspect of the resolution. In this regard, would Lebanon please provide the CTC with the number of suspicious transactions reports (STRs) received by the Special Investigation Commission and/or other competent authorities, with particular regard to STRs from bureaux de change, money remittance/transfer services and jewellery businesses. Please also indicate the number of STRs analysed and disseminated as well as the number of these which have led to investigations, prosecutions or convictions.

Response:

Pursuant to article 7 of the Combating of Money-laundering Act No. 318 of 20 April 2001, all institutions, whether or not subject to banking secrecy, are required to report immediately to the Special Investigation Commission the details of any transactions suspected of concealing money-laundering, including transactions relating to terrorist activities or the financing of terrorism.

Article 4 of the Act lists some of the many examples of institutions which are not subject to banking secrecy and which are required to report suspicious transactions. Although this article makes no direct reference to lawyers and accountants, they are under the same reporting obligation as those who fall within the scope of the laws and regulations governing their respective areas of work.

Under article 5 (f) of Act No. 318/2000 and article 13 (2) of the Regulations on the Monitoring of Financial and Banking Transactions to Combat Money-laundering, the financial monitoring officer at the bank or financial institution is required to report immediately to the Governor of the Banque du Liban, in his capacity as chairman of the Special Investigation Commission, any violation of the provisions of the Act or the Regulations.

Thus far, the Special Investigation Commission has received nine reports from bureaux de change, one report from the gold business sector and, excluding banks and financial institutions, no reports from remittance institutions (Western Union). All these reports, however, are unrelated to transactions suspected of being linked to terrorism or the financing of terrorism; they related solely to forged or bounced cheques and led to no prosecutions and consequently to no judicial rulings.

Question No. 1.5:

In the context of the effective implementation of paragraph 1 of the resolution, has Lebanon adopted measures to prevent terrorists and other criminals from having unfettered access to wire transfers for moving their funds, with regard to:

- monitoring of the compliance of financial institutions with rules and regulations governing wire transfers (cross-border and domestic);
- detecting such misuse when it occurs, in particular by ensuring that basic information on the originator of wire transfers is immediately available to relevant authorities?

Response:

Pursuant to article 10 et seq. of the Regulations on the Monitoring of Financial and Banking Transactions to Combat Money-laundering, issued by the Banque du Liban by Decision No. 7818 of 18 May 2001, as amended, all banks and financial institutions operating in Lebanon are required to establish specialized administrative committees and units to monitor financial and banking operations in order to combat money-laundering, including operations involving proceeds derived from or aimed at financing terrorism. Some of their many tasks are identified and, within their respective areas of competence, these committees and units, as well as all concerned officers at the bank or financial institution, are required to follow the procedures set forth for monitoring and combating money-laundering operations in order to pre-empt their occurrence.

Banks and financial institutions therefore each have a specialized committee which is entrusted with a number of tasks, including the review of reports referred to it by the Verification Unit and the Internal Auditing Unit concerning suspicious transactions and high-risk accounts in regard to deposits, cash withdrawals and transfers and their linkage with economic activities.

The tasks of the Verification Unit include the review of the daily and weekly cash transaction and transfer reports received from the directorates and branches concerned, as well as the combined monitoring of client accounts and transactions.

The Internal Auditing Unit performs the tasks of auditing cash transactions, transfers and account movements and periodically reporting any changes to the approved monitoring officer.

The tasks of the officer in charge of monitoring branch accounts include the monitoring of cash transactions and transfers and the reporting of any suspicious transactions to the Verification Unit.

As for the officer in charge of the Transfers Division, his tasks include those of auditing incoming transfers to customer accounts, particularly electronic transfers which do not include the name of the person ordering the transfer and which are over a certain amount and unusual in character, and reporting to the Verification Unit any transfers thought to involve suspicious transactions.

Specific tasks are also assigned to cashiers, officers in charge of the Cheques Division and branch managers.

A special unit, known as the Compliance Unit, was also established as part of the Special Investigation Commission. Its tasks are, inter alia, to ascertain and check on an ongoing periodic basis the performance by banks, financial institutions and all concerned establishments of their respective obligations under the Combating of Money-laundering Act No. 318/2001 and such regulations as may be issued in that regard by the Banque du Liban or directly by the Commission. It also makes recommendations to the Commission, through its secretary, on ways of bringing internal auditing methods to the attention of all sectors, in particular the agricultural, industrial, commercial and service sectors, with a view to combating any potential money-laundering through any one of them.

We also wish to point out that, under the Combating of Money-laundering Act and the Regulations on the Monitoring of Financial and Banking Transactions to Combat Money-laundering, all concerned institutions are required immediately to report to the Special Investigation Commission any suspicious transactions, including transfers thought to conceal suspicious transactions, in particular transfers about which there are doubts concerning the identity of the beneficiary and so on.

Effectiveness of Counter-Terrorism Machinery

Question No. 1.6:

Effective implementation of 1373-related legislation covering all aspects of the resolution requires States to have in place effective and coordinated executive machinery, as well as create and utilize adequate national and international antiterrorist strategies. In this context, does Lebanese counter-terrorist strategy and/or policy targeting, at the national and/or subnational levels, deal with the following forms or aspects of counter-terrorist activity:

- criminal investigation and prosecution;
- counter-terrorist intelligence (human and technical);
- special forces operations;
- physical protection of potential terrorist targets;
- strategic analysis and forecasting of emerging threats;
- analyses of efficiency of anti-terrorist legislation and relevant amendments;
- border and immigration control;
- control preventing the trafficking in drugs, arms, biological and chemical weapons, their precursors and the illicit use of radioactive materials.

Without compromising any sensitive information, could Lebanon please outline its legal provisions, administrative procedures and best practices in this regard?

Response:

A. *Criminal investigation and prosecution*

The Lebanese judiciary and its assistant security agencies are constantly on the alert to uncover and pre-empt any terrorist activity by arresting the would-be perpetrators and taking the appropriate measures stipulated in Lebanese laws against those who perpetrate, aid, abet or act as accomplices in such activity, as in the case of the action taken against the defendants in the attack on the network of United States restaurants.

B. *Counter-terrorist intelligence (human and technical)*

The human and technical resources in all security agencies are on permanent alert to monitor and track any terrorist activity.

C. *Special forces operations*

All security agencies have special counter-terrorism forces which, in most areas of Lebanon, have carried out raids and arrested terrorist elements and entities who were handed over to the competent judicial authority.

D. *Physical protection*

By a decision of the Central Security Council, which is headed by the Minister of the Interior and Municipalities, security was stepped up in order to protect all places that are a potential target for attack, such as Government offices, vital centres and foreign embassies, agencies and establishments.

E. *Strategic analysis and forecasting of emerging threats*

The security agencies have experts at their disposal who analyse security information, prepare assessment reports and propose measures to prevent terrorist plans from being carried out.

F. *Analyses of efficiency of anti-terrorist legislation and relevant amendments*

The Lebanese Penal Code comprises articles identifying precisely the criminal acts which are included within the meaning of terrorism. These acts are punishable with stringent penalties that are commensurate with the gravity of the act, the role of those involved and the ensuing consequences. Such penalties range from temporary hard labour to the death sentence.

Currently under consideration is a draft amendment to these articles that will widen the scope of such acts and provide for harsher penalties in accordance with the evolution of the new global concept of terrorism and the directives of the United Nations pursuant to resolution 1371 (2001).

G. *Border and immigration control*

In addition to the internal laws governing the entry and exit process in Lebanon, the Lebanese State has concluded several international agreements to limit illegal immigration, including but not limited to:

- An agreement between Lebanon and Romania on illegal immigration and the readmission of illegal residents;
- An agreement between Lebanon and Bulgaria on the readmission of illegal residents;

– An agreement between Lebanon and the People's Republic of China on traffic in persons and illegal immigration.

The Directorate-General for Public Security is responsible for strengthening border monitoring and control, prosecuting persons who violate Lebanon's rules on entry and residence, pursuing networks involved in the traffic of persons, arresting the members of such networks and bringing them before the competent authorities.

H. *Control preventing traffic in drugs, arms, biological and chemical weapons, their precursors and the illicit use of radioactive materials*

Article 3.I, paragraphs 3 and 4, of the Arab Convention for the Suppression of Terrorism, signed in Cairo on 22 April 1998, which the Lebanese Government was authorized to conclude pursuant to Act No. 75 of 31 March 1999, provides that the Contracting States shall endeavour:

> "To develop and strengthen systems for the detection of the movement, importation, exportation, stockpiling and use of weapons, munitions and explosives and of other means of aggression, murder and destruction as well as procedures for monitoring their passage through customs and across borders in order to prevent their transfer from one Contracting State to another or to third-party States other than for lawful purposes;
>
> "To develop and strengthen systems concerned with surveillance procedures and the securing of borders and points of entry overland and by air in order to prevent illicit entry thereby".

Item IV, section I (Implementing programmes), paragraphs 21 and 22, of the plan for the third implementation phase of the Arab counter-terrorism strategy, which runs for a three-year period, beginning on 16 January 2004 and ending on 15 January 2007, also urges the member States of the Council of Arab Ministers of the Interior to form response teams to cope with the potential disruption to medical centres, hospitals and security agencies caused by the use of biological and chemical weapons by terrorist entities and with the injuries and psychological repercussions produced by these dangerous weapons. It further urges those States to train security personnel and devote more attention to the monitoring and prevention of biological and chemical terrorism.

Articles 56 to 75 of the Narcotics, Psychotropic Substances and Precursors Act No. 673 of 16 March 1998 contain special provisions on importation, exportation and transit in connection with the international trade in the plants, substances and preparations included under the Act, as well as provisions applicable to commercial carriage operations and postal shipments.

Question No. 1.7:

The CTC would be grateful if Lebanon could provide it with information regarding its counter-terrorist efforts including, for example, an outline of any targeted programmes, the agencies involved and any mechanism aimed at ensuring inter-agency coordination in the various areas specified in paragraphs 2 and 3 of the resolution. The CTC is particularly interested in the following areas:

- the recruitment to terrorist groups;
- the tracing of links between criminal activity (in particular, drug trafficking) and terrorism;
- the denial of safe havens to terrorists and of any other forms of passive or active support for terrorists or terrorist groups, including, inter alia, logistical support.

Response:

A. *Recruitment to terrorist groups*

The intelligence networks to which the security agencies have access are engaged in tracing, pursuing and monitoring all terrorist elements. As a result, terrorists have been arrested and handed over to the competent judicial authority, and terrorist cells have been destroyed and prevented from recruiting new elements.

B. *Links between criminal activity (in particular drug trafficking) and terrorism*

The Lebanese security agencies set about destroying all prohibited crops and raiding drug-manufacturing centres. Through such raids, they were able to arrest several members of networks involved in the smuggling and manufacture of drugs. The investigations conducted, however, showed no link between drug-smuggling networks and terrorist organizations.

C. *Denial of safe havens to terrorists and of any other forms of support, including logistical support*

The intelligence surveillance of all territory by the security agencies led to raids on sites and places providing shelter to terrorists and the arrest of elements from terrorist groups, who were handed over to the competent judicial authority.

The Palestinian camps, however, offer a potential refuge for extremist elements, including even those who are under close investigative and intelligence surveillance.

Question No. 1.8:

In the context of the effective implementation of subparagraph 2 (e), could Lebanon please inform the CTC as to the number of persons prosecuted for:

- terrorist activities;
- the financing of terrorist activities;

- recruitment to terrorist groups;
- providing or inviting support to terrorists or terrorist organizations.

Response:

We are awaiting the reply of the Minister of Justice, which we shall transmit as soon as we receive it.

Question No. 1.9:

With regard to effective implementation of subparagraphs 1 (a), 2 (e) and 3 (a) of the resolution, the CTC would be grateful for an outline of Lebanese legal procedures and administrative mechanisms in place to ensure adequate cooperation and information-sharing among the different Government agencies which may be involved in the investigation of terrorist activities, particularly the financing of terrorism. Do the legal provisions in place authorize the administrative authorities to share both public and non-public information concerning counter-terrorism with their domestic and foreign counterparts? If yes, please outline.

Response:

Internally, there is a mechanism for cooperation among the various judicial authorities and the competent administrative authorities that is governed by the laws and regulations on security departments and forces. This cooperation takes place among the Directorate-General for Public Security, the Directorate for Internal Security Forces, the Directorate for Lebanese Army Intelligence and the Customs Administration. The Office of the Public Prosecutor at the Court of Cassation has the central power as a judicial enforcer and through its supervision of all offices of the public prosecutor and of the security forces operating under its authority.

The Combating of Money-laundering Act also provides the opportunity for cooperation between the Special Investigation Commission and the Office of the Public Prosecutor at the Court of Cassation in freezing accounts containing proceeds derived from terrorist activities and offences involving drugs and traffic in weapons, after banking secrecy has been lifted; the Office of the Public Prosecutor is notified to conduct the necessary investigations with a view to bringing the offenders to trial and thus seeking the confiscation of proceeds derived from terrorist activities and other offences stipulated in the Combating of Money-laundering Act.

In regard to the financing of terrorism at the internal level, information is exchanged in writing or electronically with the concerned organizations, departments and agencies (security, administrative, judicial and customs). An electronic system has been set up for communication between the Commission and the relevant security and customs units, through which information is exchanged with the requisite speed. At 31 December 2003, the Commission had received seven local reports on persons linked with terrorism.

Externally, the Lebanese State is a member of Interpol, within the framework and regulations of which it provides other requesting States with such information as it may have on persons suspected of supporting or financing terrorist activities. Under supervision of the Office of the Public Prosecutor at the Court of Cassation, the competent security agencies conduct the investigations required to obtain such information in accordance with the provisions of the Code of Criminal Procedure.

The Lebanese Government is committed to the full implementation of the 10 international conventions and protocols to which it has thus far acceded and which now have the force of law.

The Government is also bound by the Arab Convention for the Suppression of Terrorism, to which it acceded pursuant to Act No. 99/57 and which makes detailed provision for cooperation among the Contracting States in order to prevent and combat terrorist offences through the exchange of information, expertise and evidence, as well as through investigations, judicial assistance and judicial cooperation.

Under supervision of the Office of the Public Prosecutor at the Court of Cassation, the competent security and judicial authorities engage in such cooperation within the context of the provisions of the above-mentioned international conventions and protocols, as well as in accordance with Lebanon's internal laws.

In accordance with Act No. 318/2001, the Special Investigation Commission of the Banque du Liban receives reports from institutions subject to banking secrecy, from institutions not subject to banking secrecy, from various foreign financial intelligence units and from official authorities, both Lebanese and non-Lebanese. These reports are either submitted in writing or electronically, particularly since the Commission is a member of the Egmont Group, comprising 69 foreign financial intelligence units which are electronically linked.

In regard to the written or electronic exchange of information with the competent foreign authorities, at 13 December 2003, the Commission had received 172 reports from foreign sources, including 57 relating to names and persons connected with terrorism.

It is worth mentioning that inquiries were made at banks and financial institutions operating in Lebanon about accounts belonging to the persons concerned and that no such accounts were found to exist, with the exception of one account held by one of those persons and containing approximately US$ 2. Banking secrecy was lifted from the account, which was frozen. The concerned parties were notified accordingly.

The Ministry of Foreign Affairs and Emigrants is responsible for coordination and the exchange of information with all security authorities and competent investigation commissions. It also transmits the required information to the competent foreign bodies in Beirut or to a mission of Lebanon abroad and from there to the competent authorities abroad.

Question No. 1.10:

Regarding the implementation of subparagraphs 1 (a) and (d) of the resolution, as well as article 5 of the International Convention for the Suppression of the Financing of Terrorism, could Lebanon please provide the CTC with statistics on the number of cases in which sanctions, whether criminal, civil or administrative, were imposed on entities and/or organizations for supporting terrorists or terrorist organizations? Please outline the procedures used to proscribe foreign terrorist organizations (other than those featuring in lists drawn up by the Security Council of the United Nations), as well as data in regard to the number of such organizations and/or the relevant examples. How long does it take to proscribe a terrorist organization at the request of or based on the information of another State? In this regard, please indicate how many persons have been prosecuted for inviting and/or providing support for:

- proscribed organizations; and
- other terrorist groups or organizations?

Response:

A. *Sanctions imposed on entities and/or organizations for supporting terrorists*

Through the competent security agencies and at the request of foreign authorities or the United Nations, the Office of the Public Prosecutor at the Court of Cassation has carried out investigations on the strength of information received about activities of entities and organizations suspected of supporting terrorist activities. It took no legal action in these cases, however, either because it had no proof that such information was genuine and reliable or because these entities and organizations support terrorist activities as construed under Lebanese law. Consequently, no criminal, administrative or other sanctions have been imposed on any entity or organization.

B. *Procedures used to proscribe foreign terrorist organizations featuring in the list drawn up by the United Nations or otherwise*

Since the formation of illegal and clandestine organizations constitutes an offence punishable under the Lebanese Penal Code, the recruitment of members, the collection of funds or the solicitation of other forms of support for terrorist acts and terrorist activities in and outside Lebanon each constitute an offence. Such acts constitute either incitement to or complicity in the offence of forming an illegal (or clandestine) organization. On that basis, it can be said that the current Lebanese legislative enactments are legislative measures that fulfil the purpose of combating terrorism, particularly in association with international conventions guaranteeing coordination in that regard.

As for practical measures, under the supervision of the competent judicial authority, specifically the Office of the Public Prosecutor at the Court of Cassation, the different types of security agency coordinate with Interpol in mobilizing all of their resources in order to exchange information or data. They also conduct investigations and inquiries concerning persons suspected of engaging in underhand or bogus activities, such as recruitment under the guise of teaching or the collection of funds through organizations which may be a front for terrorist activities. The security agencies consequently report the findings of such investigations to the competent authorities in the requesting States and take the necessary action in regard to the suspects in the event that there is sufficient evidence and the legal elements required to incriminate them.

The time needed to detect and arrest the elements of a terrorist group at the request of another State cannot, however, be specified, as it depends on the facts and ramifications of each case and the potential difficulties faced by the competent authorities.

C. *Number of persons prosecuted*

As for the number of persons prosecuted for belonging to proscribed groups or other terrorist organizations, we also enclose the list containing the names of persons prosecuted for the offence of belonging to terrorist organizations or of having perpetrated terrorist acts, which was transmitted to Interpol and the United Nations at their request (see appendix 1).

Question No. 1.11:

With regard to the effective implementation of subparagraph 3 (g) of the resolution please indicate whether Lebanon applies the "prosecute or extradite" (*aut dedere aut judicare*) principle of international law. In other words, in the event of Lebanon refusing to extradite a person based on the application of a provision of Lebanese law, does Lebanon proceed to prosecute that person for the offence or offences for which that person's extradition was originally sought? Are claims of political motivation grounds for refusing extradition in the case of terrorist acts? The CTC would appreciate receiving a report on the steps which Lebanon has taken or intends to take in order to fully comply with this aspect of the resolution.

Response:

I. The provisions of article 23 of the Penal Code, which relate to the principle that Lebanese law is universally applicable, stipulate as follows:

> "Lebanese law shall apply to any foreigner present on Lebanese territory who, as a principal, instigator or accessory, set about the commission of an offence abroad that is not provided for under articles 19, 20 and 21, if his extradition has not been requested or accepted."

On the basis of the provisions of this article and in the event that Lebanon refuses to extradite a person, such person is prosecuted by the Lebanese judiciary for the misdemeanour or felony which is the subject of the request for extradition.

These provisions are consistent with the principle of "prosecute or extradite" set forth in resolution 1373 (2001).

II. Where there is a bilateral or multilateral international legal agreement governing the extradition of persons having perpetrated terrorist offences, the provisions of such agreement are applied.

Where there are no such international agreements, the provisions of the Lebanese Penal Code are applicable. Article 34 of the Code provides that extradition shall be refused if the request for extradition arises out of a political crime or if it appears to be for a political purpose. This provision applies regardless of the type and nature of the offence which is the subject of the extradition request, without excluding terrorist offences.

Question 1.12:

The CTC notes from page 9 of the third report of Lebanon that Lebanon is currently considering amending the Penal Code of 1943 and will take into account all matters relating to the combating of terrorism. The CTC would be pleased to be informed of the outcomes of this process. Could Lebanon please provide the CTC with progress report on:

- the implementation in domestic law of the international instruments relating to terrorism which Lebanon has ratified with particular regard to the penalties prescribed for offences created as required under the conventions and protocols;
- the ratification by Lebanon of the remaining conventions or protocols among the 12 international Conventions and Protocols relating to terrorism referred to in the resolution to which Lebanon has yet to become a party.

Response:

(a) At the current time, a committee composed of assistant magistrates and senior judges is drafting amendments to the Lebanese Penal Code. The committee includes the Public Prosecutor at the Court of Cassation. This draft will notably incorporate legal provisions on penalties for the offences stipulated in the international conventions and protocols to which Lebanon has acceded and which have been duly ratified by the Chamber of Deputies, the aim being to ensure consistency with the provisions of those conventions.

(b) As for ratification of the international conventions and protocols on terrorism which Lebanon has not yet ratified, this is a matter for the legislature.

Question No. 1.13:

Could Lebanon please provide the CTC with the progress report of adoption and promulgation by the Chamber of Deputies of the draft Law No. 318 of 20 April 2001, as well as of the amendment of Article 315 of the Lebanese Penal Code? Please also outline the relevant provisions of those which criminalize financing of terrorism.

Response:

In view of the growing concern over money-laundering, the Group of 7 meeting, held in Paris in 1989, decided to establish the Financial Action Task Force on Money Laundering (FATF). In April 1990, FATF published a report comprising 40 Recommendations constituting a full plan of action to combat money-laundering. In February 2000, on the basis of those Recommendations, FATF published a report specifying 25 criteria for identifying the rules and practices which obstruct international cooperation to combat money-laundering. On the basis of those criteria, FATF analysed the anti-money-laundering systems in a number of countries. In June 2000, 15 States, *including Lebanon*, were told that they had been added to the list of non-cooperative countries in the fight against money-laundering. In FATF's view, Lebanon's stringent banking secrecy regime impedes access to the information needed by the administrative authorities and the bodies charged with the conduct of investigations. Lebanon's cooperation at the international level was deemed by FATF to be unsatisfactory.

In the face of this situation and with the aim of preserving its reputation as a regional financial centre, Lebanon promulgated the Combating of Money-laundering Act No. 318 of 20 April 2004 (leaving the Banking Secrecy Act intact).

In accordance with that Act, the Banque du Liban also issued Decision No. 7818 of 18 May 2001 regulating the monitoring of financial and banking transactions to combat money-laundering.

Article 1 of Act No. 318 defines what is meant by illicit proceeds from the commission of certain offences and what is considered to be money-laundering, including money derived from the terrorism offences stipulated in articles 314, 315 and 316 of the Lebanese Penal Code.

Pursuant to Act No. 547 of 30 October 2003, article 1 of Act No. 318/2001 was amended by the addition of a provision relating to the financing or contribution to the financing of terrorism or terrorist acts or organizations in accordance with the meaning of terrorism stipulated in the Lebanese Penal Code.

Act No. 318/2001 imposes penalties of up to seven years' imprisonment and pecuniary fines on any person who undertakes, aids or abets money-laundering operations. An independent commission named the Special Investigation Commission, which has a judicial character and a juridical personality, was established at the Banque du Liban. Its activities are not subject to the authority of the latter and its function is to investigate operations suspected of constituting money-laundering offences, determine the seriousness of the evidence for any such offence and monitor compliance with the rules and procedures stipulated in the Combating of Money-laundering Act. The Commission has the exclusive authority to lift banking secrecy from any suspicious account or accounts, including credit accounts opened at banks or financial institutions, for the benefit of the competent judicial authorities. It is also the Commission which decides that accounts should be temporarily or permanently frozen and its decisions are not subject to any means of ordinary, extraordinary, administrative or judicial review, including a review for transgression of authority.

It should be noted that the Combating of Money-laundering Act stipulates a penalty of up to one year's imprisonment and a pecuniary fine for all institutions, whether or not subject to banking secrecy, which fail to perform their obligations to check the identity and addresses of their clients and ascertain their fulfilment of the obligations incumbent on them under the Act. It also stipulates that movable and immovable assets shall be forfeited to the State where it is demonstrated by a final judgement that they are connected with money-laundering offences. Under the Act, the Commission is also permitted to exchange information with the concerned domestic and foreign authorities.

It should be mentioned that the Combating of Money-laundering Act protects the chairman, members, employees and delegates of the Commission by granting them immunity within the scope of their work insofar as none of them can be sued or prosecuted for any civil or criminal liability in connection with the performance of his or her duties, including offences provided for under the Banking Secrecy Act. It also protects banks and their employees by granting them immunity when performing the duties incumbent on them under that Act or in accordance with the decisions of the Commission.

As a result of the efforts of the various concerned Lebanese organizations and departments, in June 2002, FATF *removed Lebanon from the list of non-cooperative countries in the fight against money-laundering*. During October 2003, FATF set about ending the monitoring period for Lebanon in that regard.

In regard to the amendment of article 315 of the Lebanese Penal Code, it was substituted pursuant to Act No. 553 of 20 October 2003 by the addition of a provision to the Code, namely that of article 316 *bis*, the text of which is as follows:

> "Under this Code, illicit assets shall be construed to mean all assets derived from the commission of any of the following offences:
>
> 1. The cultivation, manufacture or traffic of drugs;
>
> 2. Acts by members of a conspiracy provided for in articles 335 and 336 of the Penal Code and regarded as internationally organized crime;
>
> 3. The terrorist offences provided for in articles 314, 315 and 316 of the Penal Code;
>
> 4. The financing or contribution to the financing of terrorism, terrorist acts or terrorist organizations in accordance with the meaning of terrorism as provided for in the Lebanese Penal Code;
>
> 5. Illicit traffic in weapons;
>
> 6. The theft or embezzlement of public or private funds or the seizure of such funds by deception, falsification or abuse of a position of trust in banks and in the financial and other institutions listed in article 4 of this Code or in areas within the scope of their activity;
>
> 7. The counterfeiting of currency, credit cards, charge cards, public securities or commercial bonds, including cheques."

Question No. 1.14:

The CTC would be grateful to be informed of the legal or other measures which enable the Lebanese authorities to provide assistance in the matter of criminal investigation and judicial proceedings as required under subparagraph 2 (f) of the resolution. Is there a law in Lebanon which provides for mutual assistance in criminal investigations and judicial proceedings? Could Lebanon outline its mutual legal assistance provisions in general and with particular regard to requests for the freezing, seizure and confiscation of property or valuables?

Response:

Requests from abroad for investigations through the judicial police or for judicial assistance through the judiciary are acted upon either in accordance with the provisions of the relevant judicial agreement, where one exists, or in accordance with the principle of reciprocity and international cooperation in the event that there is no judicial agreement governing the matter. Such action is subject to the legal rules governing the procedure. Requests for the seizure and confiscation of movable or immovable property or assets are subject to the provisions of the international judicial agreement, where one exists, failing which they are subject to the provisions of international law.

Question No. 1.15:

The CTC notes from the reply to questions No 1.7 and 1.9 (at pages 7 and 8 of the third report) that Lebanon has no legal provisions in place to enable prosecution of a foreign national who is in Lebanon and has committed a terrorist act outside Lebanon against a State other than Lebanon or against that State's citizens. In this regard could Lebanon indicate the steps it intends taking in order fully to comply with those aspects of the resolution?

Response:

Under the provisions of article 23 of the Penal Code, the Lebanese judiciary may prosecute a foreigner on Lebanese territory who set about committing a terrorist act abroad against a foreign State or its citizens, provided that the act in question constitutes a "terrorist" act in accordance with the definition previously specified in Lebanon's first report, which was transmitted to the United Nations on 13 December 2001.

Effectiveness of Customs, Immigration and Border Control

Question No. 1.16:

Implementation of paragraphs 1 and 2 of the resolution requires the operation of effective customs and border controls with a view to preventing and suppressing the financing of terrorist activities. Does Lebanon impose controls on the cross-border movement of cash, negotiable instruments and/ or precious stones and metals by imposing, for example, an obligation to declare assets or to obtain prior authorization before any movement of these takes place? Please provide information concerning relevant monetary or financial thresholds. Could Lebanon provide the CTC with a common legal framework for preventing gold, diamonds and other high value items from being utilized by terrorists?

Response:

The response will be provided in the report to be submitted by Lebanon before October 2004 in accordance with Security Council resolution 1540 (2004) on preventing access to weapons of mass destruction by non-State actors.

Question No. 1.17:

As stated in Lebanon's third report (at page 8), Lebanese law does not specifically prohibit commerce in official travel documents or identification documents. Are there plans to introduce adequate prohibitions? With regard to Lebanon's reference in page 8 of its third report to "precise and stringent measures" which "the Directorate-General for Public Security of the Lebanese Ministry of the Interior has adopted to verify the forgery or sale of any documentation, in particular identity papers and travel documents", please outline Lebanese legal and administrative provisions regarding the issuance and use of national passports, particularly those which prevent:

- counterfeiting or alteration of a genuine passport by criminal and other elements who need a passport to establish a new identity or citizenship,
- obtaining a passport by deception, using falsified, stolen or genuine documents not one's own (identity theft),
- the theft and completion of a genuine blank passport document, and
- malfeasance of passport authority employees in the issuance of passports.

Response:

A. *Commerce in official travel documents and identity papers, in particular the counterfeiting or alteration of a genuine passport by criminal and other elements who need a passport to establish a new identity or citizenship*

Article 453 of the Lebanese Penal Code punishes any deliberate distortion of facts or data of which there is documentary proof in the form of a deed or manuscript.

In accordance with the Lebanese Code of Civil Procedure, the concept of a document covers any written document intended to substantiate a right, an undertaking, an event or a status and includes passports inasmuch as they are used as proof of identity, nationality or the right of travel. Consequently, the alteration of any such document is an offence punishable under article 453 of the Penal Code.

In addition to punishing the counterfeiter, article 454 of the same Code provides for punishment of persons who knowingly use the counterfeiter, meaning that a third party who knowingly uses a forged passport is deemed to be an accomplice of the counterfeiter and is punishable by same penalty. It should be pointed out, however, that the Directorate-General for Public Security issued a new type of Lebanese passport in conformity with the standards of the International Civil Aviation Organization (ICAO), according to which the passport photograph and information must be printed electronically on a plastic cover by state-of-the-art machines, thus making it impossible to forge a passport or to affix a photograph which differs from that of the passport holder. No forgeries have yet occurred since the date when this type of passport first came into use.

B. *Obtaining a passport by deception, using falsified, stolen or genuine documents not one's own*

Article 462 of the Penal Code punishes any person who knowingly presents a forged or counterfeit document to a public department in order to obtain a Lebanese passport (affidavit of identity, affidavit of domicile or witness testimony). Where there is doubt as to the authenticity of such documents, the judicial and administrative files are consulted and the person proven to have presented the forged document is arrested and handed over to the competent judicial authority to be prosecuted for the offence of forgery.

C. *The theft and completion of a genuine blank passport document*

It is impossible for blank passports to be stolen; they are produced abroad, after which they are delivered to a special committee appointed to the task of checking and making a record of the number of passports and their serial numbers.

They are then stored at the Banque du Liban in a special safe and the requisite number is removed once a month, or as necessary, by the Directorate-General for Public Security (the Lebanese Passport Office, which is in turn responsible for keeping the passports safely under lock and key where they are inaccessible to anyone other than the competent authority responsible for their due issuance).

D. *Malfeasance of passport authority employees in the issuance of passports*

Under article 461 of the Penal Code, any public servant who is required to keep records and who falsifies such records must be punished. The Directorate-General for Public Security imposes a heavier penalty on employees who are proven to have committed acts prohibited by laws and directives and hands them over to the competent judicial authority for the appropriate criminal measures to be taken against them.

We should also mention that that between 19 and 28 May 2003, the ICAO auditing team audited the safety procedures in place at Beirut International Airport, checked their compliance with the international standards required under annex 17 and submitted a report on its task to ICAO.

Question No. 1.18:

Effective implementation of subparagraphs 2 (c) and (g) of the resolution requires the operation of efficient customs, immigration and border controls to prevent the movement of terrorists and the establishment of safe havens. In this regard, please outline the legal and administrative procedures developed by Lebanon to protect port facilities, ships, persons, cargo, cargo transport units, off-shore installations and ship's stores from the risks of terrorist attacks. Have the competent Lebanese authorities put appropriate procedures in place to enable them to review and update Lebanese transport security plans as appropriate? If yes, please outline.

Response:

We are still awaiting the reply from the competent authority.

Question 1.19:

In the context of the implementation of subparagraphs 2 (b) and (j), has Lebanon implemented the ICAO standards and recommendations as described in annex 17? Could Lebanon inform the CTC when the ICAO safety audit of Lebanon's international airports has been completed?

Response:

As already mentioned in the response to question No. 1.17, between 19 and 28 May 2003, the ICAO auditing team carried out a safety audit of the procedures in place at Beirut International Airport, checked their compliance with the international standards required under annex 17 and submitted a report on its task to ICAO. It also made various comments, to which the Directorate-General of Civil Aviation and the senior management of the Safety Department at Beirut International Airport responded in the form of a letter setting out the immediate action taken in respect of some of those comments and the action planned in regard to the other comments (a copy of letter No. 8813/2 dated 22 December 2003 and of the attached comments is appended hereto—appendix 2).

Effectiveness of Controls Preventing Access to Weapons by Terrorists

Question No. 1.20:

Effective implementation of subparagraph 2 (a) of the resolution requires each Member State to have in place, inter alia, appropriate mechanisms to deny access to weapons to terrorists. Please outline the legal provisions which Lebanon has put in place to prevent terrorists from acquiring, by legal or illegal means, hazardous materials, such as radiological, chemical and biological materials, their waste products, as well as of nuclear, chemical and biological weapons. Has Lebanon established a national reporting or auditing procedure to detect the loss or theft of hazardous materials mentioned above, whether held by government or private bodies?

Response:

The terms and conditions for the importation and manufacture of ordinary pharmaceutical preparations (under a scientific name) are subject to the provisions of a series of laws and decisions promulgated by the executive concerning intensive monitoring by the Ministry of Health, the Customs Administration and all security agencies in order to prevent the entry, circulation or manufacture of toxic or illegal chemical and biological substances.

There are no special procedures in place for detecting the theft or concealment of the above-mentioned hazardous materials. The security and customs authorities, however, take such action as is required to ensure that laws and decisions are implemented and that such unlawful acts are prevented.

Under the Weapons and Munitions Act No. 137 of 12 June 1959, as amended, it is prohibited to manufacture, trade in or circulate nuclear weapons. Compliance with the provisions of this Act is monitored by all security and customs authorities.

In addition, article 6 of the Offences against Internal State Security and Terrorism Act of 11 January 1958 provides that: "Any person who, with intent to perpetrate or facilitate the perpetration of any of the felonies mentioned in this Act or any other felony against the State, manufactures, procures or is in possession of explosive or incendiary materials, toxic or inflammable products or parts used in the assembly or manufacture thereof shall be punished with hard labour for life."

Question 1.21:

Could Lebanon please outline its mechanism and procedures in place to legally prohibit and/or control the exportation of goods, the transfer of technologies, the provision of technical assistance overseas and activities connected with trade in controlled goods, with a view to preventing terrorists from gaining access to weapons or hazardous materials. The CTC would appreciate it if Lebanon could provide it with statistics on the use of legal provisions to prevent terrorists from gaining access to weapons.

Response:

Please refer to the response to question No. 1.16, as the response to this question is the same.

Question No. 1.22:

The CTC is aware that Lebanon may have covered some or all of the points in the preceding paragraphs in reports or questionnaires submitted to other organizations involved in monitoring international standards. The CTC would be content to receive a copy of any such report or questionnaire as part of Lebanon's response to these matters, as well as details of any efforts to implement international best practices, codes and standards which are relevant to the implementation of resolution 1373.

Response:

A copy of the report transmitted in accordance with Security Council resolution 1455 (2003) to the Security Council Committee established pursuant to paragraph 6 of resolution 1267 (1999) is appended hereto (appendix 3).

DOCUMENT NO. 14

LEBANON'S 2006 REPORT TO THE UN ON ITS COUNTER-TERRORISM EFFORTS

United Nations Security Council
S/2006/424

June 22, 2006

Distr.: General
22 June 2006

Original: English

Letter dated 21 June 2006 from the Chairman of the Security Council Committee established pursuant to resolution 1373 (2001) concerning counter-terrorism addressed to the President of the Security Council

The Counter-Terrorism Committee has received the attached fifth report from Lebanon submitted pursuant to paragraph 6 of resolution 1373 (2001) (see annex). I would be grateful if you could arrange for the present letter and its annex to be circulated as a document of the Security Council.

(*Signed*) Ellen Margrethe **Løj**
Chairman
Security Council Committee established pursuant to
resolution 1373 (2001) concerning counter-terrorism

Annex

Note verbale dated 16 June 2006 from the Permanent Mission of Lebanon to the United Nations addressed to the Chairman of the Counter-Terrorism Committee

[Original: Arabic]

The Permanent Mission of Lebanon to the United Nations in New York presents its compliments to the Counter-Terrorism Committee Executive Directorate and, with reference to its letter dated 31 January 2006, has the honour to transmit herewith the following documents:

- The fifth report on counter-terrorism submitted by Lebanon pursuant to paragraph 6 of resolution 1373 (2006);
- The reply of the Lebanese Government to the questions relating to measures adopted for the implementation of resolution 1624 (2005).

The Permanent Mission of Lebanon takes this opportunity to convey to the Directorate the renewed assurances of its highest consideration.

The Lebanese Republic

Ministry of Foreign Affairs and Emigrants

Directorate of Political and Consular Affairs

Fifth Report of Lebanon

1. Implementation Measures

1.2 What plans does Lebanon have to specifically criminalize the provision or collection of funds with the intent that they should be used in the commission of a terrorist act, regardless of where the act is intended to take place and whether it is attempted or completed?

Reply: (Provided by the Banque du Liban, the report of which is annexed hereto)

On 20 October 2003, the National Assembly passed Act No. 533, pursuant to which the Lebanese Penal Code enacted on 1 March 1943 was supplemented by article 316 bis, the text of which is as follows:

> Article 316 bis:
>
> **Financing of terrorism**
>
> Anyone who, by direct or indirect means, intentionally finances or contributes to the financing of terrorism, terrorist activities or terrorist organizations shall be punished by a term of hard labour of not less than three years

and not more than five years, and by a fine of not less than the amount paid [for financing] and not more than three times that amount.

Article 1 of the Money-Laundering Act No. 318/2001 was also repealed by Act No. 547/2003, pursuant to which it was replaced with another provision stipulating that, for the purposes of the Act, "illegal assets" means assets derived from the offence of financing or contributing to the financing of terrorism, terrorist activities or terrorist organizations in accordance with the meaning of terrorism as defined in Lebanese law.

Note: The text of Act No. 553 of 20 October 2003 is set forth in annex 1.1 of the report of the Banque du Liban and the text of Act No. 547 of 20 October 2003, which replaces article 1 of Act No. 318/2001, is set forth in annex 2.1 of the report.

1.3 The Committee takes note of Lebanon's statement that a new draft amendment to the Money-Laundering Act was to be submitted to the National Assembly (formerly the Chamber of Deputies) in 2003–2004 (third report, p. 3) and would appreciate an update on the status of this draft amendment.

Reply: (Provided by the Banque du Liban, the report of which is annexed hereto)

On 20 October 2003, the National Assembly passed Act No. 547, which repealed article 1 of the Money-Laundering Act No. 20 April 2001, replacing it with the following text:[1]

New article 1:

For the purposes of this Act, "illegal assets" means any assets derived from any of the following offences:

1. Cultivation or manufacture of, or trafficking in, narcotic drugs;

2. Acts committed by criminal associations, as provided for in articles 335 and 336 of the Penal Code and internationally regarded as organized crimes;

[1] Before the amendment, article 1 provided that:

For the purposes of this Act, "illegal assets" means any assets derived from any of the following offences:

1. Cultivation or manufacture of, or trafficking in, narcotic drugs;

2. The acts of conspiracy provided for in articles 335 and 336 of the Penal Code and internationally regarded as organized crimes;

3. The terrorist offences provided for in articles 314, 315 and 316 of the Penal Code;

4. Illegal trafficking in arms;

5. The theft or embezzlement of public or private funds or the appropriation of such funds by fraudulent means for which Lebanese law imposes a criminal penalty;

6. The counterfeiting of currency or public securities.

3. The terrorist offences provided for in articles 314, 315 and 316 of the Penal Code;

4. Financing or contributing to the financing of terrorism, terrorist activities or terrorist organizations in accordance with the meaning of terrorism as defined in the Lebanese Penal Code;

5. Illegal trafficking in arms;

6. The theft or embezzlement of public or private funds or the appropriation of such funds by fraudulent means, forgery or abuse of a position of trust in any of the banks, financial institutions and establishments enumerated in article 4 of the present Act or in matters within the scope of their activity;

7. The counterfeiting of currency, or of credit, debit or charge cards, or of public securities or commercial bonds, including cheques.

1.4 Could Lebanon please provide examples of cases in which, after auditing bank accounts to or from which funds had been transferred, the Special Investigation Commission decided to place an immediate freeze on an account balance (fourth report, p. 5)?

Reply: (Provided by the Banque du Liban, the report of which is annexed hereto)

The Banque du Liban entrusted us with three cases of persons suspected of involvement in terrorist activities whose accounts with a number of banks operating in Lebanon were frozen after investigation by the Special Investigation Commission of the transactions suspected of constituting terrorist financing offences. These three cases are set forth in annexes 1.4, 2.4 and 3.4 of the letter from the Banque du Liban.

1.5 The Committee would welcome an example of a suspicious transaction report (STR) by the financial monitoring officer of a bank or financial institution. Are non-financial intermediaries such as lawyers, accountants and notaries public also subject to a reporting obligation?

Reply: (Provided by the Banque du Liban, the report of which is annexed hereto)

The Banque du Liban has no STRs by the financial monitoring officer of any agent banks or financial institutions in Lebanon that relate to the financing of terrorism.

As to whether lawyers, accountants and notaries public are subject to a reporting obligation, article 4 of Act No. 318/2001 mentions a non-exhaustive number of institutions and companies that are under obligation to report details of operations suspected of concealing money-laundering. It does not explicitly mention lawyers, accountants or notaries public but does state that such persons are liable to the penalties stipulated in article

13 of the Act should they fail to report operations suspected of concealing money-laundering operations.

We should point out that, under the regulations issued by the Banque du Liban on the monitoring of financial and banking transactions in order to combat money-laundering, monitoring officers in banking institutions are required to report transactions suspected of concealing money-laundering, which include terrorist financing.

1.6 The fourth report makes various references to Act No. 318/2000 and Act 318/2001, both on money-laundering. Are these two different acts? The Committee would appreciate a copy of the(se) instrument(s).

Reply: (Provided by the Banque du Liban, the report of which is annexed hereto)

Act No. 318/2000 is the same as Act 318/2001. Act No. 318/2000 was a typographical error that appeared in one of the items of correspondence. As stated at the beginning of the reply to question 1.3, the National Assembly passed Act No. 318 dated 20 April 2001. Article 1 of Act No. 318 was then replaced pursuant to Act No. 547 dated 20 October 2003. In its letter annexed hereto, the Banque du Liban sets forth Act No. 318 of 20 March 2001 and Act No. 547 of 20 October 2003.

1.7 Could Lebanon please provide a list of investigations by its financial intelligence unit (FIU), the Special Investigation Commission?

Reply: (Provided by the Banque du Liban, the report of which is annexed hereto)

In its report annexed hereto, the Banque du Liban sets forth a list of cases relating to terrorism and the financing of terrorism submitted to and investigated by the Special Investigation Commission.

1.8 What is the specific mandate of the Special Investigation Commission? Does it include matters related to the financing of terrorism?

Reply: (Provided by the Banque du Liban, the report of which is annexed hereto)

Article 6, paragraph 4, of Act No. 318 provides that the functions of the Special Investigation Commission are to conduct investigations in connection with transactions suspected of constituting money-laundering offences, determine the seriousness of the direct and circumstantial evidence that one or more such offence has been committed and decide whether to lift banking secrecy and ultimately freeze the suspected accounts.

Article 1 of Act No. 318/2001 (as amended pursuant to Act No. 547 dated 20 October 2003) also provides that, for the purposes of the Act, "illegal assets" means assets derived from the offences specifically listed in that article, including offences involving the financing of terrorism.

Article 1 provides that:

> For the purposes of this Act, "illegal assets" means any assets derived from any of the following offences:
>
> 1. Cultivation or manufacture of, or trafficking in, narcotic drugs;
>
> 2. Acts committed by criminal associations, as provided for in articles 335 and 336 of the Penal Code and internationally regarded as organized crimes;
>
> 3. The terrorist offences provided for in articles 314, 315 and 316 of the Penal Code;
>
> 4. Financing or contributing to the financing of terrorism, terrorist activities or terrorist organizations in accordance with the meaning of terrorism as defined in the Lebanese Penal Code;
>
> 5. Illegal trafficking in arms;
>
> 6. The theft or embezzlement of public or private funds or the appropriation of such funds by fraudulent means, forgery or abuse of a position of trust in any of the banks, financial institutions and establishments enumerated in article 4 of the present Act or in matters within the scope of their activity;
>
> 7. The counterfeiting of currency, or of credit, debit or charge cards, or of public securities or commercial bonds, including cheques.

1.9 The Committee takes note of the information provided by Lebanon regarding the regulation of alternative money transfer systems and would appreciate a copy of the relevant provisions and details on their scope of application.

Response (provided by the Banque du Liban—report annexed):

Reference has been made in previous reports to the fact that alternative money transfer systems such as hawala, for instance, are non-existent in Lebanon and that money transfer operations are governed by the laws and regulations in force in Lebanon. Such operations may be effected only through banks and financial institutions by prior authorization of the Banque du Liban, which has the discretionary power to grant or deny such authorization depending on whether it deems it to be in the public interest.

Article 1, together with article 3 of the Banque du Liban's Basic Decision No. 7548 of 30 March 2000 provides that electronic transfers are to be made through banks, financial institutions, financial intermediary institutions, investment companies, money-changing establishments, or any other institution that has obtained prior authorization from the Banque du Liban.

In the annexed report, the Banque du Liban has provided a copy of the legal and regulatory provisions requiring banking institutions that conduct transfers to obtain prior authorization from the Banque du Liban. These include:

- Banque du Liban Report Annex 9.1: Basic Decision No. 7548 of 30 March 2000 on electronic financial and banking operations;
- Banque du Liban Report Annex 9.2: Articles 128–131 of the Code of Money and Credit, relating to conditions for establishing banks in Lebanon;
- Banque du Liban Report Annex 9.3: Act No. 234 of 10 June 2000 regulating the financial intermediary profession;
- Banque du Liban Report Annex 9.4: Act No. 347 of 6 August 2001 regulating the money-changing profession in Lebanon;
- Banque du Liban Report Annex 9.5: Act No. 706 of 9 December 2005 (regulating collective investment schemes in securities and other financial instruments);
- Banque du Liban Report Annex 9.6: Articles 208, 209 and 210 of the Code of Currency and Credit, which provides for administrative penalties applicable to banks, financial institutions, financial intermediary institutions, collective investment schemes, money-changing establishments, and any other entity or institution that has obtained prior authorization from the Banque du Liban, when such institutions are in violation of any of the provisions of laws and regulations in force.

1.10 The Committee takes note of the statement in the fourth report (p. 5) that informal currency and asset transfer systems, such as hawala, do not exist in Lebanon and would like to know what measures have been implemented or are planned in order to ensure that such systems are not employed.

Response (provided by the Banque du Liban—report annexed):

Article 1 of Act No. 133 of 26 October 1999 defines the functions of the Banque du Liban as follows: They shall include "in addition to those defined in article 70 of the Code of Currency and Credit, the development and regulation of the following:

- Payment procedures and systems, and in particular transactions conducted by means of automated teller machines and debit, charge or credit cards;
- Currency transfers, including electronic transfers;
- Clearance and settlement transactions based on various means of payment and financial instruments including commercial stocks and bonds and other negotiable instruments."

The Banque du Liban monitors transfers conducted by institutions that have obtained its prior authorization. If it becomes evident that parties are engaging in transfers without having obtained the required authorization it refers the case to the competent judicial authorities to take the necessary steps.

The Banque du Liban has provided annexed copies of article 10 of the Code of Currency and Credit and Act No. 133 of 26 October 1999.

1.11 The Committee takes note of the legislation regarding the regulation of charitable organizations and would be pleased to receive a copy of the investigation reports prepared by Lebanon's security agencies by order of the Office of the Public Prosecutor at the Court of Cassation (fourth report, p. 5).

The Ministry of Foreign Affairs and Emigrants will forward the response to this question to the CTC when it has been received from the Ministry of Justice.

1.12 The Committee notes that Lebanon has no specific law on mutual assistance in criminal matters (third report, p. 8) and that such assistance is therefore contingent on the existence of a treaty between the States concerned. The Committee notes that, pursuant to paragraphs 2 (e) and (f) of resolution 1373 (2001), States should have specific legislation covering the modalities for mutual assistance in criminal matters, such as the transfer of criminal proceedings or of sentenced persons; the execution of letters rogatory; and the recognition and validity of foreign criminal judgements. The Committee would appreciate an outline of any existing legal provisions that cover these modalities. In their absence, please outline what steps Lebanon intends to take in order to introduce such provisions into its domestic law.

Response (provided by the Ministry of the Interior and Municipalities): The issue of amendment of current legal provisions is before Parliament.

1.13 The Committee takes note of the information provided with respect to the basis for cooperation with other countries under its domestic law. Could Lebanon please provide a few examples of cooperation to illustrate the effectiveness of existing mechanisms? The Committee would also appreciate a list of past instances of mutual legal assistance involving Lebanon, information on extraditions carried out and any additional information on planned measures for expanded cooperation with other countries.

Response:

The Ministry of Foreign Affairs and Emigrants will forward the response to this question to the CTC when it has been received from the Ministry of Justice.

1.14 With respect to the remaining international counter-terrorism conventions to which Lebanon is not a party, the Committee wishes to remind Lebanon, in connection with its reference to the Arab Convention on the Suppression of Terrorism, that accession to regional counter-terrorism conventions cannot be viewed as an alternative to becoming a party to and implementing in domestic law all the international conventions and protocols related to terrorism. In this regard, the Committee recalls that paragraph 3 (d) of resolution 1373 (2001) calls upon all States "to become parties as soon as possible to the relevant international conventions and protocols relating to terrorism, including the International Convention for the Suppression of the Financing of Terrorism of 9 December 1999". Therefore, the Committee would like to receive a progress report on the status of the legal procedures for Lebanon's becoming a party to the International Convention for the Suppression of Terrorist Bombings and the International Convention for the Suppression of the Financing of Terrorism (second report, p. 20).

Response (the Ministry of Foreign Affairs and Emigrants):

The minutes of the Cabinet meeting held on 1 December 2005 record the Cabinet's decision to postpone discussion of Lebanon's accession to the International Convention for the Suppression of the Financing of Terrorism. According to the minutes of the meeting, the Ministry of Finance had reservations concerning the provisions of article 2, paragraph 1 (b) in connection with the struggle against foreign occupation.

With regard to the International Convention for the Suppression of Terrorist Bombings, Decree No. 15510 of 19 October 2005, signed by His Excellency the President of the Lebanese Republic, has been issued and referred to Parliament with a view to authorizing the Government to accede to that Convention.

1.15 The Committee would appreciate it if Lebanon would share with it any assessments or evaluations carried out by international or regional institutions or organizations, including those related to operational measures, in connection with implementation of resolution 1373 (2001).

Response (Ministry of Foreign Affairs and Emigrants):

Lebanon views implementation by regional and international institutions of resolution 1373 (2001) as an ongoing process. The effort to achieve practical implementation of all clauses of the resolution must be pursued continuously in order to attain the goal of that resolution and of other relevant resolutions related to combating and suppressing terrorism.

Regionally

In view of Lebanon's membership and distinctive role in the regional organization of the League of Arab States, Lebanon considers it important to draw attention to the steps taken and decisions adopted by the Council of the League in the field of cooperative contributions to international counter-terrorism efforts. In this regard, the Council of the League, at the ministerial level, at its 125th regular session held in March 2005, took up the subject of establishing an Arab expert group charged with following up the implementation of resolution 1373 (2001) as an Arab counter-terrorism mechanism, including changing its name to the Arab Group of Experts on Counter-Terrorism, which would include all Arab States in its membership and whose reports and recommendations would be submitted to the Council of the League. In this regard Lebanon also sees a need to continue dialogue and contacts between the League of Arab States and the Security Council Counter-Terrorism Committee in order to overcome such difficulties as might stand in the way of implementing certain clauses, and affirms in this regard the recommendations issued by the Arab Group of Experts regarding proposed ways of overcoming difficulties and consequences arising from the implementation of resolution 1373 (2001).

Among procedural means relating to the implementation of resolution 1373 (2001), the Lebanese security agencies (the Directorate-General of the Internal Security Forces—service and operations branch) proposes the following measures for achieving the desired goals in the area of combating terrorist acts and stopping and preventing the funding thereof:

- Mobilizing Interpol and effecting genuine coordination among all States to collect as much information as possible on terrorist individuals and organizations;
- Establishing a specific mechanism to coordinate all efforts between all national and international security agencies and the international institutions involved in this issue;
- Orienting the media towards this goal, in view of their influence on the public and the major role they play in awareness-raising and education.

2. Implementation of Resolution 1624 (2005)

Paragraph 1

2.1 What measures does Lebanon have in place to prohibit by law and to prevent incitement to commit a terrorist act or acts? What further steps, if any, are under consideration?

Response:

The Ministry of Foreign Affairs and Emigrants will forward the response to this question to the CTC when it has been received from the Ministry of Justice.

2.2 What measures does Lebanon take to deny safe haven to any persons with respect to whom there is credible and relevant information giving

serious reasons for considering that they have been guilty of incitement to commit a terrorist act or acts?

Response (the Ministry of the Interior and Municipalities):

The Directorate-General of Public Security takes a series of measures with respect to persons about whom there is information linking them to terrorist activity. These range from preventive measures in cases where the information is unconfirmed (such as providing information on cross-border movements or placing under surveillance after entering the country) to operational measures in cases where the information is confirmed (such as barring entry, detention, and interrogation). All measures are taken in coordination with the competent judicial authority.

Paragraph 2

2.3 How does Lebanon cooperate with other States in strengthening the security of its international borders with a view to preventing those guilty of incitement to commit a terrorist act or acts from entering their territory, including by combating fraudulent travel documents and, to the extent attainable, by enhancing terrorist screening and passenger security procedures?

Response (the Ministry of the Interior and Municipalities):

The Directorate-General of Public Security is cooperating with other States to strengthen the security of international borders through the implementation of measures circulated by Interpol, measures to bar entry on the basis of confirmed and verified information from credible security agencies, and a training course for public security officers and personnel on the detection of fraudulent documents, part of which is conducted in conjunction with accredited embassies in Lebanon. There are investigative branches at border posts, including at the Rafik Hariri International Airport, whose task it is to ensure that no suspicious activity takes place and that no security lapses or attempts to violate the security of travellers occur.

The Directorate-General of Public Security is also continuing its efforts to achieve comprehensive border control by establishing a biometric programme after the necessary support has been secured.

2.4 What international efforts is Lebanon participating in or considering participating in/initiating in order to enhance dialogue and broaden understanding among civilizations in an effort to prevent the indiscriminate targeting of different religions and cultures?

Response (Ministry of Foreign Affairs and Emigrants):

Because of its distinctive historical, geographical and structural situation, Lebanon plays a central role and combines a number of contradictions. Freedom of expression and speech is a basic component and among the cornerstones of political and media activity in Lebanon. In spite of the polarization into which Lebanese society might fall, the result in Lebanon has always been to resort to dialogue. Lebanon has a firm faith that the process of dialogue will repudiate violence, terrorism and extremism.

Because of the foregoing, in the midst of political differences between extremes, Lebanon established a process of national dialogue that began in March 2006 and continues to seek a common denominator and produce a formula for political cooperation. The report of the Secretary-General of the United Nations of 18 April 2006 (S/2006/248) and Security Council resolution 1680 of 17 May 2006 commended this dialogue process, as exemplified in one of the resolution's preambular paragraphs: "Expressing full support for the Lebanese National Dialogue and commending all Lebanese parties for its conduct and for the consensus reached in this context on important matters."

At the same time, Lebanon is also diverse religiously, and out of bitter previous experience has established an Islamic-Christian Dialogue Committee in which all religions and sects are represented and which conducts awareness-raising activities and seminars on dialogue among religions and civilizations in Lebanon and abroad.

2.5 What steps is Lebanon taking to counter incitement of terrorist acts motivated by extremism and intolerance and to prevent subversion of educational, cultural and religious institutions by terrorists and their supporters?

Paragraph 4

Response (Ministry of Foreign Affairs and Emigrants):

A committee made up of prominent judges and Members of Parliament is working to establish legislation to amend the Lebanese Penal Code in order to bring it into line with international counter-terrorism protocols and resolutions. Articles 317–318, in conjunction with articles 217–218 of the Penal Code cover penalties for incitement to crimes that undermine national unity, harm the good of the nation, or lead to terrorist acts.

2.6 What is Lebanon doing to ensure that any measures taken to implement paragraphs 1, 2 and 3 of resolution 1624 (2005) comply with all of its obligations under international law, in particular international human rights law, refugee law, and humanitarian law?

Response (the Ministry of the Interior and Municipalities):

The Ministry of the Interior and Municipalities has instructed the Directorate-General of Public Security to enforce the laws in force protecting human rights. This applies to all detainees regardless of the grounds for arrest, whether terrorism charges or otherwise.

E. EUROPE'S APPROACH TO LEBANON

DOCUMENT NO. 15

EUROPEAN COUNCIL: EURO-MEDITERRANEAN AGREEMENT ESTABLISHING AN ASSOCIATION BETWEEN THE EUROPEAN COMMUNITY AND ITS MEMBER STATES AND THE REPUBLIC OF LEBANON

Decision and Association Agreement 7293/02
Council of the European Union

Brussels, 18 April 2002

LEGISLATIVE ACTS AND OTHER INSTRUMENTS

Subject: Euro-Mediterranean Agreement establishing an association between the European Community and its Member States, of the one part, and the Republic of Lebanon, of the other part

– Decision and Association Agreement

COUNCIL DECISION

of

on the signing, on behalf of the Community of a Euro-Mediterranean Agreement establishing an Association between the European Community and its Member States, of the one part, and the Republic of Lebanon, of the other part,

THE COUNCIL OF THE EUROPEAN UNION,

Having regard to the Treaty establishing the European Community, and in particular Article 310 in conjunction with the first sentence of the first subparagraph of Article 300, paragraph 2 thereof,

Having regard to the proposal from the Commission,

Whereas:

(1) The Council adopted the Directives on 2 October 1995 for the Commission to open negotiations for a Euro-Mediterranean Association

Agreement between the European Community and its Member States, of the one part, and the Republic of Lebanon, of the other part.

(2) These negotiations have been concluded and the Agreement has been initialled on 10 January 2002 and the Agreement should therefore be signed on behalf of the Community,

HAS DECIDED AS FOLLOWS:

Article 1

The signing of the Euro-Mediterranean Agreement establishing an Association between the European Community and its Member States, of the one part, and the Republic of Lebanon, of the other part, is hereby approved on behalf of the Community, subject to the Council Decision concerning the conclusion of the said Agreement.

The text of the Agreement is attached to this Decision.

Article 2

The President of the Council is hereby authorised to designate the person(s) empowered to sign the Agreement on behalf of the Community subject to its conclusion.

Done at Brussels,

For the Council

The President

Euro-Mediterranean Agreement Establishing an Association Between The European Community and its Members States, of the One Part, and The Republic of Lebanon, of the Other Part

THE KINGDOM OF BELGIUM,

THE KINGDOM OF DENMARK,

THE FEDERAL REPUBLIC OF GERMANY,

THE HELLENIC REPUBLIC,

THE KINGDOM OF SPAIN,

THE FRENCH REPUBLIC,

IRELAND,

THE ITALIAN REPUBLIC,

THE GRAND DUCHY OF LUXEMBOURG,

THE KINGDOM OF THE NETHERLANDS,

THE REPUBLIC OF AUSTRIA,

THE PORTUGUESE REPUBLIC,

THE REPUBLIC OF FINLAND,

THE KINGDOM OF SWEDEN,

THE UNITED KINGDOM OF GREAT BRITAIN AND NORTHERN IRELAND,

Contracting Parties to the Treaty establishing the European Community, hereinafter referred to as the "Member States", and

THE EUROPEAN COMMUNITY, hereinafter referred to as "the Community",

of the one part, and

THE REPUBLIC OF LEBANON, hereinafter referred to as "Lebanon",

of the other part,

CONSIDERING the proximity and interdependence which historic links and common values have established between the Community, its Member States and Lebanon;

CONSIDERING that the Community, its Member States and Lebanon wish to strengthen those links and to establish lasting relations, based on reciprocity, solidarity, partnership and co-development;

CONSIDERING the importance which the Parties attach to the principles of the United Nations Charter, particularly the observance of human rights, democratic principles and economic freedom, which form the very basis of the Association;

CONSIDERING recent political and economic developments both on the European continent and in the Middle East, and the resulting common responsibilities with regard to the stability, security and prosperity of the Euro-Mediterranean region;

CONSIDERING the importance for the Community and Lebanon of free trade, as guaranteed by the General Agreement on Tariffs and Trade of 1994 (GATT) and by the other multilateral agreements annexed to the Agreement establishing the WTO;

CONSIDERING the difference in economic and social development existing between Lebanon and the Community and the need to strengthen the process of economic and social development in Lebanon;

CONFIRMING that the provisions of this Agreement that fall within the scope of Part III, Title IV of the Treaty establishing the European Community bind the United Kingdom and Ireland as separate Contracting Parties, and not as part of the Community, until the United Kingdom or Ireland (as the case may be) notifies Lebanon that it has become bound as part of the Community in accordance with the Protocol on the position of the United Kingdom and Ireland annexed to the Treaty on European Union and the Treaty establishing the European Community. The same applies to Denmark, in accordance with the Protocol annexed to those Treaties on the position of Denmark,

DESIROUS of fully achieving the objectives of the association between them by implementing the relevant provisions of this Agreement to bring the levels of economic and social development of the Community and Lebanon closer to each other;

CONSCIOUS of the importance of this Agreement, which is based on reciprocity of interests, mutual concessions, cooperation and dialogue;

DESIROUS of developing a regular political dialogue on bilateral and international issues of mutual interest;

TAKING ACCOUNT of the Community's willingness to provide Lebanon with support in its endeavours to bring about economic reconstruction, reform and adjustment and social development;

DESIROUS of establishing, maintaining and intensifying cooperation, sustained by regular dialogue, on economic, scientific, technological, social, cultural and audiovisual issues in order to achieve better mutual understanding;

CONVINCED that this Agreement will create a climate conducive to growth in economic relations between them, more particularly in the trade and investment sectors which are essential to the success of the economic reconstruction and restructuring programme and to technological modernisation,

HAVE AGREED AS FOLLOWS:

Article 1

1. An association is hereby established between the Community and its Member States, of the one part, and Lebanon, of the other part.

2. The aims of this Agreement are to:

(a) provide an appropriate framework for political dialogue between the Parties, allowing the development of close relations in all areas they consider relevant to such dialogue,

(b) establish the conditions for the gradual liberalisation of trade in goods, services and capital,

(c) promote trade and the expansion of harmonious economic and social relations between the Parties, notably through dialogue and cooperation, so as to foster the development and prosperity of Lebanon and its people,

(d) promote economic, social, cultural, financial and monetary cooperation.

(e) promote cooperation in other areas which are of mutual interest.

Article 2

Relations between the Parties, as well as all the provisions of this Agreement itself, shall be based on respect of democratic principles and fundamental human rights as set out in the Universal Declaration on Human Rights, which guides their internal and international policy and constitutes an essential element of this Agreement.

Title I
Political Dialogue

Article 3

1. A regular political dialogue shall be established between the Parties. It shall help build lasting links of solidarity between the partners which will contribute to the prosperity, stability and security of the Mediterranean region and bring about a climate of understanding and tolerance between cultures.

2. Political dialogue and cooperation are intended in particular to:

(a) facilitate rapprochement between the Parties through the development of better mutual understanding and regular coordination on international issues of common interest:

(b) enable each Party to consider the position and interests of the other;

(c) contribute to consolidating security and stability in the Mediterranean region and in the Middle East in particular;

(d) promote common initiatives.

Article 4

Political dialogue shall cover all issues of common interest to the Parties, examining in particular the conditions required to ensure peace and security through support for cooperation. The dialogue shall also seek to create new forms of cooperation directed towards common objectives.

Article 5

1. Political dialogue shall take place at regular intervals and whenever necessary, notably:

(a) at ministerial level, mainly in the framework of the Association Council;

(b) at senior official level of Lebanon, on the one hand, and of the Presidency of the Council and of the Commission on the other;

(c) by taking full advantage of all diplomatic channels including regular briefings by officials, consultations on the occasion of international meetings and contacts between diplomatic representatives in third countries;

(d) where appropriate, by any other means which would make a useful contribution to consolidating dialogue and increasing its effectiveness.

2. A political dialogue shall be established between the European Parliament and the Lebanese Parliament.

Title II
Free Movement of Goods Basic Principles

Article 6

The Community and Lebanon shall gradually establish a free trade area over a transitional period not exceeding twelve years from the entry into force of this Agreement according to the modalities set out in this Title and in conformity with the provisions of the General Agreement on Tariffs and Trade of 1994 and of the other multilateral agreements on trade in goods annexed to the Agreement establishing the World Trade Organisation (WTO), hereinafter referred to as the GATT.

Chapter 1
Industrial Products

Article 7

The provisions of this Chapter shall apply to products originating in the Community and Lebanon falling within Chapters 25 to 97 of the Combined Nomenclature and of the Lebanese Customs tariff with the exception of the products listed in Annex 1.

Article 8

Imports into the Community of products originating in Lebanon shall be allowed free of customs duties and of any other charge having equivalent effect.

Article 9

1. Customs duties and charges having equivalent effect applicable on import into Lebanon of products originating in the Community shall be progressively abolished in accordance with the following schedule:

- five years after the date of entry into force of this Agreement each duty and charge shall be reduced to 88% of the basic rate,
- six years after the date of entry into force of this Agreement each duty and charge shall be reduced to 76% of the basic rate,
- seven years after the date of entry into force of this Agreement each duty and charge shall be reduced to 64% of the basic rate,
- eight years after the date of entry into force of this Agreement each duty and charge shall be reduced to 52% of the basic rate,
- nine years after the date of entry into force of this Agreement each duty and charge shall be reduced to 40% of the basic rate,
- ten years after the date of entry into force of this Agreement each duty and charge shall be reduced to 28% of the basic rate,
- eleven years after the date of entry into force of this Agreement each duty and charge shall be reduced to 16% of the basic rate,
- twelve years after the date of entry into force of this Agreement the remaining duties and charges shall be abolished.

2. In the event of serious difficulties for a given product, the schedule applicable under paragraph 1 above may be reviewed by the Association Committee by common accord on the understanding that the schedule for which the review has been requested may not be extended in respect of the product concerned beyond the maximum transitional period of twelve years. If the Association Committee has not taken a decision within thirty days of an application by Lebanon to review the schedule, Lebanon may suspend the schedule provisionally for a period which may not exceed one year.

3. For each product concerned, the basic duty to be gradually reduced as provided in paragraph 1 shall be the rates referred to in Article 19.

Article 10

The provisions concerning the abolition of customs duties on imports shall also apply to customs duties of a fiscal nature.

Article 11

1. Exceptional measures of limited duration which derogate from the provisions of Article 9 may be taken by Lebanon in the form of an increase or reintroduction of customs duties.

2. These measures may only concern new and infant industries, or sectors undergoing restructuring or facing serious difficulties, particularly where these difficulties entail major social problems.

3. Customs duties on imports into Lebanon of products originating in the Community that are introduced by such exceptional measures may not exceed 25% *ad valorem* and shall maintain an element of preference for products originating in the Community. The total value of imports of the products which are subject to these measures may not exceed 20% of the yearly average of total imports of industrial products from the Community during the last three years for which statistics are available.

4. These measures shall be applied for a period not exceeding five years unless a longer duration is authorised by the Association Committee. They shall cease to apply at the latest on the expiry of the maximum transitional period of twelve years.

5. No such measures can be introduced in respect of a product if more than three years have elapsed since the elimination of all duties and quantitative restrictions or charges or measures having equivalent effect concerning that product.

6. Lebanon shall inform the Association Committee of any exceptional measures it intends to adopt and, at the request of the Community, consultations shall be held on the measures and sectors concerned before they are implemented. When adopting such measures Lebanon shall provide the Committee with a schedule for the elimination of the customs duties introduced under this Article. This schedule shall provide for a phasing-out of these duties in equal annual instalments starting no later than the end of the second year following their introduction. The Association Committee may decide on a different schedule.

7. By way of derogation from provisions of paragraph 4, the Association Committee may exceptionally, to take account of the difficulties involved in setting up new industries, endorse the measures already taken by Lebanon pursuant to paragraph 1 for a maximum period of three years beyond the twelve year transitional period.

Chapter 2
Agricultural, Fisheries and Processed Agricultural Products

Article 12

The provisions of this Chapter shall apply to products originating in the Community and Lebanon falling within Chapters 1 to 24 of the Combined

Nomenclature and of the Lebanese Customs tariff and to the products listed in Annex 1.

Article 13

The Community and Lebanon shall progressively establish a greater liberalisation of their trade in agricultural, fisheries and processed agricultural products, of interest to both parties.

Article 14

1. Agricultural products originating in Lebanon listed in Protocol 1 on importation into the Community shall be subject to the arrangement set out in that Protocol.

2. Agricultural products originating in the Community listed in Protocol 2 on importation into Lebanon shall be subject to the arrangement set out in that Protocol.

3. Trade in processed agricultural products falling under this chapter shall be subject to the arrangements set out in Protocol 3.

Article 15

1. Five years after the entry into force of this Agreement, the Community and Lebanon shall assess the situation in order to determine measures to be applied by the Community and Lebanon one year following the revision of this Agreement, in accordance with the objective set out in Article 13.

2. Without prejudice to the provisions of paragraph 1 and taking account of the volume of trade in agricultural, fisheries and processed agricultural products between the two Parties and the particular sensitivity of such products, the Community and Lebanon shall examine on a regular basis in the Association Council, product by product and on an orderly and reciprocal basis, the possibility of granting each other further concessions.

Article 16

1. In the event of specific rules being introduced as a result of the implementation of its agricultural policy or of any alteration of the current rules or in the event of any alteration or extension of the provisions relating to the implementation of its agricultural policy, the Party concerned may amend the arrangements resulting from this Agreement in respect of the products concerned.

2. The Party carrying out such modification shall inform the Association Committee thereof. At the request of the other Party, the Association Committee shall meet to take due account of the interest of the other Party.

3. If the Community or Lebanon, in applying paragraph 1, modifies the arrangements made by this Agreement for agricultural products, they shall accord imports originating in the other Party an advantage comparable to that provided for in this Agreement.

4. Any modification of the arrangements made by this Agreement shall be the subject, at the request of the other Party, of consultations within the Association Council.

Article 17

1. Both Parties agree to cooperate to reduce the potential for fraud in the application of the trade provisions of this Agreement.

2. Notwithstanding other provisions of this Agreement, where one Party finds that there is sufficient evidence of fraud such as a significant increase in trade products by one party to the other party, beyond the level reflecting economic conditions such as normal production and export capacities, or failure to provide administrative cooperation as required for the verification of evidence of origin by the other Party, both Parties shall enter into consultations immediately to find an appropriate solution. Pending such a solution, the Party concerned may take the appropriate measures it deems necessary. In the selection of the measure priority must be given to those which least disturb the functioning of the arrangements established in this Agreement.

Chapter 3
Common Provisions

Article 18

1. No new customs duties on imports or exports or charges having equivalent effect shall be introduced in trade between the Community and Lebanon, nor shall those already applied upon entry into force of this Agreement be increased unless this Agreement provides otherwise.

2. No new quantitative restriction on imports or measure having equivalent effect shall be introduced in trade between the Community and Lebanon.

3. Quantitative restrictions on imports and measures having equivalent effect in trade between Lebanon and the Community shall be abolished upon the entry into force of this Agreement.

4. Neither the Community nor Lebanon shall apply to exports between themselves either customs duties or charges having equivalent effect, or quantitative restrictions or measures of equivalent effect.

Article 19

1. For each product the basic rate to which the successive reductions laid down in Article 9(1) are to be applied shall be that actually applied vis-à-vis the Community on the day of conclusion of the negotiations.

2. In the event of the accession of Lebanon to the WTO, the applicable rates for imports between the Parties shall be the WTO bound rate or lower effectively applied rate enforced as of the date of the accession. If, after the accession to the WTO, a tariff reduction is applied on an *erga omnes* basis, the reduced rate shall apply.

3. The provision laid down in paragraph 2 is of application for any tariff reduction applied after the day of conclusion of the negotiations on a *erga omnes* basis.

4. The Parties shall communicate to each other their respective applied rates on the day of conclusion of the negotiations.

Article 20

Products originating in Lebanon shall not enjoy more favourable treatment when imported into the Community than that applied by Member States among themselves.

Article 21

1. The Parties shall refrain from any measure or practice of an internal fiscal nature establishing, whether directly or indirectly, discrimination between the products of one Party and like products originating in the territory of the other Party.

2. Products exported to the territory of one of the Parties may not benefit from repayment of indirect internal taxation in excess of the amount of indirect taxation imposed on them either directly or indirectly.

Article 22

1. This Agreement shall not preclude the maintenance or establishment of customs unions, free trade areas or arrangements for frontier trade except in so far as they alter the trade arrangements provided for in this Agreement.

2. Consultations between the Parties shall take place within the Association Committee concerning agreements establishing such customs unions or free trade areas and, where requested, on other major issues related to their respective trade policies with third countries. In particular, in the event of a third country acceding to the Community, such consultations shall take place so as to ensure that account can be taken of the mutual interests of the Community and Lebanon.

Article 23

If one of the Parties finds that dumping is taking place in trade with the other Party in line with prevailing international rules as defined in Article VI of the General Agreement on Tariffs and Trade (GATT) 1994 and related internal legislation, it may take appropriate measures against this practice in accordance with the WTO Agreement on the implementation of Article VI of the GATT 1994 and related internal legislation.

Article 24

1. Without prejudice to Article 35, the WTO Agreement on Subsidies and Countervailing Measures shall apply between the Parties.

2. Until the necessary rules referred to in Article 35(2) are adopted, if either Party finds that subsidy is taking place in trade with the other Party in line with prevailing international rules as defined in Articles VI and XVI of the General Agreement on Tariffs and Trade (GATT) 1994 and related internal legislation, it may invoke appropriate measures against this practice in accordance with those rules as defined by the WTO Agreement on Subsidies and Countervailing Measures and related internal legislation.

Article 25

1. The provisions of Article XIX of the GATT 1994 and the WTO Agreement on Safeguards and related internal legislation are applicable between the Parties.

2. Before applying safeguard measures as defined by international rules, the Party intending to apply such measures shall supply the Association Committee with all relevant information required for a thorough examination of the situation with a view to seeking a solution acceptable to the Parties.

In order to find such a solution the Parties shall immediately hold consultations within the Association Committee. If, as a result of the consultations, the Parties do not reach an agreement within thirty days of the initiation of the consultations on a solution to avoid the application of the safeguard measures, the Party intending to apply safeguard measures may apply the provisions of Article XIX of the GATT 1994 and the WTO Agreement on Safeguards.

3. In the selection of safeguard measures pursuant to this article, the Parties shall give priority to those, which cause least disturbance to the achievement of the objectives of this Agreement.

4. Safeguard measures shall be notified immediately to the Association Committee and shall be the subject of periodic consultations within the Committee, particularly with a view to their abolition as soon as circumstances permit.

Article 26

1. Where compliance with the provisions of Article 18(4) leads to:

(a) re-export to a third country against which the exporting Party maintains, for the product concerned, quantitative export restrictions, export duties or measures or charges having equivalent effect, or

(b) a serious shortage, or threat thereof, of a product essential to the exporting Party,

and where the situations referred to above give rise, or are likely to give rise, to major difficulties for the exporting Party, that Party may take appropriate measures under the conditions and in accordance with the procedures laid down in paragraph 2.

2. The difficulties arising from the situations referred to in paragraph 1 shall be submitted for examination to the Association Committee. The Association Committee may take any decision needed to put an end to the difficulties. If it has not taken such a decision within thirty days of the matter being referred to it, the exporting Party may apply appropriate measures on the exportation of the product concerned. The measures shall be non-discriminatory and shall be eliminated when conditions no longer justify their maintenance.

Article 27

Nothing in this Agreement shall preclude prohibitions or restrictions on imports, exports or goods in transit justified on grounds of public morality, public policy or public security; of the protection of health and life of humans, animals or plants; of the protection of national treasures of artistic, historic or archaeological value; of the protection of intellectual industrial and commercial property; of rules relating to gold and silver and conservation of exhaustible natural resources. Such prohibitions or restrictions shall not, however, constitute a means of arbitrary discrimination or a disguised restriction on trade between the Parties.

Article 28

The concept of "originating products" for the application of the provisions of the present Title and the methods of administrative cooperation relating thereto are laid down in Protocol 4.

Article 29

The Combined Nomenclature of goods shall be applied to the classification of goods for imports into the Community. The Lebanese customs tariff shall be applied to the classification of goods for imports into Lebanon.

Title III
Right of Establishment and Supply of Services

Article 30

1. Treatment granted by either Party to the other with respect to the right of establishment and the supply of services shall be based on each Party's commitments and other obligations under the General Agreement on Trade in Services (GATS). This provision shall take effect from the date of the final accession of Lebanon to the WTO.

2. Lebanon undertakes to provide a schedule of specific commitments on services, prepared in accordance with Article XX of the GATS, to the European Community and their Member States as soon as it is finalised.

3. The Parties undertake to consider development of the above provisions with a view to the establishment of an "economic integration agreement" as defined in Article V of the GATS.

4. The objective provided for in paragraph 3 shall be subject to a first examination by the Association Council one year after the entry into force of this Agreement.

5. The Parties shall not, between the date of entry into force of this Agreement and Lebanon's accession to the WTO, take any measures or actions which render the conditions for the supply of services by Community or Lebanese service suppliers more discriminatory than those existing on the date of entry into force of this Agreement.

6. For the purposes of this Title:

(a) "service suppliers" of a Party means any juridical or natural person that seeks to provide or provides a service;

(b) a "juridical person" means a company or a subsidiary, set up in accordance with the laws either of a Member State of the Community or of Lebanon and having its registered office, central administration or principal place of business in the territory either of the Community or of Lebanon. Should the juridical person have only its registered office or central administration in the territory either of the Community or of Lebanon, it shall not be considered as either a Community or a Lebanese juridical person, unless its operations possess a real and continuous link with the economy either of the Community or Lebanon;

(c) "subsidiary" means a juridical person which is effectively controlled by another juridical person;

(d) "natural person" means a person who is a national either of a Member State of the Community or of Lebanon according to their respective national legislations.

Title IV
Payments, Capital, Competition and Other Economic Provisions

Chapter 1
Current Payments and Movement of Capital

Article 31

Within the framework of the provisions of this Agreement, and subject to the provisions of Articles 33 and 34, there shall be no restrictions between the Community of the one part, and Lebanon of the other part, on the movement of capital and no discrimination based on the nationality or on the place of residence of their nationals or on the place where such capital is invested.

Article 32

Current payments connected with the movement of goods, persons, services or capital within the framework of this Agreement shall be free of all restrictions.

Article 33

1. Subject to other provisions in this Agreement and other international obligations of the Community and Lebanon, the provisions of Articles 31 and 32 shall be without prejudice to the application of any restriction which exists between them on the date of entry into force of this Agreement, in

respect of the movement of capital between them involving direct investment, including in real estate, establishment, the provision of financial services or the admission of securities to capital markets.

2. However, the transfer abroad of investments made in Lebanon by Community residents or in the Community by Lebanese residents and of any profit stemming therefrom shall not be affected.

Article 34

Where one or several Member States of the Community or Lebanon face or risk facing serious difficulties concerning balance of payments, the Community or Lebanon respectively may, in conformity with the conditions laid down within the framework of the GATT and Articles VIII and XIV of the Statutes of the International Monetary Fund, take restrictive measures with regard to current payments if such measures are strictly necessary. The Community or Lebanon, as appropriate, shall inform the other Party immediately thereof and shall provide as soon as possible a timetable for the removal of such measures.

Chapter 2
Competition and other Economic Matters

Article 35

1. The following are incompatible with the proper functioning of this Agreement, insofar as they may affect trade between the Community and Lebanon:

(a) all agreements between undertakings, decisions by associations of undertakings and concerted practices between undertakings which have as their object or effect the prevention, restriction or distortion of competition, as defined by their respective legislation;

(b) abuse by one or more undertakings of a dominant position in the territories of the Community or Lebanon as a whole or in a substantial part thereof, as defined by their respective legislation.

2. The Parties will enforce their respective competition legislation and shall exchange information taking into account the limitations imposed by the requirements of confidentiality. The necessary rules for cooperation in order to implement paragraph 1 shall be adopted by the Association Committee within five years of entry into force of this Agreement.

3. If the Community or Lebanon considers that a particular practice is incompatible with the terms of paragraph 1 of this Article, and if such practice causes or threatens to cause serious prejudice to the other Party, it

may take appropriate measures after consultation within the Association Committee or after thirty working days following referral for such consultation.

Article 36

The Member States and Lebanon shall progressively adjust, without prejudice to their commitments respectively taken or to be taken under the GATT, any State monopolies of a commercial character, so as to ensure that, by the end of the fifth year following the entry into force of this Agreement, no discrimination regarding the conditions under which goods are procured and marketed exists between nationals of the Member States and of Lebanon. The Association Committee will be informed about the measures adopted to implement this objective.

Article 37

With regard to public enterprises and enterprises to which special or exclusive rights have been granted, the Association Council shall ensure that as from the fifth year following the date of entry into force of this Agreement there is neither enacted nor maintained any measure distorting trade between the Community and Lebanon to an extent contrary to the Parties' interests. This provision should not obstruct the performance in law or in fact of the particular tasks assigned to these enterprises.

Article 38

1. Pursuant to the provisions of this Article and of Annex 2, the Parties shall ensure adequate and effective protection of intellectual, industrial and commercial property rights in conformity with the highest international standards, including effective means of enforcing such rights.

2. The implementation of this Article and of Annex 2 shall be regularly reviewed by the Parties. If problems in the area of intellectual property protection affecting trading conditions occur, urgent consultations shall be undertaken, at the request of either Party, with a view to reaching mutually satisfactory solutions.

Article 39

1. The Parties shall take as their aim a reciprocal and gradual liberalisation of public procurement contracts.

2. The Association Council shall take the steps necessary to implement paragraph 1.

Title V
Economic And Sector Cooperation

Article 40
Objectives

1. The two Parties shall together establish the strategies and procedures needed to achieve cooperation in the fields covered by this Title.

2. The Parties undertake to intensify economic cooperation in their mutual interest and in the spirit of partnership which is at the root of this Agreement.

3. The aim of economic cooperation shall be to support Lebanon's own efforts to achieve sustainable economic and social development.

Article 41
Scope

1. Cooperation shall be targeted first and foremost at areas of activity suffering the effects of internal constraints and difficulties or affected by the process of liberalising Lebanon's economy as a whole, and more particularly by the liberalisation of trade between Lebanon and the Community.

2. Similarly, cooperation shall focus on areas likely to bring the economies of the Community and Lebanon closer together, particularly those which will generate growth and employment.

3. Preservation of the environment and ecological balances shall constitute a central component of the various fields of economic cooperation.

4. The Parties may agree to extend the economic cooperation to other sectors not covered by the provisions of this Title.

Article 42
Methods and Modalities

Economic cooperation shall be implemented in particular by:

(a) a regular economic dialogue between the Parties, which covers all areas of macroeconomic policy;

(b) regular exchange of information and ideas in every sector of cooperation including meetings of officials and experts;

(c) transfer of advice, expertise and training;

(d) implementation of joint actions such as seminars and workshops;

(e) technical, administrative and regulatory assistance;

(f) the dissemination of information on cooperation.

Article 43
Education and Training

Cooperation aims at:

(a) defining the means to appreciably improve the situation in the field of education and training, particularly in vocational training;

(b) encouraging the setting up of strong links between agencies specialised in joint actions, and the exchange of experiences and know-how, essentially, the exchange of youth, exchanges between universities and other educational institutions, so as to bring cultures closer together;

(c) particularly encouraging access of the female population to education, including technical and higher education, and vocational training.

Article 44
Scientific, Technical and Technological Cooperation

The aim of cooperation shall be to:

(a) encourage the establishment of permanent links between the Parties' scientific communities, notably by means of:

- providing Lebanon with access to Community research and technological development programmes in accordance with Community rules governing non-Community countries' involvement in such programmes;
- Lebanese participation in networks of decentralised cooperation;
- promoting synergy between training and research;

(b) improve Lebanon's research capabilities; and its technological development;

(c) stimulate technological innovation and the transfer of new technology and dissemination of know-how;

(d) study the ways Lebanon can participate in European framework programmes for research.

Article 45
Environment

1. The Parties shall encourage cooperation in preventing deterioration of the environment, controlling pollution and ensuring the rational use of natural resources, with a view to ensuring sustainable development.

2. Cooperation shall be centred upon:

(a) water quality in the Mediterranean, and control and prevention of marine pollution,

(b) waste management, particularly that of toxic waste,

(c) salinisation,

(d) environmental management of sensitive coastal areas,

(e) environmental education and awareness,

(f) the use of advanced instruments for environmental management and monitoring, and in particular the use of the environment information system and studies on environmental impact,

(g) the effect of industrial development on the environment in general and on the safety of industrial plant in particular,

(h) the effect of agriculture on soil quality and water quality,

(i) soil preservation and conservation,

(j) rational management of water resources,

(k) joint research and monitoring activities as well as programmes and projects.

Article 46
Industrial Cooperation

The aim of cooperation shall be to:

(a) encourage cooperation between the Parties' economic operators, including cooperation in the context of access for Lebanon to Community business networks;

(b) support the effort to modernise and restructure Lebanon's public and private sector industry (including the agri-food industry);

(c) foster an environment which favours private initiative, with the aim of stimulating and diversifying output for the domestic and export markets;

(d) enhance Lebanon's human resources and industrial potential through better use of policy in the fields of innovation and research and technological development;

(e) facilitate access to capital markets to finance productive investment.

(f) encourage the development of SMEs, particularly by:

- promoting contacts between enterprises, partly by using Community networks and instruments for the promotion of industrial cooperation and partnership,

- facilitating credit access for financing investment,
- making information and support services available,
- enhance human resources to encourage innovation, and setting up projects and economic activities.

Article 47
Promotion and Protection of Investment

1. Cooperation shall aim at increasing the flow of capital, expertise and technology to Lebanon through, inter alia:

(a) appropriate means of identifying investment opportunities and information channels on investment regulations;

(b) providing information on European investment regimes (technical assistance, direct financial support, fiscal incentives, investment insurance, etc.) related to outward investment and enhancing the possibility of Lebanon to benefit from them;

(c) examining the creation of joint ventures (especially for small and medium-sized enterprises), and when appropriate the conclusion of agreements between the Member States and Lebanon;

(d) establishing mechanisms for encouraging and promoting investments;

(e) the development of a legal framework conducive to investment between the two Parties, through the conclusion by Lebanon and the Member States of investment protection agreements, where appropriate, and agreements preventing double taxation.

2. Cooperation may extend to the planning and implementation of projects demonstrating the effective acquisition and use of basic technologies, the use of standards, the development of human resources and the creation of jobs locally.

Article 48
Cooperation in Standardisation and Conformity Assessment

The Parties shall cooperate in:

(a) reducing divergences in standardisation, metrology, quality control and conformity assessment;

(b) developing the updating of Lebanese laboratories;

(c) negotiating mutual recognition agreements as soon as the conditions for them are met;

(d) strengthening the Lebanese institutions responsible for standardisation, quality, and intellectual, industrial and commercial property.

Article 49
Approximation of Legislation

The Parties shall use their best endeavours to approximate their respective laws in order to facilitate the implementation of this Agreement.

Article 50
Financial Services

The aim of cooperation shall be to achieve closer common rules and standards in areas including the following:

(a) developing the financial markets in Lebanon;

(b) improving accounting, auditing, supervision and regulation of financial services and financial monitoring in Lebanon.

Article 51
Agriculture and Fisheries

The aims of cooperation shall be:

(a) to support policies aiming to diversify production;

(b) to reduce food dependency;

(c) to promote a form of agriculture which pays due regard to the environment;

(d) to establish closer relations between enterprises, groupings and professional organisations of the two Parties;

(e) to provide assistance and technical training; support for agronomic research, advisory services, agricultural education and technical training of staff in the agricultural sector;

(f) to harmonise phytosanitary and veterinary standards;

(g) to support integrated rural development, including improvement of basic services and development of ancillary economic activities, particularly in the regions affected by the eradication of illicit crops;

(h) cooperation between rural areas, exchange of experience and know-how on rural development;

(i) development of sea fishing and aquaculture;

(j) development of packaging, storage and marketing techniques; and the improvement of distribution channels;

(k) to develop agricultural water resources;

(l) to develop the forestry sector, especially in the fields of reafforestation, forest fire prevention, forest pasture and combating desertification;

(m) to develop agricultural mechanisation and promotion of agricultural service cooperatives;

(n) to strengthen the agricultural credit system.

Article 52
Transport

The aim of cooperation shall be to:

(a) restructure and modernise road, rail, port and airport infrastructure linked to the main trans-European lines of communication of common interest;

(b) establish and enforce operating and safety standards comparable to those prevailing in the Community;

(c) upgrade technical equipment to Community standards for multimodal transport, container traffic and transshipment;

(d) improve road, maritime and multimodal transit and the management of ports, airports, sea and air traffic control, railways and navigation aids;

(e) reorganise and restructure of the mass transport sector including public transport.

Article 53
Information Society and Telecommunications

1. The Parties recognise that information and communication technologies constitute a key element of modern society, vital to economic and social development, and a cornerstone of the emerging information society.

2. Cooperation in this field shall aim at:

(a) a dialogue on the various aspects of the information society, including telecommunications policies,

(b) exchanges of information and technical assistance on regulatory matters, standardisation, conformity tests and certification as regards information technology and telecommunications technology,

(c) dissemination of new information and telecommunications technology, and of updated facilities for advanced communications, information services and technology,

(d) promotion and implementation of joint projects for research, technical development and industrial applications in information technologies, communications, telematics and the information society,

(e) the participation of Lebanese organisations in pilot projects and European programmes within the established frameworks,

(f) interconnection and interoperability between Community telematic networks and services and those of Lebanon,

(g) a dialogue on regulatory cooperation on international services, including aspects relating to protection of data and privacy.

Article 54
Energy

Cooperation shall focus on:

(a) promotion of renewable energy;

(b) promotion of energy-saving and energy efficiency;

(c) applied research relating to networks of databases linking the two Parties' economic and social operators;

(d) supporting modernisation and development of energy networks and the interconnection of such networks with Community networks.

Article 55
Tourism

Cooperation shall aim to:

(a) promote investment in tourism,

(b) improve the knowledge of the tourist industry and ensure greater consistency of policies affecting tourism,

(c) promote a good seasonal spread of tourism,

(d) highlight the importance of the cultural heritage for tourism,

(e) ensure that the interaction between tourism and the environment is suitably maintained,

(f) make tourism more competitive through support for increased standards and professionalism,

(g) enhance information flows,

(h) intensify training activities in hotel management and administration, and training in other hotel trades,

(i) organise exchanges of experience so as to ensure balanced, sustainable development of tourism, notably through exchanges of information, exhibitions, conventions and publications on tourism.

Article 56
Customs Cooperation

1. The Parties shall develop customs cooperation to ensure that the provisions on trade are observed. For this purpose they shall establish a dialogue on customs matters.

2. Cooperation will focus in particular on:

(a) the simplification of controls and procedures concerning the customs clearance of goods,

(b) the possibility of interconnection between the transit systems of the Community and of Lebanon,

(c) the exchange of information among experts and vocational training;

(d) technical assistance where appropriate.

3. Without prejudice to other forms of cooperation provided for in this Agreement, particularly in the fields of combating drug abuse and money laundering, the Contracting Parties' administrative authorities shall provide mutual assistance in accordance with the terms of Protocol 5.

Article 57
Cooperation in Statistics

The aim of cooperation shall be to harmonise methodology used by the Parties and to put to use data, including data-banks, on all areas covered by this Agreement for which statistics can be collected.

Article 58
Consumer Protection

Cooperation in this field should be geared to making consumer protection schemes in the Community and Lebanon compatible and should, as far as possible, involve:

(a) increasing the compatibility of consumer legislation in order to avoid barriers to trade,

(b) establishment and development of systems of mutual information on dangerous food and industrial products and interconnecting them (rapid alert systems),

(c) exchanges of information and experts,

(d) organising training schemes and supplying technical assistance.

Article 59
Cooperation in Reinforcement of Institutions and Rule of Law

The Parties reiterate the importance of the rule of law and the proper functioning of institutions at all levels in the areas of administration in general, and law enforcement and the machinery of justice in particular. An independent and effective judiciary and well-trained legal profession are of particular importance in this context.

Article 60
Money Laundering

1. The Parties agree on the necessity of making every effort to cooperate to prevent the use of their financial systems for laundering of proceeds from criminal activities in general and drug offences in particular.

2. Cooperation in this area may include administrative and technical assistance aimed at establishing effective standards and their efficient implementation in the area of combating money laundering in line with international standards.

Article 61
Prevention and Fight Against Organised Crime

1. The Parties agree to cooperate in order to prevent and fight organised crime, in particular in the following fields: human trafficking; exploitation for sexual purposes; corruption; the counterfeit of financial instruments; the illicit traffic of prohibited, counterfeited or pirated products and of illegal transactions concerning in particular industrial refuse or radioactive material; the trafficking of firearms and explosives; computer criminality; stolen cars.

2. Parties shall cooperate closely in order to establish appropriate mechanisms and standards.

3. Technical and administrative cooperation in this field will include training and the strengthening of the effectiveness of the authorities and structures responsible for fighting and for preventing criminality and the formulation of measures for crime prevention.

Article 62
Cooperation on Illicit Drugs

1. Within their respective powers and competencies, the Parties shall cooperate to ensure a balanced and integrated approach towards drugs. Drug

policies and actions shall be aimed at reducing the supply, trafficking and demand of illicit drugs as well as at a more effective control of precursors.

2. The Parties shall agree on the necessary methods of cooperation to attain these objectives. Actions shall be based on commonly agreed principles along the lines of the five basic principles endorsed at the United Nations General Assembly Special Session on Drugs of 1998 (UNGASS).

3. Cooperation between the Parties may comprise technical and administrative assistance in particular in the following areas: drafting of national legislation and policies; establishment of institutions and information centres; training of personnel; drug related research; and the prevention of diversion of precursors used for the illicit manufacture of drugs. The Parties may agree to include other areas.

Title VI
Cooperation in Social and Cultural Matters

Chapter 1
Dialogue and Cooperation in the Social Field

Article 63

The two Parties shall decide together on the methods needed to achieve cooperation in the fields covered by this Title.

Article 64

1. The Parties shall conduct regular dialogue on any social matter which is of interest to them.

2. This dialogue shall be used to find ways to achieve progress in the field of movement of workers and equal treatment and social integration of Lebanese and Community nationals legally residing in the territories of their host countries.

3. The dialogue shall notably cover all issues related to:

(a) the living and working conditions of the migrant communities;

(b) migration;

(c) illegal immigration;

(d) schemes and programmes to encourage equal treatment between Lebanese and Community nationals, mutual knowledge of cultures and civilisations, the furthering of tolerance and the removal of discrimination.

Article 65

1. With a view to consolidating cooperation between the Parties in the social field, projects and programmes shall be carried out in any area of interest to them, including:

(a) improving living conditions, particularly in disadvantaged areas and areas whose population has been displaced;

(b) promoting the role of women in the economic and social development process, particularly through education and the media;

(c) bolstering and developing Lebanon's family planning and mother and child protection programmes;

(d) improving the social security and health insurance systems,

(e) improving the health care system, notably through cooperation in the field of public health and prevention, health security and medical training and management;

(f) implementing and financing exchange and leisure programmes for mixed groups of Lebanese and European young people, youth workers, youth NGO representatives, and other experts in the youth field residing in the Member States, with a view to promoting mutual knowledge of their respective cultures and fostering tolerance.

2. The Parties shall engage in a dialogue on all aspects of mutual interest, and particularly on social problems such as unemployment, rehabilitation of the less able-bodied, equal treatment for men and women, labour relations, vocational training, safety and health at work.

Article 66

Cooperation schemes may be carried out in coordination with Member States and relevant international organisations.

Chapter 2
Cooperation in Cultural Matters, Audiovisual Media and Information

Article 67

1. The Parties agree to promote cultural cooperation in fields of mutual interest and in a spirit of respect for each other's cultures. They shall

establish a sustainable cultural dialogue. This cooperation shall promote in particular:

(a) conservation and restoration of historic and cultural heritage (monuments, sites, artefacts, rare books and manuscripts, etc.),

(b) exchange of art exhibitions and artists,

(c) training of persons working in the cultural field.

2. Cooperation in the field of audiovisual media shall seek to encourage cooperation in such areas as co-production and training. The Parties shall seek ways to encourage Lebanese participation in Community initiatives in this sector.

3. The Parties agree that existing cultural programmes of the Community and of one or more of the Member States and further activities of interest to both sides, can be extended to Lebanon.

4. The Parties shall in addition, work to promote cultural cooperation of a commercial nature, particularly through joint projects (production, investment and marketing), training and exchange of information.

5. The Parties shall, in identifying cooperation projects, programmes and joint activities, give special attention to young people, self-expression, heritage conservation issues, the dissemination of culture, and communication skills using written and audiovisual media.

6. Cooperation shall be implemented in the way set out in Article 42.

Chapter 3
Cooperation for the Prevention and Control of Illegal Immigration

Article 68

1. The Parties agree to cooperate in order to prevent and control illegal immigration. To this end:

(a) each of the Member States agrees to readmit any of its nationals present on the territory of Lebanon, upon request by the latter and without further formalities once such persons have been positively identified as such,

(b) Lebanon agrees to readmit any of its nationals illegally present on the territory of a Member State, upon request by the latter and without further formalities once such persons have been positively identified as such.

The Member States and Lebanon will also provide their nationals with appropriate identity documents for such purposes.

2. In respect of the Member States of the European Union, the obligation in this Article applies only in respect of those persons who are to be considered their nationals for Community purposes in accordance with the Treaty establishing the European Community.

3. In respect of Lebanon, the obligation in this Article applies only in respect to those persons who are considered Lebanese in accordance to the Lebanese legal system and all the relevant laws concerning citizenship.

Article 69

1. After the entry into force of this Agreement, the Parties, at the request of any of them, shall negotiate and conclude bilateral agreements with each other, regulating specific obligations for the readmission of their nationals. These agreements shall also cover, if deemed necessary by any of the Parties, arrangements for the readmission of third country nationals. Such agreements will lay down details about categories of persons covered by these arrangements as well as the modalities of their readmission.

2. Adequate financial and technical assistance to implement these agreements may be provided to Lebanon.

Article 70

The Association Council shall examine what other joint efforts can be made to prevent and control illegal immigration.

Title VII
Financial Cooperation

Article 71

1. With a view to full attainment of this Agreement's objectives, financial cooperation shall be considered for Lebanon in line with the appropriate financial procedures and resources.

2. These procedures shall be adopted by mutual agreement between the Parties by means of the most suitable instruments once this Agreement enters into force.

3. In addition to the areas covered by Titles V and VI of this Agreement, cooperation may entail inter alia:

(a) facilitating reforms aimed at modernising the economy,

(b) rebuilding and updating economic infrastructure,

(c) promoting private investment and job creation activities,

(d) taking into account the effects of the progressive introduction of a free trade area on the Lebanese economy, in particular where the updating and restructuring of the affected economic sectors, especially industry, is concerned,

(e) flanking measures for policies implemented in the social sectors, particularly for reform of social security.

Article 72

Within the framework of Community instruments intended to buttress structural adjustment programmes in the Mediterranean countries—and in close coordination with the Lebanese authorities and other contributors, in particular the international financial institutions—the Community will examine suitable ways of supporting structural policies carried out by Lebanon to restore financial equilibrium in all its key aspects and create an economic environment conducive to boosting growth, while at the same time enhancing social welfare.

Article 73

In order to ensure a coordinated approach to dealing with the exceptional macroeconomic and financial problems which could stem from the progressive implementation of this Agreement, the Parties shall closely monitor the development of trade and financial relations between the Community and Lebanon as part of the regular economic dialogue established under Title V.

Title VIII
Institutional, General and Final Provisions

Article 74

1. An Association Council is hereby established which shall meet at ministerial level when circumstances require, on the initiative of its Chairman and in accordance with the conditions laid down in its rules of procedure.

2. The Association Council shall examine any major issues arising within the framework of this Agreement and any other bilateral or international issues of mutual interest.

Article 75

1. The Association Council shall consist of the members of the Council of the European Union and members of the Commission of the European

Communities, on the one hand, and of members of the Government of Lebanon, on the other.

2. Members of the Association Council may arrange to be represented, in accordance with the provisions laid down in its rules of procedure.

3. The Association Council shall establish its rules of procedure.

4. The Association Council shall be chaired in turn by a member of the Council of the European Union and a member of the Government of Lebanon in accordance with the provisions laid down in its rules of procedure.

Article 76

1. The Association Council shall, for the purpose of attaining the objectives of this Agreement, have the power to take decisions in the cases provided for therein.

2. The decisions taken shall be binding on the Parties, which shall take the measures necessary to implement the decisions taken. The Association Council may also make appropriate recommendations.

3. The Association Council shall draw up its decisions and recommendations by agreement between the two Parties.

Article 77

1. Subject to the powers of the Association Council, an Association Committee is hereby established which shall be responsible for the implementation of this Agreement.

2. The Association Council may delegate to the Association Committee, in full or in part, any of its powers.

Article 78

1. The Association Committee, which shall meet at the level of officials, shall consist of representatives of members of the European Union and of the Commission of the European Communities, on the one hand, and of representatives of the Government of Lebanon, on the other.

2. The Association Committee shall establish its rules of procedure.

3. The Association Committee shall normally meet alternately in the Community and in Lebanon.

Article 79

1. The Association Committee shall have the power to take decisions for the management of this Agreement as well as in the areas in which the Association Council has delegated its powers to it.

2. The Association Committee shall draw up its decisions by agreement between the Parties. These decisions shall be binding on the Parties, which shall take the measures necessary to implement the decisions taken.

Article 80

The Association Council may decide to set up any working group or body necessary for the implementation of this Agreement. It shall define the terms of reference of any such working group or body that shall be subordinated to it.

Article 81

The Association Council shall take all appropriate measures to facilitate cooperation and contacts between the European Parliament and the Lebanese Parliament, and between the Economic and Social Committee of the Community and its counterpart in Lebanon.

Article 82

1. Each of the Parties may refer to the Association Council any dispute relating to the application or interpretation of this Agreement.

2. The Association Council may settle the dispute by means of a decision.

3. Each Party shall be bound to take the measures involved in carrying out the decision referred to in paragraph 2.

4. In the event of it not being possible to settle the dispute in accordance with paragraph 2, either Party may notify the other of the appointment of an arbitrator; the other Party must then appoint a second arbitrator within two months. For the application of this procedure, the Community and the Member States shall be deemed to be one Party to the dispute.

The Association Council shall appoint a third arbitrator.

The arbitrators' decisions shall be taken by majority vote.

Each Party to the dispute must take the steps required to implement the decision of the arbitrators.

Article 83

Nothing in this Agreement shall prevent a Party from taking any measures:

(a) which it considers necessary to prevent the disclosure of information contrary to its essential security interests;

(b) which relate to the production of, or trade in, arms, munitions or war materials or to research, development or production indispensable for defence purposes, provided that such measures do not impair the conditions of competition in respect of products not intended for specifically military purposes;

(c) which it considers essential to its own security in the event of serious internal disturbances affecting the maintenance of law and order, in time of war or serious international tension constituting threat of war or in order to carry out obligations it has accepted for the purpose of maintaining peace and international security.

Article 84

In the fields covered by this Agreement, and without prejudice to any special provisions contained therein:

(a) the arrangements applied by Lebanon in respect of the Community shall not give rise to any discrimination between the Member States, their nationals, or their companies or firms,

(b) the arrangements applied by the Community in respect of Lebanon shall not give rise to any discrimination between Lebanese nationals or its companies or firms.

Article 85

As regards direct taxation, nothing in this Agreement shall have the effect of:

(a) extending the fiscal advantages granted by either Party in any international agreement or arrangement by which it is bound,

(b) preventing the adoption or application by either Party of any measure aimed at preventing fraud or the evasion of taxes,

(c) opposing the right of either Party to apply the relevant provisions of its tax legislation to taxpayers who are not in an identical situation, in particular as regards their place of residence.

Article 86

1. The Parties shall take any general or specific measures required to fulfil their obligations under this Agreement. They shall see to it that the objectives set out in this Agreement are attained.

2. If either Party considers that the other Party has failed to fulfil an obligation under this Agreement, it may take appropriate measures. Before so doing, except in cases of special urgency, it shall supply the Association Council with all the relevant information required for a thorough examination of the situation with a view to seeking a solution acceptable to the Parties.

3. In the selection of the appropriate measures referred to in paragraph 2, priority must be given to those which least disturb the functioning of this Agreement. The Parties also agree that these measures shall be taken in accordance with international law and shall be proportional to the violation.

These measures shall be notified immediately to the Association Council and shall be the subject of consultations within the Association Council if the other Party so requests.

Article 87

Annexes 1 and 2 and Protocols 1 to 5 shall form an integral part of this Agreement.

Article 88

For the purposes of this Agreement, "Parties" shall mean, on the one hand, the Community, or the Member States, or the Community and its Member States, in accordance with their respective powers, and Lebanon, on the other hand.

Article 89

1. This Agreement shall be concluded for an unlimited period.

2. Either Party may denounce this Agreement by notifying the other Party. This Agreement shall cease to apply six months after the date of such notification.

Article 90

This Agreement shall apply, on the one hand, to the territories in which the Treaty establishing the European Community is applied and under the conditions laid down in that Treaty and, on the other hand, to the territory of Lebanon.

Article 91

This Agreement is drawn up in duplicate in the Arabic, Danish, Dutch, English, Finnish, French, German, Greek, Italian, Portuguese, Spanish, and Swedish languages, each of these texts being equally authentic. It shall be deposited with the General Secretariat of the Council of the European Union.

Article 92

1. This Agreement shall be approved by the Parties in accordance with their own procedures.

2. This Agreement shall enter into force on the first day of the second month following the date on which the Parties notify each other that the procedures referred to in paragraph 1 have been completed.

3. Upon its entry into force, this Agreement shall replace the Cooperation Agreement between the European Economic Community and the Republic of Lebanon and the Agreement between the Member States of the European Coal and Steel Community and Lebanon, signed in Brussels on 3 May 1977.

Article 93
Interim Agreement

In the event that, pending the completion of the procedures necessary for the entry into force of this Agreement, the provisions of certain parts of this Agreement, in particular those relating to the free movement of goods, are put into effect by means of an Interim Agreement between the Community and Lebanon, the parties agree that, in such circumstances, for the purposes of Titles II and IV of this Agreement and Annexes 1 and 2 and Protocols 1 to 5 thereto, the terms "date of entry into force of this Agreement" mean the date of entry into force of the Interim Agreement in relation to obligations contained in these Articles, Annexes and Protocols.

DOCUMENT NO. 16

EUROPEAN COUNCIL: EURO-MEDITERRANEAN AGREEMENT ESTABLISHING AN ASSOCIATION BETWEEN THE EUROPEAN COMMUNITY AND ITS MEMBER STATES AND THE REPUBLIC OF LEBANON

Final Act 7293/02 ADD 2
Council of the European Union

Brussels, 18 April 2002

LEGISLATIVE ACTS AND OTHER INSTRUMENTS

Subject: Euro-Mediterranean Agreement establishing an Association between the European Community and its Member States, of the one part, and the Republic of Lebanon, of the other part – Final Act

Final Act

The Plenipotentiaries of:

THE KINGDOM OF BELGIUM,

THE KINGDOM OF DENMARK,

THE FEDERAL REPUBLIC OF GERMANY,

THE HELLENIC REPUBLIC,

THE KINGDOM OF SPAIN,

THE FRENCH REPUBLIC,

IRELAND,

THE ITALIAN REPUBLIC,

THE GRAND DUCHY OF LUXEMBOURG,

THE KINGDOM OF THE NETHERLANDS,

THE REPUBLIC OF AUSTRIA,

THE PORTUGUESE REPUBLIC,

THE REPUBLIC OF FINLAND,

THE KINGDOM OF SWEDEN,

THE UNITED KINGDOM OF GREAT BRITAIN AND NORTHERN IRELAND,

Contracting Parties to the Treaty establishing the European Community and the Treaty on European Union, hereinafter referred to as "the Member States", and of

THE EUROPEAN COMMUNITY, hereinafter referred to as "the Community",

of the one part, and

the Plenipotentiaries of THE REPUBLIC OF LEBANON, hereinafter referred to as "Lebanon"

of the other part,

meeting in .... on .... in the year two thousand and two for the signature of the Euro-Mediterranean Agreement establishing an Association between the European Community and its Member States, of the one part, and the Republic of Lebanon, of the other part, hereinafter referred to as "the Agreement",

have at the time of signature adopted the following texts:

the Agreement,

its Annexes 1 and 2, namely:

ANNEX 1 List of agricultural and processed agricultural products falling under HS chapters 25 to 97 referred to in articles 7 and 12

ANNEX 2 Intellectual, industrial and commercial property referred to in Article 38 and Protocols 1 to 5, namely:

PROTOCOL 1 concerning arrangements applicable to imports into the Community of agricultural products originating in Lebanon referred to in Article 14(1)

PROTOCOL 2 concerning arrangements applicable to imports into Lebanon of agricultural products originating in the Community referred to in Article 14(2)

PROTOCOL 3 on trade between Lebanon and the Community in processed agricultural products referred to in Article 14(3)

ANNEX 1 concerning arrangements applicable to imports into the Community of processed agricultural products originating in Lebanon

ANNEX 2 concerning arrangements applicable to imports into Lebanon of processed agricultural products originating in the Community

PROTOCOL 4 concerning the definition of the concept of "originating products" and methods of administrative cooperation

PROTOCOL 5 on mutual administrative assistance in customs matters

The Plenipotentiaries of the Member States of the Community and the Plenipotentiaries of Lebanon have also adopted the following Declarations attached to this Final Act:

JOINT DECLARATIONS

Joint Declaration relating to the Preamble of the Agreement

Joint Declaration relating to Article 3 of the Agreement

Joint Declaration on Article 14 of the Agreement

Joint Declaration relating to Article 27 of the Agreement

Joint Declaration relating to Article 28 of the Agreement

Joint Declaration relating to Article 35 of the Agreement

Joint Declaration relating to Article 38 of the Agreement

Joint Declaration relating to Article 47 of the Agreement

Joint Declaration relating to Article 60 of the Agreement

Joint Declaration relating to Workers (Article 65 of the Agreement)

Joint Declaration relating to Article 67 of the Agreement

Joint Declaration relating to Article 86 of the Agreement

Joint Declaration relating to visas

DECLARATIONS BY THE EUROPEAN COMMUNITY

Declaration by the European Community on Turkey

Declaration by the European Community relating to Article 35 of the Agreement

Joint Declarations

Joint Declaration Relating to the Preamble of the Agreement

The Parties declare their awareness of the fact that liberalisation of trade between them implies measures to adapt and restructure the Lebanese economy which may have effects on budgetary resources and the speed of Lebanon's reconstruction.

Joint Declaration Relating to Article 3 of the Agreement

The Parties reiterate their intention to support efforts to achieve an equitable, comprehensive and lasting peace settlement in the Middle East.

Joint Declaration on Article 14 of the Agreement

Both Parties agree to negotiate with a view to granting each other concessions in the trade of fish and fishery products on the basis of reciprocity and mutual interest, with the objective of reaching agreement on the details no later than two years after the signature of this Agreement.

Joint Declaration Relating to Article 27 of the Agreement

The Parties confirm their intention to prohibit the export of toxic waste and the European Community confirms its intention to assist Lebanon in seeking solutions to the problems posed by such waste.

Joint Declaration Relating to Article 28 of the Agreement

In order to take account of the time-scale necessary for setting up the free trade areas between Lebanon and the other Mediterranean countries, the Community undertakes to give favourable consideration to requests presented to it for anticipated application of the diagonal cumulation with those countries.

Joint Declaration Relating to Article 35 of the Agreement

The implementation of cooperation mentioned in Article 35 paragraph 2 is conditional upon the entry into force of a Lebanese competition law and of the taking up of the duties of the authority responsible for its application.

Joint Declaration Relating to Article 38 of the Agreement

The Parties agree that for the purpose of the Agreement, intellectual, industrial and commercial property includes in particular copyright, including the copyright in computer programmes, and neighbouring rights, the rights relating to databases, the rights relating to patents, industrial designs, geographical indications, including designations of origin, trademarks and service marks, topographies of integrated circuits, as well as protection against unfair competition as referred to in Article 10 Bis of the Paris Convention for the Protection of Industrial Property and protection of undisclosed information on know-how.

The provisions of Article 38 shall not be interpreted in a manner to oblige either Party to accede to international conventions other than those referred to in Annex 2.

The Community will grant technical assistance to the Lebanese Republic in its endeavour to comply with its obligations under Article 38.

Joint Declaration Relating to Article 47 of the Agreement

The Parties recognise the need to modernise the Lebanese productive sector in order to adapt it better to the realities of the international and of the European economy.

The Community may give its support to Lebanon in implementing a support programme for the industrial sectors which are to benefit from restructuring and modernisation in order to cope with difficulties which may stem from the liberalisation of trade and in particular the dismantling of tariffs.

Joint Declaration Relating to Article 60 of the Agreement

The Parties agree that the standards established by the Financial Action Task Force (FATF) are part of the international standards referred to in paragraph 2.

Joint Declaration Relating to Workers (Article 65 of the Agreement)

The Parties reaffirm the importance they attach to fair treatment of foreign workers legally employed on their territory. The Member States agree that, if Lebanon so requests, they are each prepared to negotiate bilateral Agreements relating to the working conditions, remuneration, dismissal and social security rights of Lebanese workers legally employed on their territory.

Joint Declaration Relating to Article 67 of the Agreement

The Parties declare that special attention will be accorded to protection, conservation and restoration of sites and monuments.

They agree to cooperate in seeking to ensure the return of those parts of the Lebanese cultural heritage illegally removed from the country since 1974.

Joint Declaration Relating to Article 86 of the Agreement

(a) The Parties agree, for the purpose of the correct interpretation and practical application of the Agreement, that the term "cases of special urgency" in Article 86 means a case of the material breach of the Agreement by one of the Parties. A material breach of the Agreement consists in:

- repudiation of the Agreement not sanctioned by the general rules of international law,

- violation of the essential element of the Agreement, namely its Article 2.

(b) The Parties agree that the "appropriate measures" referred to in Article 86 are measures taken in accordance with international law. If a Party takes a measure in a case of special urgency as provided for under Article 86, the other Party may avail itself of the procedure relating to settlement of disputes.

Joint Declaration Relating to Visas

The Parties agree to study the simplification and acceleration of visa issue procedures, in particular with regard to bona-fide persons active in the implementation of the Agreement, including inter alia business persons, investors, academics, trainees, government officials; spouses and minor children of persons legally resident in the territory of the other Party shall also be considered.

Declarations by the European Community

Declaration by the European Community on Turkey

The Community recalls that according to the Customs Union in force between the Community and Turkey, this country has the obligation, in relation to countries which are not members of the Community, to align itself on the Common Customs Tariff and, progressively, with the preferential customs regime of the Community, taking the necessary measures and negotiating agreements on mutually advantageous basis with the countries concerned. Consequently, the Community invites Lebanon to enter into negotiations with Turkey as soon as possible.

Declaration by the European Community Relating to Article 35 of the Agreement

The European Community declares that, in the context of the interpretation of Article 35(1), it will assess any practice contrary to that Article on the basis of the criteria resulting from the rules contained in Articles 81 and 82 of the Treaty establishing the European Community, including secondary legislation.

DOCUMENT NO. 17

EUROPEAN NEIGHBOURHOOD POLICY

EU-Lebanon Action Plan

January 19, 2007

1. Introduction

The enlargement of the European Union (EU) on 1 May 2004 has brought a historical shift for the Union in political, geographic and economic terms. The EU and Lebanon are now closer together than ever before and, as near neighbours, will reinforce their political and economic interdependence. Enlargement offers the opportunity for the EU and Lebanon to develop an increasingly close relationship, going beyond co-operation, to involve a significant measure of economic integration and deepening of political co-operation. The European Union and Lebanon are determined to make use of this occasion to enhance their relations and to promote stability, security and well-being. The approach is founded on partnership, joint ownership and differentiation.

The European Neighbourhood Policy of the European Union sets ambitious objectives based on commitments to shared values and effective implementation of political, economic, social and institutional reforms.

Lebanon is invited to enter into intensified political, security, economic and cultural relations, and shared responsibility in conflict prevention and conflict resolution.

The level of ambition of the EU-Lebanon relationship will depend on the degree of Lebanon's commitment to common values as well as its capacity to implement jointly agreed priorities, in compliance with international and European norms and principles. The pace of progress of the relationship will acknowledge fully Lebanon's efforts and concrete achievements in meeting those commitments.

The European Neighbourhood Policy is part of the European Union's response to the Government of Lebanon's Ministerial Declaration which was approved by the Parliament end of July 2005. The Government presented its broad agenda of essential political and economic reforms to the International Community in September 2005. On this basis the Government undertook to prepare a multi-annual political and economic programme containing more detailed, concrete reform measures. The challenge for the Government is to ensure the implementation of the "national agenda" of priorities and objectives through appropriate programmes of political and economic reforms. These objectives should be met through a process led by the Lebanese and reflected in Lebanon's own reform programme, and supported, where necessary by the international Community, including the European Union. The European Neighbourhood Policy offers through its Action Plan a strategic tool for the EU to accompany Lebanon in its reform process.

This Action Plan is a first step in this process. It is a political document, laying out the strategic objectives of cooperation between Lebanon and the EU. It covers a timeframe of five years. Its implementation will help fulfil the provisions in the Association Agreement (AA) and will encourage and support Lebanon's national reform objectives and further integration into European economic and social structures.

The Action Plan will be taken forward in the context of our common commitment to achieving a comprehensive, just and lasting peace in the Middle East, acknowledging the important objective of restoring Lebanon's full sovereignty and territorial integrity, in accordance with International Law and relevant United Nations Resolutions. It is also in this context that a solution to the Palestinian refugee issue in Lebanon will be found.

Implementation of the Action Plan will significantly advance the approximation of Lebanon's legislation, norms and standards to those of the European Union. It will also build solid foundations for further economic integration based on the adoption and implementation of economic and trade-related rules and regulations with the potential to enhance trade and investment with the EU. Such measures will be consistent with the efforts already being made by the Lebanese authorities, with support from the International Community to devise and implement policies and measures to promote economic growth, employment and social cohesion, to reduce poverty and to protect the environment, thereby contributing to the long-term objective of sustainable development.

The execution of the Action Plan requires a serious commitment from the political authority to endorse and implement an administrative reform that improves the efficiency and effectiveness of public administration: Special emphasis must be put on control, accountability and transparency to achieve "good governance". This requires an update of legislation; especially with regard to redefining the missions and responsibilities of the

Ministries and public agencies and consequently restructuring these organisations and mobilising competent and motivated human resources.

Lebanon and the EU will cooperate closely in implementing this Action Plan.

New Partnership Perspectives

The European Neighbourhood Policy opens New Partnership Perspectives:

- The perspective of moving beyond cooperation to a significant degree of economic integration, including through a stake in the EU's Internal Market, and the possibility for Lebanon to participate progressively in key aspects of EU policies and programmes.
- An upgrade in the scope and intensity of political cooperation in particular through a regular political dialogue.
- The opportunity for convergence of economic legislation, the opening of economies to each other, and the continued reduction of trade barriers which will stimulate investment and growth.
- Increased financial support: EU financial assistance for Lebanon will be better targeted to support the actions identified in the present document, mainly to support the political and economic reform agenda of the Lebanese Government. The Commission has furthermore proposed a new European Neighbourhood and Partnership Instrument (ENPI) for this purpose, also covering the very important aspect of cross-border cooperation. The EIB will also help support infrastructure investment and private sector development and partnership through the Facility for Euro-Mediterranean Investment and Partnership (FEMIP). Possibilities of gradual opening of or reinforced participation in relevant Community programmes, promoting i.a. cultural, educational, environmental, technical and scientific links.
- Support including technical assistance and twinning to meet EU norms and standards and targeted support and advice for legislative approximation through mechanisms such as TAIEX.
- Deepening trade and economic relations, extending them progressively to cover agriculture and the service sector, and to provide the conditions for increasing investment and exports.
- Enhanced direct cooperation between administrations based on the bodies set up by the Association Agreement in particular institutionalised thematic sub-committees.

In light of the fulfilment of the objectives of this Action Plan and of the overall evolution of EU–Lebanon relations, consideration will be given to the possibility of a new contractual relationship. The Commission has suggested that this could take the form of a European Neighbourhood Agreement. The advisability of any new contractual arrangements will be considered in due time.

Priorities for Action

This Action Plan sets out a comprehensive set of priorities in areas within the scope of the Association Agreement. Among these priorities, all of which are important, particular attention should be given to:

- Enhance political dialogue and co-operation, based on shared values, including issues such as democracy and political life promoting the protection of human rights, consolidating the freedom of media and expression.
- Continue to develop an independent and impartial judiciary and to further reinforce the administrative capacity of the judiciary.
- Establish a comprehensive human rights strategy, including protection of rights of minorities, marginalised populations and non-citizens.
- Take steps to develop further freedom of media and freedom of expression.
- Cooperate to promote cross-cultural dialogue and understanding.
- Further promote equal treatment of women, including by preparing a plan to increase women's participation in political and economic life as well as eliminating all forms of discrimination against women.
- Strengthen political dialogue and co-operation on issues of international and regional interest including the Middle East Peace Process, the fight against terrorism and the proliferation of weapons of mass destruction.
- Take steps to bring the fiscal position to a sustainable basis while reducing the debt burden and improving public finance management.
- Take measures to improve business conditions to enhance growth, increase investment and to create jobs in Lebanon.
- Enhance Lebanon's export potential by further liberalisation of trade in goods and agriculture, simplifying and upgrading customs legislation and procedures, improving industrial standards and modernisation of the sanitary and phytosanitary systems.
- Prepare for progressive liberalisation of trade in services and right of establishment.
- Improved cooperation on the management of migratory flows and dialogue on visa issues.
- Strengthen the environmental dimension of public policy and EU-Lebanon co-operation.

- Promote sustainable development policies and actions, and design and implement a comprehensive social development strategy that contributes to poverty reduction.
- Develop the transport, energy, water and information society sectors and networks through sector liberalisation, investment in infrastructures and interconnection with EU networks.
- Strengthen co-operation on science and technology.

Progress in meeting these priorities will be jointly monitored in sub-committees established by the Association Agreement. The European Commission will issue a mid-term report on progress accomplished.

2. Actions

2.1. Political Dialogue and Reform

Democracy and Rule of Law

Work together to promote the shared values of democracy and the rule of law including good governance and transparent, stable and effective institutions.

- Pursue the ongoing reform efforts aiming at a more effective and efficient public sector, including streamlining of procedures.
- Support ongoing efforts to improve good governance and transparency in line with the relevant UN Conventions to which Lebanon is a party.
- Establish a political dialogue between the European Parliament and the Lebanese Parliament.
- Implement plans for decentralization and local government reform.

Fight against corruption

- Exchange information on ratification and implementation of the UN Convention against Corruption and other relevant international instruments.
- Strengthen measures against corruption through the effective implementation of a national anti-corruption strategy, including the institutional framework and the enforcement capacity and public awareness and advocacy.
- Promote cooperation on anti-corruption matters between the Lebanese law enforcement agencies and international organisations as well as with corresponding services of the EC and EU Member States.

Reform of the electoral law and the election framework

- Promote the establishment of a comprehensive strategy for reform of the system of political representation and the election framework, including fair representation of women, taking into account the recommendations set out in the final report of the EU Election Observation Mission.

- Strengthen the election system addressing electoral and other laws, election administration, and the election complaints system, and develop ways to improve media access.
- Develop joint cooperation and exchange of experience in the field of elections.

Further enhancement of the independence and impartiality, the capacity and efficiency of the judiciary, upgrade its quality and strengthen administrative capacity

- Develop a comprehensive strategy for judicial reform, and implement measures to strengthen the capacity and efficiency of the justice administration and of bodies entrusted with the implementation of the law; improve access to justice and competences within the court system.
- Improve detention and prison conditions to meet international standards.

Human Rights and Fundamental Freedoms

- Promote a comprehensive human rights strategy, including protection of rights of minorities, marginalised populations and non-citizens.
- Strengthen institutions guaranteeing the protection and defence of human rights.
- Ensure effective implementation of Lebanon's international commitments with respect to human rights and fundamental freedoms.
- Work towards improving the cooperation with the relevant UN treaty bodies and the implementation of their recommendations.
- Develop the human rights Ombudsman institution.
- Establish a dialogue for cooperation on Human Rights and Democratisation in the framework of the Association Agreement.
- Ensure the conduct of informal exchanges of views with representatives in the permanent missions at UN Headquarters before the meetings of the UN Human Rights Council and of the UN General Assembly where appropriate, as part of the overall Euro-Mediterranean Human Rights dialogue.
- Examine the possibility of acceding to the optional protocols and of lifting reservations regarding the core UN Human Rights Conventions to which Lebanon is a party.
- Engage in a dialogue on aspects of the death penalty, including adherence to the Second Optional Protocol to the International Covenant on Civil and Political Rights.

Support freedom of media and strengthening freedom of expression

- Intensify ongoing efforts to promote freedom of expression and independence of the media.

Support freedom of assembly, association and Development of Civil Society

- Intensify ongoing efforts to promote effective freedom of assembly and association by reforming the administrative framework.
- Promote development of civil society and strengthen its capacity to contribute more effectively to the democratic and political process and to economic and social progress.

Fight against torture including implementation of UN Conventions

- Explore the possibility of acceding to the optional protocol to the UN Convention against Torture and Other Cruel, Inhuman or Degrading treatment or punishment.
- Strengthen effective enforcement of legal provisions against torture.

Promotion and protection of the rights of women and children

- Promote the enhancement of women's participation in political, economic and social life as well as their role in the political decision-making process.
- Promote gender equality, in particular in the field of employment and reinforce the fight against discrimination and gender-based violence, including review of legislation on personal status, nationality and penal code.
- Discuss the lifting of reservations to the Convention on the elimination of all forms of discrimination against women (CEDAW) to which Lebanon is a party.
- Promote the rights of the child; apply the UN Convention on the Rights of the Child, and revise existing legislation taking into account the recommendations of the relevant UN Committee.
- Accede to the optional protocol to the UN Convention on the Rights of the Child on the Involvement of Children in Armed Conflict.
- Develop a child welfare strategy and related national action plans and formulate a child protection policy targeting neglected and abused children.
- Enhance protection of rights of children and intensify efforts to progressively eliminate child labour.

Fight against discrimination, racism, religious intolerance, xenophobia and racial hatred discourse

- Cooperate in the fight against discrimination, racism, xenophobia and racial hatred discourse.
- Cooperate to promote cross-cultural dialogue and understanding.

Promotion of fundamental social rights and decent work including core labour standards

- Develop a dialogue on fundamental social rights and decent work including the role and independence of trade unions.
- Ensure adherence to and enhance the effective implementation of core labour standards as defined in the 1998 ILO Declaration on Fundamental Principles and Rights at Work and related ILO Conventions.
- Ensure implementation of the relevant International Labour Conventions to which Lebanon is party.

Security Sector Reform

- Develop the administrative capacity of core security actors including law enforcement institutions; security management and oversight bodies, justice institutions.
- Ensure consistency of the management and operation of the security system with respect for human rights and democratic norms.

Co-operation on Foreign and Security Policy

Strengthen political dialogue and co-operation on Common Foreign and Security Policy matters

- Develop an enhanced political dialogue and regular ex-change of information on Common Foreign and Security Policy (CFSP) and European Security and Defence Policy (ESDP) matters.s
- Work with the EU to make multilateral institutions and conventions more effective, so as to reinforce global governance; strengthen coordination in combating security threats and address related development issues.
- Accede to the Rome Statute of the International Criminal Court and make the necessary legislative amendments for its implementation, while preserving its integrity.

Regional and International Issues, Conflict Prevention and Crisis Management

Strengthen dialogue and cooperation on regional and international issues, conflict prevention and crisis management and common security threats in accordance with national law

- Establish contact points and carry out exchanges of information on ESDP matters with the Secretariat of the Council and the Commission.
- Contribute to UN efforts and work together to resolve regional conflicts and promote effective multilateralism.

- Further develop co-operation in the context of the Middle East Peace Process with the ultimate objective of reaching a just, comprehensive and durable peace in accordance with the relevant UN resolutions.
- Promote the objective of reaching, once conditions are favourable, a Euro-Mediterranean Peace and Stability Charter.
- Participate in training activities on conflict prevention, crisis and natural disaster management.

Non-proliferation of weapons of mass destruction (WMD) and their means of delivery and illegal arms exports

- Cooperate on non-proliferation of weapons of mass destruction, their means of delivery and ballistic missiles, including through implementing UNSC Resolution 1540/04, ensuring full compliance with and national implementation of existing international obligations and promoting the accession to and implementation of other relevant international instruments.
- Further develop co-operation in the prevention of and fight against the illicit trafficking of WMD and their means of delivery, and related materials.
- Co-operate on developing effective systems of national export control, controlling export and transit of materials related to WMD and their means of delivery, as defined in UNSCR 1540, including WMD end-use control on dual use of goods and technologies, and effective sanctions for breaches of export controls.
- Improve overall coordination in the non-proliferation area and the scope of cooperation in addressing this challenge.
- Promote the relevant provisions on the political and security partnership of the Barcelona Declaration with the objective to pursue a mutually and effectively verifiable Middle East zone free of weapons of mass destruction and their delivery systems.
- Improve internal legislation in line with the EU Code of Conduct on Arms Exports.
- Explore the possibility of acceding, when conditions permit, to the 1997 Ottawa Convention on the Prohibition of the Use, Stockpiling, Production and transfer of Anti-Personnel Mines and on their Destruction.

Cooperation on preventing and combating terrorism

- Strengthen EU-Lebanon co-operation on the fight against and prevention of terrorism.
- Ensure respect of human rights in the fight against terrorism based on the recommendations of the relevant UN bodies.

- Cooperate to reinforce the role of the UN in the multilateral fight against terrorism, including through implementation of all relevant UNSC Resolutions and through signature, ratification and full implementation of all relevant UN Conventions.
- Ensure the implementation of the standards laid down in the recommendations of the Financial Action Task Force (FATF) on terrorist financing.
- Pursue efforts to arrive at a Comprehensive UN Convention on Combating Terrorism.
- Exchange information on terrorist groups and their support networks.
- Exchange views on means and methods used to counter terrorism, including in technical fields and training, and by exchange of experiences in respect of terrorism prevention, with the objective of promoting national capacity building in the field of terrorism prevention.
- Explore means and initiatives to foster international cooperation in the fight against and the prevention of terrorism by addressing all the factors which contribute to terrorism.

2.2. Economic and Social Reform and Sustainable Development

(a) Fiscal Policies, Monetary and Exchange Rate Policy

Short Term

Fiscal sustainability and macro-economic stability

- Pursue fiscal consolidation and enhance fiscal discipline.
- Adopt and implement a comprehensive debt reduction strategy.
- Develop and implement a national macroeconomic stabilisation programme.

Medium-Term

- Create macroeconomic conditions for sustainable growth.
- Improve the quality of public finances and introduce tools for medium term budget planning.
- Implement policies for achieving sustainable public finances addressing the issue of quasi-fiscal deficit and contingent liabilities.

(b) Functioning of Market Economy

Short-Term

- Enhance the performance and competitiveness of the Lebanese economy.
- Implement actions to improve contract enforcement and property rights.

Improve the business environment and investment climate to enable firms to invest, create jobs and expand

- Develop and implement a strategy to promote investment.
- Improve the regulatory framework and reduce the red tape.
- Implement actions to facilitate SME access to finance.

Progress with the establishment of fully functioning market economy

- Restructure public utilities, implement the privatisation programme and increase the transparency of the privatisation process;.

Improve transparency and accountability of public administration including in the area of public finance management

- Improve public finance and management in line with the recommendations of the CFAA.
- Publish complete and timely information on the budget, fiscal outcomes and audit reports.
- Continue work on methodology, scope and quality of statistics.

Medium-Term

Create conditions for an employment generating growth

(c) Social Development, Employment and Poverty Reduction

Short-Term

Accompanying social measures to economic reforms

- Engage in a dialogue on employment and social issues including the social consequences of economic reforms, with a view to developing possible measures in this field.
- Strengthen social safety nets and reform the social security system, improving their efficiency, targeting and coverage while progressively reducing subsidies, tax exemptions and economic distortions.

Medium-Term

Enhance Social development and Co-operation and address unemployment

- Adopt a comprehensive strategy for social development and poverty reduction. Improve statistical data related to poverty, among others on poverty survey, households' income and expenditures and regional disparities.
- Develop a strategy for reforming the pension system.

- Develop reform and strategic plans aiming at improving the quality of education and vocational training and their relevance to the labour market.
- Develop and implement market driven strategies, involving social partners, to address unemployment and increase the participation of women and youth in the labour force; modernise the National Employment Office.
- Strengthen social dialogue at all levels (tripartite and bipartite).
- Engage in a dialogue on programmes and initiatives aimed at fostering social inclusion and fight against discrimination, with particular attention to marginalised groups.
- Improve public service delivery particularly in health and education and other social services with access for all, and avoid the duplication of government subsidies between the public and the private sectors.

(d) Agriculture

- Identify and adopt accompanying measures providing for the structural, institutional, legal and administrative support necessary in order to ease access to export markets, including approximation of technical legislation.
- Identify and adopt measures and appropriate legislation in the sector of rural development, and at the level of the development of quality production i.e. local products, organic products, geographical indications, with the aim of encouraging the diversification of activity and the creation of new remunerative and sustainable trade flows.
- Increase co-operation in the field of international marketing standards for fruits and vegetables, and for other agricultural and processed agricultural products; promote equivalence schemes of certification for organic products.
- Develop measures to encourage private investment.
- Strengthen the administrative capacity of the land cadastre.
- Address the role of agricultural research centres in improving the productivity, food safety and quality, of agricultural and processed agricultural products; promote cooperation with European Research Centres, particularly in the areas of genetic engineering and biotechnology.
- Promote the distribution and exchange of information on the agricultural policies and contribute to the transfer of expertise and experience.
- Promote the use of modern technology in the agricultural sector and in different production phases.

(e) Fisheries

- Reinforce cooperation to implement the actions identified in the Declaration of the Ministerial Conference for the Sustainable Development of Fishery in the Mediterranean (Venice, 25–26 November 2003) in the framework of the relevant international instruments.
- Promote further the creation of fishermen associations with a view to implementing responsible fisheries; improve their capacity to be represented in international and multilateral organisations.
- Increase the scientific and technical capacity to monitoring fisheries and evaluate the state of the exploited marine resources and marine environment.
- Improve scientific cooperation with the Regional Fisheries Body and in particular the GFCM to strengthen a concerted and regional approach suited to the needs of sustainable fisheries.
- Undertake necessary marketing infrastructure upgrading to cope with market demands and standards.

(f) Regional Development

Medium-Term

Strengthening socio-economic cohesion of Lebanon's regions

- Develop a programme for Regional Development, including expanding economic activities beyond the Greater Beirut area.
- Strengthen the regional development management structures, and re-examine the role of the regional councils and funds.

(g) Sustainable Development

Promotion of sustainable development

- Develop a comprehensive strategy for sustainable development.
- Establish the administrative structures and procedures for strategic planning and coordination.
- Ensure integration of sustainable development into sectoral policies.

2.3. Trade Related Issues, Market and Regulatory Reform

2.3.1. Movement of Goods

(a) Trade Relations

Liberalisation of trade in goods

- Continue work towards the objective of WTO accession.

- Identify areas with export potential to the EU; further enhance export potentials by increasing the quality of Lebanese products and their competitiveness on international markets.
- Strengthen the capacity of the Lebanese administration on international trade relations.
- Participate in regional and sub-regional trade initiatives including conclusion and implementation of FTAs.
- Establish rules of procedure for dispute settlement under the Association Agreement on economic/trade matters.

(b) Agriculture and Fisheries

- Further progressive liberalisation of trade in agriculture, processed agricultural products and fisheries products, building on the Rabat roadmap and in coherence with the reform process in agriculture and rural development.

(c) Customs

- Further harmonisation and simplification of customs legislation and procedures in accordance with WTO rules and the Palermo recommendations, including computerisation with further upgrading and rolling out of the NAJM and NOOR systems to the whole customs territory.
- Strengthen co-operation between customs and other agencies working at the border to develop an Integrated Border Management Strategy.
- Reinforce customs controls on imports and exports of pirated or counterfeit goods.
- Adopt and implement the Pan-Euro-Med Protocol of origin allowing participation in the cumulation system; provide training on the application of the new protocol.
- Strengthen co-operation with the EU to combat irregularities and fraud in customs and related matters.
- Develop EU-Lebanon co-operation with regard to risk based customs control ensuring safety and security of goods imported, exported or in transit; define standards for certification of operators (exporters and transporters) intervening in commercial exchanges.
- Provide the customs administration with sufficient internal or external laboratory expertise.
- Adopt and implement a Customs Ethics Policy based on the Arusha Declaration.

(d) Standards and Conformity Assessment (EU Harmonised Areas)

- Implement the Palermo Action Plan for the Free Movement of Industrial Products of July 2003. Prepare for negotiations on an Agreement on Conformity Assessment and Acceptance of Industrial Products.
- Strengthen the administrative capacity of institutions in charge of implementing product legislation.
- Strengthen the administrative and technical capacity of the Lebanese Standards Institution (LIBNOR), conformity assessment bodies (including the Industrial Research Institute) and the accreditation body (COLIBAC).
- Ensure harmonisation of national standards with European and international standards for industrial products.
- Converge towards EU legislation on liability for defective products and general product safety including market surveillance.

(e) Restrictions and Streamlined Administration (EU Non-Harmonised Areas)

- Analyse legislation and administrative procedures to identify and progressively remove discrimination and restrictions against imported products.
- Designate a central contact point to facilitate information flows and co-operation with economic operators.

(f) Sanitary and Phytosanitary Issues

Increase food safety for Lebanese and European consumers and facilitate trade through reform and modernisation of the sanitary and phytosanitary sectors

- Upon accession to the WTO, implement the WTO Agreement on the Application of Sanitary and Phytosanitary measures and participate in relevant international bodies.
- Exchange information on and explore possible areas of convergence with EU practice in the field of sanitary and phyto-sanitary issues.
- Progressive fulfilment of EU requirements on animal health and for the processing of animal products (c.f.: Import Conditions—Importing Live Animals).
- In the medium-term, draw up a first list of measures for gradual convergence towards EU general food safety principles and requirements; start approximation of Lebanese legislation in this area.

2.3.2. Right of Establishment, Company Law and Services

(a) Establishment and Company Law

- Review national legislation with a view to identify measures to facilitate establishment of companies, including foreign-owned companies. Work towards the progressive removal of barriers to establishment.
- Adopt and implement new bankruptcy legislation.
- Strengthen corporate governance, in particular for public companies, in line with international standards.
- Work towards the adoption of international and EU relevant accounting and auditing standards and the promotion of a highly qualified audit profession.

(b) Services

- Pursue bilateral negotiations on services and establishment in accordance with the Association Agreement and the Marrakesh Ministerial Declaration.
- Develop a strategy to enhance the competitiveness of the Lebanese services sector including regulatory simplification and administrative facilitation for Lebanese and EU sectors.
- Facilitate the supply of services including the development of the necessary administrative structures and the removal of identified barriers.

Financial services

- Continue the implementation of the Financial Services Assessment Programme (FSAP).
- Work together to train independent authorities to ensure effective supervision.

2.3.3. Movement of Capital and Current Payments

- Provide information, and jointly assess, the national regime for capital movements and current payments (including the restrictions referred to in Art 33.1 of the Association Agreement).
- Exchange views and experiences concerning liberalization of capital movements.
- Ensure the protection of foreign investments.

2.3.4. Regional Co-operation

- Develop conditions for south-south trade and regional or sub-regional co-operation initiatives; promote trade and investment among the regional partners.

2.3.5. Other Key Areas

(a) Taxation

- Continue the modernization and simplification of the tax administration, including addressing the necessary administrative structures and procedures.
- Continue efforts to develop the network of bilateral agreements between Lebanon and EU Member States on avoidance of double taxation, taking into consideration Lebanon's specificity, including the improvement of transparency and the exchange of information in accordance with international standards.
- Gradual approximation of the national tax legislation with the principles of the EU acquis. Depending on the level of Lebanon's access to the Internal Market, adopt and comply with the principles of the Code of Conduct for Business Taxation.

(b) Competition Policy and State Aid

Antitrust

- Adopt and enforce the draft competition law and establish an independent and adequately-resourced competition authority.

State aids

- Develop a system to exchange with the EU an annual report on the total amount and distribution of State aid, based on a binding, uniform definition of State aid which is compatible with that of the EU and a national mechanism for collecting information on state aid.
- For sectors participating in the internal market ensure a State aids control regime and legislation meeting the requirements of the EU acquis.

(c) Intellectual and Industrial Property

- Ensure a level of protection of Intellectual and Industrial property rights similar to that of the EU and strengthen enforcement of legislation in accordance with Art 38 of the Association Agreement.
- Adhere, within the agreed timeframe, to the international agreements and conventions stipulated in the Association Agreement.
- Introduce new legislation, notably on trademarks and geographical indications, to ensure conformity with TRIPS requirements.
- Strengthen the administrative capacity for enforcement of legislation and implementation of sanctions.

- Reinforce the fight against counterfeiting and piracy in selected areas, notably through an increase in seizures and improve cooperation among relevant authorities involved, including the police, customs and judiciary.
- Increase awareness at both public and private level. Extend cooperation with third countries authorities, industry associations and organisations of rights holders and users of Intellectual Property.

(d) Statistics

- Ensure that legislation on official statistics is in line with the fundamental UN principles.
- Adopt a National Statistical Master Plan ensuring harmonisation with European and International standards, including means for its implementation, in the relevant areas, covered by this Action Plan (demography, national accounts, living conditions; prices and balance of payments etc).

(e) Public Procurement

- Improve the functioning of the current system; increase transparency, information, limited use of exceptions and easy access to judicial review. Extend its scope to all levels of the public sector.
- Improve training of contracting authorities and the business community.
- Initiate reform of the existing public procurement legislation with a view to adopt key EU and international principles of transparency, information, non-discrimination, open competition, and access to remedies procedures.
- Cooperation with the EU on the introduction of modern tendering procedures, including e-procurement.

(f) Enterprise Policy

- Improve business conditions including through the implementation of the Euro-Mediterranean Charter for Enterprise.
- Work towards implementation of the October 2004 strategy of the Euro-Mediterranean Working Programme on Industrial Cooperation.
- Create a dialogue between business, administration and academic institutions for the identification of priority actions for business improvement and the exchange of best practice.

(g) Public Finance Reform, Including Public Internal Financial Control

Accounting, Fight against Fraud and control of EU-funds

- Improve compliance of the public sector with international public sector accounting standards to improve efficiency, accountability, transparency and predictability.

- Fight against fraud and other irregularities affecting national and international funds; adopt a modern anti-corruption law and strengthen the relevant administrative and judicial structures.
- Ensure cooperation with the relevant EU Institutions and bodies in the management and control of EU funds.

Public Internal Financial Control

- Establish a Central Audit Coordination unit within the Ministry of Finance; develop a strategy and policy paper for the public internal financial control system (managerial accountability and decentralised internal audit).
- Establish the legislative framework for public internal financial control.
- Pursue gradual harmonization with the internationally agreed standards (IFAC, IIA, INTOSAI) and methodologies, as well as with EU best practices for the control and audit of public income, expenditure, assets and liabilities.
- Ensure and publish regular audits, along the best international standards, of the CDR, the National Social Security Fund and the Municipal Development Fund.
- Introduce internal audit units in all budgetary entities, in line with agreed strategy.

External Audit

- Further strengthen the administrative and procedural capacity of the Court of Accounts; focus its role on external audits solely (work on attest, systems-based and performance audits of public sector bodies); strengthen the independence of the Court of Accounts by ensuring that it reports to and having its budget approved by Parliament.

2.4. Co-operation in the Field of Justice, Freedom and Security

Further develop co-operation between Lebanon and EU Member States' judicial and law enforcement authorities

(a) Migration Issues (legal and Illegal Migration, Readmission, Visa, Asylum)

Establish a dialogue on migration issues with a view to maximise the benefits of migration both for Lebanon and the EU

- Develop a comprehensive and balanced dialogue on various migration-related issues of interest, including asylum, movement of persons, control of illegal migration and return, visas.

- Monitoring and analysis of migration: ensure synergy with Euro-Med initiatives on research on migration and the Consortium on Applied Research on International Migration (CARIM) in particular.
- Possible participation of Lebanon in relevant Community programmes, including the AENEAS programme.

Manage legal migration, admission policy and stay, social integration of migrants

- Establish a dialogue on legal migration to exchange information on admission policies and stay, work on offer and skills available in Lebanon, employment opportunities and procedures in Europe and the procedures and integration (including non-discrimination, protection from xenophobia, etc.).
- Provide information on the risks of smuggling and trafficking of migrants.
- Improve the linkages between migration and development: ensure dialogue and cooperation on the possible role of diasporas in the development of the country of origin, on facilitating remittance flows and their productive uses, or the impact of migration of trained persons on the country of origin.

Prevent and control illegal immigration into Lebanon and the European Union

- Exchange information and experiences on illegal migration including the scale of illegal immigration into and via Lebanon and monitor migratory movements; review policies for the return of migrants in an illegal situation; support activities to prevent and counter illegal migration, including by sea.
- Strengthen cooperation with the EU, countries of the region and countries of origin to prevent and fight illegal migration; ensure close coordination with actions concerning countries of origin.
- Exchange information and cooperate on transit migration.

Improve cooperation regarding readmission of own nationals, stateless persons and third country nationals

- Improve cooperation between the EU and Lebanon on all forms of readmission including the possibility of negotiating a readmission agreement between Lebanon and the EC and its Member States.
- Cooperate on consular affairs and issuing of travel documents.

Movement of persons

- Improve cooperation on the management of migratory flows.
- Cooperate on facilitating the movement of persons in conformity with the EU acquis, in particular examining the scope for facilitating visa

procedures for short stay for some categories of persons travelling to Europe or vice-versa.

- Cooperate to improve the security of travel documents and visas in conformity with international standards.

Initiate a dialogue on asylum and international protection issues

- Mindful of the special circumstances of the Palestinian refugee presence in Lebanon, cooperate to improve their economic and social situation.
- Start developing a comprehensive protection system, in line with international standards, to process and follow-up on asylum applications.
- Exchange information and best practices on asylum policy and international protection issues.

(b) Border Management

Enhance border management cooperation with neighbouring countries and the EU Member States

- Develop a strategy for an integrated system of Border Management, enhancing interagency cooperation, in particular with regard to the implementation of a common risk strategy and to the coordination of controls, as well as cooperation with neighbouring countries, including proper border demarcation.
- Improve the administrative capacity at border crossing checkpoints; develop effective surveillance along the green and the blue border; ensure provision of training, modern equipment, adequate infrastructure and facilities.
- Develop a comprehensive education and training strategy with regard to border management matters.
- Develop cross border and regional co-operation between relevant law enforcement agencies (police, border guards, migration and asylum services and customs).
- Initiate contacts for cooperation at the operational and technical level between Lebanon border authorities and FRONTEX.

(c) Fight Against Organised Crime (Including Trafficking in Human Beings)

Enhance international co-operation in accordance with the UN Convention against Transnational Organised Crime and its protocols on smuggling of migrants and trafficking in persons and on illicit manufacturing and trafficking of firearms

- Implement the UN Convention against Trans-national Organised Crime and its Protocols on smuggling migrants, trafficking in persons and illicit manufacturing and trafficking in firearms.

- Develop national provisions in line with relevant international standard and conventions.
- Establish a network of contact points with EU Member States' law enforcement authorities to promote co-operation, in particular to exchange information.
- Exchange expertise and experiences on best practices in combating organised crime, in particular with regard to trafficking in persons; exchange information on patterns and modus operandi, enhance public awareness, foster cooperation with countries of origin and transit, enhance police and judicial cooperation in witness protection programmes and assistance to victims.
- Develop law enforcement and judicial cooperation between the EU Member States and Lebanon in this field. Cooperate in the field of training.

Cooperate in the fight against cyber crime

- Co-operate to fight cyber crime, including child pornography.

Reinforce the fight against trafficking in human beings, especially women and children, and smuggling of illegal migrants, as well as activities to prevent trafficking in human beings and to reintegrate victims

- Promote regional and trans-border co-operation between relevant law enforcement bodies (police, border guards, customs and judiciary).
- Develop protection mechanisms, legal and social assistance and psychological support to victims aiming at their reintegration.

(d) Fight Against Drugs

Continue the fight against illicit drug trafficking, including precursor diversion, and against drug abuse in particular through prevention and rehabilitation, in accordance with the 1988 UN Convention on Illicit Traffic of Narcotic and Psychotropic Substances and with Art.58 of the AA

- Exchange information on the implementation of the 1988 UN Convention on illicit traffic of Narcotics and Psychotropic substances and on national anti-drug strategy covering drug supply and demand, including prevention programmes to combat drug addiction and programmes for treatment of drug addicts.
- Develop international cooperation in fight against trafficking narcotics and drug addiction, in particular prevention of drug abuse, treatment and rehabilitation of drug addicts.
- Cooperate on preventing drug precursor diversion.
- Cooperate on the implementation of the relevant UN Conventions.

(e) Fight Against Money laundering

Strengthen efforts and co-operation in the fight against money laundering in line with the standards laid down by the Financial Action Task Force (FATF)

- Exchange information on the existing European structures (Financial Intelligence Unit) and the existing system in Lebanon as regards the fight against money laundering.
- Intensify co-operation and promote exchange of information among law enforcement agencies and between Lebanon and international organisations, such as the Middle East and North Africa Financial Action Task Force, as well as with corresponding bodies in EU Member States.
- Strengthen Lebanon's system of financial information with particular emphasis on the monitoring of cash movements and wire transfers abroad.
- Identify administrative/technical support and training requirements for the development of the capacities of the Lebanese Financial Investigation Unit on combating money laundering.

(f) Combating Terrorism

- Implement the counter-terrorism related UN Resolutions and Conventions.
- Cooperate to implement the provisions of the Euro-Mediterranean Code of conduct on countering terrorism.
- Develop cooperation to strengthen the fight against the financing of terrorism in line with the standards laid down by the FATF recommendations on terrorism financing.
- Develop cooperation between Lebanon and EU Member States' counter-terrorism and law enforcement agencies.
- Develop judicial cooperation on combating terrorism.
- Work together to fight the use of the Internet for terrorist purposes.

(g) Judicial Cooperation

- Exchange information on ratification and implementation of relevant international conventions related to co-operation in criminal and civil matters.
- Develop judicial cooperation between Lebanon and EU Member States' courts in civil and criminal matters, in particular with regard to family law.
- Promote concrete solutions of family disputes in order to prevent and resolve conflicts with regard to custody, visiting rights and child abduction of children of mixed couples; promote mediation, judicial cooperation and judicial training.

2.5. Transport, Energy and Environment, Including Water

(a) Transport

Implement the National Transport Policy

- Further develop the national transport policy for the development of all modes of transport and related infrastructure, emphasizing the importance of sustainability. Ensure intermodality and integration of all transport modes. Examine the possibility of further approximation of legislative and regulatory frameworks with European and International standards, in particular for safety and security.
- Strengthen and if necessary establish the administrative structures to prepare specific plans for priority sectors and develop the necessary independent regulatory authorities.
- Develop an infrastructure policy to identify the priority infrastructure projects in various sectors as well as addressing financing issues.

Regional or sub-regional element

- Participate in the Euro-Mediterranean regional transport project.
- Continue participation in the development of GNSS (Galileo) in the Mediterranean region, in particular by giving an active role to the Galileo Euromed Cooperation Office based in Cairo; take part in particular in the new regional cooperation activities on satellite navigation systems.
- Participate in the planning and identification of priority regional infrastructure projects and their connection with trans-European transport networks.

Implement selected measures and reforms in the road an rail transport sectors

- Introduce a transparent regulatory process for the issue of freight and passenger transport licences and for access to the profession.
- Develop an integrated action plan on road safety including the technical control/road worthiness testing of vehicles.
- Implement the relevant international conventions, notably on dangerous goods transport.
- Develop a policy on the restoration and upgrading of the railway network, separating regulatory responsibilities from operational interests; promote multimodal services and address issues of interoperability (also with regional networks).

Implement selected measures and reforms in the aviation sector

- Implement the existing national aviation policy including the development of the airports and further reinforce administrative capacity (including the establishment of an autonomous Civil Aviation Authority as a pure regulator).

- Start negotiations on a comprehensive EU-Lebanon aviation agreement once such a negotiating mandate is given to the EU side.
- Assess and examine the possibility introducing at all airports open competition in ground-handling services.
- Reinforce the current level of liberalisation of charter and scheduled flights.
- Enhance administrative and technical capacity to fully implement jointly agreed JAA standards. Involve Lebanon in the work of EASA and for involvement in the Single European Sky.
- Co-operate on aviation security matters (common rules to combat international terrorism).

Regional or sub-regional element

- Take part in regional cooperation on safety, security and air traffic management.

Implement selected measures and reforms in the maritime sector

- Further develop and implement a comprehensive national maritime policy aiming at promoting and developing the maritime industry, increasing its competitiveness and promoting the participation of private sector in all aspects of maritime industry, including ports and port activities; strengthen maritime safety and security and develop the fleet; continue to implement the relevant international conventions; and approximate standards to EU legislation.
- Develop and implement the organisational reform of the ports sector with a view to introduction of an independent port authority responsible for regulation and control and an increase in the efficiency of ports.
- Assess and examine the possibility of introducing VTMIS (Vessel Traffic Management and Information Service).
- Ensure effective co-operation in maritime security by focusing on the SOLAS/ISPS Code implementation requirements.
- Continue enforcing effective maritime safety measures through efficient implementation of Port State Control and Flag State Implementation systems.
- Speed up the phasing-out of single-hull oil tankers and apply without exception the changes recently agreed in the IMO Marpol Convention.

Regional or sub-regional element

- Further develop co-operation with EU and Mediterranean partners in the framework of IMO, and promote the participation in the new regional project on maritime safety and security (SAFEMED).

- Participate in regional cooperation in the field of maritime policy, ports and short-sea shipping.
- Continue participating in the regional cooperation on Motorways of the Sea.

(b) Energy

Develop a long term energy strategy converging towards EU energy policy objectives

- Take steps to adopt and implement a long term energy strategy converging towards EU energy policy objectives and covering, inter alia, all subsectors, the strengthening of institutions and financing.
- Explore the medium-term possibility for participation in the Intelligent Energy-Europe programme.

Gradual convergence towards the principles of the EU internal electricity and gas market

- Further restructure and as appropriate privatise the electricity sector.
- Take steps to improve the financial and operational performance of Electricity de Liban.
- Improve bill collection rates and work towards the gradual elimination of energy price distortions, while taking due account of social consequences.
- Further assess gas import sources in line with the Declaration of Intent of 2 December 2003 on the Euro-Mashrek cooperation in the field of natural gas.
- Establish a first list of measures for gradual convergence towards the principles of the EU internal electricity and gas markets.
- Establish an energy regulatory body independent from market operators.
- In the medium term, complete electricity sector reform and start to implement measures for gradual convergence towards the principles of the EU internal electricity and gas markets.

Oil sector reform/restructuring refinery sector

- Study options for the development of the oil sector including restructuring of the refinery sector.

Progress on energy networks

- Further rehabilitate electricity transmission and distribution networks and reduce network losses.
- Assess the feasibility of developing gas distribution networks for the introduction of gas for households.

- Further develop regional energy (gas, oil, electricity) networks (eg. completion of the gas pipeline from Syria (GASYLE I) and the offshore national gas pipeline "GASYLE II") in line with the Declaration of Intent of 2 December 2003 on the Euro-Mashrek cooperation in the field of natural gas.
- Improve safety and security of energy infrastructure.
- Further develop electricity networks in rural areas.

Progress on energy efficiency and the use of renewable energy sources

- Take steps to develop an Action Plan including a financial plan for improving energy efficiency and enhancing the use of renewable energy.
- Reinforce the institutions dealing with energy efficiency and renewable energy sources.
- Pursue measures in energy efficiency and renewable energy sources.
- Progress to reach Lebanon's target to ensure that 10% of the country's energy needs are covered by the year 2015 by renewable energy sources.

Regional cooperation

- Cooperate, in the context of the Declaration of Intent of 2 December 2003 on the Euro-Mashrek cooperation in the field of natural gas including as regards the development of a regional Gas Master Plan.
- Explore possibilities for Euro-Mashrek cooperation in the electricity field.

(c) Environment, Including Water

Good environmental governance: ensure environmental security by protecting vital interests of individuals, society and natural environment from adverse human and natural impact as well as development trends that threaten sustainable functioning of ecosystems and functioning of human health

- Take steps to strengthen administrative structures, and procedures to ensure strategic planning of environmental issues, including financing strategies, and co-ordination between relevant actors.
- Finalise the National Environment Action Plan.
- Establish procedures regarding access to environmental information and public participation.
- Adopt implementing legislation on environmental assessments; reinforce structures and procedures to carry out environmental assessments.
- Prepare regular reports on the state-of-the-environment.
- Implement the environmental education and awareness plan.

- Support private sector and civil society actors as well as local authorities operating in the environmental sector.

Take active action for prevention of deterioration of the environment, protection of human health, and achievement of rational use of natural resources, in line with the commitments of the World Summit on Sustainable Development

- Develop framework and secondary (implementing) legislation and basic procedures and ensure planning for key environmental sectors (in line with the NEAP)—including e.g. water quality, waste management, nature protection).
- Strengthen administrative capacities including for issuing of permits as well as for enforcement and inspection.
- Implement national plans and programmes (e.g. the National Biodiversity Strategy and Action Plan).
- Take steps to apply methodologies and practices of integrated water management and integrated coastal zone management.
- Take steps to establish a national environmental monitoring network (e.g. air quality).

Integrated water resources management

- Improve the quantity and the quality of water supply from both surface and ground sources by developing integrated plans, programmes and projects that ensure environmental protection, social stability and welfare, and economic development.
- Enhance the management of the demand on water from all sectors (municipal and touristic, industrial, agricultural and environmental).
- Protect surface and ground water resources from all sources of pollution.
- Establish a nation-wide surface and ground water—quantity and quality—monitoring network to accurately control surface and groundwater level and quality.

Enhance co-operation on environmental issues

- Implement provisions under the UN Framework Convention on Climate Change and the Kyoto Protocol.
- Ratify the amendments to the Barcelona Convention and its Land-Based Sources and Dumping Protocols; sign the new Emergency Protocol and the Specially Protected Areas and Biodiversity Protocol.
- Possible participation in selected European Environment Agency activities.
- Participation in the De-Pollution Initiative for the Mediterranean Sea (Horizon 2020).

- Work together to address regional and transboundary water resource management issues, including within relevant international frameworks, and identify possibilities with neighbouring countries for enhanced co-operation in this regard, as well as on desertification issues.

2.6. Information Society, Media, and Science and Research

(a) Information Society and Media

Progress in the areas of electronic communications policy and regulation

- Adopt a comprehensive regulatory framework for electronic communications services and establishment of an independent regulatory authority.
- Liberalise the market for fixed voice telephony.

Progress in the areas of advanced infrastructure and services as well as in scientific cooperation

- Deploy a broadband network in order to promote widespread Internet access.
- Introduce on-line services, such as e-Government, e-Health, e-Business, e-Learning, etc.
- Ensure awareness raising for the participation of Lebanese entities in the Information Society Technologies (IST) part of the EU Research Framework Programme.

Progress in the areas of audiovisual policy and regulation

- Promote an exchange of views on audiovisual policy, including co-operation in the fight against racism, religious intolerance, and xenophobia.
- Develop a transparent, efficient and predictable regulatory system including through the establishment of an independent regulatory authority in the audiovisual sector.

(b) Science and Technology, Research and Development

Develop Lebanon's capacity in technological R&D to support the economy and society

- Develop a Research and Innovation policy relevant to the sustainable and equitable economic development policy objectives of Lebanon and its region, including reform of the scientific system and of the relevant regulatory framework.
- Reinforce human, material and institutional resources in order to improve the capacities in technological R&D; ensure adequate and increased investment in research through the public sector as well as through the private sector.

Prepare and encourage Lebanon's integration into the European Research Area and into the Community R&D Framework Programmes on the basis of scientific excellence

- Implement an appropriate information strategy to facilitate and encourage adequate participation of Lebanese research entities in the Community R&D Framework Programmes and joint projects; ensure a policy-driven dialogue to determine the particular priorities and the specific needs of Lebanon.
- Cooperate in high-level scientific exchanges; reinforce participation in international Marie Curie fellowships including support of the appropriate return mechanisms.

2.7. People-to-People Contacts

(a) Education, Training and Youth

Continue and enhance efforts to reform and modernise education and vocational training systems within the framework of Lebanese plans, in order to promote competitiveness, employability and mobility, to bring Lebanon closer to EU standards and practice

- Continue and enhance a policy dialogue between Lebanon and the EU on education and training.
- Ensure access for all, especially for the poor, to high quality education.
- Reform primary, secondary and vocational education to improve quality; ensure human resources development for teachers, professors and administrative bodies.
- Enhance the adaptation of higher and vocational education to the needs of the labour market inter alia by increasing the involvement of entrepreneurs, social partners and stakeholders from civil society.
- Reform higher education in line with the principles of the "Bologna process", in particular as regards definition and implementation of a homogeneous system of evaluation and quality assurance. Build institutional capacity for policy development and implementation. Develop new curricula for science and information technology. Promote reform of higher education and cooperation between higher education institutions in the EU and Lebanon through the TEMPUS programme.
- Enhance the capacities of institutions and organisations involved in developing and implementing quality assurance in the field of education and training, by using for example the tools offered by the TEMPUS programme.
- Encourage student mobility through participation in the Erasmus Mundus programme and the new scholarship programme.

Enhance co-operation in the field of youth and sports

- Enhance a dialogue between EU and Lebanon in the field of youth policy.
- Encourage youth mobility by promoting youth exchanges and enhance cooperation with the EU in the field of non-formal education for young people and promotion of intercultural dialogue.
- Promote a dialogue between the EU and Lebanon in the field of sports including exchange of experience with EU Member States.
- Promote the exchange of young professionals between European and Lebanese bodies.
- Ensure the successful implementation of the Euro-Med Youth programme by setting up of the relevant structures by Lebanon.

(b) Culture

Enhance cultural co-operation and dialogue between cultures

- Enhance participation in the relevant EC cultural cooperation programmes of the Euro-Med partnership.
- Exchange views on the UNESCO Convention on protection and promotion of the diversity of cultural expressions and promote the ratification and implementation of the text.
- Enhance dialogue between cultures, taking into consideration the principles embodied in the Action Programme for the Dialogue between Cultures and Civilizations, adopted by the Valencia Ministerial Meeting in April 2002 and taking advantage of the Anna Lindh Euro-Mediterranean Foundation for the dialogue between cultures.
- Encourage dialogue and exchange of information on cultural issues between the parties, inter alia at local level.

(c) Civil Society Co-Operation

- Examine the scope for further improving the legal and administrative framework for the operation of civil society organizations.
- Ensure Lebanese NGOs contributing effectively to the economic, political and social development process in accordance with national legislation.
- Empower consumers and protect their legitimate economic interests.

(d) Public Health

Improve the health sector through reform

- Pursue health sector reform (e.g. enhance national capacities, increase sector efficiency, improve primary health care, enhance access for the poor in particular in rural areas, health financing reform).

Increase the level of health security, health information and knowledge

- Exchange of information and know-how on health indicators and data collection.
- Participate, as observer, in the meetings of the Network of Competent Authorities.

Communicable Disease Surveillance and Health Security (Epidemiological Surveillance and Control)

- Participate, gradually, in the European Communicable Disease and dedicated surveillance networks.

3. Monitoring

The Action Plan will guide the work between the EU and Lebanon. Should the need arise, on the EU side, for specific measures necessitating legally binding decisions, the Commission will recommend to the Council the adoption of the necessary negotiating directives.

The joint bodies established under the Association Agreement will advance and monitor the implementation of the Action Plan on the basis of regular reports on its implementation.

A first review of the implementation of the Action Plan will be undertaken within two years of its adoption.

The Action Plan can be jointly regularly amended and/or updated to reflect progress in addressing the priorities.

Glossary

CDR: Council for Development and Reconstruction

CFAA: Country Financial Accountability Assessment

EASA: European Aviation Safety Agency

FATF: Financial Action Task Force on Money Laundering

FEMIP: Facility for Euro-Mediterranean Investment and Partnership

GFCM: General Fisheries Commission for the Mediterranean

ILO: International Labour Organisation

IMO: International Maritime Organization

ISPS: International Ship and Port Facility Security

JAA: Joint Aviation Authorities

MARPOL: International Convention for the Prevention of Marine Pollution from Ships

NAJM: Customs Clearance automated information system

NOOR: NAJM On-line operations

R&D: Research and Development

SME: Small and Medium Enterprises

SOLAS: International Convention for the Safety of Life at Sea

TAIEX: Technical Assistance Information Exchange

TRIPS: trade-related aspects of intellectual property rights

UNSC: United Nations Security Council

VTMIS: Vessel Traffic Management and Information Systems

WMD: Weapons of Mass Destruction

F. THE SPECIAL TRIBUNAL FOR LEBANON

DOCUMENT NO. 18

SECURITY COUNCIL RESOLUTION ESTABLISHING THE SPECIAL TRIBUNAL FOR LEBANON

United Nations Security Council
S/RES/1595

Distr.: General
7 April 2005

Resolution 1595 (2005)

Adopted by the Security Council at its 5160th meeting, on 7 April 2005

The Security Council,

Reiterating its call for the strict respect of the sovereignty, territorial integrity, unity and political independence of Lebanon under the sole and exclusive authority of the Government of Lebanon,

Endorsing the Secretary-General's opinion, as expressed in his letter of 24 March 2005 to the President of the Security Council, that Lebanon is passing through a difficult and sensitive period, that all concerned should imperatively behave with the utmost restraint and that the future of Lebanon should be decided strictly through peaceful means,

Reaffirming its unequivocal condemnation of the 14 February 2005 terrorist bombing in Beirut, Lebanon, that killed former Lebanese Prime Minister Rafiq Hariri and others, and caused injury to dozens of people, and *condemning* the subsequent attacks in Lebanon,

Having examined the report of the fact-finding mission to Lebanon inquiring into the circumstances, causes and consequences of this terrorist act (S/2005/203), transmitted to the Security Council by the Secretary-General following the declaration of the President of the Security Council of 15 February 2005 (S/PRST/2005/4),

Noting with concern the fact-finding mission's conclusion that the Lebanese investigation process suffers from serious flaws and has neither the capacity nor the commitment to reach a satisfactory and credible conclusion,

Noting also in this context its opinion that an international independent investigation with executive authority and self-sufficient resources in all relevant fields of expertise would be necessary to elucidate all aspects of this heinous crime,

Mindful of the unanimous demand of the Lebanese people that those responsible be identified and held accountable, and *willing* to assist Lebanon in the search for the truth,

Welcoming the Lebanese Government's approval of the decision to be taken by the Security Council concerning the establishment of an international independent investigation Commission, and *welcoming also* its readiness to cooperate fully with such a Commission within the framework of Lebanese sovereignty and of its legal system, as expressed in the letter of 29 March 2005 from the Chargé d'affaires a.i. of Lebanon to the United Nations to the Secretary-General (S/2005/208),

1. *Decides*, consistent with the above-mentioned letter from the Chargé d'affaires a.i. of Lebanon, to establish an international independent investigation Commission ("the Commission") based in Lebanon to assist the Lebanese authorities in their investigation of all aspects of this terrorist act, including to help identify its perpetrators, sponsors, organizers and accomplices;

2. *Reiterates* its call on the Lebanese government to bring to justice the perpetrators, organizers and sponsors of the 14 February 2005 terrorist bombing, and *calls upon* the Lebanese government to ensure that the findings and conclusions of the Commission's investigation are taken into account fully;

3. *Decides* that, to ensure the Commission's effectiveness in the discharge of its duties, the Commission shall:

- Enjoy the full cooperation of the Lebanese authorities, including full access to all documentary, testimonial and physical information and evidence in their possession that the Commission deems relevant to the inquiry;
- Have the authority to collect any additional information and evidence, both documentary and physical, pertaining to this terrorist act, as well as to interview all officials and other persons in Lebanon, that the Commission deems relevant to the inquiry;
- Enjoy freedom of movement throughout the Lebanese territory, including access to all sites and facilities that the Commission deems relevant to the inquiry;

– Be provided with the facilities necessary to perform its functions, and be granted, as well as its premises, staff and equipment, the privileges and immunities to which they are entitled under the Convention on the Privileges and Immunities of the United Nations;

4. *Requests* the Secretary-General to consult urgently with the Lebanese Government with a view to facilitate the establishment and operation of the Commission pursuant to its mandate and terms of reference as mentioned in paragraphs 2 and 3 above, and *requests also* that he report to the Council accordingly and notify it of the date the Commission begins its full operations;

5. *Requests further* the Secretary-General, notwithstanding paragraph 4 above, to undertake without delay the steps, measures and arrangements necessary for the speedy establishment and full functioning of the Commission, including recruiting impartial and experienced staff with relevant skills and expertise;

6. *Directs* the Commission to determine procedures for carrying out its investigation, taking into account the Lebanese law and judicial procedures;

7. *Calls on* all States and all parties to cooperate fully with the Commission, and in particular to provide it with any relevant information they may possess pertaining to the above-mentioned terrorist act;

8. *Requests* the Commission to complete its work within three months of the date on which it commenced its full operations, as notified by the Secretary General, and *authorizes* the Secretary-General to extend the Commission's operation for a further period not exceeding three months, if he deems it necessary to enable the Commission to complete its investigation, and requests that he inform the Security Council accordingly;

9. *Requests* the Commission to report to the Council on the conclusions of its investigation and *requests* the Secretary-General to update orally the Security Council on the progress of the Commission every two months during the operations of the Commission or more frequently as needed.

DOCUMENT NO. 19

SECRETARY-GENERAL'S REPORT ON THE ESTABLISHMENT OF THE SPECIAL TRIBUNAL FOR LEBANON

United Nations Security Council
S/2006/893

November 15, 2006

Distr.: General
15 November 2006
English
Original: English/French

I. Introduction

1. In my report to the Security Council pursuant to paragraph 6 of its resolution 1644 (2005) (S/2006/176), I set out at the Council's request the nature and scope of the international assistance needed to try before a tribunal of an international character those responsible for the terrorist bombing that killed former Lebanese Prime Minister Rafiq Hariri and others. In so doing, I put forward the general principles of a tribunal of an international character, its personal and subject matter jurisdiction, composition, location and the question of financing, on the basis of consultations between the United Nations Secretariat and the Lebanese authorities.

2. By resolution 1664 (2006), the Security Council endorsed the report and requested me to negotiate an agreement with the Government of Lebanon aimed at establishing a tribunal of an international character based on the highest international standards of criminal justice, taking into account the recommendations of my report and the views that have been expressed by Council members. The Council also requested me to submit for its consideration a report on the implementation of the resolution, in particular on the draft agreement negotiated with the Government of Lebanon, including options for a funding mechanism appropriate to ensuring the continued and effective functioning of the tribunal.

3. Following initial consultations with the Lebanese authorities in Beirut on 26 and 27 January 2006 and with two senior Lebanese judges from 24 to 28 February at United Nations Headquarters in New York, negotiations on the legal framework for the establishment of the special tribunal for Lebanon on the basis of the Security Council's mandate proceeded at the expert level between members of the Office of Legal Affairs of the Secretariat and the Government of Lebanon, represented by the Lebanese judges. The two delegations met between 31 May and 1 June 2006 at Headquarters and between 3 and 7 July 2006 in The Hague. In this latest round of negotiations the two delegations benefited from the advice and wealth of knowledge and experience of two former Presidents of the International Tribunal for the Prosecution of Persons Responsible for Serious Violations of International Humanitarian Law Committed in the Territory of the Former Yugoslavia since 1991. On 6 September, the Legal Counsel travelled to Beirut and presented the initial draft agreement and statute to the Prime Minister and to the Minister of Justice of Lebanon for their consideration.

4. Requested by the Security Council in its resolution 1664 (2006) to take account of the views that have been expressed by Council members, the Secretariat has, in the course of negotiations, taken into account the views expressed by interested members of the Council on the progress of the negotiations and the principles of the legal framework for the establishment of the special tribunal. These consultations have in many ways shaped the legal choices made in the tribunal's founding instruments.

5. The present report analyses the main features of the statute of the special tribunal and the agreement between the United Nations and the Government of Lebanon. It examines the legal nature and specificities of the tribunal, its temporal, personal and subject matter jurisdiction, its organizational structure and composition, the conduct of the trial process, the location of the seat, the funding mechanism and cooperation with third States.

II. The Legal Nature and Specificities of the Special Tribunal

6. The legal basis for the establishment of the special tribunal is an agreement between the United Nations and the Government of Lebanon, to which the statute of the tribunal is attached (see annex I). As a treaty-based organ, the special tribunal is neither a subsidiary organ of the United Nations, nor is it a part of the Lebanese court system.

7. The Security Council mandated the Secretary-General to negotiate an agreement aimed at establishing a tribunal of an international character based on the highest international standards of criminal justice. Although

the features of such an international character were not specified, the constitutive instruments of the special tribunal in both form and substance evidence its international character. The legal basis for the establishment of the special tribunal is an international agreement between the United Nations and a Member State; its composition is mixed with a substantial international component; its standards of justice, including principles of due process of law, are those applicable in all international or United Nations-based criminal jurisdictions; its rules of procedure and evidence are to be inspired, in part, by reference materials reflecting the highest standards of international criminal procedure; and its success may rely considerably on the cooperation of third States. While in all of these respects the special tribunal has international characteristics, its subject matter jurisdiction or the applicable law remain national in character, however.

8. The special tribunal for Lebanon is distinguished from other international criminal tribunals established or assisted by the United Nations in two respects: (a) in the conduct of the trial process, more elements of civil law are evident than of common law; and (b) the investigative process conducted by the International Independent Investigation Commission constitutes, in fact, the core nascent prosecutor's office.

9. With the exception of the Extraordinary Chambers in the Courts of Cambodia, the conduct of the trial process as reflected in the constituent instruments of all other United Nations-based or assisted tribunals has included more common law elements. The special tribunal for Lebanon is the first United Nations-assisted tribunal to combine substantial elements of both legal systems. The applicability of the Lebanese Code of Criminal Procedure as a guiding principle alongside other reference materials reflecting the highest standards of international criminal procedure (art. 28), the enhanced powers of the Tribunal to take measures to ensure expeditious hearing and prevent any action that may cause unreasonable delay (art. 21) and the introduction of trials in absentia (art. 22) are the most notable manifestations of civil law elements.

10. The establishment of the special tribunal for Lebanon will have been preceded by the Commission established by Security Council resolution 1595 (2005) to assist the Lebanese authorities in their investigation of all aspects of the terrorist attack that killed former Prime Minister Rafiq Hariri and others. In establishing the Commission first, the investigative process has, for all intents and purposes, begun. In so doing, it will have the effect of reducing the lifespan of the tribunal and increasing the efficiency and cost-effectiveness of its operation.

III. The Jurisdiction of the Special Tribunal: Temporal, Personal and Subject Matter

A. Temporal Jurisdiction

11. In its resolution 1664 (2006), the Security Council envisaged the prosecution of those responsible for the single terrorist bombing that killed former Prime Minister Rafiq Hariri and others on 14 February 2005. The Hariri assassination, however, was committed in a context of other attacks bearing the same or similar characteristics committed between 1 October 2004 and 12 December 2005. Extending the jurisdiction of the tribunal beyond the assassination of Rafiq Hariri to other attacks is not, strictly speaking, an extension of the temporal jurisdiction of the tribunal, but rather an extension of its jurisdiction to include, within a specified period, other attacks that the tribunal might find to be connected to the Hariri assassination and similar to it in nature and gravity. The list of such attacks is included in the third report of the Commission (S/2006/161, para. 55; attached to this report as annex II).

12. The reasons for the inclusion of these other attacks are threefold:

(a) As the investigation of the Commission has progressed, potential links have emerged between the assassination of Rafiq Hariri and other attacks;

(b) The expansion of the mandate of the Commission to provide technical assistance to the Lebanese authorities in respect of the 14 other attacks is an indication of interest on the part of the Security Council in judicial accountability beyond the Rafiq Hariri assassination;

(c) Singling out for prosecution one attack in a context of other similar attacks is bound to create a perception of selective justice.

1. Linkage Among the Attacks

13. Article 1 of the statute of the special tribunal for Lebanon (see annex I, attachment) provides as follows:

> "The Special Tribunal shall have jurisdiction over persons responsible for the attack of 14 February 2005 resulting in the death of former Lebanese Prime Minister Rafiq Hariri and in the death or injury of other persons. If the Tribunal finds that other attacks that occurred in Lebanon between 1 October 2004 and 12 December 2005, or any later date decided by the Parties and with the consent of the Security Council, are connected in accordance with principles of criminal justice and are of a nature and gravity similar to the attack of 14 February 2005, it shall also have jurisdiction over persons responsible for such attacks. This connection includes but is not limited to a combination of the following elements: criminal intent (motive), the purpose behind the attacks, the nature of the victims targeted, the pattern of the attacks (modus operandi) and the perpetrators."

14. In investigating the potential links between some or all of these attacks, the Commission has identified certain potential linkages, notably the *mode of operation*, or the general pattern of using explosive devices; the *nature of the crime or the criminal intent underlying the attacks*, namely, targeting politicians or influential journalists, as well as creating widespread fear and anxiety among elements of the population by targeting public locations, destabilizing the security situation and causing damage to infrastructure; and *the identity of perpetrators*, of at least some of the attacks.[1] In its fourth report, the Commission reached the preliminary conclusion that the 14 cases were not commissioned and executed by 14 disparate and unconnected persons or groups with an equal number of separate motives. Analytically, the cases can be linked in a number of different ways and from varying perspectives, notably their similarities in the modus operandi, and their possible intent.[2]

2. The Expanded Mandate of the Commission

15. The mandate of the Commission was originally limited to the investigation of all aspects of the terrorist attack of 14 February 2005 that killed former Prime Minister Rafiq Hariri and others (resolution 1595 (2005)). On 13 December 2005, a day after the assassination of Gebran Tueni, the Government of Lebanon requested the establishment of a tribunal of an international character and the expansion of the mandate of the Commission, or the establishment of another international investigation commission, to investigate the assassination attempts and assassinations and explosions that took place in Lebanon starting with the attempt on the life of Minister Marwan Hamadeh on 1 October 2004. In response to that request, the Security Council, in its resolution 1644 (2005), expanded the mandate of the Commission to include the provision of technical assistance as appropriate to the Lebanese authorities with regard to their investigations on the terrorist attacks perpetrated in Lebanon since 1 October 2004.

16. While the resolution expands the Commission's mandate with respect to the other 14 attacks for the purpose of extending its technical assistance to the Lebanese authorities and not for the purpose of its own investigation, it is an indication nonetheless that the Security Council is interested in judicial accountability for those responsible for those attacks as well.

---

[1] In the view of the Commission, the comparable modus operandi of each attack could point to a single group of perpetrators who aimed to conduct a series of sustainable repetitive attacks with a minimum of complications (S/2006/375, para. 69).

[2] Ibid., para. 83. In its fifth report, the Commission confirmed its preliminary conclusion regarding the interconnectivity between the 14 cases and stated that, as it was developing evidence that linked the cases into differing groupings, it was anticipated that further links between the cases might become evident upon further collection of information and evidence (S/2006/760, para. 67).

3. A Perception of Fairness, Impartiality and Objectivity of the Special Tribunal

17. In establishing the temporal jurisdiction of any United Nations-based tribunal, the Organization strives to strike a balance between a temporal jurisdiction comprehensive enough to include the most serious crimes committed by those most responsible throughout the relevant period and a jurisdiction reasonably limited so as not to overburden the prosecutor's office and the tribunal as a whole. It is a balance struck, in fact, between fairness, objectivity and impartiality of the trial process, and its efficiency and cost-effectiveness.

18. In the present circumstances, singling out for prosecution the assassination of Rafiq Hariri, while disregarding a score of other connected attacks could cast a serious doubt on the objectivity and impartiality of the tribunal and lead to the perception of selective justice.

B. Personal Jurisdiction of the Special Tribunal

19. In its resolution 1664 (2006), the Security Council did not prescribe the personal jurisdiction of the tribunal, although it was mindful of the demand of the Lebanese people that all those responsible for the terrorist bombing that killed former Lebanese Prime Minister Rafiq Hariri and others be identified and brought to justice.

20. Article 1 of the statute accordingly provides that the tribunal shall have jurisdiction "over persons" responsible for the crimes falling within its subject matter jurisdiction, whose modes of criminal responsibility are further elaborated upon in article 3. Within the all-inclusive definition of the personal jurisdiction of the tribunal, the prosecutor will be free to pursue her or his prosecutional strategy and to determine the list of potential indictees according to the evidence before him or her.

C. Subject Matter Jurisdiction

21. Article 2 of the statute provides as follows:

> "The following shall be applicable to the prosecution and punishment of the crimes referred to in article 1, subject to the provisions of this Statute:
>
> > "(a) The provisions of the Lebanese Criminal Code relating to the prosecution and punishment of acts of terrorism, crimes and offences against life and personal integrity, illicit associations and failure to report crimes and offences, including the rules regarding the material elements of a crime, criminal participation and conspiracy; and

"(b) Articles 6 and 7 of the Lebanese law of 11 January 1958 on 'Increasing the penalties for sedition, civil war and interfaith struggle'."[3]

22. While the Lebanese criminal law is the applicable law, its applicability is limited to the crimes and offences provided for in article 2 of the statute. It is also subject to the provisions of the statute and therefore to the exclusion of penalties (e.g. death penalty and forced labour) otherwise applicable under Lebanese law.

23. In keeping with the Security Council mandate requesting the Secretary-General to establish a tribunal of an international character and in the circumstances of Lebanon where a pattern of terrorist attacks seems to have emerged, it was considered whether to qualify the crimes as crimes against humanity and to define them, for the purpose of this statute, as murder or other inhumane acts of similar gravity causing great suffering or serious injury to body or to mental health, when committed as part of a widespread or systematic attack directed against the civilian population.

24. Mindful of the differences in scope and number of victims between the series of terrorist attacks committed in Lebanon and the killings and executions perpetrated on a large and massive scale in other parts of the world subject to the jurisdiction of any of the existing international criminal jurisdictions, it was nevertheless considered that the 14 attacks committed in Lebanon could meet the prima facie definition of the crime, as developed in the jurisprudence of international criminal tribunals. The attacks that occurred in Lebanon since 1 October 2004 could reveal a "pattern" or "methodical plan" of attacks against a civilian population, albeit not in its entirety. They could be "collective" in nature, or "a multiple commission of acts"[4] and, as such, exclude a single, isolated or random conduct of an individual acting alone. For the crime of murder, as part of a systematic attack against

---

[3] Article 314 of the Criminal Code provides as follows:

> "The term 'acts of terrorism' includes all acts that are intended to cause a state of alarm and have been committed by means such as explosive devices, inflammable substances, toxic or corrosive products or infectious or microbial agents that are liable to pose a public threat."

Articles 6 and 7, respectively, of the 1958 law provide:

> "All acts of terrorism shall be punishable by hard labour for life. Capital punishment shall be incurred if there were human fatalities or if a building has been wholly or partially destroyed when a person was inside, or if the act results in the destruction, even partial, of a public building, industrial installation, ship or other structure or damage to communications or transport links."

> "Conspiracy to commit one of the crimes mentioned in the preceding articles shall be punishable by hard labour for life."

[4] Article 7, paragraph 2 (a), of the Rome Statute of the International Criminal Court defines an "attack directed against any civilian population" as "a course of conduct involving the multiple commission of acts . . . against any civilian population pursuant to or in furtherance of a State or organizational policy to commit such attack".

a civilian population, to qualify as a "crime against humanity", its massive scale is not an indispensable element.

25. However, considering the views expressed by interested members of the Security Council, there was insufficient support for the inclusion of crimes against humanity within the subject matter jurisdiction of the tribunal. For this reason, therefore, the qualification of the crimes was limited to common crimes under the Lebanese Criminal Code.

D. Individual Criminal Responsibility

26. Under article 3, paragraph 1, of the statute, all those who committed, participated as accomplice, organized or directed others to commit the crime, or otherwise contributed to the commission of the crime, shall be individually responsible. This is a reflection of the Lebanese Criminal Code and general criminal law principles, evidenced, inter alia, by article 2, paragraph 3, of the International Convention for the Suppression of Terrorist Bombings of 1997 (General Assembly resolution 52/164, annex). Article 3, paragraph 2, reflects the principle of command responsibility both under international law and national criminal and military codes as more fully articulated in article 28, subparagraph (b), of the Statute of the International Criminal Court. Under article 3, paragraph 3, obedience to superior order is no defence, but may be considered in mitigation of punishment.

IV. Organizational Structure of the Special Tribunal

A. The Organs of the Special Tribunal

27. The special tribunal for Lebanon will consist of the following organs: the chambers (a pre-trial judge, a trial chamber and an appeals chamber), the prosecutor, the registry and the defence office. The composition of the chambers is mixed, with a majority of international judges in the trial and the appeals chambers. An international prosecutor, assisted by a Lebanese deputy prosecutor, is responsible for the investigation and prosecution of persons who may have committed the crimes falling within the jurisdiction of the tribunal. The registrar is appointed by the Secretary-General and is a staff member of the United Nations. The establishment of the special tribunal with a majority of international judges, an international prosecutor and a registrar is consistent with the long-established United Nations position that in the establishment of any mixed tribunal a substantial international component is a guarantee for the independence, objectivity and impartiality of the trial process.

B. Pre-Trial Judge

28. Pre-trial proceedings exist in different forms in all international criminal tribunals. However, unlike the pre-trial judge of either of the ad hoc

tribunals for the former Yugoslavia and Rwanda, or of the Special Court for Sierra Leone, who is designated by the presiding judge of a trial chamber from among the members of that chamber, the pre-trial judge of the special tribunal for Lebanon is a dedicated, single international judge serving as a pre-trial judge only and not as a member of any of the chambers.

29. The role of the pre-trial judge is primarily to review the indictment and, if a prima facie case is established, to confirm the indictment. At the pre-trial phase and throughout the investigation, the pre-trial judge may issue any orders or warrants of arrest, detention or transfer of persons as may be requested by the prosecutor for the purpose of the investigation. In the decade-long experience of United Nations-based tribunals, the role of the pre-trial judge has proved crucial to ensuring the efficiency and expediency of the trial process.

C. Defence Office

30. The need for a defence office to protect the rights of suspects and accused has evolved in the practice of United Nations-based tribunals as part of the need to ensure "equality of arms", where the prosecutor's office is an organ of the tribunal and is financed in its entirety through the budget of the tribunal. The statute of the special tribunal institutionalizes the defence office. The head of the office is appointed by the Secretary-General, although, in carrying out its functions, the office is independent. The defence office of the special tribunal is to protect the rights of the defence, draw up the list of defence counsel and provide support and assistance to defence counsel and persons entitled to such legal assistance.

V. Conduct of the Trial Process

A. Due Process of Law

31. With all the specificities of the special tribunal for Lebanon, its standards of justice and guarantees of due process of law are modelled on the highest international standards of criminal justice. In addition to listing the rights of the accused, including an elaborated provision on the presumption of innocence and the burden of proof, the statute provides for the rights of suspects during investigation, including the right not to be compelled to incriminate oneself, to be informed of the charges against him or her, to have legal assistance and to be questioned in the presence of counsel. The statute also protects the rights of victims whose personal interests are affected and, while not recognizing them as *"parties civiles"*, it permits their views and concerns to be presented and considered at all stages of the proceedings.

B. Elements of Civil Law and Common Law Systems Combined

32. The proceedings before the special tribunal, while essentially adversarial, contain elements of both civil and common law systems. While distinctive features of civil law, namely, the institution of an investigating judge and the participation of victims as "*parties civiles*" are absent, the trial process before the special tribunal is inspired by the civil law system in the following two respects, the active role of the judges and the conduct of trials in absentia:

(a) The judges of the special tribunal will take a more active role in the conduct of the trial process and the examination of witnesses. Under article 20 of the statute, unless otherwise decided by the trial chamber, "examination of witnesses shall commence with questions posed by the presiding judge, followed by questions posed by other members of the Trial Chamber, the Prosecutor and the Defence". The trial chamber may also *proprio motu* "decide to call additional witnesses and/or order the production of additional evidence";

(b) The institution of trials in absentia is common in a number of civil law legal systems, including Lebanon's. In addition, in the present case, where the conduct of joint trials for some or all of the cases falling within the jurisdiction of the tribunal is likely, it would be crucial to ensure that the legal process is not unduly or indefinitely delayed because of the absence of some accused.

33. In introducing the institution of trials in absentia on the conditions that the accused has waived his or her right to be present, that he or she has not been handed over or absconded, or otherwise cannot be found, the statute of the special tribunal takes account of the relevant case law of the European Court of Human Rights, which determined the regularity of trials in absentia in full respect for the rights of the accused.[5] Accordingly, and as a supplement to the Lebanese Criminal Procedure, article 22 of the statute provides that, where hearings are conducted in the absence of the accused, the special tribunal shall ensure that the accused has designated a defence counsel to be present in the trial or that, if he or she has refused to do so, one will be assigned to him or her by the tribunal's defence office. In case of conviction, the accused shall have the right to be re-tried in his or her presence, if the accused has not designated a defence counsel of his or her choosing in the first trial. Otherwise, the conviction will stand.

[5] Case of *Krombach v. France*, European Court of Human Rights, Application No. 29731/96, Judgment, 13 February 2001; and Case of *Sejdovic v. Italy*, European Court of Human Rights, Application No. 56581/00, Judgment, 1 March 2006.

C. Receivability and Admissibility of Evidence Collected Prior to the Establishment of the Special Tribunal

34. It will be necessary to have a coordinated transition between the work of the Commission and the special tribunal. While the modalities of such transition would be determined taking into account the progress of work of the Commission, it is necessary at this stage to ensure that the work of the Commission is preserved and that evidence collected by it prior to the establishment of the tribunal is nevertheless receivable by the tribunal.

35. In this connection, the Commission noted in its fourth report (S/2006/375, para. 111), that:

> "While based on relevant international standards, the internal procedure takes into account Lebanese law and judicial procedures, as well as the practice of the Commission since its establishment. In defining the standards to be applied, the Commission considered the procedures of international criminal jurisdictions and the minimum guarantees afforded by international criminal law and international human rights law. The internal procedure will therefore help ensure that any information collected or obtained by the Commission is admissible in future legal proceedings, notably before a tribunal of an international character".

36. In the circumstances, it is necessary to provide for the receivability of evidence collected by the national authorities of Lebanon and by the Commission in accordance with its mandate, on the understanding that its admissibility and the weight to be given to such evidence shall be determined by the tribunal in accordance with international standards on the collection of evidence.

VI. Agreement Between the United Nations and the Government of Lebanon

37. The agreement between the United Nations and the Government of Lebanon would govern the terms of United Nations cooperation in establishing the tribunal. It stipulates the composition of the tribunal, the procedure for the nomination and appointment of judges (both international and Lebanese), of the international prosecutor and the Lebanese deputy prosecutor and of the registrar and other members of the tribunal, as well as the privileges and immunities to which they are entitled.

38. As a non-United Nations organ, the special tribunal would not be entitled to the privileges and immunities of the Convention on the Privileges and Immunities of the United Nations of 1946. For the special tribunal, its premises, funds, archives and all members of the tribunal, to enjoy comparable privileges and immunities, the agreement between the United Nations and the Government of Lebanon, as well as the future headquarters agreement between the United Nations, the Government of Lebanon

and the host State, will have to provide for the necessary privileges and immunities.

39. The agreement between the United Nations and the Government of Lebanon draws, for the most part, upon the agreements signed between the United Nations and the Governments of Cambodia and of Sierra Leone. The provisions relating to the location of the seat and the funding mechanism, however, are Lebanon-specific.

A. Location of the Seat

40. For a variety of reasons, the parties share the view that it would be desirable to locate the seat of the tribunal outside Lebanon. In the choice of the seat, considerations of justice and fairness, administrative efficiency, the rights of victims and proximity to witnesses, existence of suitable facilities—both for the tribunal and its detention facilities—security arrangements and affordable costs, would be fully taken into account.

41. The location of the seat outside Lebanon will require the conclusion of a headquarters agreement between the United Nations, the Government of Lebanon and the host State. It is envisaged that when an agreement, in principle, is reached on the location of the seat, the Secretariat will dispatch a United Nations planning mission to identify adequate premises and negotiate the terms of the headquarters agreement.

42. Like the "split seat" of the Office of the Prosecutor of the International Criminal Tribunal for the Prosecution of Persons Responsible for Genocide and Other Serious Violations of International Humanitarian Law Committed in the Territory of Rwanda and Rwandan Citizens Responsible for Genocide and Other Such Violations Committed in the Territory of Neighbouring States between 1 January and 31 December 1994, where the Prosecutor conducts some investigations through his office in Kigali, while the seat of the Tribunal is in Arusha, the choice of the seat of the special tribunal outside Lebanon will not affect the operation of the prosecutor's office and the conduct of investigations in Lebanon, as necessary and subject to the conclusion of appropriate arrangements with the Government of Lebanon. The arrangements governing the presence of the Commission in Lebanon under the Memorandum of Understanding between the Government of the Republic of Lebanon and the United Nations regarding the Modalities of Cooperation for the International Independent Investigation Commission, signed on 13 June 2005 (see S/2005/393), depending on the circumstances prevailing at the time of the establishment of the tribunal, may be expanded to apply, mutatis mutandis, to the presence of an office of the prosecutor in Lebanon.

43. As is customarily the case with respect to tribunals of all kinds, the possibility that the special tribunal for Lebanon will meet away from its seat when it considers it necessary for the efficient exercise of its functions is provided for in article 8, paragraph 2, of the agreement.

B. Funding Mechanism

44. In its resolution 1664 (2006), the Security Council requested the Secretary-General to submit options for a funding mechanism appropriate to ensure the continued and effective functioning of the tribunal. Without prejudice to the authority of the General Assembly in budgetary matters under Article 17 of the Charter of the United Nations, several options are, in principle, available in the determination of the funding mechanism of the special tribunal: assessed contributions in whole or in part; voluntary contributions; or assessed and voluntary contributions combined. As the Government of Lebanon has expressed its willingness to bear a substantial part of the expenses of the tribunal,[6] all options but one include a provision that 49 per cent of the expenses of the tribunal would be borne by the Government of Lebanon. An indication of possible options and a proposed corresponding article are described below.

1. Assessed Contributions

45. The merits of assessed contributions—the funding mechanism of the two ad hoc tribunals, the International Tribunal for the Former Yugoslavia and the International Criminal Tribunal for Rwanda—were debated at the time of the establishment of the Special Court for Sierra Leone. In his report to the Security Council (S/2000/915), the Secretary-General expressed the view that only regular, predictable, assessed contributions could produce a viable and sustainable mechanism affording secure and continuous funding. It was also his view (para. 70) that:

> "A financial mechanism based entirely on voluntary contributions will not provide the assured and continuous source of funding which would be required to appoint the judges, the Prosecutor and the Registrar, to contract the services of all administrative and support staff and to purchase the necessary equipment. The risks associated with the establishment of an operation of this kind with insufficient funds, or without long-term assurances of continuous availability of funds, are very high, in terms of both moral responsibility and loss of credibility of the Organization, and its exposure to legal liability."

46. Funding through assessed contributions could be either in whole or in part. If considered an expense of the Organization under Article 17 of the Charter of the United Nations, it should be financed from assessed contributions. Any voluntary contributions, including the contribution of the Government of Lebanon, would be supplemental and be used to implement specific non-core activities. It is recalled in this connection that if a decision to fund the special tribunal through assessed contributions is

[6] A firm commitment by the Government of Lebanon on defraying its share in the expenses of the tribunal would be required before the agreement could be signed by the Secretary-General.

adopted, it would be for the General Assembly, as the authority entrusted under Article 17 of the Charter with the responsibility to consider and approve the budget, to decide on the source of funding, as well as on any budgetary and administrative arrangements to be put in place. It is also recalled that funding through assessed contributions would trigger the applicability to the special tribunal of the United Nations Financial and Staff Regulations and Rules.

47. If the mechanism of assessed contributions in whole is accepted, the relevant provision of the agreement would read:

> "The expenses of the Special Tribunal shall be considered expenses of the Organization in accordance with Article 17 of the Charter of the United Nations."

48. If the mechanism of assessed contributions in part is accepted, the relevant provision in the agreement would read:

> "The expenses of the Special Tribunal shall be borne in the following manner:
>
> > "(a) Fifty-one per cent of the expenses of the Tribunal shall be considered expenses of the Organization in accordance with Article 17 of the Charter of the United Nations;
> >
> > "(b) Forty-nine per cent of the expenses of the Tribunal shall be borne by the Government of Lebanon."

2. Voluntary Contributions

49. Voluntary contributions was the funding mechanism of the Special Court for Sierra Leone and the Extraordinary Chambers in the Courts of Cambodia, although in the former case a one-time subvention was granted by the General Assembly to replenish the dwindling reserves of the Special Court. If the option of voluntary contributions, as the sole funding mechanism of the tribunal, is adopted, then the corresponding article would read:

> "The expenses of the Special Tribunal shall be borne in the following manner:
>
> > "(a) Fifty-one per cent of the expenses of the Tribunal shall be borne by voluntary contributions from States;
> >
> > "(b) Forty-nine per cent of the expenses of the Tribunal shall be borne by the Government of Lebanon."

3. Combined Funding Mechanism

50. While the Secretary-General maintains his principled position in support of assessed contributions as the funding mechanism of international criminal jurisdictions, the uniqueness of the special tribunal for Lebanon

may warrant a different approach to the establishment of the financial mechanism. The formula proposed is a combined formula of both voluntary and assessed contributions. It provides for a continuation of assessed contributions to fund investigations (as is currently the case with the Commission) and this may be considered more viable and sustainable than other options wholly reliant on voluntary contributions. If accepted, the corresponding article would read:

> "The expenses of the Special Tribunal for Lebanon shall be borne in the following manner:
>
> > "(a) The expenses incurred for investigations shall continue to be considered expenses of the Organization in accordance with Article 17 of the Charter of the United Nations;
> >
> > "(b) Fifty-one per cent of the expenses of the Tribunal, excluding those related to investigations, shall be borne by voluntary contributions from States;
> >
> > "(c) Forty-nine per cent of the expenses of the Tribunal, excluding those related to investigations, shall be borne by the Government of Lebanon."

51. With regard to the options described in paragraphs 49 and 50 above, both of which involve voluntary contributions, the sufficiency of funds must be guaranteed before the Secretary-General can be expected to commence the process of establishment of the tribunal. In any of these options, therefore, the following text should be inserted as paragraph 2 of the corresponding article:

> "It is understood that the Secretary-General will commence the process of establishing the Tribunal when he has sufficient contributions in hand to finance the establishment of the Tribunal and twelve months of its operations, plus pledges equal to the anticipated expenses of the following twenty-four months of the Tribunal's operation. Should voluntary contributions be insufficient for the Tribunal to implement its mandate, the Secretary-General and the Security Council shall explore alternate means of financing the Tribunal."

C. Cooperation with the Special Tribunal

52. Article 15 of the agreement places an obligation on the Government of Lebanon to cooperate with the tribunal at all stages of the proceedings and to comply with its requests for assistance in the identification and location of persons, service of documents, arrest and detention of persons, and the transfer of indictees to the tribunal.

53. In maintaining the logic of Security Council resolutions 1595 (2005), 1636 (2005) and 1644 (2005), under which Member States are obliged to cooperate fully with the Commission in its investigation of the Hariri assassination, the Council may wish, at the appropriate stages and as necessary,

to consider similar measures to enable the special tribunal more effectively to prosecute those responsible for the attack against Rafiq Hariri and for other attacks falling within the jurisdiction of the tribunal.

VII. Conclusion

54. On 10 November 2006, I transmitted to the Prime Minister of Lebanon the draft agreement between the United Nations and the Government of Lebanon on the establishment of a special tribunal for Lebanon, to which was annexed a draft statute for such a tribunal. By his letter to me of 13 November 2006, the Prime Minister informed me that the Lebanese Council of Ministers had agreed in its session of that date to the draft and looked forward to the completion of the remaining steps leading to the establishment of the tribunal. By a note verbale dated 14 November 2006, the Permanent Mission of Lebanon forwarded to me a copy of observations made by the President of the Lebanese Republic, including a challenge to the decision of the Council of Ministers. The negotiated instruments are now submitted to the Security Council for its consideration.

Annex I

Agreement between the United Nations and the Lebanese Republic on the Establishment of a Special Tribunal for Lebanon

Whereas the Security Council, in its resolution 1664 (2006) of 29 March 2006, which responded to the request of the Government of Lebanon to establish a tribunal of an international character to try all those who are found responsible for the terrorist crime which killed the former Lebanese Prime Minister Rafiq Hariri and others, recalled all its previous resolutions, in particular resolutions 1595 (2005) of 7 April 2005, 1636 (2005) of 31 October 2005 and 1644 (2005) of 15 December 2005,

Whereas the Security Council has requested the Secretary-General of the United Nations (hereinafter "the Secretary-General") "to negotiate an agreement with the Government of Lebanon aimed at establishing a tribunal of an international character based on the highest international standards of criminal justice", taking into account the recommendations of the Secretary-General's report of 21 March 2006 (S/2006/176) and the views that have been expressed by Council members,

Whereas the Secretary-General and the Government of the Lebanese Republic (hereinafter "the Government") have conducted negotiations for the establishment of a Special Tribunal for Lebanon (hereinafter "the Special Tribunal" or "the Tribunal"),

Now therefore the United Nations and the Lebanese Republic (hereinafter referred to jointly as the "Parties") have agreed as follows:

Article 1
Establishment of the Special Tribunal

1. There is hereby established a Special Tribunal for Lebanon to prosecute persons responsible for the attack of 14 February 2005 resulting in the death of former Lebanese Prime Minister Rafiq Hariri and in the death or injury of other persons. If the tribunal finds that other attacks that occurred in Lebanon between 1 October 2004 and 12 December 2005, or any later date decided by the Parties and with the consent of the Security Council, are connected in accordance with the principles of criminal justice and are of a nature and gravity similar to the attack of 14 February 2005, it shall also have jurisdiction over persons responsible for such attacks. This connection includes but is not limited to a combination of the following elements: criminal intent (motive), the purpose behind the attacks, the nature of the victims targeted, the pattern of the attacks (modus operandi) and the perpetrators.

2. The Special Tribunal shall function in accordance with the Statute of the Special Tribunal for Lebanon. The Statute is attached to this Agreement and forms an integral part thereof.

Article 2
Composition of the Special Tribunal and Appointment of Judges

1. The Special Tribunal shall consist of the following organs: the Chambers, the Prosecutor, the Registry and the Defence Office.

2. The Chambers shall be composed of a Pre-Trial Judge, a Trial Chamber and an Appeals Chamber, with a second Trial Chamber to be created if, after the passage of at least six months from the commencement of the functioning of the Special Tribunal, the Secretary-General or the President of the Special Tribunal so requests.

3. The Chambers shall be composed of no fewer than eleven independent judges and no more than fourteen such judges, who shall serve as follows:

(a) A single international judge shall serve as a Pre-Trial Judge;

(b) Three judges shall serve in the Trial Chamber, of whom one shall be a Lebanese judge and two shall be international judges;

(c) In the event of the creation of a second Trial Chamber, that Chamber shall be likewise composed in the manner contained in subparagraph (b) above;

(d) Five judges shall serve in the Appeals Chamber, of whom two shall be Lebanese judges and three shall be international judges; and

(e) Two alternate judges, of whom one shall be a Lebanese judge and one shall be an international judge.

4. The judges of the Tribunal shall be persons of high moral character, impartiality and integrity, with extensive judicial experience. They shall be independent in the performance of their functions and shall not accept or seek instructions from any Government or any other source.

5. (a) Lebanese judges shall be appointed by the Secretary-General to serve in the Trial Chamber or the Appeals Chamber or as an alternate judge from a list of twelve persons presented by the Government upon the proposal of the Lebanese Supreme Council of the Judiciary;

(b) International judges shall be appointed by the Secretary-General to serve as Pre-Trial Judge, a Trial Chamber Judge, an Appeals Chamber Judge or an alternate judge, upon nominations forwarded by States at the invitation of the Secretary-General, as well as by competent persons;

(c) The Government and the Secretary-General shall consult on the appointment of judges;

(d) The Secretary-General shall appoint judges, upon the recommendation of a selection panel he has established after indicating his intentions to the Security Council. The selection panel shall be composed of two judges, currently sitting on or retired from an international tribunal, and the representative of the Secretary-General.

6. At the request of the presiding judge of a Trial Chamber, the President of the Special Tribunal may, in the interest of justice, assign alternate judges to be present at each stage of the trial and to replace a judge if that judge is unable to continue sitting.

7. Judges shall be appointed for a three-year period and may be eligible for reappointment for a further period to be determined by the Secretary-General in consultation with the Government.

8. Lebanese judges appointed to serve in the Special Tribunal shall be given full credit for their period of service with the Tribunal on their return to the Lebanese national judiciaries from which they were released and shall be reintegrated at a level at least comparable to that of their former position.

Article 3
Appointment of a Prosecutor and a Deputy Prosecutor

1. The Secretary-General, after consultation with the Government, shall appoint a Prosecutor for a three-year term. The Prosecutor may be eligible for reappointment for a further period to be determined by the Secretary-General in consultation with the Government.

2. The Secretary-General shall appoint the Prosecutor, upon the recommendation of a selection panel he has established after indicating his intentions to the Security Council. The selection panel shall be composed of two judges, currently sitting on or retired from an international tribunal, and the representative of the Secretary-General.

3. The Government, in consultation with the Secretary-General and the Prosecutor, shall appoint a Lebanese Deputy Prosecutor to assist the Prosecutor in the conduct of the investigations and prosecutions.

4. The Prosecutor and the Deputy Prosecutor shall be of high moral character and possess the highest level of professional competence and extensive experience in the conduct of investigations and prosecutions of criminal cases. The Prosecutor and the Deputy Prosecutor shall be independent in the performance of their functions and shall not accept or seek instructions from any Government or any other source.

5. The Prosecutor shall be assisted by such Lebanese and international staff as may be required to perform the functions assigned to him or her effectively and efficiently.

Article 4
Appointment of a Registrar

1. The Secretary-General shall appoint a Registrar who shall be responsible for the servicing of the Chambers and the Office of the Prosecutor, and for the recruitment and administration of all support staff. He or she shall also administer the financial and staff resources of the Special Tribunal.

2. The Registrar shall be a staff member of the United Nations. He or she shall serve a three-year term and may be eligible for reappointment for a further period to be determined by the Secretary-General in consultation with the Government.

Article 5
Financing of the Special Tribunal

To be completed.

Article 6
Management Committee

The parties shall consult concerning the establishment of a Management Committee.

Article 7
Juridical Capacity

The Special Tribunal shall possess the juridical capacity necessary:

(a) To contract;

(b) To acquire and dispose of movable and immovable property;

(c) To institute legal proceedings;

(d) To enter into agreements with States as may be necessary for the exercise of its functions and for the operation of the Tribunal.

Article 8
Seat of the Special Tribunal

1. The Special Tribunal shall have its seat outside Lebanon. The location of the seat shall be determined having due regard to considerations of justice

and fairness as well as security and administrative efficiency, including the rights of victims and access to witnesses, and subject to the conclusion of a headquarters agreement between the United Nations, the Government and the State that hosts the Tribunal.

2. The Special Tribunal may meet away from its seat when it considers it necessary for the efficient exercise of its functions.

3. An Office of the Special Tribunal for the conduct of investigations shall be established in Lebanon subject to the conclusion of appropriate arrangements with the Government.

Article 9
Inviolability of Premises, Archives and all other Documents

1. The Office of the Special Tribunal in Lebanon shall be inviolable. The competent authorities shall take appropriate action that may be necessary to ensure that the Tribunal shall not be dispossessed of all or any part of the premises of the Tribunal without its express consent.

2. The property, funds and assets of the Office of the Special Tribunal in Lebanon, wherever located and by whomsoever held, shall be immune from search, seizure, requisition, confiscation, expropriation and any other form of interference, whether by executive, administrative, judicial or legislative action.

3. The archives of the Office of the Special Tribunal in Lebanon, and in general all documents and materials made available, belonging to or used by it, wherever located and by whomsoever held, shall be inviolable.

Article 10
Funds, Assets and Other Property

The Office of the Special Tribunal, its funds, assets and other property in Lebanon, wherever located and by whomsoever held, shall enjoy immunity from every form of legal process, except insofar as in any particular case the Tribunal has expressly waived its immunity. It is understood, however, that no waiver of immunity shall extend to any measure of execution.

Article 11
Privileges and Immunities of the Judges, the Prosecutor, the Deputy Prosecutor, the Registrar and the Head of the Defence Office

1. The judges, the Prosecutor, the Deputy Prosecutor, the Registrar and the Head of the Defence Office, while in Lebanon, shall enjoy the privileges and immunities, exemptions and facilities accorded to diplomatic agents in accordance with the Vienna Convention on Diplomatic Relations of 1961.

2. Privileges and immunities are accorded to the judges, the Prosecutor, the Deputy Prosecutor, the Registrar and the Head of the Defence Office in the interest of the Special Tribunal and not for the personal benefit of the individuals themselves. The right and the duty to waive the immunity in any case where it can be waived without prejudice to the purposes for which it is accorded shall lie with the Secretary-General, in consultation with the President of the Tribunal.

Article 12
Privileges and Immunities of International and Lebanese Personnel

1. Lebanese and international personnel of the Office of the Special Tribunal, while in Lebanon, shall be accorded:

(a) Immunity from legal process in respect of words spoken or written and all acts performed by them in their official capacity. Such immunity shall continue to be accorded after termination of employment with the Office of the Special Tribunal;

(b) Exemption from taxation on salaries, allowances and emoluments paid to them.

2. International personnel shall, in addition thereto, be accorded:

(a) Immunity from immigration restriction;

(b) The right to import free of duties and taxes, except for payment for services, their furniture and effects at the time of first taking up their official duties in Lebanon.

3. The privileges and immunities are granted to the officials of the Office of the Special Tribunal in the interest of the Tribunal and not for their personal benefit. The right and the duty to waive the immunity in any case where it can be waived without prejudice to the purpose for which it is accorded shall lie with the Registrar of the Tribunal.

Article 13
Defence Counsel

1. The Government shall ensure that the counsel of a suspect or an accused who has been admitted as such by the Special Tribunal shall not be subjected, while in Lebanon, to any measure that may affect the free and independent exercise of his or her functions.

2. In particular, the counsel shall be accorded:

(a) Immunity from personal arrest or detention and from seizure of personal baggage;

(b) Inviolability of all documents relating to the exercise of his or her functions as a counsel of a suspect or accused;

(c) Immunity from criminal or civil jurisdiction in respect of words spoken or written and acts performed in his or her capacity as counsel. Such immunity shall continue to be accorded after termination of his or her functions as a counsel of a suspect or accused;

(d) Immunity from any immigration restrictions during his or her stay as well as during his or her journey to the Tribunal and back.

Article 14
Security, Safety and Protection of Persons Referred to in this Agreement

The Government shall take effective and adequate measures to ensure the appropriate security, safety and protection of personnel of the Office of the Special Tribunal and other persons referred to in this Agreement, while in Lebanon. It shall take all appropriate steps, within its capabilities, to protect the equipment and premises of the Office of the Special Tribunal from attack or any action that prevents the Tribunal from discharging its mandate.

Article 15
Cooperation with the Special Tribunal

1. The Government shall cooperate with all organs of the Special Tribunal, in particular with the Prosecutor and defence counsel, at all stages of the proceedings. It shall facilitate access of the Prosecutor and defence counsel to sites, persons and relevant documents required for the investigation.

2. The Government shall comply without undue delay with any request for assistance by the Special Tribunal or an order issued by the Chambers, including, but not limited to:

(a) Identification and location of persons;

(b) Service of documents;

(c) Arrest or detention of persons;

(d) Transfer of an indictee to the Tribunal.

Article 16
Amnesty

The Government undertakes not to grant amnesty to any person for any crime falling within the jurisdiction of the Special Tribunal. An amnesty already granted in respect of any such persons and crimes shall not be a bar to prosecution.

Article 17
Practical Arrangements

With a view to achieving efficiency and cost-effectiveness in the operation of the Special Tribunal:

(a) Appropriate arrangements shall be made to ensure that there is a coordinated transition from the activities of the International Independent Investigation Commission, established by the Security Council in its resolution 1595 (2005), to the activities of the Office of the Prosecutor;

(b) Judges of the Trial Chamber and the Appeals Chamber shall take office on a date to be determined by the Secretary-General in consultation with the President of the Special Tribunal. Pending such a determination, judges of both Chambers shall be convened on an ad hoc basis to deal with organizational matters and serving, when required, to perform their duties.

Article 18
Settlement of Disputes

Any dispute between the Parties concerning the interpretation or application of this Agreement shall be settled by negotiation or by any other mutually agreed upon mode of settlement.

Article 19
Entry into Force and Commencement of the Functioning of the Special Tribunal

1. This Agreement shall enter into force on the day after the Government has notified the United Nations in writing that the legal requirements for entry into force have been complied with.

2. The Special Tribunal shall commence functioning on a date to be determined by the Secretary-General in consultation with the Government, taking into account the progress of the work of the International Independent Investigation Commission.

Article 20
Amendment

This Agreement may be amended by written agreement between the Parties.

Article 21
Duration of the Agreement

1. This Agreement shall remain in force for a period of three years from the date of the commencement of the functioning of the Special Tribunal.

2. Three years after the commencement of the functioning of the Special Tribunal the Parties shall, in consultation with the Security Council, review the progress of the work of the Special Tribunal. If at the end of this period of three years the activities of the Tribunal have not been completed, the Agreement shall be extended to allow the Tribunal to complete its work, for a further period(s) to be determined by the Secretary-General in consultation with the Government and the Security Council.

3. The provisions relating to the inviolability of the funds, assets, archives and documents of the Office of the Special Tribunal in Lebanon, the privileges and immunities of those referred to in this Agreement, as well as provisions relating to defence counsel and the protection of victims and witnesses, shall survive termination of this Agreement.

In witness whereof, the following duly authorized representatives of the United Nations and of the Lebanese Republic have signed this Agreement.

Done at _________ on _________ 2006, in three originals in the Arabic, French and English languages, all texts being equally authentic.

For the United Nations: For the Lebanese Republic:

______________ ____________

Attachment
Statute of the Special Tribunal for Lebanon

Having been established by an Agreement between the United Nations and the Lebanese Republic (hereinafter "the Agreement") pursuant to Security Council resolution 1664 (2006) of 29 March 2006, which responded to the request of the Government of Lebanon to establish a tribunal of an international character to try all those who are found responsible for the terrorist crime which killed the former Lebanese Prime Minister Rafiq Hariri and others, the Special Tribunal for Lebanon (hereinafter "the Special Tribunal") shall function in accordance with the provisions of this Statute.

Section I
Jurisdiction and Applicable Law

Article 1
Jurisdiction of the Special Tribunal

The Special Tribunal shall have jurisdiction over persons responsible for the attack of 14 February 2005 resulting in the death of former Lebanese Prime Minister Rafiq Hariri and in the death or injury of other persons. If the Tribunal finds that other attacks that occurred in Lebanon between 1 October 2004 and 12 December 2005, or any later date decided by the

Parties and with the consent of the Security Council, are connected in accordance with the principles of criminal justice and are of a nature and gravity similar to the attack of 14 February 2005, it shall also have jurisdiction over persons responsible for such attacks. This connection includes but is not limited to a combination of the following elements: criminal intent (motive), the purpose behind the attacks, the nature of the victims targeted, the pattern of the attacks (modus operandi) and the perpetrators.

Article 2
Applicable Criminal Law

The following shall be applicable to the prosecution and punishment of the crimes referred to in article 1, subject to the provisions of this Statute:

(a) The provisions of the Lebanese Criminal Code relating to the prosecution and punishment of acts of terrorism, crimes and offences against life and personal integrity, illicit associations and failure to report crimes and offences, including the rules regarding the material elements of a crime, criminal participation and conspiracy; and

(b) Articles 6 and 7 of the Lebanese law of 11 January 1958 on "Increasing the penalties for sedition, civil war and interfaith struggle".

Article 3
Individual Criminal Responsibility

1. A person shall be individually responsible for crimes within the jurisdiction of the Special Tribunal if that person:

(a) Committed, participated as accomplice, organized or directed others to commit the crime set forth in article 2 of this Statute; or

(b) Contributed in any other way to the commission of the crime set forth in article 2 of this Statute by a group of persons acting with a common purpose, where such contribution is intentional and is either made with the aim of furthering the general criminal activity or purpose of the group or in the knowledge of the intention of the group to commit the crime.

2. With respect to superior and subordinate relationships, a superior shall be criminally responsible for any of the crimes set forth in article 2 of this Statute committed by subordinates under his or her effective authority and control, as a result of his or her failure to exercise control properly over such subordinates, where:

(a) The superior either knew, or consciously disregarded information that clearly indicated that the subordinates were committing or about to commit such crimes;

(b) The crimes concerned activities that were within the effective responsibility and control of the superior; and

(c) The superior failed to take all necessary and reasonable measures within his or her power to prevent or repress their commission or to submit the matter to the competent authorities for investigation and prosecution.

3. The fact that the person acted pursuant to an order of a superior shall not relieve him or her of criminal responsibility, but may be considered in mitigation of punishment if the Special Tribunal determines that justice so requires.

Article 4
Concurrent Jurisdiction

1. The Special Tribunal and the national courts of Lebanon shall have concurrent jurisdiction. Within its jurisdiction, the Tribunal shall have primacy over the national courts of Lebanon.

2. Upon the assumption of office of the Prosecutor, as determined by the Secretary-General, and no later than two months thereafter, the Special Tribunal shall request the national judicial authority seized with the case of the attack against Prime Minister Rafiq Hariri and others to defer to its competence. The Lebanese judicial authority shall refer to the Tribunal the results of the investigation and a copy of the court's records, if any. Persons detained in connection with the investigation shall be transferred to the custody of the Tribunal.

3. (a) At the request of the Special Tribunal, the national judicial authority seized with any of the other crimes committed between 1 October 2004 and 12 December 2005, or a later date decided pursuant to article 1, shall refer to the Tribunal the results of the investigation and a copy of the court's records, if any, for review by the Prosecutor;

(b) At the further request of the Tribunal, the national authority in question shall defer to the competence of the Tribunal. It shall refer to the Tribunal the results of the investigation and a copy of the court's records, if any, and persons detained in connection with any such case shall be transferred to the custody of the Tribunal;

(c) The national judicial authorities shall regularly inform the Tribunal of the progress of their investigation. At any stage of the proceedings, the Tribunal may formally request a national judicial authority to defer to its competence.

Article 5
Non Bis in Idem

1. No person shall be tried before a national court of Lebanon for acts for which he or she has already been tried by the Special Tribunal.

2. A person who has been tried by a national court may be subsequently tried by the Special Tribunal if the national court proceedings were not impartial or independent, were designed to shield the accused from criminal responsibility for crimes within the jurisdiction of the Tribunal or the case was not diligently prosecuted.

3. In considering the penalty to be imposed on a person convicted of a crime under this Statute, the Special Tribunal shall take into account the extent to which any penalty imposed by a national court on the same person for the same act has already been served.

Article 6
Amnesty

An amnesty granted to any person for any crime falling within the jurisdiction of the Special Tribunal shall not be a bar to prosecution.

Section II
Organization of the Special Tribunal

Article 7
Organs of the Special Tribunal

The Special Tribunal shall consist of the following organs:

(a) The Chambers, comprising a Pre-Trial Judge, a Trial Chamber and an Appeals Chamber;

(b) The Prosecutor;

(c) The Registry; and

(d) The Defence Office.

Article 8
Composition of the Chambers

1. The Chambers shall be composed as follows:

(a) One international Pre-Trial Judge;

(b) Three judges who shall serve in the Trial Chamber, of whom one shall be a Lebanese judge and two shall be international judges;

(c) Five judges who shall serve in the Appeals Chamber, of whom two shall be Lebanese judges and three shall be international judges;

(d) Two alternate judges, one of whom shall be a Lebanese judge and one shall be an international judge.

2. The judges of the Appeals Chamber and the judges of the Trial Chamber, respectively, shall elect a presiding judge who shall conduct the proceedings in the Chamber to which he or she was elected. The presiding judge of the Appeals Chamber shall be the President of the Special Tribunal.

3. At the request of the presiding judge of the Trial Chamber, the President of the Special Tribunal may, in the interest of justice, assign the alternate judges to be present at each stage of the trial and to replace a judge if that judge is unable to continue sitting.

Article 9
Qualification and Appointment of Judges

1. The judges shall be persons of high moral character, impartiality and integrity, with extensive judicial experience. They shall be independent in the performance of their functions and shall not accept or seek instructions from any Government or any other source.

2. In the overall composition of the Chambers, due account shall be taken of the established competence of the judges in criminal law and procedure and international law.

3. The judges shall be appointed by the Secretary-General, as set forth in article 2 of the Agreement, for a three-year period and may be eligible for reappointment for a further period to be determined by the Secretary-General in consultation with the Government.

Article 10
Powers of the President of the Special Tribunal

1. The President of the Special Tribunal, in addition to his or her judicial functions, shall represent the Tribunal and be responsible for its effective functioning and the good administration of justice.

2. The President of the Special Tribunal shall submit an annual report on the operation and activities of the Tribunal to the Secretary-General and to the Government of Lebanon.

Article 11
The Prosecutor

1. The Prosecutor shall be responsible for the investigation and prosecution of persons responsible for the crimes falling within the jurisdiction of the Special Tribunal. In the interest of proper administration of justice, he or she may decide to charge jointly persons accused of the same or different crimes committed in the course of the same transaction.

2. The Prosecutor shall act independently as a separate organ of the Special Tribunal. He or she shall not seek or receive instructions from any Government or from any other source.

3. The Prosecutor shall be appointed, as set forth in article 3 of the Agreement, by the Secretary-General for a three-year term and may be eligible for reappointment for a further period to be determined by the Secretary-General in consultation with the Government. He or she shall be of high moral character and possess the highest level of professional competence, and have extensive experience in the conduct of investigations and prosecutions of criminal cases.

4. The Prosecutor shall be assisted by a Lebanese Deputy Prosecutor and by such other Lebanese and international staff as may be required to perform the functions assigned to him or her effectively and efficiently.

5. The Office of the Prosecutor shall have the power to question suspects, victims and witnesses, to collect evidence and to conduct on-site investigations. In carrying out these tasks, the Prosecutor shall, as appropriate, be assisted by the Lebanese authorities concerned.

Article 12
The Registry

1. Under the authority of the President of the Special Tribunal, the Registry shall be responsible for the administration and servicing of the Tribunal.

2. The Registry shall consist of a Registrar and such other staff as may be required.

3. The Registrar shall be appointed by the Secretary-General and shall be a staff member of the United Nations. He or she shall serve for a three-year term and may be eligible for reappointment for a further period to be determined by the Secretary-General in consultation with the Government.

4. The Registrar shall set up a Victims and Witnesses Unit within the Registry. This Unit shall provide, in consultation with the Office of the Prosecutor, measures to protect the safety, physical and psychological well-being, dignity and privacy of victims and witnesses, and such other appropriate assistance for witnesses who appear before the Special Tribunal and others who are at risk on account of testimony given by such witnesses.

Article 13
The Defence Office

1. The Secretary-General, in consultation with the President of the Special Tribunal, shall appoint an independent Head of the Defence Office, who

shall be responsible for the appointment of the Office staff and the drawing up of a list of defence counsel.

2. The Defence Office, which may also include one or more public defenders, shall protect the rights of the defence, provide support and assistance to defence counsel and to the persons entitled to legal assistance, including, where appropriate, legal research, collection of evidence and advice, and appearing before the Pre-Trial Judge or a Chamber in respect of specific issues.

Article 14
Official and Working Languages

The official languages of the Special Tribunal shall be Arabic, French and English. In any given case proceedings, the Pre-Trial Judge or a Chamber may decide that one or two of the languages may be used as working languages as appropriate.

Section III
Rights of Defendants and Victims

Article 15
Rights of Suspects During Investigation

A suspect who is to be questioned by the Prosecutor shall not be compelled to incriminate himself or herself or to confess guilt. He or she shall have the following rights of which he or she shall be informed by the Prosecutor prior to questioning, in a language he or she speaks and understands:

(a) The right to be informed that there are grounds to believe that he or she has committed a crime within the jurisdiction of the Special Tribunal;

(b) The right to remain silent, without such silence being considered in the determination of guilt or innocence, and to be cautioned that any statement he or she makes shall be recorded and may be used in evidence;

(c) The right to have legal assistance of his or her own choosing, including the right to have legal assistance provided by the Defence Office where the interests of justice so require and where the suspect does not have sufficient means to pay for it;

(d) The right to have the free assistance of an interpreter if he or she cannot understand or speak the language used for questioning;

(e) The right to be questioned in the presence of counsel unless the person has voluntarily waived his or her right to counsel.

Article 16
Rights of the Accused

1. All accused shall be equal before the Special Tribunal.

2. The accused shall be entitled to a fair and public hearing, subject to measures ordered by the Special Tribunal for the protection of victims and witnesses.

3. (a) The accused shall be presumed innocent until proved guilty according to the provisions of this Statute;

(b) The onus is on the Prosecutor to prove the guilt of the accused;

(c) In order to convict the accused, the relevant Chamber must be convinced of the guilt of the accused beyond reasonable doubt.

4. In the determination of any charge against the accused pursuant to this Statute, he or she shall be entitled to the following minimum guarantees, in full equality:

(a) To be informed promptly and in detail in a language which he or she understands of the nature and cause of the charge against him or her;

(b) To have adequate time and facilities for the preparation of his or her defence and to communicate without hindrance with counsel of his or her own choosing;

(c) To be tried without undue delay;

(d) Subject to the provisions of article 22, to be tried in his or her presence, and to defend himself or herself in person or through legal assistance of his or her own choosing; to be informed, if he or she does not have legal assistance, of this right; and to have legal assistance assigned to him or her, in any case where the interests of justice so require and without payment by him or her in any such case if he or she does not have sufficient means to pay for it;

(e) To examine, or have examined, the witnesses against him or her and to obtain the attendance and examination of witnesses on his or her behalf under the same conditions as witnesses against him or her;

(f) To examine all evidence to be used against him or her during the trial in accordance with the Rules of Procedure and Evidence of the Special Tribunal;

(g) To have the free assistance of an interpreter if he or she cannot understand or speak the language used in the Special Tribunal;

(h) Not to be compelled to testify against himself or herself or to confess guilt.

5. The accused may make statements in court at any stage of the proceedings, provided such statements are relevant to the case at issue. The Chambers shall decide on the probative value, if any, of such statements.

Article 17
Rights of Victims

Where the personal interests of the victims are affected, the Special Tribunal shall permit their views and concerns to be presented and considered at stages of the proceedings determined to be appropriate by the Pre-Trial Judge or the Chamber and in a manner that is not prejudicial to or inconsistent with the rights of the accused and a fair and impartial trial. Such views and concerns may be presented by the legal representatives of the victims where the Pre-Trial Judge or the Chamber considers it appropriate.

Section IV
Conduct of Proceedings

Article 18
Pre-Trial Proceedings

1. The Pre-Trial Judge shall review the indictment. If satisfied that a prima facie case has been established by the Prosecutor, he or she shall confirm the indictment. If he or she is not so satisfied, the indictment shall be dismissed.

2. The Pre-Trial Judge may, at the request of the Prosecutor, issue such orders and warrants for the arrest or transfer of persons, and any other orders as may be required for the conduct of the investigation and for the preparation of a fair and expeditious trial.

Article 19
Evidence Collected Prior to the Establishment of the Special Tribunal

Evidence collected with regard to cases subject to the consideration of the Special Tribunal, prior to the establishment of the Tribunal, by the national authorities of Lebanon or by the International Independent Investigation Commission in accordance with its mandate as set out in Security Council resolution 1595 (2005) and subsequent resolutions, shall be received by the Tribunal. Its admissibility shall be decided by the Chambers pursuant to international standards on collection of evidence. The weight to be given to any such evidence shall be determined by the Chambers.

Article 20
Commencement and Conduct of Trial Proceedings

1. The Trial Chamber shall read the indictment to the accused, satisfy itself that the rights of the accused are respected, confirm that the accused understands the indictment and instruct the accused to enter a plea.

2. Unless otherwise decided by the Trial Chamber in the interests of justice, examination of witnesses shall commence with questions posed by the presiding judge, followed by questions posed by other members of the Trial Chamber, the Prosecutor and the Defence.

3. Upon request or *proprio motu*, the Trial Chamber may at any stage of the trial decide to call additional witnesses and/or order the production of additional evidence.

4. The hearings shall be public unless the Trial Chamber decides to hold the proceedings in camera in accordance with the Rules of Procedure and Evidence.

Article 21
Powers of the Chambers

1. The Special Tribunal shall confine the trial, appellate and review proceedings strictly to an expeditious hearing of the issues raised by the charges, or the grounds for appeal or review, respectively. It shall take strict measures to prevent any action that may cause unreasonable delay.

2. A Chamber may admit any relevant evidence that it deems to have probative value and exclude such evidence if its probative value is substantially outweighed by the need to ensure a fair trial.

3. A Chamber may receive the evidence of a witness orally or, where the interests of justice allow, in written form.

4. In cases not otherwise provided for in the Rules of Procedure and Evidence, a Chamber shall apply rules of evidence that will best favour a fair determination of the matter before it and are consonant with the spirit of the Statute and the general principles of law.

Article 22
Trials in Absentia

1. The Special Tribunal shall conduct trial proceedings in the absence of the accused, if he or she:

(a) Has expressly and in writing waived his or her right to be present;

(b) Has not been handed over to the Tribunal by the State authorities concerned;

(c) Has absconded or otherwise cannot be found and all reasonable steps have been taken to secure his or her appearance before the Tribunal and to inform him or her of the charges confirmed by the Pre-Trial Judge.

2. When hearings are conducted in the absence of the accused, the Special Tribunal shall ensure that:

(a) The accused has been notified, or served with the indictment, or notice has otherwise been given of the indictment through publication in the media or communication to the State of residence or nationality;

(b) The accused has designated a defence counsel of his or her own choosing, to be remunerated either by the accused or, if the accused is proved to be indigent, by the Tribunal;

(c) Whenever the accused refuses or fails to appoint a defence counsel, such counsel has been assigned by the Defence Office of the Tribunal with a view to ensuring full representation of the interests and rights of the accused.

3. In case of conviction in absentia, the accused, if he or she had not designated a defence counsel of his or her choosing, shall have the right to be retried in his or her presence before the Special Tribunal, unless he or she accepts the judgement.

Article 23
Judgement

The judgement shall be rendered by a majority of the judges of the Trial Chamber or of the Appeals Chamber and shall be delivered in public. It shall be accompanied by a reasoned opinion in writing, to which any separate or dissenting opinions shall be appended.

Article 24
Penalties

1. The Trial Chamber shall impose upon a convicted person imprisonment for life or for a specified number of years. In determining the terms of imprisonment for the crimes provided for in this Statute, the Trial Chamber shall, as appropriate, have recourse to international practice regarding prison sentences and to the practice of the national courts of Lebanon.

2. In imposing sentence, the Trial Chamber should take into account such factors as the gravity of the offence and the individual circumstances of the convicted person.

Article 25
Compensation to Victims

1. The Special Tribunal may identify victims who have suffered harm as a result of the commission of crimes by an accused convicted by the Tribunal.

2. The Registrar shall transmit to the competent authorities of the State concerned the judgement finding the accused guilty of a crime that has caused harm to a victim.

3. Based on the decision of the Special Tribunal and pursuant to the relevant national legislation, a victim or persons claiming through the victim, whether or not such victim had been identified as such by the Tribunal under paragraph 1 of this article, may bring an action in a national court or other competent body to obtain compensation.

4. For the purposes of a claim made under paragraph 3 of this article, the judgement of the Special Tribunal shall be final and binding as to the criminal responsibility of the convicted person.

Article 26
Appellate Proceedings

1. The Appeals Chamber shall hear appeals from persons convicted by the Trial Chamber or from the Prosecutor on the following grounds:

(a) An error on a question of law invalidating the decision;

(b) An error of fact that has occasioned a miscarriage of justice.

2. The Appeals Chamber may affirm, reverse or revise the decisions taken by the Trial Chamber.

Article 27
Review Proceedings

1. Where a new fact has been discovered that was not known at the time of the proceedings before the Trial Chamber or the Appeals Chamber and that could have been a decisive factor in reaching the decision, the convicted person or the Prosecutor may submit an application for review of the judgement.

2. An application for review shall be submitted to the Appeals Chamber. The Appeals Chamber may reject the application if it considers it to be unfounded. If it determines that the application is meritorious, it may, as appropriate:

(a) Reconvene the Trial Chamber;

(b) Retain jurisdiction over the matter.

Article 28
Rules of Procedure and Evidence

1. The judges of the Special Tribunal shall, as soon as practicable after taking office, adopt Rules of Procedure and Evidence for the conduct of the pre-trial, trial and appellate proceedings, the admission of evidence, the participation of victims, the protection of victims and witnesses and other appropriate matters and may amend them, as appropriate.

2. In so doing, the judges shall be guided, as appropriate, by the Lebanese Code of Criminal Procedure, as well as by other reference materials reflecting the highest standards of international criminal procedure, with a view to ensuring a fair and expeditious trial.

Article 29
Enforcement of Sentences

1. Imprisonment shall be served in a State designated by the President of the Special Tribunal from a list of States that have indicated their willingness to accept persons convicted by the Tribunal.

2. Conditions of imprisonment shall be governed by the law of the State of enforcement subject to the supervision of the Special Tribunal. The State of enforcement shall be bound by the duration of the sentence, subject to article 30 of this Statute.

Article 30
Pardon or Commutation of Sentences

If, pursuant to the applicable law of the State in which the convicted person is imprisoned, he or she is eligible for pardon or commutation of sentence, the State concerned shall notify the Special Tribunal accordingly. There shall only be pardon or commutation of sentence if the President of the Tribunal, in consultation with the judges, so decides on the basis of the interests of justice and the general principles of law.

Annex II
Attacks Perpetrated in Lebanon Since 1 October 2004[a]

Following is an overview of the 14 cases in chronological order.

Number	*Date*	*Type of explosion*	*Area*	*Victims*
1	1 October 2004	Car bomb	Dar El-Mraisseh locality, California Street, Beirut	Marwane Hamadeh and driver wounded, bodyguard killed
2	19 March 2005	Bomb	New-Jdeidh, northern suburb of Beirut	11 persons wounded and serious material damage to buildings and cars
3	23 March 2005	Bomb	Altavista shopping centre, Kaslik, north of Beirut	3 persons killed, 7 persons wounded and serious material damage to buildings and cars
4	26 March 2005	Bomb	Sid-El-Bouchria, north-east of Beirut	6 persons wounded and serious material damage to buildings and cars
5	1 April 2005	Bomb	Plaza shopping centre, Broumana, east of Beirut	9 persons wounded and serious material damage to buildings and cars
6	6 May 2005	Bomb	"Voice of Charity" radio station, Jounieh, north of Beirut	11 persons wounded and serious material damage to buildings and cars
7	2 June 2005	Victim's car	Ashrafieh locality, Beirut	Samir Kassir killed
8	21 June 2005	Victim's car	Wata Msaytbeh, Boustany Street, Beirut	George Hawi killed
9	12 July 2005	Car bomb	Naccache area, Beirut	Elias El-Murr and 2 other persons wounded and1 person killed
10	22 July 2005	Bomb	Monot Street, Ashrafieh locality, Beirut	13 persons wounded and serious material damage to buildings and cars

[a] See S/2006/161, para. 55.

Number	*Date*	*Type of explosion*	*Area*	*Victims*
11	22 August 2005	Bomb	Zalka locality, near Promenade Hotel, north of Beirut	11 persons wounded and serious material damage to buildings and cars
12	16 September 2005	Bomb	Naoum Libki Street, Ashrafieh locality, Beirut	1 person killed and 10 persons wounded and serious material damage to buildings and cars
13	25 September 2005	Victim's car	Ghadir locality, suburb of Beirut	May Chidiac seriously wounded
14	12 December 2005	Car bomb	Mkalles, north of Beirut	Gebran Tueni and 2 other persons killed

DOCUMENT NO. 20

TRANSCRIPT FROM THE SECURITY COUNCIL MEETING ON THE SPECIAL TRIBUNAL FOR LEBANON

United Nations Security Council
Sixty-second year
S/PV.5685

May 30, 2007

Provisional

5685th meeting
Wednesday, 30 May 2007, 3 p.m.
New York

President:	Mr. Khalilzad	(United States of America)
Members:	Belgium	Mr. Verbeke
	China	Mr. Wang Guangya
	Congo	Mr. Gayama
	France	Mr. De La Sablière
	Ghana	Mr. Christian
	Indonesia	Mr. Kleib
	Italy	Mr. Spatafora
	Panama	Mr. Suescum
	Peru	Mr. Voto-Bernales
	Qatar	Mr. Al-Nasser
	Russian Federation	Mr. Churkin
	Slovakia	Mr. Matulay
	South Africa	Mr. Kumalo
	United Kingdom of Great Britain and Northern Ireland	Sir Emyr Jones Parry

This record contains the text of speeches delivered in English and of the interpretation of speeches delivered in the other languages. The final text will be printed in the *Official Records of the Security Council*. Corrections should be submitted to the original languages only. They should be incorporated in a copy of the record and sent under the signature of a member of the delegation concerned to the Chief of the Verbatim Reporting Service, room C-154A.

Agenda

The situation in the Middle East

The meeting was called to order at 3.15 p.m.

Adoption of the Agenda

The agenda was adopted.

The Situation in the Middle East

The President: I should like to inform the Council that I have received a letter from the representative of Lebanon, in which she requests Lebanon to be invited to participate in the consideration of the item on the Council's agenda. In conformity with the usual practice, I propose, with the consent of the Council, to invite the representative of Lebanon to participate in the consideration without the right to vote, in accordance with the relevant provisions of the Charter and rule 37 of the Council's provisional rules of procedure.

There being no objection, it is so decided.

On behalf of the Council, I extend a warm welcome to the Minister of Culture and Minister of Foreign Affairs ad interim of Lebanon, His Excellency Mr. Tarik Mitri.

At the invitation of the President, Mr. Mitri (Lebanon) took a seat at the Council table.

The President: The Security Council will now begin its consideration of the item on its agenda. The Council is meeting in accordance with the understanding reached in its prior consultations.

Members of the Council have before them document S/2007/315, which contains the text of a draft resolution submitted by Belgium, France, Italy, Slovakia, the United Kingdom of Great Britain and Northern Ireland, and the United States of America.

Members also have before them documents S/2007/281 and S/2007/286, containing two letters dated 15 May and 16 May 2007, respectively, addressed to the President of the Security Council from the Secretary-General.

It is my understanding that the Council is ready to proceed to the vote on the draft resolution before it. Unless I hear any objection, I shall put the draft resolution to the vote now.

There being no objection, it is so decided.

I now give the floor to those members of the Council who wish to make statements before the voting.

Mr. Al-Nasser (Qatar) (*spoke in Arabic*): I feel it incumbent upon me first and foremost to affirm our firm, established position of advocating the need to establish justice and oppose impunity, in line with the objective set out in the United Nations Charter of creating conditions under which justice and respect for the obligations arising from treaties and other sources of international law can be maintained.

Like others, we continue to call for the truth to be brought to light regarding the crime of the assassination of the former Prime Minister of Lebanon, Mr. Rafiq Hariri, pursuant to the desire of the fraternal Lebanese people, in all its factions, to punish the perpetrators of that outrageous crime.

In that spirit, we did not hesitate to support the establishment of the Independent International Investigation Committee, and voted in favour of relevant Security Council resolutions that paved the way for the establishment of the Special Tribunal for Lebanon, which enjoys the consensus endorsement of all Lebanese factions. In a letter dated 21 November 2006, addressed to the President of the Security Council, the State of Qatar clearly indicated its position on the legal aspects of the constitutional process by which agreement was reached between the Lebanese Government and the United Nations to establish the Tribunal.

The State of Qatar remains committed to helping Lebanon seek the truth, hold accountable all those involved in those crimes and bring them to justice, while placing the interests of fraternal Lebanon at the top of our priorities so as to ensure the maintenance of its independence, sovereignty, national unity and political stability.

While committed to uncovering the truth and to the establishment of the Special Tribunal to try whoever may be implicated in the crime, we feel that the draft resolution before the Council now entails legal encroachments known to all. That may not promote national détente and could further complicate the situation in a country that is at present in dire need of national cohesion and political stability.

In spite of those difficulties, we were quite willing to consider the draft resolution in a positive spirit, with the aim of arriving at a consensus formula. The State of Qatar supports the establishment of the tribunal to punish the perpetrators of that outrageous crime. However, the insistence of the sponsors to present the draft resolution under Chapter VII—although all Security Council resolutions are binding, in accordance with Article 25 of the Charter—goes beyond its designated aim of endorsing the establishment of the tribunal, especially in the light of the complicated and delicate political situation in Lebanon. We are simply apprehensive that the adoption of the draft resolution under Chapter VII will not serve to bring stability to that country.

In the light of the foregoing, we shall abstain in the voting on the draft resolution before us. At the same time, we will continue our good offices to bring points of view in Lebanon closer, in the interest of national unity and to ensure endorsement of the establishment of the tribunal through national mechanisms and in accordance with article 19 of the agreement to establish the tribunal.

Mr. Kleib (Indonesia): My delegation wishes to explain its position before the voting on the draft resolution on the special tribunal for Lebanon.

Impunity must not be tolerated; justice must prevail. Those who are found responsible for the assassination of the late Prime Minister Hariri and for other related assassinations must therefore be brought to justice. Indonesia is committed to support the pursuit of truth and justice. We support the work of the International Independent Investigation Commission and the extension of its mandate. We also have a strong commitment to making a constructive contribution to the efforts to promote peace and stability in Lebanon.

We take note of the Lebanese Prime Minister's request for the Council to take a binding decision on the establishment of a special tribunal for Lebanon. The draft resolution before us today has been based on that request. However, the Council should not fail to take into consideration that there is no unified voice among Lebanese leaders. The domestic political situation in Lebanon has created difficulty for the international community to act further on that request.

On the draft resolution, my delegation considers that it has changed the legal nature of article 19 of the agreement, which clearly states that the agreement shall enter into force on the day after the Government of Lebanon has notified the United Nations that the internal legal requirements for its entry into force have been met. If the draft resolution is adopted, it will bypass constitutional procedure and national processes.

There are no legal grounds for the Security Council to take over an issue that is domestic in nature. Article 2, paragraph 7, of the Charter of the United Nations stresses that nothing contained in the Charter shall authorize the United Nations to intervene in matters that are essentially within the domestic jurisdiction of any State. Although that provision does not prejudice the application of enforcement measures under Chapter VII, the Security Council should not be involved in an exercise of interpreting, let alone taking over, the constitutional requirements that a State should comply with in the conduct of its authorities.

Before taking action on the draft resolution, which is intended to uphold justice, the Council should fully consider the domestic situation in Lebanon. The forceful interference by the Security Council in the national constitutional process as regards the establishment of the tribunal will not serve the greater interests of the Lebanese people, namely, reconciliation, national unity, peace and stability. The search for justice should neither create new problems nor exacerbate the already intricate situation in Lebanon.

In the light of the foregoing considerations, my delegation will abstain on the voting on the draft resolution.

Mr. Kumalo (South Africa): South Africa unequivocally condemns the assassinations of the former Lebanese Prime Minister, Mr. Rafiq Hariri, and other Lebanese leaders. Indeed, there is a consensus within Lebanon and internationally on the need for the United Nations to assist the Lebanese authorities in their efforts to bring to justice those responsible for those grave crimes and to end all impunity. It is for that reason that the United Nations International Independent Investigation Commission was set up to assist Lebanon with its criminal investigation. The decision was also taken to set up a special tribunal comprised of Lebanese and international jurists and prosecutors located outside Lebanon to prosecute any persons identified by the investigation and the Lebanese authorities as suspects in the assassination of former Prime Minister Rafiq Hariri and other Lebanese leaders.

South Africa fully supports the establishment of the tribunal and expects it to operate with impartiality and in accordance with Lebanese law and the highest international standards of criminal justice. My delegation regards Lebanese ownership of the tribunal as being of paramount importance and believes that it is incumbent upon the Lebanese authorities and people to reach a consensus position on the matter. Therefore, we still hold out the hope that the Lebanese parties can use the period specified in the draft resolution—between now and 10 June 2007—to come to a political agreement on the tribunal, and not leave it to be imposed upon Lebanon.

We maintain that it is not appropriate for the Security Council to impose such a tribunal on Lebanon, especially under Chapter VII of the Charter of the United Nations. In that regard, my delegation has frequently cautioned that the Security Council should be judicious in its invocation of Chapter VII of the Charter. We also do not believe that the Council has the right to bypass the procedures required by the Lebanese Constitution for the entry into force of an agreement with the United Nations. In discarding the Lebanese Constitution the Security Council is contravening its own decision regarding the need to respect the sovereignty, territorial integrity, unity and political independence of Lebanon.

The Security Council is mandated to act with impartiality and without bias. It cannot be seen to be taking sides in internal Lebanese politics. There is a danger that the imposition of the special tribunal on Lebanon without the consent of all the parties concerned will detrimentally affect the political stability of the already fragile Lebanese State. It will also politicize international criminal law, thereby undermining the very foundations of international law.

Furthermore, we have concerns about the precedent that this draft resolution will set. The principle of national consensus in establishing international tribunals is an important aspect of peacebuilding and national reconciliation.

Therefore, regrettably, South Africa will abstain in the voting on the draft resolution before us.

Mr. Wang Guangya (China) (spoke in Chinese): The Chinese delegation will abstain on the draft resolution before us.

We deeply deplore the unfortunate assassination of Mr. Hariri, former Prime Minister of Lebanon. China has consistently supported the fair and independent investigation of the case by the United Nations International Independent Investigation Commission. We understand and support the request of all Lebanese parties for the establishment a special tribunal. We hope that that initiative will help to establish the truth as soon as possible, hold the perpetrators accountable and ensure justice for the victims.

China notes the political consensus among all Lebanese parties on the establishment of the Special Tribunal, as well as the divergence of views regarding procedural matters. We hope that political and diplomatic efforts will assist the parties in reaching a consensus as soon as possible. Only a special tribunal that enjoys universal support among all Lebanese factions can genuinely play a role in contributing to the achievement of justice and the maintenance of peace and stability in Lebanon. The point of departure and the focus of Security Council assistance should be to help to resolve real problems without further complicating an already very complex problem.

The establishment of the Special Tribunal is, in essence, Lebanon's own internal affair. Lebanon's domestic laws provide the legal basis for the operation. It is therefore only reasonable that Lebanon should, in accordance with its constitutional procedures, complete the domestic legal process required for the entry into force of the agreement. That is explicitly provided for in the agreement between United Nations and Lebanon on the establishment of the Tribunal. As a result of the special circumstances prevailing in Lebanon, that process has encountered major difficulties, which is a cause of great concern for us.

China believes that by invoking Chapter VII of the Charter, the resolution will override Lebanon's legislative organs by arbitrarily deciding on the date of the entry into force of the draft statute. This move will give rise to a series of political and legal problems that are likely to add to the uncertainty surrounding the already turbulent political and security situation in

Lebanon and create a precedent of Security Council interference in the domestic affairs and legislative independence of a sovereign State. Such actions are likely to undermine the authority of the Council, as they are not in conformity with the long-term interests of either of the parties.

During the course of deliberations on the draft resolution before us, China, together with other members of the Council, expressed the hope that the sponsors would listen attentively and respond to our concerns by further revising the draft so as to make it more balanced and prudent. Regrettably, however, our recommendations were not adopted. That being the case, China will have no choice but to abstain.

The situation in the Middle East is extremely complex and convoluted. Various factors are interlinked, and one drop in a pool of water has a big ripple effect. It is our hope that at this difficult moment the Lebanese people will stand united in maintaining the security and stability of the nation and promoting the process of national reconciliation. It is essential that the Security Council, while addressing related issues, take fully into account the unique and complex situation in the Middle East and refrain from triggering new tensions or turbulence in the region.

Mr. Churkin (Russian Federation) (*spoke in Russian*): The Russian Federation has consistently advocated establishing the truth with respect to the murder of Rafik Hariri. The perpetrators of that crime must be brought to justice. We fully share with the sponsors of the draft resolution their primary objective of preventing impunity and political violence in Lebanon. Given the fragility of the domestic situation in Lebanon, it is essential that the Council take a balanced and considered decision with a view to promoting harmonious relations among the Lebanese people.

Given the deep rift within Lebanese society and Government structures, this matter must be pursued so that the practical implementation of the draft resolution does not face serious difficulties that could lead to negative consequences for the country and the region as a whole. During consultations on the draft resolution, the Russian Federation made a number of constructive proposals that could have considerably improved the text. The draft should have focused on the implementation, under a Council decision, of the agreement between the United Nations and Lebanon, not on the entry into force of the agreement.

The arrangement chosen by the sponsors is dubious from the point of view of international law. The treaty between the two entities—Lebanon and the United Nations—by definition cannot enter into force on the basis of a decision by only one party. The constituent documents for the Tribunal, imposed by a unilateral decision of a United Nations body—that is, a Security Council resolution—essentially represent an encroachment upon the sovereignty of Lebanon.

We do not believe that the establishment of a special tribunal by decision of the Council under Chapter VII of the Charter is warranted. There is no basis for a reference to Chapter VII in the draft resolution. United Nations practice in establishing tribunals shows that Chapter VII has been invoked only for the International Criminal Tribunal for the Former Yugoslavia and for the International Criminal Tribunal for Rwanda, which deal with crimes of genocide, crimes against humanity and war crimes—that is, international crimes. The jurisdiction of the Special Tribunal for Lebanon would not cover such crimes. By its nature, the Tribunal is a mixed body with considerable Lebanese participation that operates on the basis of the applicable criminal procedures of Lebanon.

The Tribunal is being established for Lebanon, and it is important to heed the views of all the Lebanese people on this critical issue. In this regard, it would have been justifiable to have the preambular part of the draft resolution include a reference not only to the letter from the Prime Minister of Lebanon, Fouad Siniora, but also to that from the country's President, Emile Lahoud.

The language proposed by Russia has not been reflected in text of the draft resolution. Given that fact, we intend to abstain in the vote on the draft resolution. We regret the fact that putting a draft resolution with considerable legal shortcomings to a vote in such a hasty manner will not allow the Russian Federation and a number of other members of the Security Council to support it.

The President: The Council will now proceed to take a decision on the draft resolution (S/2007/315) before it.

A vote was taken by show of hands.

In favour:

Belgium, Congo, France, Ghana, Italy, Panama, Peru, Slovakia, United Kingdom of Great Britain and Northern Ireland, United States of America

Against:

None

Abstaining:

China, Indonesia, Qatar, Russian Federation, South Africa

The President: The result of the voting is as follows: ten votes in favour, none against and five abstaining. The draft resolution has been adopted as resolution 1757 (2007).

Mr. De La Sablière (France) (*spoke in French*): France welcomes the adoption of resolution 1757 (2007) which, in response to the request of the Government of Lebanon, will enter into force on 10 June 2007, unless an internal solution is found before then with respect to the provisions of the Agreement on the establishment of a Special Tribunal for Lebanon.

This is an important decision for several reasons. The first is justice, as it opens the way to the trial of those guilty of the attack that took the life of former Lebanese Prime Minister Rafik Hariri on 14 February 2005 and other terrorist attacks committed in Lebanon since October 2004. It establishes essential continuity with the International Independent Investigation Commission.

It is also important for peace in Lebanon. Justice cannot stand in the way of stability. The rejection of impunity, shared by all Lebanese, is an essential guarantee of peace.

It is, finally, an important decision for the credibility of the United Nations—and of the Security Council in particular, whose commitment to finding the truth in Lebanon has been unflagging.

The Council can take pride today in not having resigned itself to the ongoing impasse of which the Lebanese Government and the Secretary-General and his Legal Counsel had on several occasions informed it. The Council can be proud that it has shouldered its responsibility by helping Lebanon to overcome the obstacles that it was facing and to proceed along the path to recovering its independence and its sovereignty.

Sir Emyr Jones Parry (United Kingdom): The United Kingdom welcomes the adoption of resolution 1757 (2007). The proposed Tribunal is vital for Lebanon, for justice and for the region. The establishment of the Tribunal through Lebanese internal procedures had been thwarted. The Council, for its part, has been asked to adopt a binding decision to create the Tribunal.

This is not a capricious intervention or interference in the domestic political affairs of a sovereign State. It is a considered response by the Council, properly taken, to a request from the Government of Lebanon for action to overcome a continued impasse in Lebanon's internal procedures, despite long and serious efforts to find a solution within Lebanon.

It is a long-held United Kingdom view that, to make this decision binding, it was necessary for such a resolution, inter alia, to be taken under Chapter VII. The use of Chapter VII carries no connotation other than that it makes this resolution binding. That is why the United Kingdom supported this resolution. We hope that all parties in Lebanon will now be able to move forward together to take the necessary decisions to build upon this formal establishment of the Tribunal.

Mr. Voto-Bernales (Peru) (*spoke in Spanish*): Peru decided to support this resolution because of its commitment to the fight against impunity and its firm position on combating terrorism and because it is of the view that this resolution is the only way to overcome the legislative impasse regarding the establishment of the Special Tribunal for Lebanon, given the need to ensure that justice prevails, which is essential in promoting peace and security.

Peru has taken into account that the majority of the Lebanese parliament has given ample proof of its strong determination to approve the agreement establishing a special tribunal to try the persons who have been identified by the International Independent Investigation Commission as the presumed perpetrators of the politically motivated crimes executed by means of terrorist acts. Therefore, we hope that the Lebanese parliament can be convened so that it can complete the internal constitutional process for adoption and ratification within the time schedule envisaged in the resolution we have just adopted.

In supporting this resolution, given the exceptional political circumstances that exist, Peru reaffirms its respect for and commitment to international law. Thus, recognizing the particular circumstances of the case, we believe that the agreement signed between Lebanon and the United Nations by means of a resolution, in exercise of the powers of the Security Council as provided for in Chapter VII of the Charter of the United Nations, must not constitute a precedent beyond this particular case.

Mr. Verbeke (Belgium) (*spoke in French*): Belgium voted for the resolution under consideration. Through this resolution, the Security Council confirms the consistent stance that has governed its continuous commitment to stability and peace in a sovereign and independent Lebanon. The duty of justice and the fight against impunity are essential for the stability of Lebanon. This constancy has always guided the Council in its work with respect to the establishment of the International Independent Investigation Commission and of the international tribunal.

It is this same assessment that guided my delegation to support and sponsor this new resolution. This resolution does not prejudice an agreement that remains to be reached among the Lebanese and which we continue to call for. By adopting resolution 1757 (2007) today, the Security Council has provided unreserved support to the efforts of the Government to strengthen the rule of law that all Lebanese deserve.

Mr. Matulay (Slovakia): We welcome the adoption of resolution 1757 (2007). We have supported this resolution because we believe that impunity should not be allowed and tolerated. The perpetrators of any crime have to be brought to justice. The rule of law must be respected everywhere and by everybody. The establishment of the Tribunal is necessary for a thorough investigation of the cases of politically motivated violence—in fact, terrorism—and for bringing perpetrators of these outrageous crimes to justice.

As all available means have unfortunately been exhausted on an issue that could not be solved through Lebanese constitutional means, the Security

Council had to resume its responsibility and ensure the implementation of the agreement between the United Nations and the Lebanese Republic through a legally binding resolution.

We believe that the resolution of this issue will contribute to the stabilization of the situation in Lebanon and to the process of national reconciliation.

Mr. Spatafora (Italy): I just want to add my voice to the voices of the other sponsors. With this resolution, we have wanted to demonstrate a strong support for the Government of Lebanon, a strong support for the sovereignty and independence of Lebanon, and a belief that justice is a condition for the reconciliation and therefore the stability of the country. We truly hope that in the coming days and weeks the internal forces and players in Lebanon will find a way and the right path to implement the agreement.

The President: I shall now make a statement in my capacity as representative of the United States of America.

We welcome the adoption of resolution 1757 (2007) on the establishment of the Special Tribunal for Lebanon. By adopting this resolution, the Security Council has demonstrated its commitment to the principle that there shall be no impunity for political assassinations in Lebanon or elsewhere. Those who killed Rafik Hariri and so many others will be brought to justice and held responsible for their crimes. The Tribunal will also serve to deter future political assassinations. Those who might be tempted to commit similar crimes will know that there will be consequences for perpetuating political violence and intimidation in Lebanon.

We know that it was necessary and right for the Council to act now. The Council approved the Tribunal Agreement and Statute on 21 November 2006. Since that time, the legitimate and democratically elected Government of Lebanon and the parliamentary majority have tried, using every possible means, to convince the Speaker of parliament to fulfil his constitutional responsibility to convene parliament so that final action on the Tribunal could be taken, but to no avail.

Several influential parties visited Lebanon in an effort to find a framework within which parliament could be convened. These included the Arab League, United Nations Legal Counsel Nicolas Michel and the Secretary-General himself. After five months of tireless efforts to find a solution to the impasse facing his country, Prime Minister Siniora sent the Secretary-General a letter on 14 May (S/2007/281, annex) asking that the matter be put before the Security Council so that it could take a binding decision to establish the Special Tribunal. The Secretary-General endorsed the Prime Minister's request one day later, after concluding that all diplomatic efforts had been exhausted.

We would have preferred that the Lebanese ratify the Tribunal Agreement and Statute, but we know that that was not possible. No one can say that the Lebanese Government, the Secretary-General or the Security Council failed to pursue every possible option, short of Council action on the Tribunal. But those opposed to the Tribunal made sure that there were no such options available.

We have heard many voices warn of the risks to peace and stability in Lebanon. We urge all parties to act responsibly in the days ahead and to abide by their obligations to support Lebanon's sovereignty and political independence.

For our part, we concluded that failure to act in support of Lebanon was unacceptable. There can be no peace or stability without justice.

In conclusion, the United States reaffirms its support for Lebanon. With the adoption of this resolution, we are confident that the Security Council will live up to its commitment to support Lebanon in its pursuit of justice.

I now resume my functions as President of the Security Council.

I shall now invite His Excellency Mr. Tarek Mitri, Minister of Culture and Minister for Foreign Affairs ad interim of Lebanon, to make a statement.

Mr. Mitri (Lebanon) (*spoke in Arabic*): I should like, on behalf of the Government of Lebanon, to warmly thank the Security Council for expressing its constant support for the independence, sovereignty, security and freedom of Lebanon on the basis of the principles underpinning international legitimacy and the Charter of the United Nations. The Council has never hesitated—particularly over the past two years—to express its sympathy and support for and commitment to Lebanon and its independence.

Indeed, ever since the Security Council adopted resolution 1595 (2005), which established an International Independent Investigation Commission to inquire into the assassination of the late Prime Minister Rafik Hariri and members of his entourage, and in its efforts to identify the perpetrators of that terrorist crime and other political assassinations and attempted assassinations perpetrated since October 2004, the Council has consistently supported Lebanon. It has adopted important resolutions to ensure that criminals are brought to justice and that there is no impunity. Those resolutions have been binding to ensure that justice is done.

The Council has left no room for doubt in expressing its commitment to Lebanon. Last summer, the Council supported our country when we were the target of a destructive and iniquitous Israeli aggression. The Council called upon the international community to play its role by bringing an end to that aggression and providing the necessary assistance and support at various levels to protect Lebanon's sovereignty and territorial integrity. Last week, the Council reaffirmed its support for Lebanon once again by condemning terrorist acts aimed at undermining our security, stability and vitality, as well as the role played by my country—a role based on moderation, openness, democracy and freedom.

Today, the Security Council has adopted a text that forms the basis for the establishment of the Special Tribunal for Lebanon in accordance with a methodology that has been very professionally and meticulously worked out so that it meets the highest legal criteria. I wish to express our warmest thanks to the sponsors of the resolution and to those who voted in favour of it, thereby enhancing the credibility and effectiveness of the United Nations in carrying out its responsibilities and helping Lebanon to do justice and protect peace and security.

I also wish to take this opportunity to express my warmest thanks to those States that abstained in the voting. Despite the reservations that they expressed regarding the resolution just adopted by the Council, they once again reaffirmed their commitment to the paramount importance for the principle of justice of the establishment of a special tribunal for Lebanon to identify criminals and deter the undermining of our freedom and sovereignty.

Our warmest thanks go also to the Secretary-General for his personal commitment to remain seized of the situation in Lebanon and for the sympathy and interest he has shown with respect to that situation, which has been among his highest priorities, owing to his unswerving commitment to the establishment of a tribunal. We wish moreover to thank his colleagues for their efforts.

We commend the positive atmosphere that has supported the cooperation between the Secretary-General's representatives and the Government of Lebanon. We are where we are today as a result of long-term joint endeavours by the Lebanese Government and the United Nations. Every opportunity has been taken in order to adopt the Statute of the Tribunal, to implement the agreement between the United Nations and the Government of Lebanon in accordance with the provisions of the Lebanese constitution—and to ensure that that is done also by the Lebanese parliament.

We worked for the establishment of the Tribunal because unanimity existed within Lebanon, as reflected in the resolution and in our national dialogue. There was also international Arab unanimity regarding the establishment of the Tribunal, but the path that led us to the adoption of the resolution was strewn with obstacles. Parliament was unable to meet to discuss the establishment of the Tribunal, despite the fact that a majority of parliamentarians appealed for such a meeting.

This is now an opportunity for the Lebanese to recover their fundamental rights, first and foremost their right to embark on the path towards the truth. The truth must be raised up against those who have been involved in any way in terrorist crimes against our leaders, beginning with the assassination of former Prime Minister Hariri and including the murders of journalists, parliamentarians, writers and illustrious academics.

The Special Tribunal for Lebanon will certainly act as a deterrent to terrorist activities, and today's resolution will therefore serve to protect the Lebanese people, enhance our freedom, allow us to rid ourselves of such threats, and thus move forward.

Today's resolution does not reflect the victory of one party over another. Justice is the victor. Nor does it mean that one group of Lebanese now believe themselves to be stronger than the others or to enjoy the support of the international community to the detriment of others. On the contrary, the resolution will help to strengthen the rule of law and to bolster the foundations of democracy. It will enhance the independence of the judiciary vis-à-vis the political sphere, as sought by all the Lebanese people. It is therefore in the interests of all Lebanese who seek to advance justice hand in hand with stability.

No one can hope to compel the Lebanese to choose between their quest for justice and their right to peace, security and stability, nor is it acceptable under any standard for the Lebanese to be forced to choose one path over another or for responsibility for crimes perpetrated against Lebanese to be ascribed to the victims. Under the resolution adopted today and previous resolutions, the Council has expressed its commitment to justice and stability. It also recalls all the assassinations that have taken place in Lebanon and the prevailing situation there, which threatens peace and security not only in the region, but throughout the world.

Today, therefore, we can only commemorate the victims throughout Lebanon, the martyr Prime Minister Hariri and all martyrs brought low by the hands of terrorists. We say to them that truth is the path to freedom, justice and reconciliation. Therein lies the salvation of Lebanon.

The President: There are no further speakers on my list.

The Security Council has thus concluded the present stage of its consideration of the item on its agenda. The Security Council will remain seized of the matter.

The meeting rose at 4.05 p.m.

DOCUMENT NO. 21

AGREEMENT AND STATUTE OF THE SPECIAL TRIBUNAL FOR LEBANON

United Nations Security Council
S/RES/1757 (2007)

May 30, 2007

Distr.: General
30 May 2007

Resolution 1757 (2007)

Adopted by the Security Council at its 5685th meeting, on 30 May 2007

The Security Council,

Recalling all its previous relevant resolutions, in particular resolutions 1595 (2005) of 7 April 2005, 1636 (2005) of 31 October 2005, 1644 (2005) of 15 December 2005, 1664 (2006) of 29 March 2006 and 1748 (2007) of 27 March 2007,

Reaffirming its strongest condemnation of the 14 February 2005 terrorist bombings as well as other attacks in Lebanon since October 2004,

Reiterating its call for the strict respect of the sovereignty, territorial integrity, unity and political independence of Lebanon under the sole and exclusive authority of the Government of Lebanon,

Recalling the letter of the Prime Minister of Lebanon to the Secretary-General of 13 December 2005 (S/2005/783) requesting inter alia the establishment of a tribunal of an international character to try all those who are found responsible for this terrorist crime, and the request by this Council for the Secretary-General to negotiate an agreement with the Government of Lebanon aimed at establishing such a Tribunal based on the highest international standards of criminal justice,

Recalling further the report of the Secretary-General on the establishment of a special tribunal for Lebanon on 15 November 2006 (S/2006/893) reporting on the conclusion of negotiations and consultations that took place between January 2006 and September 2006 at United Nations Headquarters in New York, the Hague, and Beirut between the Legal Counsel of the United Nations and authorized representatives of the Government of Lebanon, and the letter of its President to the Secretary-General of 21 November 2006 (S/2006/911) reporting that the Members of the Security Council welcomed the conclusion of the negotiations and that they were satisfied with the Agreement annexed to the Report,

Recalling that, as set out in its letter of 21 November 2006, should voluntary contributions be insufficient for the Tribunal to implement its mandate, the Secretary-General and the Security Council shall explore alternate means of financing the Tribunal,

Recalling also that the Agreement between the United Nations and the Lebanese Republic on the establishment of a Special Tribunal for Lebanon was signed by the Government of Lebanon and the United Nations respectively on 23 January and 6 February 2007,

Referring to the letter of the Prime Minister of Lebanon to the Secretary-General of the United Nations (S/2007/281), which recalled that the parliamentary majority has expressed its support for the Tribunal, and asked that his request that the Special Tribunal be put into effect be presented to the Council as a matter of urgency,

Mindful of the demand of the Lebanese people that all those responsible for the terrorist bombing that killed former Lebanese Prime Minister Rafiq Hariri and others be identified and brought to justice,

Commending the Secretary-General for his continuing efforts to proceed, together with the Government of Lebanon, with the final steps for the conclusion of the Agreement as requested in the letter of its President dated 21 November 2006 and referring in this regard to the briefing by the Legal Counsel on 2 May 2007, in which he noted that the establishment of the Tribunal through the Constitutional process is facing serious obstacles, but noting also that all parties concerned reaffirmed their agreement in principle to the establishment of the Tribunal,

Commending also the recent efforts of parties in the region to overcome these obstacles,

Willing to continue to assist Lebanon in the search for the truth and in holding all those involved in the terrorist attack accountable and reaffirming its determination to support Lebanon in its efforts to bring to justice perpetrators, organizers and sponsors of this and other assassinations,

Reaffirming its determination that this terrorist act and its implications constitute a threat to international peace and security,

1. *Decides*, acting under Chapter VII of the Charter of the United Nations, that:

(a) The provisions of the annexed document, including its attachment, on the establishment of a Special Tribunal for Lebanon shall enter into force on 10 June 2007, unless the Government of Lebanon has provided notification under Article 19 (1) of the annexed document before that date;

(b) If the Secretary-General reports that the Headquarters Agreement has not been concluded as envisioned under Article 8 of the annexed document, the location of the seat of the Tribunal shall be determined in consultation with the Government of Lebanon and be subject to the conclusion of a Headquarters Agreement between the United Nations and the State that hosts the Tribunal;

(c) If the Secretary-General reports that contributions from the Government of Lebanon are not sufficient to bear the expenses described in Article 5 (b) of the annexed document, he may accept or use voluntary contributions from States to cover any shortfall;

2. *Notes* that, pursuant to Article 19 (2) of the annexed document, the Special Tribunal shall commence functioning on a date to be determined by the Secretary-General in consultation with the Government of Lebanon, taking into account the progress of the work of the International Independent Investigation Commission;

3. *Requests* the Secretary-General, in coordination, when appropriate, with the Government of Lebanon, to undertake the steps and measures necessary to establish the Special Tribunal in a timely manner and to report to the Council within 90 days and thereafter periodically on the implementation of this resolution;

4. *Decides* to remain actively seized of the matter.

Annex

Agreement between the United Nations and the Lebanese Republic on the Establishment of a Special Tribunal for Lebanon

Whereas the Security Council, in its resolution 1664 (2006) of 29 March 2006, which responded to the request of the Government of Lebanon to establish a tribunal of an international character to try all those who are found responsible for the terrorist crime which killed the former Lebanese Prime Minister Rafiq Hariri and others, recalled all its previous resolutions, in particular resolutions 1595 (2005) of 7 April 2005, 1636 (2005) of 31 October 2005 and 1644 (2005) of 15 December 2005,

Whereas the Security Council has requested the Secretary-General of the United Nations (hereinafter "the Secretary-General") "to negotiate an agreement with the Government of Lebanon aimed at establishing a tribunal of an international character based on the highest international standards of criminal justice", taking into account the recommendations of the Secretary-General's report of 21 March 2006 (S/2006/176) and the views that have been expressed by Council members,

Whereas the Secretary-General and the Government of the Lebanese Republic (hereinafter "the Government") have conducted negotiations for the establishment of a Special Tribunal for Lebanon (hereinafter "the Special Tribunal" or "the Tribunal"),

Now therefore the United Nations and the Lebanese Republic (hereinafter referred to jointly as the "Parties") have agreed as follows:

Article 1
Establishment of the Special Tribunal

1. There is hereby established a Special Tribunal for Lebanon to prosecute persons responsible for the attack of 14 February 2005 resulting in the death of former Lebanese Prime Minister Rafiq Hariri and in the death or injury of other persons. If the tribunal finds that other attacks that occurred in Lebanon between 1 October 2004 and 12 December 2005, or any later date decided by the Parties and with the consent of the Security Council, are connected in accordance with the principles of criminal justice and are of a nature and gravity similar to the attack of 14 February 2005, it shall also have jurisdiction over persons responsible for such attacks. This connection includes but is not limited to a combination of the following elements: criminal intent (motive), the purpose behind the attacks, the nature of the victims targeted, the pattern of the attacks (modus operandi) and the perpetrators.

2. The Special Tribunal shall function in accordance with the Statute of the Special Tribunal for Lebanon. The Statute is attached to this Agreement and forms an integral part thereof.

Article 2
Composition of the Special Tribunal and Appointment of Judges

1. The Special Tribunal shall consist of the following organs: the Chambers, the Prosecutor, the Registry and the Defence Office.

2. The Chambers shall be composed of a Pre-Trial Judge, a Trial Chamber and an Appeals Chamber, with a second Trial Chamber to be created if, after the passage of at least six months from the commencement of the functioning of the Special Tribunal, the Secretary-General or the President of the Special Tribunal so requests.

3. The Chambers shall be composed of no fewer than eleven independent judges and no more than fourteen such judges, who shall serve as follows:

(a) A single international judge shall serve as a Pre-Trial Judge;

(b) Three judges shall serve in the Trial Chamber, of whom one shall be a Lebanese judge and two shall be international judges;

(c) In the event of the creation of a second Trial Chamber, that Chamber shall be likewise composed in the manner contained in subparagraph (b) above;

(d) Five judges shall serve in the Appeals Chamber, of whom two shall be Lebanese judges and three shall be international judges; and

(e) Two alternate judges, of whom one shall be a Lebanese judge and one shall be an international judge.

4. The judges of the Tribunal shall be persons of high moral character, impartiality and integrity, with extensive judicial experience. They shall be independent in the performance of their functions and shall not accept or seek instructions from any Government or any other source.

5. (a) Lebanese judges shall be appointed by the Secretary-General to serve in the Trial Chamber or the Appeals Chamber or as an alternate judge from a list of twelve persons presented by the Government upon the proposal of the Lebanese Supreme Council of the Judiciary;

(b) International judges shall be appointed by the Secretary-General to serve as Pre-Trial Judge, a Trial Chamber Judge, an Appeals Chamber Judge or an alternate judge, upon nominations forwarded by States at the invitation of the Secretary-General, as well as by competent persons;

(c) The Government and the Secretary-General shall consult on the appointment of judges;

(d) The Secretary-General shall appoint judges, upon the recommendation of a selection panel he has established after indicating his intentions to the Security Council. The selection panel shall be composed of two judges, currently sitting on or retired from an international tribunal, and the representative of the Secretary-General.

6. At the request of the presiding judge of a Trial Chamber, the President of the Special Tribunal may, in the interest of justice, assign alternate judges to be present at each stage of the trial and to replace a judge if that judge is unable to continue sitting.

7. Judges shall be appointed for a three-year period and may be eligible for reappointment for a further period to be determined by the Secretary-General in consultation with the Government.

8. Lebanese judges appointed to serve in the Special Tribunal shall be given full credit for their period of service with the Tribunal on their return to the Lebanese national judiciaries from which they were released and shall be reintegrated at a level at least comparable to that of their former position.

Article 3
Appointment of a Prosecutor and a Deputy Prosecutor

1. The Secretary-General, after consultation with the Government, shall appoint a Prosecutor for a three-year term. The Prosecutor may be eligible for reappointment for a further period to be determined by the Secretary-General in consultation with the Government.

2. The Secretary-General shall appoint the Prosecutor, upon the recommendation of a selection panel he has established after indicating his intentions to the Security Council. The selection panel shall be composed of two judges, currently sitting on or retired from an international tribunal, and the representative of the Secretary-General.

3. The Government, in consultation with the Secretary-General and the Prosecutor, shall appoint a Lebanese Deputy Prosecutor to assist the Prosecutor in the conduct of the investigations and prosecutions.

4. The Prosecutor and the Deputy Prosecutor shall be of high moral character and possess the highest level of professional competence and extensive experience in the conduct of investigations and prosecutions of criminal cases. The Prosecutor and the Deputy Prosecutor shall be independent in the performance of their functions and shall not accept or seek instructions from any Government or any other source.

5. The Prosecutor shall be assisted by such Lebanese and international staff as may be required to perform the functions assigned to him or her effectively and efficiently.

Article 4
Appointment of a Registrar

1. The Secretary-General shall appoint a Registrar who shall be responsible for the servicing of the Chambers and the Office of the Prosecutor, and for the recruitment and administration of all support staff. He or she shall also administer the financial and staff resources of the Special Tribunal.

2. The Registrar shall be a staff member of the United Nations. He or she shall serve a three-year term and may be eligible for reappointment for a further period to be determined by the Secretary-General in consultation with the Government.

Article 5
Financing of the Special Tribunal

1. The expenses of the Special Tribunal shall be borne in the following manner:

(a) Fifty-one per cent of the expenses of the Tribunal shall be borne by voluntary contributions from States;

(b) Forty-nine per cent of the expenses of the Tribunal shall be borne by the Government of Lebanon.

2. It is understood that the Secretary-General will commence the process of establishing the Tribunal when he has sufficient contributions in hand to finance the establishment of the Tribunal and twelve months of its operations plus pledges equal to the anticipated expenses of the following 24 months of the Tribunal's operation. Should voluntary contributions be insufficient for the Tribunal to implement its mandate, the Secretary-General and the Security Council shall explore alternate means of financing the Tribunal.

Article 6
Management Committee

The parties shall consult concerning the establishment of a Management Committee.

Article 7
Juridical Capacity

The Special Tribunal shall possess the juridical capacity necessary:

(a) To contract;

(b) To acquire and dispose of movable and immovable property;

(c) To institute legal proceedings;

(d) To enter into agreements with States as may be necessary for the exercise of its functions and for the operation of the Tribunal.

Article 8
Seat of the Special Tribunal

1. The Special Tribunal shall have its seat outside Lebanon. The location of the seat shall be determined having due regard to considerations of justice and fairness as well as security and administrative efficiency, including the rights of victims and access to witnesses, and subject to the conclusion of a headquarters agreement between the United Nations, the Government and the State that hosts the Tribunal.

2. The Special Tribunal may meet away from its seat when it considers it necessary for the efficient exercise of its functions.

3. An Office of the Special Tribunal for the conduct of investigations shall be established in Lebanon subject to the conclusion of appropriate arrangements with the Government.

Article 9
Inviolability of Premises, Archives and all other Documents

1. The Office of the Special Tribunal in Lebanon shall be inviolable. The competent authorities shall take appropriate action that may be necessary to ensure that the Tribunal shall not be dispossessed of all or any part of the premises of the Tribunal without its express consent.

2. The property, funds and assets of the Office of the Special Tribunal in Lebanon, wherever located and by whomsoever held, shall be immune from search, seizure, requisition, confiscation, expropriation and any other form of interference, whether by executive, administrative, judicial or legislative action.

3. The archives of the Office of the Special Tribunal in Lebanon, and in general all documents and materials made available, belonging to or used by it, wherever located and by whomsoever held, shall be inviolable.

Article 10
Funds, Assets and other Property

The Office of the Special Tribunal, its funds, assets and other property in Lebanon, wherever located and by whomsoever held, shall enjoy immunity from every form of legal process, except insofar as in any particular case the

Tribunal has expressly waived its immunity. It is understood, however, that no waiver of immunity shall extend to any measure of execution.

Article 11
Privileges and Immunities of the Judges, the Prosecutor, the Deputy Prosecutor, the Registrar and the Head of the Defence Office

1. The judges, the Prosecutor, the Deputy Prosecutor, the Registrar and the Head of the Defence Office, while in Lebanon, shall enjoy the privileges and immunities, exemptions and facilities accorded to diplomatic agents in accordance with the Vienna Convention on Diplomatic Relations of 1961.

2. Privileges and immunities are accorded to the judges, the Prosecutor, the Deputy Prosecutor, the Registrar and the Head of the Defence Office in the interest of the Special Tribunal and not for the personal benefit of the individuals themselves. The right and the duty to waive the immunity in any case where it can be waived without prejudice to the purposes for which it is accorded shall lie with the Secretary-General, in consultation with the President of the Tribunal.

Article 12
Privileges and Immunities of International and Lebanese Personnel

1. Lebanese and international personnel of the Office of the Special Tribunal, while in Lebanon, shall be accorded:

(a) Immunity from legal process in respect of words spoken or written and all acts performed by them in their official capacity. Such immunity shall continue to be accorded after termination of employment with the Office of the Special Tribunal;

(b) Exemption from taxation on salaries, allowances and emoluments paid to them.

2. International personnel shall, in addition thereto, be accorded:

(a) Immunity from immigration restriction;

(b) The right to import free of duties and taxes, except for payment for services, their furniture and effects at the time of first taking up their official duties in Lebanon.

3. The privileges and immunities are granted to the officials of the Office of the Special Tribunal in the interest of the Tribunal and not for their personal benefit. The right and the duty to waive the immunity in any case where it can be waived without prejudice to the purpose for which it is accorded shall lie with the Registrar of the Tribunal.

Article 13
Defence Counsel

1. The Government shall ensure that the counsel of a suspect or an accused who has been admitted as such by the Special Tribunal shall not be subjected, while in Lebanon, to any measure that may affect the free and independent exercise of his or her functions.

2. In particular, the counsel shall be accorded:

(a) Immunity from personal arrest or detention and from seizure of personal baggage;

(b) Inviolability of all documents relating to the exercise of his or her functions as a counsel of a suspect or accused;

(c) Immunity from criminal or civil jurisdiction in respect of words spoken or written and acts performed in his or her capacity as counsel. Such immunity shall continue to be accorded after termination of his or her functions as a counsel of a suspect or accused;

(d) Immunity from any immigration restrictions during his or her stay as well as during his or her journey to the Tribunal and back.

Article 14
Security, Safety and Protection of Persons Referred to in this Agreement

The Government shall take effective and adequate measures to ensure the appropriate security, safety and protection of personnel of the Office of the Special Tribunal and other persons referred to in this Agreement, while in Lebanon. It shall take all appropriate steps, within its capabilities, to protect the equipment and premises of the Office of the Special Tribunal from attack or any action that prevents the Tribunal from discharging its mandate.

Article 15
Cooperation with the Special Tribunal

1. The Government shall cooperate with all organs of the Special Tribunal, in particular with the Prosecutor and defence counsel, at all stages of the proceedings. It shall facilitate access of the Prosecutor and defence counsel to sites, persons and relevant documents required for the investigation.

2. The Government shall comply without undue delay with any request for assistance by the Special Tribunal or an order issued by the Chambers, including, but not limited to:

(a) Identification and location of persons;

(b) Service of documents;

(c) Arrest or detention of persons;

(d) Transfer of an indictee to the Tribunal.

Article 16
Amnesty

The Government undertakes not to grant amnesty to any person for any crime falling within the jurisdiction of the Special Tribunal. An amnesty already granted in respect of any such persons and crimes shall not be a bar to prosecution.

Article 17
Practical Arrangements

With a view to achieving efficiency and cost-effectiveness in the operation of the Special Tribunal:

(a) Appropriate arrangements shall be made to ensure that there is a coordinated transition from the activities of the International Independent Investigation Commission, established by the Security Council in its resolution 1595 (2005), to the activities of the Office of the Prosecutor;

(b) Judges of the Trial Chamber and the Appeals Chamber shall take office on a date to be determined by the Secretary-General in consultation with the President of the Special Tribunal. Pending such a determination, judges of both Chambers shall be convened on an ad hoc basis to deal with organizational matters and serving, when required, to perform their duties.

Article 18
Settlement of Disputes

Any dispute between the Parties concerning the interpretation or application of this Agreement shall be settled by negotiation or by any other mutually agreed upon mode of settlement.

Article 19
Entry into Force and Commencement of the Functioning of the Special Tribunal

1. This Agreement shall enter into force on the day after the Government has notified the United Nations in writing that the legal requirements for entry into force have been complied with.

2. The Special Tribunal shall commence functioning on a date to be determined by the Secretary-General in consultation with the Government, taking

into account the progress of the work of the International Independent Investigation Commission.

Article 20
Amendment

This Agreement may be amended by written agreement between the Parties.

Article 21
Duration of the Agreement

1. This Agreement shall remain in force for a period of three years from the date of the commencement of the functioning of the Special Tribunal.

2. Three years after the commencement of the functioning of the Special Tribunal the Parties shall, in consultation with the Security Council, review the progress of the work of the Special Tribunal. If at the end of this period of three years the activities of the Tribunal have not been completed, the Agreement shall be extended to allow the Tribunal to complete its work, for a further period(s) to be determined by the Secretary-General in consultation with the Government and the Security Council.

3. The provisions relating to the inviolability of the funds, assets, archives and documents of the Office of the Special Tribunal in Lebanon, the privileges and immunities of those referred to in this Agreement, as well as provisions relating to defence counsel and the protection of victims and witnesses, shall survive termination of this Agreement.

In witness whereof, the following duly authorized representatives of the United Nations and of the Lebanese Republic have signed this Agreement.

Done at __________ on __________ 2006, in three originals in the Arabic, French and English languages, all texts being equally authentic.

For the United Nations: For the Lebanese Republic:

_______________ _______________

Attachment

Statute of the Special Tribunal for Lebanon

Having been established by an Agreement between the United Nations and the Lebanese Republic (hereinafter "the Agreement") pursuant to Security Council resolution 1664 (2006) of 29 March 2006, which responded to the request of the Government of Lebanon to establish a tribunal of an international character to try all those who are found responsible for the terrorist crime which killed the former Lebanese Prime Minister Rafiq Hariri and others, the Special Tribunal for Lebanon (hereinafter "the Special Tribunal") shall function in accordance with the provisions of this Statute.

Section I
Jurisdiction and Applicable Law

Article 1
Jurisdiction of the Special Tribunal

The Special Tribunal shall have jurisdiction over persons responsible for the attack of 14 February 2005 resulting in the death of former Lebanese Prime Minister Rafiq Hariri and in the death or injury of other persons. If the Tribunal finds that other attacks that occurred in Lebanon between 1 October 2004 and 12 December 2005, or any later date decided by the Parties and with the consent of the Security Council, are connected in accordance with the principles of criminal justice and are of a nature and gravity similar to the attack of 14 February 2005, it shall also have jurisdiction over persons responsible for such attacks. This connection includes but is not limited to a combination of the following elements: criminal intent (motive), the purpose behind the attacks, the nature of the victims targeted, the pattern of the attacks (modus operandi) and the perpetrators.

Article 2
Applicable Criminal Law

The following shall be applicable to the prosecution and punishment of the crimes referred to in article 1, subject to the provisions of this Statute:

(a) The provisions of the Lebanese Criminal Code relating to the prosecution and punishment of acts of terrorism, crimes and offences against life and personal integrity, illicit associations and failure to report crimes and offences, including the rules regarding the material elements of a crime, criminal participation and conspiracy; and

(b) Articles 6 and 7 of the Lebanese law of 11 January 1958 on "Increasing the penalties for sedition, civil war and interfaith struggle".

Article 3
Individual Criminal Responsibility

1. A person shall be individually responsible for crimes within the jurisdiction of the Special Tribunal if that person:

(a) Committed, participated as accomplice, organized or directed others to commit the crime set forth in article 2 of this Statute; or

(b) Contributed in any other way to the commission of the crime set forth in article 2 of this Statute by a group of persons acting with a common purpose, where such contribution is intentional and is either made with the aim of furthering the general criminal activity or purpose of the group or in the knowledge of the intention of the group to commit the crime.

2. With respect to superior and subordinate relationships, a superior shall be criminally responsible for any of the crimes set forth in article 2 of this Statute committed by subordinates under his or her effective authority and control, as a result of his or her failure to exercise control properly over such subordinates, where:

(a) The superior either knew, or consciously disregarded information that clearly indicated that the subordinates were committing or about to commit such crimes;

(b) The crimes concerned activities that were within the effective responsibility and control of the superior; and

(c) The superior failed to take all necessary and reasonable measures within his or her power to prevent or repress their commission or to submit the matter to the competent authorities for investigation and prosecution.

3. The fact that the person acted pursuant to an order of a superior shall not relieve him or her of criminal responsibility, but may be considered in mitigation of punishment if the Special Tribunal determines that justice so requires.

Article 4
Concurrent Jurisdiction

1. The Special Tribunal and the national courts of Lebanon shall have concurrent jurisdiction. Within its jurisdiction, the Tribunal shall have primacy over the national courts of Lebanon.

2. Upon the assumption of office of the Prosecutor, as determined by the Secretary-General, and no later than two months thereafter, the Special Tribunal shall request the national judicial authority seized with the case of the attack against Prime Minister Rafiq Hariri and others to defer to its competence. The Lebanese judicial authority shall refer to the Tribunal the results of the investigation and a copy of the court's records, if any. Persons detained in connection with the investigation shall be transferred to the custody of the Tribunal.

3. (a) At the request of the Special Tribunal, the national judicial authority seized with any of the other crimes committed between 1 October 2004 and 12 December 2005, or a later date decided pursuant to article 1, shall refer

to the Tribunal the results of the investigation and a copy of the court's records, if any, for review by the Prosecutor;

(b) At the further request of the Tribunal, the national authority in question shall defer to the competence of the Tribunal. It shall refer to the Tribunal the results of the investigation and a copy of the court's records, if any, and persons detained in connection with any such case shall be transferred to the custody of the Tribunal;

(c) The national judicial authorities shall regularly inform the Tribunal of the progress of their investigation. At any stage of the proceedings, the Tribunal may formally request a national judicial authority to defer to its competence.

Article 5
Non Bis in Idem

1. No person shall be tried before a national court of Lebanon for acts for which he or she has already been tried by the Special Tribunal.

2. A person who has been tried by a national court may be subsequently tried by the Special Tribunal if the national court proceedings were not impartial or independent, were designed to shield the accused from criminal responsibility for crimes within the jurisdiction of the Tribunal or the case was not diligently prosecuted.

3. In considering the penalty to be imposed on a person convicted of a crime under this Statute, the Special Tribunal shall take into account the extent to which any penalty imposed by a national court on the same person for the same act has already been served.

Article 6
Amnesty

An amnesty granted to any person for any crime falling within the jurisdiction of the Special Tribunal shall not be a bar to prosecution.

Section II
Organization of the Special Tribunal

Article 7
Organs of the Special Tribunal

The Special Tribunal shall consist of the following organs:

(a) The Chambers, comprising a Pre-Trial Judge, a Trial Chamber and an Appeals Chamber;

(b) The Prosecutor;

(c) The Registry; and

(d) The Defence Office.

Article 8
Composition of the Chambers

1. The Chambers shall be composed as follows:

(a) One international Pre-Trial Judge;

(b) Three judges who shall serve in the Trial Chamber, of whom one shall be a Lebanese judge and two shall be international judges;

(c) Five judges who shall serve in the Appeals Chamber, of whom two shall be Lebanese judges and three shall be international judges;

(d) Two alternate judges, one of whom shall be a Lebanese judge and one shall be an international judge.

2. The judges of the Appeals Chamber and the judges of the Trial Chamber, respectively, shall elect a presiding judge who shall conduct the proceedings in the Chamber to which he or she was elected. The presiding judge of the Appeals Chamber shall be the President of the Special Tribunal.

3. At the request of the presiding judge of the Trial Chamber, the President of the Special Tribunal may, in the interest of justice, assign the alternate judges to be present at each stage of the trial and to replace a judge if that judge is unable to continue sitting.

Article 9
Qualification and Appointment of Judges

1. The judges shall be persons of high moral character, impartiality and integrity, with extensive judicial experience. They shall be independent in the performance of their functions and shall not accept or seek instructions from any Government or any other source.

2. In the overall composition of the Chambers, due account shall be taken of the established competence of the judges in criminal law and procedure and international law.

3. The judges shall be appointed by the Secretary-General, as set forth in article 2 of the Agreement, for a three-year period and may be eligible for reappointment for a further period to be determined by the Secretary-General in consultation with the Government.

Article 10
Powers of the President of the Special Tribunal

1. The President of the Special Tribunal, in addition to his or her judicial functions, shall represent the Tribunal and be responsible for its effective functioning and the good administration of justice.

2. The President of the Special Tribunal shall submit an annual report on the operation and activities of the Tribunal to the Secretary-General and to the Government of Lebanon.

Article 11
The Prosecutor

1. The Prosecutor shall be responsible for the investigation and prosecution of persons responsible for the crimes falling within the jurisdiction of the Special Tribunal. In the interest of proper administration of justice, he or she may decide to charge jointly persons accused of the same or different crimes committed in the course of the same transaction.

2. The Prosecutor shall act independently as a separate organ of the Special Tribunal. He or she shall not seek or receive instructions from any Government or from any other source.

3. The Prosecutor shall be appointed, as set forth in article 3 of the Agreement, by the Secretary-General for a three-year term and may be eligible for reappointment for a further period to be determined by the Secretary-General in consultation with the Government. He or she shall be of high moral character and possess the highest level of professional competence, and have extensive experience in the conduct of investigations and prosecutions of criminal cases.

4. The Prosecutor shall be assisted by a Lebanese Deputy Prosecutor and by such other Lebanese and international staff as may be required to perform the functions assigned to him or her effectively and efficiently.

5. The Office of the Prosecutor shall have the power to question suspects, victims and witnesses, to collect evidence and to conduct on-site investigations. In carrying out these tasks, the Prosecutor shall, as appropriate, be assisted by the Lebanese authorities concerned.

Article 12
The Registry

1. Under the authority of the President of the Special Tribunal, the Registry shall be responsible for the administration and servicing of the Tribunal.

2. The Registry shall consist of a Registrar and such other staff as may be required.

3. The Registrar shall be appointed by the Secretary-General and shall be a staff member of the United Nations. He or she shall serve for a three-year term and may be eligible for reappointment for a further period to be determined by the Secretary-General in consultation with the Government.

4. The Registrar shall set up a Victims and Witnesses Unit within the Registry. This Unit shall provide, in consultation with the Office of the Prosecutor, measures to protect the safety, physical and psychological well-being, dignity and privacy of victims and witnesses, and such other appropriate assistance for witnesses who appear before the Special Tribunal and others who are at risk on account of testimony given by such witnesses.

Article 13
The Defence Office

1. The Secretary-General, in consultation with the President of the Special Tribunal, shall appoint an independent Head of the Defence Office, who shall be responsible for the appointment of the Office staff and the drawing up of a list of defence counsel.

2. The Defence Office, which may also include one or more public defenders, shall protect the rights of the defence, provide support and assistance to defence counsel and to the persons entitled to legal assistance, including, where appropriate, legal research, collection of evidence and advice, and appearing before the Pre-Trial Judge or a Chamber in respect of specific issues.

Article 14
Official and Working Languages

The official languages of the Special Tribunal shall be Arabic, French and English. In any given case proceedings, the Pre-Trial Judge or a Chamber may decide that one or two of the languages may be used as working languages as appropriate.

Section III
Rights of Defendants and Victims

Article 15
Rights of Suspects During Investigation

A suspect who is to be questioned by the Prosecutor shall not be compelled to incriminate himself or herself or to confess guilt. He or she shall have the following rights of which he or she shall be informed by the Prosecutor prior to questioning, in a language he or she speaks and understands:

(a) The right to be informed that there are grounds to believe that he or she has committed a crime within the jurisdiction of the Special Tribunal;

(b) The right to remain silent, without such silence being considered in the determination of guilt or innocence, and to be cautioned that any statement he or she makes shall be recorded and may be used in evidence;

(c) The right to have legal assistance of his or her own choosing, including the right to have legal assistance provided by the Defence Office where the interests of justice so require and where the suspect does not have sufficient means to pay for it;

(d) The right to have the free assistance of an interpreter if he or she cannot understand or speak the language used for questioning;

(e) The right to be questioned in the presence of counsel unless the person has voluntarily waived his or her right to counsel.

Article 16
Rights of the Accused

1. All accused shall be equal before the Special Tribunal.

2. The accused shall be entitled to a fair and public hearing, subject to measures ordered by the Special Tribunal for the protection of victims and witnesses.

3. (a) The accused shall be presumed innocent until proved guilty according to the provisions of this Statute;

(b) The onus is on the Prosecutor to prove the guilt of the accused;

(c) In order to convict the accused, the relevant Chamber must be convinced of the guilt of the accused beyond reasonable doubt.

4. In the determination of any charge against the accused pursuant to this Statute, he or she shall be entitled to the following minimum guarantees, in full equality:

(a) To be informed promptly and in detail in a language which he or she understands of the nature and cause of the charge against him or her;

(b) To have adequate time and facilities for the preparation of his or her defence and to communicate without hindrance with counsel of his or her own choosing;

(c) To be tried without undue delay;

(d) Subject to the provisions of article 22, to be tried in his or her presence, and to defend himself or herself in person or through legal assistance of his or her own choosing; to be informed, if he or she does not have legal assistance, of this right; and to have legal assistance assigned to him or her, in any case where the interests of justice so require and without payment by him or her in any such case if he or she does not have sufficient means to pay for it;

(e) To examine, or have examined, the witnesses against him or her and to obtain the attendance and examination of witnesses on his or her behalf under the same conditions as witnesses against him or her;

(f) To examine all evidence to be used against him or her during the trial in accordance with the Rules of Procedure and Evidence of the Special Tribunal;

(g) To have the free assistance of an interpreter if he or she cannot understand or speak the language used in the Special Tribunal;

(h) Not to be compelled to testify against himself or herself or to confess guilt.

5. The accused may make statements in court at any stage of the proceedings, provided such statements are relevant to the case at issue. The Chambers shall decide on the probative value, if any, of such statements.

Article 17
Rights of Victims

Where the personal interests of the victims are affected, the Special Tribunal shall permit their views and concerns to be presented and considered at stages of the proceedings determined to be appropriate by the Pre-Trial Judge or the Chamber and in a manner that is not prejudicial to or inconsistent with the rights of the accused and a fair and impartial trial. Such views and concerns may be presented by the legal representatives of the victims where the Pre-Trial Judge or the Chamber considers it appropriate.

Section IV
Conduct of Proceedings

Article 18
Pre-Trial Proceedings

1. The Pre-Trial Judge shall review the indictment. If satisfied that a prima facie case has been established by the Prosecutor, he or she shall confirm the indictment. If he or she is not so satisfied, the indictment shall be dismissed.

2. The Pre-Trial Judge may, at the request of the Prosecutor, issue such orders and warrants for the arrest or transfer of persons, and any other orders as may be required for the conduct of the investigation and for the preparation of a fair and expeditious trial.

Article 19
Evidence Collected Prior to the Establishment of the Special Tribunal

Evidence collected with regard to cases subject to the consideration of the Special Tribunal, prior to the establishment of the Tribunal, by the national authorities of Lebanon or by the International Independent Investigation Commission in accordance with its mandate as set out in Security Council resolution 1595 (2005) and subsequent resolutions, shall be received by the Tribunal. Its admissibility shall be decided by the Chambers pursuant to international standards on collection of evidence. The weight to be given to any such evidence shall be determined by the Chambers.

Article 20
Commencement and Conduct of Trial Proceedings

1. The Trial Chamber shall read the indictment to the accused, satisfy itself that the rights of the accused are respected, confirm that the accused understands the indictment and instruct the accused to enter a plea.

2. Unless otherwise decided by the Trial Chamber in the interests of justice, examination of witnesses shall commence with questions posed by the presiding judge, followed by questions posed by other members of the Trial Chamber, the Prosecutor and the Defence.

3. Upon request or *proprio motu*, the Trial Chamber may at any stage of the trial decide to call additional witnesses and/or order the production of additional evidence.

4. The hearings shall be public unless the Trial Chamber decides to hold the proceedings in camera in accordance with the Rules of Procedure and Evidence.

Article 21
Powers of the Chambers

1. The Special Tribunal shall confine the trial, appellate and review proceedings strictly to an expeditious hearing of the issues raised by the charges, or the grounds for appeal or review, respectively. It shall take strict measures to prevent any action that may cause unreasonable delay.

2. A Chamber may admit any relevant evidence that it deems to have probative value and exclude such evidence if its probative value is substantially outweighed by the need to ensure a fair trial.

3. A Chamber may receive the evidence of a witness orally or, where the interests of justice allow, in written form.

4. In cases not otherwise provided for in the Rules of Procedure and Evidence, a Chamber shall apply rules of evidence that will best favour a fair determination of the matter before it and are consonant with the spirit of the Statute and the general principles of law.

Article 22
Trials in Absentia

1. The Special Tribunal shall conduct trial proceedings in the absence of the accused, if he or she:

(a) Has expressly and in writing waived his or her right to be present;

(b) Has not been handed over to the Tribunal by the State authorities concerned;

(c) Has absconded or otherwise cannot be found and all reasonable steps have been taken to secure his or her appearance before the Tribunal and to inform him or her of the charges confirmed by the Pre-Trial Judge.

2. When hearings are conducted in the absence of the accused, the Special Tribunal shall ensure that:

(a) The accused has been notified, or served with the indictment, or notice has otherwise been given of the indictment through publication in the media or communication to the State of residence or nationality;

(b) The accused has designated a defence counsel of his or her own choosing, to be remunerated either by the accused or, if the accused is proved to be indigent, by the Tribunal;

(c) Whenever the accused refuses or fails to appoint a defence counsel, such counsel has been assigned by the Defence Office of the Tribunal with a view to ensuring full representation of the interests and rights of the accused.

3. In case of conviction in absentia, the accused, if he or she had not designated a defence counsel of his or her choosing, shall have the right to be retried in his or her presence before the Special Tribunal, unless he or she accepts the judgement.

Article 23
Judgement

The judgement shall be rendered by a majority of the judges of the Trial Chamber or of the Appeals Chamber and shall be delivered in public. It shall be accompanied by a reasoned opinion in writing, to which any separate or dissenting opinions shall be appended.

Article 24
Penalties

1. The Trial Chamber shall impose upon a convicted person imprisonment for life or for a specified number of years. In determining the terms of imprisonment for the crimes provided for in this Statute, the Trial Chamber shall, as appropriate, have recourse to international practice regarding prison sentences and to the practice of the national courts of Lebanon.

2. In imposing sentence, the Trial Chamber should take into account such factors as the gravity of the offence and the individual circumstances of the convicted person.

Article 25
Compensation to Victims

1. The Special Tribunal may identify victims who have suffered harm as a result of the commission of crimes by an accused convicted by the Tribunal.

2. The Registrar shall transmit to the competent authorities of the State concerned the judgement finding the accused guilty of a crime that has caused harm to a victim.

3. Based on the decision of the Special Tribunal and pursuant to the relevant national legislation, a victim or persons claiming through the victim, whether or not such victim had been identified as such by the Tribunal under paragraph 1 of this article, may bring an action in a national court or other competent body to obtain compensation.

4. For the purposes of a claim made under paragraph 3 of this article, the judgement of the Special Tribunal shall be final and binding as to the criminal responsibility of the convicted person.

Article 26
Appellate Proceedings

1. The Appeals Chamber shall hear appeals from persons convicted by the Trial Chamber or from the Prosecutor on the following grounds:

(a) An error on a question of law invalidating the decision;

(b) An error of fact that has occasioned a miscarriage of justice.

2. The Appeals Chamber may affirm, reverse or revise the decisions taken by the Trial Chamber.

Article 27
Review Proceedings

1. Where a new fact has been discovered that was not known at the time of the proceedings before the Trial Chamber or the Appeals Chamber and that could have been a decisive factor in reaching the decision, the convicted person or the Prosecutor may submit an application for review of the judgement.

2. An application for review shall be submitted to the Appeals Chamber. The Appeals Chamber may reject the application if it considers it to be unfounded. If it determines that the application is meritorious, it may, as appropriate:

(a) Reconvene the Trial Chamber;

(b) Retain jurisdiction over the matter.

Article 28
Rules of Procedure and Evidence

1. The judges of the Special Tribunal shall, as soon as practicable after taking office, adopt Rules of Procedure and Evidence for the conduct of the pre-trial, trial and appellate proceedings, the admission of evidence, the participation of victims, the protection of victims and witnesses and other appropriate matters and may amend them, as appropriate.

2. In so doing, the judges shall be guided, as appropriate, by the Lebanese Code of Criminal Procedure, as well as by other reference materials reflecting the highest standards of international criminal procedure, with a view to ensuring a fair and expeditious trial.

Article 29
Enforcement of Sentences

1. Imprisonment shall be served in a State designated by the President of the Special Tribunal from a list of States that have indicated their willingness to accept persons convicted by the Tribunal.

2. Conditions of imprisonment shall be governed by the law of the State of enforcement subject to the supervision of the Special Tribunal. The State of enforcement shall be bound by the duration of the sentence, subject to article 30 of this Statute.

Article 30
Pardon or Commutation of Sentences

If, pursuant to the applicable law of the State in which the convicted person is imprisoned, he or she is eligible for pardon or commutation of sentence, the State concerned shall notify the Special Tribunal accordingly. There shall only be pardon or commutation of sentence if the President of the Tribunal, in consultation with the judges, so decides on the basis of the interests of justice and the general principles of law.

DOCUMENT NO. 22

SECRETARY GENERAL'S UPDATING REPORT ON THE LEBANON TRIBUNAL

United Nations Security Council
S/2007/525

September 4, 2007

Distr.: General
4 September 2007

Original: English

Report of the Secretary-General Submitted Pursuant to Security Council Resolution 1757 (2007) of 30 May 2007

I. Introduction

1. The present report is submitted pursuant to paragraph 3 of resolution 1757 (2007) of 30 May 2007, by which the Security Council requested me to undertake, in coordination, when appropriate, with the Government of Lebanon, the steps and measures necessary to establish the Special Tribunal in a timely manner and to report to the Council on the implementation of the resolution within 90 days of its adoption and periodically thereafter.

2. By resolution 1757 (2007), the Security Council decided, acting under Chapter VII of the Charter of the United Nations, that the provisions of the document annexed thereto (the "Annex") on the establishment of the Special Tribunal, including the statute attached thereto (the "Statute"), would enter into force on 10 June 2007, unless the Government of Lebanon had notified the United Nations in writing that the legal requirements for entry into force had been complied with before that date.

3. On 10 June 2007, as no notification had been received prior to that date, the provisions of the Annex and the Statute entered into force. Thereafter, as mandated by the Security Council in its resolution 1757 (2007), I commenced to undertake the steps and measures necessary to establish the

Special Tribunal in a timely manner. The most immediate actions taken since 10 June relate to: (a) the location of the seat of the Special Tribunal; (b) the appointment of the judges, the Prosecutor, the Deputy Prosecutor, the Registrar and the head of the Defence Office; (c) the staffing requirements and budget of the Tribunal; (d) the funding of the Tribunal, including both its establishment and operation; (e) the Management Committee; (f) security issues; and (g) communications and outreach.

4. The present report discusses in detail the steps already undertaken towards the establishment of the Special Tribunal and provides an outline of the next steps.

II. Location of the Seat

5. Pursuant to article 8, paragraph 1, of the Annex, "[t]he Special Tribunal shall have its seat outside Lebanon". In the paragraph it is further stipulated that "[t]he location of the seat shall be determined having due regard to considerations of justice and fairness as well as security and administrative efficiency, including the rights of victims and access to witnesses, and subject to the conclusion of a headquarters agreement between the United Nations, the Government and the State that hosts the Tribunal".

6. After considering possible seats and noting that having the Special Tribunal located in the Netherlands would fully meet the criteria set forth above, on 23 July 2007, I wrote to the Prime Minister of the Netherlands inviting his Government to consider hosting the Special Tribunal. In my letter, I emphasized that the experience and knowledge gained by the Netherlands in hosting several international courts and tribunals was invaluable. I cited the unique and essential role of the Netherlands in the development of international justice and the rule of law. In a letter dated 14 August 2007, the Prime Minister of the Netherlands informed me that his Government was favourably disposed towards hosting the Special Tribunal. From 27 to 30 August 2007, the Legal Counsel of the United Nations led a delegation to The Hague to initiate discussions with the authorities of the Netherlands regarding the modalities for the establishment of the Special Tribunal. The delegation visited possible sites for the Special Tribunal, identified issues for discussion and agreed upon further steps to achieve progress in a timely manner. In the coming weeks, subsequent meetings will be held to follow up the discussions.

III. Appointment of the Judges, the Prosecutor, the Deputy Prosecutor, the Registrar and the Head of the Defence Office

7. I will describe below the appointment processes for the judges, the Prosecutor, the Deputy Prosecutor, the Registrar and the head of the Defence Office.

A. Judges

8. In accordance with article 2, paragraph 5 (c), of the Annex, the Secretary-General and the Government of Lebanon will consult on the appointment of the judges. Paragraph 5 (a) stipulates that the Lebanese judges will be appointed by the Secretary-General from a list of 12 persons presented by the Government of Lebanon upon the proposal of the Lebanese Supreme Council of the Judiciary. In accordance with paragraph 5 (b), the international judges will be appointed by the Secretary-General upon nominations forwarded by States at the invitation of the Secretary-General, as well as by competent persons. Pursuant to paragraph 5 (d), the Secretary-General will appoint all of the judges upon the recommendation of a selection panel composed of two judges, currently sitting on or retired from an international tribunal, and the representative of the Secretary-General.

9. On 10 July 2007, the Government of Lebanon forwarded to me, in a sealed envelope, a list of the 12 judges proposed by the Lebanese Supreme Council of the Judiciary. The list will remain sealed until the selection process of all judges begins. With a view to appointing both Lebanese and international judges at the same time, the Legal Counsel sent a letter on 1 August 2007 to all Member States, on my behalf, inviting them to consider submitting candidates for appointment as judges of the Special Tribunal no later than 24 September 2007.

10. In the meantime, I have begun the process of establishing the selection panel, which will take up its task by October 2007. In keeping with article 2, paragraph 5 (d) of the annex, I will indicate my intention to the Security Council before appointing the members of the panel. The selection panel will interview the candidates during the third quarter of 2007, and I hope to appoint the judges by the end of 2007.

11. Pursuant to article 17 (b) of the annex, the judges will commence their judicial functions on a date to be determined by me, in consultation with the President of the Special Tribunal, who will be elected in accordance with article 8, paragraph 2, of the Statute. In order to draft the rules of procedure and evidence of the Special Tribunal, as envisaged in article 28 of the Statute, and to address other organizational matters as set out in article 17 (b) of the Annex, the judges may be convened on an ad hoc basis prior to the commencement of their judicial duties.

B. The Prosecutor and the Deputy Prosecutor

12. Pursuant to article 3 of the Annex, the Prosecutor will be appointed by the Secretary-General upon the recommendation of a selection panel (established in the same manner as that for the international judges), in consultation with the Government of Lebanon. A Lebanese Deputy Prosecutor will be appointed by the Government of Lebanon, in consultation with the

Secretary-General and the Prosecutor, to assist the Prosecutor in the conduct of investigations and prosecutions.

13. The recruitment of the Prosecutor will begin in due course. With regard to the Deputy Prosecutor, the Government of Lebanon has forwarded to me, in a sealed envelope, a list of suggested names in preparation for her or his appointment. The list will remain sealed until the selection process begins.

14. The provisions set out in article 17 (a) of the Annex call for appropriate arrangements to be made to ensure that there is a coordinated transition from the activities of the International Independent Investigation Commission (the "Investigation Commission") to the activities of the Office of the Prosecutor. The Secretariat has initiated discussions with the Investigation Commission aimed at achieving that end and will remain in close contact with the Commission to ensure effective coordination during the period of the establishment of the Special Tribunal.

C. The Registrar

15. Pursuant to article 4 of the annex, the Secretary-General will appoint the Registrar, who will be a staff member of the United Nations. I will start the process of identifying suitable candidates before the end of the year. He or she will take office at an appropriate time in order to develop the administrative and judicial infrastructure of the Special Tribunal so as to enable it to be operational on the date of the commencement of its functioning. The Registrar will also assist with the transition from the Investigation Commission to the Special Tribunal.

D. Head of the Defence Office

16. Pursuant to article 13, of the Statute, an independent head of the Defence Office, responsible for appointing the Office staff, drawing up a list of defence counsel and providing support and assistance to defence counsel and persons entitled to legal assistance, will be appointed by the Secretary-General in consultation with the President of the Special Tribunal.

17. I will initiate the process of identifying appropriate candidates for the position before the end of the year. The head of the Defence Office will be appointed at a later stage.

IV. Staffing Requirements and Estimated Budget

18. A preliminary estimate of the staffing requirements and the budget of the Special Tribunal has been made for the three years to which reference is made in article 5, paragraph 2, of the Annex. In making the estimate, attention was paid to the experiences of other international tribunals, in

particular that of the Special Court for Sierra Leone, which shares characteristics with the Special Tribunal.

19. While it is possible to determine the organizational and operational framework of the Special Tribunal, many issues which may have significant budgetary consequences, relating, inter alia, to the premises of the Tribunal, the number of accused persons, witnesses and trials, and the level of security required, have yet to be clarified. Therefore, the budget allocation herein presented constitutes an overall estimate rather than a precise evaluation of the funding necessary to support the operation of the Special Tribunal throughout its mandate.

20. In addition, the staffing requirements and the budget were necessarily developed on the basis of a number of assumptions, many of which may vary depending on the course of events during the establishment and operation of the Special Tribunal. Those assumptions are as follows:

(a) The work of the Office of the Prosecutor will be directed by the Prosecutor, based on the efforts already being carried out by the Lebanese authorities assisted by the Investigation Commission. The Prosecutor will benefit greatly from the work of the Lebanese authorities and the Investigation Commission in that regard. However, the Prosecutor will need the necessary time to complete the investigation work, as well as to prepare and submit an indictment;

(b) The terms and conditions of service for both judges and staff will be guided by those of the judges and staff of the Special Court for Sierra Leone, with appropriate modifications;

(c) A phased-in approach to the establishment and operation of the Special Tribunal will be adopted in accordance with the chronology of the legal process;

(d) The President of the Tribunal will take up his or her full-time duties on the date on which the Special Tribunal commences functioning;

(e) There will be three working languages with regard to the trial proceedings: Arabic, English and French;

(f) An office of the Special Tribunal will be established in Lebanon.

21. At this stage, no assumption can be made concerning the cost involved in providing for a courtroom, detention facility or office accommodation for staff.

22. Consequently, mindful of the considerations addressed above, including the required estimates referred to in article 5, paragraph 2, of the Annex, and taking into account established trends, in particular at the Special Court for Sierra Leone, it is estimated that the Special Tribunal will require a staffing level of between 415 and 430 posts and a total budget of $35 million for

the first 12 months of its operations, $45 million for the second 12 months and $40 million for the third 12 months.

23. It may be necessary to consider budgeting in the second and third years of the Special Tribunal for a second Trial Chamber. As provided for in article 2, paragraph 2, of the Annex "[t]he Chambers shall be composed of a Pre-Trial Judge, a Trial Chamber and an Appeals Chamber, with a second Trial Chamber to be created if, after the passage of at least six months from the commencement of the functioning of the Special Tribunal, the Secretary-General or the President of the Special Tribunal so requests". This would entail, if required, the appointment of four additional judges and an examination of how to accommodate an additional Trial Chamber within the existing physical infrastructure. Should a second Trial Chamber be created, it is estimated at the present time that the additional annual financial requirements would be $8 million.

24. A draft budget including staffing requirements across the organs of the Special Tribunal, will be prepared in due course.

V. Funding

25. As provided for in article 5, paragraph 1, of the annex, the expenses of the Special Tribunal will be borne in the following manner:

(a) Fifty-one per cent of the expenses will be borne by voluntary contributions from States;

(b) Forty-nine per cent of the expenses of the Tribunal will be borne by the Government of Lebanon.

26. Pursuant to article 5, paragraph 2, of the Annex, "[i]t is understood that the Secretary-General will commence the process of establishing the Tribunal when he has sufficient contributions in hand to finance the establishment of the Tribunal and 12 months of its operations plus pledges equal to the anticipated expenses of the following 24 months of the Tribunal's operation".

27. On 26 July 2007, the Secretariat created a trust fund to receive contributi1ns for the establishment and activities of the Special Tribunal. A letter to Member States inviting them to contribute to the trust fund will soon be sent.

VI. Management Committee

28. In accordance with article 6 of the Annex, the United Nations and the Government of Lebanon "shall consult concerning the establishment of a Management Committee".

29. Accordingly, on 9 July 2007, the United Nations and the Government of Lebanon agreed to establish a Management Committee, which, inter alia, would (a) provide advice and policy direction on all non-judicial aspects of

the operation of the Special Tribunal, including questions of efficiency; and (b) perform other functions as agreed by the members of the Committee. They also agreed that the United Nations would be entrusted with establishing the Management Committee, including drafting the terms of reference in consultation with the Government of Lebanon.

VII. Security

30. Ensuring the security of the Special Tribunal's officials is a matter of the highest priority in order to preserve the integrity and the independence of the Tribunal. Overall security arrangements will be made in consultation with the authorities of the Netherlands and of the Government of Lebanon.

VIII. Outreach and Communications

31. The creation of the Special Tribunal has already attracted significant interest in both Lebanon and the international community. That interest will only increase as the establishment of the Special Tribunal moves forward. Therefore, a communications strategy, including an outreach programme for the region, must be developed and implemented.

32. Adopting an effective communications strategy to provide accurate information about the establishment, role and activities of the Special Tribunal is of the utmost importance. It is also crucial to ensuring that the entire process is perceived as transparent, fair and accessible.

33. A key element for the success of the Special Tribunal is not only that justice be done but also that justice must be seen to be done. As the Special Tribunal's seat will be located outside Lebanon, the development of an effective and comprehensive outreach programme bringing the activities of the Special Tribunal closer to the population of Lebanon and the wider region is a priority.

IX. Next Steps

34. In order to support the successful and timely implementation of Security Council resolution 1757 (2007), the establishment of the Special Tribunal will proceed in three phases: (a) a preparatory phase; (b) a start-up phase; and (c) the commencement of functioning.

A. Preparatory Phase

35. During the preparatory phase, which is currently under way, the following actions will be undertaken:

(a) Identifying the premises for the seat of the Special Tribunal, in coordination with the authorities of the host State, that would provide for the detention of accused persons, the conduct of trial proceedings and offices;

(b) Negotiating a headquarters agreement with the host State;

(c) Making preliminary legal and administrative arrangements with respect to the presence in Lebanon of an Office of the Special Tribunal for the conduct of investigations;

(d) Appointing the judges, the Prosecutor, the Deputy Prosecutor and the Registrar;

(e) Identifying candidates for the head of the Defence Office;

(f) Finalizing the drafting of the terms and conditions of service of judges and of the staff;

(g) Developing a draft budget, including a staffing table, for the Special Tribunal;

(h) Initiating fund-raising for the establishment and operation of the Special Tribunal;

(i) Drafting the terms of reference of the Management Committee and determining its composition, in consultation with the authorities of the Government of Lebanon and interested Member States;

(j) Formulating and implementing communications and outreach policies for the period before the Special Tribunal becomes operational.

B. Start-up Phase

36. The start-up phase will begin when the Registrar has been appointed. This phase of activity includes the following actions:

(a) Working on the preparation of the premises identified for the Special Tribunal;

(b) Beginning the process for the recruitment and appointment of staff;

(c) Establishing a core unit of Registry personnel to assist the Registrar in preparing for the Special Tribunal to become operational.

37. In addition, during the start-up phase, the Commissioner of the Investigation Commission, working together with the Registrar, should begin taking administrative measures to ensure a coordinated transition from the Investigation Commission to the Office of the Prosecutor.

C. Commencement of Functioning

38. The responsibility falls upon me to determine when the Special Tribunal will commence functioning. This can occur when sufficient financial means have been received pursuant to article 5, paragraph 2, of the Annex. In addition,

pursuant to article 19, paragraph 2, of the Annex, the Special Tribunal will commence functioning on a date to be determined by me, in consultation with the Government of Lebanon, taking into account the progress of the work of the Investigation Commission.

39. Once the Special Tribunal is ready to commence functioning, the judges, the Prosecutor and the Registrar will be sworn in and the first plenary meeting convened. The purpose of the meeting will be twofold: (a) to elect the President of the Special Tribunal; and (b) to adopt a schedule for the drafting of the rules of procedure and evidence and other necessary documents (such as the directives on the assignment of defence counsel, on the detention of persons awaiting trial or appeal and on the code of professional conduct for defence counsel). After his or her election, I will consult with the President regarding the appointment of the head of the Defence Office, pursuant to article 13 of the Statute.

40. As set out in article 17 of the annex, the judges will serve on an ad hoc basis during this initial period of operation of the Special Tribunal. I envisage that the judges of the Trial and Appeals Chambers will only commence their official judicial functions at a later stage. However, the pre-trial judge would start her or his duties earlier than the other judges in order to issue any warrants and orders required for the conduct of investigations and for the preparation of trials.

X. Final Observations

41. It is my belief that the establishment of the Special Tribunal will contribute to ending impunity in Lebanon for the crimes under the Tribunal's jurisdiction. The United Nations remains committed to assisting the Government of Lebanon and the Lebanese people towards this end by creating a tribunal of an international character grounded in the highest standards of international justice. As the process to establish the Special Tribunal advances, I will keep the members of the Security Council apprised of this important work.

DOCUMENT NO. 23

SECRETARY GENERAL'S SECOND UPDATING REPORT ON THE LEBANON TRIBUNAL

United Nations Security Council
S/2008/173

March 12, 2008

Distr.: General
12 March 2008

Original: English

Second Report of the Secretary-General Submitted Pursuant to Security Council Resolution 1757 (2007)

I. Introduction

1. Under Security Council resolution 1757 (2007), I was mandated to take, in coordination, when appropriate, with the Government of Lebanon, the steps and measures necessary to establish the Special Tribunal in a timely manner, and to report to the Security Council within 90 days and thereafter periodically on the implementation of the resolution.

2. Since my first progress report, dated 4 September 2007 (S/2007/525), substantial progress has been made in a number of areas, including (a) the location of the seat of the Tribunal; (b) the appointment of the judges, the Prosecutor, the Deputy Prosecutor, the Registrar and the Head of the Defence Office; (c) the preparation of an estimate of the staffing and financial requirements; (d) the fulfilment of the Tribunal's funding requirements; (e) the establishment of the Management Committee; (f) the transition from the International Independent Investigation Commission to the Tribunal; (g) security issues; and (h) the development of a communication and outreach programme.

3. The purpose of this report is to present the progress achieved since the last report and to provide an outline of the next steps.

II. Location of the Seat

A. Headquarters Agreement

4. On the basis of the statement of the Government of the Netherlands, described in my last report, that it was favourably disposed towards hosting the Tribunal, the Secretariat and the authorities of the Netherlands engaged in negotiations with a view to concluding an agreement concerning the headquarters of the Tribunal. Pursuant to article 8 of the annex to resolution 1757 (2007), a headquarters agreement was to be reached on a tripartite basis between the United Nations, Lebanon and the State hosting the Tribunal. However, paragraph 1 (b) of resolution 1757 (2007) provides that, if the Secretary-General reports that the headquarters agreement has not been concluded as envisioned under article 8 of the annex to the resolution, the location of the seat of the Tribunal shall be determined in consultation with the Government of Lebanon and be subject to the conclusion of a headquarters agreement between the United Nations and the State that hosts the Tribunal.

5. On 9 November 2007, I wrote to the Prime Minister of Lebanon seeking his views on the issue of concluding a headquarters agreement as envisioned under article 8 of the annex. On 12 November 2007, he responded, agreeing with my assessment that, under the prevailing circumstances, it would be difficult to pursue a tripartite headquarters agreement to be signed and ratified in a timely manner, as called for in paragraph 3 of resolution 1757 (2007). While expressing approval of the location of the seat of the Tribunal in the Netherlands, the Prime Minister asked that I continue to take all the necessary steps and measures to continue facilitating the process and finalizing a bilateral headquarters agreement.

6. On 14 December 2007, I informed the President of the Security Council of the agreement between the United Nations and the Government of Lebanon that the United Nations should pursue a bilateral headquarters agreement with the Government of the Netherlands, adding that negotiations between the United Nations and the authorities of the Netherlands had been successfully concluded. The agreement provides, inter alia, that the host State has no obligation to let persons convicted by the Special Tribunal serve their sentence of imprisonment in a prison facility on its territory. It also stipulates that the Registrar shall take all necessary measures to arrange the immediate relocation to third States of witnesses who for security reasons cannot return to their home countries after testifying before the Tribunal. On 21 December 2007, representatives of the United Nations and the Netherlands signed the Agreement between the United

Nations and the Kingdom of the Netherlands concerning the Headquarters of the Special Tribunal for Lebanon. The Agreement was subsequently submitted by the Government to Parliament for approval.

B. Premises

7. In paragraph 6 of my last report, I indicated that the Legal Counsel of the United Nations, Nicolas Michel, had initiated discussions with the authorities of the Netherlands regarding the modalities of the establishment of the Tribunal and had visited possible sites to house the Tribunal. To determine which site was most suitable, a number of technical assessments of the sites were undertaken, all of which concluded that a building located in the urban area of The Hague was suitable for the purpose of housing the Tribunal. On that basis and after consulting with States that had made significant contributions or pledges to the funding of the Tribunal, on 6 December 2007 the Legal Counsel informed the authorities of the Netherlands that the building identified was the preferred site for the Tribunal, subject to an agreement on its cost. On 7 December 2007, the authorities of the Netherlands made an offer concerning the cost of the building, which was approved by the above-mentioned States on 12 December. Plans for the refurbishment and adaptation of the premises are currently being evaluated.

III. Appointment of the Judges, the Prosecutor, the Deputy Prosecutor, the Registrar and the Head of the Defence Office

A. The Judges

8. In paragraph 9 of my previous report, I indicated that, on 10 July 2007, the Government of Lebanon had forwarded to me, in a sealed envelope, a list of 12 candidates proposed for judicial appointments by the Lebanese Supreme Council of the Judiciary, as set forth in article 2, paragraph 5 (a), of the annex to resolution 1757 (2007). I also informed you that, with a view to my appointing Lebanese and international judges at the same time, on 1 August 2007 the Legal Counsel sent a letter to all Member States, on my behalf, inviting them to consider submitting candidates for appointment as judges of the Tribunal no later than 24 September 2007. The names of 37 international candidates were submitted.

9. In mid-October 2007, after indicating my intention to the Security Council in accordance with article 2, paragraph 5 (d), of the annex, I established a selection panel. The panel was composed of Judge Mohamed Amin El Mahdi (Egypt), who served as judge of the International Tribunal for the Former Yugoslavia from 2001 to 2005, Judge Erik Møse (Norway), currently serving as judge of the International Criminal Tribunal for Rwanda, where he was President of the Tribunal from 2003 to 2007, and the Legal Counsel.

10. In October and November 2007, the Secretariat held consultations with the Government of Lebanon in accordance with article 2, paragraph 5 (c), of the annex, which provides that the Government and the Secretary-General shall consult on the appointment of judges.

11. On 4 December 2007, having interviewed the short-listed candidates, the selection panel made its recommendations to me, which I subsequently accepted. Mindful of security considerations, I will proceed with the formal appointments of the judges and announce their names at an appropriate time in the future. The judges will assume their functions on a date to be determined by me, in consultation with the President of the Special Tribunal, as provided in article 17, paragraph (b), of the annex.

B. The Prosecutor and the Deputy Prosecutor

12. With a view to identifying candidates for consideration for the position of Prosecutor and taking into account the sensitivity of the matter, from June to September 2007, informal consultations were held with experts in the field. In October 2007, the selection panel (composed of the same members as that for the judges) interviewed candidates for this post. Early in November 2007, the Government of Lebanon was consulted on the appointment of the Prosecutor, pursuant to article 3, paragraph 1, of the annex to resolution 1757 (2007). On 8 November 2007, the selection panel recommended to me that Daniel Bellemare (Canada) be appointed as the Prosecutor. I subsequently accepted the recommendation.

13. On 14 November 2007, I appointed Mr. Bellemare as the Prosecutor of the Special Tribunal pursuant to my authority under article 3 of the annex. He will, however, commence his official duties as the Prosecutor at a later date in keeping with the provisions of the annex. On the same day, after the Security Council took note of my intention, I also appointed Mr. Bellemare to succeed Serge Brammertz as Commissioner of the Investigation Commission. I am of the view that, as called for in article 17, paragraph (a), of the annex, this approach will ensure a coordinated transition from the activities of the Investigation Commission to those of the Office of the Prosecutor of the Special Tribunal.

14. With respect to the Deputy Prosecutor, as I noted in paragraph 13 of my last report, the Government of Lebanon forwarded to me, in a sealed envelope, a list of candidates for the position. In December 2007, pursuant to consultations held between the Government of Lebanon, the Prosecutor-designate of the Special Tribunal and myself, a Deputy Prosecutor was identified. The appointment of the Deputy Prosecutor falls within the authority of the Government of Lebanon, in accordance with article 3, paragraph 3, of the annex.

C. The Registrar

15. On 13 November 2007, the Legal Counsel sent a letter to Member States on my behalf inviting them to submit nominations for appointment as Registrar of the Special Tribunal by no later than 14 December 2007. Pursuant to that letter, a total of 14 nominations were submitted by States.

16. In accordance with article 4, paragraph 2, of the annex to resolution 1757 (2007), the Registrar will be a staff member of the United Nations. On the basis of the recommendation of the selection panel that I established, on 10 March 2008, I appointed Mr. Robin Vincent as Registrar of the Special Tribunal for a period of three years to commence at a later date, to be determined in the light of the progress achieved in establishing the Tribunal.

D. The Head of the Defence Office

17. I am in the process of recruiting a Head of the Defence Office. Since my last report, a vacancy announcement for this position has been prepared and is being advertised. In accordance with article 13, paragraph 1, of the statute, I will appoint the Head of the Defence Office in consultation with the President of the Special Tribunal as soon as the latter has been identified.

IV. Staffing and Financial Requirements

18. My previous report provided preliminary estimates of the staffing and financial requirements of the Tribunal for three years. In arriving at these global estimates, attention was paid to the experience of other international tribunals, in particular the Special Court for Sierra Leone, which shares characteristics with the Tribunal. A number of issues which may have significant budgetary consequences, such as those relating to the premises of the Tribunal, the terms and conditions of service for judges and staff, the number of accused persons, witnesses and trials, and the level of security required, have yet to be clarified.

19. The assumptions outlined in paragraph 20 of my previous report remain an important basis for the staffing and financial requirements. However, two additional considerations regarding the conditions of service for the judges and staff of the Tribunal have been raised:

(a) As stated in paragraph 20 (b) of my initial report, the terms and conditions of service for both judges and staff will be guided by those of the judges and staff of the Special Court for Sierra Leone, with appropriate modifications. Specific modifications to those conditions of service are currently under review with due consideration of host country social security requirements and of the Tribunal's location at a family duty station;

(b) Article 17 (a) of the annex to resolution 1757 (2007) provides for appropriate arrangements to be made to ensure that there is a coordinated transition from the activities of the Investigation Commission to the Office of the Prosecutor of the Special Tribunal. As noted by the Commission in its ninth report to the Security Council (S/2007/684, para. 98), transitional activities also rely on the institutional memory and experience gained by its staff. Whereas a principal aspect of the Tribunal's capacity to attract staff of the highest standards depends on competitive compensation practices, consideration is being given to aligning the conditions of service of staff with those prevailing in the United Nations common system in order to maintain a degree of continuity between the staff of the Commission and the Tribunal.

20. Except for the Registrar, who is a United Nations staff member, the terms and conditions of service of staff as described above apply uniformly to all staff recruited by the Tribunal.

21. It was stated in paragraph 21 of my previous report that, at that time, no assumptions could be made concerning the costs involved in providing for a courtroom, detention facility or office accommodation for staff. As the premises of the Tribunal have now been identified, estimated costs in those areas may be integrated into overall financial requirements.

22. The annual rental cost for the building will amount to approximately $5 million and will be paid for the first years by the host State, whose generosity in this regard I applaud. Operating costs for the building are estimated at $1 million per year. Refurbishment packages are currently under review. The packages provide for basic or advanced adaptations of the building in respect of security, holding cells, courtroom and offices.

V. Funding

23. Pursuant to article 5, paragraph 1, of the annex to resolution 1757 (2007), 49 per cent of the expenses of the Special Tribunal shall be borne by the Government of Lebanon, while 51 per cent shall be borne by voluntary contributions from States. According to paragraph 2 of the aforementioned article, the Secretary-General will commence the process of establishing the Tribunal when he has sufficient contributions in hand to finance the establishment of the Tribunal and 12 months of its operations plus pledges equal to the anticipated expenses of the following 24 months of the Tribunal's operation.

24. As mentioned in paragraph 27 of my previous report, on 26 July 2007 the Secretariat created a trust fund to receive contributions for the establishment and activities of the Tribunal. On 8 October 2007, I sent a letter to all Member States inviting them to contribute to the trust fund. As at

27 February 2008, the total amount deposited in the trust fund is $29,430,872.15, with firm pledges totalling $16,408,637.34. I am confident that the contributions received, together with other expected contributions, will meet the budgetary requirements for the establishment and the first 12 months of operations of the Tribunal. On 5 December 2007, the States that had made significant contributions or pledges to the funding of the Tribunal unanimously agreed that funds should be managed directly by the Tribunal, as is the case with the Special Court for Sierra Leone, rather than through a United Nations trust fund. I will continue to seek the necessary funds from Member States and urge all to support the Tribunal and assist in this effort.

VI. Management Committee

25. As stated in paragraph 29 of my previous report, on 9 July 2007 the United Nations and the Government of Lebanon agreed to establish a Management Committee. They further agreed that the United Nations would be entrusted with the establishment of the Management Committee, including the drafting of its terms of reference, in consultation with the Government of Lebanon.

26. Accordingly, in November 2007, the Secretariat prepared, in consultation with the Government, a draft of the terms of reference of the Management Committee and discussed the draft informally with the States that had made significant contributions or pledges to the funding of the Tribunal.

27. As agreed with the Government of Lebanon on 13 February 2008, I formally established the Management Committee and invited the Legal Counsel to facilitate its first meeting.

28. Pursuant to article IV of its terms of reference, the Management Committee will, inter alia: (a) receive and consider progress reports of the Special Tribunal and provide policy direction and advice on all non-judicial aspects of its operations, including questions of efficiency; (b) review and approve the Tribunal's annual budget, take any other necessary financial decisions, and advise the Secretary-General on these matters; (c) ensure that all organs of the Tribunal are operating in as efficient, effective and accountable a manner as possible, and that optimum use is made of resources contributed by donor States, without prejudice to the principle of judicial independence; (d) assist the Secretary-General in ensuring that adequate funds are available for the operation of the Tribunal including the development of fund-raising strategies, in close consultation with the Registrar; (e) encourage all States to cooperate with the Tribunal; and (f) report

on a regular basis to meetings of representatives of the Group of Interested States for the Special Tribunal.

29. Article VIII of the terms of reference also provides that the Management Committee will organize regular meetings of representatives of the Group of Interested States and may invite, when it deems appropriate, other interested parties to submit their views regarding the work of the Tribunal.

VII. Transition from the Investigation Commission to the Special Tribunal

30. Article 17 (a) of the annex to resolution 1757 (2007) calls for appropriate arrangements to be made to ensure a coordinated transition from the activities of the Investigation Commission to the Office of the Prosecutor of the Special Tribunal. Since my last report, a series of measures have been taken and ongoing consultations held between the Secretariat and the Commission aimed at achieving this objective.

31. The possibility of ensuring a transition of personnel from the Investigation Commission to the Office of the Prosecutor has been considered with a view to preserving to the greatest extent possible institutional memory and experience gained by staff.

VIII. Security

32. The provision of appropriate security measures for personnel and property remains one of the key pillars of the successful establishment of the Tribunal. To that end, the Secretariat is working in close cooperation with the relevant authorities of the Netherlands and Lebanon.

33. In addition, the Secretariat, the Investigation Commission and experts from the International Tribunal for the Former Yugoslavia and the Special Court for Sierra Leone have been working together on developing a strategy for the protection of witnesses. Consultations were recently held to discuss the practical implementation of such measures.

IX. Communication and Outreach

34. The Secretariat has conducted extensive consultations with experts from other international tribunals and a comprehensive communication and outreach strategy was developed. A key objective of the strategy is to ensure that the Tribunal is correctly perceived as a truly independent and impartial judicial body, which functions in accordance with the highest standards of justice. Public documents that provide comprehensive information on the Tribunal are being finalized for the purposes of wide dissemination within Lebanon, the region and the public at large. In addition,

work on the establishment of an initial communications capacity for the Tribunal is under way, including the creation of a website.

X. Next Steps

35. In paragraph 34 of my previous report, I had identified three phases in the establishment of the Tribunal: a preparatory phase; a start-up phase; and the commencement of functioning.

A. Preparatory Phase

36. As described above, all the actions relating to the preparatory phase have been undertaken, if not completed:

(a) The Headquarters Agreement has been signed;

(b) The premises for the Special Tribunal have been identified;

(c) The judges, the Prosecutor and the Registrar have been selected;

(d) The Management Committee has been established;

(e) The recruitment process for the Head of the Defence Office has begun;

(f) A draft budget, including a staffing table, has been developed and will be submitted soon to the Management Committee for consideration;

(g) Communication and outreach policies have been prepared.

B. Start-Up and Commencement of the Special Tribunal's Functioning

37. The start-up phase has now commenced. Work on the preparation of the premises and on the organization of a coordinated transition between the Independent Commission and the Tribunal is being conducted. Once the Registrar starts operating in that capacity, a core unit of Registry personnel will be established in The Hague to assist the Registrar in his functions.

38. The Tribunal will commence functioning in successive phases. I anticipate that early informal consultations among the judges will facilitate the drafting of the rules of procedure and evidence and other necessary documents (such as directives on the assignment of defence counsel, on the detention of persons awaiting trial or appeal, and the code of professional conduct for defence counsel). In addition to the Registrar, the Prosecutor, followed by the pre-trial judge, will start their duties earlier than the other senior officials in order to perform their tasks in an effective and coordinated manner. The President of the Tribunal will also take up his or her duties on a full-time basis at an earlier date to ensure the efficient management and functioning of the Tribunal. The judges of the Trial and Appeals Chambers, as stated in article 17, paragraph (b), of the annex to resolution 1757 (2007), will take office on a date to be determined by me, in consultation

with the President of the Tribunal. Until they are called to work on a full-time basis, they will serve on an ad hoc basis to perform their duties.

XI. Final Observations

39. I wish to assure you that the Secretariat is dedicated to continuing to make progress in the establishment of the Special Tribunal for Lebanon in a timely manner as mandated by the Security Council. In this regard, we rely on the generosity and support of Member States. I trust that our common efforts will assist the Government and people of Lebanon towards this important common goal of restoring justice and the rule of law in Lebanon.

SUBJECT INDEX

Doc/Pg

Arms Proliferation

Counterterrorism

European Union

Human Rights

Intelligence

International Cooperation

Doc/Pg

Middle East

Military – Role of

Terrorism – Criminal Prosecution

Terrorism – Financing of

Terrorism – International

Doc/Pg

Terrorism – Policy

Terrorist Incidents

Terrorist Organizations

United Nations – Security Council Resolutions

Doc/Pg

www.ingramcontent.com/pod-product-compliance
Ingram Content Group UK Ltd.
Pitfield, Milton Keynes, MK11 3LW, UK
UKHW051048150926
475595UK00005B/173